READING HUME ON HUMAN UNDERSTANDING

Reading Hume on Human Understanding

ESSAYS ON THE FIRST *ENQUIRY*

edited by Peter Millican

CLARENDON PRESS · OXFORD

OXFORD
UNIVERSITY PRESS

Great Clarendon Street, Oxford OX2 6DP

Oxford University Press is a department of the University of Oxford.
It furthers the University's objective of excellence in research, scholarship,
and education by publishing worldwide in

Oxford New York

Auckland Bangkok Buenos Aires Cape Town Chennai
Dar es Salaam Delhi Hong Kong Istanbul Karachi Kolkata
Kuala Lumpur Madrid Melbourne Mexico City Mumbai Nairobi
São Paulo Shanghai Singapore Taipei Tokyo Toronto

with an associated company in Berlin

Oxford is a registered trade mark of Oxford University Press
in the UK and certain other countries

Published in the United States
by Oxford University Press Inc., New York

British Library Cataloguing in Publication Data
Data available

Library of Congress Cataloging in Publication Data
Data available

ISBN 0-19-875211-3
ISBN 0-19-875210-5 (Pbk.)

1 3 5 7 9 10 8 6 4 2

Typeset by SNP Best-set Typesetter Ltd., H.K.
Printed in Great Britain by
Biddles Ltd, Guildford & Kings Lynn

CONTENTS

NOTES ON CONTRIBUTORS

PETER MILLICAN is Senior Lecturer in Philosophy and Computing at the University of Leeds, where he is also Head of ACOM (Computing for All), teaching interdisciplinary Computing and IT across the University, and Director of the Electronic Text Centre. Most of his recent research has focused on epistemological topics from Hume, especially the philosophy of induction and probability, but he has also published in philosophical logic, ethics, philosophy of religion, and artificial intelligence. Other interests include the theory of academic assessment and classification (for which Leeds University recently adopted his new system), and correspondence chess (in which he is an ICCF International Grandmaster, and was British Champion in 1990). He is joint editor, with Andy Clark, of two volumes on *The Legacy of Alan Turing* (Oxford University Press, 1996).

M. A. STEWART is Research Professor in the History of Philosophy in the Universities of Lancaster and Aberdeen, and Senior Research Fellow at Harris Manchester College, Oxford. He is General Editor of the Clarendon Locke Edition and joint General Editor of the Clarendon Hume Edition. He works in British intellectual history of the seventeenth and eighteenth centuries, with a particular interest in philosophy in the Dissenting tradition. His edited collections include *Studies in the Philosophy of the Scottish Enlightenment* (Oxford University Press, 1990), *Studies in Seventeenth-Century European Philosophy* (Oxford University Press, 1997), *English Philosophy in the Age of Locke* (Oxford University Press, 2000), and, with John P. Wright, *Hume and Hume's Connexions* (Edinburgh University Press, 1994).

JONATHAN BENNETT, after a career spent mainly at Cambridge University, the University of British Columbia, and Syracuse University, now lives in retirement on Bowen Island in British Columbia. His two-volume work *Learning from Six Philosophers* was published by Oxford University Press in 2001.

MARTIN BELL taught philosophy at the University of York from 1969 to 1995, since when he has been Professor of Philosophy at Manchester Metropolitan University. His publications include an edition of Hume's *Dialogues concerning Natural Religion* (Penguin Classics, 1990), and studies of Hume's accounts of causation and of religion. He is especially interested in the relations between philosophy and its writing.

JUSTIN BROACKES is Associate Professor of Philosophy at Brown University. He has published on Aristotle, Descartes, and Hume, and on topics in metaphysics and the philosophy of mind. He is completing a study of the theory of colour and perception from the Ancient Greeks to Wittgenstein.

EDWARD CRAIG is the Knightsbridge Professor of Philosophy in the University of Cambridge, and a Fellow of the British Academy. His principal interests lie in the history of modern philosophy (especially Hume and Kant) and the theory of knowledge, and he also has a special interest in issues of epistemic privacy and linguistic meaning. He was the editor of the journal *Ratio* from 1988 to 1992, and is General Editor of the 10–volume *Routledge Encyclopedia of Philosophy*, published in 1998 and now the leading encyclopedia of philosophy in English. His other publications include *The Mind of God and the Works of Man* (Oxford University Press, 1987) and *Knowledge and the State of Nature* (Oxford University Press, 1990). He is now writing *A Very Short Introduction to Philosophy*, for the *Very Short Introductions* series published by Oxford University Press.

GALEN STRAWSON is Professor of Philosophy at the University of Reading, having until recently been a Fellow and Tutor at Jesus College, Oxford. He is the author of *Freedom and Belief* (Oxford University Press, 1986), *The Secret Connexion* (Oxford University Press, 1989), and *Mental Reality* (MIT Press, 1994). He has also published a number of articles on the philosophy of mind, moral philosophy and other subjects, and is currently writing a book about the idea of the self.

SIMON BLACKBURN is Professor of Philosophy at the University of Cambridge. Until recently he was Edna J. Koury Distinguished Professor of Philosophy at the University of North Carolina, Chapel Hill, and from 1969 to 1989 a Fellow and Tutor at Pembroke College, Oxford. He edited the journal *Mind* from 1984 to 1990. His books (all with Oxford University Press) include *Spreading the Word* (1984), *Essays in Quasi–Realism* (1993), *The Oxford Dictionary of Philosophy* (1994), *Ruling Passions* (1998), *Think* (1999), *Truth* (co-edited with Keith Simmons, 1999), and *Being Good* (2001).

GEORGE BOTTERILL has been a lecturer in the Department of Philosophy at the University of Sheffield since 1988. In addition to the history of philosophy from Descartes to Hume, his main research interests are in the philosophy of mind, the philosophy of science, and the sort of interdisciplinary work on cognition supported by Sheffield's *Hang Seng Centre for Cognitive Studies*, of which he is a founder member. His most important publication to date is *The Philosophy of Psychology* (Cambridge University Press, 1999), co-authored with Professor Peter Carruthers. His name may also be familiar to some people from the field of chess, in which he is a FIDE International Master, was British Champion in 1974 and 1977, and is a well-known author.

DON GARRETT is Kenan Distinguished Professor for Teaching Excellence in the Department of Philosophy at the University of North Carolina at Chapel Hill, and has previously taught at Harvard University, Johns Hopkins University, and the University of Utah. He is the author of *Cognition and Commitment in Hume's Philosophy* (Oxford University Press, 1997) and of articles in the history of modern philosophy. He is also the editor of *The Cambridge Companion to Spinoza* (Cambridge University Press, 1996), the North American editor of the journal *Archiv für Geschichte der Philosophie*, and a past editor of *Hume Studies*.

DAVID OWEN teaches at the University of Arizona in Tucson. His book *Hume's Reason* was published by Oxford University Press in 1999. He is currently working on theories of judgement and assent in the early modern period.

J. C. A. GASKIN is a graduate of Oxford University. He spent most of his professional life in Trinity College Dublin where he was Professor of Naturalistic Philosophy. His *Hume's Philosophy of Religion* is widely regarded as the primary philosophical examination of all the main issues. He is also author of *The Quest for Eternity* and editor of Hobbes's *Elements of Law*, *Leviathan* and Hume's *Dialogues and Natural History of Religion* for Oxford World's Classics. *The Dark Companion*, a collection of ghost stories, is to be published in 2001. He was awarded a D. Litt in 1997.

DAVID FATE NORTON is Professor of Philosophy Emeritus, McGill University, and Adjunct Professor of Philosophy, University of Victoria. He is also a Fellow of the Royal Society of Canada. He is author of *David Hume: Common–Sense Moralist, Sceptical Metaphysician* (Princeton University Press, revised edition 1984), editor of *The Cambridge Companion to Hume* (Cambridge University Press, 1993), co–author of *The Hume Library* (Edinburgh Bibliographical Society, 1996), and co–editor of Hume's *Treatise of Human Nature* for both the Oxford Philosophical Texts series (2000) and the Clarendon Edition of the Works of David Hume (forthcoming).

ABBREVIATIONS FOR WORKS BY HUME

A   *Abstract of a Book lately published, entituled, A Treatise of Human Nature, etc.* (1740), repr. in *T* 641–62, and in this collection pp. 399–411
    [Marginal figures are paragraph numbers and page numbers from *T*]

App.   Appendix to *T*

D   *Dialogues concerning Natural Religion* (1779), ed. N. Kemp Smith, 2nd edn. (Edinburgh: Nelson, 1947)

E   *An Enquiry concerning Human Understanding* (1748)

M   *An Enquiry concerning the Principles of Morals* (1751)
    References to both *Enquiries* are to page numbers in *Enquiries concerning Human Understanding and concerning the Principles of Morals* (1777), ed. L. A. Selby-Bigge, 3rd edn. rev. P. H. Nidditch (Oxford: Clarendon Press, 1975). However all quotations have been corrected to the critical text of the Clarendon editions ed. Tom L. Beauchamp (Oxford: Clarendon Press, 2000 and 1998 respectively).

Essays   *Essays, Moral, Political, and Literary* (1741–83), ed. E. F. Miller, 2nd edn. (Indianapolis: Liberty Classics, 1987)

HL   *The Letters of David Hume*, ed. J. Y. T. Greig, 2 vols. (Oxford: Oxford University Press, 1932)

L   *A Letter from a Gentleman to his Friend in Edinburgh* (1745; assembled by Henry Home), ed. Ernest C. Mossner and John V. Price (Edinburgh: Edinburgh University Press, 1967)

'Life'   'My Own Life' (1777), repr. in this collection pp. 393–8. The text is from the 1777 publication, but with wording corrected against Hume's original manuscript
    [Marginal figures are paragraph numbers]

NHL   *New Letters of David Hume*, ed. R. Klibansky and E. C. Mossner (Oxford: Clarendon Press, 1954)

NHR   *The Natural History of Religion* (1757), repr. in *Dialogues concerning Natural Religion and The Natural History of Religion*, ed. J. C. A. Gaskin (Oxford: Oxford University Press, 1993)

PE   *Philosophical Essays concerning Human Understanding*, 1st edn. (London, 1748; repr. Hildesheim, 1986)

T   *A Treatise of Human Nature* (1739), ed. L. A. Selby-Bigge, 2nd edn. rev. P. H. Nidditch (Oxford: Clarendon Press, 1978). References are to page numbers

PREFACE AND
ACKNOWLEDGEMENTS

There has never been a better time to study Hume's first *Enquiry*, a work whose literary elegance is generally admired but whose philosophical depth has often been lost in the glare of his more superficially dazzling *Treatise*. Beauchamp's new student edition (Oxford Philosophical Texts, 1999) has recently made available—at a reasonable price—a reliable critical text, backed up by an accessible introduction, notes, and glossary, while his critical edition (Clarendon Press, 2000) provides for the first time the detailed textual comparisons, lists of emendations and variants, bibliography, and references needed by serious scholars of the text. All this leaves a gap, however, for the student who has progressed beyond Beauchamp's introduction (and is now ready to move on to consider alternative views and detailed interpretative debates) or for the researcher who wishes to dig deeper into the philosophy of the *Enquiry* (in a context where the secondary literature on Hume beyond the most introductory level has hitherto been dominated by his *Treatise*). It is this gap that the current volume is intended to fill, primarily by bringing together a range of contrasting interpretations in essays by respected Hume scholars (covering all the main topics of the *Enquiry*), but also by combining these with editorial materials designed to set them in context and convey a broad appreciation of the variety of opinions represented elsewhere in the literature. Whereas the essays, including my own, all advocate particular—and sometimes directly opposed—interpretations, the Introduction (pp. 1–26) and Critical Survey of the Literature (pp. 413–72) aim to present a relatively detached overview of how the various positions either harmonize or conflict, with the Introduction focusing specifically on the essays in this volume while the Critical Survey relates them to the wider literature. I hope that these editorial additions have succeeded in enhancing the coherence and self-sufficiency of the whole, so as to give it a value even greater than the sum of its parts.

Note that the Critical Survey of the Literature is available on the Hume Project website hosted by the Leeds Electronic Text Centre at www.etext.leeds.ac.uk/hume/ where it will from time to time be updated to take account of the expanding secondary literature. This website also holds a reliable text of the 1777 edition of the *Enquiry* (with other Hume editions planned in due course) and various other related study and research aids, including an index of all the citations of Hume's works made by the essays within this collection, which should prove particularly useful for cross–referencing between them.

The detailed aims of this volume are set out in the Introduction, which outlines the principal themes of each essay and relates them to each other. But relatively inexperienced readers may also appreciate some prior guidance on which pieces to read first, and which to postpone, bearing in mind their various levels of philosophical difficulty. Such readers are probably best to start with a general sketch of Hume's main views and targets (Chapter 1 §1), before reading his own *Abstract* of the *Treatise* (pp. 399–411 below) on which Chapter 1 (§§6–7) provides a general commentary in the course of giving a section–by–section summary of the *Enquiry*; one which claims, controversially, to detect within it a fairly systematic manifesto for inductive science. The remainder of Chapter 1, and Stewart's Chapter 2, are not difficult and will be of particular interest to those who wish to know more about Hume's life and works, but they are less essential for gaining a basic philosophical understanding of the *Enquiry* itself.

Forearmed with a general grasp of the structure and central themes of the *Enquiry*, its main individual topics are perhaps best approached initially as follows. Chapter 4 §§1–3 and §§11–12 give an outline of Hume's 'sceptical doubts' in Section IV and his 'sceptical solution of these doubts' in Section V, together with an interpretation of their significance. Hume's discussion of our causal ideas in Section VII presupposes some understanding of his Copy Principle, which he explains fairly straightforwardly in the short Section II. Craig's Chapter 7 §1 then provides a commentary on Hume's application of this principle in his search for the impression of necessary connexion, highlighting some of the interpretative puzzles that it raises. The main metaphysical, religious, and epistemological implications of all this are spelt out by Hume in Sections VIII, X, XI, and XII, which are discussed respectively by Botterill (Chapter 10), Garrett (Chapter 11), Gaskin (Chapter 13), and Norton (Chapter 14).

Having worked through all these, even the relatively inexperienced student should now be well placed to go back and address the more philosophically intricate discussions in the volume, such as those on the theory of ideas and belief involving Bennett, Bell, and Broackes (Chapters 3, 5, and 6); my debate with Garrett on induction (Chapter 4 and the Appendix to Chapter 11); the 'New Hume' causal realism controversy involving Craig, Strawson, and Blackburn (Chapters 7, 8, and 9); and Owen's Bayesian consideration of Hume's argument on miracles (Chapter 12). A preliminary orientation on each issue can be gleaned from the Introduction, which indicates the main thrust of each contribution and how they relate to each other. The Critical Survey of the Literature may also prove useful in this respect (even if its references are not followed up), by sketching some of the alternative positions that have been proposed by other writers, and thus setting the views advocated in these essays within a wider context. The various interpretative debates are highly interconnected, often tracing back to general differences of perspective on Hume's fundamental intentions. So discussion of Hume's philosophy in the *Enquiry* needs ultimately to be informed by an understanding of its historical context within his life and writings, as outlined in the central sections of Chapter 1 (§§2–5) and examined in more detail in Stewart's Chapter 2. Both of these chapters make reference to Hume's short but fascinating autobiography 'My Own Life', which is also included in the collection (pp. 393–8).

I should like to end by warmly thanking all those who have helped, either directly or indirectly, in bringing this project to fruition. My first thanks must go to the contributors, both for their excellent essays—some of which have undergone various adaptations to enable them to complement each other so well—and for their considerable patience while the volume was taking shape. Both the anonymous readers and editorial staff of Oxford University Press have given valuable advice that greatly helped to shape it, while Charlotte Jenkins in particular has demonstrated both great patience and consideration in helping a hitherto inexperienced scholarly editor to complete what turned out to be an unexpectedly complex project. I am also very grateful to the Press for compiling the draft index.

My own interest in the *Enquiry* dates back many years, driven largely by the conviction that Hume's dissatisfaction with his earlier *Treatise* was real and well–founded, and that therefore his mature philosophical views should be sought, as he himself urged, in the later works. Most of my research over the past decade has accordingly been focused on two central puzzles which I felt needed to be solved if a coherent philosophy was to be found within the *Enquiry*. First, how is Hume's consistent advocacy of a disciplined and discriminating inductive science (notably in the later sections of the *Enquiry*) to be reconciled with his 'sceptical doubts' about induction? Secondly, how can he combine such a positive attitude to science with an apparently devastating scepticism about the notion of matter? In addressing first one puzzle and then the other, I have been helped immeasurably by the opportunity to present my work at the annual conferences of the Hume Society, and by the reactions and discussions of many of its members. Attempting to list all those who have provided useful feedback or suggestions would be invidious, so I would here like to express general thanks to them all. But for sustained and stimulating debate and discussion, textual advice, or particular assistance with this volume, special thanks must go at least to Tom Beauchamp, Martin Bell, Lorne Falkenstein, Don Garrett, David Norton, David Owen, Paul Russell, Sandy Stewart, and John Wright. I would also like to thank Jane McIntyre and Tony Pitson, my two co–directors of the 1998 Hume Conference at Stirling University, which had the *Enquiry* as its principal theme. It was largely thanks to discussions at Stirling that my thoughts on the second central 'puzzle' crystallized, reaching conclusions which I outlined at the final session of that conference and are here published for the first time in Chapter 1. It remains to be seen whether this account will prove any more persuasive, to those Hume scholars whose contributions have influenced it, than did my earlier attempted resolution of the 'puzzle' concerning induction (provoking the debate which is here continued in Chapter 4). But either way, I look forward to many more stimulating and instructive hours of discussion with them at future Hume conferences.

My final and deepest acknowledgement must be to my wife Pauline, who—over a period when for various reasons life has been extremely demanding and stressful for both of us—has patiently tolerated sharing a huge proportion of our limited free time (including virtually every family holiday) with Hume and his *Enquiry*. I dedicate this book to her and to our children David, Katie, and Jonathan, with love and gratitude.

Introduction

Peter Millican

Hume's *Enquiry concerning Human Understanding* (standardly referred to as the first *Enquiry*) has long been recognized as one of the best available 'classics' for introducing students to the study of philosophy; indeed in this role probably only Descartes's *Meditations* enjoys a comparable popularity. The *Enquiry* is therefore well known, but tends to be considered rather lightweight—a useful stepping-stone for those approaching epistemology for the first time, or those wishing to sample Hume's philosophy in a relatively undemanding way, but a work destined to be put on one side once the reader has graduated to the more serious business of his earlier *Treatise of Human Nature*. No doubt for the same reason, the *Enquiry* tends to be viewed as an unsystematic work, a sequence of essays on loosely related topics chosen to interest and provoke the general reader, but lacking the impressive structure, the theoretical depth, or the analytical rigour of the *Treatise*. For both more advanced students and professional philosophers, therefore, the *Enquiry* has served mainly as a convenient source of material on Humean topics, and as a back-up reference for scholars on issues where the *Treatise* is unclear. Very rarely has it been considered seriously as a major work of philosophy in its own right.[1]

Against this background, this volume's general aims (which are highly interrelated, and in no particular order) can be summarized as follows:

1. To establish the significance of the *Enquiry*, as a work of philosophy in its own right.
2. To provide a general overview of the *Enquiry*, especially for those (whether students or professional philosophers) approaching it for the first time.
3. To explain recent developments in Hume scholarship that are relevant to the *Enquiry*.
4. To elucidate, analyse, and assess the philosophy of the *Enquiry* (both what Hume said and what—arguably—he *should have* said).

---

[1] Antony Flew's book *Hume's Philosophy of Belief* (London: Routledge & Kegan Paul, 1961) is a conspicuous exception, but Flew's treatment, though a major contribution at the time, is now very dated and does not attribute Hume with a consistent or plausible overall position.

5. To clarify the interpretation of controversial parts of the *Enquiry* (whether by appeal to scholarly, philosophical, biographical, or literary considerations).
6. To draw attention to differences between the *Treatise* and the *Enquiry*, and to suggest what may lie behind these changes.

Some of these aims (notably the first and second) explicitly inform only a few of the essays in the collection; others (for example the fifth) are in evidence almost throughout. To help the reader who has particular aims in mind, I shall allude to them below as the occasion arises, in the course of giving a brief description of each of the various papers that constitute the collection.

THE CONTEXT, AIMS, AND STRUCTURE OF HUME'S FIRST ENQUIRY (MILLICAN)

The first aim of this volume is to establish the genuine significance of the *Enquiry*, as a relatively unified and systematic presentation of Hume's epistemology, and arguably as a more faithful representation of his considered opinions than the *Treatise*. So in my own initial essay (which is unashamedly partisan on the issue) I suggest that Hume was neither insincere nor misguided in asking his printer in 1775 to prefix, to the volume containing the *Enquiries* (together with *A Dissertation on the Passions* and *The Natural History of Religion*), his notorious 'Advertisement':

MOST of the principles, and reasonings, contained in this volume, were published in a work in three volumes, called *A Treatise of Human Nature*: A work which the Author had projected before he left College, and which he wrote and published not long after. But not finding it successful, he was sensible of his error in going to the press too early, and he cast the whole anew in the following pieces, where some negligences in his former reasoning and more in the expression, are, he hopes, corrected. . . . Henceforth, the Author desires, that the following Pieces may alone be regarded as containing his philosophical sentiments and principles. (*E* 2)

My paper stresses the *Enquiry*'s unity, and claims to detect within it a clear and coherent overall purpose, but also more controversially a significant move away from the philosophy of the *Treatise* (especially from its associationism) and an underlying systematic development of specific inductive principles. If I am right in this last claim, then the sequence of topics that Hume discusses has been chosen not only with a view to his overall purpose (namely, vindicating empirical science against 'superstition' and rationalist metaphysics), but also to provide a framework for the introduction of particular principles of scientific inference covering such things as hidden causes, reasoning from analogy, and probability. On this interpretation, therefore, the *Enquiry* presents a unified manifesto for inductive science, and its scepticism, so far from being in conflict with that aim (as so often supposed), importantly paves the way for legitimate 'science and enquiry' by demonstrating the impotence and even incoherence of any supposed alternative (such as theistic metaphysics, or rationalistic insight into the nature of the material world).

The second aim of this volume, related to the first, is to provide a general overview of the *Enquiry*, especially for those (whether students or professional philosophers) who are approaching it as a serious subject of study for the first time. For these readers in particular, even if they are left entirely unconvinced by my more controversial claims, I hope that my discussion of Hume's intentions, and of his profound disagreements with rationalists such as Descartes, will help to provide a context for better appreciating the *Enquiry*'s central themes. These themes are then outlined in the final part of the paper, which discusses in turn each section of the work, drawing comparisons with Hume's *Abstract* of the *Treatise* published in 1740 (and which is also included in the collection at pp. 399–411). The *Abstract* provides both a fascinating historical document, illuminating Hume's own view of his performance in the *Treatise*, and also perhaps the best short introduction to his philosophy, whether that be studied through the *Treatise* itself or through the *Enquiry*.

TWO SPECIES OF PHILOSOPHY: THE HISTORICAL SIGNIFICANCE OF THE FIRST ENQUIRY (STEWART)

The third aim of this volume is to provide readers with an appreciation of some of the major developments and debates that have taken place in Hume scholarship over the last two decades or so, which have profoundly transformed our view of central aspects of his philosophy. Sandy Stewart has been a prominent contributor to historical studies of Hume for many years, and in his essay (Chapter 2) turns his attention to the circumstances surrounding the *Enquiry*'s composition. The 'two species' of his title refers to Hume's distinction, in Section I, between 'easy' and 'abstruse' philosophy, the one preaching virtue 'in an easy and obvious manner . . . to please the imagination, and engage the affections' (*E* 5), and the other regarding 'human nature as a subject of speculation', examining it 'with a narrow scrutiny . . . in order to find those principles, which regulate our understanding, excite our sentiments, and make us approve or blame' (*E* 6). Stewart finds in Hume's discussion clear allusions to the events of 1745, when he was turned down for the chair of moral philosophy at Edinburgh University through the combined opposition of the clergy and the influential moralist Francis Hutcheson. The *Treatise* (published in 1739–40) had been accused by Hutcheson of 'lacking warmth in the cause of virtue', and by the clergy of being sceptical and atheistic. Section I can thus be seen as Hume's reply to Hutcheson—no doubt the 'easy' philosophy has its merits, but Hume's 'abstruse' attempt at accurate, dispassionate enquiry also has value and should not be condemned on the inappropriate ground of failing to preach virtue. For its purpose is quite different, just as the role of an anatomist is fundamentally different from that of a painter.

According to Stewart, the scars of Hume's anger and disappointment over the Edinburgh chair are to be found not only in Section I, but also in particular at the beginning of Section V and throughout Section XI. In reviewing the overall construction of the *Enquiry* (and thus providing a significant contribution to this collection's second aim, of providing such an overview), Stewart also identifies many other historical references and various lingering traces of the work's original form as a collection of 'Philosophical Essays'. Taken together, therefore, these first two papers in the collection present strongly contrasting views of the *Enquiry*, while at the same time being more complementary than conflicting. My own paper stresses Hume's underlying unity of philosophical purpose (with relatively little biographical reference), while Stewart brings out numerous historical details that help to explain why the *Enquiry* took the particular form that it did (in the context of a less systematic conception of Hume's distinctive philosophical aims here). Readers who approach the *Enquiry* with these themes and historical details in mind will find it to be a vastly richer and more fascinating work than might be suspected by those who have taught or studied it purely as an introductory text.

EMPIRICISM ABOUT MEANINGS (BENNETT)

The fourth aim of this volume is to discuss and assess the philosophy of the *Enquiry*, and this is unequivocally the focus of Jonathan Bennett's essay (Chapter 3) which deals with Hume's arguments in Section II (subsequent papers will in turn work fairly systematically through the principal issues arising in the remainder of the *Enquiry*). Bennett's paper is very much older than the others in the collection, being a slightly modified version of a chapter from his book *Locke, Berkeley, Hume: Central Themes*, published in 1971. Much work of that vintage now tends to be criticized in scholarly circles as historically insensitive (no doubt often with justification), but it is salutary to be reminded that understanding Hume's attempts to solve some deep and enduring problems may require serious philosophical grappling with the problems themselves at least as much as it requires historical knowledge. Perhaps the clearest example in the *Enquiry* is the problem of *meaning*, which for Hume is inextricably bound up with the nature of our 'ideas', since he takes the meaning of a word to be determined by the idea that it represents (e.g. *E* 21–2). 'Ideas' are also the material of our thoughts (e.g. *E* 18), and are to be understood in the standard empiricist fashion as quasi-sensory images (indeed for Hume, as direct copies of sensory or internal impressions). This 'theory of ideas', which Hume inherits fairly uncritically from Locke, thus leads him into a misguided identification of *thinking* and *meaning* with *having images*, so that his entire discussion of the issue is infected by a fundamental category mistake.[2] Despite this, Bennett suggests, Hume's philosophical acuity sometimes leads him towards insights that reveal the theory's limitations, but because he is so fully in its grip that he cannot reject it or transcend its vocabulary, he instead stretches it in directions quite contrary to its spirit.[3] When this happens, we can expect to find gaps or incoherences appearing in his theory, but these sorts of difficulty may not be best illuminated by primarily historical or scholarly study, for such study may only unearth more instances (in either Hume's work or that of his contemporaries) of the same underlying errors. If so, light is more likely to be shed by *philosophical* investigation of the issues, which can aim to identify the impact of those errors and to reveal the insights towards which Hume himself might have been groping. Bennett claims that Hume's treatment of the issue of meaning is a case in point. And given the clear inadequacy of his theory of ideas for dealing with the issue, and the difficulties which arise for him as a result, this claim deserves serious consideration.

Fortunately the defects of the theory of ideas have relatively little impact in the *Enquiry*, which omits most of the dubious applications that occupy so much of the *Treatise* (e.g. concerning our ideas of space and time) and explicitly brackets others (e.g. the treatment of belief in *Enquiry* V. ii). The one important remaining aspect of the theory, central to Hume's discussion of meaning, is what is commonly known as his *Copy Principle*, that 'all our ideas or more feeble perceptions [i.e. thoughts] are copies of our impressions or more lively ones [i.e. sensations or feelings]' (*E* 19). This principle, which Hume presents as a refinement of Locke's denial of innate ideas (*E* 22 n.), is destined to be invoked just once in the *Enquiry*, when in Section VII (*E* 62 ff.) it initiates his search for

---

[2] Stock objections to the theory of ideas include the following: (*a*) Much of our thinking is not even *accompanied* by mental images (consider the thought that 'prudence is a virtue'). (*b*) Even when our thinking *is* accompanied by imagery, it is not *constituted by* that imagery, as shown by the fact that one and the same image can accompany many different thoughts. (*c*) *Understanding* cannot be a matter of mental imagery, for it involves communication with others, and mental imagery would not be communicable. (*d*) Mental actions (e.g. seeing that some tree is tall, thinking or believing that it is tall, wondering whether it is tall) are to be distinguished not in terms of their objects, but in terms of the mind's *activity* and *attitudes*; the mind is not just a passive spectator of 'perceptions' on a mental stage. The third of these objections plays a major role in Bennett's essay, and the last in Broackes's, which also usefully spells out objections in the spirit of (*a*) and (*b*), and discusses at some length the particular difficulties in Hume's theory arising from its attempt to account for the different mental attitudes in terms of variation along a single dimension of 'force and vivacity' (see below pp. 191–5).

[3] A clear example of this is Hume's treatment of general terms in *Treatise* I. i. 7, which sees their meaning as determined not only by the particular idea which accompanies them on each occasion, but also by an 'attendant custom, reviv'd by the general or abstract term' which brings to mind other associated ideas when reasoning using the term (*T* 21).

the impression of *necessary connexion*, in order to reveal that concept's meaning. Such use of the Copy Principle, as a tool for examining and clarifying the meaning of words in terms of their 'empirical cashability', implies a form of 'meaning-empiricism' which is far more persuasive than the uncharacteristically poor arguments of Section II by which Hume attempts to establish the Copy Principle itself. Bennett suggests, therefore, that this may be one of those cases in which Hume is best seen as groping towards a genuine philosophical insight *despite* the inappropriate idiom of the theory of ideas in which he develops and expresses it. This insight concerns the impossibility of a term's having meaning unless it can in some way be connected with experience, and its true justification has nothing to do with mental imagery, but derives from the need for public criteria to ground understanding of linguistic communication. Bennett's reconstruction of Hume's theory of meaning on this basis may indeed superficially be highly anachronistic, but if he is right, it articulates a genuine Humean insight, and one which can potentially relieve his philosophy in the *Enquiry* of its most significant dependence on an indefensible theory of ideas.

HUME'S SCEPTICAL DOUBTS CONCERNING INDUCTION (MILLICAN)

The fifth aim of this volume is to clarify the interpretation of Hume's own thoughts as expressed in the *Enquiry*, by reference to appropriate scholarly and philosophical considerations. This implies a combination of both historical and philosophical perspectives, which indeed is shown in most of the papers in the collection, albeit in very different proportions according to their subject-matter (from Stewart's at one extreme, to Bennett's at the other). No significant interpretative issues arise in the short Section III of the *Enquiry*, and nor does it contain anything of great philosophical interest.[4] So the next essay in the collection moves straight on to Section IV, and to Hume's most famous argument, for the conclusion that factual inference to the unobserved, now generally called *induction*, 'is not founded on reason'. The interpretation of this conclusion is highly controversial, and has profound implications for the understanding of Hume's philosophy as a whole. The principal aim of my paper (Chapter 4) is therefore interpretative, but much of it is devoted to teasing out the logical structure of Hume's reasoning, which strongly constrains the range of plausible

---

[4] However, the principles of association will merit discussion in the context of Hume's theory of belief, as in the papers by Martin Bell and Justin Broackes (see below, pp. 176–80, 190–1). Looking ahead to the other two sections of the *Enquiry* which do not have essays devoted specifically to them, Section VI (on probability) is discussed in the two papers on miracles, by Don Garrett and David Owen (Chs. 11 and 12), while Section IX (on the reason of animals) is touched on both by Garrett and by my own paper in Chapter 4.

readings. In particular, I claim that his argument structure makes no sense if 'reason' is understood here in the deductivist way ascribed by most previous generations of commentators, and his argument seems equally incoherent if 'reason' is understood in what is now a more fashionable way, as our natural inferential faculty.[5] Instead my own favoured interpretation takes 'reason' to signify a supposed faculty of rational *perception*, taken for granted by almost all previous philosophers, but here undermined. Hume's famous argument thus turns out to be radically sceptical, in denying that any of our factual inferences to the unobserved are founded on any perception of evidential connexions. Instead, they are founded on 'custom', a non-rational instinct (introduced in Section V Part i), which leads us unreflectively to expect inductive uniformity, so that our presumed evidential connexions are 'read into the world' rather than being 'read off it' (a Copernican reversal intimately entwined with Hume's theory of causation). The paper then sketches how this 'Sceptical Solution' to Section IV's 'Sceptical Doubts' is able to provide the basis for an inductive science which can discriminate between good and bad factual reasoning: having identified the true foundation of such reasoning, consistency with that foundation then becomes the appropriate norm (and the Humean notion of 'reason' is accordingly reinterpreted). Thus, paradoxically, inductive scepticism paves the way for a thoroughly inductive Humean science.

Although most of the paper is closely focused on Hume's main argument of Section IV, other relatively self-standing topics discussed in particular sections, which may be useful for independent reference, include Descartes's and Locke's 'perceptual' view of reason (§2), Hume's notion of aprioricity (§4.1), the senses in which he is, and is not, a 'causal realist' (§9.2), and his understanding of 'reasoning concerning matter of fact' (§3.1) and of 'demonstration' (§7.1).

BELIEF AND INSTINCT IN HUME'S FIRST ENQUIRY (BELL)

The sixth and final aim of the collection is to identify and account for substantial changes between the *Treatise* and the *Enquiry*. This is of clear significance for the interpretation of both works, since it can shed light on Hume's motivation for including, or omitting, the relevant material. But it may be of particular additional interest to those many students and professional philosophers who

---

[5] This is the way in which 'reason' is interpreted by Don Garrett in his book *Cognition and Commitment in Hume's Philosophy* (Oxford: Oxford University Press, 1997), from which his paper on miracles in this volume (Ch. 11) is taken. That paper briefly outlines Garrett's view of Hume on induction and explains in detail how he takes it to fit with Hume's general epistemological stance. But to fill out his interpretation as an alternative to my own, he has developed the two most relevant sections from his book chapter entitled 'Reason and Induction' to provide an appendix to Chapter 11.

are already familiar with the *Treatise*, not least because such experience can make it very hard indeed to read the *Enquiry* with fresh eyes, and to keep in mind exactly what Hume has said there and what he has not. Martin Bell's essay (Chapter 5) bears on a central topic to which this particularly applies, namely Hume's theory of belief.

In the *Treatise* Hume's account of causal inference based on custom had given a unified answer to two different questions: why do such inferences lead to the particular beliefs that they do, and what is the nature of belief? In the *Enquiry*, however, the two issues are separated, with custom being dealt with in Section V Part i and Hume's theory of the nature of belief in Section V Part ii. Moreover the latter is explicitly bracketed, as being intended only for readers who 'love the abstract sciences' (*E* 47). Bell's paper seeks to explain these changes in a principled way (and thus implicitly contests the relatively crude hypothesis, espoused in my own Chapter 1, that Hume had simply lost confidence in the details of his associationist psychology and anyway now saw these details as relatively unimportant).

Hume's theory of belief in the *Treatise* centres on the conveying of force and vivacity from a present impression to an associated idea, through an associative relation set up by the observation of a constant conjunction. Thus his explanation of causal inference in terms of custom, and his account of the nature of belief in terms of the vivacity of ideas, go hand in hand. There is, however, a problem with the latter account, because causation is just one of three associative relations capable of conveying vivacity to ideas (the others being resemblance and contiguity, as at *E* 24), so if Hume's theory were correct, it would seem anomalous that of these three relations only causation can generate belief. Hume grapples with this problem in *Treatise* I. iii. 9, moving away somewhat from his initial simple definition of belief in terms of force and vivacity, and explaining how it involves the incorporation of ideas into two systems of *realities*, one involving ideas of the memory and senses, and the other involving ideas that arise from custom (*T* 108). In the Appendix to the *Treatise* (published with Book III in 1740) he dilutes still further his commitment to the 'force and vivacity' definition, describing belief as a *feeling* which 'I endeavour to explain by calling it a superior *force*, or *vivacity*, or *solidity* . . .', but which is in fact indefinable—it can be understood only by experiencing it, and 'its true and proper name is *belief*, which is a term that every one sufficiently understands in common life' (*T* 629). He reproduces this account, largely verbatim, in the *Enquiry* (*E* 48–50), and thus avoids his earlier problem since he is now able to assert, without implying any associationist anomalies, that we observe this feeling to arise only from causation (*E* 53–4). All this, however, leaves a theoretical gap, since there is no evident connexion between the indefinable feeling arising from custom, and what it is to conceive something as *really existing*.

Conception of this kind is automatically generated by the impressions of the memory and senses, and so the gap can be filled by re-emphasizing the link (present both in Hume's initial associative account, and in *Treatise* I. iii. 9) between belief and such impressions. Thus our instinctive tendency to ascribe reality to what we perceive (described later at *E* 151–2) provides a basis for explaining why our other fundamental instinct, to make inferences by custom, also issues in real belief (cf. *E* 45–6). However, the instinctive tendency to trust our senses cannot stand up to detailed critical scrutiny: as Hume discovers in *Treatise* I. iv. 2 and I. iv. 4 (echoed at *E* 151–5), deep analysis of our sensory beliefs leads to the conclusion that not only do they lack any ultimate rational foundation (just like our inductive beliefs), but more seriously, they are incoherent and therefore false. An unbelievable sceptical paradox such as this would be completely unhelpful to Hume's purposes in the *Enquiry*, particularly given his desire to make this work (unlike the *Treatise*) suitable for a general audience. Bell's suggestion is that this change in his literary aims explains Hume's reluctance to take his readers into the murky foundations of his theory of belief, and hence the bracketing of the second part of Section V.

HUME, BELIEF, AND PERSONAL IDENTITY (BROACKES)

Justin Broackes's essay (Chapter 6) also deals with Hume's theory of belief, but from a very different perspective. Where Bell sees Hume as bracketing the details of his theory for strategic reasons, to avoid getting into sceptical complications concerning the external world that would perplex and repel the general reader, Broackes sees the bracketing as a symptom of philosophical dissatisfaction arising from a continuing instability in the theory, largely due to Hume's difficulty of making it consistent with his views on personal identity and the ontological independence of perceptions. Thus both Bell and Broackes attribute key features of Hume's theory of belief to the lingering effect of sceptical theses developed in the *Treatise* but either downplayed in the *Enquiry* (as in the case of the external world) or omitted entirely (as in the case of personal identity).[6] In developing these claims, moreover, both papers examine interesting and important links between the *Treatise* and the *Enquiry*, many of which

---

[6] Along with personal identity, there is one other major sceptical argument that Hume drops from the *Enquiry*, namely, his radical 'scepticism with regard to reason' of *Treatise* I. iv. 1. In this case, however, there is clear evidence of his having changed his view of its significance, since at the beginning of *Enquiry* XII he dismisses such 'antecedent . . . universal doubt . . . of our very faculties' as incurably futile (*E* 149–50). Moreover, this sceptical argument never resurfaces in any other of Hume's writings (unlike the argument about personal identity, which is at least echoed at *D* 159, though without stressing any radical ontological implications).

have a significance far wider than the specific interpretations of Hume's theory of belief that they are here used to support.

Most of Broackes's paper is devoted to exploring a number of apparent inconsistencies in Hume's account of belief as it developed over time, and detects three distinct views competing for attention. Belief is variously defined as:

(A) a steady and vivid *idea*,
(B) a steady and vivid *conception of an idea*,
(C) a *feeling* (of steadiness and vivacity) annexed to an idea.

Of these only the first is entirely in the spirit of the theory of ideas, according to which the activity of the mind is determined purely by its contents, with these contents taking the form of 'perceptions'. But Hume freely combines this first view with both the second and the third, without ever explicitly acknowledging the tensions between them. One major pressure to renounce view (A) comes from the difficulty of accounting for belief as a mere variation in 'force and vivacity', where this is understood as the very same characteristic of perceptions that distinguishes impressions from ideas. View (B) provides far more flexibility, in allowing for variation along two dimensions—the level of vivacity of the perception itself, and the vivacity of the mind's conception of it (so now the mere contemplation of a very vivid idea can be clearly distinguished from the firm belief in a dull one). Often in the *Treatise* Hume expresses himself in a way that seems ambivalent between (A) and (B), though there is at least one passage (at *T* 105–6) that can be interpreted only in the latter way, and both seem to play a role in his thinking. However, in the Appendix to the *Treatise* and the *Enquiry*, view (C) comes to prominence (though (A) and (B) still remain in the background). (C) has its own difficulties, not least because the 'feeling' to which it refers should presumably itself be a perception of the mind, and yet Hume's arguments seem to rule out its being either an idea or an impression. In discussing these issues Hume seems to be driven back towards view (B), with the 'feeling' being interpreted not as an independent perception, but as an aspect of the mind's conception of the idea concerned.

Of the three views Broackes identifies, (A) and (C) seem subject to major objections of which Hume was at least to some extent aware, and his discussions of both seem to lead him in the direction of (B), which is philosophically by far the strongest. Why, then, did Hume not adopt (B) wholeheartedly, rather than continuing to vacillate between all three? Broackes suggests that what lies behind this is Hume's conviction in the ontological independence and self-sufficiency of perceptions, and his rejection of what he took to be the unacceptably Cartesian notion of a mind standing in distinct relation to, and thus separate from, the ideas which it conceives. If Broackes is right, then the discussion of belief in the *Enquiry* evinces Hume's continuing commitment, either consciously or unconsciously, to some major metaphysical themes of the *Treatise* that make no explicit appearance in the later work.[7]

THE IDEA OF NECESSARY CONNEXION (CRAIG)

With the three essays by Edward Craig, Galen Strawson, and Simon Blackburn we move on to the most prominent interpretative debate in recent Hume studies—whether Hume is, or is not, a 'causal realist'—presented from the point of view of three of its major participants. Craig's paper (Chapter 7) sets the scene for this debate by explaining the background and general shape of Hume's discussion of causation in *Enquiry* VII, but in doing so he develops a conception of Hume's purposes that fits very comfortably with the 'New Hume' favoured by Strawson and other proponents of the causal realist interpretation,[8] but far less comfortably with the 'positivist' Hume beloved of the twentieth-century analytic tradition.

The first chapter of Craig's book *The Mind of God and the Works of Man*[9] argues that the 'dominant philosophy' of the early modern period was the idea that man is made in the image of God and thus has a semi-divine status above nature rather than just part of it. The second chapter, from parts of which Craig's paper here has been adapted, then presents an interpretation of Hume's philosophy which takes this 'Image of God' doctrine to be his primary target. Although the doctrine can be seen as influencing thought over a wide range, including the philosophy of perception, action, and morality, its most significant impact was to inspire a rationalistic conception of human reason, viewing this as our pre-eminent faculty which radically distinguishes us from the animals and gives us a form of insight which in its essential nature, if not its extent, approximates to the transparent perception attributed to God. The prevalence of such a conception can explain why intuition and

---

[7] Bell's and Broackes's discussions, along with my own Chapter 1, thus present three quite different perspectives on the differences between the *Treatise* and the *Enquiry*, focusing on belief and its relation to scepticism. Bell sees the changes as primarily strategic, to avoid leading Hume's intended audience down paths that they would find uncongenial and off-putting. Broackes too sees the underlying fundamentals as broadly the same in both works, though suggesting that Hume has lost confidence in the details of his theory of belief without being able to correct it. I see the *Enquiry* as fundamentally different in orientation from the *Treatise*, so that the details of that theory cease to matter, and I also speculate (in n. 37) that Hume's underlying metaphysics may have radically changed through loss of commitment to his Separability Principle. All three papers make clear why interpretative controversies such as these can only properly be approached in the context of an overall understanding of Hume's intentions.

[8] Another who deserves particular mention alongside Craig and Strawson is John Wright, whose book *The Sceptical Realism of David Hume* (Manchester: Manchester University Press, 1983), ch. 4, first brought the 'sceptical realist' interpretation of Hume to prominence.

[9] (Oxford: Clarendon Press, 1987).

demonstration—the most plausible examples of transparent rational perception—were so widely taken to be the paradigms of reason's activity, and this, Craig suggests, somewhat justifies a tendency on Hume's part to view reason in a 'deductivist' manner (a tendency commonly attributed to him, though contested in my own Chapter 4, as remarked above).[10]

Against this background Craig sees Hume's main concern in Section VII as being unambiguously epistemological, to undermine the rationalist claim that our reason gives us insight into causal relations, and to replace this with a naturalistic conception of causal reasoning based on the instinctive associative mechanisms of the 'imagination'. This has the implication that the real point of most of Hume's arguments is to re-emphasize the conclusions of Sections IV and V, even though his investigation is here superficially presented very differently, not as an enquiry into the foundation of our causal inferences, but instead as an analytical quest into the origin (and hence the nature) of our idea of necessary connexion. Ostensibly this analytic strand may indeed dominate, but in practice epistemology plays the major role, as becomes evident from the examination of Hume's arguments at E 63–9, where he considers and rejects in turn a variety of possible sources for the idea in question. In each case Hume's form of argument is the same: some impression is proposed as the source of our idea of necessity (in accordance with his Copy Principle), but that impression is then summarily rejected on the ground that it cannot yield a priori knowledge of the resulting effect. But despite the confidence with which Hume repeatedly wields this argument, its basis is extremely unclear, for Hume nowhere explains why he feels entitled to assume that a perception can count as an impression of necessary connexion only if it is such as to sanction an a priori causal inference. Even more confusing, when Hume eventually discovers, at E 75, what he takes to be the genuine impression of necessary connexion (namely, the 'customary transition of the imagination from one object to its usual attendant'), it apparently itself falls foul of the very 'aprioricity' criterion which he has used to dismiss all other contenders, though he mysteriously completely fails to remark on this.[11] Craig sees this 'muddle' as symptomatic of a general confusion

---

[10] Craig's thesis that the dominant notion of reason was modelled on the ideal of divine insight can stand independently of his suggestion regarding Hume's deductivist tendency. Although the thesis is obviously weakened to some extent if rational insight is allowed to be fallible (and hence less plausibly Godlike), it could potentially derive strong support from evidence for the ubiquity of the Image of God doctrine in other fields, such as Craig provides in the first chapter of his book. There is much interesting work waiting to be done on the historical development of the concept of reason since ancient times, and the extent to which it was affected at different periods by religious thinking.

[11] Since this is one of the most perplexing pieces of argumentation in the entire *Enquiry*, it is worth noting that there are possible rationalizations which might reduce the impression of confusion (Blackburn also makes some relevant comments, mentioned later). For example, perhaps Hume is taking for granted that the impression of necessary connexion must be an impression of *connexion*, and must therefore provide some link between 'cause' and 'effect' (cf. E 77 n.). No such link is perceivable in

between analysis and epistemology, resulting from a partly unrecognized conflict between, on the one hand, a conventional Lockean emphasis on the nature and origin of our ideas (which initially encouraged Hume to present his work as building on the theory of ideas) and, on the other hand, Hume's own far more fundamentally sceptical interests (which repeatedly led him to give his overtly analytical arguments an underlying epistemological thrust).

Hume's discussion of the idea of necessary connexion is rounded off with two 'definitions of cause', in which he has traditionally been understood to be spelling out the nature of the idea of cause (and hence the meaning of the word 'cause') by reference to the impression of necessary connexion which he has finally tracked down. The two definitions, which seem to define causation in objects as mere regularity, have long been a source of interpretative debate because they do not seem to be equivalent, and this apparent confusion provides further grist for Craig's mill. The final part of his paper, in line with his general theme, challenges the assumption that Hume's notion of a definition is to be understood in the traditional analytical manner, and argues that the two 'definitions' are best seen instead as attempts to specify the conditions under which a belief in a causal connexion arises, with 'one concentrating on the outward situation, the other on the state of the believer's mind that those outward facts induce' (p. 227). Hume's definitions thus amount to a summing up of his discussion of the epistemology of causation rather than the outcome of a piece of conceptual analysis, even though his explicit approach to the problem via his theory of ideas might naturally lead a modern reader to expect the latter. Craig concludes his paper by hinting that this lesson applies more generally: even when Hume makes claims in explicit analytical or ontological language, it is often more illuminating to read these claims epistemologically because that is where his true interests lie. So when he presents his definitions of 'cause', or states that the self is a bundle of perceptions (another example explored in detail in Craig's book), these are best read not as claims about what 'cause' *means*, or what selves *really are*, but instead as claims about causes, or selves, 'so far as [these] can concern, or be known to, or pointfully investigated by, the human mind' (p. 228). It is this point of view which underlies the interpretation of Hume as a 'sceptical realist'.

any one instance, and the point of Hume's 'aprioricity' criterion may be to *prove* this, on the ground that perception can give no certain knowledge of causal relations. (This supposed 'proof' appears to rest on the assumption that a priori or perceptual evidence should yield certainty if it yields any link whatever, but ascription of such an assumption to Hume is not gratuitous for it seems to play a role in his argument concerning induction.) Thus the crucial difference with Hume's own candidate for the impression of necessity would be that it arises from experienced repetition (*E* 74–6) and is in that sense a posteriori. It is able to confer the required link between 'cause' and 'effect' by reference to this past experience, and hence is absolved from any need to pass the 'aprioricity' criterion.

DAVID HUME: OBJECTS AND POWER (STRAWSON)

Galen Strawson's paper (Chapter 8) is a forthright presentation of the 'New Hume' sceptical realist interpretation, marshalling the relevant arguments from his book *The Secret Connexion*[12] with a particular focus on the *Enquiry*, which Strawson takes to be both Hume's authoritative statement, and far more clearly committed to causal realism than the *Treatise*. Strawson has also added some responses to criticisms of his book made in Blackburn's paper in this volume, so that the two papers together give a good understanding of the ongoing debate surrounding this contentious issue.

Strawson begins from the kind of distinction emphasized by Craig, between an epistemological claim:

(E) All we can ever know of causation is regular succession,

which Hume accepts, and a positive ontological claim:

(O) All that causation actually is, in the objects, is regular succession,

which is easily confused with the former, but which Strawson takes Hume to deny. He therefore ascribes to Hume a belief in some form of causation in objects which is more than regular succession (capitalized 'Causation' for short). Hume has traditionally been presumed to make the move from (E) to (O) by means of the theory of ideas, but Strawson, like Craig, casts doubt on this, adding some new points to those already considered above. He starts by arguing that a definite claim such as (O) is 'violently at odds with Hume's scepticism . . . with respect to knowledge claims' (p. 236). The *denial* of (O) might also seem to conflict with scepticism, but Strawson points out that this only applies if the denial is a claim to *knowledge*: there is no inconsistency in a 'strict sceptic' supposing that we have a 'natural belief' in Causation which falls short of knowledge.

Strawson then proceeds to take on the traditional assumption that as far as Hume is concerned, the theory of ideas renders the notion of Causation unintelligible (and therefore incoherent and unrealizable) because there is no impression from which any such idea could be derived. Here Strawson invokes a notion from Hume's discussion of the idea of external existence (*Treatise* I. ii. 6) to argue that his principles allow us to have a 'relative idea' of Causation as 'that in reality in virtue of which reality is regular in the way that it is' (p. 240). Such 'relative ideas', Strawson suggests, fall short of the 'positively contentful' ideas that are copies of impressions, but they have the considerable virtue of

---

[12] (Oxford: Clarendon Press, 1989).

being able to succeed in referring without the requirement for any correspond-ing impression to give them content. Thus Hume is able to maintain a belief involving the relative idea of 'Causation in objects' without there being an impression of any such thing. On this interpretation, therefore, his investiga-tion into the idea of 'cause' in *Enquiry* VII, with its accompanying search for the impression from which that idea is derived, does not give an analysis of what we mean by 'cause', but simply shows that our idea of it as something in objects is 'merely relative' rather than 'positively contentful'.

Strawson also presents a selection of quotations from the *Enquiry* and the *Dialogues* to illustrate his claim that Hume is in fact a believer in Causation. Though many of these are controversial in detail,[13] they together add up to a very substantial case for supposing that Hume believes in some sort of 'hidden powers'—powers that exist but of which we are ignorant—and Strawson argues strongly that such powers cannot be interpreted as mere undiscovered regular-ities, but must involve Causation that outruns regular succession. He finds par-ticular support for this view in Hume's comments on his two definitions of cause, where he describes our causal ideas as 'so imperfect . . . that it is impos-sible to give any just definition of *cause*, except what is drawn from something extraneous and foreign to it' (*E* 76), and goes on to imply that the specific nature of this 'inconvenience' is that the definitions cannot 'point out that circum-stance in the cause, which gives it a connexion with its effect' (*E* 77). Appealing both to Craig's discussion of the definitions, and to a contemporary treatise by Burke, Strawson interprets Hume's definitions not as any sort of attempt to give the *meaning* of 'cause', but rather as a record of 'human understanding's best take on . . . the nature of the phenomenon' (p. 255).

To sum up, Strawson's strategy can be seen as falling into two parts. First, he aims to weaken the case for the traditional interpretation by casting doubt on Hume's strict adherence to the theory of ideas which seems to make the idea of Causation impossible. Part of this weakening involves appeal to a theory of 'relative' ideas which, though it does not appear in the *Enquiry*, has the merit of having played a parallel role in the *Treatise* in regard to the belief in external objects. The second part of Strawson's strategy is then to produce evidence, both from the nature of Hume's scepticism and from the particular passages in which he expresses it, to indicate that he was in fact a believer in Causation. Before making a brief further comment on this overall case, I shall consider a paper whose main object is to oppose it.

---

[13] Those from *Enquiry* IV and V are particularly disputable because of the footnote at *E* 33 n., as explained in §9.2 of Chapter 4, while those from the *Dialogues* can obviously be interpreted as express-ing only the views of Hume's characters rather than his own.

HUME ON THICK CONNEXIONS (BLACKBURN)

Simon Blackburn's paper (Chapter 9) is in direct response to Craig and Strawson, arguing that Hume is not a causal realist, though the position that Blackburn takes him to have espoused is not traditional positivism but rather a form of 'anti-realism' or 'quasi-realism' (the latter being the term that Blackburn coins for his own position as developed in his book *Essays in Quasi-Realism*[14] from which this paper is taken). On this account, the rejection of genuinely objective causal powers in objects, as traditionally ascribed to Hume, need not imply either the renouncing of causal language and thought, or its positivist redefinition in explicitly non-realist terms. Blackburn's quasi-realist instead aspires to continue speaking and thinking in much the same ways as the naive objectivist, but without presuming that such objectivist language presupposes a realist metaphysics. The quasi-realist project as a whole thus aims to vindicate our attachment to truth claims and factual language in a variety of fields (e.g. morality, intentionality, modality, and probability, as well as causation) where sceptical enquiry in a Humean spirit has cast doubt on their supposed metaphysical foundations.

Blackburn's first object of attack is the conception of 'relative' ideas attributed to Hume by Strawson (and, in his book, by Craig). He sees Hume as having a very dismissive view of such 'ideas', even in the context of Treatise I. ii. 6 where he invokes them, and as denying their ability to provide a notion of sufficient objectivity and perception-independence to ground realism. Strawson's paper responds at some length to this attack (pp. 243–5), and the points made on both sides illustrate the genuine difficulty of establishing on textual grounds even what the *Treatise* account of the relative idea of external existence amounts to, let alone how far Hume would have been prepared to deploy or develop a parallel account in the service of causal realism.

Blackburn then goes on to draw a distinction between two different notions of causal realism, which he thinks Strawson somewhat conflates under the single term 'Causation'. The first is the idea of a causal 'nexus' between two events, meaning some kind of dependency or connexion between them which is more than mere regular succession, and which makes it the case that when the first happens the second must follow. The second notion is that of a 'straitjacket', something which guarantees that the causal order of the universe will remain the same, so that the same causal nexuses which applied in the past will continue to apply in the future. Hume's argument concerning induction seems to distinguish clearly (at *E* 36–8) between a nexus and a straitjacket, showing how the supposition of 'secret powers' (i.e. hidden nexuses) behind our past observa-

---

[14] (Oxford: Oxford University Press, 1993).

tions does nothing to indicate that those powers will remain the same (i.e. does not provide a straitjacket). Nevertheless, Blackburn suggests that the distinction is in some respects unstable, and that some of the oddities of Hume's argumentation at E 63–9 in Section VII (earlier remarked on by Craig) may have arisen from his losing track of it in that context. But even if so, Hume's use of the nexus–straitjacket distinction in Section IV at least partially draws the sting of one argument which featured quite prominently in Strawson's book, that without Causation the uniformity of the universe would appear to be a 'pure fluke'. For it indicates that *nothing* could account for uniformity over time or (in Blackburn's words) 'smooth away inductive vertigo'—if this implies a continuing outrageous fluke, then it is one that, on Hume's principles, we are simply stuck with.[15]

Blackburn sees Hume's main interest in causation as being to refute the idea that we could ever apprehend a straitjacketing fact, or make any sense of what such a fact would be. It even seems dubious to attempt to form a 'relative' notion of such a fact, especially in the light of Hume's theory of abstract ideas which requires that we can form a general idea only if we have specific examples to build on. Blackburn is less hostile to the idea of a nexus, and sketches an account whereby such an idea, of a 'thick' connexion between events, could naturally arise when, after the observation of constant conjunctions, we come to make predictions on the assumption that those conjunctions will continue. He sees a close parallel here between Hume's views on causation and on morality—in each case, our apprehension of neutral facts arouses certain inclinations and passions, which we then have a tendency to objectify. Blackburn is therefore confident that attacks on causal anti-realism (e.g. the claim that it cannot account for our use of realist language) can be deflected by responses that are already familiar from the moral sphere. He ends by suggesting that the loss of realism about causation is far less serious than might be expected, for the inferential behaviour of a 'Bare Humean', who has no such belief, could be effectively indistinguishable from that of the rest of us.

The debate between Craig, Strawson, and Blackburn has brought to light many interesting points about Hume's theory of causation, and will enrich the understanding of anyone who studies it. But the gladiatorial context of the Strawson–Blackburn confrontation in particular can be misleading, masking a number of important respects in which their positions need not be so very far apart. Strawson emphasizes Hume's commitment to powers and forces in nature of which we are ignorant, and draws the conclusion that he is a causal

---

[15] In his paper Strawson acknowledges that Causation cannot play the role of soothing inductive vertigo (n. 36), though apparently he still sees it as explaining regularities and thus reducing the 'fluke' which a regularity account would imply (cf. n. 33 and 35).

realist. Blackburn sees causal realism as typically involving a commitment to the dubious notion of a 'straitjacket', unequivocally rejected by Hume, but sees him as comfortable with a 'nexus' between events if this is interpreted as a quasi-realist objectification of our inferential practices. However Strawson appears to agree that a straitjacket is not to be had, and fully recognizes Hume's insistence that our only 'positively contentful' idea of causation is derived from our tendency to make inductive inferences. Meanwhile Blackburn would surely be happy to allow (cf. his note 14) that the quasi-realist account which he favours must, if it is to reflect Hume's repeated endorsements of Newtonian science, accommodate the idea of *quantitative* powers and forces in nature which are at least in some sense 'out there to be discovered' (as, for example, when we experiment to find out 'whether the force of a body in motion be as its velocity, or the square of its velocity'; *E* 77 n.). 'Where then, cry I to both these antagonists, is the subject of your dispute?' (*D* 218). Maybe this debate can be largely resolved, while accommodating the insights of both sides, by paying due regard to the intended role of Hume's notion of force, power, or necessity within quantitative empirical science (for a sketch along these lines, and some relevant quotations, see §9.2 of Chapter 4, in which I discuss *Enquiry* IV, a section whose true relevance to this debate has perhaps not been sufficiently explored).

HUME ON LIBERTY AND NECESSITY (BOTTERILL)

George Botterill's essay (Chapter 10) turns to Section VIII of the *Enquiry*, and aims to clarify the arguments presented in that section, to distinguish them clearly from those in the corresponding section of the *Treatise*, and to set the record straight regarding Hume's contribution to the 'compatibilist' tradition. Philosophers in this tradition, since Hobbes, have argued for the compatibility of the *Principle of Determinism* (Hume's 'doctrine of necessity', that all events are entirely the result of prior causes) with the *Free Will Assumption* (Hume's 'doctrine of liberty', that people have the capacity to act freely and are therefore morally responsible for their actions). The most popular argument for their compatibility has been the *Contrastive Argument*, which maintains that although the concept of freedom indeed involves a contrast between actions that are freely performed and those that are not, nevertheless the contrast here is not the same as that between free actions and *caused* ones, and hence there is no contradiction between causation and freedom. One of Botterill's principal conclusions is that Hume does not himself advance this Contrastive Argument, although he has frequently been misrepresented as doing so, not least by fellow members of the compatibilist tradition.

Botterill begins, however, with the differences between Hume's accounts of 'liberty and necessity' in *Treatise* II. iii. 1–2 and in *Enquiry* VIII. What he calls the 'striking difference' is that in the *Treatise* Hume advocates the 'doctrine of necessity' and denies the 'doctrine of liberty', whereas in the *Enquiry* he presents an overtly compatibilist 'reconciling project' to unite the two. But behind this difference lie deeper similarities, the first of which is that in pressing the case for the doctrine of necessity, in both works, his account of the idea of necessity (from *Treatise* I. iii. 14 and *Enquiry* VII) plays a starring role, which Hume sees as his most distinctive contribution to the issue.[16] This account implies that we have no notion of necessity beyond observed regularity and our tendency to make inferences accordingly; but both regularity and inference, Hume argues, are as applicable to human affairs as they are to the physical world. Hence when we encounter what appear to be irregularities in people's behaviour, we should attribute these to 'the secret operation of contrary causes' (*E* 87), just as we would with irregularities in the behaviour of physical objects. Botterill draws attention to a number of problems with Hume's arguments for the doctrine of necessity, perhaps the most serious of which arise from his apparent wish to establish that the doctrine applies in particular to the connexion between motives and actions. Such *psychological determinism* seems to rule out the secret operation of purely *physical* causes in determining our behaviour, and hence falls far short of what could reasonably be established by any analogy between physical science and human affairs.[17]

Fortunately the deficiencies in Hume's arguments for the doctrine of necessity do not undermine his contribution to compatibilism, for a compatibilist need not be committed to the truth of determinism. Moving on, then, to the 'doctrine of liberty', Botterill notes that the 'striking difference' between the *Treatise* and the *Enquiry* is more apparent than real, since in the former Hume takes the doctrine to imply that our actions are uncaused—Botterill calls this liberty₁—whereas in the latter he interprets the doctrine as stating that we have *'a power of acting or not acting, according to the determinations of the will'* (*E* 95)—liberty₂. Both of these are to be distinguished from liberty₃, the absence of unwelcome restrictions affecting our choice of action, which in the *Treatise* Hume refers to as 'liberty of *spontaneity* . . . the most common sense of the word; and [the only] species of liberty, which it concerns us to preserve'

---

[16] This role is not mentioned in the discussion of Hume's causal realism above, nor in any of the three papers devoted to that topic, though it is arguable (Ch. 1, pp. 58–9) that it provides a crucial motivation for his discussion of the idea of necessity, and in particular for his desire to encapsulate the results of that discussion in the two definitions of 'cause'.

[17] Hume certainly does not rule out the impact of physical causes in determining our behaviour, and to this extent the term *psychological determinism* might seem infelicitous: 'A person of an obliging disposition gives a peevish answer: But he has the toothake, or has not dined.' (*E* 88). But when Hume goes on to say that 'the conjunction between motives and voluntary actions is as regular and uniform, as that between the cause and effect in any part of nature', he seems to be implying that physical causes can have such an impact only indirectly, in virtue of affecting our motives.

(T 407–8). In both works Hume's view, if not the language in which he expresses it, is much the same. As we have seen, he denies that we have liberty$_1$ (which in the *Treatise* he calls 'liberty of *indifference*'), and he bolsters this denial with an important argument (T 410–12 and E 97–9) that such indifference, so far from being essential to morality, would actually be incompatible with it (hence morality presupposes the 'doctrine of necessity'). In the *Enquiry* Hume then points out that we clearly do have liberty$_2$, which 'is universally allowed to belong to every one, who is not a prisoner and in chains' (E 95), and he goes on to argue that this too is just as well, because liberty$_2$ is obviously essential to morality (E 99). Regarding liberty$_3$ Hume says very little in either work, and moreover its well-known mention in the *Treatise*, quoted above (and given far too much emphasis by commentators), occurs only in the context of alleging a confusion between it and liberty$_1$.

Summing up, Botterill finds virtually no evidence of the traditional Contrastive Argument in either the *Treatise* or the *Enquiry*, and this is to Hume's credit, for that argument typically involves a conflation between liberty$_2$ and liberty$_3$, whose difference from each other is at least as important as the distinction between liberty$_1$ and liberty$_3$ which the argument misleadingly emphasizes. Botterill sees Hume's emphasis, on the other hand, as being in exactly the right place, focusing on liberty$_2$ or intentional agency ('what it is about an agent in virtue of which he may be held responsible for his actions'), and arguing that this 'is not only consistent with those actions being caused, but actually requires them to be caused—by psychological states of the agent' (p. 299). It is this important argument, that causation is a necessary condition of responsible agency, which constitutes Hume's major, and very significant, contribution to compatibilism.

HUME ON TESTIMONY CONCERNING MIRACLES (GARRETT)

Don Garrett's essay (Chapter 11) is an adapted chapter from his book *Cognition and Commitment in Hume's Philosophy*.[18] It conforms to the general strategy which Garrett follows in that book, of identifying difficulties and controversial issues in the interpretation of Hume, and then giving his own account of how they are to be resolved. Such an approach is particularly helpful in relation to Section X of the *Enquiry*, for here Hume's arguments are more than usually subject to misunderstanding, not so much because of any special lack of clarity in his writing, but rather because of a perceived fundamental clash between his

---

[18]   (Oxford: Oxford University Press, 1997), ch. 7.

basic philosophical principles and his case against the credibility of miracles. The clash centres on Hume's attitude to induction and probability, which in *Enquiry* IV is denied any basis in reason, but then in Section X is apparently appealed to as a touchstone of reasonableness. Garrett's interpretation of Hume has the great merit of being able to resolve this clash, and so his paper can usefully be seen not only as a clarification of Hume's views on miracles, but also as a spelling out of an alternative position on induction to that developed in my own paper on Section IV.[19]

Garrett identifies six 'apparent inconsistencies' in Hume's discussion of miracles. The first concerns the meaning of 'experience', which sometimes seems to be restricted to that of an individual, but sometimes seems to include reported experiences of others. The second involves Hume's references to 'laws of nature', which are hard to interpret in a way that makes sense of his argument. The third casts doubt on the basis of the distinction between the 'miraculous' and the merely 'marvellous', which Hume uses to rebut a potential objection. The fourth concerns the difficulty of reconciling his talk of 'superior proofs' and 'greater miracles' with passages in which 'proofs' and 'miracles' appear to be defined by reference to an absolute standard. The fifth draws attention to Hume's talk of the 'absolute impossibility' of miracles, which seems hard to square with his views on induction and causation. The sixth and final apparent inconsistency is the most fundamental—having denied that the uniformity of nature has any basis in reason, how can Hume then rely on it to argue against the credibility of miracles?

Garrett's responses to these six difficulties are conveniently collected together near the end of his paper, and it would be inappropriate here to attempt to summarize what effectively amounts to a sophisticated working out of Hume's norms of inductive reasoning. Garrett's intervening discussion covers most of the principal arguments of *Enquiry* X, and although his main emphasis is on Part i, where most of the controversial issues arise, he also usefully outlines the so-called 'a posteriori' arguments of Part ii. Throughout, his focus is on the interpretation of Hume, but the position that emerges is epistemologically rich, and suggestive of further reflections on the central notion of probability. Garrett ends by drawing attention to the most obvious direction that such further reflections might take, towards Bayesian considerations of the sort that provide the topic of the next paper.

[19] To provide further background for this alternative view, an appendix to Garrett's paper contains a development of the two sections from *Cognition and Commitment in Hume's Philosophy*, ch. 4, where he presents his own position on induction (most of the rest of that chapter is concerned with the criticism of others' views, mainly the 'deductivist' and 'anti-deductivist' interpretations on which he and I very largely agree, and which are dealt with in a very similar spirit in Chapter 4 of this volume).

HUME VERSUS PRICE ON MIRACLES AND PRIOR PROBABILITIES (OWEN)

David Owen's essay (Chapter 12) examines Hume's argument concerning miracles in a Bayesian light, and finds in the contemporary objections of Richard Price a fascinating anticipation of modern discussions of probability and evidence. Although the paper is not seriously technical, some readers might find it helpful to begin with a brief explanation of Bayes's Theorem.

Suppose that we are considering whether some hypothesis H is true, and that prior to our investigation we take the view that its probability is 0.2—this we call its *prior probability*, and represent by the symbol $P(H)$. We then observe some evidence E which bears on H, and wish to establish what impact that evidence has on the probability of H itself. In order to assess this, we need to have some idea of whether the truth of H would make the occurrence of E more, or less, probable. So let us suppose, for the sake of the illustration, that E has a 0.9 probability of occurring if H is true, but only a 0.1 probability of occurring if H is false; this seems to imply that observation of E should substantially raise the probability of H. But by how much? The answer is given by Bayes's Theorem. Representing the *conditional probability that H is true given that E is true* by the symbol $P(H \mid E)$, and the other conditional probabilities correspondingly, we have:[20]

$$P(H \mid E) = \frac{P(H) \times P(E \mid H)}{P(H) \times P(E \mid H) + P(\neg H) \times P(E \mid \neg H)}$$

and substituting: $\quad P(H \mid E) = \dfrac{0.2 \times 0.9}{0.2 \times 0.9 + 0.8 \times 0.1} = 0.69.$

Here an initially improbable hypothesis has been rendered probable through the observation of strongly supporting evidence.

Interpreted in a straightforward Bayesian manner, Hume's argument in Section X Part i claims that the prior probability of any miracle is so low (because it is by definition a violation of a law of nature) that no testimonial evidence could possibly raise its probability above 0.5. Owen gives some illustrations to show that this interpretation is indeed in the spirit of Hume's argument, and broadly yields what he would presumably have seen as appropriate results. The essence of the argument, therefore, is to emphasize the impact of prior probabilities on the assessment of evidence: the more unlikely the hypothesis,

---

[20]   The formula is less fearsome than it looks, for its numerator simply represents the prior probability that *both H and E* are true, while the denominator represents the prior probability that *E* is true. Intuitively this makes sense, because what we seek is the probability that the actual state of affairs lies within the 'logical space' in which *both H and E* are true, *given that* we know it to lie within the 'logical space' in which *E* is true.

the stronger the evidence must be to establish it. Understood in this way, miracles simply provide a limiting case, in which the hypothesis is maximally unlikely, so that the demands on the evidence cannot be met.

All this might be suspected of anachronism, but in fact Bayes's Theorem was known in Hume's lifetime, and the contemporary objections of Richard Price bear a striking resemblance to points made by Jonathan Cohen in a fairly recent debate concerning the appropriateness of using Bayes's Theorem in the assessment of testimony. Owen's discussion of Price's and Cohen's objections to Hume's Bayesian approach brings to light a number of important points, principal among these being a distinction between *credibility of testimony* on the one hand, and *reliability of the witnesses* on the other. The first of these represents the probability that an event occurred as reported, while the latter represents the probability that the event would be reported truly if it had occurred. Armed with this distinction, Owen defends Hume from Price and Cohen, and sets out to vindicate his argument concerning miracles as a powerful anticipation of modern work in probability theory and cognitive science.

RELIGION: THE USELESS HYPOTHESIS (GASKIN)

John Gaskin's well-known book *Hume's Philosophy of Religion*[21] provided a comprehensive treatment of Hume's writings on religion, but, given the enormous range of these writings, was able to devote relatively little space to the generally neglected Section XI of the *Enquiry*. In his essay here (Chapter 13) Gaskin fills this gap, both discussing the section in its relation to the rest of the *Enquiry* (Section X in particular), and examining its arguments in detail. He starts by explaining how Sections X and XI are to be read together as two complementary parts of a systematic attack on the Christian apologetic tradition, the first challenging the supposed validation through miracles of the specific Christian revelation, and the second undermining the most popular argument from *natural* theology (i.e. independent of revelation) for belief in a provident God. Gaskin shows that both of these targets were indeed flourishing in the eighteenth century, and for a long time before and since. He then goes on to discuss the significant connexions between Section XI and the other parts of the *Enquiry*, including Section I, which declares Hume's anti-theological purposes, Section IV, which establishes experience as our only guide to matter of fact, and Section XII, which rounds off his attack on natural theology by demolishing the a priori arguments for God's existence.

Section XI itself is focused on the revered Design Argument and is presented as a dialogue, no doubt to enable Hume to distance himself from his most

---

[21] (Basingstoke: Macmillan, 1978, 1988).

dangerous views. Gaskin divides the discussion into four main phases, of which the first is concerned with religious scepticism and toleration (a phase on which considerable biographical light is shed by Stewart's paper, Chapter 2). The second phase presents the main argument of the section—that it is illegitimate to argue first from the world to God and then back again, drawing new conclusions about the world beyond those that can be observed within it. The third phase deals with the effects of belief upon conduct, and adds more argument for religious toleration. The fourth and final phase brings what appears to be a fundamental objection to the Design Argument, that cause and effect relations can be identified only where two *species* of objects have been found conjoined, and hence no causal reasoning can apply in the unique case of the world and its supposed creation.

In his analysis of Hume's discussion Gaskin first concentrates on the epistemological arguments of phases two and four. Regarding the former, he agrees with Hume in emphasizing the unsolvability of the 'Inference Problem of Evil'—the problem of inferring a perfect God from a world which appears to be far from perfect. As Hume points out, this prevents the theist from arguing that the world requires the hypothesis of a perfectly good Creator, and then arguing back from the supposed perfect goodness of that Creator to conclude (for example) that the world must exhibit perfect justice in regions hitherto unknown. Gaskin also sees considerable force in the 'Unique Cause' objection which Hume puts forward in phase four, despite what might seem to be a modern counter-example to this, that modern physicists regularly discuss, and purport to draw rational conclusions about, a unique first event, namely the Big Bang. Gaskin suggests a distinction here between 'internal' and 'external' causes, where an internal cause such as the Big Bang is inferable through extrapolation from known regularities, whereas an external cause such as God is supposed to be entirely different from any known entity, and therefore cannot be so inferred.

Moving on to the practical arguments of phase three, Gaskin shows the close relationship between *Enquiry* XI and some of the central doctrines of the *Enquiry concerning the Principles of Morals* (he also makes frequent reference to the *Dialogues concerning Natural Religion*). He ends by stressing the important role of Section XI, and Hume's assault on natural theology, in his philosophy as a whole. So far from being (as some have claimed) a mischievous addition to the *Enquiry* of little philosophical relevance, Section XI is crucial to the work's practical focus and its revolutionary implications.

OF THE ACADEMICAL OR SCEPTICAL PHILOSOPHY (NORTON)

David Norton's essay (Chapter 14) provides a systematic commentary on Section XII of the *Enquiry*, explaining its themes and aims within the context of the interpretation of Hume's scepticism that he developed in his book *David Hume: Common-Sense Moralist, Sceptical Metaphysician.*[22] This interpretation sees Hume as a 'mitigated sceptic', favouring a moderate form of scepticism associated with the later philosophers of Plato's Academy (so-called 'academic scepticism').

Hume's discussion proceeds through a survey of various different forms of scepticism. His first distinction is between *antecedent* and *consequent* scepticism, which depends on whether the doubts about our faculties arise in advance of any examination of their deliverances, or as a result of such an examination. Antecedent scepticism can come in either an extreme or a moderate form, and Hume dismisses the former (e.g. Cartesian) variety while expressing considerable sympathy with the latter. Moderate antecedent scepticism is useful for 'weaning our mind from . . . prejudices', and involves the sort of careful, reflective enquiry which alone can enable us to 'attain a proper stability and certainty in our determinations' (*E* 150).

Hume then considers various types of consequent scepticism, focusing first on those raising doubts about our senses, including two arguments taken from the *Treatise*. The first of these denies our ability to prove the existence of external objects resembling our perceptions, while the second indicates that our very concept of an external object possessing so-called 'primary qualities' (e.g. physical size and solidity) is dubiously coherent. In Part ii of Section XII Hume moves on to scepticism about our reasoning faculty, distinguishing between reasoning concerning abstract relations of ideas, and that concerning matter of fact and existence. Scepticism about abstract reasoning is mainly centred around the traditional problems of infinite divisibility, whereas scepticism about 'moral' reasoning (i.e. induction), at least in its stronger 'philosophical' form, involves Hume's own famous argument of Section IV. The weaker, 'popular', form of such scepticism (which Hume calls Pyrrhonian) is, however, dismissed as excessive and futile, producing no conviction and being easily overcome by the 'more powerful principles of our nature' (*E* 159). Even this excessive scepticism can leave a positive result, however, by moderating our inclination to be dogmatic and inspiring us 'with more modesty and reserve' as a consequence of our recognizing 'the strange infirmities of human understanding, even in its most perfect state' (*E* 161).

Part iii of Section XII goes on to develop further this positive aspect of the sceptical arguments, by suggesting that they can also inspire 'another species of *mitigated* scepticism, which may be of advantage to mankind', namely, 'the limitation of our enquiries to such subjects as are best adapted to the narrow capacity of human understanding' (*E* 162). It is not so much that this limitation is *supported by* the sceptical arguments, but rather that the arguments will tend to

---

[22] (Princeton: Princeton University Press, 1982).

bring it about by moderating our confidence, and thus changing the way we think. Indeed Norton sees this emphasis on the *causal*, rather than purely intellectual, impact of scepticism as being a significant theme in Hume's account. For although Hume (unlike Descartes) takes belief to be involuntary, and hence denies that the sceptical arguments can persuade us of their negative conclusions,[23] nevertheless he also (again unlike Descartes) sees doubt as compatible with belief, so that the incredibility of the sceptical arguments does not rule out their moderating the *nature* of our commitments. Doubt is voluntary even if belief is not, for the form of doubt that Hume advocates is not palpable uncertainty or suspension of belief, but *philosophical* doubt, a matter of attending to the counter-evidence and counter-arguments to what we believe, avoiding precipitate judgement, and taking note of our faculties' limitations. Such doubt does not attempt to destroy our belief, but to mitigate it, and for this reason Norton concludes that Hume's scepticism, unlike the extreme 'Pyrrhonian' varieties criticized in Section XII, is practically viable.

Norton rounds off his paper by linking Section XII of the *Enquiry* with the discussions in various earlier sections, notably IV, X, and XI, and in doing so he effectively sketches an overview of the *Enquiry* and its purposes which has important points of both similarity and difference with those presented in the initial two papers in this volume, by myself and Stewart (Chapters 1 and 2). Norton and I are apparently in agreement in viewing the work as having a greater underlying unity of philosophical purpose than Stewart suggests. But, like Stewart, Norton sees Hume's battle against intolerance as a primary theme of the work (a view which gains considerable circumstantial support from Stewart's historical investigations), whereas I lay more stress on Hume's desire to provide a *rational* basis for distinguishing inductive science from the pseudo-sciences of theology and rationalist metaphysics.[24] But perhaps after all such disagreements amount to no more than a difference in emphasis, for all three views undoubtedly contain a substantial element of truth, and what we have seen running right through this volume is an appreciation of the rich variety of themes and arguments that combine to make Hume's *Enquiry* such a rewarding and stimulating work.

[23] Here Norton emphasizes connexions between Hume's theory of belief and Section XII, which was also an important topic of Bell's paper (Ch. 5), though interestingly his emphasis was in the opposite direction.

[24] Hence I find significance both in Hume's contrasting attitudes to inductive and sensory scepticism, and also in the final flourish of Section XII, which seems prima facie to be problematic for Norton (though he suggests an attractively ingenious interpretation of it as a deliberately ironic response to religious intolerance).

The Context, Aims, and Structure of Hume's First *Enquiry*

Peter Millican

1. HUME'S PHILOSOPHICAL TARGETS

To interpret any philosopher's work appropriately, it is important to understand the concerns that motivate him: unless we have some appreciation of what views he is opposing, and thus what points he is most concerned to prove, it can be hard to distinguish between those claims that are central to his philosophy and those that he merely took for granted because they were not at the time significantly in dispute. A striking instance of the sort of anachronism that can result from a failure to see Hume in context was the tendency, common in the middle years of the twentieth century, to see his theory of meaning as the hub of his philosophy, when in fact it plays a fairly small role in most of his principal arguments (especially in his later works) and is anyway not particularly original. More recent work on Hume has moved away from this tendency to see him as a proto-linguistic philosopher, and it is no coincidence that his reputation as a thinker who deserves to be taken seriously in contemporary debate has correspondingly flourished. Hume's arguments indeed have considerable relevance for contemporary discussion in many areas from epistemology to ethics, but we must beware of assuming that his central interests correspond with those of any particular group of more recent philosophers, even when some of these philosophers (notably the logical positivists) have derived inspiration from him and claimed him as their spiritual father. One good way of avoiding such anachronistic assumptions is to see which thinkers Hume himself viewed as his principal targets.

Writing to Michael Ramsay in August 1737 while returning from France, where he had been working on his *Treatise of Human Nature* for three years, Hume offered his friend some advice on what he might usefully read in preparation for receiving the manuscript: 'le Recherche de la Verité of Pere Malebranche, the Principles of Human Knowledge by Dr Berkeley, some of the more metaphysical Articles of Bailes Dictionary; such as those [of] Zeno, & Spinoza. Des-Cartes Meditations would also be useful . . . These books will make you easily comprehend the metaphysical Parts of my Reasoning'.[1] We can add to these the highly influential work which provides the background both for George Berkeley's *Principles* and for a number of central arguments in the *Treatise*, namely John Locke's *Essay concerning Human Understanding*, to which Hume alludes in the *Treatise*, *Abstract*, and *Enquiry* more than to any other (I. xvii. n., 2 n., 35 n., 81 n., 157 n., A646, 648, E 7, 22 n., 56 n., 64 n., 73 n.). Thus we have five authors whose writings are particularly valuable for setting Hume's 'metaphysical' philosophy in context, namely the 'empiricists' Locke and Berkeley, the 'rationalists' René Descartes and Nicolas Malebranche, and the pious sceptic Pierre Bayle. The last of these we can here put on one side, because the undogmatic and unsystematic Bayle provided neither a stable target nor a solid base on which to build, and Hume used his famous *Dictionary* primarily as a secondary source (on the views of various sceptics, for example, and of Spinoza) and as a compendium of sceptical objections and paradoxes which could be used for attacking the dogmas of others.[2] As for Locke and Berkeley, there is truth in the traditional perception of Hume as their heir in the British empiricist tradition, most notably in that he took over from them, relatively uncritically, the framework of the 'theory of ideas' within which many of the arguments in the *Treatise*, and some in the *Enquiry*, are situated. He proceeded to draw conclusions from that framework very different from those that his predecessors would have countenanced, but nevertheless his philosophy remains far more in the spirit of Locke and Berkeley than it is in the spirit of Descartes and his disciple Malebranche. Hence it is to these 'rationalists' that we must turn to get a clearer view of Hume's primary targets.

Malebranche's influence on Hume was immense, no doubt owing to his enduring reputation in France where so much of the *Treatise* was written. Unfortunately, however, his writings are relatively little known in the English-speaking world, so here I shall focus exclusively on his mentor Descartes, whose *Meditations* provides perhaps the best single yardstick against which to measure the significance of Hume's work. There is insufficient space here for a detailed comparison of the two philosophers' views, but it is highly illuminating to put

---

[1] This letter, dated 26 Aug. 1737, is reproduced in the Textual Supplements to E. C. Mossner, *The Life of David Hume*, 2nd edn. (Oxford: Clarendon Press, 1980), 626–7.

[2] App. C to ch. 14 of N. Kemp Smith, *The Philosophy of David Hume* (London: Macmillan, 1941) provides a useful first point of reference for the influence of Bayle on Hume, mentioning both of the specific articles (on Zeno of Elea and Spinoza) that Hume recommends in his letter to Ramsay.

side by side, in summary form, a list of Descartes's principal claims in the *Meditations* and of Hume's (explicit or implicit) responses to them. Such a contrast makes very clear how radical was Hume's rejection of the whole Cartesian project, and sheds a great deal of light on his critical intentions. We can divide these claims and responses into three main groups:[3]

1.1 Hume versus Descartes on the Power of Reason

According to Descartes, (1) *we have an infallible faculty of clear and distinct perception* which, if properly exercised, (2) *is able to grasp various general causal principles a priori* and, moreover, (3) *can establish the essence of mind (namely, thinking) and of body (namely, extension) by pure intellectual insight*, yielding further and more specific (4) *a priori knowledge about the behaviour of minds and of physical things*. Through such clear and distinct perception our reason also (5) *can demonstrate from our ideas alone that God must exist*, and (6) *can prove with certainty the real existence of an external, physical world* consisting of extended objects. In all of these ways, (7) *reason can defeat scepticism*.

Hume totally disagrees: (1) *we cannot prove that any of our faculties is infallible*, while (2) *all of our knowledge of causation is based on experience and is therefore uncertain*. Also (3) *our understanding of the nature of mind and matter is entirely obscure*, providing no basis for inference about anything, and hence (4) *we can learn about the behaviour of mind and matter only through observation and experience*. Moreover, (5) *neither God nor anything else can be proved to exist a priori*, from our ideas alone (indeed we have good empirical grounds to deny the existence of any benevolent deity), while (6) *we have no good argument of any sort, a priori or empirical, to justify our (purely instinctive) belief in an external world*. Taking these points together, it is clear that (7) *scepticism cannot be defeated by reason*.

1.2 Hume versus Descartes on Mind, Reason, and Imagination

Descartes argues that (8) *the mind consists of immaterial substance*, and so (9) *can survive the body's death*. (10) *Pure reason is the mind's primary function*, but as the mind is non-material, (11) *reason is outside the realm of causal determination* which governs purely physical things, being (12) *a faculty of intellectual insight which fundamentally distinguishes us from the (purely mechanistic) animals*. (13)

---

[3] Most of these points are fully set out in the *Meditations* and the *Enquiry*, but there are a few exceptions. For the contrastive component of Descartes's claim (12), concerning the mechanistic status of animals, see for example his *Discourse on Method*, pt. 5. For Hume's responses (8) and (17), see the *Treatise of Human Nature* I. iv. 5 ('Of the Immateriality of the Soul') and I. iv. 6 ('Of Personal Identity') respectively, and for more on (8) and his response (9), see the posthumous essay 'Of the Immortality of the Soul' (which probably originated as part of the manuscript of the *Treatise* though if so it was excised prior to publication).

The faculty of imagination is distinct from reason, since it depends on the body. Though many of our ideas are derived from the imagination and the senses, (14) *the mind contains some purely intellectual 'innate' ideas such as those of God, mind and extension.* (15) *The workings of the intellect are transparent to introspection* and so (16) *the mind is better known than the body.* (17) *The 'self' revealed through introspection is an indivisible unity whose essence is simply to think.*

Hume again differs on every point: (8) *the notion of substance, let alone that of an immaterial substance, is confused,* and (9) *the mind cannot survive the body's death.* (10) *Very little if any of the mind's activity is governed by 'reason' in the Cartesian sense,* while most of what we call (12) *'reason' is essentially an animal instinct* which like everything else that we do is (11) *subject to causal determination.* In fact (13) *most of our 'reasoning' is based on the imagination,* while (14) *all of our ideas are ultimately derived from the senses.* (15) *The operations of the mind are based on many hidden causal mechanisms,* far less familiar to us than some of the relatively obvious physical interactions of bodies, and so (16) *the workings of the mind are if anything less well known than those of physical things.* (17) *Introspection reveals no simple and indivisible 'self', but only a bundle of perceptions.*

1.3 Hume versus Descartes on Belief and Volition

In his quest for certainty Descartes claims that (18) *I should not accept anything which is at all uncertain,* and thus presupposes that (19) *belief is a voluntary activity.* More generally, he uses the principle that (20) *the operations of the intellect are subject to the will* both to claim that (21) *God is not responsible for my false beliefs,* and also to argue (22) *that involuntary ideas must have external causes.* He accepts that some beliefs, namely those that are clear and distinct, compel his assent, but sees this as no problem on the ground that such (23) *assent-compulsion is a guarantee of truth.*

Hume's attitude to belief is entirely different, since he claims that as a general rule, (20) *the operations of the mind are not subject to the will,* and, in particular, (19) *belief is involuntary.* Because of this, (18) *I cannot avoid accepting many things that are uncertain,* and thus (23) *the fact that I am unable to doubt something is no guarantee of its truth.* As for ideas, (22) *an involuntary idea is no guarantee of an external cause.* But even if all belief and thought were entirely voluntary, still (21) *God could not escape responsibility for our cognitive (or indeed moral) errors,* since (11) *all that we do, and believe, is causally determined.*

1.4 The Core of Hume's Attack on Rationalism

If the central theme of Hume's attack on rationalism were to be encapsulated in one sentence it might be something like this: Hume, unlike Descartes and most of the other philosophers of the seventeenth and eighteenth centuries, sees man as just a part of the natural world, rather than as a semi-divine being quite different in kind from the animals. Such a theme can be discerned in most of Hume's philosophical writings, but it is particularly prominent in his epistemology, where he consistently attacks the idea that we have a Cartesian faculty of 'reason' which gives us a transparent and Godlike insight into the essence of things, and he displaces this rationalist picture with a naturalistic account of human thinking based mainly on instinct and the 'imagination'.[4]

This perspective on Hume is borne out by the catalogue of Cartesian claims and Humean responses listed above: in nearly every case Hume is either setting limits to our intellectual capabilities (implying in particular that we lack the sort of reliable 'clear and distinct perception' which Descartes presupposes), or else he is putting forward an account of man and his faculties which places them squarely within the natural world. For Hume, virtually all of our beliefs are based ultimately on irresistible animal instinct, which operates not on pure intellectual concepts but on the quasi-sensory impressions and ideas provided exclusively through experience by our physical organs. Our mind is not above nature but is part of it, being entirely dependent on our mortal body and causally determined like everything else, through many hidden mechanisms which again can be known only by experience. Of those instinctive mechanisms which supply our beliefs about the world, the most important is custom or habit, which leads us simple-mindedly to expect in the future patterns of events similar to those we have observed in the past, even though we can give no deeper rational account of those observations nor the slightest good reason for supposing that past correlations will continue. So our beliefs about both the behaviour of objects in the external world, and the operations of our own mind, are founded on a naive assumption of uniformity, a blind reliance on the past, rather than on any sort of supernatural insight into why things work as they do.

This, then, is the overall thrust of Hume's thought, with strong currents of anti-rationalism, naturalism, empiricism, and secularism very evident in most of his writings. But although this general picture is clear enough, the details of how his thought developed through his major philosophical works is far less clear and a source of significant controversy. So let us now turn to consider some of these works, and the relation between them.

2. *THE* TREATISE OF HUMAN NATURE

Hume's assault on the rationalist view of man opened with his first, and certainly his most famous, work: the *Treatise of Human Nature*, published in

---

[4] In the *Enquiry* Hume uses the faculty term 'imagination' relatively rarely, and focuses attention instead on 'custom', which he introduces in the *Treatise* as 'a principle of association . . . operating upon the imagination' (*T* 97, 103; cf. *E* 48). The crucial point emphasized in both works, however, is not custom's relationship to the *imagination*, but rather, that it is *not* a principle of *reason*.

1739–40. But it perhaps reached its climax in the *Enquiry concerning Human Understanding* (initially published in 1748 under the title *Philosophical Essays concerning Human Understanding*), a 'recasting' of the first part of the *Treatise* which is, I shall argue, a far more reliable indicator of Hume's mature position. Although our main concern here is indeed with the *Enquiry*, it is nevertheless appropriate to make some general comments about the *Treatise*, not least because this is commonly assumed to be Hume's definitive statement, and most writers on Hume have accordingly taken it as their principal source.

As Hume recounts in 'My Own Life' (paragraph 5), most of the *Treatise* was written while he was on 'retreat' at La Flèche in Anjou, where Descartes had studied more than a century earlier. Hume returned to Britain in 1737, and in due course published the completed *Treatise* anonymously in two parts, Book I 'Of the Understanding' and Book II 'Of the Passions' in January 1739, and Book III 'Of Morals' nearly two years later, in November 1740. The subtitle of the *Treatise* declares it to be 'an attempt to introduce the experimental method of reasoning into moral subjects', but we should note that when Hume speaks of 'moral' subjects or 'moral' philosophy, he is using the word not in its restricted modern sense (meaning morality, or ethics), but in its far wider eighteenth-century sense, meaning the study of man in general, and including not only 'morals' but also 'logic' (consisting mainly of what we would now call epistemology and psychology), 'politics' (political theory, economics, history, sociology) and 'criticism' (aesthetics). As Hume makes clear in the Introduction to the *Treatise*, however, he hopes that his investigation will have still wider implications, because 'all the sciences . . . Even *Mathematics, Natural Philosophy, and Natural Religion*, are in some measure dependent on the science of MAN; since they lie under the cognizance of men, and are judged of by their powers and faculties' (*T* xv). Hume therefore aims, in explaining 'the principles of human nature', to 'propose a compleat system of the sciences, built on a foundation almost entirely new' (*T* xvi). This foundation has four principal elements:

The sole end of logic is to explain the principles and operations of our reasoning faculty, and the nature of our ideas: morals and criticism regard our tastes and sentiments: and politics consider men as united in society, and dependent on each other. In these four sciences of *Logic, Morals, Criticism, and Politics*, is comprehended almost every thing, which it can any way import us to be acquainted with, or which can tend either to the improvement or ornament of the human mind. (*T* xv–xvi)

The three books of the *Treatise* are intended to lay the foundations for the first two of these pillars of knowledge, with criticism and politics to follow in due course—the youthful Hume was certainly not lacking in ambition!

Hume's new science of man was to be distinguished from most of its predecessors by being thoroughly empirical ('experimental')—based on 'experience and observation' (*T* xvi) rather than on metaphysical argument or speculations about the 'ultimate original qualities of human nature' (*T* xvii). Hume's dismissal of such 'conjectures and hypotheses' (*T* xviii) in favour of the empirical method clearly echoes Newton's famous dictum 'hypotheses non fingo' ('I feign no hypotheses'), and indeed the whole tenor of the Introduction to the *Treatise* suggests that Hume wishes to see himself as the Newton of the moral sciences.[5] The *Treatise*, then, is intended to be an empirical investigation into the workings of the human mind: its cognitive faculty (or 'understanding') in Book I, its non-moral 'passions' in Book II, and its 'moral sense' in Book III.

In view of these stated aims, Hume's prodigious philosophical talents, and the primitive state of psychological theory, it is not surprising that the *Treatise* contains a liberal mixture of sophisticated philosophical argument and relatively crude psychological explanation. Most of Hume's accounts of human thinking revolve around the association of ideas, a grand unifying theme which was initially a source of pride but later perhaps a mild embarrassment. We can judge Hume's early high opinion of this aspect of his performance from the fascinating *Abstract* of the *Treatise* (outlined in §7 below), which he published anonymously in March 1740 in an attempt to provoke interest and boost sales: 'Thro' this whole book, there are great pretensions to new discoveries in philosophy; but if any thing can intitle the author to so glorious a name as that of an *inventor*, 'tis the use he makes of the principle of the association of ideas, which enters into most of his philosophy.' (*A* 661–2).[6] Our opinion today is unlikely to tally with this—the psychological explanations in the *Treatise* are often just too crude to be convincing, while Hume's efforts to force others into the straitjacket of associationism make them appear tortuous and contrived. By contrast Hume's philosophical arguments, many of which were to be repeated and developed in the *Enquiry* (and will therefore be discussed below), are highly original, deep, stimulating, and extremely wide-ranging, combining to make the *Treatise* a magnificent contribution to philosophy if not to psychology. In Book I alone Hume deals with the nature and origin of ideas in general and the ideas of space and time in particular, knowledge and belief, probability,

---

[5] For a discussion of the methodological principles that Hume may have drawn from his understanding of Newton, see J. Noxon, *Hume's Philosophical Development* (Oxford: Clarendon Press, 1973), which also contains a very interesting examination of the development of Hume's thought after the *Treatise*. For more recent scholarship on Hume's knowledge of the contemporary scientific culture, emphasizing influences other than Newton, see M. Barfoot, 'Hume and the Culture of Science in the Early Eighteenth Century', in M. A. Stewart (ed.), *Studies in the Philosophy of the Scottish Enlightenment* (Oxford: Clarendon Press, 1990), 151–90.

[6] In a famous passage in the *Treatise* itself which again reveals his Newtonian ambitions, Hume compares the association of ideas with gravitation, suggesting a close analogy between his own theory of the mind and Newtonian physical science: 'Here is a kind of ATTRACTION, which in the mental world will be found to have as extraordinary effects as in the natural . . .' (*T* 12–13; cf. *T* 289).

causation, perception, personal identity, and several varieties of scepticism, while his discussions of many of these topics are more thorough and sophisticated than any that had previously been given. For all its flaws, Hume's *Treatise of Human Nature* is unquestionably a masterpiece.

3. HUME AND RELIGION

Although the *Treatise* contains a great deal, it was originally intended to contain yet more. Writing to his friend Henry Home, later Lord Kames, in December 1737, Hume states that 'I am at present castrating my work, that is, cutting off its nobler parts, that is, endeavouring it shall give as little offence as possible, before which, I could not pretend to put it into the Doctor's [Joseph Butler's] hands.' *(HL* i. 25). It is not known exactly which 'nobler parts' Hume removed from the *Treatise*, though these almost certainly included 'some *Reasonings concerning Miracles*' mentioned in the same letter (presumably an earlier version of Section X of the *Enquiry*), and probably also a sceptical discussion of the immortality of the soul (the topic of a 1755 essay which was prudently withdrawn from publication and eventually appeared posthumously).[7] It seems that Hume, either in the hope of winning Butler's good opinion or for other prudential reasons (e.g. to avoid the risk of prosecution for heresy or criminal blasphemy), removed those sections of the *Treatise* that were most explicitly sceptical about religious topics, but his interest in religion can still be discerned in what remains. In the Introduction (*T* xv), for example, Hume singles out 'Natural Religion' (the 'science' that aims to prove God's existence from nature and reason alone, without resort to revelation) as a subject which might be particularly improved using the results of his science of man. And many later sections of the *Treatise* have very clear sceptical implications both for the traditional theistic arguments[8] and for various Christian doctrines such as transubstantiation, the immortality of the soul, and the goodness of God.[9]

---

[7] J. C. A. Gaskin (*Hume's Philosophy of Religion*, 2nd edn. (Basingstoke: Macmillan, 1988), 170, 182) gives strong grounds for the conjecture that the manuscript of *Treatise* I. iv. 5, 'Of the immateriality of the soul', originally contained arguments that were to appear in the essay 'Of the immortality of the soul'.

[8] *Treatise* I. ii. 6 and I. iii. 7 anticipate Kant's famous objection to the Ontological Argument that 'existence is not a predicate'. I. iii. 3 undercuts the Cosmological Argument by denying that the Causal Maxim is demonstratively certain. I. iii. 6 lays the foundation for Hume's devastating critique of the Design Argument in *Enquiry* XI and in the *Dialogues concerning Natural Religion*, since it implies that causes (e.g. the cause of order in the universe) can be known only by experience.

[9] *Treatise* I. iv. 3 attacks the theory of substance and accidents, the basis of the Roman Catholic doctrine of transubstantiation. I. iv. 5 and I. iv. 6 undermine the traditional notion of the soul, and thus the doctrine of its immortality. II. iii. 1 and II. iii. 2 have fatal consequences for the popular Free Will Defence to the Problem of Evil (as Hume later spells out in *Enquiry* VIII). Finally the entire moral framework of Book III is naturalistically based on human 'sentiment', and as such repudiates the claim that morality is dependent upon God's will, and also throws doubt on the very notion of a good God. (That Hume was

The anti-religious orientation of the *Treatise* was evident enough to Hume's contemporaries,[10] and was soon to deprive him of the chance to be appointed as professor of moral philosophy at Edinburgh University (a controversy which provoked the writing of *A Letter from a Gentleman to his Friend in Edinburgh* (1745) in his defence). But many commentators have neglected this aspect of Hume's thought, partly no doubt because the philosophy of religion has been relatively unfashionable, but also because for many years it was commonly supposed that Hume's writings on religion were published only for the sake of achieving fame and notoriety rather than for any serious philosophical purpose.[11] Such accusations were partly encouraged by what Hume himself says in 'My Own Life', where he admits to having being disappointed when the *Treatise* 'fell *dead-born from the press* without reaching such distinction, as even to excite a murmur among the zealots', and he also intimates that 'love of literary fame' has been his 'ruling passion' ('Life', 6, 21). These quotations were taken by Hume's critics, out of context, to suggest that he must have included the provocative Sections X and XI in the *Enquiry* in order to ensure that this time the 'zealots' would be suitably roused. Such accusations have long ago been very thoroughly answered,[12] but some of their influence still lingers. However the truth about Hume's treatment of religion is almost exactly the reverse of what they allege. So far from being one of his peripheral interests, included in his later works solely to provoke controversy, religion was instead a lifelong concern informing much of his thought, and one whose relative absence from the *Treatise* was due entirely to the prudence of its author, who as we have seen reluctantly 'castrated' his work shortly before it was published.

It is important even when studying the relatively forthright *Enquiry* to appreciate how often Hume's discussions of religion are influenced by the dictates of prudence. He does not feel able to state his sceptical views explicitly, so he frequently resorts to irony and other devices to get his message across. In Section

well aware of the consequences of his moral theory is clear from a letter of 16 Mar. 1740 to Francis Hutcheson, in which he says that he feels forced to conclude 'that since Morality, according to your Opinion as well as mine, is determin'd merely by Sentiment, it regards only human Nature & human Life' (*HL* i. 40). He also in this letter alludes to Hutcheson's prosecution for teaching heresy by the Glasgow Presbytery in 1737 for his own, relevantly similar, opinions on morality.)

[10] P. Russell ('Skepticism and Natural Religion in Hume's *Treatise*', *Journal of the History of Ideas*, 49 (1988), 247–65) argues that attacks on John Locke's and Samuel Clarke's Christian rationalism in particular are clearly implicit in the arguments of the *Treatise*, and would have been recognized as such by Hume's contemporaries.

[11] The 1893 introduction to Selby-Bigge's edition of the *Enquiries* contains a strong attack on Hume along these lines. It is regrettable that this has been retained in the modern revisions without any editorial comment on its manifest unreliability.

[12] The two classic refutations of these charges are Kemp Smith, *The Philosophy of David Hume*, ch. 24, and E. C. Mossner, 'Philosophy and Biography: The Case of David Hume', *Philosophical Review*, 59 (1950), 184–201; repr. in V. C. Chappell (ed.), *Hume* (London: Macmillan, 1968), 6–34.

VIII, for example, we are told that the difficulties of reconciling the existence of evil with the existence of a perfect God are 'mysteries, which mere natural and unassisted reason is very unfit to handle; and whatever system she embraces, she must find herself involved in inextricable difficulties, and even contradictions, at every step which she takes with regard to such subjects' (*E* 103). Here Hume ironically uses the language of piety to convey to those who can discern it the message that God and evil are incompatible, but this language provides an excellent protection against possible accusations of blasphemy. Again, at the end of Section X Hume famously concludes

that the CHRISTIAN religion not only was at first attended with miracles, but even at this day cannot be believed by any reasonable person without one. Mere reason is insufficient to convince us of its veracity: And whoever is moved by *Faith* to assent to it, is conscious of a continued miracle in his own person, which subverts all the principles of his understanding, and gives him a determination to believe what is most contrary to custom and experience. (*E* 131)

Here too the sceptical message is clearly visible behind the pious talk: anyone who believes in miracle stories is entirely unreasonable, his 'understanding' having been subverted by faith.[13] In Section XI Hume uses a different technique to cover his tracks: engaged on the dangerous project of criticizing the respected Design Argument for God's existence, he resorts to a dialogue form, putting most of the objections into the mouth of 'a friend who loves sceptical paradoxes' of whose principles, Hume tells us, he 'can by no means approve' (*E* 132).[14] This was a ploy Hume was later to use again in his celebrated *Dialogues concerning Natural Religion*, and to such good effect that there has even been a fair amount of dispute over which character in the *Dialogues* most represents his views. On the basis of the mixed evidence provided by his sceptical arguments on the one hand, and his protestations of faith on the other, some commentators maintain that Hume was unequivocally an atheist while others insist that he was merely opposed to abuses of religion and to religious metaphysics. The best extensive recent discussion of Hume's philosophy of religion charts a middle course, arguing that he was an 'attenuated deist' who believed only in some

---

[13] Though as Kemp Smith points out in his edition of the *Dialogues* (*D* 47), Hume's tongue-in-cheek description of the workings of faith is not so very different from the orthodox teaching of the reformed churches of his day!

[14] A third tactic Hume uses to disguise his intentions is to attack the various pillars of religious orthodoxy one by one, while piously appealing to those that he is not currently disputing. Thus in the *Natural History of Religion* he compares monotheism unfavourably with polytheism on every count except its reasonableness in the light of the Design Argument (*NHR* II, IX–XV); in the *Dialogues* he then attacks the Design Argument, and this time relies on revelation to safeguard his orthodox credentials (*D* 227–8). Meanwhile, *Enquiry* X has already indicated his negative view of revelation, but this does not prevent him appealing to it again in 'Of the Immortality of the Soul' (*Essays* 590, 598). All this illustrates how Hume's various statements on religion should not be naively taken at face value.

indeterminate 'ordering agent' behind the universe, an agent about which (or perhaps 'whom') nothing of any religious significance can be known.[15]

There is insufficient space here to do justice to the debate over Hume's personal attitude to religious beliefs and to religious practices, but since both are of fundamental importance to the understanding of the aims of the *Enquiry*, and vital for situating it in the context of his later writings, I shall briefly record my own opinion and draw attention to some of the relevant evidence.[16] Hume was, to all intents and purposes, an atheist, and he certainly did not believe in anything like the Christian God. Although he sometimes speaks approvingly of 'true religion', this does not correspond to any of the 'popular' religious systems, and indeed it seems that he attaches little content to the phrase other than at most a minimal metaphysical belief (that the cause of order in the universe probably bears 'some remote inconceivable analogy to the other operations of nature, and among the rest to the œconomy of human mind and thought'; *D* 218) and an entirely non-theological moral commitment (to the sort of enlightened and secular morality which he himself endorses in his moral writings).[17] His reason for using the phrase is largely prudential: by drawing a contrast between 'true' and 'popular' religion, he can freely attack the excesses of the latter without exposing himself as an atheist. The most notable example of this move is in the final section of the *Dialogues*, where Hume's principal spokesman, Philo, suddenly makes a volte-face and accepts the existence of God, having previously argued powerfully, throughout the *Dialogues*, that the arguments for God's existence which Cleanthes and Demea had proposed totally fail. This section is notoriously difficult to interpret, and has been the subject of much discussion, but I shall confine my comments to just two observations. First, it is Philo's acceptance of 'true religion' (*D* 219) which liberates him to launch a devastating attack on all 'vulgar superstition' (undoubtedly intended to include the various Christian denominations),

---

[15] Gaskin, *Hume's Philosophy of Religion*, 219–23.

[16] The importance of Hume's other religious writings to the interpretation of the *Enquiry* goes well beyond the obvious relevance of the *Dialogues* to *Enquiry* XI. For example, the first section of the *Dialogues* (originally written about 1751) provides Hume's only direct critical discussion of the sort of mitigated scepticism that he had advocated in Section XII of the *Enquiry*, published only three years before (see n. 42 below). The other writings to be mentioned here not only have clear relevance to specific parts of the *Enquiry* (and of the companion *Enquiry concerning the Principles of Morals*, dating from 1751) but also more generally give substance to the claims of writers such as Stewart and Norton (Chapters 2 and 14 in this volume), who see the *Enquiry's* principal theme (manifested most clearly in Sections I, V, and XI, but also in VIII, X, and XII) as being opposition to religious dogmatism.

[17] In fact these two aspects of 'true religion' are in some tension, because Hume clearly does not believe that the cause or causes of order in the universe bear any analogy whatever to human moral qualities (*E* 138–9, 141–2, *D* 211–12, 219) and this suggests (contrary to Gaskin, *Hume's Philosophy of Religion*, 187–8) that Hume's references to 'true religion' do not identify any single coherent position, but are simply tactical devices.

without thereby contradicting his earlier pieties and expressions of faith. Secondly, Philo's acknowledgement of the existence of God is so attenuated as to amount to virtually nothing at all. He suggests that 'the whole of natural theology . . . resolves itself into one simple, though somewhat ambiguous, at least undefined proposition, *that the cause or causes of order in the universe probably bear some remote analogy to human intelligence*' (*D* 227), and he indeed seems happy to endorse this. But we should read this passage together with an earlier one, where Philo remarks that 'there [is] a certain degree of analogy among all the operations of nature, in every situation and in every age; [that] the rotting of a turnip, the generation of an animal, and the structure of human thought . . . probably bear some remote analogy to each other' (*D* 218).[18] Put crudely, Philo's view (and hence presumably Hume's) seems to be that the ultimate cause of order in the universe (call it 'God' if you will; *D* 142) probably bears as much analogy to human thought as does the rotting of a turnip!

Hume's interest in, and antagonism towards, religion were both genuine and profound, and reveal themselves in many of his works. He thought of religion, at least in its 'popular' forms, as a thoroughly evil and pernicious influence, which is born out of superstitious fears (*NHR* ii, iii, and vi; 'Of Superstition and Enthusiasm'), corrupts morality in a variety of ways (*NHR* xiv; 'Of Superstition and Enthusiasm'; 'Of Suicide'), and in particular recommends spurious 'monkish virtues' (*M* 270, *NHR* x), promotes intolerance (*NHR* ix), and encourages the vices of hypocrisy ('Of National Characters' 204 n.), self-deception (*NHR* xiii), and simple-minded credulity (*E* 117–8, *NHR* xi–xii). Hume's *History of England* is full of examples to bear out his suggestion that 'If the religious spirit be ever mentioned in any historical narration, we are sure to meet afterwards with a detail of the miseries which attend it.' (*D* 220), and indeed it seems likely that his increasing antipathy towards organized religion during his life was fuelled by such historical discoveries.[19] Hume's objections to religion were ethical at least as much as they were philosophical, and it is moral repugnance rather than mischief which motivates his attacks.

Hume evidently believed that his assault on the intellectual foundations of religion could undermine its power over his discerning readers:[20]

---

[18] The similarity in wording here is most unlikely to be coincidental, for the phrase 'remote analogy' occurs nowhere else at all in the whole of Hume's surviving philosophical writings, nor in his letters, nor in his *History of England*. Hence it is of particular significance that the 'rotting turnip' paragraph is, in the words of M. A. Stewart ('The Dating of Hume's Manuscripts', in P. Wood (ed.), *The Scottish Enlightenment* (Rochester, NY: University of Rochester Press, 2000), 267–314), Hume's 'dying testament to posterity' (p. 303), having been added in 1776.

[19] D. T. Siebert (*The Moral Animus of David Hume* (London: Associated University Presses, 1990), ch. 2) explores the development of Hume's attitude to religion in his *History of England*.

[20] Hume makes very similar remarks in Section I of the *Enquiry* (*E* 12–13).

One considerable advantage that arises from philosophy, consists in the sovereign anti-dote which it affords to superstition and false religion. All other remedies against that pestilent distemper are vain, or at least uncertain. Plain good sense, and the practice of the world, which alone serve most purposes of life, are here found ineffectual: history, as well as daily experience, furnish instances of men endowed with the strongest capacity for business and affairs, who have all their lives crouched under slavery to the grossest superstition. . . . But when sound philosophy has once gained possession of the mind, superstition is effectually excluded; and one may fairly affirm, that her triumph over this enemy is more complete than over most of the vices and imperfections incident to human nature [because superstition is] founded on false opinion. ('Of Suicide', first paragraph)

But he is not at all optimistic about the prospects of ridding humanity in general of religion and superstition. At the beginning of *Enquiry* X (*E* 110), for example, he expresses the hope that his argument against the credibility of miracles will help to protect 'the wise and learned' from 'superstitious delusion', but he simultaneously suggests that others will be beyond its help, since he feels sure that stories of miracles and prodigies will be propagated 'as long as the world endures'. A similar anti-religious ambition, combined with pessimism, is revealed in the fascinating letter (reprinted in *D* 243–8; cf. *D* 2) from Hume's close friend Adam Smith to William Strahan, his printer, which Smith wrote soon after Hume's death in order to proclaim to the world the exemplary moral character of this notorious atheist.[21] In this letter Smith recounts a deathbed conversation with Hume, where Hume jokingly speculates about the reasons he might offer to Charon, the boatman who ferries souls to Hades across the River Styx, for giving him longer to live:

But I might still urge, 'Have a little patience, good Charon, I have been endeavouring to open the eyes of the Public. If I live a few years longer, I may have the satisfaction of see-ing the downfall of some of the prevailing systems of superstition.' But Charon would then lose all temper and decency. 'You loitering rogue, that will not happen these many hundred years. Do you fancy I will grant you a lease for so long a term? Get into the boat this instant, you lazy, loitering rogue.'

This letter suggests that Hume saw a major part of his life's work as the under-mining of 'superstition', and demonstrates that his antipathy to religion con-tinued unabated until his death.[22] The same message is conveyed by Hume's

---

[21] It was then commonly taken for granted that moral behaviour depends on religious belief, and in particular the belief in divine reward and punishment, heaven and hell. Thus many people who knew Hume only for his sceptical religious views would have assumed that he was a rogue, and this misappre-hension Smith is keen to remedy.

[22] In his edition of the *Dialogues* (*D* 76–9) Kemp Smith also includes an interesting essay by James Boswell, describing his own deathbed interview with Hume, in which Hume is quoted as saying that 'he never had entertained any belief in Religion since he began to read Locke and Clarke', and that 'the Morality of every Religion was bad'. Boswell was disappointed that Hume's disbelief in the afterlife

anxious precautions, in the days before his death, to ensure that his anti-religious masterpiece, the *Dialogues*, would be published (see *D* 88–92). We can conclude that Hume's writings on religion are anything but frivolous: they are motivated by his earnest desire to 'open the eyes of the public' to what in his view is, and has been historically, one of the world's greatest evils.

4. HUME'S INTENTIONS IN THE ENQUIRY, AND ITS RELATION TO THE TREATISE

It should now be clear that at least as regards its concern with religion, the *Enquiry* is a far more faithful record of Hume's thinking than is the 'castrated' *Treatise*. But this alone cannot explain why Hume in his later life disowned the *Treatise* and requested (through a letter to his printer William Strahan in October 1775, *HL* ii. 301) that an 'Advertisement' should be attached to the volume containing his two *Enquiries* (together with his *Dissertation on the Passions* and *The Natural History of Religion*), stating that these works should 'alone be regarded as containing his philosophical sentiments and principles' (*E* 2). Most writers on Hume have overlooked or systematically ignored this request, some no doubt simply because the *Treatise* contains a wealth of material which is far too interesting to pass over, but many because they have tended to look on the *Enquiry* as merely a watered-down version of Book I of the *Treatise*, a more elegant and less taxing easy-read edition for the general public, with the technical details omitted and a few controversial sections on religion added to whet their appetite and provoke the 'zealots'. Quite apart from its misjudgement of the seriousness of Hume's concern with religion, this traditional view of the two works—according to which the *Treatise* gives the more faithful picture of his central philosophical position, and the *Enquiry* merely a more palatable selection—seems to me highly implausible.[23] The 'Advertisement' was written when Hume had already achieved great fame as a historian and essayist, and after some months of experiencing distressing symptoms from the cancer that would shortly kill him ('Life', p. 20). He was no longer a struggling author desperate for recognition but a respected man of letters mindful of how he wished to be

was maintained even as his death approached, and was deeply unsettled by Hume's evident equanimity at the prospect of his total annihilation (see also Mossner, *The Life of David Hume*, 605–6).

[23] Many of the points summarized in the remainder of this paragraph are spelled out by J. O. Nelson ('Two Main Questions concerning Hume's *Treatise* and *Enquiry*', *Philosophical Review*, 81 (1972), 333–7), who goes on to propose that it is the *Treatise*'s contamination with 'metaphysics', of the kind Hume would later condemn, which provides a genuine philosophical basis for his repudiation of it. I shall later (in n. 37) propose something in a similar spirit, concerning Hume's loss of confidence in his Separability Principle and its implications. But this is not I think the whole story, and might not be even a principal theme. For criticism of Nelson's thesis, see P. D. Cummins, 'Hume's Disavowal of the *Treatise*', *Philosophical Review*, 82 (1973), 371–9.

remembered, and in an ideal position to promote the *Treatise* both to his contemporaries and to posterity had he wished to do so.[24] Hence his striking repudiation of it, as 'a juvenile work' which should not be taken to represent his
philosophical principles, demands to be taken seriously. Nor can this be dismissed as the peevishness of an old man looking back at his unsuccessful first
work from the perspective of later acclaim, because he had expressed very similar views in a letter written to Gilbert Elliot of Minto in spring 1751, nearly twen-
ty-five years earlier:

> I believe the philosophical Essays [i.e. the first *Enquiry*] contain every thing of Conse-
> quence relating to the Understanding, which you woud meet with in the Treatise; & I
> give you my Advice against reading the latter. By shortening & simplifying the Ques-
> tions, I really render them much more complete. *Addo dum minuo.* ['I add while reduc-
> ing.'] The philosophical Principles are the same in both: But I was carry'd away by the
> Heat of Youth & Invention to publish too precipitately. So vast an Undertaking, plan'd
> before I was one and twenty, & compos'd before twenty five, must necessarily be very
> defective. I have repented my Haste a hundred, & a hundred times. (*HL* i. 158)

So we are left with the question why Hume thought the *Enquiry* superior to the
Treatise, and whether this can be explained away as merely his judgement on
their respective literary merits, or whether it reflects a substantial philosophical
difference. The former might seem to be suggested by his comment to Elliot that
'the Philosophical Principles are the same in both', and also by a well-known
passage from 'My Own Life' ('Life', 8): 'I had always entertained a notion, that
my want of success in publishing the Treatise of Human Nature, had proceeded
more from the manner than the matter . . . I, therefore, cast the first part of that
work anew in the Enquiry Concerning Human Understanding'. On the other
hand, his letter to Elliot also makes points of philosophical substance, that the
Enquiry contains 'every thing of Consequence relating to the Understanding',
and that his work is rendered 'much more complete' by being better focused.
Moreover, in the 1775 letter to Strahan which accompanied the 'Advertisement'
Hume comments that 'It is a compleat Answer to Dr Reid and to that bigotted
silly Fellow, Beattie.' (*HL* ii. 301). Both Thomas Reid and James Beattie had
criticized the *Treatise* primarily for its scepticism and implausible metaphysics,
and very little for its literary style, so again Hume seems to be implying that the
Enquiry differs significantly from the *Treatise* in content as well as in style. Let us
now examine what these significant differences might be.

---

[24] That Hume was seriously concerned about how he would be remembered and his work transmitted to posterity is very clear from the autobiographical 'My Own Life' (whose nuances are sensitively
explored in Siebert, *The Moral Animus of David Hume*, ch. 5), and also from the care that Hume took to
revise his works during his final illness and to ensure that the *Dialogues* would be published (for which,
see Kemp Smith's app. c: *D* 87–96).

As we saw above, the *Treatise* is primarily an attempt to introduce 'the experimental method of reasoning' into the moral sciences, and to erect on that basis an associationist psychological theory. This is not to say, of course, that it contains only constructive 'cognitive science', and indeed there is famously a great deal of virulent philosophical scepticism in the *Treatise*, particularly in Part iv of Book I. But the main use of this scepticism is in the service of Hume's science of man, as for example when the sceptical argument regarding induction is brought to bear in I. iii. 6 to dismiss the complacent presumption that factual beliefs are founded on insights of 'reason', only to be followed immediately in I. iii. 7 and I. iii. 8 by Hume's alternative, associationist, account of belief and factual inference which attributes them instead to 'the imagination' (this one central example of Hume's typical procedure in the *Treatise* is repeated in the *Enquiry*, Sections IV and V). The primary purpose of Hume's sceptical arguments in the *Treatise* is to clear away the rationalist view of man which he is attempting to displace, to make room for his own naturalistic accounts of human thinking. Thus critical philosophy is primarily the means rather than the end, for it is the construction of an associationist psychology which is Hume's ultimate goal.

There is evidence, however, that after the publication of the *Treatise* Hume quickly became increasingly dissatisfied with its psychological theories. Compare, for example, his enthusiastic remarks about the power and range of the principle of association, quoted earlier from the *Treatise* and the *Abstract*, with the first paragraph of his essay 'The Sceptic' (1742). It is hard to believe that the author of this paragraph, a philosopher noted for his reflexive thinking,[25] could have failed to have in mind its obvious relevance to the author of the *Treatise*:

I HAVE long entertained a suspicion, with regard to the decisions of philosophers upon all subjects, and found in myself a greater inclination to dispute, than assent to their conclusions. There is one mistake, to which they seem liable, almost without exception; they confine too much their principles, and make no account of that vast variety, which nature has so much affected in all her operations. When a philosopher has once laid hold of a favourite principle, which perhaps accounts for many natural effects, he extends the same principle over the whole creation, and reduces to it every phænomenon, though by the most violent and absurd reasoning. Our own mind being narrow and contracted, we cannot extend our conception to the variety and extent of nature; but imagine, that she is as much bounded in her operations, as we are in our speculation. (*Essays* 159–60)

There is also a brief but perhaps significant echo of this 'suspicion' in Section I of the *Enquiry*: 'Moralists . . . have sometimes carried the matter too far, by

---

[25] The theme of reflexivity in Hume's work has been particularly emphasized by Annette Baier, for example in her influential book *A Progress of Sentiments* which is appropriately subtitled 'Reflections on Hume's *Treatise*' (Cambridge, Mass.: Harvard University Press, 1991).

their passion for some one general principle' (*E* 15).[26] Neither of these passages makes any explicit reference to associationism in particular, and they are no doubt susceptible of alternative interpretation, but apart from their evident appropriateness to the *Treatise* a strong reason for reading them as in part self-directed is the independent evidence for Hume's general disillusionment with his early associationist psychology, namely, the surprisingly minor place which he gives to that theory in his later works and especially in the two *Enquiries*. Thus, for example, Section III of the *Enquiry*, 'Of the Association of Ideas', was reduced in the 1777 edition to only three paragraphs, and even before that pruning it contained in addition only a few pages of discussion on the relevance of associationism to the understanding of literature, rather than any systematic analysis of the associationist theory.[27] The only significant applications of associationism later in the *Enquiry* appear in Part ii of Section V, where Hume presents his account of the mechanism of belief, and in Section VI, where he develops that account to deal with probability. But even in this central theory of belief, of which he had made so much in the *Treatise* and the *Abstract*, Hume's presentation seems lacking in confidence. He omits much of the detail of his earlier account, and repeatedly states that he is now doing no more than suggesting 'analogies' (*E* 47, 50, 54) or giving 'hints' to 'excite the curiosity of philosophers' (*E* 59). Moreover he tells the reader quite explicitly that his theory of belief is entirely inessential for the comprehension of the remaining sections of the book: 'the following enquiries may well be understood, though it be neglected' (*E* 47). In the *Enquiry concerning the Principles of Morals* Hume's distancing from his former associationism goes even further, clearly implying that his former associationist account of his central notion of *sympathy* (e.g. in *Treatise* II. i. 11, II. ii. 9, and III. iii. 1) is not only irrelevant to the purpose at hand but probably false:

It is needless to push our researches so far as to ask, why we have humanity or a fellow-feeling with others. . . . No man is absolutely indifferent to the happiness and misery of

---

[26] I do not wish to claim that Hume's criticism of this passion for single principles is *exclusively* self-directed, for at *M* 298 he attacks in similar terms philosophers who attempt to reduce all human motivation to selfishness: 'All attempts of this kind . . . seem to have proceeded entirely from that love of *simplicity* which has been the source of much false reasoning in philosophy.' Even here, however, there is a marked contrast with the tone of the *Treatise*, where he comments approvingly on 'that simplicity, which has been hitherto [my system's] principal force and beauty' (*T* 367).

[27] Indeed the discussion is introduced with the dismissive comment that such an analysis 'would lead into many useless subtilties', and ends by modestly disclaiming any systematic ambition for itself: 'These loose hints . . . thrown together, in order to excite the curiosity of philosophers, and beget a suspicion . . . that many operations of the human mind depend on the connexion or association of ideas, which is here explained.' The entire discussion is omitted from the Selby-Bigge edition of the *Enquiry*, but can be found in paragraphs 3.4 to 3.18 of the recent student edition by T. L. Beauchamp, which is based on the 1772 text (Oxford: Oxford University Press, 1999). The quotations in this note are from paragraphs 3.3 and 3.18 of the latter.

others. The first has a natural tendency to give pleasure; the second, pain. . . . *It is not probable, that these principles can be resolved into principles more simple and universal, whatever attempts may have been made to that purpose.* But if it were possible, it belongs not to the present subject . . . (*M* 220 n., my emphasis)

Why might Hume have lost confidence in his associationist theory, and chosen to downplay it so much in his later work? One obvious possibility, suggested by the earlier quotation from 'The Sceptic', is that he began to see it as being unconvincingly 'violent and absurd' in its efforts to reduce all mental phenomena to one 'favourite principle'. But another major factor was probably the particular difficulties that he encountered in trying to build an associationist account of human thought that is even self-consistent, difficulties which are already very apparent in Part iv of Book I of the *Treatise*, and which become even more explicit in the Appendix to the *Treatise* (published with Book III).[28] Some of these again concern the details of his theory of belief. But even more threatening are the intractable paradoxes involving our beliefs in the external world and in our own self: in each case Hume sets out to explain an important aspect of our mental lives, but in both his analysis ultimately leaves him not with a benign psychological explanation of the belief concerned, but instead with a sceptical quandary that casts doubt on it.

To take the external world first, Hume begins *Treatise* I. iv. 2, entitled 'Of Scepticism with regard to the Senses', by posing the question 'What causes induce us to believe in the existence of body?' and explicitly ruling out any sceptical doubts: ''tis vain to ask, *Whether there be body or not?* That is a point, which we must take for granted in all our reasonings' (*T* 187). However, by the end of this section the nature of Hume's explanation of our belief in body based on the apparently 'trivial' operations of the faculty of imagination ('the fancy') threatens to undermine that belief completely:

I begun this subject with premising, that we ought to have an implicit faith in our senses . . . But to be ingenuous, I feel myself *at present* of a quite contrary sentiment . . . I cannot conceive how such trivial qualities of the fancy, conducted by such false suppositions, can ever lead to any solid and rational system. . . . 'Tis impossible upon any system to defend either our understanding or senses; and we but expose them farther when we endeavour to justify them in that manner. . . . Carelessness and in-attention alone can afford us any remedy. (*T* 217–18)

It is bad enough that our belief in the external world should be rationally indefensible, but two sections later (in *Treatise* I. iv. 4, 'Of the modern philosophy') Hume appears to go even further, concluding that causal reasoning shows the

---

[28] Here I shall focus only on the more dramatic problems for Hume's associationism, but for an excellent more detailed account of some of Hume's other difficulties and his apparent progressive disillusionment, see J. Passmore, *Hume's Intentions*, 3rd edn. (London: Duckworth, 1980), ch. 6.

belief in body to be not merely groundless but fundamentally incoherent: 'Thus there is a direct and total opposition betwixt our reason and our senses; or more properly speaking, betwixt those conclusions we form from cause and effect, and those that persuade us of the continu'd and independent existence of body.' (*T* 231).

Turning now from the external to the internal world, Hume begins the section 'Of personal identity' (I. iv. 6) with an attack on the supposed Cartesian concept of a perfectly simple, unified, and persisting self, quickly replacing it with his own famous 'bundle theory', according to which a person is 'nothing but a bundle or collection of different perceptions, which succeed each other with an inconceivable rapidity, and are in a perpetual flux and movement' (*T* 252). Most of the rest of this section is devoted to the diagnosis of an alleged pervasive cognitive error: how it is that through the association of ideas we commonly confuse the idea of genuine identity with the idea of 'a succession of related objects' (*T* 253), and the implications of this confusion for our concepts of identity in general and of personal identity in particular. Since the mind is constantly in flux rather than uniform over time, its supposed identity can only be 'fictitious' (*T* 259), but Hume identifies a variety of associative principles which seduce our imagination into making this fiction almost irresistible. Hume's alternative 'bundle' concept of the self initially appears to survive unscathed from his critique,[29] but in the Appendix he famously expresses despair even about that:

Upon a more strict review of the section concerning *personal identity*, I find myself involv'd in such a labyrinth, that, I must confess, I neither know how to correct my former opinions, nor how to render them consistent. (*T* 633)

There is a major interpretative puzzle here about just what the big problem with his theory is supposed to be,[30] but what is clear is that Hume has again found himself in an unpleasant and potentially embarrassing sceptical morass.

How embarrassing these problems are for Hume depends, however, on what he is up to. If, as critics from Reid and Beattie onwards have alleged, he is primarily an exponent of unsystematic 'careless [i.e. carefree] scepticism' in the style attributed to his character Philo in the *Dialogues* (*D* 128), then paradoxes and contradictions should be grist to his mill, serving to emphasize 'the whimsical condition of mankind' (*E* 160). Some sections of the *Treatise* (notably those

---

[29] At *T* 366 Hume contrasts conjectures about external bodies, which inevitably involve 'contradictions and absurdities', with conclusions about 'the perceptions of the mind', which being 'perfectly known' should provide the means to 'keep clear of . . . contradictions'.

[30] D. Garrett (*Cognition and Commitment in Hume's Philosophy* (Oxford: Oxford University Press, 1997), ch. 8) gives a clear critical review of various proposed solutions to this puzzle, before preferring an interesting solution of his own.

just mentioned and I. iv. 1) may indeed lend themselves to such an interpretation, but thoroughgoing scepticism provides an unconvincing basis for any would-be science of man, and the supposition that sceptical bewilderment is Hume's objective seems hard to square with the apparently genuine dismay and concern for consistency evinced in the Appendix and in the Conclusion to Book I (e.g. *T* 268).[31] But whatever our view of the *Treatise*, it is clear that by the time he came to write the *Enquiry* Hume was very far from revelling in the excesses of scepticism—in this 'recasting' of his work he plays down the problem of the external world, he omits his previously all-embracing 'scepticism with regard to reason' of *Treatise* I. iv. 1 and summarily dismisses such 'antecedent scepticism' as futile and unreasonable (*E* 149–50), while he fails even to mention his labyrinthine problem of personal identity. Of course this is not to deny that much of the *Enquiry*, like Book I of the *Treatise*, is infused with sceptical thinking, but here, as a rule, the sceptical doubts are satisfactorily answered or at least supplied with a 'sceptical solution' that lays them to rest. So whatever Hume's purposes in the *Enquiry* may be, they do not appear to harmonize well with the radical sceptical paradoxes of Book I Part iv of the *Treatise*, and presumably the prominence of these paradoxes in his earlier work provides at least a part of his motive for 'recasting' it.

All this still leaves us with the question of what Hume's primary aim in the *Enquiry* might be, if it is neither to promote the associationist psychology of the *Treatise* nor to preach scepticism. The obvious place to look for an answer is Hume's own introduction to the work, Section I, whose predominant flavour can be conveyed by the quotation of a few key passages:

we shall now proceed to consider what can reasonably be pleaded in [metaphysics'] behalf. (*E* 9)

Here indeed lies the justest and most plausible objection against a considerable part of metaphysics, that they are not properly a science; but arise either from the fruitless efforts of human vanity, which would penetrate into subjects utterly inaccessible to the understanding, or from the craft of popular superstitions, which, being unable to defend themselves on fair ground, raise these intangling brambles to cover and protect their weakness. . . . But is this a sufficient reason, why philosophers should desist from such researches, and leave superstition still in possession of her retreat? Is it not proper to draw an opposite conclusion, and perceive the necessity of carrying the war into the most secret recesses of the enemy? . . . The only method of freeing learning, at once, from these abstruse questions, is to enquire seriously into the nature of human understanding, and show, from an exact analysis of its powers and capacity, that it is by no means fitted for such remote and abstruse subjects. We . . . must cultivate true

---

[31] The interpretation of the final section of Book I of the *Treatise* is notoriously difficult, and it would take us too far afield to explore it here. Two excellent but contrasting attempts to make good sense of it are those of Baier, *A Progress of Sentiments*, ch. 1, and Garrett, *Cognition and Commitment*, ch. 10.

metaphysics with some care, in order to destroy the false and adulterate. . . . Accurate and just reasoning is the only catholic remedy . . . and is alone able to subvert that abstruse philosophy and metaphysical jargon, which, being mixed up with popular superstition . . . gives it the air of science and wisdom. (*E* 11–13)

Besides this advantage of rejecting, after deliberate enquiry, the most uncertain and dis-agreeable part of learning, there are many positive advantages, which result from an accurate scrutiny into the powers and faculties of human nature. . . . may we not hope, that philosophy, if cultivated with care, . . . may . . . discover, at least in some degree, the secret springs and principles, by which the human mind is actuated in its operations? (*E* 13–14)

Happy, if we can [reconcile] profound enquiry with clearness, and truth with novelty! And still more happy, if . . . we can undermine the foundations of an abstruse philoso-phy, which seems to have hitherto served only as a shelter to superstition, and a cover to absurdity and error! (*E* 16)

Here we find a clear enough purpose, which harmonizes perfectly with the con-tent of the later sections of the *Enquiry* and which moreover makes excellent sense of its differences from the *Treatise*. For if Hume's primary aim is to attack 'superstition' and 'false metaphysics' to clear the way for properly empirical sci-ence, then he is well advised to avoid giving hostages to fortune in the form of either unconvincingly convoluted associationist hypotheses or irresoluble sceptical conundrums. Strained reasoning of either sort would provide an obvi-ous target for criticism from self-appointed defenders of 'common sense' such as Reid and Beattie, and it may be that part of Hume's reason for describing the *Enquiry* as a 'compleat answer' to them is that in it his associationist theories are presented as inessential speculations, while his scepticism takes only a 'mitigated' form. Moderating his scepticism also usefully sidesteps a favourite tactic of fideists such as Bayle, who were fond of using paradoxes— notably those involving infinite divisibility—to subvert confidence in human reason and thus make room for faith. This was a tactic familiar to Hume, having been advocated also in the influential 'Port Royal Logic' (*The Art of Thinking*).[32] And that Hume has it explicitly in mind is suggested by a footnote in the *Enquiry*, where he proposes a method of avoiding mathematical paradoxes using the theory of abstract ideas that he had developed in the *Treatise*:

It seems to me not impossible to avoid these absurdities and contradictions, if it be admitted, that there is no such thing as abstract or general ideas, properly speaking; but that all general ideas are, in reality, particular ones, attached to a general term . . . *It cer-tainly concerns all lovers of science not to expose themselves to the ridicule and contempt of*

[32] Antoine Arnauld and Pierre Nicole, *L'Art de penser* (1662), trans. as *The Art of Thinking* by J. Dickoff and P. James (Indianapolis: Bobbs-Merrill, 1964), which is explicitly mentioned by Hume in both the *Treatise* (*T* 43) and the *Abstract* (*A* 647), advises the reader to study paradoxes 'since such efforts diminish his self-conceit and remove from him the impudence that makes him oppose—on the ground that he cannot understand them—truths propounded by the church' (pt. IV, ch. 1, p. 301).

the ignorant by their conclusions; and this seems the readiest solution of these difficulties.'
(*E* 158 n., my emphasis)

In short the *Enquiry*, through its omission or at least parenthesizing of the details of Hume's associationist theory, and through the significant mitigation of its scepticism, provides only minimal exposure to potential 'ridicule and contempt' from Hume's opponents. By giving them so little scope for counterattack, and in conspicuous contrast to the *Treatise*, it effectively forces them to look instead to their own defences.[33]

5. HUME'S INTELLECTUAL LEGACY: THE TREATISE OR THE ENQUIRY?

All this might prompt the question to what extent Hume's changes in the *Enquiry* are *merely* strategic: might it be that his real philosophical commitments are unchanged from those of the *Treatise*, and that the sidelining of his associationism and the mitigation of his scepticism in the later work are only ploys to make it less vulnerable to attack? Might it be, in other words, that in assessing Hume's primary philosophical legacy we should ignore his last-minute bequest of the *Enquiry* and focus on the *Treatise* instead?

This suggestion, though it has obvious attractions for anyone who is rightly fascinated by the intricate philosophy of the *Treatise*, seems implausible to me for at least four reasons. First, we have seen that there is clear evidence of Hume's being genuinely dissatisfied with the *Treatise* and of various changes of mind, evidence provided most emphatically by the Appendix to the *Treatise* and by his letters, though there are plenty of corroborative hints in the body of the *Treatise* and in the two *Enquiries*. Secondly, Hume had very good reason to be dissatisfied with the *Treatise*, in respects which correspond well to his later self-criticisms—when he reformulates his theory of belief, for example, or attacks extreme 'antecedent scepticism' as futile, or expresses doubts about his account of personal identity, he seems indeed to have put his finger on seriously prob-

---

[33] If it is so important to Hume's purposes that his scepticism in the *Enquiry* is not too extreme or potentially 'ridiculous', then this raises the major question *whether he has any right*, on his own principles, to 'mitigate' the more radical scepticism of the *Treatise* (e.g. to advocate at *E* 162 a limitation of our enquiries to common life, when *T* 271 seems to imply that no such limitation is possible). If the *Enquiry* indeed provides a legitimate sanction for such mitigation, then this is of considerable philosophical significance, and might well provide a further explanation of Hume's preference for the later work. Two possible mitigating factors are mentioned in the discussion below, first, his apparent dropping of (or at least greatly reduced reliance on) the Separability Principle, which lay behind many of his more extravagant conclusions in the *Treatise*; and secondly, his consistent emphasis on inductive systematization, which seems to provide a relatively solid and down-to-earth basis for theorizing about the world of common life without any dependence on—and even despite the ultimate incoherence of—our notion of matter (and perhaps of other metaphysical notions also).

lematic areas of his earlier philosophy. Thirdly, and related to this, the judgement of history has broadly confirmed Hume's implicit assessments of quality in selecting the individual essays which constitute the *Enquiry*. Thus, for example, his argument concerning the non-rational basis of induction (Sections IV and V), his analysis of causation (Section VII), his compatibilism (Section VIII) and his critique of natural theology (Sections X and XI) are all universally accepted as philosophical classics worthy of serious overall consideration on their own merits, whereas by contrast the detailed associative psychology of the *Treatise*, including Hume's baroque explanations of our ideas of space and time and our beliefs in the external world and in the self, are generally taken seriously only by specialist scholars or by those (notably university teachers and their students) who are content to mine them for interesting philosophical nuggets. This correspondence is no coincidence, for Hume was a man of excellent philosophical judgement which not surprisingly matured over time.

My final point will take rather longer to develop, because it concerns Hume's philosophy as a whole and the overall significance of the *Treatise* and of the *Enquiry*. Earlier we identified some of Hume's main philosophical opponents, and looked in particular at a wide range of issues on which he argued comprehensively against the rationalist position of Descartes. From our own historical perspective this contest may look very one-sided, with Hume the obvious victor on most if not all points, but in the mid-eighteenth century things would have looked very different, for rationalistic doctrines were then still being confidently propagated and vigorously defended by many writers. Such doctrines, even if not explicitly concerned with the existence or nature of God, typically had a theological motivation—the intrinsic inertness of matter, for example, was a favourite topic not only of Berkeley and the continental occasionalists (following Malebranche),[34] but also of various English and Scottish philosophers concerned to prove the impossibility of thinking matter and hence to rule out any mechanistic conception of man.[35] Thus in opposing 'abstruse philosophy and metaphysical jargon . . . mixed up with popular superstition' (*E* 12) Hume is actively contributing to contemporary debates not only in natural theology but also in scientific metaphysics; that he has such debates in mind is made evident in a footnote on the inertness issue in Section VII of the *Enquiry*, where he

---

[34] According to Malebranche God is the only true cause, and so for example when one billiard ball strikes another, it does not really *cause* the other to move; rather, the collision provides an *occasion* on which God exercises his power to make the balls move as though they had causally interacted. Hume elegantly summarizes this theory at *E* 70–1, before strongly criticizing it at *E* 71–3.

[35] See J. W. Yolton, *Thinking Matter* (Minneapolis: University of Minnesota Press, 1983), ch. 5, for a useful discussion of such philosophers, notably Andrew Baxter, who in the 1720s lived near Hume and his friend Kames in the Scottish Borders, and who corresponded with Kames about the Newtonian concept of matter.

bemoans the occasionalism 'so prevalent among our modern metaphysicians' (*E* 73 n.). Now given this context it is pertinent to ask which aspects of his 'metaphysical' philosophy Hume himself would probably have considered most central and important, and which appear by contrast relatively peripheral; the answer, I suggest, corresponds quite closely with the distinction between what he included in the *Enquiry* and what he omitted. Again this suggestion can be backed up with our earlier list of Cartesian claims and Humean responses. Only with respect to the self, and perhaps the immateriality of the soul,[36] does the transition from the *Treatise* to the *Enquiry* in any way dilute Hume's position, but the omission from the *Enquiry* of any direct reworking of *Treatise* I. iv. 5 and I. iv. 6 (presumably due to dissatisfaction with his account of personal identity) is more than compensated by the addition of a range of powerful arguments in Section VII (*E* 64–9), which emphasize—more explicitly than the *Treatise* ever had—the total impossibility of aprioristic knowledge of the mind's workings.

Although I have made this case in respect of Hume's disagreements with Descartes in particular, a similar conclusion could be drawn in respect of his disagreements with other rationalistic philosophers too. In all such debates, I suggest, the *Enquiry* is a far more potent weapon than Book I of the *Treatise*, owing to the greater focus of its sceptical attacks and the omission from it of unconvincing (albeit sometimes ingenious) psychological theorizing which has limited relevance to the task at hand. Most of the material that Hume deletes in moving from the earlier to the later work falls into one of three categories: (*a*) detailed taxonomy of our impressions and ideas (*Treatise* I. i. 2–6, I. iii. 5), (*b*) investigation of our ideas of space and time in particular (I. ii. 1–5), and (*c*) associationist accounts of cognitive errors, some of which have extreme sceptical implications (I. iii. 9, I. iii. 13, I. iv. 1–6). But none of this is of any central significance in Hume's attack on rationalism, some of it provides obvious and vulnerable targets for his opponents, and some of it—notably his discussion of space and time—even itself smacks of rationalistic metaphysics.[37] Thus if Hume's permanent philosophical importance lies overwhelmingly in

[36] Hume's arguments on immateriality are not forgotten, however, for they resurface in summary form at the beginning of the posthumous essay 'On the Immortality of the Soul' mentioned earlier. Moreover the main points of those arguments, that the notion of substance is confused and indeterminate, and that no causal principles can be known a priori, are very clearly present in the *Enquiry*, so this part of the essay can be seen as merely spelling out fairly obvious corollaries of Hume's established principles.

[37] The most rationalistic parts of the *Treatise* are those where Hume argues from the nature of perceptions to the nature of objects by making use of his 'Separability Principle' (i.e. whatever is different is distinguishable and hence separable by thought) or its converse. So it is very noteworthy that in the *Enquiry*: (*a*) the Separability Principle makes no appearance; (*b*) there is no explicit discussion of the simple–complex distinction which is arguably the Separability Principle's foundation (Garrett, *Cognition and Commitment in Hume's Philosophy*, 68); and (*c*) as already mentioned, there is no developed theory of the structure of space and time, which in the *Treatise* is not only crucially based on

his consummate defeat of rationalism, as I believe it does, rather than in his tortured attempts to construct an associationist cognitive science, and if Hume correctly perceived this, then his preference for the *Enquiry* is both understandable and fully vindicated. Not only do the sections of the *Enquiry*, taken individually, include Hume's best and most lasting contributions to 'metaphysical' philosophy, but also the *Enquiry* as a whole provides a brilliant synthesis of his primary objective in that philosophy, the refutation of rationalistic metaphysics.

None of this implies that the mature Hume has in any way lost his earlier commitment to the application of 'the experimental method of reasoning' to 'moral subjects'—far from it, for as he repeatedly emphasizes, his defeat of aprioristic metaphysics leaves empirical observation and experiment as the only legitimate basis of scientific investigation, and as we shall see shortly, the *Enquiry* has much to say about the principles which should properly govern such empirical research. Hume's apparent loss of confidence in the psychology of the *Treatise* does not even imply that he has begun to feel doubts about the prospects for a thoroughgoing *associationist* psychology, though it does suggest that he no longer sees himself as the Newton of the moral sciences, and has acquired a more realistic perspective on *his own* achievements in that area. In the *Enquiry* he accordingly retains his stake to a reputation as a psychologist only in a muted way, suggesting 'explications and analogies' which others might take further but without risking the credit of his philosophical work should his associationism fail to stand the test of time. It has not stood that test, and modern cognitive scientists pay no heed to it, though of course they do pursue their work in the thoroughly empirical way that he advocated. So again Hume's judgement in distancing himself from his juvenile psychology has proved astute: his permanent contributions to the advancement of learning have indeed turned out to lie primarily in his philosophical assault on the heart of rationalism rather than in the associationism for which that assault was, in the *Treatise*, designed to clear the ground. And precisely because his appreciation of the relative merits of these aspects of his work was ultimately correct, it is clear that modern cognitive scientists, following him methodologically but not in his associationism, are unequivocally to be numbered among his true intellectual

the Separability Principle but also plays an important role in facilitating the simple–complex distinction by providing ultimate simples (ibid. 74). Given how neatly this links together some of the hitherto puzzling differences between the two works (differences which, in default of any more principled explanation, have generally been attributed to the 'shortening and simplifying' described by Hume to Elliot), it is tempting to speculate that *all* of Hume's major deletions between the *Treatise* and the *Enquiry* might be accounted for by a loss of confidence both in associationism (as discussed earlier) and in the Separability Principle. If so, this would I believe be a tribute to his good philosophical judgement, and would also be an additional nail in the coffin of the view of the *Enquiry* as merely a simplified *Treatise*.

heirs. The foundation of modern, empirical, cognitive science is indeed part of the legacy of Hume the philosopher, but not of Hume the psychologist.

6. THE INTEGRITY AND STRUCTURE OF THE FIRST ENQUIRY

I have argued for a controversial conclusion: that Hume's *Enquiry concerning Human Understanding* was correctly judged by its author to be philosophically superior to Book I of his *Treatise of Human Nature*. Not all will be convinced, and indeed it would be unrealistic to suppose that a brief discussion such as this should persuade even a significant proportion of the great majority of philosophers and scholars who have taken a contrary view. However, I trust that what has been said above has at least been sufficient to establish with confidence a more modest conclusion. Namely, that whatever the truth may be regarding Hume's later rejection or continued acceptance of the distinctive philosophy and psychology of the *Treatise*, and whatever our judgement on which of these works is philosophically the more powerful, Hume's first *Enquiry* deserves to be read and studied *on its own terms*, and not merely as an afterthought or addendum to his earlier masterpiece. For the *Enquiry* is a serious philosophical work in its own right, with a fundamentally different approach from the *Treatise* and a distinct—or at least a more focused—primary objective. It makes no attempt to establish an associationist science of man, but neither does it presuppose the details of any such science; instead, it presents an independent and integrated assault on the credentials of rationalistic metaphysics, with material chosen appropriately to that end. Thus although nearly all of the detailed psychological explanation from Book I of the *Treatise* is omitted, significantly reducing the bulk of the work as a whole, there are significant additions too. Prominent among these are not only the religious topics in Sections X and XI, and the discussion of mitigated scepticism in Section XII, but also major improvements and extensions to the arguments concerning induction, causation, and free will in Sections IV, VII, and VIII respectively. These three sections (together with Part i of Section V) constitute the theoretical heart of Hume's anti-rationalist case, and the development of these central arguments, together with their streamlining and liberation from the psychologistic context of the *Treatise*, would alone be sufficient to make the *Enquiry* an indispensable source for the anti-rationalist theme in Hume's philosophy even without the distinctive religious and other material which has no precedent in the *Treatise*.

The greater focus of the *Enquiry* is apparent not only in its content but also in its structure, which interestingly follows quite closely that of the 'single and concise . . . chain of reasoning' (A 643) which Hume presents in the earlier *Abstract*, and refers to in its subtitle as 'The CHIEF ARGUMENT' of the *Treatise*.

Since the *Abstract* seems to have been mostly written in October to November 1739, this suggests that within barely nine months of publication of the first two books of the *Treatise* Hume was already rethinking the structure of his work and isolating its most important lines of argument in a way that would finally bear fruit in the *Enquiry*, and which (perhaps significantly) corresponds far less well with the distribution of material in the *Treatise* itself.[38] For this reason the *Abstract* provides at least as good an introduction to the *Enquiry* as it does to the *Treatise*, and any student of Hume is well advised to read it for a general outline of his intentions before moving on to either of the larger works. Hence I shall end with an overview of the shared structure of the *Abstract* and the *Enquiry*, to help orientate such readers and to enable them to identify clearly the general thrust of Hume's 'chief argument'. Where the two works diverge significantly in their presentation of this argument, I shall follow the order of treatment in the *Enquiry*, taking care, however, to make reference to any corresponding passages in the *Abstract*. Indeed every section of the *Enquiry* will be mentioned below, albeit some only briefly, because as we shall see, nearly all of them have a significant part to play in the development of Hume's 'chief argument', making the *Enquiry* a far more integrated work than has usually been appreciated. The ultimate aim of this overview, therefore, is to show that the *Enquiry* is very far from being merely a collection of related essays or edited highlights from the *Treatise*—it can, and should, be read as a systematic exposition of Hume's mature anti-rationalist and thoroughly empiricist philosophy.

7. AN OUTLINE OF HUME'S 'CHIEF ARGUMENT' IN THE ABSTRACT AND THE ENQUIRY

Hume begins both the *Abstract* and the *Enquiry* with introductory material contrasting two types of philosophy, which in Section I of the *Enquiry* he calls the 'easy' and the 'abstruse' respectively. He then explains his own commitment to the latter, a conception of philosophy which values scientific accuracy above popular eloquence. In Section II, as in the *Abstract*, he begins his 'abstruse' investigation with some definitions that provide the basis of his theory of ideas, but he draws attention to only one crucial result of that theory (*A* 647–8, *E* 19), the so-called 'Copy Principle' that all our 'ideas' (the materials of our thought) are

---

[38] See Mossner, *The Life of David Hume*, 121–9, for a discussion of the *Abstract* in the context of the public reception of the *Treatise*. Although the 'chief argument' of the *Abstract* indeed provides the backbone of the *Enquiry*, there are also important relevant differences between the two works, yielding further evidence regarding the development of Hume's views. Thus in March 1740, when the *Abstract* appeared, it seems that Hume was not yet feeling the doubts about personal identity which, as we have seen, were manifested in the Appendix only eight months later. His theory of geometrical ideas is also singled out for special mention in the *Abstract*, whereas in the *Enquiry* what little remains of it is relegated to footnotes. Accordingly neither of these topics will be mentioned in the following overview.

copied from 'impressions' (sensations or feelings). Hume commends this as a tool for identifying bogus ideas that lack corresponding impressions (A 648–9, E 22), and in this capacity it is destined to play an important role within his analysis of causation in Section VII. Apart from this principle, however, and the observation that impressions are distinguished from ideas in having more 'force and vivacity' (A 647, E 17–18), his theory of ideas has little relevance to what follows, so in the *Abstract* he develops it no further, while in the *Enquiry* he completes his treatment with a cursory summary of the principles of association (in Section III) before quickly moving on to his main business, the investigation of causation and of reasoning 'concerning matter of fact' (i.e. what is now usually called 'induction').[39]

In the *Treatise* the topics of causation and induction had been very closely intertwined, with Hume setting out (in *Treatise* I. iii. 2) to analyse our idea of cause and effect, then resolving this into its components, and eventually coming to consider induction only while 'beat[ing] about . . . neighbouring fields' (*T* 78) in the course of his search for the origin of the most perplexing of those components, the idea of necessary connexion. Given the *Abstract*'s role as a summary of the *Treatise* it not surprisingly follows the same general order of treatment, though now the discussions of causation and induction are far less entangled, and they already show clear signs of a shift in Hume's thinking from an analytical to an epistemological perspective. These changes are completed in the *Enquiry*, where induction is introduced as a purely epistemological issue in Section IV and separated entirely from the analysis of causation, which is now treated in a single continuous discussion in Section VII (bringing the definition of 'cause' in terms of its components together with the search for the impression of necessity).[40] Moreover, even the latter section, despite its declared purpose of clarifying ideas, is given an emphasis which is at least as much epistemological as analytical. Between Sections IV and VII are inserted discussions of belief and of probability: the theory of belief in Section V provides Hume's 'sceptical solution' to the problem of induction raised in Section IV, while his treatment of probability in Section VI extends this theory to deal with cases of inference

---

[39] With the exception of the special case of 'custom', the *Abstract* does not even mention the principles of association until the final paragraph, where as we saw earlier they are emphasized quite strongly and rhetorically. The obvious explanation for this last-minute flourish is the *Abstract*'s intended role in promoting the *Treatise*, which is full of associationist psychology, but it is clear that already by late 1739 Hume had come to appreciate that his main philosophical results could be presented independently of this psychology.

[40] The *Enquiry* also differs from the *Treatise* and *Abstract* in its detailed account of the components of the idea of 'cause', with contiguity no longer being considered as essential to it (compare *T* 75 and *A* 649 with *E* 76). One motive for this change might have been to accommodate the possibility of gravitational action at a distance (which *E* 30 suggests is probably for us an 'ultimate cause'), but another likely motive is to permit causal relations between 'perceptions, which . . . exist no where' (*T* 236).

based on inconsistent experience. These topics also appear in the same order in the *Abstract* (albeit probability only very briefly), placed between the material on induction and the search for the impression of necessity.

Hume's argument in Section IV and Section V Part i of the *Enquiry*, and in the corresponding paragraphs of the *Abstract*, starts from a fundamental question about the foundation of our 'reasonings concerning matter of fact' (*A* 649, *E* 26): 'what is the nature of that evidence, which assures us of any real existence and matter of fact, beyond the present testimony of our senses, or the records of our memory' (*E* 26). Most of our knowledge, from history to the laws of physics, depends on such factual inference (for which Hume uses a variety of terms including 'moral' and 'probable' reasoning), and yet he observes that it has tended to be neglected by philosophers both ancient and modern (*A* 646–7, *E* 26). These philosophers have instead focused most of their attention on 'demonstration'—that is, on the sort of reasoning used in algebra, arithmetic, geometry or formal logic, whose validity can be logically guaranteed because it depends only on 'relations of ideas' (*E* 25) and not at all on how things stand in the world. Factual reasoning clearly lacks this kind of security, because whatever evidence we might have for believing facts beyond our present experience (e.g. my beliefs that the sun will rise tomorrow, that my desk will not evaporate, or that my pen will fall if I throw it up in the air), it is always *conceivable* that such a belief should turn out to be mistaken: logic alone or 'relations of ideas' cannot guarantee its truth. So what basis do I have for making any factual inferences beyond my direct experience, and how can I ever have confidence in a belief thus inferred? Hume's answer is that such inferences can never be based entirely on rational considerations, but always presuppose something which cannot be independently justified, namely, that the world's ways of working are uniform and hence that correlations observed in the past will continue into the future. This assumption enters our factual reasonings through the operation of 'custom', a non-rational instinct which leads us to expect in the future what we have observed in the past, even though we cannot give the slightest good reason for such an expectation. The centrality of custom in our thoughts is easy to overlook precisely because it is so strong and immediate (*E* 28–9): it enters into our factual inferences without our ever being aware of it, and indeed in everyday life such inferences are characteristically immediate and unreflective, with custom acting quietly but irresistibly to extrapolate beliefs from past experience as soon as we make a relevant observation. Thus, for example, I have uniform experience that balls in the air fall to earth, and so as soon as I see a ball thrown above me, I immediately believe that it too will fall:

This belief is the necessary result of placing the mind in such circumstances. It is an operation of the soul, when we are so situated, as unavoidable as to feel the passion of love, when we receive benefits; or hatred, when we meet with injuries. All these operations are a species of natural instincts, which no reasoning or process of the thought and understanding is able, either to produce, or to prevent. (*E* 46–7)

But the importance of custom is not confined to these everyday inferences. Even our reflective scientific reasonings (for example, when we infer a future eclipse from equations describing the motions of sun, earth, and moon) would be quite impossible without the presupposition of uniformity which custom provides.

Having established the role of custom in factual reasoning, Hume adds some 'speculations' (*E* 47) about the nature and causes of belief, which in the *Enquiry* are placed in Section V Part ii and thus separated from the main flow of his argument. He starts (*A* 652, *E* 47) by addressing a question which other philosophers have overlooked, namely, what is it that distinguishes the mere conception of some proposition (e.g. that the ball will fall) from belief that the proposition is true? His answer is that belief cannot arise merely from addition to, or rearrangement of, the ideas involved in such a conception (for if it did then we would be able to change our beliefs at will); instead it must involve a (typically involuntary) difference in the manner of conception: 'belief is nothing but a more vivid, lively, forcible, firm, steady conception of an object, than what the imagination alone is ever able to attain' (*E* 49; cf. *A* 654). This characterization of the distinction between belief and mere conception, however, is highly reminiscent of that between impressions and ideas in terms of 'force and vivacity', and suggests some 'analogies' (*E* 54; cf. *A* 655, *E* 50) among the operations of the mind which in the *Enquiry* he goes on to explore, but in the *Abstract* only alludes to briefly. Again the contrast between both of these works and the *Treatise* is striking, because what he presents at this point even in the *Enquiry* is merely a faint echo of what initially (*Treatise* I. iii. 8–13) had been an explicit theory of belief formation. According to this theory (e.g. *T* 98, 122) belief comes about through the literal transfer of force and vivacity from a present impression (e.g. of a ball in the air) to an associated idea (e.g. that the ball will fall), with this force and vivacity being conveyed—in a way apparently directly analogous to the communication of impulse in a hydraulic system—along channels of association carved out by previous experience (e.g. observations of balls in the air subsequently falling), and thus converting the idea, through the resulting increase in its force and vivacity, from a mere conception into a belief. In the *Enquiry* Hume still evinces some lingering affection for this theory but far less confidence in it: not only does he take it less literally, as a speculative source of mere 'explications and analogies' rather than as a reliable account of genuine causal laws governing the transfer of force and vivacity, but also he states clearly that his philosophical conclusions are quite independent of it (*E* 47).

Hume's account of 'probability'—reasoning in which we draw tentative conclusions from inconsistent past experience as opposed to firm conclusions from uniform past experience—is presented very briefly in Section VI of the *Enquiry*, and is given only one short paragraph in the *Abstract* (*A* 655). Hume's main aim here seems to be to emphasize how comfortably his theory of belief can accommodate such reasoning: just as a uniform experience of *A*s followed by *B*s can lead us, on observing an *A*, to conceive *B* in a forceful manner (i.e. to believe that a *B* will occur), so an inconsistent experience of *A*s followed sometimes by *B*s and sometimes by *C*s can lead us, on observing an *A*, to conceive both *B* and *C*, each with a force proportionate to its past frequency. Again, however, Hume avoids any commitment to the literal 'hydraulic' interpretation of this theory which had dominated in the *Treatise* (e.g. *T* 129–30, 134, 142), attributing probabilistic belief instead to 'an inexplicable contrivance of nature' (*E* 57). He also emphasizes again how peripheral such details are to his main business, commenting that he will 'think it sufficient, if the present hints excite the curiosity of philosophers' (*E* 59).

The digressions on his theory of belief now completed, Hume in Section VII comes to the second central topic of his 'chief argument', namely the analysis of causation and of the idea of necessary connexion. Here a number of themes come together and are intermingled (arguably even confused). First, Hume announces his objective of clarifying the important idea of 'power, force, energy, or necessary connexion' (*E* 62; cf. *A* 656) in accordance with his Copy Principle of Section II, by searching for an impression from which this idea might be derived.[41] Then he examines various putative sources of such an impression (notably our external perception of causal interactions, our internal perception of the operations of our will, and our idea of God), dismissing each of these in turn on the ground that nothing we perceive in any of these cases can yield any a priori understanding of the causal sequences involved—we can know only from experience what causes what, in either the external or the internal arena, and this implies that power or necessary connexion is simply not something that we can perceive. The Copy Principle, however, tells us that all genuine ideas are copies of impressions, so in the apparent absence of any corresponding impression, 'the necessary conclusion *seems* to be, that we have no idea of connexion or power at all, and that these words are absolutely without any meaning' (*E* 74). But Hume manages to avoid this sceptical result, for by turning his attention from passive perception to the active operation of the mind in factual reasoning, he after all succeeds in finding an impression to vindicate the crucial idea. As he has previously explained in Sections IV and V, after we have seen *A*s repeatedly and reliably followed by *B*s (what he calls a 'constant

---

[41] Although at *E* 62 Hume initially makes reference to the 'ideas' of '*power, force, energy,* or *necessary connexion*', he then (*E* 63–4) seems to treat them as a single idea, as he had also in the *Treatise* on the ground that they are 'nearly synonimous' (*T* 157).

conjunction' between *A* and *B*), any subsequent observation of an *A* leads us by custom to expect a *B*. He now draws his conclusion: 'This connexion, therefore, which we *feel* in the mind, this customary transition of the imagination from one object to its usual attendant, is the sentiment or impression, from which we form the idea of power or necessary connexion.' (*E* 75; cf. *A* 657). Hume rounds off this discussion in the *Enquiry* (but not in the *Abstract*) with two 'definitions of cause' (*E* 76–7) before a final 'recapitulation' (*E* 78–9). Such presenting of definitions accords well with the analytical objective announced at the beginning of the section, but nevertheless the real significance of most of the arguments that he has given in the meantime seems rather to be epistemological. Most of these arguments are focused on the impossibility of the sort of 'understanding' of causation that would yield causal knowledge independently of induction, and as such they serve primarily to reinforce the conclusions of Section IV. Even the most overtly analytical paragraphs of Section VII—where the genuine impression of necessity is finally identified and 'cause' defined (*E* 74–7)—have a similar epistemological tendency, for their central message is that we have absolutely no understanding of 'power' or 'necessary connexion' independently of our own inferential behaviour. When we try to contemplate any supposed connexion in nature, in the sense of an objective basis for causal inferences between events, not only do we lack any conception of such a connexion, but we lack 'even any distinct notion what it is we desire to know, when we endeavour at a conception of it' (*E* 77). One of Hume's motives for emphasizing this total lack of understanding of any supposed necessity in nature is indeed thoroughly epistemological, to refute the claims to knowledge of those such as Cartesians and 'modern metaphysicians' (*E* 73 n.) who claim to know by rational insight what types of thing can have which types of power. But Hume also has another motive which perhaps crucially accounts for the overt and otherwise puzzling analytical emphasis in Section VII: this motive becomes apparent only in Section VIII.

Hume's own view of the significance of his account 'of liberty and necessity' can be gauged from the fact that in the *Abstract* this is the only topic from Book II of the *Treatise* (II. iii. 1–2) to merit more than a brief mention, and is given no less than four paragraphs, more than any other single topic except induction (which is easily the longest) and belief. Likewise in the *Enquiry* it is the only Book II topic to find a place, with Hume astutely relocating it from its *Treatise* context within his treatment of the passions to a far more appropriate and conspicuous position immediately after his explication of the idea of necessary connexion. At the same time he considerably refines and extends his original discussion, whose limited main theme supporting the 'doctrine of necessity' is well summarized in the *Abstract* (*A* 660–1). In 'recasting' this for the *Enquiry* Hume redefines its objectives, modifies its terminology, improves its structure, strengthens its arguments, and incorporates within it observations regarding the use of inductive and probabilistic reasoning about both the physical world and human behaviour, in particular an important paragraph on scientific method and the search for hidden causes, copied verbatim from earlier in the *Treatise* (*T* 132, *E* 86–7). The section 'Of Liberty and Necessity' which results is not only the longest but one of the most philosophically important sections of the *Enquiry*, and one which accordingly deserves far more scholarly attention than it has hitherto been given. A striking instance of its relative neglect is the extent to which this section has been widely ignored in the recently fashionable debate over Hume's alleged 'causal realism'. And there is a major irony here, because if the suggestion at the end of my last paragraph is correct, then Hume's overtly analytical emphasis in his discussion of the idea of necessity—an emphasis whose interpretation is at the very heart of the 'causal realism' debate—is motivated very largely, perhaps even predominantly, by his need to prepare the ground for his resolution of the free will issue in Section VIII.

The ancient problem of free will and determinism arises from a perceived conflict between, on the one hand, the common-sense supposition that some human actions are genuinely free ('the doctrine of liberty'), and, on the other hand, the scientifically inspired belief that the world is governed by deterministic causal laws ('the doctrine of necessity'). Hume ascribes the 2,000 years' lack of progress on this issue to conceptual ambiguities (*E* 80–1), and accordingly sets out to remove these ambiguities, with the aim of showing 'that all men have ever agreed in the doctrines both of necessity and of liberty, according to any reasonable sense, which can be put on these terms' (*E* 81). The first stage of this clarification appeals directly to the results of Section VII: our idea of necessity is derived only from the customary transition of thought which is conditioned in us by the observation of a constant conjunction, and so 'Beyond the constant *conjunction* of similar objects, and the consequent *inference* from one to the other, we have no notion of any necessity, or connexion.' (*E* 82; cf. *A* 661). It follows that the doctrine of necessity, as it applies to human action, can amount to no more than the two claims that human actions follow consistent patterns, and that we draw inferences about them accordingly; both, Hume thinks, can be established beyond reasonable dispute (*E* 83–8 and 88–91 respectively). Turning now to the second stage of his 'reconciling project', Hume argues that 'By *liberty* . . . we can only mean *a power of acting or not acting, according to the determinations of the will*'—a degree of freedom 'universally allowed to belong to every one, who is not a prisoner and in chains' (*E* 95). Again Hume appeals to Section VII to back up his position, this time to dismiss as 'unintelligible' any rival conception of liberty which takes it to involve some form of non-necessitating causation (*E* 96). His own interpretations of the doctrines of 'necessity' and 'liberty' are, he concludes, the only ones that are tenable and coherent—and thus interpreted the two doctrines are not only manifestly consistent with each other, but true. This is not quite the end of the matter, however, because the doctrine of necessity in particular has traditionally been thought to be subversive of morality, and with this in mind Hume proceeds in Part ii of Section VIII to defend his account against any such accusation. So far from posing any danger to morality, he argues that both the doctrine of necessity and the doctrine of liberty, as he interprets them, are essential to it. Moreover, the 'moral sentiments' (E 102) which lead us to ascribe blame and merit are left quite unaffected by any such metaphysical niceties. Hume carefully refrains, however, from stating that the doctrine of necessity is harmless to religion, and he is content to leave unstated what is by then the obvious negative consequence regarding God's supposed goodness (E 103).

With Section IX of the *Enquiry* we move beyond the core of Hume's 'chief argument' to material which has no parallel in the *Abstract*, although it does correspond to a section in the *Treatise*, the identically named 'Of the reason of animals' (I. iii. 16). Despite its brevity this discussion has an important role in Hume's anti-rationalist campaign, firmly placing man's faculties within rather than above nature. But the paragraph with which it starts is also independently significant, making explicit an important general principle about analogical reasoning which has hitherto been at best implicit (cf. E 30–1, 72), and which will in due course be invoked within the argument of Section XI (E 143–6). This principle is, that since inductive inference involves the extrapolation of observed regularities—the prediction of similar effects from similar causes—it follows that the strength of such inference is crucially dependent on the degree of similarity involved. Thus where inferences are made regarding things that are not *exactly* similar to those previously observed, 'the analogy is less perfect, and the inference is less conclusive; though still it has some force, in proportion to the degree of similarity and resemblance' (E 104). This principle has a clear application to the reasoning of animals and of ourselves: animals are in many ways similar to us though not entirely, and so although it cannot be guaranteed that our cognitive processes will be the same as theirs, nevertheless an inference drawn from facts about animal reasoning to conclusions about human reasoning preserves enough analogy to have significant force. And this confirms Hume's account of induction, for animals, like us, clearly learn from experience, and since they evidently do not do this on the basis of abstruse arguments but through the operation of unreflective instinct—by simply taking for granted that past patterns will continue into the future—this strongly supports by analogy Hume's claim that the same is true of ourselves.

Sections X and XI have no parallel in the *Treatise* (or therefore in the *Abstract*), owing as we saw earlier to Hume's prudence in 'castrating' his first work through the removal of his most explicit attacks on religion. Both sections discuss popular arguments for God's existence, respectively the Argument from Miracles and the Design Argument, and the general philosophical theme which justifies their place in the *Enquiry* is common to both. Namely, that these revered arguments, though they (either implicitly or explicitly) depend on inductive reasoning, in fact violate the principles of that reasoning as established by the earlier analyses in Sections IV, V, VI, VIII, and IX. However, Sections X and XI should not be seen merely as applications of an already completed inductive 'theory'; rather, they serve as important illustrations of a general theoretical framework which at the same time provide Hume with the opportunity to develop that framework further, first in the direction of inferences involving conflicting probabilities, and then in the direction of inferences involving proportion and analogy. Hence these sections, though admittedly not part of the core of Hume's 'chief argument', are certainly more than mere appendices to it.

To take the case of miracles first, Hume has previously shown that induction, which is our only available method of 'reasoning concerning matter of fact', is founded on a basic simple assumption of uniformity. But this assumption does not imply that we should crudely extrapolate into the future those superficial and typically imperfect regularities which most immediately strike us. On the contrary, it should actively encourage a systematic search for initially less obvious, but more reliable, *underlying* regularities, so as to reveal more uniformity in the world's workings than is apparent at first glance (here the important paragraph at *E* 86–7, mentioned earlier, is particularly pertinent). Where we are unable to trace inconsistent phenomena to fully uniform underlying regularities, however, we have to make do with merely probable inferences drawn from this experience in the manner explained in Section VI: the wise man accordingly 'considers which side is supported by the greater number of experiments' and 'proportions his belief to the evidence' (*E* 110–11). If we apply these principles to reports of miracles, we shall find that the most consistent regularities, and those therefore that merit most inferential weight, are not those that tell in favour of the truthfulness of such reports but quite the reverse. For although we indeed have experience of a general correlation between reports of events and the truth of those reports, nevertheless this experience is by no means uniform and is subject to all sorts of familiar distortions (particularly when religious belief is involved), while on the other hand we inevitably have much more consistent experience that miraculous events—events contrary to the generally observed course of nature—just do not happen (or if they do, happen so rarely that any particular miracle report will always be far more likely to be false than true).

Hume's treatment of the Design Argument in Section XI draws attention in turn to three respects in which that argument violates the principles of inductive reasoning. The first, to which the majority of the section is devoted, involves a principle of proportionality: 'When we infer any particular cause from an effect, we must proportion the one to the other, and can never be allowed to ascribe to the cause any qualities, but what are exactly sufficient to produce the effect.' (*E* 136). This clearly rules out the traditional theologian's trick of first inferring the existence of a designer from the perceived order of nature, and then immediately arguing back from the inferred qualities of this designer (e.g. perfect goodness and justice) to draw *new* conclusions about nature (e.g. that the world must be better and more just than it appears). However, the principle does not rule out bringing additional evidence to bear, and so is not insurmountable except in cases where a cause is known *only* by the effect in question. In common life this will not usually be a problem, because the causes we infer are typically similar to others that we have previously experienced, enabling us at the very least to reason by analogy as discussed in Section IX. But the second difficulty with the Design Argument (*E* 143–6) is that in this case the analogy is just too distant to carry any force—indeed the remoteness of the analogy between man and God suggests a third and even more radical difficulty (*E* 148). For God is understood as being entirely unique, falling under no known species, and we have seen (from Sections IV and VII) that causal laws can be learned only through the observation of constant conjunctions between species of objects. Hence it follows that inductive causal inference, the only type of reasoning available for drawing any conclusions beyond mere 'relations of ideas', can have no legitimate application in attempting to prove God's existence.

The final section of the *Enquiry*, 'Of the Academical or Sceptical Philosophy', is the most difficult to interpret, presenting a wide variety of sceptical arguments whose ultimate purpose is sometimes hard to discern, and with subject-matter that goes well beyond the scope of Hume's 'chief argument' concerning induction and causal reasoning. There is nevertheless a corresponding passage in the *Abstract*, one which usefully highlights the three major themes of *scepticism*, *empiricism*, and *naturalism* which run through Hume's philosophy in the *Treatise*:

> By all that has been said the reader will easily perceive, that the philosophy contain'd in this book is very sceptical, and tends to give us a notion of the imperfections and narrow limits of human understanding. Almost all reasoning is there reduced to experience . . . Our author . . . upon the whole concludes, that we assent to our faculties, and employ our reason only because we cannot help it. Philosophy wou'd render us entirely *Pyrrhonian*, were not nature too strong for it. (*A* 657)

'The strange infirmities of human understanding' (*E* 161) also provide the first and most prominent theme of Section XII of the *Enquiry*, with Hume drawing the moral that we should be cautious and undogmatic in our reasoning and should confine 'our enquiries to such subjects as are best adapted to [our] narrow capacity' (*E* 150, 161–2). The naturalistic theme mentioned in the *Abstract* passage also plays a significant role throughout Section XII, for what saves us from Pyrrhonism (i.e. extreme scepticism) is not intellectual reflection but natural instinct, which determines us both to reason inductively despite the absence of any rational basis for so doing (*E* 159) and to believe in an external world even though that belief is groundless and dubiously coherent (*E* 151–5). Hume does not spell out exactly how all this scepticism is supposed to mesh with the generally scientific and constructive spirit of his 'chief argument' (represented by the empiricist theme in the quotation from the *Abstract* above), and he has thus left his interpreters with a difficult puzzle. But a personal view of what I take to be Hume's overall position would go roughly as follows.

Natural instinct gives us a belief in inductive uniformity which we find irresistible however strong the sceptical objections to it might be, so any attempt to displace or to doubt it would be quite futile. This being so, the wise response is simply to accept it and to reason accordingly, systematically following out its logical implications such as those revealed by the explorations in Sections VIII to XI—notably the principles of reasoning concerning hidden uniformities (*E* 86–7), analogy (*E* 104), conflicting evidence (*E* 110–11), proportionality (*E* 136), and unique causes (*E* 148). These provide a sufficient basis not only for everyday reasoning but also for empirical science, which indeed is 'nothing but the reflections of common life, methodized and corrected' (*E* 162) and whose only proper aspiration is 'to reduce the principles, productive of natural phaenomena, to a greater simplicity, and to resolve the many particular effects into a few general causes, by means of reasonings from analogy, experience, and observation' (*E* 30). Any more profound scientific ambition would be misguided because no form of rationalistic understanding of the world appears to be possible, and anyway the frailty of our faculties gives no ground for confidence when they attempt to draw conclusions beyond the range of the natural beliefs over which we have no choice. Even our fundamental belief in physical matter cannot provide any basis for a non-inductive science (although it is just as instinctive and irresistible as our belief in uniformity and therefore equally worthy of unquestioned acceptance), for it is far too confused, indeterminate, and even paradoxical to enable any deeper conclusions about the nature of things to be drawn from it with any security.

Thus inductive reasoning, founded on natural instinct, is vindicated as our only possible means of scientific progress, but appreciation of its relatively lowly foundation should inspire us with due humility in applying it: 'there is a degree of doubt, and caution, and modesty, which, in all kinds of scrutiny and decision, ought for ever to accompany a just reasoner' (*E* 162). An even more significant moral is 'the limitation of our enquiries to such subjects as are best adapted to the narrow capacity of human understanding' (*E* 162), a limitation whose basis is left rather unclear in the *Enquiry*, but is spelt out much more fully in Part I of the *Dialogues concerning Natural Religion*, in a long speech by Philo:

[W]hen we look beyond human affairs and the properties of the surrounding bodies: When we carry our speculations . . . into the creation and formation of the universe; the existence and properties of spirits . . . We must be far removed from the smallest tendency to scepticism not to be apprehensive, that we have here got quite beyond the reach of our faculties. So long as we confine our speculations to trade, or morals, or politics, or criticism, we make appeals, every moment, to common sense and experience, which strengthen our philosophical conclusions, and remove (at least, in part) the suspicion, which we so justly entertain with regard to every reasoning that is very subtile and refined. But in theological reasonings, we have not this advantage; while at the same time we are employed upon objects, which, we must be sensible, are too large for our grasp, and of all others, require most to be familiarised to our apprehension. We are like foreigners in a strange country, to whom everything must seem suspicious . . . We know not how far we ought to trust our vulgar methods of reasoning in such a subject; since, even in common life and in that province which is peculiarly appropriated to them, we cannot account for them, and are entirely guided by a kind of instinct or necessity in employing them.

All sceptics pretend [i.e. claim], that . . . we could never retain any conviction or assurance, on any subject, were not the sceptical reasonings so refined and subtile, that they are not able to counterpoise the more solid and more natural arguments, derived from the senses and experience. But it is evident, whenever our arguments lose this advantage, and run wide of common life, that the most refined scepticism comes to be on a footing with them, and is able to oppose and counterbalance them. The one has no more weight than the other. The mind must remain in suspense between them; and it is that very suspense or balance, which is the triumph of scepticism. (*D* 134–6)

Philo's position here seems to be identical with that taken by Hume in the *Enquiry*, but provides a much clearer rationale of the recommended limitation of our epistemic ambitions.[42]

---

[42] However, it is intriguing that Cleanthes' response to Philo (*D* 136–7) then raises serious questions about the adequacy of this rationale, indicating that Hume himself may ultimately have found it less than convincing. Certainly in the *Dialogues* he does not rely on it, but rejects the arguments of natural theology by showing in detail how they fail on their own terms to establish their conclusion, rather than on the general ground that they run wide of common life. A letter to Gilbert Elliot of Minto dated 18 Feb. 1751, just when the *Dialogues* were being composed, suggests that this may represent a conscious shift of principle: 'in Metaphysics or Theology . . . Nothing . . . can correct bad Reasoning but good Reasoning: and Sophistry must be oppos'd by Syllogism'. Hume then mentions various religions, and comments that 'no thinking man can implicitly assent to any of them; but from the general Principle, that as the Truth in these Subjects is beyond human Capacity, & that as for one's own Ease he must adopt some Tenets, there is more Satisfaction & Convenience in holding to the Catechism we have been first taught. Now this I have nothing to say against. I woud only observe, that such a Conduct is founded on the most universal & determin'd Scepticism, join'd to a little indolence. For more Curiosity & Research gives a direct opposite Turn from the same Principles.' (*HL* i. 151–2). The first draft of the *Dialogues* is explicitly discussed in Hume's next letter to Elliot, dated only twenty days later (*HL* i. 153–7).

The *Enquiry* itself draws to a close with a brief discussion of the appropriate limits. First, the scope of demonstrative methods is severely restricted, *except* in mathematics, by the lack of clear and precise relationships between our ideas—hence as far as reasonings of any significant intricacy are concerned, 'the only objects of the abstract sciences or of demonstration are quantity and number' (*E* 163). But induction from experience is the only other type of reasoning available, and thus it follows that the 'proper subjects of science and enquiry' (*E* 163) reduce to only those involving either 'abstract reasoning concerning quantity or number' or 'experimental reasoning concerning matter of fact and existence'. Anything else, such as 'divinity or school metaphysics, for instance', must be fanciful and fallacious, and so the *Enquiry* ends with Hume's famous verdict on the work of his theological and rationalist opponents: 'Commit it then to the flames: For it can contain nothing but sophistry and illusion' (*E* 165)!

Two Species of Philosophy: The Historical Significance of the First *Enquiry*

M. A. Stewart

Hume's *Enquiry concerning Human Understanding* was originally published under the title *Philosophical Essays concerning Human Understanding* in 1748. The title reference to 'Human Understanding' sets up one set of associations for the modern reader, but the opening sentence sets up another: we find ourselves reading about *moral* philosophy. In fact, the opening section as a whole locates the work within a particular topical controversy. To understand how that is so, we have to look both at Hume's career and at the nature of philosophy teaching at the time. The relevant events must be seen in the context of his relations in the 1740s with his fellow philosopher Francis Hutcheson and the Hutcheson circle; but those must be seen in turn against a broader background of the influence of the writings of Anthony Ashley Cooper, third Earl of Shaftesbury, in the early decades of the century.

In April 1745 Hume entered upon his first paid employment at the age of almost 34. Nearly twenty years earlier he had tried briefly but feebly to settle to the study of law, and nine years after that, equally briefly and feebly, started training as a merchant. When employment finally came, it was not the employment he wanted. Hume wrote to a friend of 'the Secrecy, with which I stole away from Edinburgh, & which I thought necessary for preserving my Interest there' (*HL* i. 60). The interest in question was his candidacy for the post of professor of moral philosophy at the University of Edinburgh.[1] The job he got while that candidacy was pending, and the position with which he had to console himself

---

[1] A full account of this episode is provided in M. A. Stewart, *The Kirk and the Infidel* (Lancaster: Lancaster University, 1995), where acknowledgement is also made to other recent studies.

when the candidacy failed, was that of tutor to George Johnstone, Marquess of Annandale. The marquess was a young Scots aristocrat of unstable mind, who had taken a temporary let of Weld Hall in Hertfordshire.

By early June 1745 Hume knew he was out of the running for the Edinburgh post. Looking to the future, he wrote to Henry Home of Kames, 'I intend to continue these philosophical & moral Essays, which I mention'd to you' (*NHL* 18). On leaving the marquess's employment in April 1746, Hume went briefly to London. A month later he had sent his baggage home, but it was nearly a year before he caught up with it. He was unexpectedly signed up as secretary to James St Clair, commander-elect of a projected escapade against French Canada; there was a four-month delay before the force was authorized to sail, and then it was to Brittany (*HL* i. 90, 94–8). During his enlistment Hume appears to have left his manuscripts for safe keeping with his parliamentarian friend James Oswald.[2] When he returned home in spring 1747, he finalized work on the *Philosophical Essays* and showed the manuscript to Henry Home, who considered it 'indiscreet' (*HL* i. 106). Hume persisted in his plans to publish: 'in the first place, I think I am too deep engaged to think of a retreat. In the second place, I see not what bad consequences follow, in the present age, from the character of an infidel; especially if a man's conduct be in other respects irreproachable.' (*HL* i. 106). Next winter Hume was again in London while the first edition of *Philosophical Essays* and the third edition of *Essays, Moral and Political* (including three new essays) were in the press. In mid-February 1748 he was once more with St Clair, on an embassy to Turin (*HL* i. 111). The works just mentioned came out during his absence, *Philosophical Essays* in April 1748 and the new edition of his other *Essays* in November.[3] Clearly, these had been the imminent projects mentioned in the letter to Home in June 1745.

Thus Hume had begun work on the *Enquiry* before his defeat for the Edinburgh post, but a certain amount of the writing was completed in the aftermath of that defeat. The proximity of the two events is confirmed by his adaptation of some of the very language of the *Enquiry* in a letter that he wrote to John Coutts, one of his principal backers, at the height of the crisis in Edinburgh. This letter, which formed the basis of part of *A Letter from a Gentleman to his Friend in Edinburgh*, an intended defence of the *Treatise* hastily thrown

---

[2] *HL* i. 106. In Hume's diary for a part of the expedition is a record of his own and his commander's luggage, including 'One Box Mr Hume's Books | Box Paper Mr Hume' (British Library, Add. MS 36638), so he may also have kept some study materials to occupy free moments.

[3] *Philosophical Essays* was extensively advertised in the London press in April. The records of the printer, William Strahan, show that the printing and publishing were, uncharacteristically, in the same month (British Library, Add. MS 48800, fo. 65). It is thus uncertain if Hume was around to see the proofs, and the edition appeared without any errata. Publication of the new edition of *Essays, Moral and Political* was delayed because Hume gave his friend Lord Tinwald discretion to determine its overall composition (*HL* i. 111–13).

together by Henry Home in May 1745, incorporates material from the footnote about the different traditions in natural philosophy that was to appear at the end of Section VII Part i of the *Enquiry*.[4] This overlap is significant. If we know the accusations against his philosophy that cost Hume the appointment, and the intellectual climate in which the accusations arose, much of the detail takes on a new interest and importance. First, however, we must trace the earlier history of some important metaphors that recur in Section I of the work, and show how they are related to his intellectual development and to the sequence of Hume's publications over the whole decade 1739–48.

I

When the first volumes of *A Treatise of Human Nature* appeared in 1739, sales and notices were disappointing. Hume consulted Hutcheson about the impending Book III, but failed to exercise the prudence on this occasion that he had exercised when he had hoped for Joseph Butler's opinion of the previous books (*HL* i. 25). Hutcheson, an Ulster Scot, was professor of moral philosophy at Glasgow and the leading Scottish philosopher of his generation, and had given civil acknowledgement to Books I–II of the *Treatise* on publication.[5] Hume would have known Hutcheson at this time only through his early, 1720s writings,[6] and seems to have underestimated the extent to which they were on a collision course over Book III. There followed both an exchange of letters and a face-to-face meeting; Hume tried meanwhile to promote the earlier volumes with his *Abstract* (1740). In 1741–2 came two sets of *Essays, Moral and Political*, some of which had been in preparation since before the completion of the *Treatise*. In 1745 the private correspondence that became public through the printing of *A Letter from a Gentleman* returned to the themes of the *Treatise*, but had a

---

[4] *L* 28–9; *PE* 118–19 n., rev. at *E* 73 n. There are a few other parallels, but none of the others so obviously suggests that Hume had the parallel narrative actually in front of him. The suggestion that Pyrrhonism is 'a Kind of *Jeu d'esprit*' (*L* 19–20) anticipates the comments at the end of Section XII Part ii (*PE* 247–9, *E* 159–60); and in both writings the distinctive example of 'a Horse' to illustrate a thesis on general ideas (*L* 26; *PE* 244–5 n., rev. and abridged at *E* 158 n.) reflects the great familiarity with horses and horse-riding that leads Hume to use them as examples in a number of different contexts. I assume, as one must, that in his letter Hume was cannibalizing the already drafted *Philosophical Essays*, not that in the latter work he copied from a letter that he had thrown off in a morning and is unlikely to have kept a copy of. Significantly, he did not find it relevant to include in his letter the reference to 'our modern Metaphysicians' (now generally supposed to include Andrew Baxter) which would be included in the footnote in *Philosophical Essays*.

[5] Henry Home served as intermediary. Later Hutcheson would help secure a continental review of Hume's work. See I. S. Ross, 'Hutcheson on Hume's *Treatise*: An Unnoticed Letter', *Journal of the History of Philosophy*, 4 (1966), 69–72; M. A. Stewart and J. Moore, 'William Smith (1698–1741) and the Dissenters' Book Trade', *Bulletin of the Presbyterian Historical Society of Ireland*, 23 (1993), 20–7.

[6] Francis Hutcheson, *An Inquiry into the Original of our Ideas of Beauty and Virtue; in Two Treatises* (1725 and later editions); *An Essay on the Nature and Conduct of the Passions and Affections. With Illustrations on the Moral Sense* (1728 and later editions).

negligible circulation; and in 1748 appeared *Philosophical Essays concerning Human Understanding*.

Hume had taken up privately Hutcheson's criticisms on a number of substantive topics in the *Treatise*: on teleology, motivation, the distinction between natural and artificial virtues, and abstract ideas (*HL* i. 33–5, 39).[7] To the charge that the concluding volume 'wants a certain Warmth in the Cause of Virtue' Hume responded that the mind, like the body, can be studied in different ways. The anatomist studies it 'to discover its most secret Springs & Principles', the painter 'to describe the Grace & Beauty of its Actions'. These are incompatible perspectives:

> Where you pull off the Skin, & display all the minute Parts, there appears something trivial, even in the noblest Attitudes & most vigorous Actions: Nor can you ever render the Object graceful or engaging but by cloathing the Parts again with Skin & Flesh, & presenting only their bare Outside. An Anatomist, however, can give very good Advice to a Painter or Statuary: And in like manner, I am perswaded, that a Metaphysician may be very helpful to a Moralist; tho' I cannot easily conceive these two Characters united in the same Work. (*HL* i. 32–3)

There is no reason to suppose Hume ever attended a dissection, but he would have heard as a student of the usefulness of anatomy to natural religion. In spite of its lasting importance to him as a source of analogy, he did not count it among the top sciences: it calls for assiduity rather than genius.[8] When he studied natural philosophy in his final year at college in 1724–5, he could have found in the class library Vesalius' graphically illustrated textbook of human anatomy.[9] More useful than this, however, would have been a compilation called *The Natural History of Animals*, where the authors distinguished the perception of the anatomist and the anatomical illustrator from that of the painter. The painter represents what is seen, which in many animals disguises rather than reveals their 'true' characteristics. The anatomist penetrates behind the

---

[7] He also responded publicly, without answering Hutcheson by name, in the sense that he made significant changes not simply to the Conclusion but across the whole of Book III. On the evidence of the correspondence, this included the removal of material that was gratuitously hostile to religious opinion (*HL* i. 34, 37); otherwise Hume seems to have been more concerned to reconstruct his defences than to concede anything to Hutcheson's views. At least one item in the Appendix, and therefore possibly more, is traceable to these exchanges (*HL* i. 39, *T* 637). See J. Moore, 'Hume and Hutcheson', in M. A. Stewart and J. P. Wright (eds.), *Hume and Hume's Connexions* (Edinburgh: Edinburgh University Press, 1994). In an earlier paper Moore has speculated that Hutcheson too revised his own publications in the light of his encounter with Hume: see 'The Two Systems of Francis Hutcheson', in M. A. Stewart (ed.), *Studies in the Philosophy of the Scottish Enlightenment* (Oxford: Clarendon Press, 1990), 58.

[8] Stewart, *Studies*, Introduction, 8.

[9] Andreas Vesalius, *De Humani Corporis Fabrica* (1543, 1555); this and the next work are listed in *The Physiological Library. Begun by Mr. Steuart, and some of the Students of Natural Philosophy in the University of Edinburgh* (1725), Edinburgh University Library, De 10.127. On this, see M. Barfoot, 'Hume and the Culture of Science in the Early Eighteenth Century', in Stewart, *Studies*.

appearance and learns to see what 'should be' represented: in the case of a bear, for example, 'there is no one which do's not find it wholly *Difforme*, when the Skin being flead off, it's true shape and Figure may be seen, without any hindrance or obstruction'.[10]

Painters themselves marked the distinction less sharply, having recognized ever since Leonardo's *Treatise on Painting* that a knowledge of anatomy, notably of bone relationships and musculature, was necessary for the effective depiction of motion, effort, even static poses. French theorists had stressed the connection in the seventeenth century, and it was familiar to British readers in the eighteenth century through the writing of Jonathan Richardson.[11] The painters naturally believed that painting was of equal service to anatomy. But by Hume's day anatomists had started to contest this; and a later eighteenth-century Scot, the surgeon John Bell, argued as forcefully as Hume for the separation of functions:

Even in the first invention of our best anatomical figures, we see a continual struggle between the anatomist and the painter; one striving for elegance of form, the other insisting upon accuracy of representation. It was thus that the celebrated Titian consented to draw for Vesalius: Though it is but too plain that there can be no truth in drawings, thus monstrously compounded betwixt the imagination of the painter, and the sober remonstrances of the anatomist, striving for accurate anatomy, where the thing cannot be; for those figures, which are supposed to be drawn truly from the anatomical table, are formed from the imagination of the painter merely; sturdy and active figures, with a ludicrous contrast of furious countenances, and active limbs, combined with ragged muscles, and naked bones, and dissected bowels, which they are busily employed in supporting, forsooth, or even demonstrating with their hands.[12]

Whether or not Hume was the first to appropriate the relationship between anatomy and painting in a metaphorical sense, the separate terms of the relation had had a long history as metaphors. Bacon had generally described his reformist programme as that of a husbandman cultivating the resources of the mind by curing its distempers. But in Book I of *The Advancement of Learning* he claimed to have 'described and opened, as by a kind of dissection, those peccant

---

[10] *The Natural History of Animals containing the Anatomical Description of several Creatures, Dissected by the Royal Academy of Sciences at Paris* (1702), sig. b3ʳ and p. 43.

[11] Leonardo da Vinci, *Trattato della pittura* (posth., 1651; French edn. 1651; Eng. edn. 1721); Roger de Piles, *Abrégé d'anatomie, accommodé aux arts de peinture et de sculpture* (1667; pseud. François Tortebat); id., *Cours de peinture par principes* (1708), 38, 153–8, trans. as *The Principles of Painting, under the Heads of Anatomy* (1743), 23, 95–8; Charles Alphonse Dufresnoy, *De Arte Graphica*, with French trans. and comm. R. de Piles (posth., 1668), Eng. trans. under the same title with additional essays by John Dryden (1695), precept VII; Jonathan Richardson, *An Essay on the Theory of Painting* (1715), 22, 136–7.

[12] John Bell, *Engravings of the Anatomy of the Bones, Muscles and Joints* (1794), p. vi. Among modern anatomists who had by Hume's day begun to repudiate 'the interference of painters in a subject degrading to their highest art', Bell mentions Bidloo (1708), Morgagni (1720s), Albinus (1725), and Cheselden (1726).

humours . . . which have not only given impediment to the proficience of learning, but have given also occasion to the traducement thereof'. Hobbes, in the opening chapter of his *Human Nature*, had distinguished the 'anatomy' of the powers of the body from a comparable study of the powers of the mind. For more than a century authors published 'anatomies' of psychological subjects,[13] to the point where Swift briefly satirized the idea of a 'Dissection of Human Nature' in *A Tale of a Tub*. Blackmore, in a poetic adaptation of the latest philosophy to promote natural religion, captured Locke's uncertainty about a correct division of the mental faculties:

> The Learned, who with Anatomic Art
> Dissect the Mind, and thinking Substance part,
> And various Pow'rs and Faculties assert;
> Perhaps by such Abstraction of the Mind
> Divide the Things, that are in Nature joyn'd.[14]

On the other side, a friendly rivalry between the advocates of painting and poetry as to which was the superior profession, particularly in its moral effectiveness, did not prevent them from adopting one another's vocabulary; writers generally, but poets in particular, were portrayed as 'painting' when they described scenes in a way calculated to move the reader or hearer.[15]

Hume was not just cashing in on other people's metaphors to make an *ad hominem* point to Hutcheson. He had already identified his project as that of 'the accurate anatomy of human nature' when he was writing Book I (*T* 263), and this terminology occurs again in his self-projection in the *Abstract* (*A* 646). In the discussion of the passions in Book II an ingenious parallel is drawn from physical anatomy, to suggest that the analogy between animal and human structures which provides the *raison d'être* for animal experimentation can be applied also to the 'anatomy of the mind' (*T* 325–6).

---

[13] John Lyly, *Euphues: The Anatomy of Wit* (1578); Simion Grahame, *The Anatomy of Humors* (1609); Robert Burton, *The Anatomy of Melancholy* (1621); Ephraim Huit, *The Anatomy of Conscience* (1626); Silvester Jenks, *An Essay upon the Art of Love, containing an Exact Anatomy of Love and all the other Passions which Attend it* (1702). The terminology of 'anatomy' and 'dissection' was also applied to social, political, and ecclesiastical commentary. Those engaged in the literal study of physical anatomy had an alternative metaphor for their own work: they saw themselves as 'geographers' who produced 'atlases' of the body.

[14] Richard Blackmore, *The Creation* (1712), VII. 560–4. Blackmore explained his project, in terms reminiscent of Shaftesbury, as an attempt 'to bring Philosophy out of the secret Recesses of the Schools, and strip it of its uncouth and mysterious Dress, that it may become agreeable, and admitted to a general Conversation'. His theistic counterblast to Lucretius was commended by Addison (*The Spectator*, no. 339): 'The Reader cannot but be pleased to find the Depths of Philosophy enlivened with all the Charms of Poetry, and to see so great a Strength of Reason, amidst so beautiful a Redundancy of the Imagination.'

[15] Thus, for the poet as painter, see Edward Young in *The Guardian*, no. 86 (19 June 1713), James Arbuckle in *The Dublin Weekly Journal*, no. 13 (26 June 1725); for the painter as poet, Steele in *The Spectator*, no. 226 (19 Nov. 1711). For broad comparisons between painting and poetry, see Dryden, 'A Parallel betwixt Painting and Poetry', in *De Arte Graphica*, citing classical precursors; Richardson, *Essay*, 21–2; Jean-Baptiste Dubos, *Réflexions critiques sur la poësie et sur la peinture* (1719; Eng. trans. 1748).

Right at the outset of the *Treatise* Hume had warned readers against expecting that the painstaking analysis he was engaged in was going to be 'so very easy and obvious'. 'For if truth be at all within the reach of human capacity, 'tis certain it must lie very deep and abstruse' (*T* xv, xiv). By the early part of Book III this deep analysis appears to have brought him to endorse the Hutchesonian thesis that moral distinctions are 'deriv'd from a moral sense' (*T* 470). But the agreement is cosmetic. Although this moral sense is in some way rooted in our nature, Hume quickly rejects the suggestion that it operates as a kind of natural instinct without regard to other considerations. By the Conclusion, which he revised in the light of his correspondence with Hutcheson, these other considerations have usurped the stage in a direct challenge to Hutcheson's presentation. Hume's final position is that 'sympathy is the chief source of moral distinctions' (*T* 618; cf. *T* 579). 'Those who resolve the sense of morals into original instincts of the human mind, may defend the cause of virtue with sufficient authority; but want the advantage, which those possess, who account for that sense by an extensive sympathy with mankind.' (*T* 619). For it is only through the operation of sympathy that we have the 'interest', either in the individual or society, that evokes the approbation we feel at the virtuous conduct both of others and of ourselves. 'All lovers of virtue'—whom Hume had addressed in the epigraph on the title-page of Book III—'must certainly be pleas'd to see moral distinctions deriv'd from so noble a source, which gives us a just notion both of the *generosity* and *capacity* of our nature.' (*T* 619).

Much of the intervening discussion, as so often in the *Treatise*, had been concerned with the complex mechanisms by which the particular faculty ('so noble a source') actually operates. These are now exploited in order to show that, and why, this operation of sympathy is inherently satisfying to us—and how, through it, the moral sense is simultaneously both disinterested and engaged. In a way that might be construed as too self-centred, Hume momentarily warms to the way that this reciprocity of interest brings individual happiness, but then checks himself, taking a public stand on the distinction he had previously expressed privately to Hutcheson:

I forbear insisting on this subject. Such reflexions require a work a-part, very different from the genius of the present. The anatomist ought never to emulate the painter: nor in his accurate dissections and portraitures of the smaller parts of the human body, pretend to give his figures any graceful and engaging attitude or expression. There is even something hideous, or at least minute in the views of things, which he presents; and 'tis necessary the objects shou'd be set more at a distance, and be more cover'd up from sight, to make them engaging to the eye and imagination.

Again, however, the anatomist can help the painter, who 'must have an exact knowledge of the parts' before he can 'design with any elegance or correctness'.

And thus the most abstract speculations concerning human nature, however cold and unentertaining, become subservient to *practical morality*; and may render this latter science more correct in its precepts, and more persuasive in its exhortations. (*T* 620–1)

Hume himself, however, was not going to take matters that far.

It is natural to think we know what is in contention here, from the evidence of Hutcheson's biographers. His colleague William Leechman was to testify to Hutcheson's 'rational enthusiasm', which 'animated him at all times', and which led him on occasion to abandon the confining 'character of the didactic teacher'.[16]

He apprehended that he was answering the design of his office as effectually, when he dwelt in a more diffusive manner upon such moral considerations as are suited to touch the heart, and excite a relish for virtue, as when explaining or establishing any doctrine, even of real importance, with the most philosophical exactness: he regarded the culture of the heart as a main end of all moral instruction: he kept it habitually in view, and he was extremely well qualified for succeeding in it, so far as human means can go: he had an uncommon vivacity of thought and sensibility of temper, which rendered him quickly susceptible of the warmest emotions upon the great subjects of morals and religion: this gave a pleasant unction to his discourses, which commanded the attention of the students, and at the same time left strong impressions upon their minds.[17]

The effect was that, when Hutcheson 'described the several virtues exercised in real life, as beautiful in themselves, as the noblest employment of our rational and moral powers, as the only sources of true dignity and happiness to individuals and to communities', his students were reputedly 'charmed with the lovely forms, and panted *to be* what they beheld'.

This is more than the conventional party defences of an obituarist—though it is that too. It represents the professional preacher's ideal, and it is no surprise that natural religion should loom large in Leechman's account of its application. But neither Hutcheson nor Leechman was a 'declamatory' preacher, and Hutcheson had been scornful of those who deliberately manipulate the emotions:

A Habit of this kind is soon contracted, and the Effect of it very charming to many Minds, and indeed it is a much more easy Task than to gain the rational Approbation of Gentlemen of Virtue and Discernment. But alas need I say of what vast Prejudice this

---

[16] Some recent commentators have identified 'warmth' with 'didacticism' (R. B. Sher, 'Professors of Virtue', and P. B. Wood, 'Science and the Pursuit of Virtue in the Aberdeen Enlightenment', both in Stewart, *Studies*), but in 18th-century usage these were contrasted. On Leechman, see M. A. Stewart, 'Leechman, William', in J. W. Yolton *et al.*, *The Dictionary of Eighteenth-Century British Philosophers*, 2 vols. (Bristol: Thoemmes Press, 1999), ii. 543–4.

[17] William Leechman, Preface to Francis Hutcheson, *A System of Moral Philosophy*, 2 vols. (Glasgow, 1755), vol. i, pp. xxxi–ii; but see pp. xxvi–xxxiii, throughout. Other friends and students left similar testimonies to Hutcheson's singular effect as a moralist and communicator both in and out of the classroom. See Sher, 'Professors of Virtue', 97–8.

would be to all elegant and valuable Studies? and what is much more to be considered a very great Loss to the Interests of true Religion and Virtue?[18]

If we look for passages in Hutcheson's own writing which evince the attitudes he failed to find in Hume, they do not jump off the page. One can point to the conclusion to Book I of his moral 'Compend', translated as 'Some practical considerations to excite and preserve the study of virtue', and the conclusions to the first and third books of his *System of Moral Philosophy*.[19] These publications postdate the debate with Hume. If we look for something that Hutcheson missed in Hume's writing but could already point to in his own, then we shall probably identify it with a stress on the good in human nature, and on the peace and pleasure that come both to others and to ourselves from a life lived in conformity with, rather than against, the designs of nature. In VI. 1–2 of the 'Inquiry concerning Virtue', Hutcheson set out to 'consider the *moral Pleasures . . .* as they are the *most delightful Ingredient* in the ordinary Pleasures of *Life*'. He did this by sketching a number of scenarios in which various pleasures are present or absent while the 'moral Pleasures' of love and friendship are added or subtracted, to show that 'a *Mixture* of the *moral Pleasures* is what gives the *alluring Relish*'. And in VI. 2 of his 'Essay on the Passions', Hutcheson reinforces the point that this is no mere exercise of the study: 'If these Studies be only matter of *Amusement* and *Speculation*, instead of leading us into a constant *Discipline* over our selves, to correct our Hearts, and to guide our Actions, we are not much better employed, than if we had been studying some useless Relations of *Numbers*, or Calculations of *Chances*.'[20]

To help avoid too intellectual an approach, Hutcheson stressed the great use of poetry in appealing to the moral sense. Epic and tragedy, by concentrating so largely on character depiction, 'give a vastly greater Pleasure than the Writings of *Philosophers*, tho both aim at recommending *Virtue*'; while the use of moral epithets in the graphic personification of qualities and agencies creates 'a greater Beauty in this manner of Representation, this Imagery, this Conjunction of *moral Ideas*, than in the fullest Narration, or the most lively natural Description'.[21]

That Hume, for his part, should stand his ground and wish to defend the autonomy of metaphysics at the end of the *Treatise* is not surprising. To do otherwise would have been inconsistent with the stance he had taken at the outset. Hume was to present in this work a 'science of MAN' which would be the

---

[18] [Hutcheson,] *Considerations on Patronages* (1735), 20–1.

[19] *A Short Introduction to Moral Philosophy* (1747; Latin edns. 1742, 1745), ch. 7; *A System of Moral Philosophy*, i. 221–6, ii. 376–80.

[20] *An Essay on the Nature and Conduct of the Passions and Affections* (1728), 173–4.

[21] *An Inquiry into the Original of our Ideas of Beauty and Virtue* (1725), 240–4. The moral function of poetry had already been identified by Bacon.

'only solid foundation' for all the other sciences, from those which 'more intimately concern human life' (which include 'Logic, Morals, Criticism, and Politics'), to those which 'are the objects of pure curiosity' (which include 'Mathematics, Natural Philosophy, and Natural Religion'); and it would have the necessary limitations of any study based on experiment (*T* xv–xvi). Because the *Treatise* was a foundational study, it was never going to deal comprehensively even with those branches of philosophy that are addressed within it. Hutcheson should not have been so surprised at the omissions, but Hume probably misjudged the omissions complained of. By identifying 'Warmth' with 'an Air of Declamation' he seems to be placing Hutcheson in the tradition whose best-known Scottish exponents would be George Turnbull, Thomas Blackwell the younger, and David Fordyce, a succession of teachers at Marischal College, Aberdeen. They had not yet published, but all found a common inspiration in the rhapsodic style of the third Earl of Shaftesbury. Hume himself was to parody this style in three essays depicting the non-Sceptic sects ('The Epicurean', 'The Stoic', 'The Platonist').

In emphasizing in the *Treatise* that his researches must 'lie very deep and abstruse', Hume contrasted his 'anatomical' approach with the 'indolent' acceptance of a philosophy which is 'natural and entertaining'. The latter he regarded as the superficial refuge of those who see only the weak foundations of competing systems, for whom 'Amidst all this bustle 'tis not reason, which carries the prize, but eloquence; and no man needs ever despair of gaining proselytes to the most extravagant hypothesis, who has art enough to represent it in any favourable colours.' (*T* xiv). Later he notes the way that verbal painting—'in all the colours of eloquence'—plays upon the imagination and induces belief (*T* 123) or influences passion (*T* 387, 426–7). But the effect is unreal compared with that of direct experience or causal reasoning. 'There is something weak and imperfect amidst all that seeming vehemence of thought and sentiment, which attends the fictions of poetry.' (*T* 631).

II

Hume had suffered in his late teens from too much competing eloquence about virtue.[22] He had read intensively in the ancient moralists, which induced a nervous crisis. He recovered, but kept his distance thereafter from this mode of philosophizing. He suggested in his letter to Hutcheson that it would be a breach of 'good Taste' to combine the anatomist's and painter's roles in the same work, and that this would not help the cause in question. Even if he could not

[22] M. A. Stewart, 'The Stoic Legacy in the Early Scottish Enlightenment', in M. J. Osler (ed.), *Atoms, Pneuma, and Tranquillity* (Cambridge: Cambridge University Press, 1991).

easily have found the combination, as he portrayed it, in Hutcheson, he could in Shaftesbury, who had recommended just the kind of regimen in the ancient moralists that had destroyed Hume's mental equilibrium. Shaftesbury had his anatomical moments, as Hume acknowledged (*T* xviin.). But by having publicly identified himself with Shaftesbury's substantive philosophy, and then privately advocated 'Warmth in the cause of Virtue' to Hume, Hutcheson had probably sent him the wrong signals.

Hume acquired his third-edition set of Shaftesbury's *Characteristicks* in 1726.[23] This was a compilation very much in the Bayle mould (Bayle and Shaftesbury had been friends), where the message has to be followed through a trail of references.[24] The philosophical heart of the work is its second volume, containing the narrative treatise 'An Inquiry concerning Virtue, or Merit' and the dialogue 'The Moralists'. The first volume discusses literary and philosophical method in some rather rambling essays and the third volume, 'Miscellaneous Reflections', adopts the standpoint of an independent commentator on his own work. Style and tone are in permanent flux as Shaftesbury variously assails, cajoles, and engages the sympathies of a readership of gentlemen, virtuosi, persons of political standing or literary talent, who share his concern for religion and virtue and his impatience with priests, cloistered scholastics, and mad enthusiasts. He sought by his methods to unite opposites—gentlemen and scholars, virtuosi and persons of virtue—through a programme of reflection that was predominantly Stoic in inspiration. He admired the Stoics for what he considered their life of action as well as their rational religion, and for their identification with nature as the ground of morality and society; the main alternative he identified with Epicureanism, which he considered both shallow and hostile to all Stoicism's lofty ambitions. The key to Stoic success was, however, an intense programme of self-reflection, aided through conversation with one's philosophical peers.

At some time between Hume's reading in Shaftesbury and 1729,

There was another particular, which contributed more than any thing, to waste my Spirits & bring on me this Distemper, which was, that having read many Books of Morality, such as Cicero, Seneca & Plutarch, & being smit with their beautiful Representations of

---

[23] University of Nebraska Library, SPEC 108n Sh1c, v.1–v.3.

[24] For a superb account of Shaftesbury's method and his impact on different communities of 18th-century readers, see I. Rivers, 'Shaftesburian Enthusiasm and the Evangelical Revival', in J. Garnett and C. Matthew (eds.), *Revival and Religion since 1700: Essays for John Walsh* (London: Hambledon Press, 1993); ead., *Reason, Grace and Sentiment: A Study of the Language of Religion and Ethics in England, 1660–1780*, 2 vols. (Cambridge: Cambridge University Press, 1991–2000), ii: *Shaftesbury to Hume*. Rivers highlights the elements of Shaftesburian parody in Hume's *Essays*, and notes significant divergences between Hutcheson's and Shaftesbury's positions. On the latter, see also S. Darwall, *The British Moralists and the Internal 'Ought'* (Cambridge: Cambridge University Press, 1995).

Virtue & Philosophy, I undertook the Improvement of my Temper & Will, along with my Reason & Understanding. I was continually fortifying myself with Reflections against Death, & Poverty, & Shame, & Pain, & all the other Calamities of Life. These no doubt are exceeding useful, when join'd with an active Life; because the Occasion being presented along with the Reflection, works it into the Soul, & makes it take a deep Impression, but in Solitude they serve to little other Purpose, than to waste the Spirits, the Force of the Mind meeting with no Resistance, but wasting itself in the Air, like our Arm when it misses its Aim. (*HL* i. 13–14)

Hume's prosecution of this regimen left him not only in turmoil—other factors contributed, like a loss of religious conviction—but predisposed towards the Epicurean alternative, which by the early eighteenth century shared a certain amount of common ground with scepticism.[25] The *Treatise* was the great working out of this synthesis, but in the short term it failed.

For some months before he received and responded to Hutcheson's criticism of his performance as a moralist in 1739, Hume had been experimenting with his own alternative to abstract reasoning. This was the writing of popular philosophical essays, primarily for the improvement of coffee-table and tea-table conversation, after the manner of the *Tatler* and *Spectator*. Of those which were published in the two collections of *Essays, Moral and Political* of 1741–2, some were quickly dropped, including one 'Of Essay Writing' which tells us how Hume saw his alternative role at the time. He had resolved to help develop a Shaftesburian 'League betwixt the learned and conversible Worlds', by introducing into literary essays a distillation of such philosophical insights and literary and historical learning as might assist or stimulate those who 'join to a sociable Disposition, and a Taste of Pleasure, an Inclination to the easier and more gentle Exercises of the Understanding, to obvious Reflections on human Affairs, and the Duties of common Life, and to the Observation of the Blemishes or Perfections of the particular Objects, that surround them'.[26] At the same time he wished to discourage reading in subjects that attracted bombastic writers, whose works induced warm passions among the ladies.

In another short-lived and over-gallant essay, 'Of the Study of History', he considered three possible literary genres for promoting virtue. These are the three 'parts of human learning' identified in Book II of Bacon's *Advancement of Learning*—history, poetry, and philosophy, which for Bacon related respectively to the faculties of memory, imagination, and reason. Taking an opposite line to Hutcheson's, Hume came down on the side of history:

---

[25]   Moore, 'Hume and Hutcheson'.

[26]   *Essays* 553–5. Cf. Blackmore, *The Creation*, and Addison, *The Spectator*, no. 339. For useful studies of Hume's early essays, see N. Smith, 'Hume's "Rejected" Essays', *Forum for Modern Language Studies*, 8 (1972), 354–71; M. A. Box, *The Suasive Art of David Hume* (Princeton: Princeton University Press, 1990), ch. 3.

Poets can paint virtue in the most charming colours; but, as they address themselves entirely to the passions, they often become advocates for vice. Even philosophers are apt to bewilder themselves in the subtility of their speculations; and we have seen some go as far as to deny the reality of all moral distinctions. But I think it a remark worthy the attention of the speculative, that the historians have been, almost without exception, the true friends of virtue, and have always represented it in its proper colours, however they may have erred in their judgments of particular persons. (*Essays* 567)[27]

Hume's own historical writing was still some years away. But the attempt to write moral essays at the level of popular journalism soon palled and the essays concerned were gradually withdrawn. He turned to the more up-market model of *The Craftsman* and to writings directed to those he considered his social and intellectual peers. A transitional paper which found its way into the permanent canon was 'The Sceptic', one of a tetralogy of pieces on alternative philosophical stances. This presents a succinct picture of the nature and limits of moral enquiry within the context of philosophical scepticism: it makes plain Hume's own conviction that philosophy—any philosophy—has little direct impact on living, and his 'doubts concerning all those exhortations and consolations, which are in such vogue among speculative reasoners' (*Essays* 171). In a long footnote he identifies a limited role for inductive experience in the formation of moral maxims. That this is consistent with, and not a retraction of, the stance of a 'sceptical moralist' is clear from its reappearance in the 'sceptical solution' of the sceptic's doubts in *Philosophical Essays* (*PE* 74–6 n., *E* 43–5 n.).

Once the slighter early essays drop from the canon, a number of relatively isolated pieces remain, but the majority of Hume's *Essays* consist in groups of loosely related pieces. There is, for example, not just the cluster of papers on philosophical sects, but another on government and parties; then a later cluster on monetary matters, and a further group on politics. *Philosophical Essays concerning Human Understanding* was first presented to the public as another anonymous collection 'By the AUTHOR of the ESSAYS MORAL and POLITICAL', both title and content suggesting that it was originally conceived after the same plan. In the first three editions (1748, 1750–1, 1756), what we now know as the 'sections' of the *Enquiry* were individually numbered 'essays', a usage that still survives in the critical literature in references that have continued since Hume's day to the 'essay' on miracles. At the heart of the whole seems to be an attempt, like that of 'The Sceptic', to present in revised form some selected but related

---

[27] Thus Machiavelli 'discovers a true sentiment of virtue in his history of FLORENCE'. History is, for Hume, the discipline which *par excellence* studies cause and effect in human behaviour (see the original version of Essay III, 'Of the Connexion of Ideas', in *Philosophical Essays*), and so—as he sees it—the consequences of different forms of motivation (see also the long footnote to Essay V). On history versus poetry, which Hume continued to associate with the Baconian faculties of memory and imagination respectively, cf. *T* 630–1.

elements of Hume's philosophy in as straightforward a way as the subject-matter allowed, avoiding the ancillary detail that had given the *Treatise* its systematic character but defeated virtually all readers.

On the surface, Essay I is a general essay on philosophical writing, just as Essay I of the 1742 *Essays* was a general essay on essay writing, but I shall come back to this in a moment. Essays II–III jointly lay the foundations and supply the raw materials that will be needed by the remaining pieces. If Essay II does not fit the essay mould as happily as some of the others, it is nevertheless more tightly organized than the discursive opening sections of the *Treatise* on which it is modelled; it comes to a more decisive climax, with a decision procedure for identifying sense and nonsense in metaphysics. In Essay III a summary account of the association of ideas is used as a preface to 'some of the Effects of this Connexion upon the Passions and Imagination' (*PE* 33); but with the posthumous deletion of the last two-thirds of this section, the residue now remaining in most modern editions takes on a different role as preface to the argument of Sections IV–V, especially V. ii.[28]

Essays IV–VI sketch the constructive scepticism which Hume sees as the natural outcome of the account of our faculties in Essays II–III. The flamboyant opening of Essay V, denouncing Stoic hypocrisy, disrupts the continuity and is a legacy of the format which once gave a degree of literary autonomy to the individual sections. Essays VII–XI apply the preceding philosophy to a small group of central topics in moral psychology and the philosophy of action—the primary interest of Essays VII–IX—and to problems in the foundations of revealed and natural religion—Essays X–XI. In spite of their cognate subject-matter, both VII and VIII begin *de novo* with a moral about the need for verbal exactness in philosophy, echoing the peroration of Essay II: this again suggests their status as originally separate pieces rather than sections of a single evolving narrative, with the break in continuity particularly evident at the beginning of VII. The pieces on religion are striking for their combined length, which would be out of proportion in a work that had been genuinely conceived as a single narrative on the operations of the understanding. 'Of Miracles' was indeed once planned as a section of the *Treatise* and retains some of the enigmatic character of the longer work; in its original form it probably consisted in only the first part.[29] The other piece, originally titled 'Of the Practical Consequences of Nat-

---

[28]   Green and Grose, whose edition of the *Enquiry* was appropriated by Hendel, identify three sample editions in which the complete text of Section III occurs during Hume's lifetime, but there were in fact ten—*all* the editions up to and including the last one which Hume himself saw through the press (1772). The lifetime text is reinstated in T. L. Beauchamp's new Clarendon edition.

[29]   The epistemology and psychology of Part i fit with the epistemology and psychology of the *Treatise*, but there is an escalation in Hume's critical interest in the institutions and social circumstances of religion in the post-*Treatise* period. I include his manuscript memoranda in that period.

ural Religion' and now known under its later title 'Of a Particular Providence and of a Future State', is a complex literary exercise: both titles are a smokescreen, along with the pretence of a dialogue, deflecting attention from the primary content. And the final essay, 'Of the Academical or Sceptical Philosophy', provides an exposition and assessment which are largely independent of, though not inconsistent with, the presentation in the preceding essays.

That the whole collection might be presented as something more than the sum of its constituent essays seems to have occurred to Hume first around 1758, when he retitled it *An Enquiry concerning Human Understanding*. This signalled that the work was in future to be seen as some sort of counterweight to the more recent *Enquiry concerning the Principles of Morals*, but tells us nothing about how it was first conceived.[30] It was at least partly a device to streamline the organization of Hume's multifarious collections for a one-volume omnibus edition, but it may also signal a continuing shift in his conception of the essay genre. In his 1741 *Essays* (pp. iii, v) Hume had stressed that in any set of essays the pieces are individually self-standing. That extreme position does not suit the limited interdependence of the component parts of what would become the two *Enquiries*.

There is no great significance in Hume's having already recommended his *Philosophical Essays* in preference to the *Treatise* in his letters to Gilbert Elliot in 1751 and to John Stewart in 1754 (*HL* i. 158, 187): these need only be taken as saying that *Philosophical Essays* contained the relevant substance of his philosophy on those matters (such as causation) that Elliot and Stewart were contesting. It is in the last year of his life—in the late 'Advertisement' to the second volume of his collected *Essays and Treatises*, which he sent to his printer in October 1775, and in 'My Own Life' which he wrote in April 1776 for posthumous publication—that Hume is finally explicit that the first *Enquiry* was a recasting of Book I of the *Treatise*. This was the line he wished to promote to posterity, for reasons that must have been in part prudential. He either did not wish to be remembered for a relative failure, or wished to gloss over changes of mind since 1740, or genuinely believed that the *Enquiries* preserved enough of his philosophy in a form that did not give unnecessary hostages to his critics. It was, nevertheless, a rationalization. The drastic change made in the posthumous role of Section III is consistent with this—a change in philosophical conception at the expense of literary balance.

The original full-length Essay III goes well beyond the rudimentary thoughts on poetry and history in the Appendix to the *Treatise* (*T* 630–2) and the early

---

[30] The moral *Enquiry* also was originally projected as a set of essays: the evidence for this is in the first-edition errata, where two survivals of 'Essay' for 'Section' are identified and corrected. But Hume decided on the title change here ahead of publication, and did not bring the first *Enquiry* into line with it until two editions later.

Essays, but is by no means the only point of major divergence between *Treatise* and *Philosophical Essays*. Two essays, as I have noted, are distinctive for their theological emphasis. But in fact nearly half of the constituent pieces cover ground which is somewhat different from that covered in *Treatise* I, although clearly indebted to the same general philosophy; and significant elements of Hume's moral philosophy are incorporated in Essays I, V, VII, and XII. It was intended as a coherent collection that would take the reader into religion and morals, and into history and aesthetics, as well as psychology and metaphysics.

Thus Essay II concludes with a brisk resolution of one of the contested questions in moral philosophy: if we define our terms precisely, there is no reason to dispute the existence of either natural or innate passions. Essay III, in its original form, concentrates largely on how a writer creates the unity of action which moves the reader or hearer of poetry and history. The techniques of the poet are again assimilated to those of the painter. In Essay V, where custom is identified as a 'natural Instinct' or 'mechanical Tendency' of the mind, its influence is traceable alike in science, history, and morals. There are cross-references from physical to moral subjects in both Essay IV (Part i) and Essay V (especially the long footnote in Part i). Essay VII deals relatively summarily with the celebrated problems of the definition of cause, preceding this with a substantial discussion of our defective sense of human agency and of the hollowness of occasionalism's attribution to the Deity of operations we do not understand in ourselves. If only moral subjects could have the precision of mathematical ones! That develops into a three-way comparison between mathematics, morals (with metaphysics appended), and natural philosophy—and all as an elaborate lead-in to the obscurity of power as an idea in what is indifferently called 'Metaphysics' and the 'moral Sciences'. The next essay, 'Of Liberty and Necessity', concentrates on the intimate connexion between our knowledge of motivation and our sense of voluntary action. Here, the obscurity is less endemic in the subject-matter than in the sophistry of philosophers: but this at least is a topic which has a resolution, and whose resolution is equally assumed in history, politics, morals, and criticism. It is unlike those topics 'that lie entirely beyond the Reach of human Capacity, such as those concerning the Origin of Worlds, or the Oeconomy of the intellectual System or Region of Spirits' (*PE* 130, *E* 81). This comment prepares us for the impending discussions of revealed and natural religion in the essays to come. But the discussion of miracles turns out to be less a discussion in the philosophy of religion than in the philosophy of history.

This is not, then, a narrow study of 'human understanding'. It is the application of a theory of the understanding across most of the disciplinary fields where anyone in the eighteenth century would expect to find it applied; and they all come under the umbrella of 'moral philosophy' broadly conceived.

III

We have seen that Hume's writing of his *Philosophical Essays* overlapped his stay at Weld Hall in 1745–6, and that this coincided with the final crisis in the unsuccessful campaign of his friends in Edinburgh to secure for him the vacant chair of moral philosophy. The post was formally in the gift of the town council, but they faced pressures from political and other quarters. Hutcheson led the academic opposition from outside, recommending several alternative candidates, one of whom (William Cleghorn) was successful. His opposition was supported by Leechman, an Edinburgh graduate who was now professor of divinity at Glasgow but had personal and professional links with Edinburgh. Inside the university and among the clergy, the attack on Hume was led by the principal, William Wishart, a lifelong follower of Hutcheson, who as a young divine had once participated in the election of Hutcheson to the corresponding Glasgow chair in 1729.[31] He now sank his differences with the evangelical ministers of Edinburgh to mount a near-united front to Hume's candidacy. For both Hutcheson and Wishart, moral philosophy was a consortium of studies that culminated in natural religion, and even the liberal theologians of the day had to teach within the broad framework of the Westminster Confession.

Wishart signally misunderstood the *Treatise*, but he exploited Hume's reputation in finding in it incipient signs of unbelief. His objections to the work had been leaked to Hume some weeks before the ministers of the Edinburgh churches vetoed the nomination and prevented its being formally brought before the council. Hume had answered the charges in his private letter to ex-Provost Coutts, and Henry Home had tried to head off the ministers' adverse vote by bringing together Wishart's charges and Hume's informal response in the unavailing *Letter from a Gentleman*. Hume's input into the *Letter* had not been intended for print. But the criticisms and his ensuing defeat rankled to the point where they left a permanent mark on the character and argument of what he *was* preparing to print. His *Philosophical Essays*, therefore—that is, the first *Enquiry*—is effectively his public attempt to rebut the accusations of his opponents. Not that that is all it is, or was meant to be—it was, indeed, a point of principle with Hume not to respond directly to critics at all.[32] Rather, a work

---

[31] On Wishart, see M. A. Stewart, 'William Wishart, an Early Critic of *Alciphron*', *Berkeley Newsletter*, 6 (1982–3), 5–9; id., 'Academic Freedom—Origins of an Idea', *Bulletin of the Australian Society of Legal Philosophy*, 16 (1991–2), 1–31; id., *The Kirk and the Infidel*; id., 'Principal Wishart (1692–1753) and the Controversies of his Day', *Records of the Scottish Church History Society*, 30 (2000), 60–102.

[32] Or so he liked to maintain. But at *HL* i. 265 Hume indicates that he would have been tempted into debate with William Warburton if he had had a more temperate antagonist. My claim that the first *Enquiry* is effectively a response to Hume's critics of 1745 was previously made in *The Kirk and the Infidel*, and has been misunderstood by Annette Baier, 'Hume: The Reflective Women's Epistemologist?', in A. J. Jacobson (ed.), *Feminist Interpretations of David Hume* (University Park: Pennsylvania State University Press, 2000), 32. Baier thinks I was showing that the *Enquiry* was published to try to secure the Edinburgh chair; but it was, of course, published three years after that incident.

that he had already partially conceived took on this added dimension in the charged circumstances of its composition. This is why the work as a whole, and not just the two essays on religion, left Hume 'too deep engaged to think of a retreat' (*HL* i. 106).

It is in this context that we are to understand the otherwise overdrawn opening of Essay V, with its apparently unprovoked attack on Stoicism, and its defence of scepticism against 'so much groundless Reproach and Obloquy' and 'public Hatred and Resentment': 'By opposing so many Vices and Follies, it raises to itself abundance of Enemies, who stigmatize it as libertine, prophane, and irreligious' (*PE* 70–1, *E* 41). Christian Stoicism was still the dominant philosophy in the colleges of the day, and Hutcheson its leading proponent.[33] Hume had just had to face the 'accusation of Heresy, Deism, Scepticism, Atheism &c &c &c' which 'was supported by the pretended Authority of Mr Hutcheson & even Mr Leechman' (*HL* i. 57–8). He was incensed at what he perceived as a self-interested party zeal in favour of established moral and religious values masquerading as moral objectivity, and his reference to 'the supine Indolence of the Mind, its rash Arrogance, its lofty Pretensions, and its superstitious Credulity' is an attack on the complacent propagation of those values by the academic establishment in the 1740s (*PE* 70, *E* 41).

Three essays later Hume reiterates a complaint against typecasting first made in the *Treatise*.

> There is no Method of Reasoning more common, and yet none more blameable, than in philosophical Debates, to endeavour the Refutation of any Hypothesis, by a Pretext of its dangerous Consequences to Religion and Morality. When any Opinion leads into Absurdities, 'tis certainly false; but 'tis not certain an Opinion is false, because 'tis of dangerous Consequence. Such Topics, therefore, ought entirely to be forborn, as serving nothing to the Discovery of Truth, but only to make the Person of an Antagonist odious. (*PE* 152–3, revised at *E* 96; cf. *T* 409)

Not that he concedes there is anything in his account—in context this is his account of 'liberty and necessity'—which can get in the way of morality. Such problems as face Hume's system face any system which contemplates the reconciliation of morality with natural religion. The Stoic view of suffering, which construes human ills as cosmic goods—Hutcheson was a contemporary promoter of the same doctrine—is the view of the cloistered theoretician. It gives no alleviation to the individual racked by pain, and is more likely to aggravate than calm his passions (*PE* 159–62, *E* 101–3).

That Hume has contemporary targets, and particularly ecclesiastical targets, in mind at this time is made the more likely by a celebrated passage from

---

[33] Stewart, 'Stoic Legacy'.

another work of the same date. The essay 'Of National Characters' is one of those which was added to the new edition of *Essays, Moral and Political* which went through the press in the same year as *Philosophical Essays*. It contains a diatribe against the clerical profession, out of all proportion to the needs of an essay on 'national characters'. Not all clergy are subjected to the same degree of censure, but it is difficult not to see Hume's own experience behind the complaint that they tend to overawe the populace and to form a self-interested faction, united to preserve their professional standing against antagonists whom they identify as 'impious and prophane' (*Essays* 199–201 n.). Although he is partly targeting priestcraft, and thus the practices of episcopalian cultures, Hume may still have been provoked by the publication in 1746 of Leechman's *The Temper, Character and Duty of a Minister of the Gospel*; an alienated reader could see this as depicting the ministerial character as contrived and based in self-interest.

Wishart's accusations against Hume's *Treatise* were summed up in six heads preserved for us in *A Letter from a Gentleman*:[34]

1. Universal Scepticism.
2. Principles leading to downright Atheism, by denying the Doctrine of Causes and Effects.
3. Errors concerning the very Being and Existence of a God.
4. Errors concerning God's being the first Cause, and prime Mover of the Universe.
5. He is chargable with denying the Immateriality of the Soul, and the Consequences flowing from this Denial.
6. With sapping the Foundations of Morality, by denying the natural and essential Difference betwixt Right and Wrong, Good and Evil, Justice and Injustice.

The charge of 'universal scepticism' is answered by Hume in *Philosophical Essays* in the final essay, which is more explicit than any of his previous writings on the distinction between Pyrrhonian and academic scepticism, and repeats the point already anticipated in *A Letter from a Gentleman* that Pyrrhonism is a form of intellectual diversion. But it is also addressed at a number of other points, for instance at the beginning of Essay V, where Hume is careful to stress that scepticism is a theoretical rather than a practical stance. At both references he responds to the popular stereotype of the sceptic as an enemy of religion.

---

[34] Paul Russell, 'Wishart, Baxter and Hume's *Letter from a Gentleman*', *Hume Studies*, 23 (1997), 245–76, has challenged whether the accusations were Wishart's. His objections to the identification are sophistical and involve a cumulatively inconsistent strategy to discredit even Hume's testimony on the matter. He fails to establish his central claim that the accusations come from a follower of Samuel Clarke, and his hypothesis that they might have been orchestrated from overseas by such a follower who kept Hume's *Treatise* in his luggage is whimsical. In judging Wishart's concerns to be alien to the accusations, he has not taken into account either the nature of the curriculum or the eclectic philosophical character of Wishart's own literary promotions during his period as principal. See Stewart, 'Principal Wishart'.

That he 'denies' the existence and all-pervasiveness of causal connexion is answered by the analysis he actually provides of causal connexion in Essays VII–VIII. The attacks on his religious conformity were clearly harder to counter, and Hume seems to have decided that the best tactic here was to come clean (cf. *HL* i. 106). As in some other works, he will assent to the existence of something like an ultimate cause, without being prepared to get into any meaningful description of it. He knew that the constraints he placed on reason would be seen as undermining natural, and even revealed, religion, and he does not need to have been unduly ironic in placing religious faith beyond the help of philosophy. In *Philosophical Essays* Hume does not go over the same ground on the soul or the self as in the *Treatise*, but in Essay VIII he denies that we have any knowledge of its nature; and his assimilation of human to animal intelligence in Essay IX (though the sentiments are not new) has an obvious relevance to the subject. In XI the topic of immortality is subsumed under a more general discussion of natural religion, in the course of which Hume through the mouth of the ancient Epicurean questions the moral argument for immortality and the immortality argument for morality. Essay VIII discusses the conditions of moral action, and concludes by rejecting the suggestion that anyone's sense of morals can be at risk from his speculative opinions.

IV

That true religion and morality can withstand sceptical enquiry is Hume's official stance throughout the work. But so far the evidence of topical allusions in the narrative is still circumstantial. To clinch my interpretation I concentrate in conclusion on two essays, I and XI. Essay I, 'Of the Different Species of Philosophy', merits particularly close attention. Only two species are under discussion, but they are not 'species' in the sense of branches of philosophy, as ordinarily understood.[35] They are two forms or styles of a single branch, namely moral philosophy, the subject Hume had just been declared unfit to teach. Moral philosophy included ethics, which is why I have been highlighting Hume's allusions to morals in other parts of the work. But it also included the all-important preparatory studies that we would now characterize as philosophy of mind and psychology of action: this was commonly called 'pneumatology', or the science of spirits or minds. For most practitioners it extended to, and indeed started from, the knowledge of God, and led to the study of all forms of human social arrangements within a framework of natural religion. Hume's exploration of the powers and operations of the mind, of the nature of willed action and its

---

[35] Metaphysics is, however, called a 'Species' of philosophy in this other sense, in the third paragraph of Essay VII.

relation to morals, and of the foundations of natural and revealed religion, are all part of moral philosophy as it was then conceived; but for him natural religion was not intrinsic but extrinsic to the enquiry—it was one of the things that the enquiry itself put under scrutiny.

Of the two styles of moral philosophy, he says, each has its uses. The one's primary concern is with conduct: it considers man 'chiefly as born for Action; and as influenc'd in his Actions by Taste and Sentiment'. The other's primary concern is with the mind: it considers man 'rather as a reasonable than an active Being, and endeavour[s] to form his Understanding more than cultivate his Manners'.

The advocates of the first style, who influence action by moulding sentiment, are masters of literary technique:

Virtue, of all Objects, is the most valuable and lovely; and accordingly this Species of Philosophers paint her in the most amiable Colours, borrowing all Helps from Poetry and Eloquence, and treating their Subject in an easy and obvious Manner, such as is best fitted to please the Imagination, and engage the Affections. They select the most striking Observations and Instances from common Life; place opposite Characters in a proper Contrast; and alluring us into the Paths of Virtue, by the Views of Glory and of Happiness, direct our Steps into these Paths, by the soundest Precepts and most illustrious Examples. They make us *feel* the Difference betwixt Vice and Virtue; they excite and regulate our Sentiments; and so they can but bend our Hearts to the Love of Probity and true Honour, they think, that they have fully attain'd the End of all their Labours. (*PE* 1–2, *E* 5–6)

If this sounds sufficiently like Leechman's depiction of Hutcheson in his more popular mode, which Hume subsequently identifies with the poet and the preacher, the alternative technique must remind us of the author of the *Treatise* and any who think like him:

They regard Mankind as a Subject of Speculation; and with a narrow Scrutiny examine human Nature, in order to find those Principles, which regulate our Understandings, excite our Sentiments, and make us approve or blame any particular Object, Action, or Behaviour. They think it a Reproach to all Literature, that Philosophy should not yet have fixt, beyond Controversy, the Foundation of Morals, Reasoning, and Criticism; and should for ever talk of Truth and Falshood, Vice and Virtue, Beauty and Deformity, without being able to determine the Source of these Distinctions. . . . Tho' their Speculations seem abstract and even unintelligible to common Readers, they please themselves with the Approbation of the Learned and the Wise; and think they are sufficiently compensated for the Labours of their whole Lives, if they can discover some hidden Truths which may contribute to the Instruction of Posterity. (*PE* 2–3, *E* 6)

The philosophy which engages in moral painting is 'easy and obvious'; it is more popular with the run of mankind, because it impinges more upon 'common Life', engages their feelings, and thereby informs their conduct. It gives them, or seems to give them, what they are looking for without taxing their minds. The other is 'accurate and abstruse' and tends to lose its impact when it attempts to 'enter into Business and Action'. The painter who makes an error in his depictions may still re-engage people's feelings; the 'abstract Reasoner' who wanders off course is apt to disappear into obscurity.

The painter was identified in the *Treatise* with the non-Humean philosopher, and the 'deep', 'abstruse', or 'abstract' metaphysician with the Humean. Is Essay I, therefore, rueful autobiography, or has Hume changed sides since his first exchanges with Hutcheson? Something, to be sure, has evolved, because the 'declaiming' moralist who was the painter in the *Treatise* period has softened into the 'easy' moralist of polite literature. One can still portray this as a transition from one Shaftesburian persona to another. Even those who have not sensed the significance of Hume's aligning metaphysicians of the calibre of Aristotle, Malebranche, and Locke—some of the most formative influences on his own thought—against moralists like Cicero, La Bruyère, and Addison should notice that these comments foreshadow the defence of scepticism later in the *Philosophical Essays* and that Hume soon rallies to the side of metaphysics.[36] The 'accurate and abstract Philosophy' *subserves* the 'easy and humane' (*PE 7, E 9*): that does not mean it is subordinate to it, but rather that the easy and humane depends on the accurate and abstract.[37] Hume elaborates again, as he had done in the Conclusion to the *Treatise* (where the same reference to 'subservience' occurs), on the ways, both literal and metaphorical, in which the accurate knowledge of the anatomist is absolutely necessary to the

---

[36] It is sometimes suggested that Hume sought to emulate Addison's style. Contemporaries understood him to be critical of that style and to have heavily corrected his own set of *The Spectator*. See John MacLaurin, *Apology for the Writers against the Tragedy of Douglas* (1757), 4. There is no record of annotation in the catalogued set of *The Spectator* from the Hume library: see D. F. Norton and M. J. Norton, *The David Hume Library* (Edinburgh: Edinburgh Bibliographical Society, 1996), item 16.

[37] There is an echo here of Henry Grove's essay on our moral nature, in *The Spectator*, no. 588 (1 Sept. 1714). Grove had been tutor at the Presbyterian academy at Taunton. 'Man may be considered in two Views,' he wrote, 'as a Reasonable, and as a Sociable Being; capable of becoming himself either happy or miserable, and of contributing to the Happiness or Misery of his Fellow-Creatures.' Our exercise of the latter capacity is not only 'extreamly serviceable to' our exercise of the former, but the former is also dependent upon the latter: 'And, indeed, 'tis obvious to remark, that we follow nothing heartily, unless carried to it by Inclinations which anticipate our Reason, and, like a Biass, draw the Mind strongly towards it.' The last phrase is further echoed in Hume's depiction of 'Nature' as pulling the run of mankind away from the extremes of pure reasoning and mere conviviality to the middle ground of the moderate active life, having 'secretly admonish'd them to allow none of these Byasses to *draw* too much, so as to incapacitate them for other Occupations and Entertainments' (*PE 6, E 9*). Grove had been concerned to dispel the opposition between those who traced human motivation to self-love and those who traced it to benevolence. An equal interest in ourselves and others is, he claimed, necessary to human nature, and both interests have been designed by the Creator to be compatible. Someone motivated exclusively by self-love is a cold reasoner: but reason alone, though it may detect the prudence of seeking the general happiness as a means to one's own, is a poor motivator; and only someone who responds unselfishly to the interests of others can satisfy also the demands of self-love. Hume has redefined the reasoning and sociable natures for his own purposes.

painter (*PE* 7–8; *E* 9–10). Nor are the moral painters the only other professionals who can improve their performance by mastering something of the accuracy of the metaphysician. Even if they could not, the metaphysician should be allowed the healthy enjoyment of his intellectual exercise—a thesis that runs counter to what we found in Hutcheson.

The apparent pessimism at the beginning about the chances for metaphysics thus gives way to a confident defence, and one of the primary reasons for the pessimism—the metaphysician's tendency to construct straw schemes—is scrutinized. The fault is not with the discipline itself, but with the robber barons who have usurped the accurate philosopher's position. They draw their armoury from 'popular Superstition', and overwhelm the unguarded with 'religious Fears and Prejudices'; furthermore, 'many Persons find too sensible an Interest in perpetually recalling such Topics'.[38]

> The only Method of freeing Learning, at once, from these abstruse Questions, is to enquire seriously into the Nature of human Understanding, and shew, from an exact Analysis of its Powers and Capacity, that it is, by no means, fitted for such remote and abstruse Subjects. We must submit to this Fatigue, in order to live at Ease ever after: And must cultivate true Metaphysics with some Care, in order to destroy the false and adulterate. (*PE* 11–12, *E* 12)

Hume comments on some of the powers and faculties that are worth investigating, and notes by way of illustration, in a lengthy footnote omitted from modern editions, how Hutcheson had lately advanced our understanding of moral perception and Butler our understanding of the passions (*PE* 14–16 n.). But whatever Hutcheson's personal contribution to one side in the debate, the culture to which Hutcheson belonged is located in the treacherous 'Forests', where the 'stout' philosopher has 'remitted his Watch' and capitulated to the religious interest by letting his imagination carry him deeper than his experience warrants (*PE* 10; *E* 11). So Hume now has a dual target: not just the superficiality of the easy philosophy, but the misdirectedness of adverse allies who have seen the need to give the easy philosophy respectable foundations but compromised themselves by a tendentious agenda.

So far there is little doubt that Hume remains firmly on the side of the anatomist—explicitly identified with the metaphysician—against the painter,

---

[38] This position is more fully developed in Hume's *Natural History of Religion* (1757). In Section xi of that work he argues that popular theism attracts philosophical support because it appears to share the same conclusion as a rational theism. But the passions that lead to popular theism have a stronger hold than the reason that leads to speculative theism. People need mystery and darkness; it is therefore an obfuscating, degraded philosophy, such as the scholastic, that partners their superstitions. This scenario was first sketched in Hume's essay 'Of Superstition and Enthusiasm' in the 1741 collection. Superstition motivated by fear fills the gap left by ignorance of the true processes of causation. In Hume's view, popular beliefs about the occurrence of miracles and the iniquity of suicide also contain superstitious elements.

and that the very retention of that imagery reinforces his old view that the two functions cannot cohere in the same work. It is sometimes claimed that they cohere in the second *Enquiry*, which is closer in format to early Hutcheson than anything else Hume wrote; but I do not believe that they were seen by Hume as cohering, in terms of the distinction as he himself had drawn it. Certainly he depicts, even paints, the virtuous life in laudatory terms in Section IX of that work, and might be thought finally to have responded to the injunction set out in the epigraph from Lucan prefixed to Book III of the *Treatise* ('Ask for a model of the honourable man'). But the whole purpose of this depiction is to solve the 'anatomical' (analytical) questions he has set himself about the foundation of morals; it is with a view not to influencing his readers' behaviour, but to gaining their intellectual assent. There are a number of passages even in the second *Enquiry* where he continues to identify himself with the anatomist: *M* 177–8, 287, 297–8, 322.[39] Contemporaneously with that work Hume introduced a distinction between 'shallow' and 'abstruse' thinkers in the essay 'Of Commerce' (in his *Political Discourses* of 1752) and defended the abstruse. In the same period again, in the prologue to the *Dialogues*, Hume put a form of the distinction into the mouth of Pamphilus, who, as the unsophisticated pupil of Cleanthes, gives his side's game away in recommending that the complexities of natural religion should be pursued through the untaxing medium of informal and easy conversation.

Hume's newest conflict with the Hutchesonian party had reopened old sores and prompted a revival of the old rhetoric, but it also brought home to him that there were deeper issues than he had once appreciated. For purposes of public presentation he was prepared to use the good reputation of Hutcheson as he was of Butler to help promote the cause of moral science, though from 1756 onwards, when all prospects of academic preferment had evaporated, he abandoned this dependence. There is no reason to think he did not genuinely appreciate the contributions he took them to have made in their more austerely 'anatomical' writing. But his reference to the *Sermons* also calls to mind Butler's second edition Preface, which actually pioneered the distinction between easy and abstruse approaches to moral subjects. Butler had opted uncompromisingly for the abstruse as that which alone is fit to engage serious people's minds and lead them to truth, and had expressed a preference for enquiries into 'what the particular nature of man is, its several parts, their economy or constitution' as the principal but not the only component of such a study.[40]

---

[39] Hume's view that *moral philosophy*, in his preferred sense, does not trade upon human sociality is not to be confused with his conviction that *morality itself* does.

[40] I owe this reference to R. G. Frey. A more sympathetic picture of 'easy' studies had been put forward by Shaftesbury, in part I of 'The Moralists', where we may find a more plausible model for the Hume of

If the associations of the 'easy' philosophy are derogatory and anti-intellectual—though its content varies—then the ascription to Hume himself of the dictum of 'Nature' must be a reversal of his intended sense.[41] 'Be a Philosopher; but amidst all your Philosophy, be still a Man' (*PE* 7; *E* 9) is the *poet's* attitude to philosophy that he repudiates. It comes at the conclusion of a passage where Hume has been describing a popular picture of the socially desirable conversationalist—someone who moves at ease between books and business and occupies an intermediate position between the extremes of what is conceived by the rest of the world as the philosophical depressive and the loutish ignoramus. Such an individual avoids the kind of intellectual challenge that could upset anything. The irony in Hume's depiction is clear, and the reference to 'students' whose minds have not been stretched in the acquisition of all-purpose maxims is a likely reflection on the type of moral instruction the college teacher was expected to distil:

In order to diffuse and cultivate so accomplisht a Character, nothing can be more useful than Compositions of the easy Style and Manner, which draw not too much from Life, require no deep Application or Recess to be comprehended, and send back the Student among Mankind full of noble Sentiments and wise Precepts, applicable to every Emergence of human Life. (*PE* 5–6, modified at *E* 8)

The result will be to make 'Virtue . . . amiable, Science agreeable, Company instructive, and Retirement entertaining'—but at the cost of eliminating the primary sciences like natural philosophy and medicine,[42] and confining study to 'such as may have a direct Reference to Action and Society'. If those who had these limited horizons dealt civilly with those who did not, we might just leave each to 'his own Taste and Sentiment'. But life is not like that: 'the Matter is often

---

'Of Essay Writing'. Shaftesbury's aim was to rescue philosophy from 'Colleges and Cells' and restore it to educated conversation (i. i; cf. Hume, *Essays* 534). The literary representation of this he termed 'Moral Painting'. A similar disparagement of unworldly learning occurs in 'Soliloquy: or Advice to an Author', III. iii.

[41] Typical of this reversal are E. C. Mossner, *The Life of David Hume* (Edinburgh: Nelson, 1954; 2nd edn. Oxford: Clarendon Press, 1980), title-page; A. G. N. Flew, *Hume's Philosophy of Belief* (London: Routledge & Kegan Paul, 1961), 9; P. Jones, 'David Hume', in D. Daiches *et al.* (eds.), *A Hotbed of Genius* (Edinburgh: Edinburgh University Press, 1986), 66; N. Capaldi, *Hume's Place in Moral Philosophy* (New York: Peter Lang, 1989), 24; D. T. Siebert, *The Moral Animus of David Hume* (London: Associated University Presses, 1990), 45; J. V. Price, 'Hume, David', in Yolton *et al.* (eds.), *The Dictionary of Eighteenth-Century British Philosophers*, i. 446. The appeal to 'Nature' is derived from Shaftesbury, 'Soliloquy', III. iii, while the sentiments of the dictum carry echoes of Pope. Cf. 'Epistle to James Craggs', 13; 'Essay on Criticism', 523 (I owe the latter references to M. A. Box). In the course of his grading of the pleasures in the 'Essay on the Passions', 173, Hutcheson characterized morals, politics, and religion as 'manly Studies' which influence our dispositions and affections. It is a perversion of 'the Learned' to find their pleasures in abstruse analysis that terminates 'upon the *Knowledge* itself' rather than in virtuous application.

[42] In Essay XII Hume includes 'natural Philosophy, Physic, Chymistry, &c.' among 'the Sciences, which treat of general Facts'.

carry'd farther, even to the absolute rejecting all profound Reasonings or what is commonly call'd *Metaphysics*' (*PE* 6–7, modified at *E* 9). It is at this point that Hume swings round to defend metaphysics against predators.

. . . is this a just Cause why Philosophers should desist from such Researches, and leave Superstition still in Possession of her Retreat? Is it not reasonable to draw a direct contrary Conclusion, and perceive the Necessity of carrying the War into the most secret Recesses of the Enemy? In vain do we hope, that Men, from frequent Disappointments, will at last abandon such airy Sciences, and discover the proper Province of human Reason. For besides, that many Persons find too sensible an Interest in perpetually recalling such Topics; besides this, I say, the Motive of blind Despair can never reasonably have place in the Sciences; since, however unsuccessful former Attempts may have prov'd, there is still room to hope, that the Industry, Good-fortune, or improv'd Sagacity of succeeding Generations may reach Discoveries unknown to former Ages. (*PE* 11, modified at *E* 12)

This will subvert the 'adulterate' form of the abstruse philosophy which 'seems to have serv'd hitherto only as a Shelter to Superstition and a Cover to Absurdity' and which is eventually going to be branded as fit for the flames. Hume hopes to eliminate it—in the final paragraph of the essay—by an exercise which may yet 'unite the Boundaries of the different Species of Philosophy' (*PE* 19, *E* 16). This naturally suggests again Hume's offer to Hutcheson to try to bring the painter and anatomist into harmony. But it is not the *painting* of virtue that he is offering to salvage from the easy philosophy. It is lucidity and comprehensibility. He recognizes that the abstruse philosophy can defeat itself by its complexity and he will therefore reduce the degree of detail to the minimum necessary. So it is the *manner* of the essay and the *matter* of the treatise that Hume is going to reconcile in these *Philosophical Essays*, and this has involved him in concessions two ways: his original treatise manner is now as unacceptable to him as his original essay content. But his aim is still the same: to make his philosophy intelligible to the minority who are capable of judging it.

When we turn to Essay XI, there are more substantial matters to interest the reader. It is an important document in the moral defence of the sceptical philosophy, but there are also topical signals.

Hume begins by contrasting what he regards as the 'bigotted Jealousy and Persecution' of his day with the liberty of thought and belief allowed to 'the Professors of every Sect of Philosophy' in antiquity. In Greek and Roman times there were no 'Creeds, Confessions, or penal Statutes'—and hence, of course, no Westminster Confession. The priests ministered to 'the Vulgar and Illiterate' and left 'the Learned and Wise' to their own devices. The 'pertinacious Bigotry' of his own day is again to be identified with the false metaphysics of Essay I; for it is philosophy's offspring, which, after 'allying with Superstition' and becoming involved with 'speculative Dogmas and Principles of Religion, the present

Occasions of such furious Dispute', becomes 'her most inveterate Enemy and Persecutor' (*PE* 206–7, *E* 132–3). Hume questions in his own name whether the civil magistrate should be concerned with the moral consequences of the professor's unbelief—it was the magistrates of Edinburgh who had led the movement to appoint Hume as their professor and the clergy who blocked them—and he replies through his alter ego:

I know . . . that in Fact these Persecutions never, in any Age, proceeded from calm Reason, or any Experience of the pernicious Consequences of Philosophy; but arose entirely from Passion and Prejudice. But what if I should advance farther, and assert, that if *Epicurus* had been accus'd before the People, by any of the *Sycophants* or Informers of those Days, he could easily have defended his Cause, and prov'd his Principles of Philosophy to be as salutary as those of his Adversaries, who endeavour'd, with such Zeal, to subject him to the public Hatred and Jealousy? (*PE* 208, modified at *E* 134)

Seeing himself in the role of Epicurus, Hume responds that the public assembly—an alias for the town council before whom the philosopher has been 'impeach'd by furious Antagonists'—should limit itself to 'Questions of public Good and the Interest of the Commonwealth' and not be 'diverted to the Disquisitions of speculative Philosophy'. Questions about 'the Origin and Government of Worlds' are 'entirely indifferent to the Peace of Society and Security of Government'; as 'the most speculative, of all Philosophy', this subject is a potential topic for the Schools, but both here and in the following essay there is a strong hint that it may be found beyond the scope of reason. Those who try to 'establish Religion upon the Principles of Reason'—for example, those who try to establish a natural religion based on the Design Argument, as the Hutchesonian party consistently did—will be defeated by the weakness of their own faculties; and once again we come back to the image of the painter. 'They paint, in the most magnificent Colours, the Order, Beauty, and wise Arrangement of the Universe; and then ask, if such a glorious Display of Intelligence and Wisdom could proceed from the fortuitous Concourse of Atoms, or if Chance could produce what the highest Genius can never sufficiently admire.' (*PE* 210, *E* 135).[43] But sound reasoning will ascribe to the Deity no more attributes than are strictly necessary to account for 'the present Scene of Things, which is so full of Ill and Disorder'. It is the profession of 'Priests and Poets' to extol the creation, but if philosophers follow suit, 'they have aided the Scale of Reason by the Wings of Imagination' (*PE* 213–14, *E* 137–8). No argument from experience can show that there are rewards and punishments in another life for virtue and vice in this, let alone that they are individually computed; but there is abundant experience to show that in *this* life

---

[43] Hume actually rejected the cosmology of chance. His Epicurean adopts the stance of a follower of Strato debating the Stoics' Design Argument before the Athenian public, which had been depicted by Pierre Bayle in his *Continuation des Pensées diverses* (1705), sect. 106.

Virtue is attended with more Peace of Mind than Vice; and meets with a more favourable Reception from the World. I am sensible, that, according to the past Experience of Mankind, Friendship is the chief Joy of human Life, and Moderation the only Source of Tranquillity and Happiness. I never balance betwixt the virtuous and vicious Course of Life; but am sensible, that, to a well-dispos'd Mind, every Advantage is on the Side of the former. (*PE* 217, *E* 140)

If it is experience that guides us in private and public life, it should equally be experience that guides us 'in the School, or in the Closet' (*PE* 220, *E* 142). Our religion will not be like popular religion. Its foundations will be empirical, because if it has any credibility at all, it is 'nothing but a Species of Philosophy'. 'No new Fact can ever be infer'd from the religious Hypothesis; no Event foreseen or foretold; no Reward or Punishment expected or dreaded, beyond what is already known by Practice and Observation' (*PE* 226–7, *E* 146). Although Hume sees religion here as less consistently corrupting than he does in *The Natural History of Religion*—it can be socially useful, by imposing a certain restraint on our passions—he will not permit its contestable claims to impinge on the liberty of the individual.

I think the State ought to tolerate every Principle of Philosophy; nor is there an Instance of any Government's suffering in its political Interests by such Indulgence. There is no Enthusiasm among Philosophers; their Doctrines are not very alluring to the People; and no Restraint can be put upon their Reasonings, but what must be of dangerous Consequence to the Sciences, and even to the State, by paving the Way for Persecution and Oppression in Points, wherein the Generality of Mankind are more deeply interested and concern'd. (*PE* 228, modified at *E* 147)

At the turn of a new century we are more used to the ideal, if not the reality, of a separation of higher education from political and ecclesiastical management, and can no doubt see the force of Hume's argument for academic freedom in philosophy. But Hume himself was too close to events to present an unimpassioned picture of the circumstances of his day.[44] 'Bigotry' and 'zealotry' were the standard terms of opprobrium to hurl at the evangelical opponents of any liberal position. But it was not the extremists who went to such lengths to block Hume's chances. It was the leading liberals, opposing one systematic philosophy to another. To make complete sense of the conflict requires a more extensive study of the other side, who have been represented here too much by brief rhetorical excerpts and an adverse portrayal by their opponent. But what

---

[44] He was also too glib, in supposing that if you identify the non-rational bases of someone's beliefs you will not influence their beliefs. On Hume's stance on academic freedom, see Stewart, 'Academic Freedom—Origins of an Idea', and *The Kirk and the Infidel*; on the European context of the debate, id., 'Libertas Philosophandi: From Natural to Speculative Philosophy', *Australian Journal of Politics and History*, 40 (1994), suppl., 29–46.

is important is that the philosophy under review in the first *Enquiry* is a much less narrow one than traditional commentary has recognized. The mechanics of human understanding are indeed there, but so is their application across the main fields of human thought. To realize not only that this is so, but why it is so, is an important step to rehabilitating an uneven but interesting work, which has come to be underestimated at least in part through its author's own misguided attempt to regulate its posthumous reputation.

The first *Enquiry* is an exposition and defence of scepticism as the only philosophy compatible with a true knowledge of the human mind. Hume probably believed honestly if speciously that its applications are intellectual rather than practical, because the *practitioner*, even when devoid of knowledge, will be guided by beliefs founded in experience and in the necessities of human nature. He considered the case to be slightly different with religion and morality: here it cannot affect our practice but only improve our understanding, to know that these domains are outside the province of human reason except so far as either of them is dependent on causal reasoning. Scepticism is therefore an enemy only of vested interests; but it was such interests, in Hume's view, that had corrupted even the most moral elements of his society.

3

Empiricism about Meanings

Jonathan Bennett

IDEAS AND IMPRESSIONS

Hume inherited from Locke a certain theory about what it is for a general word to have a meaning, or at least about what makes a general word have one meaning rather than another. According to this theory, what a person means by a given general term depends upon what (kind of) idea he regularly associates it with; and for both philosophers this is linked with the view that all intellectual activities consist in the mental manipulation of ideas. Locke also used 'idea' to stand for quasi-sensory states: he thought of ideas as mental items that come into or are present to one's mind when one sees, hears, or feels things, and also when one hallucinates and when one imagines—seeing something in the mind's eye or hearing it in the mind's ear. This double use of 'idea' is a vehicle for Locke's substantive assimilation of the intellectual side of our nature to the sensory side, as though *thinking about* a state of affairs, for example, were on some kind of continuum with *experiencing* it.

Where Locke has the single word 'idea', Hume has three: for the genus of items that Locke calls 'ideas' Hume reserves the term 'perceptions', and for the two species that comprise that genus he uses 'idea' and 'impression'. The word 'perception' really is being used here to cover the whole range of mental events, as is the cognate verb: 'To hate, to love, to think, to feel, to see; all this is nothing but to perceive.' (*T* 67).

Hume's line between 'ideas' and 'impressions' is really two lines which he wrongly thinks coincide with one another. (i) There is the line drawn by his official explanation of the difference between the two: impressions are strong, lively, vivacious, intense, while ideas are weak, faded, washed out, faint, languid.

This is a revised version of Jonathan Bennett, *Locke, Berkeley, Hume: Central Themes* (Oxford: Clarendon Press, 1971), ch. 9.

(ii) Impressions are what we have in sense-experience, while ideas are the raw materials of thinking, understanding, and meaning. Here is Hume introducing (i) and showing that he expects it to coincide with (ii):

Those perceptions, which enter with most force and violence, we may name *impressions*; and under this name I comprehend all our sensations, passions, and emotions, as they make their first appearance in the soul. By *ideas* I mean the faint images of these in thinking and reasoning . . . (*T* 1; see also *T* 319)

And again in the *Enquiry*:

We may divide all the perceptions of the mind into two classes or species, which are distinguished by their different degrees of force and vivacity. The less forcible and lively are commonly denominated THOUGHTS or IDEAS. The other species [may be called] IMPRESSIONS . . . By the term *impression*, then, I mean all our more lively perceptions, when we hear, or see, or feel, or love, or hate, or desire, or will. And impressions are distinguished from ideas, which are the less lively perceptions, of which we are conscious, when we reflect on any of those sensations or movements above-mentioned. (*E* 18)

In fact, the distinctions (i) and (ii) come nowhere near to coinciding. Hume's assumption that they do involves the view that thinking about or 'reflecting on' a state of affairs is like feebly experiencing it—with the colours unsaturated and dim, the sounds low, and so on. Yet, despite the manifest falsity of this position, Hume was able to do some real work with it, using it as his vehicle for expressing and defending his meaning-empiricism—a potent and conspicuous doctrine which launches the *Treatise* and dominates Section II of the first *Enquiry*. According to meaning-empiricism, the limits on what one can understand or make sense of are set by the limits on what one has experienced.

The seeds of this are to be found in Locke, but the doctrine is more naturally thought of in connexion with Hume because it plays a more active role in his work than in Locke's—presumably because Hume saw more clearly its potential as a weapon of destructive criticism, or had a greater will to use it as such. Confronted by an expression which his theory implies to be meaningless, Locke's usual response is not to condemn the expression but to soft-pedal on the theory. Hume tries to do better than this, and never shrinks from following the argument wherever it honestly seems to him to lead. I am not sure whether this difference between the two philosophers is one of insight or one of nerve.

Since 'impressions' are by definition nothing but forceful perceptions, Hume can reasonably think that all our sensory intake in experience of the objective realm consists of 'impressions'; but he ought also to allow an 'impression' status to much of what occurs in vivid dreams, hallucinations, etc. Sometimes, however, he uses 'impression' as though it covered only the data of ordinary experience of the objective realm (e.g. *T* 19). This narrowing tendency, although Hume explicitly disavows it, and although it conflicts with his view that there are impressions of reflection as well as sensation, is strongly manifested in his preparedness to treat meaning-empiricism as a view about understanding in relation to experience of the objective realm, while always expressing it as a thesis about understanding in relation to impressions. I'll return to this in a moment.

Hume believes that thought is a transaction with ideas; but his definition of 'idea' as 'faint perception' ought to discourage him from saying conversely that every transaction with ideas is a case of thinking—unless of course he follows Descartes and Locke in using 'thought' etc. to sprawl over the whole range of the mental. Yet he calls ideas 'the faint images of [impressions] in thinking and reasoning' and 'the less lively perceptions, of which we are conscious, when we reflect on [our impressions]'. These turns of phrase strongly suggest that any having of ideas is to count as 'thinking' in some fairly normal sense of that word.

Returning now to his tendency to equate 'impressions' with 'perceptions of the objective realm': when that is combined with Hume's official account of the idea–impression distinction, the result is to equate 'experience of the objective realm' with 'intense or violent sensory states'. Considered as an account of what it is to perceive something objective or outer, this is simple to the point of idiocy.

Hume was capable of such optimistic simplifications; but this is because of a defect in his peripheral vision, so to speak, and not because he could not deal in complex depth with a problem when he had it in focus. I have accused him of one simplification about thinking and another about objectivity. Since he did not see that 'thinking and reasoning' presents a philosophical problem in its own right, Hume's stray remarks about it seldom rise above the level of the quoted passage. But in *Treatise* I. iv. 2 he did address himself squarely to the analysis of objectivity concepts, and his treatment of them, although deeply flawed, is a peerless example of disciplined depth and complexity.

HUME'S MEANING-EMPIRICISM

'[A]ll our simple ideas . . . are deriv'd from simple impressions, which are correspondent to them, and which they exactly represent' (*T* 4). Hume adopts Locke's distinction between 'complex' and 'simple' ideas, the former linked with definable words, the latter with words whose meanings—Hume thinks—must be learned through confrontation with examples. The simple–complex antithesis has worked much mischief in the theory of meaning generally, but I shall not harry it here.

Each time Hume defends his meaning-empiricism, he claims to have two arguments for it.[1] First, everyone who has a given simple idea also has one or

---

[1] See *T* 3–5, *E* 19–20.

more impressions that are 'correspondent' to it, i.e. which resemble it in everything but strength. This cannot be coincidence: 'Such a constant conjunction, in such an infinite number of instances, can never arise from chance; but clearly proves a dependence of the impressions on the ideas, or of the ideas on the impressions.' (*T* 4–5). Furthermore, the impressions must cause the ideas, and not vice versa, since the ideas never come first. Our simple ideas, therefore, are copies of impressions—i.e. they are caused by impressions and resemble them. Secondly: 'If it happen, from a defect of the organ, that a man is not susceptible of any species of sensation, we always find, that he is as little susceptible of the correspondent ideas. A blind man can form no notion of colours; a deaf man of sounds' (*E* 20; see also *T* 5). It is clear that this will yield only a special case of the first argument.

If we take this at face value, as a theory about the preconditions for having unlively 'perceptions' or quasi-sensory states, what evidence can Hume have for it? He may claim to know about his own ideas by 'reflection', but what of the ideas of others? He reports on the ideas of the blind and the deaf, asserts that 'A LAPLANDER or NEGROE has no notion of the relish of wine' (*E* 20), and confidently uses 'we': 'That idea of red, which we form in the dark . . .' (*T* 3), 'we find, that any impression . . . is constantly followed by an idea, which resembles it' (*T* 5), 'when we analyze our thoughts or ideas . . . we always find, that they resolve themselves into such simple ideas as . . .' (*E* 19). How could he know?

A related question: what would count as evidence against the theory when so construed? Of his thesis that every simple idea is preceded by a correspondent impression Hume says:

Every one may satisfy himself in this point by running over as many [ideas] as he pleases. But if any one should deny this universal resemblance, I know no way of convincing him, but by desiring him to shew . . . a simple idea, that has not a correspondent impression. If he does not answer this challenge, as 'tis certain he cannot, we may from his silence and our own observation establish our conclusion. (*T* 3–4)

The theory's truth is, indeed, to depend solely upon whether anyone can 'shew' or 'produce' a simple idea not preceded by a correspondent impression:

Those who would assert, that this position is not universally true nor without exception, have only one, and that an easy method of refuting it; by producing that idea, which, in their opinion, is not derived from this source. It will then be incumbent on us, if we would maintain our doctrine, to produce the impression, or lively perception, which corresponds to it. (*E* 19–20)

To be able to assess the theory, then, we must know how to go about 'producing' an idea.

Clearly, Hume will not bow to any fool or knave who claims to have a counter-example, any congenitally blind man who says 'I have an idea of purple'. To 'produce' an idea one must not merely *say* but *show* that one has it; and Hume is confident that his challengers will fail in this larger task, e.g. that a congenitally blind man who says 'I have an idea of purple' won't be able to give us reasons for believing him.

But the blind man might well satisfy us that he is not lying, and then Hume's only resort would be to say that the blind man did not know what 'purple' means. This, I suggest, is the source of his confidence: he is sure that the congenitally blind man would not be able to 'produce' an idea of purple because he would not be able to satisfy us that he knew what 'purple' means. In short, no one is to count as having an idea of purple unless he knows the meaning of 'purple' or a synonym of it in some other language.

Now, what of the people whose ideas Hume counts as positive evidence for this theory? He has not asked them what ideas they have, and even if he did, why should he believe their answers? He must say: 'Well, they clearly understand the word "purple", and that is good enough for me.' If he does not say this, then it is perfectly obscure how he can have any positive evidence for his theory as applied to anyone but himself. If he does say it, then anyone counts as having an idea of purple if he understands 'purple' or a synonym of it in some other language.

Combining the two results: someone counts as having an idea of purple if and only if he understands 'purple' or a synonym thereof. Hume's theory is not that *ideas* pre-require impressions, but that *understanding* pre-requires impressions. Although he believes that the two go together, he is in fact confronted by the parting of their ways, and he does in fact go along the path of understanding, not the path of washed-out sensory presentations.

I could have *jumped* to this conclusion. I could have said: 'When Hume speaks of "ideas" his real topic is meaning and understanding, for his analysis of these is basically Lockean.' The longer route, however, displays more of the logical structure. The salient points are that when Hume's theory is taken at face value, we cannot bring evidence to bear upon it; that the evidence he would probably have allowed has the effect of turning the theory into one not about ideas but about understanding; and that this transformation solves the evidence problem only because understanding consists not in having Humean ideas but in something for which there are public criteria.

So we should see Hume as having a theory about how impressions are pre-required for understanding—with 'understanding' properly understood. His official equation of 'understanding' with 'having ideas', since it dictates his wording of the theory and also affects details in his handling of it, cannot be neglected; but the theory ought not to be seen as primarily one about ideas.

It comes down to this. We may say, in shorthand, that Hume accepts (1) 'Ideas follow impressions', (2) 'Understanding is having ideas', (3) 'Understanding follows impressions'. If we see (3) as inferred from (1) and (2), then (1) stands on its own feet and so cannot be assessed, and the meaning of (3) is dictated by (2), so that (3) cannot be assessed either. So we shall do better to take (3) as accepted on its own merits, i.e. as a theory that really is about understanding. This credits Hume with knowing what understanding really is, and of course he does know this. His theoretical acceptance of (2)—which leads him to express (3) as (1)—is belied by his preparedness to identify cases of understanding on the basis of the criteria we ordinarily do employ—criteria that lie in the public domain and do not concern 'ideas'. There is nothing mysterious, or even unusual, about a philosopher's misdescribing a concept that he is well able to use properly.

Taking Hume's theory to have the form 'You cannot understand W unless you have first . . .', we still have difficulties with it. I now present three of them.

Understanding is having certain linguistic abilities; we can tell whether someone understands a given word; and we could discover a case of understanding that was not preceded by impressions of the sort demanded by Hume's theory. What someone understands now is not logically tied to what he underwent earlier: the account of 'newly born' adults in Shaw's *Back to Methuselah* is a perfectly consistent fantasy. Hume himself sees his theory as refutable by counter-evidence, yet he will not retract it at the drop of a hat. After denying that he has ever had an impression of a necessary connexion in the outer world, he writes:

[Should I therefore] assert, that I am here possest of an idea, which is not preceded by any similar impression? This wou'd be too strong a proof of levity and inconstancy; since the contrary principle has been already so firmly establish'd, as to admit of no farther doubt; at least, till we have more fully examin'd the present difficulty. (*T* 77)

Elsewhere he is even stubborner, as when he argues that we cannot attach sense to 'time during which nothing happens':

But that we really have no such idea, is certain. For whence shou'd it be deriv'd? Does it arise from an impression of sensation or of reflexion? . . . [I]f you cannot point out *any such impression*, you may be certain you are mistaken, when you imagine you have *any such idea*. (*T* 65)

Here and elsewhere Hume seems to treat meaning-empiricism as knowable a priori, as not after all vulnerable to counter-examples. A well-tested empirical theory has some power to discredit an occasional putative counter-example: 'Delicious though that pie looks, I doubt if it is because this bakery never seems to produce nice pies.' But Hume thinks his theory can fatally discredit whole classes of alleged counter-examples: he mainly uses it, indeed, to argue that nobody has an 'idea' of eventless time, objective necessary connexion, the self, etc. Why can't his opponents say that these are precisely the classes of 'ideas' for which the theory is false?

There is a second difficulty about Hume's position. If a congenitally blind man showed that he understood 'purple', Hume's theory would be refuted, and this would deprive him of his main argument for saying that certain expressions are meaningless. In such an eventuality he would be committed to conceding that perhaps those expressions are meaningful after all, and yet it seems clear that such a concession would really be misplaced: whether 'eventless time' and the rest make sense cannot depend on the linguistic abilities of a blind Patagonian.

A third difficulty: Hume is concerned with whether certain expressions make sense, or whether we understand anything by them, and he thinks that these questions have some importance. But if it really does matter *now* whether a given expression makes sense, then its making sense or not ought to show *now*: we ought to be able to settle the question by attending to the present and the future. Yet Hume, in trying to answer the question through his theory, implies that it is best answered by looking to the past—as though the best way of assessing a baker were by considering his country of birth.

Summing up these three matters: Hume offers an empirical theory as though he knew it to be true a priori; and the theory that he offers turns out to be largely irrelevant to the matters that he wants it to illuminate. I now proceed to explain why.

THE GENETIC NATURE OF HUME'S THEORY

The crucial trouble is that Hume's theory is genetic rather than analytic: he expresses it as a theory about what must occur *before* there can be understanding, rather than about what understanding is, or about what it is for an expression to have a meaning.

He would have done better to say something like the following. An expression E in our public language has a meaning only if we can tell whether a given person understands it, and our evidence for that must consist in how he uses it. Suppose he uses it correctly in statements whose truth-value does not depend upon the state of his environment at the time of speaking—in verbal definitions, necessary truths, contingent generalizations, etc. This will assure us of his understanding of E if, but only if, we know that he understands the other words used in those statements. Someone's saying 'Red things tend to irritate bulls' or 'Red things are always coloured' is not evidence of his understanding 'red' if his grasp of 'bulls' or 'coloured' is seriously in doubt. This looks like a vicious circle; and our only escape from it is through the fact that 'using E correctly' may involve relating E correctly not only to other expressions but also to bits of the objective world. The basis for our common understanding of a language is our ability to agree on statements of the form 'That is a . . .', where 'that' refers to something accessible to all of us; and E cannot be accounted as meaningful unless it is—or connects with expressions that are—usable in statements of that kind. The connexions may be lengthy and tenuous, and of course they need not consist in strings of verbal definitions; but if there is to be the possibility of evidence for or against the claim that somebody understands E, then there must be some coherent way of connecting E with the empirical world—the world given to us through our impressions.

That would preserve the empiricist spirit of Hume's theory, while turning it from a genetic into an analytic one. That would solve each of my three difficulties, as I now explain.

The analytic theory would say what it is for an expression to be understood or to have a meaning, and it could be refuted only by philosophical argument. An alleged counter-example to it would be a putatively meaningful expression E that was denied to be connectable with the world in the required way; and a friend of the theory would have to challenge E's meaningfulness or supply it with empirical connexions. If he could do neither—that is, if E turned out to have a meaning and to lack empirical connexions—that would refute Hume's meaning-empiricism. It would have been refuted, however, not by the actual existence of E but just by its bare possibility. That is how we refute conceptual doctrines, namely by adducing possibilities that clash with them. So the analytic theory really is knowable a priori if it is knowable at all. The first difficulty has gone.

If the analytic theory were false, it would obviously be reasonable to demand a retrial for the other expressions that had been condemned on the strength of the theory—which removes the second difficulty. Furthermore, the scrutiny of a supposed counter-example would not be an exercise in personal biography: the decisive facts lie in the present and future, not in the past; which removes the third difficulty.

Much of what Hume says in deploying his meaning-empiricism can be modelled over into a theory that is not genetic and—harking back to the first theme of the preceding section—not about ideas. This can be done, indeed, too far for it to be a coincidence. I do not say that Hume 'really meant' to offer an analysis of meaning and understanding; but I do suggest that what he said about ideas as copied from impressions is explained, somewhat and somehow, by the fact that his remarks can be 'translated' into analytic truths about meaningfulness in relation to empirical cashability. Let us examine one striking example of how far such modelling or 'translating' can go.

To get a protracted sound from a tuning-fork you must rap it hard in the first place; and, analogously, Hume could think it obvious that the first in a series of similar 'perceptions' must be 'lively' or 'vivacious' if it is to linger on in the form of conjured-up perceptions on later occasions. He certainly does take 'vivacity' to be a quantum that is transmitted, with some loss, from an impression to the ideas that follow it:

[W]hen any impression has been present with the mind, it again makes its appearance there as an idea; and this it may do after two different ways: either when in its new appearance it retains a considerable degree of its first vivacity, and is somewhat intermediate betwixt an impression and an idea; or when it intirely loses that vivacity, and is a perfect idea. (T 8; see also T 98, T 144, E 54)

Now, this view of 'vivacity', that comes right from the heart of Hume's theory considered as a theory about the origins of ideas, implies a reason for saying that any simple idea must be preceded by a lively perception. But I have remarked that he tends to equate 'impression' with 'sensory intake from the objective world': he does not care whether a blind man could have a vivid hallucination of something purple. Let us translate 'lively' into 'pertaining to the objective realm', as well as turning Hume's theory into one about understanding rather than ideas, and construing it as analytic rather than genetic. Under this threefold 'translation', the statement 'Ideas must be preceded by *lively* perceptions' becomes 'What is understood must be connectable with experience of the *objective* realm'. The stress on 'lively', which was encouraged by the primitive face-value form of the theory, reappears as a stress on 'objective'. The latter stress can be justified within the triply transformed version of the theory: you cannot know that I understand E unless there is something that you and I can both connect with E—that is, something interpersonal and thus objective.

(I do not offer these transformations as an act of fond indulgence towards Hume. The point is simply that it is profitable to look at Hume in the light of these 'updating' transformations—they throw light on his text, and help to bring to the surface many instructive complexities. Some indulgences towards great philosophers of the past are not like this: they rescue the subject from some difficulty at the price of making his thought bland, vague, or ambiguous. *They* are not worth doing.)

I have not laboured to present a fully articulated theory about meaningfulness in relation to empirical cashability, for I do not think that Hume's sort of meaning-empiricism is much helped by a precise, general theory. Berkeley, for example, in his excellent criticisms of the veil of perception theory, needs no magisterial principles about the limits on intelligibility. He shows that Locke's doctrine fails to answer the set questions, to draw the needed distinctions, to explain the relevant facts, to connect helpfully with other philosophical problems, or to bear in any way upon possible experience. His case would not have been stronger or more interesting if he had adduced a general theory of meaning to justify the further conclusion '. . . and therefore Locke's doctrine is meaningless'.

Hume, too, often proceeds by detailed, down-to-earth argument rather than by blanket applications of his meaning-empiricism; and often enough he is not arguing for a conclusion about meaninglessness at all, but is trying to see *what* an expression means by seeing *how* it connects with the empirical world.

It is fortunate that Hume's work is not too deeply rooted in his theory; for whenever the latter is taken as sufficient in itself, the results are calamitous. For example, his discussion of 'empty space' and eventless time is badly warped by his simple-minded search for 'impressions of', and by his trust in the spurious simple–complex dichotomy.[2] From the defensible premiss that nothing could count as an impression of empty space or of empty time, Hume infers that neither 'empty space' nor 'empty time' has a meaning. I think that there could be empty space and that there could be empty time; but, whether I am right or wrong about that, these are certainly separate issues that require different arguments.

That was about the theory's ostensible concern with 'ideas'. It seems to suffer less harm from its genetic nature.

It is worth noting that these two principal defects in Hume's statement of meaning-empiricism are connected: in two distinct ways, the stress on 'ideas' is a positive encouragement into geneticism.

First, superficially, it is tempting to think of ideas as copies of impressions, and therefore to think that impressions must come first. With 'ideas' replaced by 'capacities to use words correctly' or the like, this temptation disappears. The second way in which 'idea' encourages geneticism lies deeper. Hume wants to settle controversial questions of the form 'What, if anything, does *E* mean?' Because his answers are controversial he must argue for them; but if his arguments appealed explicitly to criteria having to do with the use of *E*—criteria on which, no doubt, he silently relies in uncontroversial cases—he would be forced to see and admit that his equation of meaning with ideas is hopelessly wrong. So he has to tackle these controversial questions in a way that draws our attention, and his own, away from *E* itself and towards issues about 'antecedent impressions' which are in fact irrelevant to the matter in hand. Taking them to be relevant is espousing a genetic rather than an analytic form of meaning-empiricism.

---

[2] See *Treatise* I. ii. 3.

4

Hume's Sceptical Doubts Concerning Induction

Peter Millican

1. INTRODUCTION

Section IV of Hume's first *Enquiry*, entitled 'Sceptical Doubts concerning the Operations of the Understanding', contains the third and most extensive presentation of his massively influential argument concerning induction, the foundation stone of his philosophical system.[1] However despite being one of the best known and most widely read texts in the entire canon of Western philosophy, the interpretation of this argument has been much debated, and there is still no established consensus even on the question of what exactly Hume is attempting to prove with it, let alone on the philosophical merits of his attempt.

It may seem astonishing that the interpretation of an argument so familiar, and from a writer so clear and elegant, can be subject to such debate and apparent uncertainty. Some of this can be put down to the prejudices of previous generations of commentators, many of whom dismissed Hume as an extreme 'deductivist' sceptic (and hence read his argument as a dogmatic rejection of any reasoning that fails to meet deductive standards), while others claimed him as a spiritual father (and hence read his argument anachronistically as an anticipation of twentieth-century concerns).[2] But a deeper

[1] The first and most studied presentation of the argument is in the *Treatise of Human Nature* I. iii. 6, *T* 86–92, to which frequent reference will be made below, and the second in the *Abstract* of the *Treatise*, *A* 649–52. The first stage of the argument, following its *Enquiry* presentation in Section IV Part i, appears for yet a fourth time, elegantly summarized in the *Dialogues* (*D* 145–6; see §4.1 below).

[2] Notable examples of the former group are A. Flew, *Hume's Philosophy of Belief* (London: Routledge & Kegan Paul, 1961), D. C. Stove, 'Hume, Probability, and Induction', *Philosophical Review*, 74 (1965), 160–77 (repr. in V. C. Chappell (ed.), *Hume* (London: Macmillan, 1968), 187–212), and D. C. Stove, *Probability and Hume's Inductive Scepticism* (Oxford: Clarendon Press, 1973), and of the latter group,

explanation of the extent of the interpretative controversy, even among sympathetic and historically sensitive scholars, is provided by the central place
that the argument occupies within Hume's system, and the tensions within
that system which it generates and reflects.[3] The most fundamental of these
tensions is between Hume the inductive sceptic, and Hume the apostle of
empirical science. For while his famous argument concludes that induction
has no basis in reason (commonly interpreted as implying that induction is
completely unreasonable), nevertheless Hume's other writings consistently
preach the virtues of inductive science, repeatedly emphasizing its superiority
over non-empirical 'divinity or school metaphysics' (E 165), and even
advocating explicit inductive criteria of rationality (e.g. T 173–5, E 57–8,
86–7, 104–7, 110–11, 136–7).

With the development of recent Hume scholarship, and much wider appreciation of his constructive philosophical purposes, it has become increasingly
fashionable to relieve this apparent tension in his philosophy by reinterpreting
the aims of his argument concerning induction. For although Hume's repeated
statements of his conclusion render it relatively uncontroversial that the overt
purpose of his argument is to prove that induction 'is not founded on reason',
nevertheless this leaves considerable scope for different views about what 'reason' means here, and whether it is a notion to which Hume himself is committed. Thus some scholars have interpreted Hume's 'reason' to mean *reasoning*,
accordingly taking his conclusion to have nothing to do with the rational credentials of inductive inference but only with its *computational mechanism* or
causation (i.e. that it does not involve, or is not brought about by, reasoning or
ratiocination).[4] Meanwhile, other scholars have continued to interpret 'reason'
as a normative (though usually deductivist or narrowly rationalistic) notion,
but have treated Hume's argument as a *critique* of that notion, purely intended
to reveal its impotence rather than to imply any genuine sceptical concerns

A. J. Ayer, *Language, Truth and Logic* (London: Gollancz, 1936) and K. R. Popper, *Conjectures and Refutations* (London: Routledge & Kegan Paul, 1963).

   [3] The centrality of the argument within Hume's system is evident from the logic and structure of the
Enquiry in particular, but is made most explicit in the *Abstract*, whose title-page declares its purpose as
being to illustrate and explain 'The CHIEF ARGUMENT' of the *Treatise* (A 641), and which then devotes
more space to induction than to any other topic.

   [4] For example, D. Garrett, *Cognition and Commitment in Hume's Philosophy* (Oxford: Oxford Univer-
sity Press, 1997), H. W. Noonan, *Hume on Knowledge* (London: Routledge, 1999), and D. Owen, *Hume's
Reason* (Oxford: Oxford University Press, 1999). A similar line on the *point* of Hume's argument is taken
by R. Connon, 'The Naturalism of Hume Revisited', in D. F. Norton, N. Capaldi, and W. L. Robison (eds.),
McGill Hume Studies (San Diego, Calif.: Austin Hill Press, 1979), 121–45, and by J. Broughton, 'Hume's
Skepticism about Causal Inferences', *Pacific Philosophical Quarterly*, 64 (1983), 3–18, repr. in D. W. D.
Owen (ed.), *Hume: General Philosophy* (Aldershot: Ashgate, 2000), 149–64, who, however, interpret 'rea-
son' as a deductivist normative notion rather than as our actual faculty of reasoning.

about induction.[5] Both of these groups of scholars, therefore, see Hume's argument as being almost totally non-sceptical from his own point of view.

My aim in this paper is to develop and defend an interpretation of Hume's argument which reconciles its apparent sceptical thrust with his positive purposes, while denying neither. So, on the one hand, I shall maintain (against the recent trend) that Hume's 'Sceptical Doubts' are genuinely *sceptical*, while on the other hand, I shall explain (against his traditional critics) why Hume nevertheless feels able to use his argument as the basis for a constructive inductive science. My discussion will focus almost entirely on the version of the argument which appears in the *Enquiry*, partly because it represents Hume's considered view and is greatly superior to the earlier versions,[6] but also because I am more confident of how it is to be interpreted. The argument in the *Treatise*, largely because of its brevity and structural defects, is open to a far wider range of relatively plausible readings. And although my own inclination is to see it as an immature expression of the argument in the *Enquiry*, it is of course conceivable that Hume's view changed significantly between writing the two works. Hence I shall here attempt as far as possible to defend my interpretation by reference to the *Enquiry* alone, and it is fortunate that this gives an ample textual basis for constraining quite tightly the range of plausible readings. As we shall see, the detailed logic of *Enquiry* IV reveals a very great deal about Hume's intentions— enough, I believe, to refute both the traditional 'deductivist' and the more recent non-sceptical interpretations. The picture of his famous argument that eventually emerges is altogether more coherent and defensible than his traditional critics have alleged, while at the same time carrying far more sceptical force than his recent defenders have acknowledged.

The remainder of this paper is structured as follows. §2 discusses what I describe as the 'perceptual view of Reason' (using a capital R to signify the intellectual faculty which Hume, like many others, also calls 'the understanding'). This conception of Reason dates back to the birth of philosophy, but my principal aim here is to show that it dominated modern thought in the century prior

---

[5] For example, T. Beauchamp and T. Mappes, 'Is Hume Really a Sceptic about Induction?', *American Philosophical Quarterly*, 12 (1975), 119–29, T. Beauchamp and A. Rosenberg, *Hume and the Problem of Causation* (Oxford: Oxford University Press, 1981), N. S. Arnold, 'Hume's Skepticism about Inductive Inference', *Journal of the History of Philosophy*, 21 (1983), 31–55, and A. C. Baier, *A Progress of Sentiments: Reflections on Hume's Treatise* (Cambridge, Mass.: Harvard University Press, 1991). The papers by Connon and Broughton mentioned in the previous footnote also get close to this sort of 'anti-deductivist' interpretation of Hume's argument in *Treatise* I. iii. 6, though Broughton believes that in the *Enquiry* 'Hume does treat the analogue of the I. iii. 6 argument as delivering skeptical results' (p. 15).

[6] For instance the *Treatise* version of the argument is mixed in rather haphazardly with Hume's analysis of causation; has a highly psychologistic emphasis (on 'impressions', 'ideas', and mental processes instead of on inferential relations between propositions); is structurally convoluted (partly owing to its failure to connect causal with 'probable' reasoning from the outset); and omits a number of important stages (such as the proof that the Uniformity Principle cannot be founded on sensation or intuition).

to Hume, and was taken for granted equally by those of both 'rationalist' and 'empiricist' inclinations. Particular attention is given to Locke, whose logical framework was largely inherited by Hume, and whose perceptual view of 'probable' reasoning provides, I believe, the principal target of Hume's 'Sceptical Doubts'. §3 begins the analysis of Section IV of the *Enquiry* by looking briefly at the distinction known as Hume's Fork, between what he calls 'relations of ideas' and 'matters of fact'. Then §3.1 aims to clarify what exactly Hume understands by the form of inference which he calls 'probable', 'moral' or 'reasoning concerning matter of fact', but which is now usually called 'induction'. Here I introduce some unambiguous terminology which will be presupposed in the remainder of the paper, henceforth using the phrase 'factual inference to the unobserved' to refer to this form of inference, which is the topic of Hume's famous argument. The argument itself is briefly sketched in §3.2, which most importantly introduces what I call the 'Uniformity Principle', the principle of resemblance between past and future which plays a central role in Hume's discussion. Then §§4 to 9.3 work in detail through the text of his argument, establishing its logical structure by careful attention to his precise words. I believe that the interpretative structure which emerges in §10 (and is presented in detail in the appendix to the paper) can make sense of every paragraph and of every inferential step in *Enquiry* IV, something which cannot truly be said, as far as I am aware, of any alternative interpretation that has hitherto been proposed.

While working through Hume's argument, I shall address en route some major related interpretative issues, including his understanding of aprioricity (§4.1) and of 'demonstrative' inference (§7.1), and the evidence from Section IV regarding his alleged causal realism (§9.2). I shall also identify (§7.2) a major gap in his argument, namely, his failure to address the (admittedly highly questionable) possibility that induction might be given a rational foundation using mathematical probabilistic reasoning from a priori principles.

With all these preliminaries completed, §10 presents a detailed analysis of the *logic* of Hume's argument, starting with his 'founded on' relation (§10.1), then dealing with the role and nature of the Uniformity Principle (§10.2), and finally showing (§10.3) how the logic of his reasoning strongly supports the claim that his target is indeed the perceptual view of 'probable' reasoning advocated by Locke. Then §11 sketches Hume's alternative and totally non-perceptual account of inductive reasoning, explaining how, almost paradoxically, his profoundly sceptical argument about inductive inference, by highlighting the central role of 'custom' in our thinking, is able to provide the basis for his positive theory of inductive science. §12 discusses the implications of all this for Hume's own understanding of the notion of 'Reason', and stresses its revolutionary significance for scientific practice and aspiration. Rationalistic insight is shown to be an impossible dream, leaving the modest Humean search for inductive order as our only recourse.

2. DESCARTES, LOCKE, AND THE ANCIENT TRADITION OF PERCEPTUAL REASON

People in general, but no doubt philosophers in particular, have long taken pride in their intellectual powers, which more than any other feature of humankind seem to elevate us above the beasts (and, perhaps equally attractively to some, philosophers above the common herd!). But the spectacular successes of the scientific revolution, in which metaphysicians such as Descartes and Leibniz were major participants alongside Galileo, Newton, and many other 'natural philosophers', apparently reinforced this hubris even more. The human faculty of thinking, which was proving so amazingly effective in unravelling nature's secrets, widely came to be seen as our pre-eminent and essential characteristic, a view most famously advocated by Descartes: 'thought; this alone is inseparable from me. . . . I am . . . in the strict sense only a thing that thinks; that is, I am a mind, or intelligence, or intellect, or reason . . .'.[7] Descartes also influentially distinguished (in his Sixth Meditation) between the pure intellectual faculty on the one hand, and on the other hand those faculties, notably the senses and the imagination, that contribute to our thinking but are nevertheless contaminated by the body. Only pure intellect was generally supposed capable of yielding true insight and knowledge, and being so special and unique to humankind (indeed our whole essence, according to the Cartesians), was piously viewed as a manifestation of the divine image.[8]

Our intellectual faculty was called by a variety of names, most commonly 'the understanding' or 'reason'. The former emphasized this faculty's function of providing us with *insight*—genuine understanding of things and *perception* of their nature, rather than mere thought about them. The latter emphasized instead its function of providing *reasons*—the basis of rational inference and *reasoning*. These two aspects, though different, are closely related, since full understanding of a truth, unless it be known immediately through direct 'intuition' (as, for example, that 1 + 1 = 2), requires the apprehension of one or more inferential steps, and also of the reasons which ground them. But whatever their relation, most philosophers of the early modern period treated the

---

[7] René Descartes, *Meditations on First Philosophy* (1641), included with six sets of *Objections and Replies* in *The Philosophical Writings of Descartes*, trans. J. Cottingham, R. Stoothoff, D. Murphy, and A. Kenny, 3 vols. (Cambridge: Cambridge University Press, 1984), ii. 18.

[8] E. J. Craig, *The Mind of God and the Works of Man* (Oxford: Clarendon Press, 1987), chs. 1 and 2, argues that the idea of human reason as the 'image of God' within us was even the 'dominant philosophy' of the entire early modern period, and interprets this as Hume's principal target.

two names as equivalent, and Hume appears to have followed this practice to the extent of alternating between 'reason' and 'the understanding', within the same section and sometimes even within the same sentence, for the sake of mere elegant variation.[9]

Philosophers of course differed in their detailed view of this faculty (which I shall henceforth usually call 'Reason'), but there was general agreement, following ancient tradition, that it was essentially a faculty of *perception*. Descartes frequently speaks of it as 'the natural light' and of 'seeing clearly and distinctly' by that light,[10] and perceptual language was standardly used both by his followers (notably Malebranche) and by other rationalists. Price provides a British example, writing within the decade after the first publication of the *Enquiry*:

> sense and understanding are faculties of the soul totally different . . . The one not discerning, but suffering; the other not suffering, but discerning; and signifying the soul's Power of surveying and examining all things, in order to judge of them; which Power, perhaps, can hardly be better defined, than by calling it, in Plato's language, the power in the soul to which belongs . . . the apprehension of Truth.[11]

Here the language may be non-Cartesian in flavour, but the meaning is much the same as Descartes's. Our senses, according to Price, do not so much perceive as 'suffer' sensation, while the function of our Reason is to 'survey', 'examine', 'discern', and thus to 'apprehend Truth'.[12]

However, a perceptual view of Reason was not by any means confined to those we now class as 'rationalists', for it also dominates the thinking of the 'empiricist' Locke, whose stature in British philosophy was unrivalled throughout the period of Hume's career.[13] Locke's *Essay concerning Human Under-*

---

[9] For examples from the *Treatise*, see *T* 88, 92, 150, 180, 186–7, 193, 211, 218, 268, 413–17, 463–4, 468, and compare *T* 117 n. and 371 n. For the *Enquiry*, see *E* 25, 55, 76, and 104. L. A. Selby-Bigge, *British Moralists*, 2 vols. (Oxford: Clarendon Press, 1897) is perhaps the most widely available source for other writers of the period, among whom an identification of 'reason' and 'the understanding' was evidently commonplace, as illustrated in his numbered sections §48, §450, and §§590–4 (respectively Shaftesbury, *An Inquiry concerning Virtue* (1699, 1732), Hutcheson, *Illustrations upon the Moral Sense* (1728, 1742), and Price, *A Review of the Principal Questions in Morals* (1758, 1787); in each case the dates are those of the first edition and of the edition used by Selby-Bigge).

[10] Hobbes questioned the light metaphor in the Third Set of Objections to the *Meditations*, with Descartes replying: 'As everyone knows, a "light in the intellect" means transparent clarity of cognition' (*Philosophical Writings*, ii. 134–5).

[11] Selby-Bigge, *British Moralists*, §593.

[12] Hume, like Price, was echoing standard practice when in the *Treatise* he stated that 'Reason is the discovery of truth or falsehood.' (*T* 458; cf. his note at *E* 14 in the first edition: 'That Faculty, by which we discern Truth and Falshood . . .'). But this general agreement on the function of that faculty, and the 'obvious' and equally conventional distinction between it and 'the will' (*E* 14; cf. Hutcheson in Selby-Bigge, *British Moralists*, §§448, 450) clearly does not imply any deep agreement on its nature.

[13] That the perceptual metaphor was flourishing within British non-rationalist thought right up to the time of Hume's *Treatise* is illustrated by Butler's *Analogy of Religion* (1736), of which Hume thought highly (see E. C. Mossner, *The Life of David Hume*, 2nd edn. (Oxford: Clarendon Press, 1980), 111–12), and which refers to 'speculative reason' and 'moral understanding' as 'our speculative [and] practical faculties of perception' (I. vi. 19).

standing (hereafter simply the *Essay*) does not always follow the usual contemporary practice of treating 'reason' and 'the understanding' as equivalent, but tends to reserve the former for *reasoning* or *inference*, leaving direct 'intuition' of immediately apprehended truths (e.g. that $1 + 1 = 2$) as part of 'the understanding' but not of 'reason' proper.[14] This might lead us to expect, in his discussion of the latter sub-faculty, that the standard perceptual metaphor would be relatively muted, but in fact it figures prominently:

> *Inference* . . . consists in nothing but the Perception of the connexion there is between the *Ideas*, in each step of the deduction, whereby the Mind comes to see, either the certain Agreement of Disagreement of any two *Ideas*, as in Demonstration, in which it arrives at Knowledge; or their probable connexion, on which it gives or with-holds its Assent, as in Opinion. (*Essay* IV. xvii. 2)

Locke sees this sub-faculty of reason as yielding two main types of reasoning, 'demonstrative' and 'probable'. Both have the same general structure, typically involving one or more intermediate steps between premiss and conclusion, with these intermediate steps taking the form of 'Ideas' which may be fully formed propositions but apparently need not be.[15] To avoid unnecessary complexity, however, I shall assume in what follows that the 'Ideas' involved in inferences are indeed propositional, since this is logically more coherent and corresponds better with Hume's own language in the *Enquiry*.[16]

Locke coins the term 'proofs' for the intermediate ideas that connect the premiss of any inference with its conclusion, so the structure of an argument with two such intermediate ideas would be as follows:

[14] It would be a mistake to read much into this, however, because Locke himself (*Essay* II. xxi. 17–20) forthrightly ridicules the language of 'faculties', criticizes it as a source of philosophical error, and declares himself inclined to forgo it completely were it not that faculty words are so much in fashion that 'It looks like too much affectation wholly to lay them by' (ed. P. H. Nidditch (Oxford: Clarendon Press, 1975), 243). In his view, when we refer to man's 'understanding', all we can properly mean is that man has a power to understand, and it is a serious mistake to speak of our faculties 'as so many distinct Agents' (p. 243). Accordingly he seems to care little about where faculty boundaries are drawn or how they are named: 'the understanding, or reason, whichever your lordship pleases to call it' (*First Letter to Stillingfleet*, III. 70).

[15] See paragraph 6 of *Essay* IV. xvii. 4 (p. 673), in which non-propositional ideas such as 'God the punisher' and 'just Punishment' serve as intermediate steps. Locke is vague about the logical structure of inferences, for example sometimes calling a proposition an 'Idea' but most often treating a proposition as made up of two 'Ideas'. Unfortunately with Locke, as later with Hume, a dislike of Aristotelian syllogism seems to have led to a regrettable distaste for logical precision, and his account of reasoning is as a result seriously problematic. For instance it is unclear how his 'chain of ideas' model of reasoning could deal with inferences involving multiple premisses and/or quantified propositions (e.g. 'All *A*s are *B*s or *C*s; All *B*s are *D*s; All *C*s are *D*s; ∴ All *A*s are *D*s' is valid, but not easily reducible to a single chain of ideas; moreover the corresponding inference with 'Some . . .' would be invalid, despite the similarity of the 'Ideas' involved). For a brief contextual overview of Locke's 'logic', see Peter Millican, 'Logic', in D. Garrett and E. Barbanell (eds.), *Encyclopaedia of Empiricism* (Westport, Conn.: Greenwood Press, 1997), 215–17.

[16] Although Hume still sometimes lapses into Lockean talk of 'interposing ideas' (*E* 37), the core of his argument in Section IV of the *Enquiry* is expressed in the (logically far preferable) language of 'propositions' (e.g. *E* 34). Hence I disagree with Owen's claim (*Hume's Reason*, 119–20) that the Lockean 'chain of ideas' model of inference is essential for properly understanding Hume's argument (cf. §10.3 below).

Premiss → Proof$_1$ → Proof$_2$ → Conclusion

Whether this counts as 'demonstrative' or 'probable' reasoning will depend entirely on the strength of the inferential connexions, the 'links in the chain of ideas' here shown as arrows. If these links are all 'intuitive'—providing an immediate, transparently clear, and visibly certain connexion—then the inference as a whole is demonstrative, meaning that the conclusion follows from the premiss with absolute certainty. If any of the links are merely 'probable', then the inference itself is only probable (which would seem to allow the possibility of a 'probable' inference consisting of only a single link).[17]

It is worth re-emphasizing two key points about Locke's account of inference. The first of these, which will prove relevant to clarifying the force of Hume's famous argument, is that Locke's distinction between 'demonstrative' and 'probable' reasoning has nothing to do with formal structure, but depends entirely on the strength of the relevant inferential connexions:

As Demonstration is the shewing the Agreement, or Disagreement of two *Ideas*, by the intervention of one or more Proofs, which have a constant, immutable, and visible connexion one with another: so *Probability* is nothing but the appearance of such an Agreement, or Disagreement, by the intervention of Proofs, whose connexion is not constant and immutable, or at least is not perceived to be so, but is, or appears for the most part to be so, and is enough to induce the Mind to *judge* the Proposition to be true, or false, rather than the contrary. (*Essay* IV. xv. 1)

The second key point, confirming Locke's place within the ancient tradition which clearly dominated early modern philosophy (and much else before and since), is that in all of its operations, and hence in Lockean probable reasoning as well as demonstrative, Reason's primary function is one of *perception*:[18]

In both [demonstrative and probable reasoning] the Faculty which finds out the Means, and rightly applies them to discover Certainty in the one, and Probability in the other, is that which we call Reason. For as Reason perceives the necessary, and indubitable con-

---

[17] However, it does not follow that the conclusion of a 'probable' inference is *itself* probable (i.e. likely to be true), even if the premiss is true, for each merely probable connexion in a long chain will gradually erode the probability of the whole, and there may besides be other probable inferences that weigh on the other side. Locke is aware that judging the overall probability of a proposition will typically require the balancing of opposing considerations, as he makes clear in a passage (*Essay* IV. xv. 5) which interestingly anticipates Hume's argument against the credibility of miracle reports in *Enquiry* X.

[18] This point is made in terms of Reason rather than the more narrowly inferential 'reason proper', to emphasize Locke's place in the tradition. But it will be no surprise that Reason's main non-inferential operation, that of intuition, is explained by Locke in totally perceptual terms: 'This part of Knowledge is irresistible, and like the bright Sun-shine, forces it self immediately to be perceived, as soon as ever the Mind turns its view that way; and leaves no room for Hesitation, Doubt, or Examination, but the Mind is presently filled with the clear Light of it' (IV. ii. 1). It is interesting to note that, whether consciously or unconsciously, Hume would later use strikingly similar language to characterize the irresistibility of inductive 'proofs' (e.g. his reference to sunshine at *T* 183, and the phrase 'no room for doubt' at *E* 56 n.), despite his total rejection of the perceptual model of inductive reasoning.

nexion of all the *Ideas* or Proofs one to another, in each step of any Demonstration that produces Knowledge; so it likewise perceives the probable connexion of all the *Ideas* or Proofs one to another, in every step of a Discourse, to which it will think Assent due. . . . [Where] the Mind does not perceive this probable connexion; where it does not discern, whether there be any such connexion, or no, there Men's Opinions are not the product of Judgment, or the Consequence of Reason; but the effects of Chance and Hazard . . . (*Essay* IV. xvii. 2)

As his language of 'perception' and 'discovery' imply, Locke considers probability to be a thoroughly objective matter: depending on the evidence that we have for it, 'so is any Proposition in it self, more or less probable' (*Essay* IV. xv. 6; cf. IV. xx. 5). Accordingly, forming a 'right Judgment' about such propositions is 'to proportion the *Assent* to the different Evidence and Probability of the thing' (*Essay* IV. xvi. 9) and where there is mixed evidence for and against the proposition in question, to 'take a true estimate of the force and weight of each Probability; and then casting them up all right together, chuse that side, which has the over-balance' (IV. xvii. 16; cf. n. 17 above).

The extent to which Locke's thinking is infused with the perceptual view of Reason is illustrated by how he takes pains to address, and then deals with, a problem which arises precisely because he holds that view: if probable reasoning involves the *perception* of probabilities, then how is it that people ever disagree regarding what is, and is not, probable? Locke devotes an entire chapter (nearly four times the length of the earlier one on probability!) to this artificial problem of 'Wrong Assent, or Errour', just as Descartes had devoted his entire Fourth Meditation, and their solutions to it have significant similarities.[19] Neither takes seriously the possibility of falsehood or illusion in the basic perceptual deliverances of Reason, and both instead attribute error mainly to ill-informed, dogmatic, or precipitate judgement. Even though Locke, unlike Descartes at this point, explicitly recognizes that some people have a weaker intellectual faculty than others, this turns out not to be due to any failure to perceive correctly the appropriate component probabilities, but rather, an inability to 'carry a train of Consequences in their Heads, nor weigh exactly the preponderancy of contrary Proofs and Testimonies, making every circumstance its due allowance' (*Essay* IV. xx. 5). It is in memory, attentiveness, concentration, and thoroughness that weak reasoners fall short, rather than in the rational perception of individual probabilities.

[19] Though they importantly disagree on a related matter, namely the ethics of belief. Descartes maintains that we are free to withhold assent to any judgement except when we have clear and distinct perception of its truth (e.g. *Philosophical Writings*, ii. 25, 41), whereas Locke, like Hume after him, acknowledges that belief is involuntary even in many cases of merely probable evidence: 'we cannot hinder . . . our Assent, where the Probability manifestly appears upon due Consideration of all the Measures of it . . . a Man can no more avoid assenting, or taking it to be true, where he perceives the greater Probability' (IV. xx. 16)—note yet again the perceptual metaphor.

Locke's treatment of error might well seem to be straining the perceptual view of Reason potentially to breaking-point. In deductive disciplines such as mathematics and logic, and even calculable games such as chess, talk of 'seeing' truths and inferential connexions may indeed come naturally, almost irresistibly.[20] But the same is not true in non-deductive areas, where truth and evidential relationships are less clear-cut and often controversial, so that visual metaphors seem far less appropriate—here the language of 'opinion' and 'estimation' is likely to be preferred, with disagreements being ascribed to differences in personal judgement rather than 'error'. It is interesting to speculate whether this might in part explain the reluctance of earlier philosophers, held captive by the perceptual ideal, to accommodate probability within their theories. Descartes, for example, attempts rather unconvincingly to force the scientific practice with which he is familiar into a broadly deductive pattern, rejecting the notion of 'mere' probability and instead characterizing differences between acceptable levels of theory confirmation only in terms of varying degrees of 'certainty' (so that a theory which is actually at best highly probable might be described by him as 'morally certain').[21] It is hard to say whether this reluctance to recognize the notion of probability was indeed significantly conditioned by the perceptual metaphor. But if it was, then some of the differences between the 'rationalist' Descartes and the 'empiricist' Locke may be less to do with a contrast in 'rationalistic' outlook than with their relative willingness to acknowledge the messy truth about scientific and everyday inferential practice at the price of accepting tensions within their theory of Reason. Locke, at any rate, was prepared to pay that price, and it was his explicit recognition of probable reasoning, and his incorporation of it within the domain of perceptual Reason, that set the scene for Hume's sceptical attack.[22]

---

[20] In an early draft of the *Essay* Locke even went so far as to identify demonstration with intuition on the basis of its visual nature: 'we . . . looke for noe greater certainty then what our eyes can afford us, the whole evidence of this assurance being noe more then what the word *Demonstration* doth naturaly import; which is to shew any thing as it is & make it be perceived soe that in truth what we come to know this way is not by proofe but intuition, all the proofe that is used in this way of knowledg being noe thing else but shewing men how they shall see right . . . without useing arguments to perswade them that they are soe' (John Locke, *Draft B of the Essay concerning Human Understanding*, in *Drafts for the Essay concerning Human Understanding, and Other Philosophical Writings*, ed. P. H. Nidditch and G. A. J. Rogers (Oxford: Clarendon Press, 1990), i. 153).

[21] See D. M. Clarke, *Descartes's Philosophy of Science* (Manchester: Manchester University Press, 1982), 134–59, especially 137–8 and 158–9, for a useful account of Descartes's treatment of theory confirmation and the relative certainty of theories, and references to his negative comments on probability.

[22] It is perhaps significant that Hume's two most extensive discussions of inductive inference in the *Enquiry* (Sections IV and X) deal respectively with what Locke states to be the two 'grounds of Probability', namely, 'conformity with our own Experience' and 'the Testimony of others Experience' (*Essay* IV. xv. 4, section heading). Locke's discussion of these two 'grounds' is extremely cursory, and he never spells out how they are supposed to condition the perception of probable connexions.

3. THE TOPIC AND OVERALL STRUCTURE OF HUME'S ARGUMENT

Hume begins Section IV of the *Enquiry* by distinguishing between two kinds of proposition, which he calls 'relations of ideas' and 'matters of fact'. The former comprise 'the sciences of Geometry, Algebra, and Arithmetic; and in short, every affirmation, which is either intuitively or demonstratively certain'. These are discoverable 'by the mere operation of thought', without consulting experience, because as the classification implies, they concern only the internal relations between our ideas themselves, and therefore have no 'dependence on what is any where existent in the universe' (*E* 25). Knowledge of relations of ideas thus fits comfortably within the perceptual model of Reason, and Hume accordingly here sees no need to dispute or modify the conventional Lockean picture. Indeed he is essentially in broad agreement with Locke to this point: knowledge of relations of ideas is to be had either directly through immediate intuition, or indirectly through demonstrative reasoning, which itself consists of chains of intuitive links.

3.1 *Hume's Quarry: The Basis of Factual Inference to the Unobserved*

It is the basis of our assurance of 'matters of fact' which Hume wishes to explore further, since this is of a fundamentally different character and far less transparent than our knowledge of 'relations of ideas':

Matters of fact . . . are not ascertained in the same manner; nor is our evidence of their truth, however great, of a like nature with the foregoing. The contrary of every matter of fact is still possible; because it can never imply a contradiction, and is conceived by the mind with the same facility and distinctness, as if ever so conformable to reality. *That the sun will not rise to-morrow* is no less intelligible a proposition, and implies no more contradiction, than the affirmation, *that it will rise.* We should in vain, therefore, attempt to demonstrate its falsehood. Were it demonstratively false, it would imply a contradiction, and could never be distinctly conceived by the mind.

It may, therefore, be a subject worthy of curiosity, to enquire what is the nature of that evidence, which assures us of any real existence and matter of fact, beyond the present testimony of our senses, or the records of our memory. (*E* 25–6)

So the aim of Hume's investigation in the remainder of Section IV will be to examine the foundation of our beliefs about matters of fact which are *absent*: those that are not immediately 'present' to our senses or memory.[23] Hume will

---

[23] Hume sometimes speaks simply of 'matters of fact', but he is clearly not concerned here with those that are immediately available to us through sensation or memory, since he raises no sceptical doubts about these faculties at this point. It has been suggested (by J. Bennett, *Locke, Berkeley, Hume: Central*

argue that the only possible foundation for such beliefs is provided by extrapolative inferences from things that we have observed to those that we have not, these inferences operating on the assumption that the unobserved will resemble the observed.[24] In the *Treatise* and *Abstract* Hume usually follows Locke in calling these 'probable' reasonings or arguments, whereas in the *Enquiry* he tends to prefer the expression 'reasonings concerning matter of fact' (though he still uses the term 'probable', and sometimes 'moral'). However, since they are now generally termed 'inductive' inferences, Hume's argument is most commonly referred to as his argument concerning *induction*.

Unfortunately the terms 'probable', 'moral', 'inductive', and even 'reasoning concerning matter of fact' all carry some risk of misunderstanding, so it is important to keep in mind that Hume is here discussing everyday factual inferences, of the kind that we use whenever we draw a conclusion about any empirical state of affairs which is neither directly observed nor remembered. Scientific inferences fall into the same category, because although these may be distinguished by the care and precision that are exercised in making them (their 'exacter and more scrupulous method of proceeding'; *D* 134), nevertheless Hume maintains that they are essentially 'nothing but the reflections of common life, methodized and corrected' (*E* 162). So taken as a class, the inferences that Hume is concerned with are not in any way unusual: they are neither particularly technical, nor involve any distinctive subject-matter, nor have any specific grammatical form. When he calls them 'probable', he is using this term in its Lockean sense of being less than certain, which does not imply that they need be *probabilistic* in any mathematical sense. When he calls them 'moral', he is using this term in the eighteenth-century sense in which 'moral evidence' means 'evidence which is merely probable and not demonstrative' (*Oxford English Dictionary*), and this does not imply that they need have anything to do with *morality* or *ethics* or even with the 'moral sciences' (such as economics, politics, etc.). And when we today call these inferences 'inductive', all we should mean is that they involve extrapolation from what has been experienced to something which has not been experienced, not that they need be 'inductive' in the Aristotelian sense of involving an inference to *universal* laws.[25]

Themes (Oxford: Clarendon Press, 1971), 245) that Hume tends to count something as a 'matter of fact' only if it is 'absent'. But this seems too strong a conclusion to draw from Hume's admittedly sometimes careless omission of the restriction (e.g. *T* 92, *E* 75), given that such a usage would make its common inclusion (e.g. *E* 26, 45, 159) pleonastic; would not conform to his principal criterion for 'matter of factness' (conceivability of the contrary); and would conflict outright with some of his explicit uses of the phrase (e.g. *T* 143: 'any matter of fact we remember'; *T* 469: 'Here is a matter of fact; but 'tis the object of feeling, not of reason.').

[24] However, not all factual beliefs have any such foundation, notably those based on indoctrination or 'education', which is 'frequently contrary to reason' and thus not 'recogniz'd by philosophers' (T116–7).

[25] Some Hume interpreters have apparently been misled by the Aristotelian sense of 'induction', which is ironic given that Hume himself never uses the term in this context. Flew, for example, clearly

The potential misunderstanding that arises from Hume's use of the term 'reasoning concerning matter of fact' (sometimes 'matter of fact and existence') is best explained by example. Consider any deductively valid inference that has an experiential conclusion, such as the following:[26]

Mars is red and round   *therefore*   Some round thing is coloured

Does this count as 'reasoning concerning matter of fact'? It might at first glance seem to do so, for it is surely a piece of reasoning, while both its premiss and its conclusion assert straightforward 'matters of fact' (i.e. contingent propositions knowable only through experience). But such an inference cannot possibly count as 'reasoning concerning matter of fact' as *Hume* understands that phrase, because here the link between premiss and conclusion is deductively certain rather than merely 'probable', is clearly explicable in terms of 'relations of ideas', and hence (a point whose significance will become clear later) requires no appeal to experience and no dependence on supposed causal relations. In Hume's terms, therefore, this inference is certainly not an instance of 'reasoning concerning matter of fact', and hence falls outside the scope of his main discussion.

To sum up, Hume's interest in *Enquiry* IV is in the type of inference whereby we acquire belief in matters of fact 'beyond what is immediately present to the memory and senses' (*E* 45, my emphasis), and *beyond* what can be inferred from that basis by purely deductive methods (i.e. 'demonstrative' reasoning; see §7.1 below). In other words, he is concerned with *ampliative* reasoning, whereby we draw conclusions about *new* matters of fact that are not deductively implied by those from which we start. Following Locke, Hume recognizes that such reasoning will generally yield merely 'probable' conclusions, and at best 'moral' certainty, so he accordingly calls it 'probable' or 'moral' reasoning. As we shall see, he takes all such reasoning to be based on an extrapolation from observed to unobserved, presupposing a resemblance between the two—extrapolative inference of this sort is now almost universally called *induction*. To clarify the presentation of Hume's argument, and my discussion of it, some simple and unambiguous terminology will prove helpful:

takes the Aristotelian sense as primary, defining induction as 'A method of reasoning by which a general law or principle is inferred from observed particular instances' (A. Flew, *A Dictionary of Philosophy* (London: Pan, 1979), 159); and in his *Hume's Philosophy of Belief*, 71–2, and *David Hume* (Oxford: Blackwell, 1986), 53, he interprets Hume's argument as applying only to 'inductive' arguments thus understood.

[26] Note that here and elsewhere I use the term 'deductive' in its *informal* sense, according to which an inference is deductively valid if and only if the truth of its premisses logically guarantees the truth of its conclusion (I shall argue in §7.1 below that this is essentially what Hume means by 'demonstrative'). There is no requirement that the inference should be 'valid in virtue of its form', nor that it should be reducible through substitution to a formal tautology. Hence my choice of this example, whose validity derives in part from the meanings of 'red' and 'coloured' rather than from any formal inference schema.

Factual inference	Inference that draws a conclusion about matter(s) of fact, beyond what is deductively ('demonstratively') implied by the premises (whatever those facts might be, and however that inference might operate)
Factual inference to the unobserved	*Factual inference* that moves from premises about what has been observed, to a conclusion about something which has not been observed (however that inference might operate)
Inductive inference	*Factual inference to the unobserved* that operates by extrapolation on the basis that the unobserved will resemble the observed

3.2 A Preliminary Sketch of Hume's Argument, and his Uniformity Principle

The argument of *Enquiry* IV aims to prove that factual inference to the unobserved is not 'founded on' the faculty of Reason (what exactly Hume means by all this will be the topic of §10 below). This proof falls broadly into two halves, pivoting around a principle of resemblance between observed and unobserved which I shall call the Uniformity Principle. In the first half Hume begins by arguing that all factual inference to the unobserved must be founded on experience, since only experience can tell us anything about causal relations, and causation provides our only basis for drawing inferences about things that we have not perceived. He then goes on to conclude that since all inference from experience is founded on the supposition that what we find in experience can be extrapolated beyond it (i.e. the Uniformity Principle), it follows that all factual inference to the unobserved must itself be founded on that Uniformity Principle. Hume expresses our reliance on this principle in a number of ways, sometimes in general terms but sometimes more specifically in terms of the expected uniformity of cause and effect relations:

we always presume, when we see like sensible qualities, that they have like secret powers, and expect, that effects, similar to those, which we have experienced, will follow from them. (*E* 33)

we . . . put trust in past experience, and make it the standard of our future judgment . . . (*E* 35)

all our experimental conclusions proceed upon the supposition, that the future will be conformable to the past. (*E* 35)

all inferences from experience suppose, as their foundation, that the future will resemble the past, and that similar powers will be conjoined with similar sensible qualities. (*E* 37)

The second half of Hume's argument is devoted to showing that this Uniformity Principle has no adequate foundation in Reason, since it cannot be established a priori from anything that we discover through immediate sensation; it does not follow immediately (i.e. by 'intuition') from the uniformity that we have observed within our experience; and nor can it be proved from that experience either demonstratively or by factual reasoning. Having exhausted, as he believes, all possible sources of rational foundation, Hume eventually concludes that the Uniformity Principle cannot be founded on Reason. And given the result from the first half of his argument, that all factual inference to the unobserved is founded on the Uniformity Principle, he therefore takes it to follow that no factual inference to the unobserved is founded on Reason.

Let us now explore the stages of this argument in detail, working in turn through the main propositions that Hume is concerned to establish (and which provide the main headings for §§4 to 8 below).

4. ALL FACTUAL INFERENCES TO THE UNOBSERVED ARE FOUNDED ON EXPERIENCE

Part i of Section IV of the *Enquiry* is devoted to establishing one fundamental result, that all factual inferences to the unobserved must, if they are to have any force, be based on experience. So part of the answer to Hume's original query: 'what is the nature of that evidence, which assures us of any [absent] matter of fact' (*E* 26) is that such evidence cannot be purely a priori.

4.1 What does Hume Mean by 'A Priori'?

Before examining Hume's argument for this important result, however, it will be helpful to clarify what he understands by aprioricity. For when he denies that some kind of knowledge or inference is a priori, he usually means not simply *that it requires experience*, but *that it requires experience beyond mere perception of the objects concerned*. The contrast between the more familiar 'absolute' notion of aprioricity and this Humean notion is brought out by a passage in his *Dialogues concerning Natural Religion* (henceforth the *Dialogues*) which nicely summarizes the Section IV Part i argument that we are shortly to examine:

Were a man to abstract from every thing which he knows or has seen, he would be altogether incapable, merely from his own ideas, to determine what kind of scene the universe must be, or to give the preference to one state or situation of things above another. For as nothing, which he clearly conceives, could be esteemed impossible or implying a contradiction, every chimera of his fancy would be upon an equal footing;

nor could he assign any just reason, why he adheres to one idea or system, and rejects the others, which are equally possible.

Again; after he opens his eyes, and contemplates the world, as it really is, it would be impossible for him, at first, to assign the cause of any one event; much less, of the whole of things or of the universe. He might set his fancy a rambling; and she might bring him in an infinite variety of reports and representations. These would all be possible; but being all equally possible, he would never, of himself, give a satisfactory account for his preferring one of them to the rest. Experience alone can point out to him the true cause of any phenomenon. (*D* 145–6)

In this passage the first paragraph illustrates the absolute notion of aprioricity, according to which a proposition counts as a priori only if someone could know it while 'abstracting from every thing which he knows or has seen'—that is, *without appeal to any experience whatever*. The second paragraph illustrates the more relaxed Humean notion, according to which a proposition counts as a priori if it can be known *without appeal to any experience beyond what is currently being perceived* (and hence without any appeal to memory as opposed to sensation).

It would take us too far afield to discuss the broader logical issues and difficulties associated with this Humean notion of aprioricity, but it is worth considering why Hume adopts it. In the context of his discussion of factual inference *to the unobserved* he is obviously prepared to take for granted what *is* observed (i.e. the immediate deliverances of our senses).[27] His question at this point in his discussion is what *else* can be inferred from our sensory perceptions, and his answer is that if we exclude all experience other than those perceptions themselves (and therefore exclude for the present even the evidence of memory), then *no further 'object' whatever* can be inferred: 'There is no object, which implies the existence of any other if we consider these objects in themselves, and never look beyond the ideas which we form of them.' (*T* 86–7). Hume treats present perceptual 'ideas' as a priori in order to express this point, but his doing so also seems to be part of a broader tendency to incorporate such ideas within the domain of Reason, presumably again because of their epistemological immediacy and security. At one point in the *Abstract* he even appears to suggest that Reason itself is capable of sensory perception: 'It is not any thing that *reason sees in the cause*, which make us infer the effect. Such an inference, were it

---

[27] This does not mean, however, that he is prepared to take for granted our *interpretation* of our sensory impressions. For example, when we have an experience like that of seeing, smelling, handling, and tasting bread, it is only the immediate impressions that carry the sanction of sensation. Whether those impressions are genuinely caused by a nourishing food is another matter entirely, and one that can perfectly well be subject to sceptical doubt (*E* 33–4, 37). Thus the immediate deliverances of our senses include our perception of breadlike 'sensible [i.e. sensory] qualities', but not that we are genuinely perceiving *bread*.

possible, would amount to a demonstration, as being founded merely on the comparison of ideas.' (A 650, my emphasis). The *Enquiry* is less explicit, but comes close to the same suggestion: 'When we reason a priori, and consider merely any object or cause, *as it appears to the mind*, independent of all observation, it never could suggest to us the notion of any distinct object, such as its effect' (E 31, my emphasis). Here again we have the usual contrast between, on the one hand, what is *immediately* perceived and is thus available a priori to 'the mind', and on the other hand, what has been *previously* perceived (and is now merely remembered) and is thus counted as a posteriori 'experience' or 'observation'.

There are many other echoes, throughout this section of the *Enquiry*, of the perceptual view of Reason, and indeed the entire argument of Part i can be understood as the start of a systematic assault on that view. This, I would suggest, explains why Hume expounds at such length what is logically a relatively small part of his overall argument, providing numerous examples to illustrate his central thesis that the causal powers of objects are not perceivable in any way. As he repeatedly emphasizes, all that we perceive of objects comes through the senses, and Reason is quite unable to discover, within the 'sensible qualities' of objects or the ideas that they produce in us, anything that carries any direct implication regarding those objects' future behaviour.

4.2 The Argument of Section IV Part I

The structure of Hume's argument in Part i of Section IV can be represented as follows (diagram, p. 124), with each major stage represented by a numbered proposition, and the set of arrows to any particular proposition indicating Hume's grounds for inferring that proposition (whether or not those grounds are, in fact, adequate—the aim here is to show the structure of Hume's reasoning, not necessarily to endorse it).

This diagram provides, of course, only an idealized outline, since Hume himself does not present his arguments as having any such explicit structure. Indeed it is not easy in Part i to find even a straightforward statement of its conclusion, though proposition (6) is evidently implicit both in Hume's argumentative procedure and in the summing-up which he gives in the first paragraph of Part ii (E 32).[28] Moreover, his oft-repeated explicit statements of (2) and (5) are clearly intended to be read together, and Hume apparently sees (6) as such an obvious consequence of these that it does not even need to be stated,

---

[28] For the summing up, see the beginning of §5 below. Hume's procedure of arguing for (6) via (2) and (5) is also made clear at E 27: 'If we would satisfy ourselves, therefore, concerning the nature of that evidence, which assures us of matters of fact, we must enquire how we arrive at the knowledge of cause and effect.'

124   PETER MILLICAN

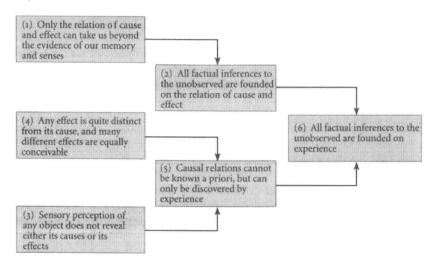

except perhaps in passing: 'nor can our reason, unassisted by experience, ever draw any inference concerning real existence and matter of fact' (E 27); 'In vain, therefore, should we pretend to determine any single event, or infer any cause or effect, without the assistance of observation and experience.' (E 30).

Hume's argument from (1) to (2) is presented very briefly at E 26: 'All reasonings concerning matter of fact seem to be founded on the relation of *Cause and Effect*. By means of that relation alone we can go beyond the evidence of our memory and senses.' He then proceeds to give some illustrations to substantiate this claim that a 'just inference from [facts about] one object to [facts about] another' (T 89) can only be based on causation: this relation alone can provide the requisite 'connexion between the present fact and that which is inferred from it', without which any such inference 'would be entirely precarious' (E 27).

Having concluded that all factual reasoning is causal, Hume now sets himself to prove that all knowledge of causal relations is a posteriori: 'I shall venture to affirm, as a general proposition, which admits of no exception, that the knowledge of this relation is not, in any instance, attained by reasonings a priori; but arises entirely from experience' (E 27). The argument for this proposition, (5) in the structure diagram, occupies the remainder of Part i. Hume provides two lines of argument for it, the first of which is initially presented using a thought experiment. Suppose that the first man, Adam, just after his creation by God, and with no previous experience to call on, had been confronted with water and fire. Simply from examining their 'sensible qualities', Adam could not possibly have inferred what effects they would have. This illustrates the general proposition (3): 'No object ever discovers, by the qualities which appear to the senses, either the causes, which produced it, or the effects, which will arise from it' (*E* 27). Hume thinks that this proposition, and what he takes to be its immediate consequence (5), appear unsurprising 'with regard to such objects, as we remember to have once been altogether unknown to us', but when an object has been very familiar to us since our birth, 'We are apt to imagine, that we could discover [its] effects by the mere operation of our reason, without experience.' (*E* 28).

To show that this natural assumption is mistaken, Hume employs a second line of argument, summarized in the diagram as proposition (4), which starts with a characteristically Humean challenge: 'Were any object presented to us, and were we required to pronounce concerning the effect, which will result from it, without consulting past observation; after what manner, I beseech you, must the mind proceed in this operation?' (*E* 29). He then goes on to claim that the challenge cannot be met: that there is no way in which pure Reason alone can discover causal connexions. For any cause and its effect are logically quite distinct; a priori there is nothing in the one to suggest the idea of the other; so in advance of experience any imagined pairing between causes and effects will appear entirely arbitrary. And even if by luck we happen to guess the correct pairing, so that we succeed in ascribing to some particular cause its actual future effect, nevertheless the conjunction of the two will still appear arbitrary from an a priori point of view, 'since there are always many other effects, which, to reason, must seem fully as consistent and natural' (*E* 30).

It is important to notice that this second line of argument is significantly different from that with which Hume is commonly attributed, most notably by Stove.[29] For Hume is not stating merely that cause and effect are logically distinct—that the one is conceivable without the other—and concluding that for this reason alone there cannot be a legitimate inference from one to the other. He is starting from a much stronger premiss, namely, that a priori there is *no discernible connexion whatever* between cause and supposed effect: in advance of experience the conjunction of the two appears 'entirely arbitrary', and the supposed effect is therefore no more 'consistent and natural' than any number of alternatives.[30] So Hume's argument here need not rely, as Stove supposes, on the deductivist assumption that an inference from cause to effect is unreasonable

[29] 'Hume, Probability, and Induction', 194; *Probability and Hume's Inductive Scepticism*, 31.

[30] There is an interesting progression in Hume's thought here. In the *Treatise* his argument does turn largely on mere conceivability, and the suggestion of arbitrariness is relatively muted: 'we might . . . have substituted any other idea' (*T* 87; cf. *T* 111–12). In the *Abstract* this suggestion is expanded: 'The mind can always *conceive* any effect to follow from any cause, and indeed any event to follow upon another' (*A* 650). By the time of the *Enquiry* arbitrariness has clearly become Hume's principal emphasis, as it remains when he repeats the argument in the *Dialogues* (*D* 145–6, quoted in §4.1 above).

unless the occurrence of the cause without the effect is logically inconceivable. It requires only the far more modest principle that if the inference from cause to effect is to be justifiable a priori, then the connexion between cause and effect must be at least to some extent non-arbitrary, and an examination of the cause must be able to yield some ground, however slight, for expecting that particular effect in preference to others. In adopting this compelling principle, Hume is not in any way committing himself to the deductivist view, that the only arguments of any kind which have any force are those that are logically conclusive.[31]

Having completed the principal arguments of Part i, Hume briefly states its conclusion: 'In vain, therefore, should we pretend to determine any single event, or infer any cause or effect, without the assistance of observation and experience.' (E 30). He then adds two paragraphs which give valuable insight into his conception of science, spelling out some implications for scientific theorizing in general and for applied mathematics in particular. First, science has absolute limits, in that it cannot possibly uncover the 'ultimate springs and principles' of nature: in other words it cannot provide pure rational insight into why things behave as they do. Such insight would require an a priori grasp of causal relations, which Hume's arguments have ruled out, so the most we can hope for is 'to reduce the principles, productive of natural phaenomena, to a greater simplicity, and to resolve the many particular effects into a few general causes' (E 30). Scientists can continue to search for systematic order in the operations of nature, but they cannot aspire to an ultimate explanation of why things are ordered in the way that they are.

Applied ('mixed') mathematics might seem to provide an exception to this rule, since it appears to consist of rational deductions from the a priori principles of geometry and arithmetic. But Hume points out that any piece of applied mathematics also presupposes certain physical laws, for example the conservation of momentum, and any such law is incurably a posteriori. So although a priori mathematical reasoning certainly has a part to play in the application of such laws, 'to determine their influence in particular instances', it remains true that 'the discovery of the law itself is owing merely to experience, and all the abstract reasonings in the world could never lead us one step towards the knowledge of it' (E 31; cf. §7.1 below).

---

[31] A suspicion might remain that the argument of *Treatise* I. iii. 6, where Hume does seem content to argue from mere conceivability, is based on a general deductivist assumption. However a more plausible explanation is that he is here taking for granted a principle made explicit in the *Abstract* (A 650, quoted in §4.1 above), that a priori evidence must yield demonstrative certainty. We shall see in §7.2 that this assumption plays a role later in the *Enquiry* version of the argument (when Hume denies the possibility of a priori non-demonstrative reasoning), but it clearly does not imply any corresponding deductivism about a posteriori evidence.

5. ALL FACTUAL INFERENCES TO THE UNOBSERVED ARE FOUNDED ON THE UNIFORMITY PRINCIPLE

The first paragraph of Part ii provides a summary of what Hume takes his argument to have established so far, and the second announces his intentions for what follows:

> When it is asked, *What is the nature of all our reasonings concerning matter of fact?* the proper answer seems to be, that they are founded on the relation of cause and effect. When again it is asked, *What is the foundation of all our reasonings and conclusions concerning that relation?* it may be replied in one word, EXPERIENCE. But if we still carry on our sifting humour, and ask, *What is the foundation of all conclusions from experience?* this implies a new question . . .
>
> I shall content myself, in this section, with an easy task, and shall pretend [i.e. claim or aspire] only to give a negative answer to the question here proposed. I say then, that, even after we have experience of the operations of cause and effect, our conclusions from that experience are *not* founded on reasoning, or any process of the understanding. (*E* 32)

Hume then embarks, in the very long third paragraph, on a slightly unfocused discussion combining two distinguishable lines of thought, the first of which can be represented as follows:

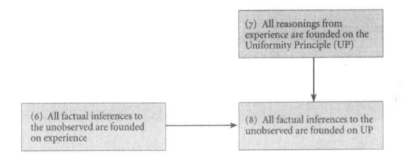

This part of Hume's argument is perhaps the least explicit of any, but, as we shall see, it can nevertheless be spelt out with reasonable confidence on the basis of what he says both before and after it.

The quotation above from the first paragraph of Part ii makes clear that Hume's motive for investigating arguments from experience is to shed light on the general nature of factual inferences to the unobserved—this will explain the inference from (6) and (7) to (8) in the structure diagram. His investigation begins negatively, with a reminder that our experiential reasonings cannot possibly be based on any perceptual knowledge of objects' 'secret powers'. But the positive account soon follows: 'notwithstanding this ignorance of natural powers and principles, we always presume, when we see like sensible qualities, that they have like secret powers, and expect, that effects, similar to those, which we have experienced, will follow from them' (*E* 33). That this is indeed Hume's positive account is made clear by an otherwise puzzling back-reference two pages later, which he makes while summarizing this part of his argument, and which cannot plausibly be interpreted as referring to anything else: 'We have said . . . that all our experimental conclusions proceed upon the supposition, that the future will be conformable to the past' (*E* 35). So Hume clearly takes himself to have stated that (7) all arguments from experience, and hence (8) all factual inferences to the unobserved (since these are all founded on experience), 'proceed upon the supposition' that nature is uniform: that similar causes will, in the future, have similar effects to those that they have had in the past. For convenient reference I am calling this supposition the Uniformity Principle.

We have here reached the pivot of Hume's argument. For most of what he has said so far has been devoted to establishing proposition (8)—that all factual inferences to the unobserved are founded on, or 'proceed upon the supposition' of, the Uniformity Principle—while most of what follows will be devoted to showing that the Uniformity Principle has no possible foundation in Reason ('the understanding'). And it is from these two results that Hume draws his famous conclusion that our beliefs in [absent] matter of fact and real existence are '*not* founded on reasoning, or any process of the understanding' (*E* 32).

6. *THE UNIFORMITY PRINCIPLE IS NOT FOUNDED ON EITHER SENSORY OR INTUITIVE EVIDENCE*

The previous section examined the first distinguishable line of thought in the long third paragraph of Section IV Part ii. It is now time to move on to the second line of thought, which can be represented as follows:

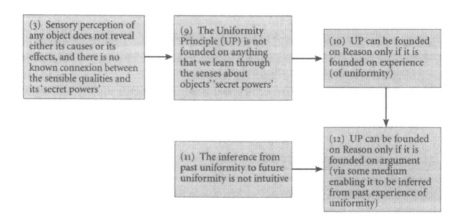

As in Part i Hume emphasizes our inability to discern an object's causes or effects by mere observation of its 'sensible qualities', but here the point of doing so is made clear only after he has sketched his positive account of experiential reasoning based on the Uniformity Principle: 'there is no known connexion between the sensible qualities and the secret powers; and consequently . . . the mind is not led to form such a conclusion concerning their constant and regular conjunction, by any thing which it knows of their nature' (E 33). This passage straightforwardly expresses the implication from (3) to (9) as represented in the structure diagram above (though (9) as stated in the diagram makes explicit the contrast which Hume apparently intends, between direct *perceptual* knowledge of object's secret powers, which he here denies, and indirect *inferential* knowledge based on past experience, which he has not yet ruled out).

Having rejected the possibility of establishing the Uniformity Principle on the basis of direct perception (i.e. grounds that are 'a priori' in the sense that was explained earlier), Hume goes on to examine whether past experience can provide any foundation for the principle. He is willing to allow that '*Experience* . . . can . . . give *direct* and *certain* information of those precise objects . . . and that precise period of time, which fell under its cognizance'. But his question is whether this gives any basis for extrapolating that experience 'to future times, and to other objects, which, for aught we know, may be only in appearance similar' (E 33–4). He spells out this logical issue very explicitly (in a passage which is here asterisked for future reference):

> (*) These two propositions are far from being the same, *I have found that such an object has always been attended with such an effect*, and *I foresee, that other objects, which are, in appearance, similar, will be attended with similar effects*. I shall allow, if you please, that the one proposition may justly be inferred from the other . . . But if you insist, that the inference is made by a chain of reasoning, I desire you to produce that reasoning. The connexion between these propositions is not intuitive. There is required a medium, which may enable the mind to draw such an inference, if indeed it be drawn by reasoning and argument. (E 34)

Past experience of uniformity might perhaps provide grounds for the Uniformity Principle, but if so, since these grounds are not intuitive, they would have to be mediated by 'reasoning and argument'. Here we seem to have a fairly clear statement of the inference from (11) to (12) in the structure diagram above.

As I have interpreted him here, Hume quickly dismisses any a priori foundation for the Uniformity Principle, and does so on the basis of propositions (3) and (9) alone. Hence after this he does not further consider the possibility of there being some a priori argument that would provide a link between observed and unobserved (i.e. an argument concluding that *whatever* has happened in the past, however irregular and chaotic that might have been, can be expected to continue into the future). Instead, he turns his attention (as proposition (10) indicates) to the possibility of an a posteriori argument for the Uniformity Principle, one based on the *actual* evidence of experience, which would appeal to the *character* of what has happened in the past (presumably its uniformity) in attempting to show that the past remains a reliable guide to the future. On this interpretation, therefore, the passage (*) quoted above makes perfect sense: Hume is challenging the reader to provide an inferential link from experienced uniformity to a prediction-warranting Uniformity Principle, and is pointing out that since this inference is not sanctioned by direct intuition, it must be mediated by reasoning involving intermediate steps if it is to provide an adequate foundation for that principle.

There is, however, a subtly different way of viewing Hume's argument which can also claim some support from the text, though it treats it less as a continuous train of thought. On this alternative view, Hume's explicit questioning of whether experience can provide a foundation for the Uniformity Principle does not signal a complete shift of interest from a priori to a posteriori reasoning; rather, he is simply raising a number of sceptical queries in no particular order, in turn highlighting difficulties in the attempt to found the principle on sensation, on experience, on intuition, and finally, on argument *of any kind*. This interpretation might seem to be favoured by one particular sentence in the text: 'The bread, which I formerly eat ['ate'], nourished me; that is, a body of such sensible qualities, was, at that time, endued with such secret powers: But does it follow, that other bread must also nourish me at another time, and that like sensible qualities must always be attended with like secret powers?' (*E* 34). On my preferred interpretation, Hume is focusing at this point on attempts to infer the Uniformity Principle from *the past experience of uniformity*, whereas at first sight this sentence gives the impression of appealing to *one particular past experience* rather than to a pattern of uniform experiences. However this impression is not decisive ('that time' can perfectly well refer to a period rather than to one occasion, as indeed would be suggested by the immediately preceding sentences) and it is strongly counterbalanced by the otherwise smooth flow of Hume's logic, and the structural similarities with his reasoning in Part i (where the discounting of sensation as an a priori source of causal knowledge signals a complete shift of attention towards reasoning from experience). Moreover the alternative interpretation requires a somewhat artificial construal of the long passage (*) quoted earlier,[32] and fails to account for the strong emphasis on past uniformity which dominates most of the remainder of the section (*E* 36–8).

---

[32] See P. J. R. Millican, 'Hume's Argument concerning Induction: Structure and Interpretation', in S. Tweyman (ed.), *David Hume: Critical Assessments*, 6 vols. (London: Routledge, 1995), ii. 91–144 (repr. in D. W. D. Owen (ed.), *Hume: General Philosophy* (Aldershot: Ashgate, 2000), 165–218), especially 109–10, which presents this alternative view, and which interprets the passage in question as treating the

7. *THE UNIFORMITY PRINCIPLE IS NOT FOUNDED ON ARGUMENT*

The stage is now set for the climax of Hume's argument concerning induction, in which he denies the possibility of any good reasoning at all that could provide a foundation in Reason for the Uniformity Principle and thus for factual inference. Many commentators have treated this part as though it were virtually the whole of Hume's argument (Fogelin,[33] for example, calls the entire argument concerning induction Hume's 'no-argument argument') so it is worth recalling that in the *Enquiry* it is not only preceded by Part i, but is also introduced by the line of thought outlined in §6 above, in which Hume takes the trouble to argue that some reasoning is necessary if the Uniformity Principle is to be founded on Reason, a point which he apparently takes more or less for granted in the *Treatise* and *Abstract*.

The structure of this most famous part of Hume's argument is admirably clear:

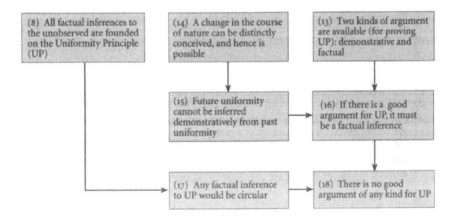

It starts with the general claim (13) that 'All reasonings may be divided into two kinds, namely, demonstrative reasoning . . . and moral reasoning, or that concerning matter of fact and existence [i.e. factual reasoning].' (*E* 35). The

Uniformity Principle as a rule of inference rather than as a proposition. When writing that earlier paper, I had not fully appreciated the relevance here of Hume's notion of apriority, and hence overlooked the structural parallel with his reasoning in Part i. Further evidence for my new interpretation comes from the *Treatise*, which explicitly focuses on arguments 'founded on past *experience*, and on our remembrance of . . . *constant conjunction*' (*T* 88; cf. *T* 87, 163 n.).

[33] R. Fogelin, *Hume's Skepticism in the Treatise of Human Nature* (London: Routledge & Kegan Paul, 1985), 46.

inference from (14) to (15) is then quickly drawn: 'That there are no demonstrative arguments in the case, seems evident; since it implies no contradiction, that the course of nature may change . . . Now whatever is intelligible, and can be distinctly conceived, implies no contradiction, and can never be proved false by any demonstrative argument or abstract reasoning *a priori*.' Propositions (13) and (15) together imply (16): 'If we be, therefore, engaged by arguments to put trust in past experience, and make it the standard of our future judgment, these arguments must be probable [i.e. factual] only'. But now the previous conclusion (8) can be appealed to in order to show (17) 'that there is no argument of this kind' (*E* 35). For (8) states that all factual inferences to the unobserved are founded on the Uniformity Principle. 'To endeavour, therefore, the proof of [the Uniformity Principle] by probable [i.e. factual] arguments . . . must be evidently going in a circle, and taking that for granted, which is the very point in question.' (*E* 35–6).

Though superficially very straightforward, there is a lot going on here beneath the surface. For example, Hume is certainly not being entirely explicit when he states that 'all reasonings' are either demonstrative or factual and goes on to rule out the possibility of either type of argument for the Uniformity Principle. For he was surely well aware that philosophers could, and would, concoct various *defective* arguments to support this principle—indeed he considers such an argument himself, at *E* 36–8. What he is denying, therefore, is that any *good* argument is available for the purpose, on the grounds: first, that all *good* arguments are either demonstrative or factual; secondly, that there cannot be a *good* demonstrative proof of the falsity of what is distinctly conceivable; and thirdly, that a *good* factual argument cannot be circular.[34] This passage is, in fact, an illustration of a general rule of Hume interpretation, that when he speaks of 'all [or no] arguments [reasonings, inferences]', the qualification 'good' is usually implied.[35]

7.1 What does Hume Mean by 'Demonstrative'?

Hume's grounds for ruling out the possibility of a good argument for the Uniformity Principle also merit some discussion, not least because they have

[34] The first of these three points will suffice if the terms 'demonstrative' and 'probable' are themselves interpreted normatively, so that an argument only *counts as* being of the appropriate type if it is a *good* instance. But Hume himself does not consistently interpret them in this way, and in the *Treatise* especially seems perfectly content to talk of 'fallacious' demonstrations (e.g. *T* 53, 80) or 'unphilosophical' probable reasonings (I. iii. 13).

[35] A related instance is at *E* 88: 'it is from past experience, that we draw all inferences concerning the future, and . . . conclude, that objects will always be conjoined together, which we find to have always been conjoined'. Hume would surely not consider this statement refuted by the irrational inferential practices of soothsayers (which may bear no relation to past experience) or by the popular 'gambler's fallacy' (which may bear a contrary relation—'I've lost every game so far, so I'm bound to win the next!'); cf. also the comment on 'education' in note 24 above. Some other examples of Hume's presupposing a restriction to *good* inferences are at *T* 81, 163, *E* 78 n., 150, 159, *D* 205, 227.

been thought by previous commentators to have significant interpretative implications. First, let us consider Hume's argument from distinct conceivability, which he uses to prove that matters of fact in general, and the Uniformity Principle in particular, cannot be established by any demonstrative reasoning:

The contrary of every matter of fact is still possible; because it can never imply a contradiction, and is [distinctly] conceived by the mind . . . We should in vain, therefore, attempt to demonstrate its falsehood. Were it demonstratively false, it would imply a contradiction, and could never be distinctly conceived by the mind. (E 25–6)

it implies no contradiction, that the course of nature may change . . . Now whatever is intelligible, and can be distinctly conceived, implies no contradiction, and can never be proved false by any demonstrative argument or abstract reasoning *a priori*. (E 35)

These passages (and others like them such as T 89, 95, A 650, 651, E 163–4) have been taken by many as decisive evidence that Hume holds the view (in Stove's words) 'that there can be no demonstrative arguments for any conclusion concerning matter of fact'. This being so, it seems to follow that Hume must mean by a 'demonstrative argument' a '(valid) argument *from necessarily true premisses*', since obviously a valid argument from mere matter-of-fact premisses might well have a matter-of-fact conclusion (whose falsehood would imply no contradiction and would be distinctly conceivable).[36] Against this popular interpretation, however, I shall now claim that Hume means by 'demonstrative' much the same as we today mean by 'deductive', in the informal sense according to which an argument is deductive (or 'deductively valid') if and only if the truth of its premisses guarantees the truth of its conclusion.[37]

The argument sketched below is deductively valid in the modern informal sense, and would I believe undoubtedly be classed by Hume as 'demonstrative':

1. The momentum of a body is equal to its mass multiplied by its velocity.
2. In any collision the total momentum of the colliding bodies (in any given direction) is conserved.
∴ If a spherical rigid body of mass 2 kg moving directly eastward at 25,000 m/s collides head-on and instantly sticks fast to a second spherical rigid body of mass 10,000 kg which is moving directly westward at 4 m/s (without any breakage, any simultaneous interaction with other

---

[36] The quotations from Stove are from *Probability and Hume's Inductive Scepticism*, 35. Similar views have been expressed by a wide range of highly respected authors, including Beauchamp and Rosenberg, *Hume and the Problem of Causation*, 43; Garrett, *Cognition and Commitment in Hume's Philosophy*, 87; J. C. A. Gaskin, *Hume's Philosophy of Religion*, 2nd edn. (Basingstoke: Macmillan, 1988), 77; and J. A. Passmore, *Hume's Intentions*, 3rd edn. (London: Duckworth, 1980), 20.

[37] I say 'much the same' to avoid commitment on fine details, for example whether an argument whose premisses are inconsistent, or irrelevant to a necessarily true conclusion, could nevertheless count as 'demonstrative'.

bodies, any change of mass, etc.), then the second body will no longer be moving westward immediately after the collision.

This is precisely the kind of applied mathematics which Hume discusses at E 31 (in a paragraph which was mentioned in §4.2 above), and it is in fact a version of his own, rather imprecisely expressed, example:[38]

it is a law of motion, discovered by experience, that the moment or force of any body in motion is in the compound ratio or proportion of its solid contents and its velocity; and consequently, that a small force may remove the greatest obstacle . . . if, by any contrivance . . . we can encrease the velocity of that force, so as to make it an overmatch for its antagonist.

Within this paragraph Hume calls such reasonings 'abstract' rather than 'demonstrative', but the ancestor of this passage in the *Treatise* makes the equation between the two explicit:

Mathematics, indeed, are useful in all mechanical operations . . . But 'tis not of themselves they have any influence. . . . Abstract or demonstrative reasoning . . . never influences any of our actions, but only as it directs our judgment concerning causes and effects . . . (*T* 413–14)

Hume is totally clear that the premisses of the argument above are contingent and known only a posteriori:[39]

Geometry assists us in the application of this law . . . but still the discovery of the law itself is owing merely to experience, and all the abstract reasonings in the world could never lead us one step towards the knowledge of it. (*E* 31)

So unless Hume is seriously inconsistent, it cannot be a defining condition of what he calls 'abstract' or 'demonstrative' reasoning that it must have necessarily true or a priori premisses.

Quite apart from his discussion of applied mathematics, there is in *Enquiry* IV another place where Hume makes clear that he is prepared to countenance the possibility of a 'demonstrative' inference from a contingent premiss (ironically, immediately before the very application of the argument from distinct conceivability which is supposed by Stove and others to require a contrary interpretation). For when at E 35 Hume canvasses the possibility of a demonstrative inference to the Uniformity Principle, he certainly appears to have in mind an argument premised on contingent past uniformity, as expressed in the

---

[38] Here the 10,000 kg body exemplifies a 'great obstacle', the 2 kg body a 'small force', and change of direction counts as 'removal'.

[39] I here gloss over the fact that one of the premisses can plausibly be seen as a *definition* of 'momentum', a subtlety that Hume does not address. The important point for present purposes is simply that the argument indeed has at least one contingent premiss.

passage (*) quoted earlier. Indeed if my interpretation in §6 above is correct, then the whole point of Hume's 'no-argument argument' is precisely to consider such *experiential* arguments for the Uniformity Principle.

If Hume is prepared to accept that a demonstrative inference can have premisses that are not necessary truths,[40] then what are we to make of his argument from distinct conceivability which is so often adduced for the opposite conclusion? I suggest that we simply need to distinguish between the plausible claim

> *that no contingent proposition can be proved demonstratively, or is demonstrable, or can be demonstrated*

and the much stronger, but highly dubious claim

> *that no contingent proposition can be the conclusion of any demonstrative inference.*

The former is both genuinely Humean and arguably true;[41] the latter is neither, and Hume nowhere asserts it, despite the frequency with which Stove and others attribute it to him. There is absolutely no difficulty, in Hume's system, with a demonstration that one matter of fact (e.g. 'Mars is red and round') implies another (e.g. 'Some round thing is coloured'), nor—which is inferentially equivalent—with an argument that starts from the one matter of fact as a known or believed premiss, and concludes demonstratively that the other is therefore also true. All such arguments may be called 'demonstrations' and described as 'demonstrative', but they are not 'demonstrations of' or 'demonstrative proofs of' any matter of fact; all they can be said to *demonstrate* is the deductive *implication* between the matters of fact concerned.[42] Hume's argument from distinct conceivability can accordingly be invoked whenever he wishes to deny such a deductive relationship, as for example when he remembers 'that such an object has always been attended with such an effect', but is denying the deducibility from it of the conclusion 'that other objects, which are, in appearance, similar, will be attended with similar effects' (*E* 34). Here the co-conceivability of the premiss and the negation of the conclusion is, as

---

[40] He is presumably even prepared to accept that a demonstration can be premised on a necessary falsehood, since he often argues by *reductio ad absurdum* (e.g. *T* 43: 'we may produce demonstrations from these very ideas to prove, that they are impossible').

[41] 'Arguably', because the details will depend on whether a 'demonstrative proof' is understood to exclude a posteriori premises, and on the interpretation of 'contingent' in the light of issues in the theory of reference associated with the work of Saul Kripke (issues very distant from any of Hume's concerns). Clearly the point will be incontrovertible if 'contingent' is equated with a posteriori, and 'prove demonstratively' (etc.) is interpreted as meaning deductive proof from a priori principles.

[42] Though it is logically rather imprecise to describe a demonstrative argument from *P* to *Q* as being a demonstration that *P* implies *Q*, the inferential equivalence between the two makes it unsurprising if Hume sometimes conflates them.

Hume points out, quite enough to wreck any such supposed deductive implication, and this fully accounts for the use of his argument from distinct conceivability.

The argument from distinct conceivability aside, I believe the only other texts that in any way support the common misinterpretation I have been criticizing are Hume's comments about the limited province of demonstration, most explicitly: 'It seems to me, that the only objects of the abstract sciences or of demonstration are quantity and number, and that all attempts to extend this more perfect species of knowledge beyond these bounds are mere sophistry and illusion.' (E 163). But as he goes on to explain immediately following this sentence, Hume is pessimistic about the extent to which demonstration can be of significant use in the 'moral sciences' not because demonstrative inferences from contingent premises are by definition impossible, but rather because most of our ideas in 'moral subjects' lack the precise and intricate relationships which enable lengthy demonstrations to be both reliable and fruitful in more quantitative disciplines (E 163; cf. E 60–1, T 71).[43] This explanation implies that the best potential source of useful demonstrative reasonings from contingent premises will be in applied mathematics, nicely corroborating our earlier example involving the conservation of momentum. It is evidently no coincidence that Hume's discussion of 'mixed mathematics' provides the crucial test case by which this interpretative dispute can be decisively settled.

7.2 The Gap in Hume's Argument

It is just as well for the cogency of Hume's argument that his category of 'demonstrative' reasonings is not confined to those that are a priori, for if it were so confined, then his insistence that the only available kinds of inference are 'demonstrative' and factual–inductive would be *manifestly* incorrect: he would quite gratuitously have left out of account any arguments that start from a posteriori premises but then proceed deductively rather than by appeal to causation and uniformity ('Mars is red and round, therefore some round thing is coloured' being a simple example). Given Hume's generally good logical instincts and philosophical competence, this provides additional corroboration of the interpretation of 'demonstrative' advanced above. Nevertheless, I believe that there is a different and genuine gap in Hume's argument at this point, not because he overlooks the possibility of a posteriori deductive inferences, but on the contrary because he overlooks the possibility of a priori non-deductive inferences—that is, inferences which are less than deductively certain, but

---

[43] This does not imply that demonstrative arguments are excluded from non-quantitative disciplines, just that these 'pretended syllogistical reasonings' are likely to be rather trivial, in some cases reducing to a mere 'imperfect definition' (E 163). But even such trivial arguments can sometimes play a useful role, as in the 'syllogism' which Philo advances in the *Dialogues* at D 142–3.

which are 'founded on' considerations of a priori probability rather than on experience.

To see how this gap emerges, consider again Hume's grounds for ruling out the possibility of either a demonstrative or a 'probable' foundation for the Uniformity Principle. The reason he is confident that no demonstrative argument can do the job is that such an argument always yields absolute certainty relative to its premises, so that the mere distinct conceivability of a change in the course of nature (14) is sufficient to show that the Uniformity Principle cannot be established by demonstration (15) no matter what our premises about the past might be. By contrast, Hume's reason for ruling out the possibility of a 'probable' foundation for the Uniformity Principle is his claim that the only good form of such reasoning potentially available for this purpose is inductive inference, which is itself founded on experience (7) and hence on the Uniformity Principle (8). Thus any inductive argument which purports to provide a foundation for the Uniformity Principle will be viciously circular, since it must be founded on the very principle for which it is attempting to provide a foundation.[44] Putting all this together, it follows that if there were a third form of reasoning that yielded merely probable inferences (rather than certainties), but did so on a priori grounds (rather than by extrapolation from past experience), then this form of reasoning would be completely immune to Hume's objections: he could not rule out the possibility of such reasoning's providing a foundation for the Uniformity Principle either on the basis of his argument from distinct conceivability or on the ground of circularity.

It is highly debatable whether a priori probabilistic reasoning (based, for example, on the Principle of Indifference, 'logical probability' measures, considerations of invariance, or other supposedly non-empirical principles) is a genuine possibility or, if it is, whether such reasoning could conceivably provide a foundation for the Uniformity Principle. But those (such as Popper) who claim that Hume himself showed this particular route to be a dead end are certainly mistaken,[45] for as we have seen, when he denies that 'probable' reasoning could perform such a role, Hume has in mind only inductive reasoning from experience, not mathematical probabilistic reasoning that is a priori.[46] There is,

---

[44] Note that this 'foundational circularity' differs from the more familiar 'deductive circularity' of an argument whose conclusion is also one of its premises. In this sense, contra Stove ('Hume, Probability, and Induction', 205), a circular argument need not be deductively valid.

[45] A point made strongly against Popper and others by Stove, 'Hume, Probability, and Induction', 189–90.

[46] Hume apparently tries to keep an open mind about the existence of other 'species' of reasoning ('I cannot find, I cannot imagine any such reasoning. But I keep my mind still open to instruction'; E 36), and may be aware that this is a weak point in his argument ('there may still remain a suspicion, that the enumeration is not compleat'; E 39). However, he is so far from conceiving of the possibility of a priori probabilistic reasoning that he virtually defines 'demonstrative' reasoning as that whose inferential steps are a priori, in calling it 'reasoning concerning relations of ideas' (E 35; cf. T 124, A 650).

then, a definite gap in Hume's argument. Whether this gap can be exploited by his opponents is an interesting and important question, and one that I have explored at length elsewhere, but there is insufficient space to address it here.[47]

8. HUME'S CONCLUSION: NO FACTUAL INFERENCE TO THE UNOBSERVED IS FOUNDED ON REASON

Having finished his 'no-argument argument', the pieces of Hume's jigsaw are all complete. In typical fashion he leaves it to his reader to slot them into place, but if the account given above is correct, the way in which they are intended to fit together is evident from the structure and flow of his argument:

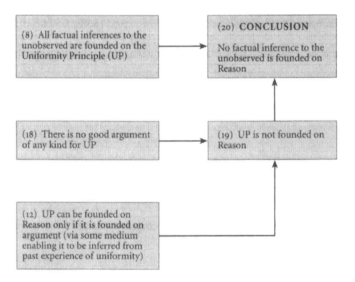

(8) All factual inferences to the unobserved are founded on the Uniformity Principle (UP)

(20) **CONCLUSION**
No factual inference to the unobserved is founded on Reason

(18) There is no good argument of any kind for UP

(19) UP is not founded on Reason

(12) UP can be founded on Reason only if it is founded on argument (via some medium enabling it to be inferred from past experience of uniformity)

The precise nature of Hume's conclusion may seem unclear from his own words. We have already seen that he anticipates it when stating his intentions at E 32: 'I say then, that, even after we have experience of the operations of cause and effect, our conclusions from that experience are *not* founded on reasoning, or any process of the understanding.' But when later summing up the section at E 39, he expresses his conclusion somewhat differently: 'it is not reasoning which engages us to suppose the past resembling the future, and to expect similar effects from causes, which are, to appearance, similar. This is the propo-

---

[47] This question is the principal focus of the second part of my doctoral dissertation ('Hume, Induction, and Probability', University of Leeds Ph.D. thesis, 1996, 101–237), which is in preparation as a book under the same title. Although the idea of a priori probability is often dismissed out of hand, the list of those who have attempted to provide such a foundation for induction is quite substantial, including Laplace, De Finetti, Harrod, D. C. Williams, Stove, Mackie, and Blackburn.

sition which I intended to enforce in the present section.' There is a subtle difference here: at *E* 32 he is saying that *our particular experiential conclusions* are
not 'founded on reasoning, or any process of the understanding', whereas at *E* 39
he seems to be saying that our supposition of *the Uniformity Principle* is not so
founded. If we move forward to the beginning of Section V, however, we can
find at *E* 41 a passage which helps to reconcile these two readings: 'we . . . conclude . . . in the foregoing section, that, in all reasonings from experience, there
is a step taken by the mind, which is not supported by any argument or process
of the understanding'. So all reasonings from experience involve a step, namely
the assumption of uniformity, which is not supported by 'any process of the
understanding'—which, indeed, *cannot* be so supported if Hume's argument is
correct. And Hume goes on in Section V to provide an alternative explanation
of why we make this step: it is entirely non-rational, and is the product not of
Reason but merely of a particular one of our brute 'natural instincts, which no
reasoning or process of the thought and understanding is able, either to produce, or to prevent' (*E* 46–7). This instinct is what 'makes us expect, for the
future, a similar train of events with those which have appeared in the past'
(*E* 44), and Hume accordingly calls it 'custom', or 'habit'. Here, then, is the
answer to his original enquiry at *E* 26 regarding 'the nature of that evidence,
which assures us of any [absent] matter of fact': 'All inferences from experience,
therefore, are effects of custom, not of reasoning. . . . Without the influence of
custom, we should be entirely ignorant of every matter of fact, beyond what is
immediately present to our memory and senses.' (*E* 43–5).

9. CODA: 'SECRET POWERS', CAUSAL REALISM, AND A PARTING SHOT

In both the *Treatise* and the *Enquiry* Hume's main argument finishes with his
circularity charge against any would-be 'probable' justification of the Uniformity Principle. But in both he goes on to refute one natural attempt that might
be made to justify induction by appeal to objects' 'powers'.[48] In the *Treatise* the
way in which Hume introduces this discussion makes very clear its status as a
rounding-off illustration of the impact of his argument, rather than as an essential component (and accordingly I call it the argument's 'coda'):

---

[48] In the *Enquiry* Hume first presents an additional new argument (but one reminiscent of *T* 88 and
163–5) designed to strengthen his claim that the continuing uniformity of causal relations cannot be
established a posteriori by Reason, on the ground that if it could be so established it would be knowable
'upon one instance' and not (as we find) only 'after a long course of uniform experiments' (*E* 36; cf. *E* 43).
This argument may indeed be quite effective against the perceptual view of Reason (since *perceived*
connexions can reasonably be expected to be unaffected by mere repetition), but Hume's inability to
imagine any kind of reasoning to which numbers of instances would be relevant suggests a (historically
unsurprising) poor grasp of statistical inference.

Shou'd any one think to elude this argument; and without determining whether our rea-soning on this subject be deriv'd from demonstration or probability, pretend that all conclusions from causes and effects are built on solid reasoning: I can only desire, that this reasoning may be produc'd, in order to be expos'd to our examination. It may, per-haps, be said, that after experience of the constant conjunction of certain objects, we rea-son in the following manner. Such an object is always found to produce another. 'Tis impossible it cou'd have this effect, if it was not endow'd with a power of production. The power necessarily implies the effect; and therefore there is a just foundation for drawing a conclusion from the existence of one object to that of its usual attendant. The past production implies a power: The power implies a new production: And the new production is what we infer from the power and the past production. (*T* 90)

The *Enquiry* version of this attempt to provide a foundation for induction is subtly different, in that instead of apparently using the existence of a cause and effect relationship to infer the existence of a power, it takes for granted from the start that objects have powers and appeals to the *constancy* of causal relations to infer a continuing 'connexion between the sensible qualities and the secret powers' (*E* 36).[49] But the forceful refutation that follows is equally decisive against either version:

When a man says, *I have found, in all past instances, such sensible qualities conjoined with such secret powers*: And when he says, *similar sensible qualities will always be conjoined with similar secret powers*; he is not guilty of a tautology. . . . You say that the one propo-sition is an inference from the other. But you must confess, that the inference is not intui-tive; neither is it demonstrative: Of what nature is it then? To say it is experimental, is begging the question. For all inferences from experience suppose, as their foundation, that the future will resemble the past, and that similar powers will be conjoined with similar sensible qualities. . . . It is impossible, therefore, that any arguments from expe-rience can prove this resemblance of the past to the future; since all these arguments are founded on the supposition of that resemblance. (*E* 37–8; cf. *T* 91)

Here we clearly have a straightforward application of Hume's central argument, rather than a significant independent addition to it. This elegant refutation does, however, help to settle an important issue concerning the relationship between Hume's reasoning about induction and his theory of causation.

9.1 The Place of Causation in Hume's Argument

In the *Treatise* Hume's argument concerning induction is presented in the con-text of his analysis of causation. This can give the impression that the one relies

---

[49] This is only to be expected, given the discussion in §6 above. Hume also considers a similar move later in the *Treatise* version at *T* 91 ('Shou'd it be said, that we have experience, that the same power con-tinues united with the same object . . .'). Hume's emphasis on 'powers' in the *Enquiry* seems to reflect an increased appreciation of their role in Newtonian science (cf. pp. 144–5 below).

heavily on the other, and many books on Hume have tended to confirm this impression by treating the two together, often within the confines of a single chapter. But the quotation above from *E* 37–8 shows clearly that Hume's case against the rational foundation of induction is quite independent of his 'regularity' analysis of causation, for even if causation is instead a matter of 'secret powers', and even if all observed *A*s have in fact been endowed with the secret power to produce *B*, this in itself can give us no reason for supposing that some hitherto *unobserved A* has been or will be similarly endowed. The point is that because the connexion between *A* and that power is not a priori, we can only justifiably infer a continued conjunction between them if we already have some justification for extrapolating from observed to unobserved. So an analysis of causation in terms of 'secret powers' (or 'natural necessities', as they might now be called) provides no answer whatever to the inductive sceptic.

Since Hume's views about induction do not depend on his own analysis of the notion of causation, this naturally raises the question of why that notion should nevertheless feature so prominently in his famous argument, and whether it plays any essential role there. Appealing to the structural analysis developed above, we can see that causation features importantly in Hume's argument at only two points: first, in Part i, where he uses it as a 'middle term' for deducing that all factual reasoning to the unobserved is based on experience (propositions (1) to (6)); and secondly, at the beginning of Part ii (*E* 33), where he appeals again to his earlier claim about our inability to perceive any connexion between objects' powers and their sensible qualities (proposition (3)), and goes on to draw the corollary that the Uniformity Principle cannot be established on the basis of such perception (proposition (9)). Taking these two together, it seems that causation plays a role in Hume's argument only to the extent of enabling him to conclude *that inferences beyond the present testimony of our memory and senses (including inferences about the Uniformity Principle) cannot be drawn a priori from our immediate perceptions and hence must be founded on past experience.* However this proposition seems just as plausible in its own right without any mention of causation, and it can moreover be supported directly by most of the examples, and much of the argumentation, that he provides in Part i.

Hume's argument, therefore, can apparently be reconstructed without any essential mention of causation (a point of which I shall take advantage in §10 below, when presenting a simplified version). And Hume himself might have welcomed such a reconstruction, for it would rid him of any dependence on his initial premiss (1), about which he seems to have some doubts later in the *Enquiry* when in Section X he turns his attention to inferences based on human testimony. When these doubts arise, it is interesting and perhaps significant that he deals with them in exactly the way that would be required to permit such a reconstruction of his Section IV argument, for he makes no attempt to defend this premiss, but instead simply remarks that it can be bypassed for his current purposes, on the ground that any testimonial inference to the unobserved, even if it is admitted to be non-causal, must nevertheless be based on experience:

> This species of reasoning, perhaps, one may deny to be founded on the relation of cause and effect. I shall not dispute about a word. It will be sufficient to observe, that our assurance in any argument of this kind is derived from no other principle than our observation of the veracity of human testimony, and of the usual conformity of facts to the reports of witnesses. (*E* 111)

This remark is tantalizing, but unfortunately we shall probably never know whether Hume ever noticed its relevance to his argument concerning induction.

9.2 Induction and Hume's Alleged Causal Realism

Hume's 'coda' can also shed light on an issue of considerable recent scholarly debate—namely, whether he was a believer in genuinely mind-independent necessities underlying the observed regularities that lead us to interpret our experience causally and to draw inductive inferences accordingly. The issue is too complex to explore in any detail here, so I shall confine myself to three points regarding the relevance of *Enquiry* IV to this debate. The first concerns the language of 'secret powers' which Hume uses throughout Part ii (especially in the coda), and which has been thought by some to show that he firmly accepts a notion of mind-independent powers in objects, quite different from any 'idea' that would be sanctioned by his empiricist 'regularity' analysis in *Enquiry* VII (*E* 62–3, 75–7).[50] For example:

> no philosopher, who is rational and modest, has ever pretended to . . . show distinctly the action of that power, which produces any single effect . . . (*E* 30)

> nature . . . conceals from us those powers and principles, on which the influence of . . . objects entirely depends. . . . but as to that wonderful force or power . . . of this we cannot form the most distant conception. But notwithstanding this ignorance of natural powers and principles, we always presume, when we see like sensible qualities, that they have like secret powers . . . (*E* 32–3)

> experience . . . teaches us, that those . . . objects . . . were endowed with such powers and forces. (*E* 37)

---

[50] See D. W. Livingston, *Hume's Philosophy of Common Life* (Chicago: University of Chicago Press, 1984), 154–6, and G. Strawson, *The Secret Connexion* (Oxford: Clarendon Press, 1989), ch. 16. Both Livingston and Strawson acknowledge the *E* 33 footnote quoted below, but seem unaware of its possible context in the debate between Hume and Kames, which I believe greatly clarifies its significance.

But these quotations show nothing of the kind, as is made clear by a footnote which Hume inserted into the 1750 edition, directly after the words 'natural powers' in the second quotation above:

The word, *power*, is here used in a loose and popular sense. The more accurate explication of it would give additional evidence to this argument. See Section 7. (*E* 33 n.)

I believe Hume added this footnote in direct response to criticisms from his long-time friend Henry Home, later Lord Kames, who in 1751 brought to publication his *Essays on the Principles of Morality and Natural Religion*,[51] including an essay 'Of our Idea of Power' which attacks what he takes to be Hume's official view, that we have no idea of causation in objects beyond mere regularity. Kames presents the 'secret power' language of Section IV as evidence that Hume himself cannot consistently accept this 'violent paradox',[52] so Hume's insertion of this footnote—apparently *expressly* to make clear that such language is to be interpreted in the light of his Section VII analysis and hence cannot conflict with it—seems strongly to suggest that Kames's interpretation of Hume's position was correct (as indeed might be expected given their intimacy and mutual philosophical interests).[53] Thus Hume's use of the language of 'powers' in Sections IV and V cannot now be brought as evidence for any departure from his Section VII view. If anything quite the reverse, because the footnote seems to confirm that he sees Section VII as revealing the 'precise meaning' (*E* 62; cf. *E* 67 n., 82) behind our causal notions even when those are used in a 'loose and popular' manner.

My second point arises from the result of Hume's coda (summarized in §9 and briefly discussed in §9.1). There he argues that the notion of an objective causal power, even if it is supposed to be coherent, can provide no escape from his sceptical conclusions, because extrapolation into the future of a past constant conjunction between (for example) *A* and *the secret power to produce B* has no more basis in Reason than extrapolation of the constant conjunction between *A* and *B* which it is invoked to explain. Hence *in so far as the supposition of secret powers is intended to provide an explanation of the consistency of objects' behaviour over time*—to remove what can otherwise seem the outrageous coincidence that the world should continue to operate according to the same laws,

---

[51] Henry Home, *Essays on the Principles of Morality and Natural Religion* (Edinburgh, 1751), published anonymously.

[52] See pp. 290–2 for the allegation of inconsistency, and p. 283 for the description of Hume's position as a 'violent paradox' (an allusion to *T* 166).

[53] See Mossner, *The Life of David Hume*, 119, for Kames's description (to Boswell) of how he had invited Hume to 'try to beat your Book [i.e. the *Treatise*] into my head'. Evidently he made considerable efforts to understand Hume, exchanged manuscripts with him prior to publication (notably that of the *Enquiry* or *Philosophical Essays*, see *HL* i. 106, 111), and particularly discussed causation with him over many years. For background on Hume's relationship with Kames, see also Mossner, pp. 58–62, 410–12.

microsecond after microsecond, for billions of years—*that supposition is entirely useless*. If Hume is right, there is no way that the uniformity of the laws of nature over time can be accounted for, whether in terms of underlying metaphysical 'necessities' or anything else, and if this implies that we have no option but to accept an outrageous coincidence as fact, then so be it. At any rate, Hume's forceful reasoning clearly indicates that he himself would be quite unmoved by any argument for the existence of objective powers based on the avoidance of inductive coincidence.[54]

My final point contrasts somewhat with the first two, and suggests a possible middle ground in the causal realist debate by identifying a sense in which Hume is indeed committed to accepting the ascription of powers to objects, while neither denying the subjective origin of our corresponding idea, nor appealing to any underlying metaphysical necessity of the type that we have just seen rejected. Consider three passages, the first of which is from his important paragraph on 'mixed mathematics' discussed above in §7.1:

it is a law of motion, discovered by experience, that the moment or force of any body in motion is in the compound ratio or proportion of its solid contents and its velocity . . . (*E* 31)

We find by experience, that a body at rest or in motion continues for ever in its present state, till put from it by some new cause; and that a body impelled takes as much motion from the impelling body as it acquires itself. These are facts. When we call this a *vis iner-tiae*, we only mark these facts, without pretending to have any idea of the inert power; in the same manner as, when we talk of gravity, we mean certain effects, without comprehending that active power. It was never the meaning of Sir ISAAC NEWTON to rob second causes of all force or energy . . . (*E* 73 n.)

the idea of *power* is relative as much as that of *cause*; and both have a reference to an effect, or some other event constantly conjoined with the former. When we consider the *unknown* circumstance of an object, by which the degree or quantity of its effect is fixed and determined, we call that its power: And accordingly, it is allowed by all philosophers, that the effect is the measure of the power. But if they had any idea of power, as it is in itself, why could not they measure it in itself? The dispute whether the force of a body in motion be as its velocity, or the square of its velocity . . . needed not be decided by comparing its effects in equal or unequal times; but by a direct mensuration and comparison. (*E* 77 n.)

Expressed using a variety of notions—*moment, force, power, energy*—which Hume sees as being 'all nearly synonimous' with *necessity* (*T* 157),[55] these

---

[54] Such an argument seems to be the main theme of Strawson, *The Secret Connexion*, ch. 5, though Strawson here does not entirely distinguish between invoking causal powers to explain uniformity *over time* (which I am here denying that Hume would accept) and invoking causal powers to explain regular patterns of behaviour *at a time* (which, in the sense discussed below, Hume might accept).

[55] Cf. *A* 656 and *E* 62, 77 n. The virtual synonymy of 'power' and 'necessary connexion' is made particularly explicit in the original title of *Enquiry* VII: 'Of the Idea of Power, or Necessary Connexion'.

passages strongly suggest that he recognizes the *legitimacy* of such notions if properly understood. The only content that we can give to any notion of force, power, or necessity (i.e. our only *idea* of it) is in terms of the observable regular behaviour of objects and our tendency to draw inferences accordingly, but nevertheless once we have such an idea it can quite *properly* be ascribed to objects themselves, since only thus can it feature in quantitative scientific explanations. Such explanations form the heart of Newtonian science, serving 'to reduce the principles, productive of natural phaenomena, to a greater simplicity, and to resolve the many particular effects into a few general causes' (*E* 30). So the ascription of powers to objects has considerable instrumental value, even if it sits rather uneasily with Hume's insistence that the corresponding idea has a subjective source. Indeed his own ultimate position remains philosophically rather elusive, appearing to be more than mere instrumentalism (else why insist on finding an impression to clarify the idea?) but at the same time seeming to deny the literal meaningfulness of ascribing that clarified idea to objects (e.g. *T* 164–8, 266–7, *E* 77, 93). Whether there is a coherent position here is certainly debatable, for literal ascription to objects appears to be required in order to reap the scientific rewards (a disanalogy with the easier cases of secondary and moral qualities, where objective ascription plays no such instrumental role). All this perhaps explains why the exegetical debate has proved so intractable: Hume's position combines elements that seem to imply literal ascription of powers to objects with other elements that seem to contradict it.

9.3 The Reasoning of Peasants, Infants, and Brute Beasts

Having completed his abstract philosophical arguments for the thesis that factual inferences are not founded on Reason, Hume ends Section IV with a relatively down-to-earth parting shot:

> It is certain, that the most ignorant and stupid peasants, nay infants, nay even brute beasts, improve by experience, and learn the qualities of natural objects, by observing the effects, which result from them. . . . If you assert, therefore, that the understanding of [a] child is led [to draw inferences about the future] by any process of argument or ratiocination, I may justly require you to produce that argument . . . You cannot say, that the argument is abstruse, and may possibly escape your enquiry; since you confess, that it is obvious to the capacity of a mere infant. If you hesitate, therefore . . . or . . . produce any intricate or profound argument, you . . . give up the question, and confess, that it is not reasoning which engages us to suppose the past resembling the future, and to expect similar effects from causes, which are, to appearance, similar. This is the proposition which I intended to enforce in the present section. (*E* 39)

This is effective rhetoric, but its philosophical significance is less clear, for of course the inductive rationalist is unlikely to claim that infants base their expectations on Reason. Rather, he will concede that infants are supplied (by God, perhaps) with appropriate instincts which initially govern their thinking, but he will maintain that these instincts are, or can be, supplanted by Reason as that faculty develops. Hume's parting shot, then, has little force unless it is supplemented by other considerations such as the desirability of a simple and uniform theory of all human and animal reasoning. It is therefore worth noting that precisely this point is emphasized by Hume later in the *Enquiry*, in the important but relatively neglected Section IX, 'Of the Reason of Animals' (itself a descendant of the similarly titled section I. iii. 16 of the *Treatise*).

10. *THE LOGIC OF HUME'S ARGUMENT*

We can now at last put together a complete detailed structure diagram of Hume's argument in Section IV of the *Enquiry*, which is shown in the appendix to this paper followed by a table setting out, for each numbered proposition in the structure diagram, those precise passages of the *Enquiry* text that I have interpreted as stating (or in two cases merely implying) that very proposition. The diagram and table together prove clearly, I hope, that the interpretation I am advancing is based squarely on Hume's text.[56]

The purpose of the present section, however, is to analyse the underlying logic of Hume's argument, and for this it will be more fruitful to consider a simplified version of its structure (albeit one that is straightforwardly derived from the detailed diagram), in which all of the principal stages are expressed in terms of Hume's 'founded on' relation. This also facilitates easy reference to these stages through semi-formal abbreviation, using symbols which will I hope be fairly self-explanatory.

This diagram (p. 147) shows how Hume's argument pivots around the Uniformity Principle, and also reveals clearly its fundamental dependence on the logic of the 'founded on' relation, which underlies all of its major stages. This logic is manifested in the following four conditional formulae, which together fully account for the inferential structure represented in the diagram.

(f1) $FO(f,e) \& FO(e,u) \rightarrow FO(f,u)$
(f2) $FO(f,u) \rightarrow \neg FO(u,f)$
(f3) $\neg FO(u,s) \& \neg FO(u,i) \& \neg FO(u,d) \& \neg FO(u,f) \rightarrow \neg FO(u,R)$
(f4) $FO(f,u) \& \neg FO(u,R) \rightarrow \neg FO(f,R)$

The third of these carries obvious implications for Hume's notion of Reason, which will be discussed later (in §10.3). But the other three formulae seem to

---

[56] For a detailed comparison with Stove's well-known (but seriously deficient) structure diagram, see Millican, 'Hume's Argument concerning Induction', 118–24. The same article goes on (pp. 124–6) to discuss and criticize Stove's formal interpretation of Hume's conclusion.

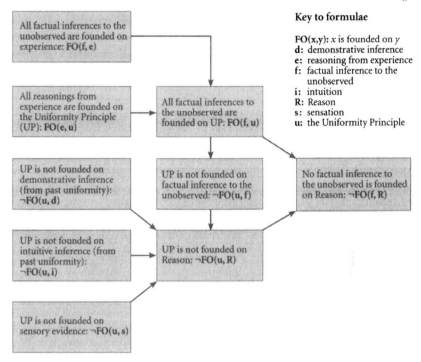

Key to formulae

FO(x,y): *x* is founded on *y*
d: demonstrative inference
e: reasoning from experience
f: factual inference to the
   unobserved
i: intuition
R: Reason
s: sensation
u: the Uniformity Principle

A logical sketch of Hume's argument in *Enquiry* IV

exemplify more general logical properties of the 'founded on' relation, providing important constraints on its interpretation. Let us take these in turn, before going on to discuss what that relation might mean in the light of these constraints.

10.1 The Logic of Hume's 'Founded On' Relation

(f1), the first formula listed above, appears to be a straightforward instance of *transitivity*, indicating that Hume takes 'founded on' to be in general a transitive relation,[57] just as we might expect given the nature of the foundational metaphor. Moreover, this transitivity is clearly the key inferential mechanism in the first half of Hume's argument, which instantiates a typical transitive chain: factual inference is founded on causal reasoning, which is founded on reasoning from experience, which is founded on the Uniformity Principle, and from

---

[57] A relation is *transitive* if whenever *x* bears the relation to *y*, and *y* to *z*, it follows that *x* bears the relation to *z*. Examples of transitive relations include equivalence relations (e.g. 'equal in height to'), weak ordering relations (e.g. 'no greater than', 'at least as tall as'), and strict ordering relations (e.g. 'less than', 'heavier than', 'descended from').

this Hume takes it to follow that factual inference is founded on the Uniformity Principle.

(f2) is equally straightforward and unsurprising, indicating that Hume takes the 'founded on' relation to be *asymmetric*,[58] which again is just what would be expected from the foundational metaphor. Indeed given the transitivity of the 'founded on' relation, its asymmetry follows immediately from the fact that nothing can be founded on itself (i.e. the 'founded on' relation is *irreflexive*).[59] This evidently provides the logical basis for Hume's denial that the Uniformity Principle can be founded on factual inference, for it explains why such a breach of asymmetry would imply a breach of irreflexivity, and hence would be 'going in a circle, and taking that for granted, which is the very point in question' (E 36).

Formula (f4), however, is altogether more perplexing, since although it may appear at first glance to have a broadly transitive character, in fact the pattern of inference that it instantiates seriously conflicts with transitivity and asymmetry,[60] and is anyway not one that Hume accepts in general. To see this, consider a similar formula but with reasoning from experience (e) substituted in place of Reason (R):

$$FO(f,u) \& \neg FO(u,e) \rightarrow \neg FO(f,e).$$

Hume would certainly accept the antecedent of this conditional, that factual inference is founded on the Uniformity Principle and that the Uniformity Principle is not founded on reasoning from experience.[61] But he would equally certainly deny its consequent, which contradicts his frequent claim that all factual inference is founded on (reasoning from) experience. So unlike the relatively straightforward (f1) and (f2), formula (f4) leaves us with a genuine puzzle about what is going on in the logic of Hume's argument. It might seem that he must be guilty of an error here, perhaps mistaking the logic of his 'founded on' relation or failing to apply it consistently, or perhaps equivocating on the relation's meaning, in which case presumably his argument might be vitiated by this

---

[58] A relation is *asymmetric* if whenever x bears the relation to y, it follows that y *does not* bear the relation to x. Examples of asymmetric relations include those in which the two relata fall into different categories (e.g. 'husband of') and strict ordering relations. Transitivity and asymmetry together imply that 'founded on' is itself a strict ordering relation.

[59] If a relation is not asymmetric, then there is at least one pair x and y such that x bears the relation to y and also y bears the relation to x. But if this is so, then the transitivity of the relation would immediately imply that x bears the relation to x, and y to y, which would mean that the relation could not be irreflexive.

[60] Even if the three substituted terms are required to be distinct, it generates an inconsistency with asymmetry whenever one term is founded on two others or (given transitivity) whenever one term is founded on a second which is in turn founded on a third.

[61] That the Uniformity Principle is not founded on reasoning from experience follows immediately from the asymmetry of the 'founded on' relation, given that reasoning from experience is founded on the Uniformity Principle.

ambiguity in its central notion. Fortunately, however, the puzzle can be resolved by investigating just what Hume means by the relation, and this resolution will turn out to be more subtle and far less damaging than these unpalatable alternatives would suggest.

Hume talks of the 'founded on' relation as connecting a wide range of different types of thing—beliefs, conclusions, principles, relations, inferences, types of inference, faculties, even 'experience'—and he himself provides a variety of different paraphrases for it. He repeatedly states, for example, that:

(1) All factual inferences 'are founded on the relation of cause and effect' (*E* 27, 32; cf. *E* 35). This is paraphrased in terms of such reasoning requiring 'knowledge of cause and effect' (*E* 27; cf. *E* 35).

(2) All our reasonings and conclusions concerning cause and effect 'are founded entirely on experience' (*E* 164; cf. *E* 32). This is paraphrased as 'our knowledge of [cause and effect] is derived entirely from experience' (*E* 35).

(3) All inferences from experience 'are founded on the supposition of [the] resemblance of the past to the future' (*E* 38; cf. *E* 104). This is paraphrased as 'all our experimental conclusions proceed upon the supposition, that the future will be conformable to the past' (*E* 35).

(4) Factual inferences 'are *not* founded on reasoning, or any process of the understanding' (*E* 32). This is paraphrased by saying that in all such inferences, 'there is a step taken by the mind, which is not supported by any argument or process of the understanding' (*E* 41).

What seems to be in common to all of these is the issue of the *source of authority* for the beliefs, theories, inferences, and inferential methods whose foundation is in question. Accordingly, when Hume states that one thing 'is founded on' another, I suggest he means that it *derives its authority* from that other. This suggestion is corroborated by his sometimes using precisely this sort of language to express his familiar claim that all factual inferences are 'founded on' experience:

None of [the sciences or arts] can go beyond experience, or establish any principles which are not founded on that authority. (*T* xviii)

It is experience only, which gives authority to human testimony; and it is the same experience, which assures us of the laws of nature. (*E* 127)

Moreover, if this is indeed what Hume means by 'founded on', then it explains why he should take for granted that it is a transitive relation, because if *X* derives its authority from *Y*, and *Y* derives its authority from *Z*, then it will indeed be true that *X* derives its authority, albeit indirectly, from *Z*—authority is (so to speak) passed down the chain, a metaphor which Hume himself uses in a related context:

> 'Tis obvious all this chain of argument or connexion of causes and effects, is at first founded on those characters or letters, which are seen or remember'd, and that without the authority either of the memory or senses our whole reasoning wou'd be chimerical and without foundation. Every link of the chain wou'd in that case hang upon another; but there wou'd not be any thing fix'd to one end of it, capable of sustaining the whole; and consequently there wou'd be no belief nor evidence. (*T* 83; cf. *E* 46)

So the 'transitive' part of Hume's reasoning follows straightforwardly: if factual inference derives its authority from reasoning concerning cause and effect, and that derives its authority from experiential reasoning, and that derives its authority from the Uniformity Principle, then it will indeed be true that factual inference derives its authority (albeit indirectly) from the Uniformity Principle.

It is equally easy, on these terms, to explain the 'asymmetric' part of Hume's reasoning represented by formula (**f2**), for clearly two things cannot each derive their authority from the other. But as we have seen, this simple logic changes when Hume comes to consider, later in the argument, the question of whether the Uniformity Principle (and hence factual inference) is founded on, or derives its authority from, Reason. This happens, I suggest, because Reason is here the *ultimate source* of the relevant authority, so that an assertion or denial of its sanction is very naturally understood as implying more than a mere assertion or denial of possible derivative authority. The subtle shift of meaning can be illustrated by spelling out examples of the two types of assertion side by side:

(1) Factual reasoning is founded on the Uniformity Principle

means Factual reasoning derives its authority from the Uniformity Principle

which means Factual reasoning derives *whatever authority it possesses* from the Uniformity Principle.

(2) The Uniformity Principle is founded on Reason

means The Uniformity Principle derives its authority from Reason

which means The Uniformity Principle *has authority* derived from Reason.

This important but subtle difference fully legitimizes Hume's reasoning, and without supposing him to be guilty of any crude equivocation in his use of the 'founded on' relation. For thus interpreted the step in his argument represented by formula (**f4**) turns out to be clearly valid:

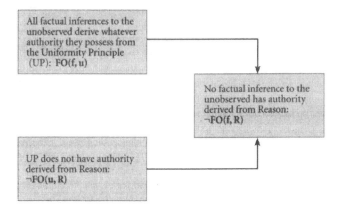

Interpreting Hume's 'founded on' relation in terms of the derivation of rational authority—a manifestly normative notion—thus fully explains the logic of his argument, which as we shall see (in §10.3) provides strong grounds for preferring an unambiguously normative interpretation of that argument to the recently fashionable alternatives.

10.2 The Role and Nature of the Uniformity Principle

Before moving on to this larger topic, however, let us consider the role of the Uniformity Principle within the argument, a question which has been debated by commentators in terms of what kind of 'presupposition' for induction Hume takes the principle to provide. The discussion above provides a clear, though partial, answer: induction 'presupposes' the Uniformity Principle in the sense that any rational authority which inductive inferences have must be derived from that principle—in other words, *inductive inferences can be rationally founded only if the Uniformity Principle is itself rationally founded*. This answer, however, leaves undetermined both what Hume understands by rational foundedness, and also what account he might give of the supposed dependence of induction on the Uniformity Principle.

Historically by far the most popular account of these matters is that Hume operates with a deductivist conception of Reason, and accordingly takes the Uniformity Principle to be presupposed by inductive inferences in the sense of its being an implicit premiss which is required to transform them into deductions. As Stove puts it: 'Inductive arguments are all invalid as they stand, and it would be necessary, in order to turn them into valid arguments, to add to their premises a proposition which asserts that unobserved instances resemble observed ones.'[62] The central thrust of Hume's argument, on this account, is that

---

[62] Stove, *Probability and Hume's Inductive Scepticism*, 43.

the non-provability of the Uniformity Principle—and hence the non-availability of this essential implicit premiss—exposes any inductive inference as 'a broken-backed syllogism, crippled for lack of a suitable middle term'.[63]

Despite its popularity with commentators, however, this account has little to recommend it. First, it is questionable whether Hume sees the Uniformity Principle as functioning as a missing *premiss* of inductive reasoning—in the *Treatise*, not only does he deny that it typically plays any relevant psychological role:

the understanding or imagination can draw inferences from past experience, without reflecting on it; much more without forming any principle concerning it, or reasoning upon that principle (*T* 104)

but also, he seems to deny that this lack is inferentially problematic:

we may exert our reason without employing more than two ideas, and without having recourse to a third to serve as a medium betwixt them. We infer a cause immediately from its effect; and this inference is not only a true species of reasoning, but the strongest of all others, and more convincing than when we interpose another idea to connect the two extremes. (*T* 96 n.)

Secondly, even if Hume does indeed see the Uniformity Principle as an implicit 'medium' connecting the observational premiss of an inductive inference with its conclusion,[64] this does not in the least imply that the resulting connexion must be *deductive*, for as we saw in §2 above, the Lockean 'logic' that Hume inherited employed the notion of a 'medium' or 'proof' as much within 'probable' as within 'demonstrative' reasoning.[65] Thirdly, the Uniformity Principle as Hume presents it in the *Enquiry* (quoted in §3.2 above) is anyway far too vague to serve as a plausible *deductive* link between the premisses and conclusion of an inductive inference.[66] Fourthly, it seems extremely unlikely that Hume intended the principle to provide any such deductive (and hence infallible) connexion, for he clearly recognizes that inductions are incurably fallible *even on the supposition that nature is uniform*, since we can never be certain that we

[63] Flew, *Hume's Philosophy of Belief*, 81.

[64] Although Flew (ibid. 70–1) takes Hume to be speaking of the Uniformity Principle as providing such a 'medium', in fact Hume uses the term only in the context of demanding an argument *for* the Uniformity Principle based on past experience (*E* 34, 37; cf. §6 above).

[65] As further corroboration, Locke uses the term 'probable *Mediums*' at Essay IV. xvii. 16, and at *D* 143 Hume speaks of 'mediums' that 'reach no farther . . . than experience [revised at one stage to "moral evidence"] and probability'. The tendency of commentators to jump to a deductivist interpretation of Hume's argument simply because they take the Uniformity Principle to be functioning as an unavailable 'medium' is thus seriously anachronistic given the 18th-century background of Lockean 'logic'—if anything it reveals their own deductivist prejudices (presumably inherited from Aristotle via Frege) rather than Hume's.

[66] The more explicit principle of the *Treatise* (quoted in the next footnote) might seem to be capable of providing such a link, but only if it were so specific as to be clearly false in general, given that (as Hume recognized) inductions are incurably fallible.

have taken all relevant causal factors into account (e.g. T 175, E 86–7). Finally, as we shall see below (in §10.3), there are strong independent grounds for denying that Hume employs a deductivist concept of Reason within his famous argument, since in one of its main stages (propositions (13) and (16) in the structure diagram) he explicitly canvasses the possibility of a 'probable' argument for the Uniformity Principle.

Perhaps the best way to approach an alternative account of the role of the Uniformity Principle is to ask ourselves the very question to which Hume takes that principle to be the answer: what exactly *is* being 'presupposed' by someone who performs a factual inference from observed to unobserved? One modest and presumably fairly uncontroversial answer to this question is as follows: when we inductively extrapolate from observed to unobserved (for brevity, from 'past' to 'future'), we are presupposing that past instances are *evidentially relevant* to future instances, or in other words, that the nature of past instances gives some evidence concerning the nature of future instances. This is not all, however, for we also suppose that the evidence provided by past instances is *positively* relevant, in that future instances are likely to *resemble* past instances rather than, for example, contrasting with them. Hence any inductive inference takes for granted that past instances have a *positive evidential relevance* to future instances. This presupposition can very naturally, though loosely, be expressed by saying that *future instances can be expected to resemble past instances* (cf. T 89), that *the future will be conformable to the past* (E 35), that *the past is a rule for the future* (cf. E 38), and so on. I suggest, therefore, the following interpretation: when Hume claims that inductive inferences are founded on the Uniformity Principle, he is simply making the straightforward point that any inductive argument, *by its very nature*, treats past instances as *positively evidentially relevant* to future instances. This interpretation makes good sense of Hume's claim and the various ways in which he expresses it, explains why he thought it too obvious to require further elaboration, and also neatly reconciles his denial of the Uniformity Principle's conscious psychological role (T 104, quoted above) with his claim that it nevertheless represents 'a step taken by the mind . . . in all reasonings from experience' (E 41).[67] The Uniformity Principle functions

---

[67] The *Treatise* is less committal about whether the Uniformity Principle is typically involved at all in inductive inference, stating only that '*If* reason determin'd us' to make such inferences, *then* 'it wou'd proceed upon that principle' (T 89, my emphasis). I suggest that this is because Hume here views the principle as being an explicit proposition 'that instances, of which we have had no experience, must resemble those, of which we have had experience, and that the course of nature continues always uniformly the same' (T 89)—a proposition which he rightly takes to play no conscious role within most inductive inference. His more subtle approach in the *Enquiry*, which treats the presumption of uniformity as a relatively vague evidential principle whose adoption is *manifested* in our inferential practice (rather than as an explicit proposition which may or may not be consciously contemplated) fits nicely with his discussion of the idea of necessity, which even in the *Treatise* he had accounted for in an almost exactly corresponding way (as presaged by his suggestion at T 88 that 'the necessary connexion depends on the inference').

within inductive inference not so much as a propositional premiss (whether implicit or explicit), but rather as the underlying rationale of any such inference, a principle whose adoption we *manifest* every time we treat the past as positive evidence regarding the future.[68]

10.3   The Logic of 'Reason' in Hume's Argument

We are now at last in a position to address and, I hope, to settle conclusively what is perhaps the most important interpretative controversy surrounding Hume's argument concerning induction: what does Hume mean by 'reason' within that argument, and in particular within its celebrated conclusion that induction 'is not founded on reason'? It will come as no surprise that I take Hume to be employing here the traditional perceptual notion of Reason, and accordingly interpret his conclusion as essentially a denial that induction is based on any form of *rational perception*, whether direct or mediated by inference. The most obvious evidence in favour of this interpretation is simply the contemporary dominance of this perceptual notion (as sketched in §2 above) together with the appropriateness of Hume's argument as a means of undermining it—for example, his emphasis on the impossibility of 'seeing' the effect within the cause (§4.1), and his conclusion that induction is founded on the instinctive operation of custom rather than on any perceptible rational connexion (§8). Another significant virtue of this interpretation is to explain why Hume should have singled out *induction* in particular for this type of sceptical treatment. He was well aware that a Cartesian challenge could be mounted against intuition, demonstration, and sensation (*E* 149–50, 152–4), and that the impossibility of a non-circular justification of our faculties is by no means peculiar to induction. His special interest in induction, I suggest, is accounted for by his feeling able to prove conclusively of it alone—and without recourse to any extreme Cartesian scepticism about our faculties in general—that it is utterly beyond the reach of any form of *perceptual* justification.[69]

---

[68]   This interpretation also removes what can seem an inconsistency in Hume's thought, by distinguishing between the Uniformity Principle (which *cannot* itself be founded on experience, on pain of circularity) and the superficially similar principle that 'The same cause always produces the same effect', which Hume says 'we derive from experience' and can then use as a basis for drawing a general conclusion even from a single, carefully controlled experiment (*T* 173–4; cf. *T* 104–5, 131, *E* 107 n.). The latter principle is concerned with the *consistency* of events within our experience rather than the *evidential relevance* of observed to unobserved. But without the presupposition of evidential relevance, such consistency could not of course be extrapolated from past to future.

[69]   In the *Treatise* (IV. i. 1 and IV. i. 2 respectively) Hume does apply a somewhat similar sceptical treatment to demonstration and sensation, and draws a similar moral, that these are based on the instinctive idea-enlivening operations of the imagination rather than on rational perception (a point emphasized at *T* 265). It is an interesting question whether the moderation of such scepticism in the *Enquiry* is philosophically or merely strategically motivated, but certainly his inductive scepticism in the *Enquiry* has proved to be far more pointed and effective for being dissociated from scepticism about these other, more perceptual, cognitive operations.

Although these considerations show that Hume's argument makes good sense interpreted as an assault on the Lockean perceptual view of 'probable' Reason, they do not by themselves rule out alternative interpretations. What I now intend to show is that the structure and logic of Hume's argument, as examined above, are seriously inconsistent with the various alternative interpretations that have hitherto been proposed. The most prominent of these alternatives are: (*a*) the 'deductivist' interpretation most strongly advocated by Flew and Stove, according to which Hume's argument is intended to show that induction cannot yield the absolute certainty characteristic of deductive Reason; (*b*) the 'anti-deductivist' account of Beauchamp *et al.*, Arnold, and Baier, which sees the argument as following a similar logic but with the intention of undermining that deductivist concept of Reason rather than endorsing it; and (*c*) the 'no argument' interpretation of Garrett and Noonan, which takes the argument to be denying that our use of the method of inductive inference is caused by any higher-level *reasoning* (i.e. argument or ratiocination) about that method.[70] All of these imply that Hume's denial of a rational foundation for induction is in some way limited—in the case of (*a*) and (*b*), by restricting attention to forms of evidence that yield absolute certainty, and in the case of (*c*), by focusing only on forms of evidence that involve inference. Hence all of them fail to provide a full account of the structure of that part of Hume's argument which was explored in §§6 and 7 above, and represented in §10 by the formula

(f3) $\neg FO(u,s) \ \& \ \neg FO(u,i) \ \& \ \neg FO(u,d) \ \& \ \neg FO(u,f) \rightarrow \neg FO(u,R)$.

As this formula indicates and as we saw in detail earlier, when Hume discusses the rational credentials of the Uniformity Principle he in turn rules out *four* potential sources of evidence: sensation, intuition, demonstration, and factual inference. The first two of these are directly perceptual rather than inferential (and should therefore be irrelevant to his purposes if the 'no argument' interpretation were correct), while the last of them can yield at best 'probability' (and should therefore be irrelevant if either the 'deductivist' or the

---

[70] As well as the 'meta-reasoning' variant of this interpretation, emphasized here, there is a 'computational' variant which takes Hume to be arguing that our inductive inferences are typically immediate and unreflective rather than involving intermediate steps or significant ratiocination. Garrett (*Cognition and Commitment in Hume's Philosophy*) and Noonan (*Hume on Knowledge*) favour the meta-reasoning variant, Connon ('The Naturalism of Hume Revisited'), Broughton ('Hume's Skepticism about Causal Inferences), and Owen (*Hume's Reason*) the computational (Garrett's position in this volume, pp. 332–4, combines elements of both). 'No argument' is potentially a misleading nickname for the interpretation, given that in Hume's day 'argument' could mean not only 'process of reasoning' but also 'proof', 'evidence', or 'reason' (*Oxford English Dictionary*), so when he writes that induction is not founded on 'argument', we cannot take for granted that he is using the word in its primary modern sense. 'No ratiocination' would be a more precise nickname for what is intended.

'anti-deductivist' interpretation were correct). Defenders of these interpretations might be tempted to dismiss this sort of objection by alleging carelessness or superfluity in Hume's discussion, but a highly significant passage from *A Letter from a Gentleman to his Friend in Edinburgh*, written by Hume in exactly the period when he was working on the *Enquiry*, strongly indicates that on the contrary, his selection of these four potential sources of evidence is entirely deliberate: 'It is common for Philosophers to distinguish the Kinds of Evidence into *intuitive, demonstrative, sensible, and moral*' (*L* 22). Hume's argument is carefully designed to rule out *every* potential 'kind of evidence' for the Uniformity Principle that might be thought to be available on the conventional, perceptual view of Reason. And so the kinds of evidence that he considers are not restricted either to those that yield absolute certainty, or to those that are inferential.[71] For convenient reference, we might therefore appropriately call this the 'no reason whatever' interpretation.

So far I have made the case in favour of this interpretation on the basis of what Hume *does* say in his argument, but it can also be pressed strongly on the basis of what he *does not* say. To take the 'deductivist' and 'anti-deductivist' interpretations first, *if* (as these interpretations would imply) Hume's concern in *Enquiry* IV were simply to deny that induction can yield absolute deductive certainty, *then* it would be astonishing that he should have overlooked the possibility of proving this concisely and elegantly in almost a single step, using his argument from distinct conceivability. For given any factual inference to the unobserved, no matter what its observational premises might be, we can always distinctly conceive a change in the course of nature which would result in the falsehood of its hitherto unobserved conclusion; and this conceivability is by itself more than sufficient on Humean principles to rule out immediately any prospect of finding a deductive guarantee for such an inference. This simple proof is so characteristically Humean in structure, style, and content (cf. *E* 35, 164, *D* 189) that it surely could not have escaped the great sceptic's notice had it been sufficient for his purposes. So the fact that he instead develops an argument of considerable sophistication, in which he takes such pains to explore and dismiss in turn a variety of possible sources of inductive warrant including at least one (namely 'probable' reasoning) which on deductivist principles is patently worthless, provides compelling evidence that the conclusion which he seeks goes well beyond the reach of this crude deductivist 'hole in one'.[72]

---

[71] Moreover, the context of the *Letter* does make clear that Hume uses 'evidence' here in its modern sense, as referring to a source of epistemic support, for on the same page he talks of an opinion's being 'supported by *moral Evidence*'. Hence I disagree with Garrett's claim (*Cognition and Commitment in Hume's Philosophy*, 228) that 'Hume . . . consistently uses ["evidence"] to mean "evidentness"—that is, as equivalent to "belief", "assurance", or "vivacity", construed as properties of ideas.' This is arguable as an interpretation of that term in the *Treatise*, but seems quite wrong in relation to the *Enquiry*, for example Hume's use of the term at *E* 26–7 and throughout Section X.

[72] In addition to the criticisms presented in this section, I have already extensively attacked (in §10.2)

Turning now to the 'no argument' interpretation, on this account the most surprising omission from Hume's discussion is any serious consideration of *faulty* (e.g. incomplete, question-begging, or simply fallacious) arguments on which the Uniformity Principle, and hence our use of induction, might be founded. For if, as this interpretation maintains, Hume's purpose is purely to deny that we are caused to reason inductively through the influence of some higher-level argument or ratiocination, then to restrict his attention here to *good* arguments, as though only these could possibly have any causal influence upon us, would seem to manifest a most un-Humean rationalist prejudice.[73] And indeed it is hard to see why he should presume that this causal impact of our belief in the Uniformity Principle (whether mediated by means of a good or a bad argument) should in any way imply that it itself is founded on some *further* argument.[74] To illustrate these points, here are a few higher-level reasonings that might, for all that is said in Hume's famous argument, cause us either to reason inductively or to accept the Uniformity Principle:

(1) (I just happen to find myself believing that) the future will resemble the past. But if the future resembles the past, then induction can be relied on. Therefore induction can indeed be relied on.

(2) God has implanted in me a belief that the future will resemble the past. God is no deceiver. Therefore the future will resemble the past.

(3) In the past, it has always turned out that hitherto unobserved objects tended to resemble previously observed objects. Hence in the future it can be expected that unobserved objects will resemble observed objects.

(4) The observed regular behaviour of objects indicates that they have intrinsic essences which necessitate them to behave and to appear as they do. Given that such essences exist, it follows that there must be a

the 'unavailable deductive medium' view of the Uniformity Principle which constitutes a central plank of both the 'deductivist' and 'anti-deductivist' interpretations as these are usually presented. Hence I shall devote most attention here to the 'no argument' interpretation.

[73] Likewise, on what I have called the 'computational' variant of the 'no argument' interpretation, it is hard to understand why Hume should restrict his attention to 'intermediate ideas' that are well-founded. The Uniformity Principle can potentially play such a role in ratiocination however it may have come into our minds, so if Hume's primary concern in his argument is to deny that it (or any other intermediate idea) does so, then his discussion of the possible sources of evidence for it is largely irrelevant except on the extremely un-Humean assumption that we are incapable of having irrational or inferentially unfounded beliefs. Note the contrast here between these *purely* causal notions of Reason and the implicitly normative perceptual notion, for which a restriction to genuinely 'visible' inferential links is relatively unproblematic.

[74] Noonan (*Hume on Knowledge*) tries to fill the resulting hole in what he takes to be Hume's argument as follows: 'We could not be caused to engage in the practice of inductive inference by our acceptance of an argument, a premiss of which was the Uniformity Principle, unless we also had available an argument *for* the Uniformity Principle (for we could not believe in the Uniformity Principle, antecedently to acquiring a disposition to engage in inductive inference, except on the basis of argument)' (pp. 119–20). But on Humean principles, both of Noonan's 'could not' claims seem to be entirely gratuitous.

consistent relationship between objects' appearances and their behaviour. Hence the relationships observed in the past will continue into the future.

Hume's reaction to all of these is entirely predictable, and he would, of course, be quite unimpressed. In the first case he would refuse to accept our belief in uniformity as a bare fact, and would express his 'sifting humour' by questioning its foundation (E 32–3). In the second, he would no doubt criticize the 'unexpected circuit' of our reliance on God's veracity, perhaps on the ground that if induction 'be once called in question, we shall be at a loss to find arguments, by which we may prove the existence of that Being or any of his attributes' (E 153). In the third case, he would certainly object to the argument's circularity (E 35–6). In the fourth, he would reject our talk of intrinsic necessitating 'essences' as incomprehensible (A 649, E 73–7) and would go on to point out that the extrapolation of objects' causal powers into the future, in the context of an argument for induction, then becomes question-begging (E 36–8). But on the 'no argument' interpretation, all of these predictable responses would be completely beside the point, for although they indeed identify logical inadequacies in the proffered arguments,[75] they do nothing whatever to prove that such arguments can play no *causal* role in the explanation of (some, if not all, of) our inductive behaviour. Moreover the author of *Treatise* I. iii. 9–13 and of *Enquiry* VII could hardly fail to appreciate this, for he, of all people, could never suppose it to be an a priori truth that only good arguments can influence us (cf. T 110–17, 143–7), nor could he consider it appropriate to investigate any issue of psychological causation through abstract discussion of arguments' merits rather than concrete empirical observation (cf. E 67–9).[76]

A related objection to the logic of the 'no argument' interpretation can be developed by reference to the discussion of Hume's 'founded on' relation in §10.1 above. Here the two most relevant formulae are these:

---

[75] That Hume has his eye set firmly on questions of rational warrant rather than merely causal explanation, even in the *Treatise*, is particularly clear in his response to (4) above, in what I have called (in §9) the 'coda' to his argument. There, at T 90–1, he speaks for example of 'solid' and 'weak' reasoning, discusses whether one proposition 'can' (or 'can never') 'prove' another, and gives the fact that 'the foregoing reasoning had no just foundation' as a decisive ground for concluding that the reasoning in question cannot constitute a basis in Reason for our inductive inferences.

[76] Hume's discussions of induction do admittedly include what would be on this interpretation two highly appropriate empirical observations. First, at T 103–4 (cf. E 54), where he remarks that we characteristically draw inductive conclusions immediately and unreflectively, even in cases where we have never before reflected on the relevant uniformity. And secondly, at E 39 (in what §9.3 above calls his 'parting shot'), where he points out that infants and animals universally make use of inductive prediction even though they are clearly in no position to understand, let alone to frame for themselves, higher-level arguments about it (cf. also T 178, E 106). In both cases these observations follow the statement of his famous argument, and he draws the moral that they corroborate the conclusion of that argument, but there is no sign that he views them as constituting essential, or even significant, parts of it.

(f1) FO(f,e) & FO(e,u) → FO(f,u)
(f4) FO(f,u) & ¬FO(u,R) → ¬FO(f,R).

On the 'no argument' interpretation, the 'founded on' relation is supposed to involve only causation rather than any derivation of rational authority, so 'FO(f,e)' is presumably to be read as 'Factual inference to the unobserved is caused by reasoning from experience'. However, an abstraction such as the Uniformity Principle is not the sort of thing that can have direct causal influence, so if 'founded on' is to be understood in this way, it follows that 'u' cannot be taken as standing for the Uniformity Principle itself, but must instead mean something like *reasoning that invokes the Uniformity Principle*. Translating accordingly, the causal variant of formula (f1) turns out like this:

> (f1c) If factual inference to the unobserved is caused by reasoning from experience, and reasoning from experience is caused by reasoning that invokes the Uniformity Principle, then factual inference to the unobserved is caused by reasoning that invokes the Uniformity Principle.

This might seem satisfactory, because the transitivity which is characteristic of causal relations makes (f1c) plausibly true (and the corresponding variant of formula (f2) is equally unproblematic). But moving on now to formula (f4), we must find a way of rendering '¬FO(u,R)' and '¬FO(f,R)' in appropriate terms. The latter is the ultimate conclusion of Hume's famous argument, and so consistency with the 'no argument' interpretation requires us to interpret these expressions as denials that the form of reasoning in question (respectively reasoning that invokes the Uniformity Principle, and factual inference to the unobserved) is itself caused by (further) reasoning.[77] Hence we reach:

> (f4c) If factual inference to the unobserved is caused by reasoning that invokes the Uniformity Principle, and reasoning that invokes the Uniformity Principle is not caused by (further) reasoning, then factual inference to the unobserved is not caused by (further) reasoning.

However, (f4c) is logically quite inadequate to play its required role. First, it does nothing to solve the 'puzzle' mentioned in §10.1, for it provides no apparent explanation of why the form of conditional

FO(x,y) & ¬FO(y,z) → ¬FO(x,z),

---

[77] Here again I focus on the meta-reasoning variant of the 'no argument' interpretation, though essentially the same problem arises for the computational variant—simply replace '(further) reasoning' by 'inference via intermediate steps' to see roughly how the objection would proceed. Put crudely, it is hard to see why Hume might suppose that a lack of *inferential* foundation for UP itself should be 'inherited' by conclusions that are themselves *inferred* on the basis of UP.

which cannot in general be valid on Humean terms, should be thought acceptable in this instance. Secondly, it can seriously be questioned whether (f4c) as
stated actually provides a legitimate instantiation of this (at least *superficially*
plausible) form, because in the two propositions 'reasoning that invokes the
Uniformity Principle is not caused by (further) reasoning' and 'factual inference to the unobserved is not caused by (further) reasoning', the phrase '(further) reasoning' evidently refers to something different—in the former case it
means *further reasoning beyond that which invokes the Uniformity Principle*, and
in the latter it means *further reasoning beyond the factual inference to the unobserved*. Thirdly, and disastrously for the 'no argument' interpretation, the result
of this equivocation is to make (f4c) not only invalid, but almost self-refuting.
For if factual inference to the unobserved is caused by reasoning that invokes
the Uniformity Principle, then it immediately follows that factual inference to
the unobserved is indeed caused by '(further) reasoning'—namely, that very
reasoning which invokes the Uniformity Principle![78]

The upshot of all this is that the structure of Hume's argument concerning
induction is no more comprehensible on the 'no argument' interpretation than
it is on the 'deductivist' and 'anti-deductivist' interpretations. The latter are
unable to explain why Hume's reasoning is so complex, and in particular, why
he takes the trouble even to consider the possibility of a 'probable' foundation
for the Uniformity Principle. But on the 'no argument' interpretation a great
deal of Hume's discussion, including even his overall strategy of throwing light
on inductive reasoning by examining its foundation through the Uniformity
Principle, turns out to be not only irrelevant but also seriously fallacious. Given
this damning verdict, it might naturally be wondered at this point whether my
discussion of these rival interpretations has been somehow unfair or incomplete, overlooking some alternative way of understanding Hume's language
which would make good sense of everything he says in the appropriate terms. To
address this possibility I can think of no better response than a Humean challenge: *if* anyone claims that there is some consistent and plausible way of understanding the logic of Hume's argument in deductivist, anti-deductivist,
meta-reasoning, or computational terms, *then* let them spell out its logic in
detail, making clear how the 'founded on' relation is to be understood, what
logical properties (e.g. transitivity, asymmetry) this relation has, and how the
structure of Hume's argument, represented by the diagram in the appendix
and/or formulae (f1) to (f4), can be made sense of in those terms. I hope I have

---

[78] Note that there is no way round this problem by somehow trying to identify the two types of reasoning (e.g. by deeming that factual inference to the unobserved itself indirectly invokes the Uniformity
Principle). For quite apart from any logical difficulties that would then arise elsewhere, the two relata of
the 'founded on' relation must clearly be distinct if it is supposed to be interpreted in causal terms.

proved that the interpretation presented here, which understands the 'founded on' relation in terms of the derivation of rational authority, and Reason as a supposed faculty that perceives evidential connexions (whether sensory, intuitive, demonstrative, or 'probable'), is fully able to meet this challenge. But I am not aware of any other interpretation that even comes close to doing so.

11. THE NATURE OF HUME'S INDUCTIVE SCEPTICISM

It is clear that Hume saw the conclusion of his argument concerning induction as a sceptical result. The very title of Section IV, 'Sceptical Doubts concerning the Operations of the Understanding' strongly suggests this, and he then confirms it by providing an unambiguously 'negative answer' (E 32) to the doubts that he there raises (at E 158 he also refers back to the argument as presenting 'sceptical objections to *moral* evidence'). Moreover, if my analysis of the argument's logic is correct, it proceeds by undermining every possible source of rational evidential authority for the Uniformity Principle, a principle which is itself presented as being the only potential source of such authority for inductive inferences. Hence it is no surprise to find Hume expressing his conclusion in words that are entirely consonant with the 'no reason whatever' interpretation that I have advocated:[79]

I say then, that, even after we have experience of the operations of cause and effect, our conclusions from that experience are *not* founded on reasoning, or any process of the understanding. (E 32)

in all reasonings from experience, there is a step taken by the mind, which is not supported by any argument or process of the understanding . . . (E 41)

we cannot give a satisfactory reason, why we believe, after a thousand experiments, that a stone will fall, or fire burn . . . (E 162)

Similar statements occur in the *Treatise*, including most emphatically:[80]

---

[79] Note that Hume's sceptical conclusion is not confined to the general practice of induction, but applies, as these quotations make clear, to each individual inductive inference. Hence it must be read as meaning that *every such inference* lacks a 'foundation' or 'support' in Reason or the understanding, which tells strongly against the 'no argument' interpretation given that Hume repeatedly stresses the role of explicit *ratiocination* in many, or even most, such inferences (T 133, 175, E 86–7, 107 n.). He sees *all* inductive inferences as lacking a foundation in *Reason*, but only *some* as being immediate, unreflective, and independent of *reasoning*.

[80] See also T 91: 'not only our reason fails us in the discovery of the *ultimate connection* of causes and effects, but even after experience has inform'd us of their *constant conjunction*, 'tis impossible for us to satisfy ourselves by our reason, why we shou'd extend that experience beyond those particular instances, which have fallen under our observation'. Both this and the passage from T 139 (also A 652, 655–6) bear out Stove's claim (*Probability and Hume's Inductive Scepticism*, 32, 58–9) that Hume's conclusion about factual inferences *from* experience is intended to echo his conclusion about factual inferences *prior to* experience (i.e. inferences that are 'a priori' in the Humean sense discussed in §4.1 above). The latter is

Let men be once fully perswaded of these two principles, *That there is nothing in any object, consider'd in itself, which can afford us a reason for drawing a conclusion beyond it*; and, *That even after the observation of the frequent or constant conjunction of objects, we have no reason to draw any inference concerning any object beyond those of which we have had experience*; I say, let men be once fully convinc'd of these two principles, and this will throw them so loose from all common systems, that they will make no difficulty of receiving any, which may appear the most extraordinary. (*T* 139)

Here Hume stresses that the negative conclusion of his famous argument, that 'we have no reason to draw any [inductive] inference', is sufficiently striking to 'throw men loose from all common systems'. So he clearly cannot have understood this conclusion as being only a relatively modest result, such as a denial of the claim that induction has deductive warrant, or a denial that our use of induction is caused by higher-level argument. Neither of these claims was any part of the established Lockean orthodoxy, which as we have seen (in §2 above) fully acknowledged the fallibility of 'probable' reasoning,[81] and attributed our judgements of probability to the perception of probable connexions rather than to higher-level ratiocination.[82] So to make sense of his own assessment of it, Hume's conclusion must be significantly more radical than what is attributed to him by either the 'anti-deductivist' or the 'no argument' interpretation.

However, at the other extreme, if the conclusion of his famous argument is to be at all consistent with his other discussions of inductive reasoning, that conclusion cannot be quite as radical as the 'deductivist' interpretation maintains. For deductivism would have the implication that all factual inferences to the unobserved are completely worthless, or, in Stroud's memorable phrase, that 'as far as the competition for degrees of reasonableness is concerned, all possible beliefs about the unobserved are tied for last place'.[83] And this would obviously make a nonsense of Hume's efforts, in both the *Treatise* and the *Enquiry*, to develop a theory of scientific reasoning whose whole point is to distinguish between good and bad inductive inferences. Focusing here on the *Enquiry*,[84]

clearly a *sceptical* conclusion, and this gives a further ground for taking the former to be sceptical also. In the *Enquiry* a similar echo occurs implicitly in the quotation above from *E* 32, and also between the two paragraphs at *E* 42.

[81] See also *Essay* IV. xv. 2 for Locke's clear recognition of the fallibility of probable reasoning, and *Essay* IV. iii. 9–17, 21–9, and IV. vi. 7–16 for his views on the very narrow limits of certain 'knowledge'.

[82] The idea that our practice of induction might be founded on higher-level reasoning also seems profoundly un-Lockean in spirit, given his view of Reason in general as having a God-given 'native Faculty' to perceive evidential connexions directly and thus avoid any dependence on meta-inferential formal rules (*Essay* IV. xvii. 4).

[83] B. Stroud, *Hume* (London: Routledge & Kegan Paul, 1977), 54.

[84] For a corresponding discussion focusing primarily on the *Treatise*, see Millican, 'Hume's Argument concerning Induction', 128–34. This draws attention to several passages in which Hume clearly implies that 'probable' arguments can vary in force (e.g. *Treatise* I. iii. 11–12, *T* 31, 173–5, 181–2), and it also outlines his attempt (*Treatise* I. iii. 9–13, *T* 225–6) to develop a systematic theory of factual inference based on 'gen-

perhaps the clearest denial of undiscriminating inductive scepticism comes in Section X, which explicitly relies on the principle that factual inferences can vary in force according to their conformity with experience, thus implying that they are not all worthless: 'One, who, in our climate, should expect better weather in any week of JUNE than in one of DECEMBER, would reason justly, and conformably to experience ... A wise man ... proportions his belief to the evidence.' (*E* 110). Hume goes on to apply this general principle to inferences from testimony in particular, and thus erects what becomes the central pillar of his celebrated argument concerning miracles: 'the evidence, resulting from ... testimony, admits of a diminution, greater or less, in proportion as the fact is more or less unusual' (*E* 113). But this argument of Section X is not a special case—indeed much of the *Enquiry* can be seen as developing a general and fairly systematic theory of how inductive inferences should be made and judged. Some highlights of this theory appear at *E* 86–7 (recommending a search for hidden causes), *E* 104–5 (on reasoning from analogy), *E* 107 n. (giving some hints on experimental method), *E* 56–9 and 110–11 (dealing with probability in cases of inconsistent experience), and *E* 136–7 (proposing norms of proportionate inference). Whether these passages add up to anything approaching a comprehensive theory may be debatable, but it cannot seriously be denied that Hume in the *Enquiry* makes numerous comparative judgements about inductive inferences which are clearly inconsistent with thoroughgoing deductivist scepticism.

What kind of scepticism is it, then, that on the one hand denies that we have *any reason whatever*, or *any kind of evidence*, to ground our reliance on induction, but on the other hand proposes a theory of inductive inferences which draws normative distinctions among them, and recommends that we rely on them in proportion to 'the evidence'? An answer emerges if we contrast the Lockean account of induction, which Hume rejects, with the alternative that he develops in *Enquiry* V, his so-called 'Sceptical Solution' to his earlier 'Sceptical Doubts'.

Hume's 'Sceptical Solution', as the term implies, 'solves' his problem of the foundation of inductive inference, but does so in a way that is consistent with the sceptical conclusion of his argument concerning induction. That conclusion remains entirely intact:

in all reasonings from experience, there is a step taken by the mind, which is not supported by any argument or process of the understanding (*E* 41).

eral rules' and on the distinction within the imagination between those principles that are 'permanent, irresistable, and universal' and those that are 'changeable, weak, and irregular'. Notoriously, however, this distinction breaks down in the conclusion of *Treatise* Book I (*T* 267–8), apparently plunging Hume more deeply into scepticism than ever occurs in the *Enquiry*.

But the point of Hume's 'solution' is to deny that this negative result will, or should, have any effect on our tendency to infer inductively, because the crucial 'step taken by the mind' whose foundation it questions—the assumption of uniformity between past and future—is one that we cannot help making:

If the mind be not engaged by argument to make this step, it must be induced by some other principle of equal weight and authority . . . (E 41)

This principle is CUSTOM or HABIT. . . . By employing that word, we pretend not to have given the ultimate reason of such a propensity. We only point out a principle of human nature, which is universally acknowledged, and which is well known by its effects. Perhaps, we can push our enquiries no farther, or pretend to give the cause of this cause; but must rest contented with it as the ultimate principle, which we can assign, of all our conclusions from experience. (E 43)

[Belief arising from inference through custom] is the necessary result of placing the mind in such circumstances. It is an operation of the soul, when we are so situated, as unavoidable as to feel the passion of love, when we receive benefits; or hatred, when we meet with injuries. All these operations are a species of natural instincts, which no reasoning or process of the thought or understanding is able, either to produce, or to prevent. (E 46-7)

Thus inductive inference has after all a foundation of sorts, though clearly not of the kind that Hume had previously been seeking. For although 'custom' is explicitly described here as a source of 'authority' (corroborating the interpretation of the foundational relation developed in §10.1 above), this is obviously nothing like the *rational* authority that Locke had purported to find in the perception of objective probable connexions. Quite the contrary, for Hume's theory implies a Copernican reversal of this explanatory order: inductive evidential connexions, so far from being 'read off the world' as Locke had implied, turn out instead to be 'read into it' (in the guise of causal relations) by our entirely non-rational assumption of inductive uniformity. In terms of the traditional theory of perceptual Reason, this reversal is therefore *profoundly* sceptical.[85] Nevertheless, it need not mean that as far as factual inference is concerned, 'anything goes'—that any such inference is as good (or as bad) as any other. For as Hume forcefully demonstrates in the remainder of the *Enquiry*, the

---

[85] Hume's Copernican revolution, though less celebrated, is epistemologically far more radical than Kant's later version, because of its *non-rational* basis. So far from being sceptical, Kant used this sort of explanatory reversal to try to *rescue* a priori knowledge of matters of fact from the Humean critique, by appeal to a supposed a priori knowledge of our own minds' synthetic capacities (a supposition which Hume, quite correctly, would never have allowed, as made clear by E 64-9). Hume may have woken Kant from his dogmatic slumbers, but as Bertrand Russell quips, Kant 'soon invented a soporific which enabled him to sleep again' (*A History of Western Philosophy* (London: George Allen & Unwin, 1946), 731).

universality and irresistibility of this new foundation for induction enables such undiscriminating scepticism to be very effectively opposed through an insistence on what Noxon calls 'methodological consistency'.[86] Thus, for example, the superstitious theist may appeal to a reported miracle to ground his faith, but *the very same* inductive principles that underlie his confidence in the truth of the miracle report can be shown to tell more strongly in the opposite direction. When fully informed and faced with the balance of empirical evidence, therefore, his beliefs will be pressured to change through the force of custom operating within him. Perhaps neither the rationalist nor the undiscriminating sceptic will initially be impressed with this kind of *ad hominem* appeal to an admittedly non-rational and potentially deceitful instinct.[87] But since they too, just like the theist, are irresistibly governed by this instinct (whether they like it or not), their own inferential tendencies can likewise be harnessed to persuade them in the direction of sound empirical science. Many, no doubt, will resist such a following through of the consequences of inductive thinking, perhaps by refusing to listen to the evidence proposed or to examine its full implications. Others may be intellectually incapable of the kind of careful analysis involved, which may require 'that nice distinctions be made, just conclusions drawn, distant comparisons formed, complicated relations examined, and general facts fixed and ascertained' (*M* 173).[88] But such refusal or incapacity is unambiguously a failing of *rationality*, thus providing an entirely appropriate basis for normative judgement. So Hume is fully justified in drawing a distinction between 'the wise' and 'the vulgar' on this basis, between those who systematically pursue the consequences of our irresistible assumption of uniformity, and those who do not. The *Enquiry* shows how such a systematic pursuit involves searching for hidden causes, careful design of experiments, disciplined reasoning from analogy and probability, and so forth. All this effectively vindicates the methods of Humean empirical science, by demonstrating that they are 'nothing but the reflections of common life, methodized and corrected' (*E* 162).

Philo in the *Dialogues* sums up nicely how Hume's view of induction, as founded on non-rational custom, can be comfortably combined with a healthy respect for systematic empirical science (i.e. natural *philosophy*):

---

[86] J. Noxon, *Hume's Philosophical Development* (Oxford: Clarendon Press, 1973), 180–7.

[87] 'Nothing leads us to [inductive] inference but custom or a certain instinct of our nature; which it is indeed difficult to resist, but which, like other instincts, may be fallacious and deceitful' (*E* 159).

[88] In this quotation from the *Enquiry concerning the Principles of Morals* Hume is expressing how Reason enters into *moral* rather than inductive decisions, but there is a great similarity between his views in these two fields, as indicated by the long quotation from the *Dialogues* below. Both involve building on fundamental principles which are themselves non-rational, although the working out of their consequences is nevertheless answerable to Reason.

To whatever length any one may push his speculative principles of scepticism, he must act, I own, and live, and converse like other men; and for this conduct he is not obliged to give any other reason than the absolute necessity he lies under of so doing. If he ever carries his speculations farther than this necessity constrains him, and philosophises, either on natural or moral subjects, he is allured by a certain pleasure and satisfaction, which he finds in employing himself after that manner. He considers besides, that every one, even in common life, is constrained to have more or less of this philosophy; that from our earliest infancy we make continual advances in forming more general principles of conduct and reasoning; that the larger experience we acquire, and the stronger reason we are endowed with, we always render our principles the more general and comprehensive; and that what we call *philosophy* is nothing but a more regular and methodical operation of the same kind. To philosophise upon such subjects is nothing essentially different from reasoning on common life; and we may only expect greater stability, if not greater truth, from our philosophy, on account of its exacter and more scrupulous method of proceeding. (*D* 134)

12. *HUME'S REINTERPRETATION OF 'REASON'*

We have now seen that there is a sense in which Hume is genuinely sceptical about induction, and another sense in which he is not. We can very crudely encapsulate the sceptical and non-sceptical aspects of his position, each within a single sentence, as follows:

> We can see *no reason whatever* for supposing that the past gives any evidence at all regarding what will happen in the future, and hence *no reason whatever* why induction should be a reliable method of inference.

> We cannot help taking for granted that the past is a reliable guide to the future and making inferences on that basis, and there is no other method of factual inference which has this irresistibility; hence we should treat induction as our norm of factual reasoning.

The first of these uses the idiom of the perceptual view of Reason, and aims to express Hume's 'sceptical doubts' concerning the operations of that faculty as thus conceived. But the second suggests a very different, naturalistic, view of human Reason, relieving it of the futile attempt to understand and predict matters of fact through pure perceptual insight, and steering it instead in the direction of a relatively modest inductive science. Hume himself adopts this latter view in most of his writings, counting inductive inference as a genuine operation of Reason, and even (as we have seen in §11) distinguishing it as the normative criterion by which all 'reasoning concerning matter of fact and existence' is to be judged. This can seem paradoxical or confused, for while in his famous argument he very explicitly denies that induction is founded on Reason, and moreover seems to deny that it is itself an operation of

Reason,[89] elsewhere he very clearly states that inductive causal inference is one of Reason's most central operations:

The understanding exerts itself after two different ways, as it judges from demonstration or probability ... reason is nothing but the discovery of [causal] connexion ... (*T* 413–14)

reason, in a strict and philosophical sense, can have an influence on our conduct only after two ways: Either when it excites a passion by informing us of the existence of something ... or when it discovers the connexion of causes and effects ... (*T* 459)

reason [is] ... sufficient to instruct us in the pernicious or useful tendency of qualities and actions ... Reason judges either of *matter of fact* or of *relations*. (*M* 286–7)

However, this apparent inconsistency is not seriously problematic, and its basis is fairly evident. Hume naturally enough begins by using the word 'reason' in a way that is (so to speak) *extensionally* consistent with that of his contemporaries as described in §2 above: he means by it the faculty by which we judge of truth and falsehood.[90] In his argument concerning induction he also uses the word in a way which is *intensionally* consistent with the usage of his contemporaries, meaning a faculty whose operations are all founded on *perception*. But clearly in the aftermath of that argument, he *cannot* continue to use the word in a way that is *both* extensionally *and* intensionally consistent with the standard usage. Given his sceptical conclusion, *either* he must relinquish the idea that we have a faculty of Reason capable of factual inference, *or* he must cease to treat Reason as the conventionally presumed faculty of rational insight. Hume not surprisingly chooses the second option, continuing to acknowledge a faculty of Reason that embraces 'probable' inference, but reinterpreting its nature.[91] His notion of

---

[89] A denial that induction is an operation of Reason is, for example, clearly implicit in two passages from Section V, where Hume recapitulates his argument: 'though he should be convinced, that his understanding has no part in [an inductive inference]' (*E* 42); 'Reason is incapable of any such variation [i.e. the variation with experience that is characteristic of inductive inference]. . . . All inferences from experience, therefore, are effects of custom, not of reasoning.' (*E* 43; cf. n. 48 above).

[90] Though often the word is restricted, by both Hume and his contemporaries, to imply the *appropriate* operation of that faculty, so in this sense *faulty* reasoning or judgement does not count as deriving from Reason. Don Garrett ('Ideas, Reason, and Skepticism: Replies to my Critics', *Hume Studies*, 24 (1998), 171–94, esp. 186–7) argues quite persuasively in response to two of my earlier papers ('Hume's Argument concerning Induction', and 'Hume on Reason and Induction: Epistemology or Cognitive Science?', *Hume Studies*, 24 (1998), 141–59) that such normative usage by itself should not be taken to imply any straightforward ambiguity in the faculty term, so here I have retreated somewhat from the explicit 'multiple senses' interpretation that I previously espoused. (However, my critical view of Garrett's own interpretation is essentially unchanged, as will be clear in particular from §10.3 above.)

[91] Not only is the second option preferable given the obvious association of 'reason' and 'reasoning', but also it enables Hume to retain the faculty word for honorific purposes, to distinguish the proper conclusions of well-disciplined inductive inference from the 'whimsies and prejudices' of the imagination. This motivation is apparent in the footnote at *T* 117, which distinguishes a wide sense of 'imagination' (encompassing all operations that involve the vivacity of ideas) from a narrow sense which excludes demonstration and induction on the ground that they are sufficiently epistemologically respectable to

Reason therefore remains coextensional with Locke's, but behind this façade of similarity hides a philosophical revolution.

The extent of Hume's revolution, though anticipated in Section IV, does not become fully apparent until very nearly the end of the *Enquiry*. By that stage Section VII has emphasized the impossibility of aprioristic knowledge even of our own minds, and has shown that we have absolutely no conception of necessity or power in objects independent of our own inferential tendencies. Section XII then mobilizes a range of further sceptical arguments, the most important of which serve to demonstrate both the weakness of our grounds for any claim to knowledge of the physical world, and also how little we understand of its nature (*E* 151–5). Our belief in body, just like our confidence in induction, turns out to be an irresistible natural instinct with no basis in rational insight. But unlike induction, this instinct yields no promise of scientific progress, for the deeper we try to go in understanding the nature of matter (e.g. by invoking the popular distinction between primary and secondary qualities), the more confusion and absurdity we encounter. Only now can the radical implications of Section IV be fully appreciated. The comfortable idea that the behaviour of matter is somehow 'comprehensible', inspired by the 'naturalness' of Newtonian physics (cf. *T* 111–12), has turned out to be an illusion. Even the effect of colliding billiard balls, widely supposed to be a paradigm of rational understanding, is no more predictable a priori than any other causal interaction. So in place of the seductive but illusory ideal of a science built on perceptual Reason, our *only* recourse is to Humean Reason, modestly looking for correlations in the phenomena without any pretence to ultimate rational insight:

> the utmost effort of human reason is, to reduce the principles, productive of natural phaenomena, to a greater simplicity, and to resolve the many particular effects into a few general causes, by means of reasonings from analogy, experience, and observation. But as to the causes of these general causes, we should in vain attempt their discovery . . . These ultimate springs and principles are totally shut up from human curiosity and enquiry. Elasticity, gravity, cohesion of parts, communication of motion by impulse; these are probably the ultimate causes and principles which we shall ever discover in nature; and we may esteem ourselves sufficiently happy, if, by accurate enquiry and reasoning, we can trace up the particular phaenomena to, or near to, these general principles. The most perfect philosophy of the natural kind only staves off our ignorance a little longer . . . (*E* 30–1)

Hume's Reason is *inductive* Reason, not because we have any rational ground for expecting induction to be reliable, but simply because its irresistibility

---

be counted instead among the operations of 'reason'. See Millican, 'Hume on Reason and Induction', 145–7, for a discussion of this arguably very significant footnote.

makes it the best we have left once the bogus ideal of perceptual insight has been swept away. And so paradoxically, in an age of continuing rationalistic ambition among 'our modern metaphysicians' (*E* 73 n.), induction's greatest sceptic becomes also its foremost champion.

APPENDIX

Hume's Argument Concerning Induction (from Section IV of the *Enquiry Concerning Human Understanding*)

HUME'S OWN STATEMENT OF THE PROPOSITIONS IDENTIFIED IN THE STRUCTURE DIAGRAM

(1) By means of [*Cause and Effect*] alone we can go beyond the evidence of our memory and senses. (*E* 26)

(2) All reasonings concerning matter of fact seem to be founded on the relation of *Cause and Effect*. (*E* 26)

. . . all arguments concerning existence are founded on the relation of cause and effect . . . (*E* 35)

. . . all our evidence for any matter of fact, which lies beyond the testimony of sense or memory, is derived entirely from the relation of cause and effect . . . (*E* 159)

(3) No object ever discovers, by the qualities which appear to the senses, either the causes, which produced it, or the effects, which will arise from it . . . (*E* 27)

It is allowed on all hands, that there is no known connexion between the sensible qualities and the secret powers . . . (*E* 33)

(4) . . . every effect is a distinct event from its cause. It could not, therefore, be discovered in the cause, and . . . the conjunction of it with the cause must appear . . . arbitrary; since there are always many other effects, which, to reason, must seem fully as consistent and natural. (*E* 30)

(5) . . . the knowledge of [cause and effect] is not, in any instance, attained by reasonings *a priori*; but arises entirely from experience . . . (*E* 27)

. . . *causes and effects are discoverable, not by reason, but by experience* . . . (*E* 28)

In vain, therefore, should we pretend to . . . infer any cause or effect, without the assistance of observation and experience. (*E* 30)

(6) . . . nor can our reason, unassisted by experience, ever draw any inference concerning real existence and matter of fact. (*E* 27)

In vain, therefore, should we pretend to determine any single event . . . without the assistance of observation and experience. (*E* 30)

(7) . . . we always presume, when we see like sensible qualities, that they have like secret powers, and expect, that effects, similar to those, which we have experienced, will follow from them. (*E* 33)

We have said, that . . . all our experimental conclusions proceed upon the supposition, that the future will be conformable to the past. (*E* 35)

. . . all inferences from experience suppose, as their foundation, that the future will resemble the past, and that similar powers will be conjoined with similar sensible qualities. (*E* 37)

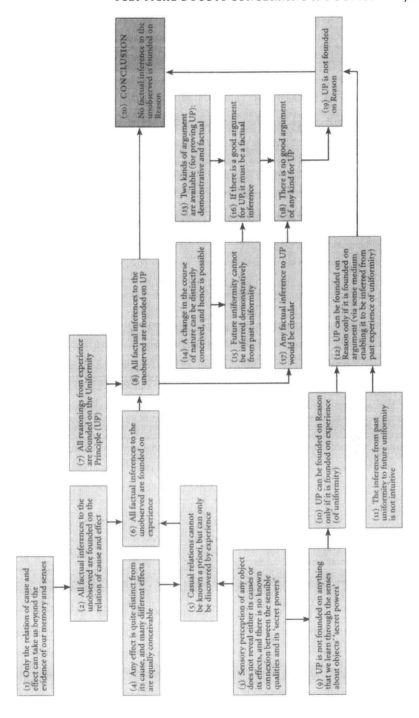

(8) *[This proposition is implicit in the inferential sequence:]* We have said, that all arguments concerning existence are founded on the relation of cause and effect; that our knowledge of that relation is derived entirely from experience; and that all our experimental conclusions proceed upon the supposition, that the future will be conformable to the past. (*E* 35)

(9) . . . the mind is not led to form such a conclusion concerning [sensible qualities' and secret powers'] constant and regular conjunction, by any thing which it knows of their nature. (*E* 33)

(10) *[This proposition is implicit in Hume's transition from considering 'a priori' evidence for the Uniformity Principle to considering experiential arguments for it:]* As to past *Experience*, it can be allowed to give *direct* and *certain* information of those precise objects only, and that precise period of time, which fell under its cognizance: But why this experience should be extended to future times, and to other objects, which, for aught we know, may be only in appearance similar; this is the main question on which I would insist. (*E* 33–4)

(11) The connexion between these propositions [*I have found that such an object has always been attended with such an effect* and *I foresee, that other objects, which are, in appearance, similar, will be attended with similar effects*] is not intuitive. (*E* 34)

(12) There is required a medium, which may enable the mind to draw such an inference, if indeed it be drawn by reasoning and argument. (*E* 34)

(13) All reasonings may be divided into two kinds, namely, demonstrative reasoning, or that concerning relations of ideas, and moral reasoning, or that concerning matter of fact and existence. (*E* 35)

(14) . . . it implies no contradiction, that the course of nature may change . . . May I not clearly and distinctly conceive [such a thing]? (*E* 35)

(15) That there are no demonstrative arguments in the case, seems evident . . . (*E* 35)

. . . whatever is intelligible, and can be distinctly conceived, implies no contradiction, and can never be proved false by any demonstrative argument or abstract reasoning *a priori*. (*E* 35)

(16) If we be, therefore, engaged by arguments to put trust in past experience, and make it the standard of our future judgment, these arguments must be probable only, or such as regard matter of fact and real existence . . . (*E* 35)

(17) To endeavour, therefore, the proof [that the future will be conformable to the past] by probable arguments, or arguments regarding existence, must be evidently going in a circle, and taking that for granted, which is the very point in question. (*E* 35–6)

(18) . . . it may be requisite . . . to show, that none of [the branches of human knowledge] can afford such an argument. (*E* 35)

. . . we have no argument to convince us, that objects, which have, in our experience, been frequently conjoined, will likewise, in other instances, be conjoined in the same manner . . . (*E* 159)

(19) . . . it is not reasoning which engages us to suppose the past resembling the future, and to expect similar effects from causes, which are, to appearance, similar. (*E* 39)

. . . nothing leads us to [infer that constant conjunctions will continue] but custom or a certain instinct of our nature . . . (*E* 159)

(20) I say then, that, even after we have experience of the operations of cause and effect, our conclusions from that experience are *not* founded on reasoning, or any process of the understanding. (*E* 32)

. . . in all reasonings from experience, there is a step taken by the mind, which is not supported by any argument or process of the understanding . . . (*E* 41)

All belief of matter of fact or real existence [is due merely to] a species of natural instincts, which no reasoning or process of the thought and understanding is able, either to produce, or to prevent. (*E* 46–7)

5

Belief and Instinct in Hume's First *Enquiry*

Martin Bell

INTRODUCTION

At the end of Part i of Section V of the *Enquiry concerning Human Understanding* Hume arrives at a conclusion about belief. This is an outcome of his investigation of probable reasoning, a central theme around which much of the work revolves. The sections which follow, about necessary connexion, liberty and necessity, miracles, divine providence, and scepticism, all depend on the arguments of Sections IV and V Part i. After stating the conclusion, Hume goes on in Section V Part ii to some 'farther researches' about the nature and causes of belief. But these further enquiries, we are told, are not needed for understanding subsequent arguments, and can be omitted by readers who have no taste for 'the abstract sciences' (*E* 47).

This is an interesting move. What significance does this bracketing of discussion of the nature of belief have for our reading of the *Enquiry*, and for our understanding of the relations between the *Enquiry* and *A Treatise of Human Nature*?

It is an interesting move for at least this reason. In the *Treatise*, as David Owen has recently stressed,[1] Hume's account of probable reasoning, as based on custom, not rational insight into nature, has, as a corollary, the explicit rejection (*T* 96–7 n.) of earlier theories (Owen discusses Descartes and Locke among others) of what it is to have a belief. On these earlier theories, to have a belief is, in part, to form in the mind an idea of a special kind—a judgement—whose content is structurally and relationally different from ideas formed by mere conception. Very roughly, in the theories Hume rejected belief and conception

---

[1] David Owen, *Hume's Reason* (Oxford: Oxford University Press, 2000), ch. 7.

are different propositional attitudes partly because they are attitudes to different kinds of content. In contrast, in his own theory the content of an idea that is believed by one person and an idea that is conceived but not believed by another can be exactly the same. As a result, he has the task of answering a new question: how does belief differ from mere conception, given that the contents can be the same?

In the *Treatise* Hume seems to take pride both in discovering a novel question and in providing an answer. There does not seem to be any suggestion that the topic is unimportant. In the *Enquiry* the question is bracketed, as if to lessen its importance. This is therefore an interesting difference. What could it suggest about the differences in general between the *Treatise* and the *Enquiry*?

I

Hume's theory of empirical belief is focused on beliefs in 'real existence and matter of fact, beyond the present testimony of our senses, or the records of our memory' (*E* 26). The theory has to answer two questions. First, when we acquire such beliefs, why do they have the specific contents that they do? Why, in particular circumstances, do we come to believe *this* rather than *that*? Secondly, what is it for a certain content to be believed? Why, in particular circumstances, do we come to *believe* something? As has just been noted, for Hume the second question gets its urgency because of the way he answers the first. In the *Treatise*, at least in the main text, Hume ties his answers closely together by invoking the principles of association: resemblance, contiguity, and causation. The first question was answered by his account of probable reasoning as a process in which the mind is not 'determin'd by reason' but by 'a certain association and relation of perceptions' (*T* 88–9). It is custom which produces cases of the natural relation of causation between perceptions, and which therefore explains why, given as input a particular impression of sense or memory, the imagination is 'determined' to conceive the particular idea it does as the output.

In developing this theory, in *Treatise* I. iii. 6 Hume has already started to answer the second question, why the output is believed. At the end of that section he concludes that 'we may establish this as one part of the definition of an opinion or belief, that 'tis *an idea related to or associated with a present impression*' (*T* 93). In the next section he completes the definition of what it is for a certain idea to be believed: 'An opinion, therefore, or belief may be most accurately defin'd, A LIVELY IDEA RELATED TO OR ASSOCIATED WITH A PRESENT IMPRESSION.' (*T* 96). Finally, in *Treatise* I. iii. 7 he explains why the idea that is the conclusion of a causal inference is enlivened, by appealing to 'a general maxim in the science of human nature, *that when any impression becomes present to us, it not only transports the mind to such ideas as are related to it, but likewise com-*

municates to them a share of its force and vivacity' (*T* 98). The *Treatise* account of belief reads as a continuous development of answers to both questions about belief, connected by repeated appeals to the principles of human nature, in particular, the principles of the association of perceptions.

II

The treatment of these topics in the *Enquiry* deliberately breaks the continuity we find in the *Treatise*. The account of the processes of probable reasoning, which explains why the content of a belief in a matter of fact beyond the evidence of sense and memory is what it is, is given first in Section IV and Section V Part i. In these passages Hume refers to the conclusions of probable inferences as 'beliefs' only occasionally (*E* 26, 46, 47), and at no point raises the second question. When he does raise it, in the part bracketed for a restricted audience, we note that his treatment of it is much closer to the second thoughts about belief which Hume added in the Appendix of the *Treatise* (*T* 623–7), and to the summary he gives in the *Abstract* (*A* 653–5).

This might suggest an explanation of the significance of the differences between the two texts which would go roughly like this. In the passages just mentioned, in the Appendix and the *Abstract* where Hume expresses second thoughts about the nature and causes of belief, we find two features that contrast with the main text of the *Treatise*. First, the second thoughts are expressed somewhat tentatively, as if Hume were encountering some problem not fully resolved. Secondly, particularly in the *Abstract* (*A* 655), Hume already draws back from engagement with the detail of his associationist theory of the transference of vivacity. These features are also found in the *Enquiry*: the discussion in Section V Part ii is an investigation 'which, however accurate, may still retain a degree of doubt and uncertainty' (*E* 47), and in any case can 'be neglected' (*E* 47) by most readers. The suggested explanation, then, is that certainly by the time of writing the *Enquiry*, and probably already before then, Hume had both lost some confidence in the detail of his associationist theory and also ceased to regard it as so central to his philosophical purposes. Thus, in the *Enquiry* he merely invites readers who have a 'taste' for it to try their hands at formulating a more satisfactory account of the nature of belief; and he implies that getting a better theory is not essential for the arguments of the rest of the work. The account of the nature of belief is left as a tentative speculation because Hume does not have a more satisfactory and detailed theory to offer, and—since in general the *Enquiry* does not depend on the associationist theory to the extent that the *Treatise* does—because the rest of the work does not need it. That explains the bracketing, and in a way that fits easily with a straightforward reading of the text.

The hypothesis of this paper agrees with the suggestion above to the extent of looking to the revisions Hume made to his initial theory of the nature and causes of belief for a clue to the difference between the *Treatise* and the *Enquiry*. It differs, however, in suggesting that Hume bracketed part of his discussion of belief in the *Enquiry* not because he thought the revised theory was inadequate, or because he had lost confidence in the explanatory power of the association-ist theory, but as a tactical move made appropriate by his overall strategy in the *Enquiry*. This hypothesis suggests that we should hear the note of tentativeness and lack of concern which Hume sounds at this point with a degree of suspi-cion. On this approach, the bracketing of *Enquiry* V. ii is interpreted as a rhetori-cal device whose purpose can be understood in terms of two factors: the need for and nature of Hume's revisions to his initial theory in the *Treatise* of the nature and causes of belief, on the one hand, and, on the other, the differences between the *Treatise* and the *Enquiry* with respect to their intended audiences and aims.

III

Beginning with the revisions to the theory of the nature and causes of belief, let us remind ourselves of the problem which Hume had already confronted in the *Treatise*. In the main text he claims that, given that the difference between belief and simple conception does not consist in a difference in content, it can consist only in a different amount of force and vivacity: 'When you wou'd any way vary the idea of a particular object, you can only encrease or diminish its force and vivacity. If you make any other change on it, it represents a different object or impression.' (*T* 96).

Force and vivacity is the feature by which perceptions are distinguished into ideas and impressions, and ideas of memory are distinguished from ideas of the imagination. Hume's first thought, then, was that the same thing distinguishes beliefs from simple conceptions. Beliefs, too, are more forceful and lively thoughts than ideas of the imagination, although they are less forceful than ideas of memory (*T* 153). Beliefs are ideas related to present impressions, as the explanation of causal inference shows, and they are also more lively than ideas simply conceived by the imagination. In this way the accurate definition of what a belief is was obtained (*T* 96).

The definition is not repeated in the *Enquiry*. Instead of saying that the dif-ference between belief and simple conception can consist only in a difference in force and liveliness, Hume there speaks first of all of the difference as one of 'some sentiment or feeling' (*E* 48). This is following the revisions that Hume made in the Appendix to the *Treatise*. To the passage from the main text quoted above, where the only possible difference between belief and simple conception is said to be a difference in the liveliness of the idea, Hume added a reference to the place in the Appendix where he said that there is an 'error' in the main text,

> where I say, that two ideas of the same object can only be different by their different degrees of force and vivacity. I believe there are other differences among ideas, which cannot properly be comprehended under these terms. Had I said, that two ideas of the same object can only be different by their different *feeling*, I shou'd have been nearer the truth. (*T* 636)

Why was this an error? In both the *Treatise* and the *Enquiry* Hume proposes that beliefs are ideas with a distinctive character, ideas which are conceived in a distinctive manner. He claims that this manner of conception is explicable by reference to a general maxim of the theory of human nature. The general maxim is that when objects are associated in the imagination by any of the three principles of association, and when one object is presented to the mind in sense or memory, then the idea of the associated object is enlivened by the associated impression of the sense or idea of the memory (*T* 98, *E* 50–1).

In the exposition of the theory of belief in the two texts there is a significant difference in the moment at which this maxim is invoked. *Treatise* I. iii. 7 is called 'Of the Nature of the Idea, or Belief', and the next section, where the general maxim is stated, is called 'Of the Causes of Belief'. This suggests that the nature of belief had already been established before Hume turned to examining its causes. Yet all that had been said about the nature of belief was in the definition, 'a lively idea related to or associated with a present impression'. That is, all that had been said about the nature of ideas that are believed was that they are more lively than ideas merely conceived by the imagination, where 'lively' simply invokes the notion of force and vivacity as employed generally in the theory of human nature.

When, in *Treatise* I. iii. 8, Hume at once appeals to the general maxim, he therefore generates a difficulty to which he himself draws attention in the following section, 'Of the Effects of Other Relations and Other Habits'. The problem is that, according to the maxim, ideas can be enlivened by association with the data of sense and memory by any of the three principles of association. Yet 'we find by experience, that belief arises only from causation' (*T* 107), and not from resemblance or contiguity. If all there is to the nature of belief is the enlivening of ideas by objects presented by sense or memory, and if the general maxim is correct, then 'it shou'd follow, that that action of the mind [belief] may not only be deriv'd from the relation of cause and effect, but also from those of contiguity and resemblance' (*T* 107).

Hume's solution involves a move away from the definition of belief as merely a lively idea. Instead, in *Treatise* I. iii. 9 he gives a lengthy description of how just certain perceptions—sense-impressions, ideas of memory, and ideas inferred from these by custom—are 'comprehended' together as 'systems' of 'realities' (*T* 107–10). Believed ideas are ideas comprehended as realities, and they have a characteristic feeling to the mind, for each such idea 'takes its place in the imagination, as something solid and real, certain and invariable'. In contrast, for example, to be reminded of a friend by seeing a picture of him is indeed to have one's idea enlivened, but it is not to acquire a belief in his real existence. There is a difference between 'the conviction of any opinion' and 'the vivacity of any conception'. These *feel* different, and that difference is not captured by a definition in terms of the theoretical dimension of force and vivacity. It is a difference which can only be given a phenomenological description.

In Section V Part ii of the *Enquiry* Hume makes sure that this problem does not arise. He does not define belief in terms of force and vivacity, but at once provides a phenomenological description of the mental act which the reader already identifies as 'belief', 'which is a term, that every one sufficiently understands in common life' (*E* 49). Only having done so does Hume then refer to the general maxim of the enlivening of ideas by any of the principles of association, and he stresses that this allows an explanation of the causation of belief only by analogy. He had, indeed, said in the *Treatise* that the general maxim was used only to provide an analogy (*T* 107); but now in the *Enquiry* he is in a position to avoid the objection that the cases are not analogous, but the same phenomenon. The same examples of the effects of resemblance and contiguity, as well as causation, are used in both texts; but armed with the prior phenomenological description of belief, identified as in 'common life' instead of theoretically defined, Hume can be safely explicit: 'We may observe, that, in these phaenomena, the belief of the correlative object is always presupposed; without which the relation could have no effect. The influence of the picture supposes, that we *believe* our friend to have once existed. Contiguity to home can never excite our ideas of home, unless we *believe* that it really exists.' (*E* 53–4).

In the *Enquiry*, therefore, Hume avoids the problem he had in the *Treatise* when he claimed that beliefs are nothing but ideas enlivened by association. He is committed to the view that what distinguishes belief is a feeling or sentiment, and that this is not a separable impression distinct from the idea which is believed. But also it is not enough simply to invoke the general phenomenon of transference of vivacity. The feeling of belief characterizes the way, or 'manner', in which believed ideas occur in the imagination. Can anything more be said beyond this phenomenological description?

Throughout the investigation of the nature of probable reasoning in Section IV and Section V Part i of the *Enquiry* Hume takes it as obvious that the conclusions of such inferences are beliefs in matters of fact. When he speaks of 'matters of fact', he frequently speaks also of 'real existence' (for example, *E* 26, 27, 35, 42, 164). Indeed, in the *Treatise* he defines a conclusion about a matter of fact as one 'concerning the existence of objects or of their qualities' (*T* 94).

As noted before, the conclusions of inferences, which previous philosophers had called judgements and thought of as having a distinctive structure, are, for Hume, merely conceptions. The immediate conclusion of a simple causal inference is an idea, a conception. Any such idea has an object, in the intentional sense, that of which it is an idea. But the possibility of conceiving an object, for Hume, shows only that such an object is possible, not that it is actual or real. There is, however, no distinct idea of actuality or real existence: 'We have no abstract idea of existence, distinguishable and separable from the idea of particular objects. 'Tis impossible, therefore, that this idea of existence can be annex'd to the idea of any object, or form the difference betwixt a simple conception and belief.' (*T* 623).

The content of a belief is an idea, and where a certain object is the object of that idea, to believe the idea is to believe in the real existence of the object. The linguistic assertion of a belief, in an existential proposition, does not express an idea of the real existence of the object, for there is no such idea, only the idea of the object itself. Again, Hume argues that to believe in the real existence of the object of an idea is to conceive the idea of that object in a certain manner. It is this manner which Hume attempts to describe phenomenologically, by saying that it is 'a more vivid, lively, forcible, firm, steady conception of an object, than what the imagination alone is ever able to attain. This variety of terms, which may seem so unphilosophical, is intended only to express that act of the mind, *which renders realities, or what is taken for such, more present to us than fictions*' (*E* 49, my emphasis).

The question, therefore, is, why should that distinctive manner of conception which Hume has shown to be the product of custom also be the distinctive manner of conception which is what it is to believe in the real existence of an object?

Hume's answer is that the process whereby there arises the distinctive manner of conception of ideas which are conclusions of causal inferences is analogous to, but not simply a case of, the process whereby ideas are enlivened through any of the three principles of association. But what is distinctive about the conclusions of causal inferences, and what makes them beliefs in real existence, is their association with impressions of the senses and ideas of the memory. This connexion to impressions of sense and ideas of memory is important, not simply because these perceptions are more lively than mere ideas of the imagination, but because occurrences of these *particular* types of lively perceptions are instinctively and immediately taken by the mind to be presentations of real existences. This is what Hume appeals to in *Treatise* I. iii. 9 in the course of explaining why ideas enlivened by resemblance or contiguity alone are not thereby beliefs. The manner of conception which characterizes the conclusions of causal inferences is derived from impressions of sense and ideas of memory, and these are immediately and non-inferentially regarded as presenting their objects as real existences. Since, however, in causal inference the imagination, when presented with a given object by sense or memory, conceives at once the idea of some particular object, this instinctive transition 'conveys to it all that force of conception, which is derived from the impression present to the senses' (*E* 54). As a consequence, the manner in which the conclusions of causal inferences is conceived is a continuation of, because an immediate transference from, the manner in which the mind treats the objects presented to it by sense and memory. Thus sense-impressions, ideas of memory, and conclusions of causal inferences together form a system of 'realities, or what is taken for such'.

IV

The previous section reviewed some of the problems which beset Hume's early account of the nature and causes of belief in the *Treatise*, and how his revised theory, in the Appendix of the *Treatise*, the *Abstract*, and the *Enquiry*, avoids them. The revised theory makes central the connexions between real existence, impressions of sense and memory, and the conclusions of causal inferences. Just before the start of Section V Part ii Hume characterizes the way in which beliefs in real existence arise as 'a species of natural instincts' (*E* 46–7). Hume's account of belief in the *Enquiry* implicitly connects two 'instincts'. One is the instinctive belief in the real existence of the objects of ideas produced by causal inference. The other is the instinct which makes its appearance later on, in Section XII, where he discusses the 'evidence of *sense*' (*E* 151). Significantly, this evidence has already been identified, in Section V Part i, as what constitutes the 'foundation' of 'the knowledge of any real existence' (*E* 46). Here we have two instincts, and they are connected. It is this connexion which provides an answer to the question why the instinctive manner of conception of the conclusions of causal inferences is also belief in real existence and matter of fact. But the two connected instincts are not discussed together. One would have expected that they would have been, and—assuming that the account in the previous section of the revised theory of the nature and causes of belief is correct—the place to do so would have been Section V Part ii, the bracketed section. The thought here is that the reason why Hume does not at once discuss together the two instincts is also the reason for the bracketing.

In turning our attention to the second instinct, in Section XII, where Hume discusses the evidence of the senses, we are at once struck again by the difference between the *Enquiry* and the corresponding discussion, this time in *Treatise*

I. iv. 2. Both works discuss the evidence of the senses in the context of sceptical arguments. Both identify a certain initial and instinctive attitude of the mind towards the impressions of the senses. In the *Treatise* Hume describes this attitude as a 'vulgar supposition' (*T* 18); it consists in taking it that 'our perceptions are our only objects'(*T* 218). That is, it consists in an immediate acceptance of the objects of impressions as real objects, things in the world, not representations of such things. Since such real objects are believed to have 'continued' and 'distinct' existence (*T* 188), Hume offers a long and detailed explanation of how such a belief could arise on the basis of that 'vulgar supposition'.

No such account is provided in the *Enquiry*. Here Hume speaks of 'a natural instinct or prepossession, to repose faith in [our] senses', and explains that it is this 'natural faith' which leads us to treat the objects of sense-impressions as themselves real objects:

It seems also evident, that, when men follow this blind and powerful instinct of nature, they always suppose the very images, presented by the senses, to be the external objects, and never entertain any suspicion, that the one are nothing but representations of the other. This very table, which we see white, and which we feel hard, is believed to exist, independent of our perception, and to be something external to our mind, which perceives it. (*E* 151–2)

It is perfectly clear that as soon as Hume begins to examine this 'instinct' or 'natural faith' in the evidence of the senses, in both works, he does so from the standpoint of the reflective theorist of human nature, and that from this standpoint the natural faith or instinct cannot stand up to scrutiny. In the *Treatise* Hume explores the way in which a distinctively philosophical theory, according to which sense-impressions are only images which represent real objects, emerged from reflection on the 'vulgar supposition' and its consequences. But after having done so, he remarks,

I begun this subject with premising, that we ought to have an implicit faith in our senses, and that this wou'd be the conclusion, I shou'd draw from the whole of my reasoning. But to be ingenuous, I feel myself *at present* of a quite contrary sentiment, and am more inclin'd to repose no faith at all in my senses, or rather imagination, than to place in it such an implicit confidence. (*T* 217)

In the *Enquiry* he points out again the conflict he finds between the 'vulgar supposition' operative in common life, and the stance of reflective philosophy:

But this universal and primary opinion of all men is soon destroyed by the slightest philosophy, which teaches us, that nothing can ever be present to the mind but an image or perception . . . (*E* 152)

If the interpretation of this paper is correct, then Hume's revised theory must make a connexion between the nature and causes of belief and the initial natural and instinctive attitude of trust or faith in 'the testimony of the senses', and in the 'records of the memory' (by means of which sense-impressions are repeated in the imagination). The theory of the causation of belief shows that beliefs arise, as a 'necessary result', as a 'species of natural instincts' (*E* 46–7), when that initial natural instinct is in place and is unimpeded in its operation. However, according to Hume, as soon as the mind adopts the reflective standpoint of the theorist of human nature, in order to provide a detailed 'anatomy' of this 'operation of the soul', the natural instinct and with it the natural reliance upon the conclusions of probable reasoning is brought into question and subjected to sceptical doubts.

The 'anatomy' of human nature is the pursuit of one of the 'species of philosophers' Hume describes in Section I of the *Enquiry*. Such a philosopher addresses an audience 'of the learned and the wise', taking them 'in the light of a reasonable rather than an active being', and by means of 'accurate and abstruse' dissections seeks to lay bare the underlying principles of human nature. The other species of philosopher addresses a wider audience, not only the wise but also those who are 'active' in the affairs of 'common life', and the purpose of such a philosopher is (in a phrase Hume borrows from Addison, an exemplar of this species) 'only to represent the common sense of mankind in more beautiful and more engaging colours' (*E* 7).

The author of the *Treatise* belongs unequivocally to the first species. The author of the *Enquiry* aims to belong to both, and to carry out philosophy in a style which 'can unite the boundaries of the different species' (*E* 16). The method of the first species is abstract reasoning. The method of the second species (the portrait painter) is the easy and obvious depiction of human nature. Hume's aim is to do philosophy by 'reasoning in [an] easy manner' (*E* 16).

Philosophy in this easy manner is directed as much to the person engaged in common life as it is to the learned person in the study. Hume's main conclusion, that beliefs in matters of fact are a species of natural instincts, is wholly new to both, and Hume wants both to accept it. He wants all his readers to accept his account of what beliefs in matters of fact really are, but he does not want to disturb those beliefs themselves. In fact, if his theory is correct, then beliefs of this kind cannot be disturbed, provided that human nature is left to itself. Sceptical problems can affect our natural convictions, and bring everything into doubt. But if the theory is correct, such excessive scepticism cannot be long-lasting. Furthermore, no way of acquiring beliefs, other than as nature determines, can be recommended as in some way better. The deepest and most abstract dissections of human nature may for a while disturb our natural trust in senses, memory, and probable inference, but no positive alternative is forthcoming.

When Hume establishes that probable reasoning is founded on custom and not reason, he comments that, despite what this conclusion from the philosophical dissection room has revealed about probable reasonings, 'there is no danger, than these reasonings, on which almost all knowledge depends, will ever be affected by such a discovery' (E 41). Here the reflective stance of the anatomist does nothing to undermine the authority we accord to probable reasoning; it merely reveals what that authority is (E 41–3). But the dissection of the natural instinct to trust the evidence of our senses has no such benign outcome. To the conflict between the results of philosophical anatomy and the engaged consciousness of common life, 'Carelessness and in-attention alone can afford us any remedy.' (T 218).

In the one case, natural belief can be harmonized with profound reflection. The two species of philosophy can be united in a single work. But in the case of the instinct to trust our senses and memory, the lesson of the *Treatise* is that profound reflection on the nature of this instinct cannot be made to harmonize with the deliverances of nature. Hume's revised account of belief solved one problem, but because it did so by connecting the two instincts, it generated another. The new problem was a problem about how far the author of the *Enquiry*, writing in the 'easy manner' and attempting by doing so to address both the learned and the intelligent layperson, could safely report all the discoveries of the philosophical dissection room. The problem was not one of what the revised theory of belief should be, nor of what the method of investigating the theory of human nature should be, but it was a problem about writing. In the broad sense, it was a question of rhetorical strategy. Given the different audience and aims of the *Enquiry*, compared to the *Treatise*, the detailed anatomy should not be pursued too far. Better to bracket it. In this way, the connexion made by the revised theory between the two instincts becomes less obvious, and that is to be welcomed precisely because, as the anatomist knew, the two instincts differ in how they relate to everyday, engaged consciousness. In presenting the revised theory of the nature and causes of belief, Hume knew, too much abstruse analysis runs the risk of temporarily undermining natural convictions and thereby rendering the theory itself, in a mind engaged in the everyday world of business and action, merely incredible. That would be to lose the audience for the new style of philosophy that Hume intended to carry out in all his writings after the *Treatise*.

6

Hume, Belief, and Personal Identity

Justin Broackes

Hume in the *Treatise* was proud of his view of belief. 'This act of the mind has never yet been explain'd by any philosopher' (*T* 96–7 n.), he says early in the discussion; and he congratulates himself on the coherence of his views, 'the agreement of these parts, and the necessity of one to explain another' (*T* 154). But in the Appendix, only twenty-one months later, he confesses to difficulties: 'even when I think I understand the subject perfectly, I am at a loss for terms to express my meaning' (App. 628). Famous for the second thoughts on personal identity, the Appendix actually takes more than twice as long modifying the theory of belief, admitting even an outright 'error' (App. 636). By the time of the *Enquiry*, another eight years on, Hume's anxieties seem to have got the better of him altogether. Section V Part ii is introduced as containing 'speculations, which, however accurate, may still retain a degree of doubt and uncertainty'; 'the following enquiries may well be understood, though it be neglected' (*E* 47).

Abstracting from many other respects in which Hume's formulations vary,[1] I shall argue that Hume offers us three kinds of conception of belief.[2] Taking 'steadiness and vivacity' to represent the characteristic features of belief, there are three kinds of thing to which those features apply. Belief may be

---

[1] There are two other notable dimensions of variation. First, besides the terms 'vivid' and 'steady' to describe the characteristic feature of belief, Hume also uses 'lively, forcible, firm' (*E* 49), '*stronger*' and 'more *intense*' (*A* 654)—terms which we cannot assume are equivalent. (Comments in Book II of the *Treatise*, for example, suggest that Hume wanted a distinction between 'enliven[ing]' an idea and 'infix[ing]' it in the imagination; *T* 453.) Secondly, particularly in the *Treatise*, he sometimes makes it part of his definition of belief that it be 'associated with a present impression' (e.g. *T* 96), and even that it 'aris[e] only from causation' (*T* 107)—which suggests that Hume on these occasions is importing into his view of what belief consists in his view of when belief is justified. I shall say very little about these dimensions of variation. On the second, see John Passmore, *Hume's Intentions* (London: Duckworth, 1952; 3rd edn. 1980), 61–4, 94–104.

[2] The principal discussions are in *Treatise* I. iii. 7–10, App. 623–32, *A* 652–5, and *Enquiry* V. ii. As will emerge, the three views should probably not be called *theories* of belief—which would imply more systematicity and completeness than I would claim for all of them.

(*a*)   a steady and vivid *idea*,

(*b*)   a steady and vivid *conception of an idea*, or

(*c*)   a *feeling* or *sentiment* (of steadiness and vivacity) which is 'annexed to' an idea (*E* 48).

(I shall use '(A)', '(B)' and '(C)' to refer to the corresponding views of the nature of belief.) The puzzle is not so much that Hume should have changed his mind, as that neither before nor after his change of mind did Hume have a stable view. In the *Treatise* he seems to have held both (A) and (B) without any sense of tension. The Appendix officially introduces (C) and gives reasons to doubt (A); but in the *Enquiry* all three views are still in evidence. The later work shows signs of exasperation as well as uncertainty, in repeating almost verbatim more than three pages from the *Treatise* and the Appendix.[3] It is almost as though, when it came to the mechanics of belief, Hume still wanted a theory (cf. *E* 14–15); but finding himself unable to write from scratch anything he could be fully confident of, he reused material that at least took a definite view, whatever its other shortcomings.

1. THE TREATISE *AND THE* FIRST VIEW OF BELIEF

My main concern is with the place of belief within Hume's map of the mind. He calls a *perception* 'whatever can be present to the mind' (*A* 647), and he divides perceptions into *impressions* and *ideas*. Into which category then do beliefs fall?

They cannot simply be ideas. First, when one person believes what another disbelieves, they 'form all the same ideas' (*T* 95) but not the same beliefs; so 'The idea of an object is an essential part of the belief of it, but not the whole' (*T* 94). Secondly, the best candidate idea that one might annex to a conception in order to turn it into a belief is that of existence; but in fact 'the idea of existence is nothing different from the idea of any object' (*T* 94; cf. *Treatise* I. ii. 6). To think of God and to think of God as existing are one and the same thing; and it is not the same as believing that he exists. The Appendix adds a third reason: 'The mind has command over all its ideas'; it does not have control over its beliefs; so belief cannot consist merely in 'a new idea, annex'd to the conception' (App. 623–4; cf. *E* 47–8). The premiss that the mind has command over all its ideas is doubtful if 'ideas' include dreams and hallucinations (as the talk of 'disease or madness' at *E* 17 would suggest); but it makes good sense if 'ideas' are what some

---

[3] Citing page and line numbers: *E* 49.10–50.2 come almost verbatim from App. 629; *E* 50.2–50.11 from App. 625; and *E* 51.10–53.15 from *T* 99–101. There are other places in the *Enquiry* where Hume reuses earlier material, but nowhere else does it form such a high proportion of the total on a topic. Interestingly, the 'missing shade of blue', on which Hume also had reason to feel himself embarrassed, is another case where he discharged his obligations by simply copying from his earlier text. (*E* 20.27–21.26 correspond to *T* 5–6.)

people now call 'propositional contents' and Hume called 'conceptions'. We can form propositional contents at will; we cannot take up the attitude of belief towards them at will; so indeed, beliefs are not simply propositional contents.

The Appendix adds reasons why belief cannot on the other hand involve simply an additional impression: among other things, that 'nothing ever enters into our *conclusions* but ideas, or our fainter conceptions' (App. 625).

What then is the nature of belief? Hume's main argument (*T* 95–6) is this:

(1) There are cases where one person believes exactly what another person disbelieves.

(2) The only way in which two ideas may differ while still being ideas of the same object is in respect of 'force and vivacity'.

Hence (3) Belief may be defined as 'A LIVELY IDEA RELATED TO OR ASSOCIATED WITH A PRESENT IMPRESSION' (*T* 96).

Apart from the demand in the conclusion for a 'present impression',[4] the argument is close to being valid. If we supply an additional premiss,

(2') Belief and disbelief involve nothing but ideas,

then (1) and (2) imply that belief and disbelief involve nothing but ideas differing only in force and vivacity. And from there it is only a small step to the thought that of the two, beliefs must be the livelier, and hence to the conclusion that belief is, precisely, a 'lively idea'. The premises are not uncontroversial, however, and we shall see that Hume himself came to repudiate (2) explicitly, and (2') implicitly.

Even in this first exposition Hume seems to be pulled between the two views (A) and (B) which I mentioned above. Some passages suggest that in belief and disbelief there are two ideas, differing only in 'force and vivacity', as on view (A); others suggest that there is only one idea but two different attitudes towards it, as on view (B). On the first view, belief is a certain kind of idea; on the second, it is a certain kind of conception of an idea. Hume's earlier statement that the difference 'lies not in the parts or composition of the idea' but 'in the *manner*, in which we conceive it' (*T* 95) leans toward the second view, which will be considered in detail later. (Cf. *T* 96: belief 'can only change the *manner* of our conceiving [ideas]'.) But Hume comes down firmly on the side of view (A) in his definition and in many other places. He defines belief as 'A lively idea . . .' (*T* 96). He talks of how we 'vary the idea of a particular object' (*T* 96)—which presumably results in a different, if closely related, idea of the same object. And later in the *Treatise* he continues to describe belief as 'nothing but a strong and lively

---

[4] The demand may seem to come out of the blue at this point in the argument. Hume has prepared for it in the preceding section, however, in the last lines of *T* 93.

idea deriv'd from a present impression' (*T* 105), and as 'a lively idea related to a present impression' (*T* 110; cf. *T* 427).

The principal attraction of this view lies in its coherence with the rest of Hume's picture of the mind. The objects of the mind vary along a single dimension of force and vivacity. At the opening of the *Treatise* ideas and impressions are distinguished by their degrees of vivacity; memories and beliefs are later placed at intermediate positions on the same scale. Just as 'the *belief* or *assent*, which always attends the memory and senses, is nothing but the vivacity of those perceptions they present' (*T* 86), so the belief that attaches to our ideas of the unobserved consists merely in the vivacity of those ideas.[5] Perhaps the greatest attraction for Hume is that this fits so neatly into a mechanical theory of the production of beliefs. *Treatise* I. iii. 8 develops a theory of how it is by the *communication of vivacity* from an impression present to the senses or memory that our idea of the (unobserved) cause or effect comes to be a belief, rather than a mere conception. When I find a watch on a desert island (to use an example from *E* 26), and come to believe that someone has been there before, there are two processes at work—the association of perceptions, and the communication of vivacity. Given a constant conjunction of (perceptions of) watches and people, the association of ideas (a form of habit) gives me a propensity to form an idea of a person when presented with an impression of a watch. That idea is transformed into a belief, by receiving some of the vivacity that attaches to my impression of the watch: ' 'tis from some present impression we borrow that vivacity, which we diffuse over the correlative idea' (*T* 154). This communication of vivacity occurs not just between causally related ideas, but also in a lesser degree between ideas related by contiguity or resemblance (*Treatise* I. iii. 9; cf. *E* 49–54)—a process which Hume describes in marvellously picturesque terms.[6] In probabilistic reasoning, 'the vivacity of thought' can even be 'divided and split in pieces' (*T* 129; cf. *T* 134): instead of one strong belief (say, that some side or other of a die will come up), I may have six weak and unvivid beliefs that side 1 will come up, that side 2 will, and so on.

The unity of Hume's thought here extends even into his view of the passions and of morality. Suppose that I believe that another person has a headache and I offer her some aspirin. How can a pain that I do not feel serve as a spur to my

---

[5] A subsidiary argument for Hume's view of belief uses one similarity between impressions and beliefs to prove a further similarity: beliefs have similar effects to impressions; the effects of impressions are due to their vivacity; so beliefs must resemble impressions in vivacity (see *T* 119–20; cf. *T* 103). The argument rests on Hume's principle that 'The same cause always produces the same effect, and the same effect never arises but from the same cause.' (*T* 173)—a principle which leaves it obscure how we could ever say that cars break down for a variety of reasons.

[6] See the talk of vividness being conveyed 'as by so many pipes or canals' (*T* 122; cf. *T* 386), quoted below in n. 25.

own action? Hume offers a theory. 'In sympathy there is an evident conversion of an idea into an impression. This conversion arises from the relation of objects to ourself.' (*T* 320). As at all times, I have an impression of myself. ('"Tis evident, that the idea, or rather impression of ourselves is always intimately present with us'; *T* 317.) The other person is related to me by resemblance, and perhaps also contiguity. The vivacity of my impression of myself will be conveyed to related ideas—hence my idea of her pain becomes 'so inliven'd as to become the very sentiment or passion' (*T* 319). It is almost as though I feel her pain, and this impression in me (the enlivened idea of the pain) is capable of serving as an impulse to action, therefore, just as my own pains are. (For more details, see e.g. *T* 289, 317–20, 380, 386, 575–6.) As belief is central to Hume's philosophy of the understanding, so sympathy is central to his moral philosophy: it is 'the chief source of moral distinctions' (*T* 618). What is remarkable is that Hume traces both belief and sympathy to the same process: the communication of vivacity from an impression to an idea. In the *Treatise* vivacity and the communication of it are the fundamental notions of Hume's whole philosophy of mind.[7]

The simplicity of Hume's system is bound to arouse suspicion. Can such architectural symmetry have been achieved without grinding away some of the natural irregularities of the building materials? In systematizing the mind, has Hume not distorted it?[8] With the theory of belief, the most important of established lines of criticism concern (*a*) Hume's imagistic conception of thought and (*b*) his attempt to characterize the principal differences between impressions, beliefs, and mere conceptions along a single dimension—whether of force, vivacity, steadiness, or anything else. Without being able to consider these fully, it is worth taking one criticism in each category and seeing how Hume can

---

[7] Hume makes much of the analogy between the two cases: 'What is principally remarkable in this whole affair is the strong confirmation these phænomena [in the domain of the passions] give to the foregoing system concerning the understanding, and consequently to the present one concerning the passions; since these are analogous to each other.' (*T* 319; cf. *T* 380).

It is interesting to compare the fate of the two explanations in Hume's later works. In the *Enquiry concerning the Principles of Morals* Hume drops his theory of the operation of sympathy, without offering a substitute. 'We must stop somewhere in our examination of causes' (*M* 219 n.). In the *Enquiry concerning Human Understanding*, on the other hand, causal beliefs are still traced to the transference of vivacity. (*E* 54: 'The thought moves instantly towards [the idea], and conveys to it all that force of conception, which is derived from the impression present to the senses.') Given that this apparatus remains in place, we can see how uncomfortable it would have been for Hume really to suspend judgement in the *Enquiry* on the nature of belief: if impressions differ from ideas in respect of vivacity (as Section II argues), and if it is some measure of that same distinguishing feature which is communicated to an idea to turn it into a belief (as *E* 54 suggests), then a characteristic feature of beliefs must be their vivacity.

[8] 'Is this the man that Nature made? . . . This is a puppet, surely, contrived by too bold an apprentice of Nature, to mimic her work. It shows tolerably by candle light; but, brought into clear day, and taken to pieces, it will appear to be a man made with mortar and a trowel' (Thomas Reid, *Inquiry into the Human Mind* (1764), repr. in *The Works of Thomas Reid*, ed. Sir William Hamilton, 6th edn. (Edinburgh, 1863), i.103).

respond to the first round of fire, though it is doubtful how much longer he could defend his position.

A major objection is that the content of at least some beliefs could not possibly be carried simply by an image, which is what Hume conceives his ideas to be. Take, for example, the thoughts that all tomatoes are red, that the particular tomatoes now being thought of are red, and that all tomatoes if thought of are red: the differences between these thoughts can hardly be fully captured by whatever differences there are in the images they bring to mind. Hume might reply, however, using his theory of abstract ideas (from *Treatise* I. i. 7; cf. *E* 158 n.), according to which a general term 'raises up an individual idea, *along with a certain custom*' (*T* 21, my emphasis). The difference between the various tomato-thoughts lies, he might say, not just in the ideas brought to mind by the words, but in the associated customs. This opens many further questions: how far Hume can really claim to have an account of generality in thought, as well as in language; how far the theory implies that, for consistency, Hume should then be saying that the contents of our beliefs are ideas with associated 'customs', rather than simply ideas; and how far the 'ideas' really do any work once the 'customs' have been brought into play. All these are questions I shall leave aside. Whatever suspicions we may have that Hume could not answer them satisfactorily, it is worth noticing that his imagistic conception of beliefs cannot be fully assessed in isolation from his theory of abstract ideas.

An objection in the second category is this. Can the vivacity of an idea be changed without the content changing? Maybe—to build on the colour comparison in *T* 96—an idea of a blue vase can be brightened up without coming to represent a different shade of blue. But what of the idea of a *bright* blue vase? Can that be brightened up without coming to represent an even brighter blue vase? However we take the talk of force and vivacity—and there are certainly times when Hume wanted not to place too much weight on it[9]—as long as the characteristics of belief are intrinsic features of an idea, they seem liable to affect its content.

Here again preliminary replies are available. First, the experiences of looking at a scene with one eye and with two eyes may (if the case is carefully enough constructed) differ intrinsically without differing in pictorial content. It seems possible, therefore, that two images or ideas might in a similar way differ intrinsically without differing in what they represent. The question would remain, however, whether variation in that kind of respect could really constitute the

---

[9] This is especially clear in the *Enquiry*. 'I confess, that it is impossible perfectly to explain this feeling or manner of conception. . . . And in philosophy, we can go no farther than assert, that *belief* is something felt by the mind, which distinguishes the ideas of the judgment from the fictions of the imagination.' (*E* 49). But this still does not stop Hume giving a '*description* of this sentiment' which begins 'vivid, lively, forcible . . .'.

crucial difference between perception, belief, and mere conception—a question on which I can only feel considerable doubt. A second defence of Hume is also available: two photographs printed from one negative may differ in brightness (or indeed in tinge of colour) while in a perfectly good sense representing the very same scene. And we are often quite capable of adjusting to these differences so as to recognize the sameness of the properties represented, and to recognize which properties they are. The point is an important one, and Hume could have appreciated an analogue of it in the domain of painting; but it is not enough to get him out of difficulty. It may be the case that a fainter image and a darker image can be *recognized* to represent the same scene; but that requires a state of mind that consists in more than the mere *having* of the images in question (perhaps the state of mind includes also the *taking* or *treating* of each image in a certain way). Hume, however—at least when developing this first conception of belief—seems to want belief, like perception, to consist merely in the *having* of an image or idea.[10]

Hume may have imagined he could escape the challenges so far. But there is one criticism within the second category, the force of which Hume himself seems to have acknowledged. It was raised by Hume's kinsman Henry Home, a prominent advocate and writer on anthropology, criticism, and philosophy, who as a Scottish judge from 1752 took the title of Lord Kames. In the *Essays on the Principles of Morality and Natural Religion*, a sympathetic reply to much of Hume's *Enquiry*, Kames points out that vivacity cannot be enough to distinguish belief from mere conception. On Hume's view, 'credulity and a lively imagination would be always connected, which does not hold in fact. Poetry and painting produce lively ideas, but they do seldom produce belief.'[11]

It may well have been this objection that actually prompted Hume in the Appendix to the *Treatise* to renounce the view that the only way in which ideas may differ while still being ideas of the same object is in respect of 'force and

---

[10] David Pears makes beautifully clear the danger that change of image may change content. (See *Hume's System* (Oxford: Oxford University Press, 1990), 48–9; cf. 40–4.) Unlike me, however, Pears thinks Hume clearly 'wanted to avoid the notion that strength and vivacity are pictorial properties of ideas of belief' (p. 50). In support he quotes from *T* 96, where Hume is insisting that the content of a belief may be the same as that of a disbelief. Unfortunately, however, this will not establish that Hume had a non-pictorial conception of liveliness unless we also know that Hume himself was alive to the danger that any pictorial property would affect the content, and that he thought that danger could not be averted. I think he was aware of the danger, but believed that vivacity was uniquely capable of averting it; and as I have been arguing here, there are reasons—insufficient though they are—to support that view. On Pears's own understanding of force and vivacity, see the end of §1 below.

[11] Henry Home, Lord Kames, *Essays on the Principles of Morality and Natural Religion* (Edinburgh, 1751), p. II, Essay I, p. 222. (The first two editions were published anonymously; the third he acknowledged.) Kames continues later: 'Can any man doubt, who has not an hypothesis to defend, that poetry makes a stronger impression than history? Let a man, if he has feelings, attend the celebrated Garrick in the character of Richard, or in that of king Lear; and he will find, that dramatic representations make strong and lively impressions, which history seldom comes up to' (pp. 223–4).

vivacity' (premiss (2) above)—thus renouncing his first view of belief.[12] The Appendix admits that 'poetical enthusiasm' produces vivid ideas, but does not produce belief (App. 630–1). Vivacity of an idea, therefore, cannot constitute belief. 'Had I said, that two ideas of the same object can only be different by their different *feeling*, I shou'd have been nearer the truth.' (App. 636). In different ways this suggests both the second and third conceptions, which I shall take up in the sections that follow.

I have been working with a fundamentally pictorial interpretation of terms like 'force and vivacity'. I should comment briefly on two other interpretations. Some have treated force and vivacity as (i) a disposition to a certain kind of behaviour, or to a certain kind of judgment;[13] others have treated it as (ii) a disposition of the mind *to keep hold of* and *not to release* the idea in question.[14] (The first is a tendency to a certain kind of behaviour, the second a tendency to a certain kind of mental act.) On the first view, Hume would be recognizing a point stressed in Ryle: that at least some beliefs need to be understood as dispositions. This view cannot be ascribed to Hume. Hume lays great weight upon the 'Influence of belief': he devotes the whole of section I. iii. 10 in the *Treatise* to it, and treats beliefs as 'the governing principles of all our actions' (App. 629). But this tendency to influence action is not to be *identified* with 'force and vivacity'; rather, it is supposed to *derive from* it. The influence of beliefs is said to 'proceed from' their force and vivacity (*T* 119), and to 'flow from' their solidity and force (*T* 121). When Hume talks of vivacity and force, he hopes to have found an

[12]　Though Kames's *Essays* were not published until 1751, he met Hume shortly after the publication of the *Treatise*. According to Boswell, Kames 'shewed him his Objections, and David, who was not very ready to yield, acknowledged he was right in every one of them' (G. Scott and F. A. Pottle (eds), *Private Papers of James Boswell from Malahide Castle* (New York, privately printed, 1928–34), xv. 273–4; quoted in D. F. Norton, *David Hume—Common-Sense Moralist, Sceptical Metaphysician* (Princeton: Princeton University Press, 1982), 174). Unfortunately, we have no direct account of what those earlier objections were.

[13]　H. H. Price and D. M. Armstrong find this dispositional conception in Hume, though not on its own. For Price, though the occurrence conception of belief dominates, there are hints in Hume also of something like R. B. Braithwaite's view that the belief that *p* is a tendency to act as if it were true that *p*. 'It might be suggested that this is what the "forcefulness" or "strength" of the believed idea would amount to—its tendency or liability to affect one's action' (H. H. Price, *Belief* (London: Allen & Unwin, 1969), 187). Armstrong holds a similar view: Hume 'wavers between' characterizing belief by this kind of behavioural effect, and characterizing it by 'internal difference' (D. M. Armstrong, *Belief, Truth and Knowledge* (Cambridge: Cambridge University Press, 1973), 71). John Bricke raises an objection to Armstrong similar to my own, in *Hume's Philosophy of Mind* (Edinburgh: Edinburgh University Press, 1980), 122.

[14]　David Pears seems to hold this second kind of view: the vivacity of memory must be a '*behavioural property*' of the image, e.g. its being 'stubborn and difficult to alter' (*Hume's System*, 44; see also, on the force and vivacity of belief, pp. 49–50). MacNabb seems to find traces of both (i) and (ii) in Hume: he mentions the conception of belief as a disposition to assent (though MacNabb 'cannot honestly say for Hume that he clearly recognised' that this is what people 'most often' mean by belief), and he also talks of belief as being 'fix[ed] . . . in the mind to the exclusion of rival ideas'. See D. G. MacNabb, *David Hume* (London: William Collins, 1951), 75–6.

intrinsic feature of our ideas which in turn *is responsible for* that influence. Suggestion (ii) is more promising: Hume talks of belief as 'a firmer conception, or a faster hold, that we take of the object' (App. 627), and that does suggest a tendency *not to lose hold* of the idea. The difficulty here is not with the idea that this conception weighed with Hume, or that he may have had it in mind when he talked of force and solidity. The difficulty is with the idea that this can have been Hume's dominant and fundamental conception of what was distinctive of belief. The vivacity attaching to memory and beliefs is supposed to be the same (though in lesser degree) as that attaching to impressions and also the hallucinations of 'disease or madness' (*E* 17). The common feature of these vivid images can hardly be unalterability—some hallucinations are vivid but highly changeable—whereas one could easily take it to be pictorial vividness. Beliefs are being fitted into a continuum of cases already characterized by impressions on one side and 'faint images' on the other (*T* 1); the fundamental conception really does seem to be pictorial, and in applying it to belief, Hume continues to make comparisons with the 'liveliness or brightness' of a particular shade of colour (*T* 96). Hume might have been better off using a behavioural property as the 'vivacity' attaching to belief, and there are certainly hints that such a conception came to weigh with him; but it was not his fundamental conception, nor the one that plays the dominant part in his mechanisms of the mind. As we have already seen, Hume became increasingly dissatisfied with the idea of taking vivacity alone to characterize belief; but the other two suggestions discussed here would not have satisfied him as general substitutes for vivacity either.

2. THE SECOND VIEW: A VIVID CONCEPTION OF AN IDEA

We have already seen suggestions in the *Treatise* of a second view, on which belief would consist in a certain kind of conception of an idea. Belief is 'only a strong and steady conception of any idea' (*T* 96–7 n.); belief is 'a more vivid and intense conception of an idea' (*T* 103).[15] These phrases are ambiguous if we allow that 'idea' may sometimes apply not just to an idea, but (as famously in Locke) to what an idea is *of*. Hume might be saying either that belief is a more vivid conception *of an object* (i.e. a more vivid idea of that object), or that belief is a more vivid conception *of an idea of an object*. The former is the view I have already found in Hume; but, as we shall see, the latter is definitely present as well.

---

[15] Further examples are these: 'the mind . . . applies itself to the conception of the related idea with all the force and vivacity it acquir'd from the present impression' (*T* 99); 'belief is nothing but a more forcible and vivid conception of an idea' (*T* 107); and cf. *T* 119–20.

Hume often talks of belief as a 'manner of conceiving'. How does this fit with the two views so far identified? Strictly, a manner of conceiving can hardly be literally identical with either an idea or a conception of an idea. (A *manner* cannot be identical with an *individual thing*.) But they can be closely linked: conceiving in the appropriate manner may be identical with *having* an appropriate kind of idea: 'conceiving vividly' might be applied to *having a vivid idea* (i.e. thinking of an object vividly, as on view (A)) or alternatively to *having a vivid conception of an idea* (i.e. conceiving an idea of an object vividly, as on view (B)). The idiom is compatible in principle, therefore, with either view; and it is actually used in conjunction with them both. Sometimes belief varies 'the manner, in which we conceive *any object*' (*T* 96, my emphasis)—which fits with view (A). At other times belief changes 'the *manner* of our conceiving [the *ideas*]' (*T* 96), and we 'conceive *that idea* in a stronger and more lively manner' (*T* 116, my emphasis)—which fits with view (B). I shall therefore treat those passages which describe belief as a certain 'manner of conceiving' as merely a variant of the two views that have already been identified.

Hume shows no embarrassment at the ambiguity in his expression. Perhaps he thought the differences between views (A) and (B) unimportant. One passage, however, constitutes unambiguous support for the second view, and shows how radically it differs from the first. Hume has been explaining how causal reasoning results in a belief, by the communication of vivacity from an impression present to the senses or memory. An objection occurs to him: surely I can reason from a mere *idea* to a belief (e.g. from my idea of red to the belief that I once had an impression of red), using the principle that all ideas are derived from impressions. But that forces the question: where does the vivacity of the resultant belief come from, if there is no *impression* present which can have supplied it?

... to this I answer very readily, *from the present idea*. For as this idea is not here consider'd, as the representation of any absent object, but as a real perception in the mind, of which we are intimately conscious, it must be able to bestow on whatever is related to it the same quality, call it *firmness, or solidity, or force, or vivacity*, with which the mind reflects upon it, and is assur'd of its present existence. The idea here supplies the place of an impression, and is entirely the same, so far as regards our present purpose. (*T* 106)

An impression or 'vivid perception' is therefore, after all, not needed to support a belief—an idea will do as well, as long as the mind *reflects upon it* with force and vivacity. And we may presume that the vivacity associated with the resultant belief is of the same character: it is the mind's reflection upon the idea that is lively, rather than the idea itself.

This passage marks a substantial departure from the first view of belief—one that results in tension, as we shall see, with Hume's official theory of the mind.

Instead of merely one dimension of variation among perceptions, Hume is now allowing two. Instead of classifying perceptions simply as more or less vivid, he is classifying them as (*a*) more or less vivid in themselves, and (*b*) more or less vividly apprehended by the mind. As a result, he is in a position to distinguish a vivid perception faintly apprehended, from a faint perception vividly apprehended:[16] the idea of red in the example above (from *T* 106) will be an instance of the latter type, and it will be the vivacity of the mind's apprehension that is transferred to the associated idea, not the (non-existent) vivacity of the object of that apprehension.

This second view harmonizes well with Hume's description of belief as arising from a general 'disposition' of the mind, when it has been 'elevate[d] and enlivene[d]' by a present impression, which has the effect that 'every action, to which the mind applies itself, will be more strong and vivid, as long as that disposition continues' (*T* 98). The suggestion is that the mind is, so to speak, activated or 'hyped up' by the presence of an impression, and everything in the mind is thereby coloured or brightened up. The idea has its problems, in that we might end up with too many beliefs on sunny days with vivid impressions and too few on dull ones—but it has the virtue of making belief a matter more of the mind's *attitude*, than of its *object*.

This second view evidently escapes one of the main problems that faced view (A): that a change in the vivacity of an idea is liable to change its content. Jonathan Bennett puts the objection in an extreme form: Hume's view 'implies, for example, that there is no difference between believing that the Sahara is warm and entertaining the thought that it is extremely hot'.[17] This is a fair challenge to view (A), but it completely misses (B): a vivid apprehension of the idea that the Sahara is warm is clearly different from a faint apprehension of the idea that it is extremely hot. But if this second view has its advantages, it also has what Hume was bound to regard as disadvantages—to which we shall return after setting out the third view.

3. THE THIRD VIEW: A SENTIMENT OR FEELING OF BELIEF

When in the Appendix Hume abandons what I identified as premiss (2) of his main argument for the first view, he suggests a different principle: 'Had I said,

---

[16] The same apparatus may be able to provide Hume with a reply to the accusation that he cannot make a proper distinction between the idea of a hat and the idea of the idea of a hat. On the present suggestion (which is one way of developing the hint in the last paragraph of *Treatise* I. iii. 8, *T* 106), Hume could distinguish these as the vivid apprehension of a faint perception of a hat, and the faint apprehension of a faint perception of a hat. The mind boggles at the thought of how the theory might ramify.

[17] Jonathan Bennett, *Locke, Berkeley, Hume: Central Themes* (Oxford: Clarendon Press, 1971), 294.

that two ideas of the same object can only be different by their different *feeling*, I shou'd have been nearer the truth.' (App. 636). His new suggestion is that 'belief consists merely in a certain feeling or sentiment . . . When we are convinc'd of any matter of fact, we do nothing but conceive it, along with a certain feeling, different from what attends the mere *reveries* of the imagination.' (App. 624).[18]

In some ways this is a development of view (B). On Hume's conception of the mind as perfectly aware of itself,[19] we would expect that if the mind conceived an idea in a vivid manner (as on view (B)), then it would be aware of doing so, and it would therefore (as on view (C)) have a particular 'feeling or sentiment' of that vividness of conception. The terms that characterized the idea in view (A), and the conception of the idea in view (B), reappear to characterize the feeling in view (C): 'this different feeling I endeavour to explain by calling it a superior *force*, or *vivacity*, or *solidity*, or *firmness*, or *steadiness*' (App. 629). But any ascription of a view to Hume at this point is necessarily tentative. Hume's statements present problems of interpretation. (How can a feeling literally be called *force*, *vivacity*, or *solidity*? Presumably it must be a feeling *of* force, vivacity, or solidity. And how can one have a feeling of force, vivacity, or solidity *tout simple*? Force, vivacity, and solidity are properties, and it is hard to see how you can have a feeling of force, vivacity, or solidity without having a feeling of the force, vivacity, or solidity of something in particular. What then is the something? On the suggestion of this paragraph it is the *conception of the idea* that one feels to be forceful, lively, and solid, but a good measure of interpretation goes into the suggestion.) Hume himself is diffident. 'Provided we agree about the thing, 'tis needless to dispute about the terms' (App. 629). But though he thinks 'a definition of this sentiment' may be 'a very difficult, if not an impossible task' (*E* 48), this does not stop him offering 'a *description*' of it (*E* 49).

In the *Enquiry* this third view (C) is the official line: 'the difference between *fiction* and *belief* lies in some sentiment or feeling, which is annexed to the latter' (*E* 48). What is surprising is to find the other two views present as well, the first of which was effectively repudiated eight years before, in the Appendix to the *Treatise*. As on view (A), belief is described as 'a more vivid, lively, forcible, firm, steady conception of an object, than what the imagination alone is ever able to attain' (*E* 49). And Hume repeats an expression of view (B) from the Appendix:

---

[18] Are 'sentiments' impressions or ideas? Other passages suggest that Hume uses the words 'sentiment' and 'feeling' interchangeably for what he at other times calls impressions. '[W]e always find, that [our thoughts or ideas] resolve themselves into such simple ideas as were copied from a precedent feeling or sentiment.' (*E* 19). We distinguish vice and virtue 'by means of some impression or sentiment they occasion . . . tho' this feeling or sentiment is commonly so soft and gentle, that we are apt to confound it with an idea' (*T* 470; cf. *T* 472).

[19] '[S]ince all actions and sensations of the mind are known to us by consciousness, they must necessarily appear in every particular what they are, and be what they appear' (*T* 190).

'belief consists not in the peculiar nature or order of ideas, but in the *manner* of their conception, and in their feeling to the mind' (*E* 49 = App. 629). Why did Hume keep all three views in play, yet refuse to acknowledge any of them with confidence? In each case, Hume was, I think, under the influence of both a strong reason to espouse the view and a strong reason to reject it.

The problem with the first view has already been noted: there are cases of vivid ideas (for example, in poetical enthusiasm) that yet are not beliefs. But Hume was also under pressure to keep the theory. On his official view, the objects of the mind are ideas and impressions; only if beliefs are simply a special variety of idea or impression can the official view be literally sustained.

The pressures with the second view are more subtle. Its attraction lies in the idea that the difference between believing something and merely entertaining the idea of it consists, as we might say (in the modern idiom), in our attitude to the idea, or, as Hume puts it, in the way in which we conceive it. The first difficulty is relatively superficial, involving a double use of the word 'idea'. An idea may be either what one has when one has a thought, or instead the *content* of such a thought (something that can also be the object of another propositional attitude). Belief is a certain kind of idea, according to the first use—and maybe a vivid one—but it is only its content that is an idea, according to the second. A parallel problem may even arise with the word 'content'. One may ask, 'What are the contents of the mind?' and reply in Humean fashion, 'Ideas and impressions'. But then what about beliefs? They cannot *be* ideas—for one idea may be common to a belief, a disbelief, and a mere conception. On the other hand, they cannot involve anything else either—since 'there is nothing ever enters into our *conclusions* but ideas' (App. 625). So they end up involving a *way of conceiving*, or else 'a peculiar feeling', that mysteriously counts as neither an idea nor an impression. These problems arise partly from a double use of these terms. As one might say, deliberately oscillating between them: the contents of the mind are more than just contents. One can have different ideas simply by having different attitudes to the same idea. And if we then re-examine the claim that the mind consists simply of ideas and impressions, it begins to seem less of a datum: if 'idea' is used in the second sense (for *propositional contents*), then the mind will also include attitudes to ideas; and if 'idea' is used in the first sense (for *beliefs*), then the mind will contain other items (like mere conceptions and disbeliefs) too.

4. THE SECOND VIEW AND HUME'S THEORY OF PERSONAL IDENTITY

So far, this might seem to improve the chances of success for the second view. It would seem open to Hume to amend his theory to: 'the mind consists of impressions, ideas and *attitudes* to ideas (or ways of having them)'. But Hume would, I think, have been unhappy with this. For such 'ways of having ideas' would seem to involve the mind's standing in a certain relation to an idea: the mind would conceive the idea vividly, the idea would present itself to the mind in a vivid manner. And to allow an irreducible relation between the mind, on the one hand, and its ideas, on the other, would to Hume have smacked of Cartesianism. The mind that stood in this relation to ideas would be in danger of turning into a 'Cartesian' self, a substance that was merely the supposed support of the properties of the self.

I shall set out quickly the disagreement between Hume and Descartes on the nature of the self, and then investigate how deep are the difficulties that Hume's view poses for his view (B) of belief. I shall try to unearth the source of Hume's theory of the self—ironically in a misapplication of a good Cartesian principle—before ending with the suggestion that if we set aside that flawed theory of the self, then view (B) emerges, at least in structure, as an attractive conception of belief.

One of the main motivations for the theory of personal identity in the *Treatise* is Hume's desire to rebut Descartes's view of the mind—though he can hardly be said to have understood it. There are many aspects to Descartes's view.[20] But the main object of Hume's attack was the idea that the mind was a substance (or, as we might say, a 'self-sufficient thing'), and thoughts were 'modes' of it (or, as we might say, its 'properties'): a mind could have different thoughts at different times rather as a piece of wax could have different shapes at different times.[21] Hume's reply, in short, is that he is unaware of any 'self' endowed with 'perfect identity and simplicity' which somehow supports the existence of his particular perceptions; indeed,[22] whatever others may find in themselves, Hume is 'certain there is no such principle in' him (*T* 252).[23] '[S]etting aside', he says with irony, 'some metaphysicians . . . I may venture to affirm of the rest of mankind, that they are nothing but a bundle or collection of

[20]   There is a good general discussion in ch. 5 of John Cottingham, *Descartes* (Oxford: Blackwell, 1986).

[21]   See e.g. Descartes, *Principles of Philosophy*, I. lxiv.

[22]   In *The Mind of God and the Works of Man* (Oxford: Clarendon Press, 1987) Edward Craig plays down this further claim (see esp. ch. 2 §5). Hume is principally concerned, he thinks, to show that we have no good reason to believe in the existence of such a self, rather than that there is definitely no such thing. I find this very doubtful. Hume insists, over and over again, and in widely separated places, that impressions and ideas are self-sufficient existences, capable of existing on their own—which would make no sense if he believed that impressions and ideas might really, for all he knew, only be modes of a real self. The suggestion that Hume is concerned here with epistemology *rather than* metaphysics is hard also to reconcile with Hume's use of principles like 'Whatever is clearly conceiv'd may exist' (*T* 233)—for these principles seem designed precisely to bridge the gap between epistemology and metaphysics.

[23]   Hume's injustice to Descartes begins here: Descartes never claimed that one was directly aware of the mind; rather, one is aware of thoughts, recognizes that thoughts cannot exist without a thinker, and then *concludes* (as in the *cogito*) to the existence of the mind. (See Descartes, *Principles of Philosophy*, I. xi and lii.)

different perceptions, which succeed each other with an inconceivable rapidity, and are in a perpetual flux and movement' (*T* 252). The difficulty this poses for the theory of belief is that, if ideas and impressions literally 'constitute the mind' (*T* 253), then there hardly seems room to talk, as view (B) does, of the different ways in which the mind may apprehend or 'reflect upon' an idea.

Critics have pointed before to places where Hume's science of the mind threatens to conflict with the bundle theory.[24] In some cases the threat is fairly easily averted. The idea of time, like that of space, arises 'not . . . from a particular impression', but 'from the manner, in which impressions appear to the mind' (*T* 36). But there seems a good prospect of reconciling this with the bundle theory: the 'manner' in which temporally or spatially extended perceptions appear to the mind may be reducible to the (temporal and spatial) relations of perceptions (or parts of perceptions) *to other perceptions* in the bundle—rather than requiring irreducible relations of perceptions *to the mind*.

A second threat arises from Hume's talk of propensities of the mind, for example to 'spread itself on external objects' (*T* 167) and to 'feign the continu'd existence of the perceptions of our senses' (*T* 254; cf. 208). But such propensities can be reconciled with the bundle theory: we need only say, for example, that minds, that is, *bundles of ideas*, are of such a kind that when an internal impression of necessity occurs in a bundle, ideas of a corresponding necessity in external objects tend to occur in the bundle also. There is no need for this feature of ideas and impressions to be grounded in *something else* (such as a mind over and above its impressions and ideas)—it is simply a brute fact about ideas and impressions that they tend to occur in those patterns, just as the gravitational attraction of bodies is a brute fact about them (cf. *T* 12–13).

The problem with the second view of belief is more serious.[25] We cannot reinterpret the talk of the mind's relation to an idea as a matter of the patterns in

---

[24] e.g. Norman Kemp Smith, *The Philosophy of David Hume* (London: Macmillan, 1941), e.g. 49, 74; and Jane L. McIntyre, 'Is Hume's Self Consistent?', in D. Norton, N. Capaldi, and W. Robison (eds), *McGill Hume Studies* (San Diego, Tex.: Austin Hill Press, 1979).

[25] Jane McIntyre identifies another source of conflict ('Is Hume's Self Consistent?') that is also hard to resolve—harder, indeed, than she thinks. The conflict is this: 'the force of *custom* in accounting for our beliefs and complex ideas seems to presuppose the continuing existence of a self underlying perceptions' (p. 84); her proposal is that the conflict is only superficial, because the past perceptions which have given rise to a person's present associations of ideas may actually persist. A bundle of perceptions can be said to learn from experience in that earlier perceptions persist among later perceptions; and 'Perceptions that persist through various collections can, of course, influence any of the collections in which they occur' (p. 87). There is a difficulty with this. It is unfortunate to require that the earlier perceptions that set up associations of ideas always continue in existence. May I not have a habit of associating watches with people without keeping in my present bundle my earlier perceptions of watches and people, or even memories of them? (After all, 'the mind makes the transition without the assistance of the memory'; *T* 104.) McIntyre talks at one point of 'the *underlying* persistence of individual perceptions' (p. 87, my emphasis); but if underlying presence is *unconscious* presence in the mind, that itself is hard to reconcile with Hume's usual attitude that the mind is aware of those perceptions that it has. *(continued overpage)*

which ideas and impressions occur, for Hume has effectively denied that belief can be reduced to the having of impressions or ideas. Belief is not simply having an idea ('The idea of an object is an essential part of the belief of it, but not the whole.'; *T* 94), and yet it does not involve an additional idea or impression (e.g. App. 623–7). It is not even possible to interpret belief as a matter of the *relation* of an idea to the *other ideas in the bundle*. For Hume would surely insist that beliefs are 'distinct existences', which could exist on their own, just like any other perception (*T* 207, 233, App. 634)—whereas if belief consisted ultimately in the relation of an idea to the rest of the bundle, then that belief would not be capable of existing (at least as a belief) independently of the rest.

Hume has good reasons and bad reasons for rejecting the Cartesian notion of a self. There are arguments of a familiar type suggesting that our impressions could never have furnished us with an idea of mental substance (e.g. *T* 232–3). But there is a more interesting argument. The Cartesian could not even save his notion of a substance by defining it as '*something which may exist by itself*', because that definition 'will never serve to distinguish substance from accident, or the soul from its perceptions'. For, Hume insists, our perceptions are them- selves self-sufficient things, so they would themselves by that definition count as substances. '[S]ince all our perceptions are different from each other, and from every thing else in the universe, they are also distinct and separable, and may be consider'd as separately existent, and may exist separately, and have no need of any thing else to support their existence.' (*T* 233; cf. *T* 107, 244; App. 634).

Hume is leaping out of the frying-pan into the fire—abandoning an incoher- ent notion of the self for an incoherent notion of its thoughts. The idea that one of my perceptions—that pain I had on Monday morning—could exist, on its

---

I suspect in fact that if Hume has any conception of what mediates or carries the influence of experi- ence from past to present, then it is a mechanical and physical model. As the mind has repeatedly pro- ceeded from one perception to another, animal spirits have repeatedly taken a certain path in the brain, thereby opening up passages which make it easier for the animal spirits to flow along the same path again. Hume describes the communication of vivacity from impression to idea using this kind of image. 'The vividness of the first conception diffuses itself along the relations, and is convey'd, as by so many pipes or canals, to every idea that has any communication with the primary one.' (*T* 122). The same pipes figure in the mechanisms of sympathy, where 'If I diminish the vivacity of the first conception, I diminish that of the related ideas; as pipes can convey no more water than what arises at the fountain.' (*T* 386). John P. Wright has suggested that such passages are not merely figurative, but signs of a seriously meant physio- logical theory of the movement of 'animal spirits' which Hume inherited from Book II of Malebranche's *Recherche de la vérité* (see John P. Wright, *The Sceptical Realism of David Hume* (Minneapolis: University of Minnesota Press, 1983), ch. 5, esp. pp. 216 ff.). Hume could equally, of course, have found the root idea in Descartes's *Passions de l'âme* (e.g. 1. xxxiv, xxxvi) or indeed in much post-Galenic physiology. However it was first suggested to Hume, this hydraulic picture is obviously hard to reconcile with the notion that the mind is strictly only a bundle of ideas and impressions. At best Hume could take the view that per- ceptions in the mind are *causally* affected by patterns of occurrence in the brain, while being *ontologically* distinct and self-sufficient; but he would be left with the implication that the association of ideas occurs not because of intrinsic features of items in the mental realm, but because of activities at the level of the animal spirits in the brain.

own, as the one object in the world, is very probably incoherent, and Hume certainly fails in his arguments to defend it. My 'perceptions' are indeed often (though not always) independent of each other—in the sense that I could believe that *p* without believing that *q*, even though I actually believe both. But the implication that my belief that *p* is therefore a self-sufficient object independent of everything else, and capable of existing on its own, is fallacious. Two dents on a car door may be independent of each other, in that each could exist without the other; but this does not mean that either of them could exist without the door.[26]

One source of the problem is Hume's misuse of the Cartesian principle that 'Whatever is clearly conceiv'd may exist'. Descartes allowed that whatever is clearly and distinctly conceived is possible, and used it to prove the real distinction between mind and body. But he insisted that simply to be able to think of *a* without *b* is not sufficient for proving that *a* could exist without *b*—the conception has to be clear and distinct, and of *a* as a complete thing. Descartes would deny the inference to the possibility of ideas' existing on their own without the mind whose ideas they are—for we do not have a clear and distinct conception of a thought without its thinker. Thought and thinker differ, as Descartes puts it, *modally*, and not *really*.[27] Hume, on the other hand, though he usually demands a 'clear' idea, hardly treats this as a stringent additional demand: for him, whatever is distinguishable in thought (however casually) is separable, and may therefore exist separately.[28]

---

[26] Cf. John Cook, 'Hume's Scepticism with regard to the Senses', *American Philosophical Quarterly*, 5 (1968), 1–17; P. T. Geach, *Truth, Love and Immortality* (London: Hutchinson; Berkeley: University of California Press, 1979), 45–47.

[27] Cf. Descartes, *Principles of Philosophy*, 1. lx–lxi ff., and First Set of Replies, in *Œuvres de Descartes*, ed. C. Adam and P. Tannery, 11 vols., rev. edn. (Paris: Vrin/CNRS, 1964–76), vii. 120–1.

[28] There is an interesting tension between Hume's use of this principle and his views on abstract ideas. One reason for his rejection of Lockean abstract ideas is that 'the precise length of a line is not different nor distinguishable from the line itself; nor the precise degree of any quality from the quality' (*T* 18–19). In getting a general idea, say, of the length of this line (which is something it shares with various other lines), what happens is not that we manage to separate or distinguish an idea of the line's length from an idea of the line, but rather that we 'consider [the line and its length] together, since they are in effect the same and undistinguishable; but still view them in different aspects, according to the resemblances, of which they are susceptible' (*T* 25). It is a case of 'partial consideration' (*T* 43), not of separation of ideas.

This view of abstract ideas leaves Hume open to an objection to his thesis of the self-sufficiency of perceptions: just as the length of a line is inseparable from the line, so also it might be that an impression or idea is inseparable from a mind; in both cases, if we imagine that we have a clear idea of the one without the other, we are wrong—we are actually only attending to the resemblance of the mind (or line) to other minds (or other lines) in some respects and not others. Hume at one point recognizes a challenge of this kind (*T* 244–5): admitting that you cannot separate (as a self-sufficient item) the motion of a body from the body itself, he considers the objection that you similarly cannot separate a thought from its thinker— so a thought would be, in the ancient terminology, an 'action' of the soul and, in the modern, an 'abstract mode'. Hume's reply is dogmatic: 'Our perceptions *are* all really different, and separable, and distinguishable from each other, and from every thing else, which we can imagine; *and therefore* 'tis impossible to conceive, how they can be the action or abstract mode of any substance.' (*T* 245, my emphasis). He does

What Hume is trying to do is to separate *A's thought* from *A*—to abstract from *How it is for A* the *How it is*. The temptation to do this is finely described by Bernard Williams:

We can say that the general form of a question about someone's conscious state is *how is it for A?* Wondering whether *A* is in pain, I take up in imagination *A*'s point of view, and encounter from that point of view the possibilities that there is pain or not, that it does or does not hurt . . . If I then revert to the third-personal or objective point of view, and try to form a conception from there of just what is in the world when *A* is in pain, the temptation is to try to write into the world, in some hazy way, the appropriate content of *A*'s experience—as we might naturally, but too easily say: the pain. But in taking the content of *A*'s experience, and putting it into the world as a thing we can conceive of as there, we are in effect trying to abstract from *how it is for A*, the *how it is* and leave it as a fact on its own, which however has the mysterious property that it is available only to *A*, and can only be known directly to *A*.[29]

This is precisely what Hume does, and it is the main source of his problems with personal identity. Given simply a handful of *how it is*'s, there can seem no place for *A*, except as a bundle of those contents, or else as a mistake. And yet to take *A* as such a bundle would seem to make his identity both artificial and fragile. Descartes would never have had the same trouble—for *how it is for A* would from the start be a mode, dependent on, and inseparable from the substance *A*—whatever the problems his conception of that purely mental substance may have on other accounts.

Williams replies to the misconception behind Hume's move: 'The *only* perspective on the contents of *A*'s consciousness is the perspective of *A*'s consciousness.' Hence, 'What we need as an objective fact in the world, conceivable from a third-personal point of view, is not the *it is so* of *it is so for A*, but *it is so for A* itself.' The picture of self-sufficient mental contents, essentially independent of everything else in the world, such as the facts of physiology, speech, and behaviour, is very probably incoherent: 'If there were a class of autonomous

point out a difference between the cases: 'Motion to all appearance induces no real nor essential change on the body, but only varies its relation to other objects.' whereas the passage of ideas in a person over time does seem to constitute 'a radical difference'. But this difference between the cases is irrelevant to Hume's claim: change in the length of a tapeworm over time also seems a real, and not just relational, difference; yet Hume would not for that reason say that the length of the tapeworm at any one time could be separated from the tapeworm itself. In the argument of *T* 245 the idea that the successive states of the person are independent of each other seems to have been confused with the idea that they are independent *tout court*; and the idea that over time there is strictly no persisting substance may have covertly supported Hume's refusal to refer attributes to a substance even at a single time. The views on identity over time have their own problems (see e.g. T. Penelhum, 'Hume on Personal Identity', *Philosophical Review*, 64 (1955), 571–89); my present points are that they lend no real support to the views on substance at a single time, and that the latter views are themselves in conflict with what Hume says about abstract ideas.

[29] Bernard Williams, *Descartes* (Harmondsworth: Penguin, 1978), 295.

items in the world which were the contents of consciousness, then there would have to be a coherent conception of the world from which just those items had been removed, leaving all those other facts as they were.' And yet there seems no such conception.[30]

There may be a special sense in which it is fine to say 'A's thought could exist even if A did not', if we are using 'thought' for a special kind of abstract object— e.g. for a kind of belief that a may have and b may lack, and c may take a long time to acquire, which might therefore exist even if a didn't have it. (Perhaps such a notion is involved when one person says to another: 'You've obviously had that belief for longer than I have'.) But if we are using 'thought' for an individual mental content, then it cannot be separated from the person whose thought it is. The case is parallel to that of properties and their bearers: (given a suitable defence of the existence of universals or properties) *redness* might exist even if this postbox did not; but we can make no sense of the idea that *the redness of this postbox* could exist even if the postbox did not. The important point is that recognizing this dependence of thoughts on thinkers is one way to free ourselves of the image of the bare self, endowed with 'perfect identity and simplicity', which is the supposed bearer of those thoughts. It is Hume's belief in the self-sufficiency of thoughts that makes him unable to see Descartes's self as anything other than a property-less substratum, a thing intrinsically without thoughts, which yet somehow 'possesses' them by the same sort of extrinsic relation as holds between me and my briefcase.[31] That kind of conception of the self is dispensable, and indeed incoherent; in so far as Hume shies away from the second view of belief because it would commit him to just such a self standing in a relation of vivid apprehension to an idea, he is absolutely right to do so. But it is not the view that Descartes actually held.

A modern analogue of the second view can also escape Hume's worries. The second view, in its most general form, is that belief consists in one's standing in a certain relation to an idea. On a proper conception, the idea need not be a self-sufficient but essentially mental item, nor need the other term of the relation be a mysteriously simple and unchanging self. Some modern conceptions of belief as a propositional attitude can be seen then as developments of this second view.

---

[30] Ibid., 295–6.

[31] In actual fact, of course, Descartes conceived the self in no such way: it was a thing which had different thoughts at different times in the same common-or-garden way as a piece of wax has different shapes. The loss of a coherent conception of the relation of a substance to its modes and attributes (or, as we would say, of a thing to its properties) extends in British philosophy from Locke to Russell (with the notable exceptions of Kames and to some extent Reid) and it is sad that it is at least partly due to Descartes's misleading comparison of it to the relation of a person to his clothes (see e.g. Descartes, Sixth Set of Replies, in *Œuvres de Descartes*, vii. 461).

Belief might, for example, be a matter of standing in a certain relation to an idea, in the sense of *proposition* or Fregean *thought*.[32] (So different people could literally believe the same thing.) And the thing that stands in that relation to the idea could simply be a *person*—a flesh-and-blood, talking, thinking thing—not a 'Cartesian self'. This is only one of many available views; the point is that the obstacles to the second view that existed for Hume with his theory of personal identity do not rule out all varieties of such a view for everyone.

In this section I have explored the problems that Hume's second view of belief, as a vivid conception of an idea, encountered from his theory of personal identity. Hume never remarks on the conflict: my claims are (i) that there is a tension between the second view of belief and Hume's theory of personal identity;[33] (ii) (tentatively) that a dim awareness of this may explain why Hume never made a formal declaration of the advantages of view (B) over view (A), even after he was committed (by App. 628) to renouncing the detail of the latter; and (iii) that none the less, of the two views, it is the theory of personal identity that is the more problematic, with its claim that ideas and impressions are independent, self-sufficient things. Hume noticed correctly that an unchanging

---

[32] Hume does not make much of the notion of a proposition (indeed at *T* 96–7 n. he makes a virtue of eroding the distinction between propositional and non-propositional contents). But Kames, before criticizing the detail of Hume's theory, gives credit to it for making clear 'that belief is not any separate action or perception of the mind, but a modification of our perceptions, or a certain *manner of conceiving propositions*' (*Essays*, 221, my emphasis). Kames's conception of a proposition can hardly have been Frege's conception of a thought; the terms indicate a family of related views. Kames's fundamental criticism of Hume is that he should not assume that the 'modification of the idea' in question is a 'lively conception', for this is 'but one of many modifications' (p. 223).

[33] There is a question over how far the tension is present in the *Enquiry*. In the Appendix to the *Treatise* Hume had some notoriously obscure second thoughts about personal identity, which leave it obscure even what disquieted him about his earlier theory, let alone what changes he wished to make. My own view is that Hume himself was unsure what to jettison and what to keep from the theory of personal identity, and therefore no part of that theory fully ceased to have a hold on him in later years. Despite his reservations, therefore, the theory of the self will have continued to put pressure on view (B). (There are elements of the *Treatise* theory in Part IV of Hume's later work, the *Dialogues concerning Natural Religion*. Philo argues that the 'soul of man' is 'a composition of various faculties, passions, sentiments, ideas; united, indeed, into one self or person, but still distinct from each other'—and he seems to have the agreement of Cleanthes (*D* 158). But this is moderate, both in tone and in content, compared with the *Treatise*.)

It is interesting, however, that (A)—the view which most shows the pressure to make the objects of the mind vary along just the one dimension of vivacity—is dropped in the Appendix, at just the same time as Hume is backtracking on the doctrine of personal identity. It may be that Hume is more indulgent to views (B) and (C) thereafter partly because he has relaxed his commitment to that doctrine. My suggestion is that the *Treatise* doctrine of personal identity none the less continues to exercise some influence on him, and it would stop him firmly and fully espousing either (B) or—as I shall argue later—(C).

Large parts of the *Treatise*'s picture of the mind obviously survive into the *Enquiry*, for example: 'we may divide all the perceptions of the mind into two classes or species, which are distinguished by their different degrees of force and vivacity' (*E* 18). Hume does not say that the mind is literally constituted by these perceptions; but if belief itself counts as a perception, then there is already the material to make Hume uncomfortable about view (B).

thought-less bearer of thoughts would be redundant; this left open two options—to say that thoughts belong to nothing, or to say that thoughts belong to something different. Hume took the first option, which clashes with view (B) of belief. The second option seems to me the more promising, and if the bearer of thoughts is nothing more peculiar than a *person*, then it is quite compatible with Hume's aim of avoiding a mysteriously simple and unchanging self. View (B) is, however, more promising in form than content. It may be right to see belief as involving a *subject* standing in a *relation* to an *object*, but the most promising options are not the ones Hume favours. The *object* of the mind may need to be a state of affairs, a proposition, or perhaps an individual mental content, rather than Hume's imagistic 'ideas'; the *relation* in question surely cannot be force and vivacity of apprehension; and the *subject* may need to be a person, of a kind for which Hume never made provision.[34]

5. DIFFICULTIES WITH THE THIRD VIEW

The problems are more obvious with view (C), that belief is 'merely a peculiar *feeling* or *sentiment*' (App. 623). The first difficulty is whether to class the 'feeling' as an idea or an impression. It cannot be an additional idea (or else we could believe anything at will), so the natural view might seem to be that it is an additional impression. Hume immediately goes on, however, to scotch this suggestion. He produces four arguments. First, 'It is directly contrary to experience': in our beliefs, we have ideas that are 'different to the feeling; but there is no distinct or separate impression attending them' (App. 625). Secondly, 'it must be allow'd, that the mind has a firmer hold' of something it believes. So why look for anything else, 'or multiply suppositions without necessity?' (App. 626). Thirdly, we can cite causes for the 'firm conception' but not for any 'separate impression'.

---

[34] Norman Kemp Smith has also remarked on the tension between Hume's view of belief as 'a quality of this and that perception' and his view of it as 'an attitude of mind', which correspond to what I have called views (A) and (B); and he links those views respectively to Newtonian and Hutchesonian (or, roughly, mechanical and biological) elements in Hume's approach to mental phenomena (*The Philosophy of David Hume* (London: Macmillan, 1941), 74). There are at least three divergences between us. First, whereas he takes the Hutchesonian view to be 'the more fundamental in Hume's thinking' (p. 76), I find the Newtonian view and, with it, the bundle theory, to be (however unfortunately) the dominant one in Book I of the *Treatise* and, in particular, the discussion of belief. Secondly, Kemp Smith takes Hume's theory of space and time as 'manners of appearance' to be irreconcilable with the bundle theory (p. 49); I have argued above, however, that those 'manners of appearance' may be a matter simply of relations *among* perceptions, and it is only the second view of belief that really makes trouble for the bundle theory. Thirdly, Kemp Smith makes nothing of the passage at *T* 105–6 which I find the one place where Hume unambiguously commits himself to irreducible relations between the mind and its objects. Rereading Kemp Smith's discussion of this matter, however, has only served to impress upon me how much present-day discussion suffers from neglect of his work: how many striking ideas have been neither rebutted nor retained in later debate.

Fourthly, we can explain all the effects of belief as those of 'firm conception'; so we don't need to suppose anything further.

Two things are interesting here. First, though he has only just introduced view (C), he is already (with the phrases 'firm hold' and 'firm conception') talking as if this third view were equivalent to (A) or (B). Secondly, and more importantly, Hume is rebutting with these four arguments a view that seems virtually impossible to distinguish from the proposal he himself has just made. The view he is rebutting is this:

> belief, beside the simple conception, consists in some impression or feeling, distinguishable from the conception . . . It is only annex'd to it, after the same manner that *will* and *desire* are annex'd to particular conceptions of good and pleasure.[35] (App. 625)

The view he is proposing, which I label (C), is this:

> belief consists merely in a certain feeling or sentiment . . . When we are convinc'd of any matter of fact, we do nothing but conceive it, along with a certain feeling . . . (App. 624)

What is supposed to be the difference between them? Both involve a 'feeling' in some way added to an idea. One might think the difference lay in the relation of the 'feeling' to the idea: on the rejected view, the relation would be more remote (the feeling is 'only annex'd . . .'). But on the proposed view as it appears in the *Enquiry*, the sentiment or feeling is also merely 'annexed' to the belief, and the conception is only '*attended with* a feeling or sentiment' (*E* 48, my emphasis).

The essential point may be that Hume wants to distance himself from any view that makes the feeling 'distinguishable' from the conception. There would be good reasons for doing so; the problem is that, once again, there are elements in Hume's general view of the mind that make it impossible for him to do so. One reason to reject a feeling of belief 'distinguishable from the conception' and merely 'annexed' to it is that if there were such a thing, the feeling would presumably be able to occur on its own, detached from any conception. One could have feelings of belief, without there being anything believed.[36] The problem with this idea is subtle. It is not that there is no such thing as being under the impression that you have a belief, without there being anything that you believe, in the sense intended. It is that there seems no prospect of constructing the belief that *p* out of that feeling together with the mere conception that *p*. We may allow that there is a feeling of belief, in that if you believe that *p*, you will often

---

[35] Hume's rejection is shown in the sentence that follows: 'the following considerations will, I hope, be sufficient to remove this hypothesis' (App. 625).

[36] Bertrand Russell, following William James, seems to have believed in the existence of just such feelings: 'a man's soul may sweat with conviction, and he be all the time utterly unable to say what he is convinced of. It would seem that, in such cases, the feeling of belief exists unattached, without its usual relation to a content believed . . . Much of what passes for revelation or mystic insight probably comes in this way' (*The Analysis of Mind* (London: George Allen & Unwin, 1921), 252).

be aware that you believe that *p*. But that feeling is derivative from the belief, not a component part of it.

This gives us reason not to invoke a feeling of belief 'distinguishable from the conception' and merely 'annexed' to it. But what is to be the Humean alternative? The suggestion might be that belief involves a feeling or sentiment that is *intrinsically connected* with the conception, and not detachable from it. But how could Hume allow this? The general theory of the mind seems to forbid it: 'since all our perceptions are different . . . they are also distinct and separable . . . and may exist separately' (*T* 233). A feeling of belief would be distinguishable and different from the conception believed; it must therefore in Hume's view be capable of existing on its own.[37] There seems no alternative available to Hume, as long as he is ready to employ in the way he did (rather than in Descartes's more careful way) the principle that 'Whatever is clearly conceiv'd may exist' (*T* 233).

I began with the question why Hume should not only have held different views of belief at different times, but also in the *Enquiry* have seemed to hold all three views at once and rather sheepishly. The simple answer is that there are close connexions between the three kinds of view, so it was easy to slip between them. The more sophisticated answer is that Hume was under pressure from his general theory of the mind. The view of belief (A) as a vivid idea, though crude, had the virtue of simple compatibility with the picture of the mind as consisting of ideas and impressions; even after he backtracked in the face of the 'poetical enthusiasm', that picture (and many of the systematic parallels between impressions and beliefs, which Hume needed for his mechanics of belief) continued to exercise an influence on him and lead him back to the first view. The view of belief (B) as a vivid conception of an idea met some of the objections to the first view. Unfortunately, however, the suggestion of the mind's standing in a certain relation to an idea would have seemed tainted with Cartesianism: the mind would have seemed in danger of being treated as something separate from its own perceptions. So whatever the attractions of the second view, Hume always had reason to abandon it. I have argued that the root of the trouble lay in

---

[37] It is interesting to see how the atomistic conception of the world—which is as central to Hume's theory of the mind as it is to his views on causation—reaches a *reductio ad absurdum* first in the former area. Any theory which (like Hume's; see *T* 20) insists on the independence of thoughts from their objects (or what they refer to) will have difficulty making sense of intentionality and reference. As long as the referents are 'external' objects, this consequence may seem tolerable; but when the referent of the thought is itself an idea, then the logical independence of these is less tolerable; and in the case of belief, it seems quite unacceptable. In the belief that *p*, the attitude element which refers to a thought (rather as 'That's true' does) can hardly be logically independent of the thought.

David Pears develops some further worries about Hume's inability to make sense of intentionality, in *Hume's System*, 52.

Hume's mistaken theory of personal identity: a modern view of belief as a propositional attitude is in some ways parallel to the second view, but freed of Hume's view that ideas are substances, it is under no compulsion to misconstrue the mind that takes attitudes to thoughts as a thought-less bearer of thoughts. The second view has its virtues; if we ask why Hume was diffident in his affirmation of it, we need perhaps look no further than the picture of personal identity which would have led him to reject it. As for the view of belief (C) as a sentiment or feeling: Hume's problem is to stop the view from collapsing into the view that belief consists in a separable impression merely annexed to the idea. The latter is a view that Hume himself rejects, and I have added a further reason of my own (that there is no separable 'feeling of belief'); but it seems impossible finally for Hume to stop the collapse. Driven once again by his conviction of the independence and self-sufficiency of all the contents of the mind, Hume is incapable of giving a place to a feeling that cannot be logically detached from the idea to which it is directed. The third view too, therefore, was one which Hume had serious, if suspect, reasons to reject.[38]

[38] I am grateful to John Campbell, William Child, Adrian Cussins, Michael Dummett, Peter Millican, Alison Simmons, and Wayne Waxman for comments on a predecessor of this paper. The Hume Society Conference of 1994 gave me the benefit of a Reply from Wade Robison and of comments from the Program Committee and other participants; I am grateful to them all.

7

The Idea of Necessary Connexion

Edward Craig

Section VII of the *Enquiry concerning Human Understanding* is one of the most frequently read passages in Hume's entire output; at a guess, only the material of Section IV surpasses it. And since many readers come to it early in their studies one might think that its waters are fairly smooth. But not so: they are full of barely hidden turbulence, for here two streams of Hume's thought run together—and foam.

These two streams I shall call the 'analytic' and the 'epistemic'. But those are words from the twentieth-century philosopher's vocabulary, and their application to Hume's writings needs to be explained. In the first place, Hume has a theory about the content of our concepts and how it can best be investigated. Concepts, or 'ideas' as he calls them, are made by taking mental copies of sensory impressions and compounding the results. Should the content of an idea be obscure to us, the way to clarify our minds about it is therefore to seek the impression or impressions from which it was copied. As a young man Hume took this theory over from Locke more or less unchanged; he gave it pride of place right at the beginning of the *Treatise*, and twelve or so years later repeated it in Section II of the first *Enquiry*. The programme it defines is what I call his 'analytic' enterprise.

Hume is also interested in the question how we come to hold the beliefs that we do. I can't believe what I can't think, that is to say: can't represent to myself; but I can very well think all manner of things which I don't believe. If I believe something, an account of how I acquired the capacity to think it is not enough to explain the fact. Something else is needed, and Hume was keen to supply it. This is his 'epistemic' enterprise. Whatever type of belief he is currently considering, the general strategy is always much the same. There are three candidates

The two main sections of this paper have been adapted from E. J. Craig, *The Mind of God and the Works of Man* (Oxford: Clarendon Press, 1987), ch. 2 §§3 and 4.

for the production of any belief: the senses, reason, and the imagination. The first of these meant much the same to Hume as it does to us; the differences need not detain us here. The third is completely different: in Hume's usage it refers to the mechanism of association and enlivenment of ideas that he has described in earlier sections. 'Reason' is the tricky one. Hume has a tendency to equate it with deduction (as he would say, 'demonstration'), and the fashion amongst commentators has been to find this disconcertingly, perhaps question-beggingly, narrow. To understand it we need to take a wider view of the intellectual background of Hume's thought; fortunately, in doing so we can also prepare ourselves for the trickiest feature of Section VII.

Hume's immediate philosophical predecessors had in various ways evinced an intense interest in the idea, doubtless imprinted on their minds in their upbringing, that man was made in the image of God. This interest gave characteristic direction to their theory of knowledge: egged on by the enormous successes of the sciences in the seventeenth century, they nearly all took it that one (if not *the*) point of similarity between man and God lay in their cognitive powers: the human mind, after all, was evidently well suited to grasping the essential nature of God's creation, and how then could there fail to be such a likeness? But God's cognitive powers are (of course) perfect, and so philosophers were led to look for something in man which, in its own little way, might be of comparable perfection. Our grasp of 'demonstrative' connexions was one of the few obvious candidates. Here, at least, we have the impression that we could not be wrong, that everything that is relevant to the question is in full view and transparent to our intellects. This is what it must be like for God, and our business is to bring our cognitive endeavours, so far as possible, to a similar level of perfection. 'Reason' is the faculty which, properly used, is to do this work for us; it is the divine element in our cognitive make-up.[1]

If there is, driving Hume's thought, a single, quickly statable purpose, it is the extirpation of this doctrine of man as an image of God. Neither with regard to our intellectual capacities, nor with regard to our moral preferences is there in his opinion any reason to think that we bear anything more than the remotest resemblance to whatever created the universe. Reason, conceived as so infallibly penetrating a faculty, may exist in man, but its range is minute. For no more than a tiny fragment of our beliefs is there any hope of attaining the degree of insight which this misguided ideal had suggested; this tiny fragment concerns only relations between our ideas—it includes nothing at all about what is actually the case anywhere in the universe.

---

[1] These background themes are treated at length in the first chapter of Craig, *The Mind of God and the Works of Man*.

Accordingly, Hume spends much time and energy arguing that beliefs of this, that, or the other type cannot be attained by reason. The concept of reason that he chooses to work with is not, as many have recently felt, arbitrarily rigorous. Quite the contrary: it is the very concept of reason which was required by the epistemological form of the Image of God doctrine, and it was exactly what Hume needed to work with to get his attack on target.

That is, relatively speaking, an obvious effect of Hume's overarching purpose. There is another effect, rather more subtle, without a grasp of which we shall find much impenetrable mystery in the detail of Section VII. The epistemological version of the Image of God doctrine is concerned with the possibility of perfect insight into the truth of our beliefs, and that brings with it the requirement that there can be equally perfect insight into their *content*. How could our knowledge of truth be better than our knowledge of meaning? In such a climate the thought that this content is embodied in image-like items that we can call before consciousness must be very welcome, for our grasp of our own current mental states is, apart from deductive logic, the only example of infallible knowledge that can with any plausibility claim to be such.

An opponent of the Image of God ideology, by contrast, has no primary need of a theory which makes the content of thoughts transparent to the thinker. He needs a theory of content only if he requires one for his arguments about where our beliefs do and do not come from. So if we take the case of Hume and causal beliefs as our illustration, this would mean that his analytic theory has to do two things for him. The first is to guarantee that the content of causal beliefs goes beyond anything which can be fulfilled by the immediate data of sense; the second is to support the argument that reason cannot deliver them, even if fed premises which are immediately certifiable by the senses. For either of these would give us (according to the epistemological views of the time) just the kind of infallible grasp of their truth which an opponent of the Image of God doctrine will want to reject. The first of these purposes hardly calls for a *theory* of content at all. The second may, at least in Hume's case. For his argument that causal beliefs cannot be the product of reason rests on the lemma that any cause–effect correlation can be clearly and distinctly conceived to break down; and whether that is true or not must depend on what clear and distinct conception of such breakdown would be, which in turn depends upon the precise content of the thought that breakdown has occurred. To decide whether we can conceive the occurrence of the normal cause not followed by the normal effect, we must be quite clear what we are being invited to do. Hume's confidence that we can rests, I suspect, on the premiss that our 'ideas' of those events contain nothing more than his theory of their origins would allow. But be that as it may, this issue was settled—in Hume's estimation—in Section IV.

Such, I conjecture, is the background to the beginning of Section VII. In accordance with his main programme of replacing the semi-supernaturalism of the Image of God doctrine by the naturalism of his quasi-Newtonian model of the mind, Hume is out to enforce his claim that our causal beliefs are the output of the associative mechanism the 'Imagination'. His attention is therefore directed to the way in which we acquire those beliefs—the question what the 'idea' of cause may be, and how we come by it, is of interest only in so far as it has to be answered in the course of deciding that issue. But his theory of the nature of belief directs him back to the analytic component of his thought: he must find an idea of causality for the associative processes to enliven, and the theory of the origin of ideas then commits him to finding a suitable impression. And so the scene is admirably set for two questions—whence the idea? and: whence the belief?—to claim Hume's attention simultaneously. Which they do: the analytic and the epistemic strands of his thought wind themselves up into a rare old tangle.

But however great the tangle, the hypothesis that Hume's underlying concern is with the refutation of the Image of God doctrine implies that it is epistemology which will take precedence for him over analysis; the question about the genesis of beliefs will weigh heavier that the theory of impressions and ideas. The role of the latter, however vital, is still only to serve Hume's views, negative and positive, about the former. This order of precedence, I contend, really is detectable in Section VII.

1. THE HUNT FOR CAUSES

That claim might well be thought refuted almost as soon as made. After all, what is undoubtedly the kernel of Hume's thought on the subject begins with a search for the impression from which the *idea* of power is derived, and ends by *defining* a cause, activities which fall squarely in the analytic area; the search for the impression is supposed to allow us to apply Hume's 'mental microscope' (*E* 62) to the idea and so discern its exact content, while a definition is (is it not?) a statement of the content of the idea defined. Nevertheless, we shall see that the primacy of epistemology for Hume expresses itself here in two ways. One is the fact that, having approached his problem in terms of the theory of ideas and their related impressions, he soon stops taking the details of that theory at all seriously. The other is the way in which, while to all intents and purposes arguing about the origin of the idea of power, he employs as his main argument a point from the epistemological side of his thinking, the connexion of which with the analytic question (whence, if at all, do we obtain the idea of cause?) is mysterious and is allowed to remain so. The emphasis of Hume's concerns emerges clearly—more clearly than it emerged to Hume himself, it seems.

As is well known, Hume presents his investigation of causality as the search for a particular impression, that from which the idea of 'power or necessary connexion' is derived. The problem is to find the nature of the idea which corresponds to 'causes' when we think or say that *A* causes *B*. Given Hume's principles governing the origin and nature of ideas, this is equivalent to discovering the impression in which it originates, since it is simply a copy of this impression. Therefore: 'To be fully acquainted . . . with the idea of power or necessary connexion, let us examine its impression; and in order to find the impression with greater certainty, let us search for it in all the sources, from which it may possibly be derived.' (*E* 63). His first move is just what this programme leads the reader to expect: it is to ask exactly what is perceived when we observe some causal interaction. When we see one billiard ball collide with another, there is nothing, apart from the motion of the first ball and the subsequent motion of the second, that 'appears to the *outward* senses'. This overstates the case a little: there normally is a third impression, an auditory one. But the strength of Hume's point does not rest on the literal truth of the claim that there is no other impression, but rather on the fact that any others there might be would all be regarded as impressions of further events or objects, further members of the causal chain, not as the impression of the linking power or 'necessary connexion'.

So far there are no surprises. We are investigating the properties of a certain idea, so we look for the corresponding impression, the one from which it is copied. An impression is a perceptual state of a mind, so we ask what perceptual states occur when we perceive one event causing another. But with the next paragraph comes something unexpectedly different: 'From the first appearance of an object, we never can conjecture what effect will result from it. But were the power or energy of any cause discoverable by the mind, we could foresee the effect, even without experience; and might, at first, pronounce with certainty concerning it, by mere dint of thought and reasoning.' (*E* 63). Here epistemological considerations, questions about the circumstances under which we could know something, have suddenly come to the fore. But it is only reasonable to assume, from his silence on the subject, that Hume is still continuing on the same course, and giving another argument for the claim that there is no outward impression of power. If he is not, then he has abandoned the analytical question right at the beginning, and the thesis that analysis is less important to him than epistemology is already strongly confirmed. But to suppose that he has abandoned it would surely be premature: the thought appears to be that if there were an impression of power, we could then tell by inspection of the cause what effect it would have, without waiting for, or drawing on, experience. Hume then calls up one of his most famous epistemological results, shown by the argument from the conceivability of the contrary, that the effects of a cause can never be known a priori. Therefore, there is no impression of power.

What reason have we been given, however, to accept the first premiss, that if there were an impression of power, we could predict the effect a priori? One can imagine the following response from the opposition: 'We admit your point that causal truths cannot be known a priori, but what we maintain does not conflict with it. All that it shows is that the idea of causing *B* isn't part of the idea of *A*, with which we fully agree. We simply hold that sometimes, when we perceive a causal interaction, we have an impression of 'bringing about', or 'causing', as well as the impressions of the two events involved; and that this is the impression from which we copy the idea you are looking for.'

Hume has, in theory, two lines of reply. One would be to say that such an impression, because of what it is supposed to be the impression of, *would* have to make a priori knowledge of causal truths possible. This line, as we shall see, leads into deep complications. The other would be to refer back to his first argument, that there just is no such impression. That would be to admit that the second argument does no work: if the first argument succeeds, the matter is settled; if it doesn't, the second won't help.

If the second argument made just this one brief appearance, no doubt we could and probably should shrug it off. But in fact Hume now continues by presenting variants of it for several pages. Having considered the outward case, he now wants to show that the missing impression cannot be found by looking at mental causation, either when we move our body, or when 'we raise up a new idea'. There are a number of such arguments (*E* 64–9), and all of them have the same form: if there were an impression of power, we should know things which in fact we do not. Thus, if there were such an impression, we should know how the mind is able to affect matter (*E* 65), we should know a priori what we can in fact only know from experience, such as that the will can move the fingers but not the heart or liver. But why the impression of power, if it occurred, would necessarily bring all these benefits with it, we are not told. Consider this example, of the many available:

Secondly, We are not able to move all the organs of the body with a like authority; though we cannot assign any reason besides experience, for so remarkable a difference between one and the other. Why has the will an influence over the tongue and fingers, not over the heart or liver? This question would never embarrass us, were we conscious of a power in the former case, not in the latter. (*E* 65)

But why not? The position would simply be that in some cases we could exert the will, then observe the impression of power and that of the required bodily movement; whereas in others we could exert the will without either of these further impressions making any appearance. The puzzle would remain: to know why they sometimes did and sometimes did not follow upon the act of willing, depending upon which organ one willed to move. So isn't Hume imposing a gratuitously strong condition on the impression, one that suggests that his real interest is in the epistemological questions, how we know or come to believe truths about causes, and only secondarily in the content of the concept as revealed by the dictum that every idea is a copy of an impression?

What might account for this apparent (and seemingly unconscious) drift towards the epistemological, apart from the hypothesis that knowledge and belief, rather than the nature of ideas, is Hume's real focus? One suggestion I have heard can be disposed of quickly. It says that the drift is only apparent: what happened in the first argument was that Hume denied that the idea of cause might have its origin in the senses, and he is now going on to ask whether it could have its origin in reason. Two major difficulties rule this interpretation out, however. In the first place, Hume tells us clearly in the opening sentences of each of the next two paragraphs that he is still pursuing the question of what is and what is not *perceived*. In the first he is speaking of outward impressions: 'In reality, there is no part of matter, that does ever, *by its sensible qualities*, discover any power or energy' (*E* 63, my emphasis). In the second it is inner perception, what Hume calls 'impressions of reflection', that are involved: 'let us see, whether this idea be derived from reflection on the operations of our own minds, and be *copied from any internal impression*' (*E* 64, my emphasis). This stress on what is not perceived would be irrelevant to the question whether the idea of causality may not be arrived at by reasoning. And the hypothesis that it is that question which Hume is here addressing himself to faces a second difficulty at least as great. In the footnote to this passage (*E* 64 n.), where Hume really (and explicitly) is considering the possibility that the idea of power may be arrived at by reasoning, he dismisses it almost contemptuously in a couple of lines. It is not to be entertained that he was simultaneously engaged in producing, over several pages, strenuous and detailed arguments against the very same possibility.

But to go back a step: could it really be a necessary condition of an impression's being the impression of power that its mere occurrence make possible this a priori knowledge of which Hume writes? Hardly: there is no impression the mere occurrence of which gives us knowledge, since any impression can be illusory; why should this putative impression be asked to pass a test which any impression must fail? But perhaps we ought to reformulate the test: the occurrence of the impression should at least make us *believe* in the existence of some a priori knowable connexion between the cause and the effect. That would in a sense be very reasonable. For given Hume's theory of belief, wherever there is an impression of an X there ought to be belief in an X—belief, on his view, is the occurrence of a particularly vivid idea, and nothing more vivid than an impression. Arguably, then, were there on some occasion an impression of 'power or necessary connexion', there should be a belief that power was being exercised, or that some necessary connexion obtained. But even then we would still be well short of what Hume demands: not just that we believe that there is power, or necessary connexion, but that in addition we can see that it is the power of A to produce B; and in addition to *that*, that we could forecast its existence just on the basis of our idea of A—and this seems to be simply gratuitous.

Besides, this whole line is in confusing conflict with at least two features of Hume's thought. First, there is his somewhat underdeveloped epistemology of a priori knowledge, which consists, according to him, in the perception of relations between ideas, not of the two related ideas and a third. If in some cases we did know a priori that A and B were connected, we would know it by having perceived a relationship between the idea of A and the idea of B, not by having both of these accompanied by a further idea (or impression). Secondly, although there are some grounds for attributing to Hume the view that where there is an impression of an X there is *ipso facto* a belief in an X, equally there are grounds for not doing so. For the impression of a table, for Hume, appears to be a visual(?) image of a table. But to believe in a table is to believe in the presence of an independent and continuing object, and Hume elsewhere has spent a whole chapter explaining that such beliefs come about only when these images occur in an intricate context of consistency and coherence amongst our various perceptions.[2] He does not, therefore, seem to hold the general principle just stated relating impressions to beliefs; so the question returns: why should he hold it in respect of *causality* in particular?

Another feature of Hume's approach is also puzzling. Why does he speak of the idea of 'power or necessary connexion'? Does he take it that the idea of power could only be an idea of necessary connexion, where 'necessary' implies that it belongs to the kind of which a priori knowledge is possible? It seems that he does, since he never gives any indication that they might be different ideas, while the speed with which his thought passes to the topic of a priori knowledge strongly suggests that he understands 'necessary' in that sense. It looks as if he has just ignored what the modern reader will think of as an obvious prima-facie possibility, that there is a necessity stronger than concomitance but weaker than the deductive, and it is of this that we are seeking the impression and idea.

It is noteworthy that this is just the direction in which a polemical concern with the Image of God doctrine would have led. It is not hard to see how that doctrine would promote a view of causal connexions as being infallible[3] and open to the highest degree of rational insight.[4] The wording of Hume's text

---

[2] *Treatise*, I. iv. 2.

[3] A word which Hume sometimes uses: see e.g. *E* 65 line 2.

[4] For more explicit discussion of this point, see Craig, *The Mind of God and the Works of man*, ch. 1. §4 (pp. 37–44).

leaves little room for doubt that he has that type of connexion in mind; at one point its pedigree appears on the surface in full view: 'Volition is surely an act of the mind, with which we are sufficiently acquainted. Reflect upon it. Consider it on all sides. Do you find anything in it like this creative power, by which it raises from nothing a new idea, and with a kind of FIAT, imitates the omnipotence of its Maker' (E 69). That last phrase could be copied from Leibniz, among seventeenth-century philosophers possibly the most determined and certainly the most explicit proponent of the Image of God doctrine.

All that is clear here is that there is a muddle, but enough can be seen for us to make a plausible guess at what is causing it: Hume is trying to force his analytic theory about ideas and their origin in impressions into a very uncomfortable and dubious relationship with his epistemological theory about the acquisition of knowledge and the formation of belief. Whether this is a misguided attempt to gain further evidence for his claim about the idea, or a manifestation of the tendency to slip away from the theory of ideas and impressions to the area where his interests really lie, is something on which it would be premature to be confident. But there is much more in Section VII of the first *Enquiry* (and elsewhere) to favour the latter alternative—we have not yet seen anything like the full extent of the tangle between the conceptual and the epistemological in Hume's pages.

So far we have seen the tangle in Hume's choice of arguments. It is also visible in his choice of words. Such expressions as 'were we conscious of a power' (E 65) show just the right ambiguity: they can mean 'were we to have the impression of a power', but equally easily 'were we to have knowledge of a power'. Nor does the first entail the second, since presumably any impression can occur illusorily— and yet an illusory impression of power, one which occurred though no power had in fact been exercised, would do just as well as the original of someone's idea of power as would a veridical one. So one might have the idea of power by this route without any justifiable claim to knowledge. They are therefore not equivalent, and if Hume failed to notice this, then *that* fact calls for explanation, all the more so since he uses one example which ought to bring the thought of a possible illusion clearly to mind:

A man, suddenly struck with a palsy in the leg or arm, or who had newly lost those members, frequently endeavours, at first, to move them, and employ them in their usual offices. Here he is as much conscious of power to command such limbs, as a man in perfect health is conscious of power to actuate any member which remains in its natural state and condition. But consciousness never deceives. Consequently, neither in the one case nor in the other, are we ever conscious of any power. (E 66)

The key phrase here is 'consciousness never deceives'. For the argument to go through, this has to imply that if there is no power, there is no impression of power. From that we could indeed conclude, given that the palsied man and the healthy man have the same impressions, as Hume claims, that there was no impression of power in either case. But if that is what is meant by 'consciousness never deceives', it isn't true, and Hume cannot seriously have thought that it was, once he got the question into clear focus. The example in fact shows nothing at all about the immediate contents of our consciousness as they are in themselves, and so does not connect with the theory of ideas and their origin in impressions. The point that it can legitimately be used to make is an epistemological one: it is impermissible to conclude from the feeling that we have the power to move our limbs (assuming that there is such a feeling) that we do indeed have the power. At least, the conclusion is not deductively drawn, nor is it the strongest kind of induction—for Hume has just specified a factual counter-example. We find that we can (almost always) move our limbs not by deduction from the immediate presentations of consciousness, but from our (almost invariable) success in moving them. Which is exactly what Hume says in the very next sentence: 'We learn the influence of our will from experience alone.' Contrary to the author's professed intentions, this passage is not about the formation of the idea of power. It is about what we *know* and how we come to know it: not from reason operating on the deliverances of consciousness, but more mundanely from what experience tells us about the constant course of nature. Epistemology rules, and Hume's appeal to the slogan that 'consciousness never deceives' only indicates that he has not, at this stage, fully realized what he is up to.

The tendency to slough off the theory of impressions and ideas in favour of his epistemological aims emerges ever more clearly as the denouement approaches. We find ourselves facing a crisis of the analytic or conceptual kind; meaninglessness threatens, words without ideas: 'the necessary conclusion *seems* to be, that we have no idea of connexion or power at all, and that these words are absolutely without any meaning' (E 74). Hume is still hopeful, however. The belief in a causal connexion arises only from the experience of multiple instances of the conjunction of cause and effect—here he comes close to the rather optimistic assumption that we only believe causal propositions when we are justified in doing so—so, since the belief presupposes the idea, there must be something about the multiple case which is capable of generating it. What special new impression arises, then, from 'a repetition of similar instances'? Answer:

only, that . . . the mind is carried by habit, upon the appearance of one event, to expect its usual attendant, and to believe, that it will exist. This connexion, therefore, which we *feel* in the mind, this customary transition of the imagination from one object to its usual attendant, is the sentiment or impression, from which we form the idea of power or necessary connexion. (E 75)

This is extremely curious. Over the last ten pages Hume has argued repeatedly that there is no impression of power that is observed when we move our bodies or call up ideas in our minds. Now it turns out that after all there is some such feeling of connexion (a 'sentiment or impression') when an idea arises involuntarily by virtue of its association with another idea (or impression) which is already present to consciousness. Nothing is said as to how this can be, how this case can differ from the ones previously dismissed. One would have thought that both types of argument used then could be used again with the same effect. First, that there is no third impression of reflection, but just the impression of one idea followed by that of the other. Secondly, the 'feeling', if it occurs, does not allow us a priori insight into the necessity of this particular succession of ideas[5]—which was earlier deemed enough to show that no impression of power is found. So careless is he about the detail of the conceptual branch of his theory, and that at the very moment of climax when the elusive impression is (supposedly) finally being revealed.

That, however, is not the only startling feature of the passage. Hume does not just speak of the 'connexion . . . which we feel in the mind' as being the sought-after impression; he also adds, in apposition, the phrase 'this customary transition of the imagination from one object to its usual attendant'. But a transition, customary or not, is not a further impression. 'Customary transition' is simply Hume's way of referring to the fact that the impression or idea of the causing event is followed regularly in the mind by the idea of the effect. So whatever one may think about the rest of the sentence taken by itself—as we have seen, it is quite mysterious enough—the words 'this customary transition of the imagination from one object to its usual attendant' do not fit into it at all. They belong, clearly, to the epistemic side of Hume's enterprise, not the analytic; they do not go along with the theory of ideas and impressions, the hunt for an impression of which the idea of cause may be the copy, but with his associationist theory of the origin of belief. The repeated experience of a concomitance between A and B generates an association between their ideas, which results in a 'transition of the imagination' from the thought or perception of one to the thought of the other, and then in certain cases allows the first to enliven the idea of the second to the point at which it becomes a belief in the existence of its object. Thus the mind is brought 'upon the appearance of one event, to expect its usual attendant, and to believe that it will exist' (E 75). Once again the epistemology, here in the form of the theory of belief, asserts itself, and in the very sentence in which Hume is trying, albeit somewhat half-heartedly, to make the

---

[5] Something which Hume knows perfectly well, as witness T 169: 'The uniting principle among our internal perceptions is as unintelligible as that among external objects, and is not known to us any other way than by experience.'

decisive pronouncement about the theory of ideas and impressions in its application to the concept of causality.

There is, it is true, an ambiguity in the phrase 'the idea of a necessary connexion' which spans just the distinction that Hume here smudges over, that between thinking of something, and believing in its existence. It matches very closely the ambiguity of 'consciousness of a power', upon which we have already dwelt. But to try to attribute the vacillations of Section VII of the *Enquiry concerning Human Understanding* to a failure on Hume's part to perceive this ambiguity would be very shallow. When he writes on the nature of belief, he shows unmistakably how well he understands the difference between merely entertaining an idea and believing in its content; his whole approach to the subject is precisely to pose the question in what this difference may consist (*E* 47–8). Besides, the alternative hypothesis, that the weight of Hume's interests lay in the epistemological sector and that he had made something of a false start by beginning with the theory of ideas and impressions, has at least two major advantages. In the first place, it is itself explicable in terms of the preoccupations of his immediate philosophical ancestors; the prevalence of the ideal of quasi-divine insight accounts for the epistemological bias, and the contemporary prominence of Locke's *Essay on Human Understanding*, with its heavy emphasis on the nature and genesis of ideas, accounts for the attractiveness of the false start. In the second place, it can help us to find our way through other passages from his works. One such is the famous chapter 'Of Personal Identity' from the *Treatise of Human Nature*.[6] Another is very closely related to the section just discussed: Hume's notoriously disparate 'two definitions of cause'.

2. THE TWO DEFINITIONS

The problem is well known. Towards the end of the relevant sections of both the first *Enquiry* and the *Treatise of Human Nature* we find two statements, each of which is said to be a definition of cause (*T* 169–70, *E* 76–7). We are used to the idea that there may be two definitions of one concept if the alternatives are allowed to differ from each other only verbally while still counting as two, but Hume's two definitions are not like that. His *definienses* quite certainly differ in intension, and arguably in extension as well. I shall consider them as they appear in the *Treatise*, since one of the best-known discussions of the puzzle, J. A. Robinson's paper 'Hume's Two Definitions of "Cause"' and the consequent exchange between him and Thomas J. Richards, takes the *Treatise* as its basis. Here, to refresh the reader's memory, are the two definitions from *T* 170:

---

[6] For a treatment of this, see Craig, *The Mind of God and the Works of Man*, ch. 2 §5 (pp. 111–20).

(1) We may define a CAUSE to be 'An object precedent and contiguous to another, and where all the objects resembling the former are plac'd in like relations of precedency and contiguity to those objects, that resemble the latter'.

(2) A CAUSE is an object precedent and contiguous to another, and so united with it, that the idea of the one determines the mind to form the idea of the other, and the impression of the one to form a more lively idea of the other.

Robinson and Richards take their cue from Hume's statement that in the first definition cause is defined as a 'philosophical relation', in the second as a 'natural relation' (*T* 169–70). Their understanding of this distinction is, I think, quite correct: any many-placed predicate is a philosophical relation, but only those relations are 'natural' which bring about an association of the relevant ideas in the mind of an observer. Now according to Robinson, the first definition really is a definition, in the modern sense of being an analysis of the concept of cause. The second is not a definition at all, but 'simply a restatement of the proposition that the (already defined) cause–effect relation is a *natural* relation, in a somewhat elliptical formulation'.[7] Richards finds the supposed ellipse too eccentric to be credible.[8] One has to agree; Hume's command of English would have needed to fail completely for him to use the wording of (2) just to make that point. So while accepting Robinson's account of the first definition, Richards provides an alternative reading of the second: it is a statement of the conditions under which one may properly believe, or assert, that one thing causes another; the two definitions give us respectively truth conditions and assertibility conditions for causal propositions.

Robinson's response to this contains several acceptable points. He chides Richards for introducing a normative element into his reading of the second definition, holding that it is better regarded as a statement of the conditions under which belief in a causal connexion does *in fact* arise, rather than those under which it is proper to hold a causal belief. He agrees that Richards's suggestion 'certainly makes sense of the fact that Hume does state that (1) and (2) are both definitions'—(which his own version did not), but claims on the other hand that 'it surely does not make sense of Hume's further claim, that (1) and (2) are both definitions *of the same notion* ("different views of the same object")'— (whereas his version did). He continues: 'However, any attempt to sort out Hume's intentions in this matter is going to fail to make sense of *part* at least of

⁷ J. A. Robinson, 'Hume's Two Definitions of "Cause" ', *Philosophical Quarterly*, 12 (1962), 162–71; repr. in V. C. Chappell (ed.), *Hume* (London: Macmillan, 1968), 129–47. The quotation is at p. 139 of the latter.
⁸ T. J. Richards, 'Hume's Two Definitions of "Cause" ', *Philosophical Quarterly*, 15 (1965), 247–53; repr. in Chappell (ed.), *Hume*, 148–61.

what Hume said about (1) and (2) . . .'.[9] Here we diverge; this pessimism is premature. It is forced upon him by an assumption which he and Richards apparently share, namely that Hume's term 'definition' must, if at all possible, be taken in its modern sense of the exhibiting of necessary and sufficient conditions for the defined concept, much the same as that of 'analysis'. It is an offshoot of a much more general assumption, to which I have already referred: the widespread tendency to think of Hume as a foreruner of the logical positivist movement, hence to emphasize the importance in his thought of conceptual and analytical considerations and to read in that light any remarks which look as if they might be susceptible of it. The word 'definition', given its usage in twentieth-century philosophy, invites such a reading, so let us try to forget its connotations in the area of synonymy, analysis, and intensional equivalence, and locate it instead in Hume's mechanics of belief, in accordance with the general policy of emphasizing his epistemology.

We may then take a tip from Robinson's treatment of the second 'definition', and hypothesize that a definition of cause, for Hume, is a statement of the conditions under which belief in a cause–effect relationship does in fact come about. Can we not understand both definitions in this way, as two different descriptions of the conditions that generate belief? If we can, it will make sense both of Hume's assertion that they are 'different views of the same object', and of the fact that he calls them both 'definitions'.

There is, of course, a prima-facie objection to this procedure, and it looks to be a serious one: at the beginning of his first paper Robinson contends that the two definitions are not even extensionally equivalent—put less technically: there are circumstances to which one applies and the other does not. My proposal could perfectly well survive their lack of *intensional* equivalence, the fact, in other words, that they are not synonymous. The point would be that they would always apply together if they applied at all, in virtue of the way in which Hume's laws of association operate. Thus if the condition stipulated in (1) held of a given pair of objects, that would produce the association of the ideas of those objects that is described by (2). And since there is, on Hume's account, no other way to produce that type of association, the truth of (2) would, conversely, require the truth of (1). But if, on the other hand, they are not even *extensionally* equivalent, then clearly there is a problem. If one can be true when the other is not, how can they be called 'views of the same object'?

It certainly looks as if they are not extensionally equivalent. In the first place, a pair of 'objects' could satisfy the first definition without ever having been observed to do so, or even without ever having been observed at all. Presumably

---

[9] J. A. Robinson, 'Hume's Two Definitions of "Cause" Reconsidered', in Chappell (ed.), *Hume*, 162–8, at 165.

there actually are many such pairs in the world, and Hume, who sometimes speaks of 'the operation of secret causes', is far from denying it. But if the relations between the objects have not been observed, nobody will associate the idea of one with that of the other, therefore they will not satisfy the second definition. Conversely, the second may be satisfied without the first. That will happen, for instance, in cases where we *wrongly* believe some pair of events to be respectively cause and effect of each other. The associations of ideas will exist, as specified in (2), but it will not be the case that all events like the first will be followed by events like the second, so that (1) will not hold of them.

All this has to be admitted, but the problem is not insoluble so long as we approach the passage with the general principle in mind that Hume is stating the conditions which give rise to a belief in causal connexion. There is then no special difficulty about the second definition, at least: Hume is saying that, for any pair of events for which it holds, the observer in question will believe the first to be the cause of the second. He may later be disappointed in his expectations, the concomitance between events of these types may turn out to be less universal than he had thought, in which case he will revise his opinions. The first definition, however, looks more troublesome. It is clear that no belief will arise unless there is some mind that observes the regular concomitance. Definition (1) makes no mention of any observer, so it doesn't, on Hume's or anyone else's view of causality, state sufficient conditions for the formation of a causal belief.

But how much of a problem is this, really? If at this stage Hume's mind was firmly fixed on the mechanics of belief, might he not have felt the need for an observer to be so obvious that explicit mention of it would be superfluous and pedantic? All the more so since he has given a hint of it in the preceding sentence, where we were told that the two definitions differ by asking us to consider causality 'either as a philosophical or as a natural relation; either as a comparison of two ideas, or as an association between them'. To say that the first definition makes us consider causality as a comparison of *ideas* indicates that the thought of the observer is not too far away.

There is some tidying up still to be done before this reading can be accepted, but first I should like to point out that the suggestion that what Hume calls a definition is not, in our technical sense, a definition at all, is no ad hoc measure designed to deal with this one passage, nor is it wholly innovatory. It is not ad hoc because, first, it fits well with the hypothesis that Hume's prime philosophical concern was the destruction and replacement of the Insight Ideal, a hypothesis which itself fits well with the fact of the Insight Ideal's prominence in the thought of nearly all his greatest predecessors. Secondly, it is needed to solve another textual problem, this time from his writing on ethics. And it is not wholly innovatory because it actually has been used in this connexion.

That last remark refers to Antony Flew's article 'On the Interpretation of Hume',[10] in which he discusses a paper by Geoffrey Hunter.[11] Hunter had held it absurd to attribute to Hume (as is of course standard practice) the view that no *is* can entail any *ought*, since he 'thinks that Ought-propositions are logically equivalent to certain Is-propositions'.[12] This Hunter asserts on the basis of the sentence 'So that when you pronounce any action or character to be vicious, you mean nothing, but that from the constitution of your nature you have a feeling or sentiment of blame from the contemplation of it.' (quoted from *T* 469). He evidently supposes that when Hume writes 'you mean nothing but that', he is announcing a synonymy claim or analysis, involving at least logical equivalence of *definiens* and *definiendum*. But it is at least as plausible to place this terminology, which would nowadays belong firmly to *semantic* enquiry, in the context of Hume's quasi-Newtonian science of man. After the comment that Hume is often read as if his works had been written for publication in *Analysis*, Flew points this out, and closes his article by saying: '. . . Hume's choice of phrase is also, surely, significant . . . "You pronounce . . ." but "you mean nothing but that . . .". When phrases of this sort are employed the point usually is: not that this is what your words actually mean; but rather that this is what, if you would only face the facts and be honest, you would have to admit.' Even more interesting from our present point of view is another passage, this time from the first Appendix to the *Enquiry concerning the Principles of Morals* (and also mentioned by Flew), since in it we find the very word, 'define', which was at the centre of the trouble over Hume's account of cause. It runs: 'The hypothesis which we embrace is plain. It maintains that morality is determined by sentiment. It defines virtue to be *whatever mental action or quality gives to a spectator the pleasing sentiment of approbation*; and vice the contrary. We then proceed to examine a plain matter of fact, to wit, what actions have this influence' (*E* 289). If we really are to take this for a definition, as the term is nowadays understood, then it becomes quite inescapable that, for Hume, whether a given action is virtuous or vicious is 'a plain matter of fact'. Given that last sentence, the point could hardly have escaped him. Yet only two pages earlier he has based his proof that morality cannot rest on reason on the premiss that 'reason judges either of *matter of fact* or of *relations*', and challenged the opposition to produce the matter of fact or relation in which they hold morality to consist. We have the option of charging Hume with the most glaring howler, or concluding that this is not, in modern philosophical usage, a definition at all.

It seems, then, that there is good reason to be wary of reading Hume too heavily in terms of the conceptual-analytical part of his theory. Because of

[10] A. G. N. Flew, 'On the Interpretation of Hume', *Philosophy*, 38 (1963), 178–82.
[11] G. Hunter, 'Hume on Is and Ought', *Philosophy*, 37 (1962), 148–52.   [12] Ibid. 149.

recent concentration on semantic analysis, those who have written about the history of philosophy, being all too ready to find their embryonic selves in the past, have played this aspect of his thought up until the reader became prepared to find it doing all the central work; whereas in truth it belongs quite near the periphery. We shall see yet more evidence for that claim before the end of this paper.

There is a residual puzzle about the 'two definitions' passage. I have said that it is best understood as presenting two descriptions of the circumstances under which belief in a causal connexion arises, one concentrating on the outward situation, the other on the state of the believer's mind that those outward facts induce. This steers clear of the problem with which Robinson and Richards were grappling, but it does leave an important fact about the text unexplained: nowhere in the paragraph in which the two definitions are stated does Hume say anything about belief or knowledge, but he does say a great deal about *what a cause is*. Is that not the language of someone who is making an ontological point, telling us something about the way reality is, rather than an epistemological one about the genesis of our opinions?

Hume's attitude to ontological issues is complex; like that of Kant, it has at least two levels. We have already remarked that the negative aspects of his programme would lead us to expect a degree of agnosticism about the nature of reality: the claim that the real cannot be known in a certain way does not commit one to any further claims about what it is or is not like. We have also remarked, in effect, that the positive side of his endeavours would do little or nothing to reverse this tendency. They are only concerned with what is real in so far as it is necessary to account for our beliefs, for which job Hume needs no more equipment than minds and their impressions, at most. And there are in fact plenty of signs of such agnosticism. For instance: 'I am, indeed, ready to allow, that there may be several qualities both in material and immaterial objects, with which we are utterly unacquainted; and if we please to call these *power* or *efficacy*, 'twill be of little consequence to the world.' (*T* 168). There is a tradition which, spurred on by the disastrous assimilation of Hume's philosophy to logical positivism,[13] sees such passages as ironical expressions of the negative ontological thesis that there are no such qualities; but that assimilation needs to look to its own defences. In any case, it is much harder to see irony in a sentence like the following, used by Philo (and seemingly assented to by Cleanthes) in his refutation of the cosmological argument in Part IX of the *Dialogues concerning Natural Religion*: 'And . . . may it not happen, that, could we penetrate into the intimate nature of bodies, we should clearly see why it was absolutely impossible, they could ever admit of any other disposition?' (*D* 191).

---

[13] Discussed in Craig, *The Mind of God and the Works of Man*, ch. 2 §6 (pp. 120–30).

Cleanthes has just made the very similar point, that if there is a necessarily existent being, it may be matter—the contrary cannot be proved: 'It must be some unknown, inconceivable qualities, which can make [the Deity's] non-existence appear impossible, or his attributes unalterable: And no reason can be assigned, why these qualities may not belong to matter. As they are altogether unknown and inconceivable, they can never be proved incompatible with it.' (D 190). It is very hard to read these as anything other than sincere expressions of Hume's mature opinion, nor, since that should not now surprise us, is there any reason to try. But Hume has another way of using ontological language: *for us*, human beings in the natural state of mind, there *are* causes, bodies, minds that preserve an identity through time—this is a consequence of his doctrine that we cannot help having these beliefs and seeing the world accordingly. It is only to be expected, therefore, that he will sometimes speak as if he firmly took there to be causes (and the rest); and equally it is to be expected that when he sets himself to investigate the question what a cause is, he will talk about the *belief* that there are causes and the circumstances under which this belief is held. On his theory, after all, this is the only thing that can be investigated under that heading; the deep metaphysical question about what it is, ultimately, that shifts the universe from one state into the next he regards as being beyond the reach of human enquiry. In a very similar way Kant, speaking as an empirical realist, will say that there are spatio-temporal objects, causes, substances—but then investigate them by talking about the way in which our sensibility and understanding do, and must, work. So when Hume asks what an X is, and embarks on an answer rather than counselling a resigned agnosticism, we will do well to remember that there is a vague tacit clause roughly along the lines of 'so far as Xs can concern, or be known to, or pointfully investigated by, the human mind'. In fact, the clause is not even always tacit: 'And as the constant conjunction of objects constitutes the very essence of cause and effect, matter and motion may often be regarded as the causes of thought, *as far as we have any notion of that relation.*' (T 250, my emphasis). Hence the famous equation of the causal connexion with the genesis of our belief in it—no conflation of the logical and the psychological, this, but a concise and powerful statement of the heart of Hume's position: 'The necessary connexion betwixt causes and effects is the foundation of our inference from one to the other. The foundation of our inference is the transition arising from the accustom'd union. These are, therefore, the same.' (T 165). Hence, also, the less consciously provocative explanation of his procedure in the paragraph of the *Treatise* immediately preceding the 'two definitions': 'This order would not have been excusable, of first examining our inference from the relation before we had explain'd the relation itself, had it been possible to proceed in a different method. But as the nature of the relation depends so much on that of the inference, we have been oblig'd to advance in this seemingly preposterous manner . . .' (*T* 169). It should not therefore be felt as an objection to my suggested reading of the 'two definitions' that it treats statements which, prima facie, are about causality as being in the first instance concerned with what is *believed* about causes, and why. On the contrary, it is almost an argument in its favour. For since the two themes are (at any rate for purposes of serious investigation) virtually identified with each other by Hume's philosophy, it is highly likely that when he uses the language of ontology it will be illuminating to read what he says in terms of his theory of belief, a point which is not restricted to his writings on causality.

8

David Hume: Objects and Power

Galen Strawson

I

Many people think that Hume holds a straightforward 'regularity' theory of causation, according to which causation is nothing more than regular succession or constant conjunction. 'If Hume is right', Saul Kripke says, then 'even if God were to look at [two causally related] events, he would discern nothing relating them other than that one succeeds the other.'[1] 'Hume's conclusion', according to Roger Woolhouse, is 'that so far as the external objects which are causes and effects are concerned there is only constant conjunction'; so far as the 'operations of natural bodies' are concerned, 'regularity and constant conjunction are all that exist'.[2] Even now, Barry Stroud thinks that Hume's view is that 'all that ever happens in the world independently of minds is that one thing succeeds another and resembles other instances that followed similar antecedents'.[3] I will call this astonishing view the 'standard view'. I will argue that it is wrong, and that Hume believes in causal power, or 'natural necessity', or 'Causation', as I will sometimes call it.[4]

[1] S. Kripke, *Wittgenstein on Rules and Private Language* (Oxford: Blackwell, 1982), 67. According to the regularity theory of causation (and ignoring certain complications), a particular event of type A (say A_1) is the cause of a particular event of type B (say B_1) if and only if A_1 is prior to and spatio-temporally contiguous with B_1, and all events of type A are prior to and spatio-temporally contiguous with events of type B: causation is just regular succession: 'in nature one thing just happens after another' (A. J. Ayer, *The Central Questions of Philosophy* (London: Penguin, 1973), 183).

[2] R. Woolhouse, *The Empiricists* (Oxford: Oxford University Press, 1988), 149–50.

[3] B. Stroud, *The Quest for Reality* (New York: Oxford University Press, 2000), 11.

[4] Two recent critics of the 'standard' view are J. P. Wright (*The Sceptical Realism of David Hume* (Manchester: Manchester University Press, 1983) and 'Hume's Causal Realism: Recovering a Traditional Interpretation', in R. Read and K. Richman (eds.), *The New Hume Debate* (London: Routledge, 2000), 88–99) and E. J. Craig (*The Mind of God and the Works of Man* (Cambridge: Cambridge University Press, 1987), ch. 2). Cf. also N. Kemp Smith, *The Philosophy of David Hume* (London: Macmillan, 1941), 396–402.

II

If you want to know what Hume thought about causation, you have to give priority to his first *Enquiry*, which begins as follows:

MOST of the principles, and reasonings, contained in this volume, were published in a work in three volumes, called *A Treatise of Human Nature*: A work which the Author had projected before he left College, and which he wrote and published not long after. But not finding it successful, he was sensible of his error in going to the press too early, and he cast the whole anew in the following pieces, where some negligences in his former reasoning and more in the expression, are, he hopes, corrected. Yet several writers, who have honoured the Author's Philosophy with answers, have taken care to direct all their batteries against the juvenile work, which the Author never acknowledged, and have affected to triumph in any advantages, which, they imagined, they had obtained over it: *A practice very contrary to all rules of candour and fair-dealing, and a strong instance of those polemical artifices, which a bigotted zeal thinks itself authorised to employ.* Henceforth, the author desires, that the following Pieces *may alone be regarded as containing his philosophical sentiments and principles.* (*E* 2, my emphasis)

These are strong words for Hume, and they express hurt. Responding anonymously in 1745 to an early attack on the *Treatise*, he described the quotations from the *Treatise* given by his 'accuser'—which read like a summary of what many for most of the twentieth century regarded as Hume's essential views—as 'maim'd Excerpts' (*L* 3) selected with 'a Degree of Unfairness which appears to me altogether astonishing' (*L* 20). The accuser (probably William Wishart) used Hume's words, but 'pervert[ed] them & misrepresent[ed] them in the grossest way in the World' (*NHL* 15).

Hume's public response was to write the *Enquiry* (1748). He wrote it to counteract the misinterpretation of the *Treatise*, and to correct certain mistakes:

The philosophical Principles are the same in both: But I was carry'd away by the Heat of Youth & Invention to publish too precipitately. . . . I have repented my Haste a hundred, & a hundred times. (*HL* i. 158)

I . . . acknowledge . . . a very great Mistake in Conduct, viz my publishing at all the Treatise of human Nature . . . Above all, the positive Air, which prevails in that Book, & which may be imputed to the Ardor of Youth, so much displeases me, that I have not Patience to review it. (*HL* i. 187)[5]

He expected a much better reception for the *Enquiry*, in which 'the same Doctrines [are] better illustrated & exprest'—a striking remark when one is trying

---

[5] This remark about the 'positive air' is particularly poignant when one considers those who persist in thinking that Hume held an outright ontological 'bundle theory of the self' (see G. Strawson, 'David Hume: mind and self', forthcoming). The principal 'negligences in . . . expression' that Hume finds in his *Treatise* and regrets in his Advertisement to the *Enquiry* are doubtless his phrasings of epistemological points in a dramatically ontological idiom (see Craig, *The Mind of God and the Works of Man*, ch. 2 §5).

to establish Hume's views about causation, given that all the main support for the view that Hume was an outright regularity theorist derives from the *Treatise*, and vanishes in the *Enquiry*.

'But allow me to tell you, that I never asserted so absurd a Proposition as *that any thing might arise without a Cause*: I only maintain'd, that our Certainty of the Falshood of that Proposition proceeded neither from Intuition nor Demonstration; but from another Source.' (*HL* i. 187). Hume was irritated by the suggestion that he thought otherwise—that he was 'denying the Truth of [a] Proposition, which indeed *a Man must have lost all common Sense to doubt of* ' (*L* 22). He would have been equally irritated by the allegation that he asserted that regular succession is all there is to causation. The most direct proof of this is given on pp. 253–6 below.

In asking that the *Enquiry* alone should 'be regarded as containing his philosophical sentiments and principles', Hume lays a clear obligation on us. We can read the *Enquiry* back into the *Treatise*, when trying to understand his considered view; we can't go the other way. Everything in the *Treatise* that is or appears incompatible with the *Enquiry* must be discarded. Nothing in the *Treatise* can legitimately be used to throw light on any passage in the *Enquiry* unless two conditions are fulfilled: the passage in the *Enquiry* must be unclear (this is not often the case), and the passage from the *Treatise* must not be incompatible with anything in the *Enquiry* that is not in dispute. Even when a passage from the *Treatise* is called in evidence, its claim to make a contribution to interpretation must be weak when compared with competing claims from passages in the *Enquiry* other than the passage under consideration.

If we also respect Hume's insistence that 'the philosophical Principles are the same in both' the *Treatise* and the *Enquiry*, we have a further obligation. In order to understand the *Treatise*—in order, in particular, to avoid being misled by the dramatic and polemical exaggerations of the 'Ardor of Youth'— we must read the *Enquiry* back into the *Treatise* wherever possible, and give it priority. For it was written to correct the misunderstanding of the *Treatise*.

Nearly all present-day commentators ignore this obligation, and many of them have their exegetical principles exactly the wrong way round.[6] Hume deserves sympathy, for it is bad to be attacked for views one never held, and worse to be praised and famous for holding them.[7] I know of no greater abuse

---

[6] Year after year the Oxford University Examination Decrees for the *History of Philosophy from Descartes to Kant* paper specify that Hume is to be studied in connection with the *Treatise*; no mention is made of the *Enquiry*. A proposal to include the *Enquiry* was rejected by the Oxford Sub-Faculty of Philosophy in 1999.

[7] It is bad to be praised for holding views one never held even when they are right, but worse when they are absurd.

of an author in the history of philosophy.[8] Many love the *Treatise* because they love argument, and this is understandable; many excellent philosophers are condemned to the lower divisions in philosophy because, consciously or not, they are more attached to cleverness and argument than truth. Hume is not among them, however, and no one can avoid the obligations described in the preceding paragraph. It cannot be plausibly argued that there is early Hume and late Hume, that they are importantly different, and that each deserves study in his own right. Hume was at work on the *Treatise*-clarifying *Enquiry* within five years of the publication of the *Treatise* and probably earlier, and (once again) was most insistent that the philosophical principles are the same in both. We have no reason to judge him to be self-deceived on this matter.[9]

III

When Hume talks of 'objects' he usually means genuinely external objects, in a sense to be explained further below. Sometimes, however, he only means to refer to mental occurrences, or what he calls 'perceptions', and it may be suggested that this is always so: that he only means to refer to the 'immediate', mental objects of experience, in talking of objects. This suggestion is worth mentioning, because if it were correct it would be easy to understand why Hume might wish to adopt a regularity theory about causation in the 'objects'.[10] But it is not correct—Hume didn't mean to refer only to mental occurrences or perceptions, and when I use the word 'object' I will mean what he usually meant in the contexts with which I will be concerned: objects that are genuinely non-mental things, things that exist independently of our minds.[11]

I will argue for this soon. For the moment I will take it for granted, because it allows me to state the main objection to the standard view of Hume. It is that the standard view fails to distinguish clearly between two fundamentally different notions, one ontological, the other epistemological. It fails to distinguish sufficiently between the ontological notion of causation as it *is* 'in the objects', and

---

[8] Perhaps the near-exclusive focus on the *Groundwork of the Metaphysic of Morals*, in the discussion of Kant's moral philosophy, is a comparable case.

[9] See S. Buckle, 'Hume's Biography and Hume's Philosophy: "My Own Life" and *An Enquiry concerning Human Understanding*', *Australian Journal of Philosophy*, 77 (1999), 1–25, and 'British Sceptical Realism: A Fresh Look at the British Tradition', *European Journal of Philosophy*, 7 (1999), 1–29, for some excellent recent work on this issue. See also S. Buckle, *Hume's Enlightenment Tract* (Oxford: Clarendon Press, 2001).

[10] This point is discussed in G. Strawson, *The Secret Connexion* (Oxford: Clarendon Press, 1989), 45–6 and app. A, 'Cartoon-Film Causation'. On this view, Hume agrees with Berkeley about what causation is, considered as a phenomenon in the physical world, but puts things differently.

[11] Hume sometimes means events when he talks of objects. When this is so, the present claim is that he means events that involve genuinely external, mind-independent objects, not merely mental events. In *The Secret Connexion* (ch. 22.2) I point out that Hume's belief in causal power does not depend on belief in external objects, although they go naturally together. On the general question of Hume's use of the word 'object', see M. Grene, 'The Objects of Hume's *Treatise*', *Hume Studies*, 20 (1994), 163–77.

the epistemological notion of causation so far as we *know* about it in the objects.[12] But this distinction is crucial. In the end Hume's regularity theory of causation is only a theory about causation so far as we can know about it in the objects, not about causation as it is in the objects. As far as causation as it is in the objects is concerned, Hume believes in Causation.

In other words: the 'standard' view confuses Hume's epistemological claim

(E) All we can ever know of causation is regular succession

with the positive ontological claim

(O) All that causation actually is, in the objects, is regular succession.

It moves, catastrophically, from the former to the latter. The former is arguably true. The latter is fantastically implausible. It is 'absurd', as Hume might have put it.[13]

Although (E) and (O) are clearly distinct, Hume sometimes abbreviates his main claims, in the *Treatise*, in such a way that he seems to slide from (E) to (O), propelled by his theory of ideas or meaning. In these cases, the passage from the merely epistemological claim (E) to the ontological claim (O) appears to be made via the semantic claim

(S) All we can legitimately *manage to mean* by expressions like 'causation in the objects' is regular succession.

The transition is made as follows. (1) (E) is true. (2) If (E) is true, (S) is true (that's strict empiricism for you). (3) If (S) is true, (O) is true. Hence (4) (O) is true. Why does (O) follow from (S)? Because, given (S), when the phrase 'causation in the objects' comes out of our mouths or pens, or occurs in our thought, it inevitably just means regular succession. So (O) causation in the objects—here is the phrase, meaning 'regular succession'—just is regular succession. After all, regular succession is regular succession.[14]

---

[12] See J. L. Mackie, *The Cement of the Universe* (Oxford: Clarendon Press, 1974), ch. 1, and Craig, *The Mind of God and the Works of Man*, ch. 2 §§4 and 5 (cf. this volume, Ch. 7 §2).

[13] In fact nothing in the present account of Hume hangs on the claim that the regularity theory is absurd (see e.g. D. M. Armstrong, *What is a Law of Nature?* (Cambridge: Cambridge University Press, 1983), J. Foster, 'Induction, Explanation, and Natural Necessity', *Proceedings of the Aristotelian Society*, 83 (1982), 87–101, G. Strawson, 'Realism and Causation', *Philosophical Quarterly*, 37 (1987), 253–77, and *The Secret Connexion*, chs. 5, 8, 22), but I take it to be obvious that there is more to causation than regularity (it is equally obvious that this can't be conclusively proved). The regularity view is very like dogmatic phenomenalism: to suppose that regularity is all there is to causation is like supposing that objects consist merely of perceptions (actual or possible). It is a delicate matter to find the best way of saying what causation involves, over and above regularity; but there is a fundamental respect in which one has already said enough when one has granted that matter has a certain nature.

[14] The same type of argument can be made if one replaces 'causation' and 'regular succession' with 'external objects' and 'perceptions' respectively, or with 'the self' and 'a series of perceptions' respectively.

I am going to reject this view of the consequences of Hume's theory of ideas (or theory of meaningfulness). Let me raise an initial doubt. Suppose there were good grounds for thinking that Hume's theory of ideas did license the (very strange) move from (E) to (O) via (S)—and hence licensed the claim that all we can suppose a thing to be is what we can detect or experience or know of it, simply because we cannot manage to mean anything more than what we can detect or experience or know of it, when we think or talk about it. Even if this were so, the following decisive objection to attributing (O) to Hume would remain: (O), the claim that causation is definitely nothing but regular succession, and that there is definitely no such thing as Causation, makes a positive ontological assertion about the ultimate nature of reality. It is therefore violently at odds with Hume's scepticism—his scepticism with respect to knowledge claims about what we can know to exist, *or know not to exist*, in reality. As a strict sceptic with respect to knowledge claims about the nature of reality, Hume does not make positive claims about what definitely does exist (apart from mental occurrences or 'perceptions', whose existence he rightly takes as certain). But, equally clearly, he does not make positive claims about what definitely (or knowably) does not exist. For such claims are equally unwarranted, from the sceptical point of view. Ignorance, as he says, is never a 'good reason for rejecting any thing' (*E* 73). This point about Hume's scepticism is enough to refute any attribution of (O) to him: it is enough to refute the standard view.

IV

The following objection may be put. As a strict sceptic with respect to knowledge claims, Hume will not claim that we can know that there is definitely nothing like Causation in reality. Equally, though, he will not claim that there definitely is something like Causation in reality.

This is true. It requires us to take note of the distinction between knowledge and belief. Those who think that Hume is a straightforward regularity theorist with respect to causation standardly suppose that he makes a *knowledge* claim on the question, claiming that causation is definitely just regular succession, and that therefore there is definitely nothing like Causation. Such a knowledge claim is ruled out by his scepticism. The *belief* that there is some such thing as Causation is not ruled out, however. Scepticism can acknowledge the naturalness of this belief, and grant that it may well be something like the truth; it will merely insist that although we believe it, we cannot prove it to be true.

Some think that Hume cannot even admit to *believing* in the existence of anything like Causation, given his scepticism. I will discuss the motivation for this view in §§V and VI. For the moment it suffices to say that Hume is not a

Pyrrhonist.[15] This objection fails to take account of his doctrine of 'natural belief', according to which we have certain natural beliefs (for example, in the existence of external objects) which we find it practically impossible to give up. Scepticism of the Humean kind does not say that these beliefs are definitely not true, or unintelligible, or utterly contentless (see §VI). Genuine *belief* in the existence of *X* is fully compatible with strict scepticism with regard to *knowledge* claims about the existence of *X*.[16]

In fact Hume never really questions the idea that there is Causation—something in virtue of which reality is regular in the way that it is. Following Newton, he repeatedly insists on the epistemological claim that we know nothing of the ultimate nature of Causation. '[T]he power or force, which actuates the whole machine . . . of the universe . . . is entirely concealed from us' (*E* 63), and 'experience only teaches us, how one event constantly follows another; without instructing us in the secret connexion, which binds them together, and renders them inseparable' (*E* 66). We cannot know the nature of Causation. But to say that is not to doubt that Causation exists.

V

These quotations seem very clear indeed. But it may now be objected that Hume can't mean what he says. He can't mean what he says because he holds that the idea of causation as something more than regular succession—the idea of Causation—is completely *unintelligible*. What's more, he says the same about the notion of 'external objects'.

The fact that he said the same about the notion of external objects may, however, be part of the solution, not part of the problem. I will now approach the general issue of Hume's attitude to questions of meaning and intelligibility by defending the view that he was committed to the intelligibility of the realist conception of objects. This commitment is obvious in the *Enquiry*, and also in the *Treatise*, but some doubt it, believing that Hume is some sort of idealist about objects, and is forced to be so by a theory of meaning which entails that talk of external objects is unintelligible.

The central point is simple. When present-day philosophers say that something is unintelligible, they mean that it is incoherent and cannot exist. But Hume—with Locke, Berkeley, and many others—uses the word 'unintelligible' in the literal sense, which survives in the standard non-philosophical use of the word—as when we say that a message is unintelligible, meaning simply that we cannot understand it, although it exists ('Ni chredai Hume nad yw

---

[15] 'I am not such a Sceptic, as you may, perhaps, imagine'(*HL* i. 186).
[16] See Kemp Smith, *The Philosophy of David Hume*, 62–8, and ch. 21.

achosiaeth yn ddim ond cyd-ddigwyddiad rheolaidd'). When Hume says that something is unintelligible, then, he means that we cannot understand it. In particular, he means that we cannot form an idea of it or term for it that has any positive descriptive content on the terms of the theory of ideas. To say this, however, is not to say that we cannot refer to it, or that the notion of it is incoherent.

Hume's position on this matter is like Locke's position with respect to the 'real essence' of gold. Locke takes it that the real essence of gold is completely unknown to us. This leads him to say that in so far as the word 'gold' carries a 'tacit reference to the real Essence' of gold, as it does in common use, it has '*no signification at all*, being put for somewhat, whereof we have no Idea at all'.[17] In other words, the word 'gold' is *completely meaningless*—it lacks any positive descriptive content on the terms of the theory of ideas—in so far as it is taken to refer to the unknown real essence of gold. And yet it does so refer, as Locke concedes. We can perfectly well talk about the real essence of gold and take it to exist.

Berkeley makes a similar move when he proposes that the term 'notion' be used as a 'term for things that cannot be understood'. It is, he says, 'absurd for any man to argue against the existence of [a] thing, from his having no direct and positive notion of it'. He thinks that it is only where 'we have not even a relative notion of it' that we 'employ words to no manner of purpose, without any design or signification whatever' and allows that 'many things, for anything I know, may exist, whereof neither I nor any other man has or can have any idea or notion whatsoever.'[18] This is Berkeley speaking.

Kant makes a similar move. On the one hand, he says that the categories, which include the concept of cause, 'have only an empirical use, and have *no meaning whatever* when not applied to objects of possible experience'. On the other hand, he says that 'in *thinking*', and a fortiori in intelligible—hence contentful, hence meaningful—thinking, 'the categories are not limited by the conditions of our sensible intuition, but have an unlimited field. It is only *knowledge* of what we think . . . that requires intuition'.[19]

The point is routine in Hume's time. He continually stresses the fact that there may be aspects of reality of which we can form no positively descriptive

[17] See Locke, *Essay concerning Human Understanding* III. x. 19 (ed. P. H. Nidditch (Oxford: Clarendon Press, 1975); my emphasis). Cf. Mackie, *Problems from Locke* (Oxford: Clarendon Press, 1976), 93–100.

[18] G. Berkeley, *De Motu*, in *Philosophical Works*, ed. M. R. Ayers (London: Dent, 1975), §23; id., 'Three Dialogues' (1713), ibid. 177, 184.

[19] Kant, *Critique of Pure Reason*, B724 (my emphasis) (see also B298–9); B166 n. (my emphasis) (see also B309). Kant gives a clear indication of what he means by the word 'meaning' in the phrase 'no meaning whatever' on B300: when the categories are not applied to what is given in sensible intuition, he says, 'all meaning, *that is, all reference to the object*, falls away' (my emphasis).

conception on the terms of the theory of ideas, and which are in that sense wholly unintelligible by us. This is an integral part of his scepticism. It is, in fact, an integral part of any sound philosophy.

VI

The claim about Hume may still be doubted. So I will consider what happens in the *Treatise* when Hume explicitly considers the thought that talk of realist external objects is 'unintelligible', given his theory of ideas.[20] Speaking of the notion of external objects, Hume says that it is 'impossible for us so much as to conceive or form an idea of any thing *specifically different* from ideas and impressions' (*T* 67, my emphasis). By 'specifically different' he means 'of a different species or kind'; so his claim is that we cannot form any idea of anything which is of an entirely different species or kind from ideas and (sensory) impressions. Why not? Because the content of our ideas is entirely derived or copied from our impressions, and such impression-copy content can never amount to a genuine representation of something entirely different from impressions. But this means it can never amount to a genuine representation of an external object. For an external object is by hypothesis an essentially non-mental thing, and is *obviously* of an entirely different species from an essentially mental thing like an impression and an idea.[21]

Hume, then, seems to be saying that we can never conceive of or form any idea of such a thing as an external object. But he goes straight on to grant that we can after all form some sort of conception of external objects:

The farthest we can go towards a conception of external objects, when [they are] suppos'd specifically different from our perceptions, is to form a *relative* idea of them, without pretending to *comprehend* the related objects. (*T* 68, my emphasis)

This is the farthest we can go; external objects are 'incomprehensible'; we have only a 'relative' idea of them. But a relative idea of *X* is not no idea at all. An everyday example of a case in which one has a referentially efficacious but in a sense contentless and hence merely 'relative' idea of something *X* is the idea one has of something when one can refer to it only as, say, 'whatever it was that

---

[20] At this point the argument becomes a bit more complicated. The direct argument that Hume believes in Causation starts in §VII, and does not depend on the details of this section.

[21] Here I put aside an important complication. It has to do with Hume's attitude to Locke's 'resemblance' theory. Briefly, if the Lockean account of the resemblance between primary qualities of objects and ideas of primary qualities is at all defensible, then it is arguable that objects are *not* entirely (qualitatively) different from perceptions, even though they are indeed of an entirely different *species* or kind. On this view, ideas of primary qualities really can give us some genuine idea of what external objects are like; they render them at least partly 'intelligible'. Hume's final position on Locke's claim is one of agnosticism (*E* 153). See Wright, *The Sceptical Realism of David Hume*, ch. 2.

caused this appalling mess'. In this case, one may have no positive conception of the nature of X.[22]

In the case of Causation, our merely relative idea of it is 'that in reality in virtue of which reality is regular in the way that it is'; or, in Hume's terms, it is 'the power or force, which actuates the whole machine . . . of the universe' (E 63) and on which the 'regular course and succession of objects totally depends' (E 55). It is 'that circumstance in the cause, which gives it a connexion with its effect' (E 77), 'that very circumstance in the cause, by which it is enabled to produce the effect' (E 67–8). Or—to quote the *Treatise* rather than the *Enquiry*—it is that which is in fact the 'reason of the conjunction' of any two objects (T 93). This description suffices to pick Causation out in such a way that we can go on to refer to it while having no descriptively contentful conception of its nature on the terms of the theory of ideas.

Many quotations from Hume's *Dialogues* can also be called in support. The dialogue form raises certain problems of interpretation, but there is no doubt that Philo represents Hume's views.[23] Many still proceed as if the *Dialogues*—Hume's most carefully composed work of philosophy and arguably his 'greatest work of metaphysics'[24] —simply does not count when it comes to understanding Hume's views. They seem viscerally incapable of admitting that quotation from the *Dialogues* has the same weight as quotation from the *Enquiry* and the *Treatise*, and have in consequence no hope of getting Hume right. They cannot hear Hume speaking as Philo when he says,

It is observed by arithmeticians, that the products of 9 compose always 9 or some lesser product of 9; if you add together all the characters, of which any of the former products is composed. Thus, of 18, 27, 36, which are products of 9, you make 9 by adding 1 to 8, 2 to 7, 3 to 6. Thus 369 is a product also of 9; and if you add 3, 6, and 9, you make 18, a lesser product of 9. To a superficial observer, so wonderful a regularity may be admired as the effect either of chance or design; but a skilful algebraist immediately concludes it to be the work of necessity, and demonstrates, that it must for ever result from the nature of these numbers. Is it not probable, I ask, that the whole œconomy of the universe is conducted by a like necessity, though no human algebra can furnish a key which solves the difficulty? And instead of admiring the order of natural beings, may it not happen, that, could we penetrate into the intimate nature of bodies, we should clearly

---

[22] Except, perhaps, the thought that it is a physical phenomenon. But who knows? Maybe it isn't even a physical phenomenon.

[23] See G. Strawson, 'Epistemology, Semantics, Ontology, and David Hume', *Facta Philosophica*, 2 (2000), §8.

[24] J. P. Wright, Critical Review of Wayne Waxman, *Hume's Theory of Consciousness, Hume Studies*, 21 (1995), 350. Some think that Hume attacked all metaphysics. In fact he considers his own work in the first part of the *Treatise* and in the first *Enquiry* to be metaphysics (as Kant observes (*Prolegomena* (1783), trans. P. G. Lucas (Manchester: Manchester University Press, 1953), 6)), and remarks, in his essay 'Of the Rise and Progress of the Arts and Sciences', that metaphysics is one of the four principal 'branches of science. Mathematics and natural philosophy . . . are not half so valuable.' (*Essays*, 126).

see why it was absolutely impossible, they could ever admit of any other disposition? (*D* 191)

Let me return to the discussion of objects in the *Treatise*. Hume writes that

we may *suppose*, but never can *conceive* a specific difference betwixt an object and an impression (*T* 241, my emphasis).

This contrast is important. It occurs at several other points in the *Treatise* (e.g. *T* 68, already quoted), and the idea behind it, expressed in one way or another, is routine in Hume's time. Anything that is to count as a genuine *conception* of something must be descriptively contentful on the terms of the theory of ideas: it must have directly impression-based, impression-copy content. By contrast, a supposition that something exists or is the case can be a genuine *supposition*, genuinely about something, and hence intelligible in our present-day sense, without being contentful (or meaningful or intelligible) on the terms of the theory of ideas. So the natural supposition that there are external objects 'specifically different from perceptions' is an intelligible one in our sense, and may well be true. All that follows from the theory of ideas is that we cannot form any well-founded descriptively contentful conception of external objects.[25]

Here as elsewhere Hume respects the principles of his scepticism, which prohibit the claim that we can know that there *isn't* anything to which the merely 'relative' idea of objects realistically conceived might relate or refer. Hume grants that there may be such external objects, firmly believes that there are, and merely insists that there will always remain a sense in which their nature is 'perfectly inexplicable' by us (*T* 84).[26] The conclusion of the famous discussion of objects in I. iv. 2 of the *Treatise* is not that there are no external objects, or that the notion of such things is incoherent—i.e. unintelligible in our strong, modern sense. On the contrary. In the penultimate paragraph Hume remarks that he began his discussion of objects by 'premising, that we ought to have an implicit faith' in our natural, sense-and-imagination-based belief in external objects (*T* 217). He concludes that this is indeed what we ought to do, announcing in the final paragraph that he will proceed upon the 'supposition . . . [that] there is both an external and internal world' (*T* 218).

His conclusion, then, is certainly not that there are no external objects. Nor is it that the idea of external objects is incoherent (unintelligible in our strong modern sense). He has two main points, of which the first is that we can

---

[25] More precisely: we cannot do this unless Locke's resemblance claim is defensible in some form; and this too we cannot know. See n. 21. For a recent development of the point, see Craig, *The Mind of God and the Works of Man*, ch. 2 esp. §6. See also Wright, 'Hume's Causal Realism'.

[26] Either partly or wholly inexplicable, depending on the defensibility of Locke's resemblance claim. See, once again, n. 21.

supply no decent rational foundation or justification for the belief that there are external objects: 'By what argument can it be proved, that the perceptions of the mind must be caused by external objects, entirely different from them, though resembling them . . . ?' (*E* 152–3). It cannot be proved, he says. For 'It is a question of fact, whether the perceptions of the senses be produced by [such] external objects, resembling them', and if we ask 'How shall this question be determined?', the answer is 'By experience surely; as all other questions of a like nature. But here experience is, and must be entirely silent.' (*E* 153).

In other words: it is either true or false that there are external objects, but we cannot know which. A fortiori, the supposition—and natural belief—that there are external objects is intelligible, and hence meaningful. Hume himself takes it that it is true, for the belief that it is true is part of natural belief.

His second point is that there is none the less something profoundly problematic, incomplete, misleading—defective, relative, inadequate, inaccurate, imprecise, imperfect, vulgar, loose, uncertain, confused, indistinct, 'fiction'-involving (see e.g. *T* 267, 218, 160, 639, *E* 67 n., 76, 77 n.)—about any conception of external objects (or Causation) that purports to be anything more than a merely 'relative' notion of external objects. This view is a consequence of his theory of ideas, and the question he faces is then this: 'What exactly is the content of natural beliefs featuring defective conceptions of this sort?' He doesn't answer this question in any detail, however. It is a question which tormented many in the twentieth century, but it was not one about which Hume felt he needed to say any more. The point he insists on is that we are deluded if we think we have any sort of complete, adequate, accurate, precise, perfect, philosophical, tight, certain, distinct, legitimately sense-based, descriptively contentful conception of external objects (or Causation).

Suppose for a moment that the standard view is right to claim that Hume thinks that the idea of external objects has no content at all, and indeed can have no content. The argument about causation that was given in §III can be rerun for objects as follows: (1) All we can ever know or observe of external objects are perceptions. (2) So (given standard meaning-empiricist principles) all we can legitimately manage to mean by expressions like 'external object' (or 'table', or 'chair') are perceptions. (3) So the statement that external objects are nothing but perceptions must be true—because when the phrase 'external objects' is used, it inevitably just means perceptions. Hence (4) phenomenalism is true, outright ontological phenomenalism, the view that external, physical objects are definitely—provably—nothing more than perceptions. Do not suppose that the conclusion can be tamely stated as 'Even if something other than perceptions exists, we can't manage to mean this "something"'. On the present view, the quoted sentence is already a kind of nonsense, because the phrase 'something other than perceptions' cannot really manage to refer to something other than perceptions in the way it purports to do.

Fortunately, this is not Hume's view. It is, he says, a straightforward '*question of fact*, whether the perceptions of the senses be produced by *external objects . . . entirely different from them*' (*E* 153). This is *very* clear. Or consider the *Treatise* again: 'we may well suppose in general' that physical objects are different from perceptions; there is no problem with this. The problem is that it is 'impossible for us *distinctly* to conceive' this (*T* 218, my emphasis).

Certainly Hume says things that admit the interpretation I am rejecting. He wrote the *Treatise* in the 'Ardor of Youth'. He was tempted into provocative expressions he regretted (*HL* i. 187, *E* 2). Even in the *Treatise*, however, he followed Locke and Berkeley (and many others) and anticipated Kant (and many others) in making the essential move, distinguishing between what we can suppose and what we can conceive in such a way as to allow that language can intelligibly be supposed to refer to something of which we have (and can have) no impression-copy-contentful idea.

Simon Blackburn ('Hume and Thick Connexions' Ch. 9 pp. 261–3 in this volume) has argued that little weight can be placed on the fact that Hume makes a distinction between what we can suppose and what we can conceive, because Hume himself does not make much of it. But we could grant, for purposes of argument, that Hume does not make much of the distinction—although he relies on it constantly. We could grant that Hume, in the *Treatise*, in the iconoclastic ardour of youth, sees the necessity of making the distinction between what we can suppose and what we can conceive as somewhat *annoying*. The fact remains that it is something that he finds himself obliged to record, in the course of his sceptical progress. He duly does so, clearly and unambiguously.[27] It is, as remarked, a routine distinction, utterly indispensable in any serious empiricist enterprise. It immediately blocks the disastrous argument from (1) to (4) set out above, and Hume takes it for granted in the *Enquiry*, which omits nearly all the technicalities of the *Treatise*. He takes it, in particular, and to repeat, that it is a straightforward although undecidable 'question of fact, whether the perceptions of the senses be produced by external objects . . . entirely different from them, though resembling them (if that be possible)'.[28]

It is a very simple point. Hume has to grant that thought and language can reach beyond perceptions in such a way that the thought that something other than perceptions exists can be allowed to be intelligible and possibly true. For if

---

[27] Note his equally clear statement, when arguing that we can have no idea of Causation, that he is 'indeed, ready to allow, that there may be several qualities both in material and immaterial objects, with which we are utterly unacquainted' (*T* 168): the realm of existence does not necessarily cease where the realm of words or positively contentful conceptions ceases.

[28] In the last seven words of this quotation Hume adverts to the point discussed in n. 21.

he does not do this, then, once again, he is condemned to dogmatic meta-physics; to outright ontological idealism; to the view that the statement 'Percep-tions are all that exist' is *provably true*. He is landed with a form of metaphysical certainty that he cannot possibly tolerate, as a sceptic who denies the possibility of attaining knowledge about the ultimate nature of reality (other than percep-tions). This is the first, crucial component of what John Wright calls his 'scepti-cal realism'. The second is simply his endorsement of certain 'natural beliefs'. He really does believe that external objects exist, and that Causation exists (see §§VII–XI below).

Blackburn claims that it is an 'error of taste to make sceptical realism a fun-damental factor in the interpretation of Hume' (pp. 259, 267 in this volume), but this is back to front. It is a grave error of taste and judgement to think that a philosopher of Hume's sceptical profundity could have failed to adopt a scepti-cal realist attitude. Blackburn's claim (p. 262) that Hume dismisses the 'sup-poses' versus 'conceives' distinction out of hand is not supported by the text he quotes from the *Treatise*, and is controverted both by Hume's announcement (on the same page) that he will proceed on the supposition that 'there is both an external and internal world' (*T* 218), and by his earlier declaration that the exis-tence of body is something 'which we must take for granted' (*T* 187), and by his practice throughout the *Treatise* and the *Enquiry*.

Blackburn is also wrong to claim that he quotes 'the two major passages' in which the suppose–conceive distinction features, 'with enough surrounding context to matter' (p. 261). For he omits Hume's most striking employment of the distinction:

[S]ince we may suppose, but never can conceive a specific difference betwixt an object and impression; any conclusion we form concerning the connexion and repugnance of impressions, will not be known certainly to be applicable to objects (*T* 241).

Here Hume is stating that the relations we discover on the basis of our impres-sions cannot be known to apply to real objects. His closing use of the word 'objects' is straightforwardly realist, and the clause 'will not be known certainly' adds the scepticism to the realism. He goes on to say that although we cannot have certainty, we can 'by an irregular kind of reasoning from experience, dis-cover a connexion or repugnance betwixt objects, which extends not to impres-sions' (*T* 242). No one who acknowledges no distinction between objects and perceptions can say this.[29]

Blackburn's claim (p. 262) that Hume 'affirms idealism' when he says that 'we never really advance a step beyond ourselves' in our conceptions (*T* 67) is also

[29] Both Craig (*The Mind of God and the Works of Man*, 124–5) and Wright ('Hume's Causal Realism', 90) have good discussions of this passage.

false. It turns Hume into a metaphysician of exactly the sort that he was not. At this point Hume is making a routine empiricist epistemological claim about the limits of knowledge and understanding. He is directly echoing Locke who wrote, 'it seems probable to me, that the simple *Ideas* we receive from Sensation and Reflection, are the Boundaries of our Thoughts; beyond which, the Mind, whatever efforts it may make, is not able to advance one jot' (*Essay* II. xxiii. 29). And Locke—that great and paradigmatic realist—was not affirming idealism.

All in all, Hume handles this issue in just the right way. He travels to the frontier of the absurd thesis about meaning (the thesis that leads to Mad Metaphysical Phenomenalism) in accordance with his empiricist theory of ideas. Then he stops, acknowledging, correctly, that it is intelligible to suppose that things other than perceptions exist, and expressing with great force the point that we can have no (certain) knowledge of their nature:

As long as we confine our speculations to *the appearances* of objects to our senses, without entering into disquisitions concerning *their real nature and operations*, we are safe from all difficulties . . . If [however] we carry our enquiry beyond the appearances of objects to the senses, I am afraid, that most of our conclusions will be full of scepticism and uncertainty.[30]

These are the sentiments of a sceptical realist (and follower of Newton) who relies on the distinction between 'supposing' and 'conceiving' and is far from affirming idealism.

One useful thought for those who still doubt that Hume generally writes as a sceptical realist is as follows: he repeatedly distinguishes between the 'sensible qualities' of objects, on the one hand, and the objects themselves and their 'secret' or unknown nature or internal structure, on the other hand. Whenever he does so, he is *ipso facto* thinking of objects in a realist fashion as something more than perceptions (as something more than idealist or phenomenalist objects). For he holds that there is nothing hidden or unknown in perceptions: unlike genuine external bodies, perceptions have no unobservable ontic backsides or innards: 'The perceptions of the mind', he says, 'are perfectly known', whereas 'the essence and composition of external bodies are . . . obscure' (*T* 366). It follows that bodies cannot be perceptions, on Hume's view. For nothing can be both perfectly known and obscure.

I will now begin on the direct argument—it is little more than an argument by quotation—that Hume believes in Causation, after first briefly stating his view about the nature of our idea of Causation, and describing an apparent tension in his thought.

---

[30] *T* 64 n. (*T* 638–9) (second emphasis mine). This is a note Hume added in order to try to correct misunderstanding of the text. Note the restraint of 'most' and the mildness of 'scepticism and uncertainty'.

VII

The result of applying Hume's theory of ideas to the idea of Causation is clear: we have no idea of it at all, conceived of as something in the world of physical objects. Why not? Because we can form no positively descriptively contentful conception of it. Why not? Because we can form a descriptively contentful conception of something only out of impression-copy content, and there is no impression of Causation to be found in or derived from objects. Why not? Because all we ever actually observe is regular succession, one thing following another.

It follows that no term like 'power' or 'force' can ever really *manage to mean* anything in the world, on the terms of the theory of ideas. It cannot pick up descriptively on anything in the world. It can only manage to pick up descriptively on something in the mind: the feeling of determination in the mind which we come to experience on being confronted with regular succession in the world. For this, according to Hume, is the impression-source from which our actual idea of power or Causation is derived.[31]

It has been widely believed that Hume went on from the epistemological claim that we have no idea of Causation to the outright ontological claim that there is nothing like Causation, and that causation is nothing but regular succession. And it is true that Hume's empiricist theory of ideas, strictly and literally interpreted, creates some pressure on him to put things in this way (see §III). But this pressure is comfortably offset by his scepticism and realism—which one might equally well call his deep philosophical common sense—as I will shortly show by quotation. The strict and literal interpretation of Hume's theory of meaning is not Hume's interpretation,[32] and in fact he takes it for granted that there is Causation.

There is certainly a tension in Hume's expression of his thought: he uses terms like 'power' and 'force' in a way that is arguably ruled out by his theory of ideas. If we call such terms 'Causation' terms—terms that purport to refer to Causation, i.e. to causation conceived of as something essentially more than regular succession—we can state the tension as follows: Hume holds that no Causation term can manage to 'positively-contentfully' mean anything like Causation. And yet he allows in practice that they can manage to mean something like Causation, at least in the sense of genuinely *referring* to it.

Well, this is at most a tension; it is not an inconsistency. The appearance of tension arises because our understanding of words like 'meaning' and 'unintelligible' is not the same as Hume's. There is obviously no difficulty in the idea that

---

[31] See *E* 75 (and *T* 165). On *E* 67 n. Hume remarks that the experience of effort we have in pushing and pulling things (for example) also enters into the 'vulgar . . . idea of power'. See also *E* 78 n.

[32] See Craig, *The Mind of God and the Works of Man*, ch. 2 esp. §6.

we may successfully use a term to refer to something which has some manifestation in our experience, even though we have no positive conception of its nature, over and above the thought that it is something and has the manifestation that it has (see §V). The idea that we can do such a thing is correct and indispensable. (It is even more obvious that we can refer to something when we only have an 'inadequate' or 'imperfect' idea of it.)

VIII

I have claimed that Hume grants that Causation terms may reach out referentially to refer to Causation in the world, just as terms purporting to refer to external objects may reach out to external objects, and I will now try to show that he consistently uses Causation terms like 'power' and 'force' in a straightforwardly referring way. He assumes that Causation exists: it is that on which the 'regular . . . succession of objects *totally depends*' (*E* 55, my emphasis); it is 'the *reason* of the conjunction' that we observe between two (types) of objects (*T* 93, my emphasis). He takes it for granted that there must be something about the world in virtue of which the world is regular. The idea that there might be nothing—the 'Humean' view—is not a candidate for consideration. The point he cherishes and wants to drive home, spectacularly contrary to the orthodoxy of his time, is simply that we have no positive descriptive conception of the nature of causal power.[33]

At *E* 30 Hume writes that

no philosopher, who is rational and modest, has ever pretended to assign *the ultimate cause* of any natural operation, or to show distinctly the action of *that power, which produces* any single effect in the universe (my emphasis).

Following Newton, here as elsewhere, he goes on to say that we can greatly simplify our account of the laws of nature, reducing it to a 'few general causes',

But as to *the causes of these general causes*, we should in vain attempt their discovery. . . . These *ultimate springs and principles* are totally shut up from human curiosity and enquiry. (my emphasis)

But they certainly exist.

---

[33] The worst reason for attributing the 'Humean' view to Hume is probably the one considered in n. 38 below. Note that the word 'depends', in the quotation from *E* 55, cannot be supposed to indicate any sort of causal dependence. The way in which regular succession depends on powers and forces may be supposed to be something like the way the properties of a substance like mercury are held to depend on its property of having a certain atomic structure. The crucial idea is simply that there is something in the nature of things in virtue of which things are regular in the way they are, something which is therefore not just the fact of the regularity itself. One could put the point by saying that regular succession is a manifestation or aspect of Causation, and depends on it in that sense.

This natural reading is doubted by those who think that all Hume's apparently referring uses of Causation terms are really ironic, but they ignore his admiration for Newton. There is, furthermore, a serious difficulty in the idea that a book written in order to clarify misunderstanding should be loaded with irony in such a way as to be deeply misleading.

At *E* 33 Hume writes that

It is allowed on all hands, that there is no known connexion between the sensible qualities and *the secret powers* [of bodies],

for nature

conceals from us those *powers and principles, on which the influence of . . . objects entirely depends.*

And at *E* 63–4 he writes that

The scenes of the universe are continually shifting, and one object follows another in an uninterrupted succession; but *the power or force, which actuates the whole machine*, is entirely concealed from us, and never discovers itself in any of the sensible qualities of body. (all three emphases mine)

Speaking as Philo, he says that

Chance has no place, on any hypothesis, sceptical or religious. Every thing is surely governed by steady, inviolable laws. And were the inmost essence of things laid open to us, we should then discover a scene, of which, at present, we can have no idea. Instead of admiring the order of natural beings, we should clearly see, that it was absolutely impossible for them, in the smallest article, ever to admit of any other disposition. (*D* 174–5)

Some have suggested that when Hume talks of secret or concealed powers or forces, all he really means are constant conjunctions, or objects, that are too small to be detected.[34] But even if this interpretation were thought to have some plausibility for the plural uses of terms like 'power' and 'force', it would have none for the more common singular uses. When someone speaks of the 'power or force, which actuates the whole machine . . . of the universe', and says that it is 'entirely concealed' from us, it is very implausible to suppose that all he really means are all those hundreds of constant conjunctions that are too small to be seen.[35]

---

[34] See e.g. J. Broackes, 'Did Hume Hold a Regularity Theory of Causation?', *British Journal for the Philosophy of History*, 1 (1993), 100–1; K. Winkler, 'The New Hume', *Philosophical Review*, 100 (1991), 541–79.

[35] See Strawson, *The Secret Connexion*, ch. 18. At this point the following objection may be made: 'Hume talks as if Causation exists for ease of exposition. He grants its existence to his opponents for the sake of argument, so that he can then shoot home his epistemological point that even if it does exist we can know nothing about its nature. But he doesn't really believe in it at all.' This view is not strictly

At *E* 37–8, after speaking of

our natural state of ignorance with regard to the powers and influence of all objects,

Hume goes on to give an argument against the appeal to past experience in justifying induction that makes essential use of the idea that causal power exists. Although particular experiences of objects at particular times may indeed show us

that those particular objects, at that particular time, were endowed with . . . *powers and forces* (my emphasis),

still, he says, we can never be sure that the objects in question will continue to have just those same powers in the future. The reason why induction cannot be justified by appeal to past experience, therefore, is precisely that

[the] *secret nature* [of bodies], and consequently, all their effects and influence, may change (my emphasis)

—between now and the next time we observe them. So the reason why induction is not rationally justifiable by appeal to past experience is certainly not that there isn't really any power governing bodies. It is not that bodies do not really have any secret nature or powers governing their effects and influence, so that anything might happen. On the contrary. Bodies do have a secret nature which determines their effects and influence. The trouble with appeals to past experience is simply that past experience can never provide a guarantee that the secret nature of bodies will not change in the future, bringing change in their effects and influence.[36]

This clarifies something that is obvious on reflection but often misunderstood: there is *no special link between inductive scepticism and the regularity theory of causation*. The argument for inductive scepticism just quoted appeals essentially to Causation.

refutable, because it denies outright the relevance and force of all the direct evidence against it, but there is no reason to believe it. There is no reason to claim that a sceptic and follower of Newton like Hume holds that there is definitely nothing about reality in virtue of which it is regular in the way that it is, so that its regularity is an objective fluke from moment to moment. There isn't even any reason to claim that he believes that there *may* be nothing about reality in virtue of which it is regular in the way that it is, so that the regularity *may* be an objective fluke from moment to moment. Hume certainly insists that we can't know whether the 'original, inherent principle of order [lies] in thought or in matter', but he is clear on the point that there is some such principle of order, and that 'Chance has no place, on any hypothesis' (*D* 174).

[36] Blackburn thinks that I invoke fundamental physical forces 'to soothe away inductive vertigo' (p. 266 in this volume), but I have no wish to do this. Nothing could do it, as Hume's argument shows (see Strawson, *The Secret Connexion*, 113). Blackburn is equally wrong to think that I want a 'straitjacket', something that can give certainty about the future (see G. Strawson, 'The Contingent Reality of Natural Necessity', *Analysis*, 51 (1991), 209–13).

IX

When things go normally, Hume says, ordinary people suppose that they perceive

the very force or energy of the cause, by which it is connected with its effect (*E* 69, my emphasis).

They only feel the need to invoke some invisible unperceived power or principle when something happens which they think of as extraordinary. But philosophers do better, for they can see that

even in the most familiar events, *the energy of the cause* is . . . unintelligible (*E* 70, my emphasis).

They realize, that is, that we have no positive conception of its ultimate nature in any case at all—although it certainly exists. Going on to talk of the occasionalists, Hume sets out their view

that the true and direct principle of every effect is not any power or force in nature, but a volition of the Supreme Being (*E* 70).

He strongly implies that he finds their view absurd, and ill-motivated even on religious grounds. More important for present purposes, however, is the methodological argument he presents against them. First, he observes that it is precisely their acknowledgement of our ignorance of power or energy in objects that leads them to 'rob nature . . . of every power', and attribute all power to God. Next, he observes that it is awareness of 'The same ignorance' that then leads them to rob the human mind too of power, and to 'assert, that the Deity is [also] the immediate cause of the union between soul and body', e.g. when we act.

He grants that they are right about our ignorance in these departments: we are indeed

totally ignorant of the power, on which depends the mutual operation of bodies (*E* 70)

(although there must of course be some such thing); and we are

no less ignorant of that power, on which depends the operation of mind on body, or of body on mind (*E* 70)

(although of course there must be some such thing). But if it is acknowledgement of our ignorance that leads the occasionalists to attribute all power to God, then they should realize that our ignorance of any power that might be attributed to God is equally complete:

We are ignorant, it is true, of *the manner in which bodies operate on each other*: Their *force or energy* is entirely incomprehensible: But are we not equally ignorant of the manner or force by which a mind, even the supreme mind, operates either on itself or on body? (*E* 72, my emphasis)

Yes, he answers, and goes on to make a remark that again appears to suffice to refute the standard view of Hume:

Were our ignorance, therefore, a good reason for rejecting any thing, we should be led [to deny] all energy in the Supreme Being as much as in the grossest matter. We . . . comprehend as little the operations of one as of the other. (*E* 72–3, my emphasis)

Here things are very clear. Our ignorance is not a good reason for rejecting the possible existence of anything. This quotation refutes the view that Hume can be supposed to be positively denying the existence of Causation, in going on at such length about how we are ignorant of it. And he continues with a distinction between what we *mean* and what there *is* which clearly illustrates that the tension described on pp. 246–7 is unproblematic for him: 'when we talk of gravity,' he says,

we *mean* certain effects, without comprehending *that active power* [i.e. gravity itself] (*E* 73 n., my emphasis)

—which none the less exists.

Newton famously agrees: 'the cause of Gravity . . . I do not pretend to know'.[37] In a general comment on his account of forces in Definition VIII of his *Principia*, he says that he intends 'only to give a mathematical notion of those forces, without considering *their physical causes and seats*', and that he considers certain 'forces not physically, but mathematically: wherefore the reader is not to imagine that by those words [attraction, impulse, or propensity towards a centre] I anywhere take upon me to define the kind, or the manner of any action, *the causes or the physical reason thereof*, or that I attribute *forces, in a true and physical sense*, to certain centres'. Newton is quite clear that we have a merely relative idea of such forces: we can have no knowledge of their nature beyond the knowledge we have of their observable manifestations.

X

At *E* 74 a famous passage occurs which may at first seem to support the standard view. Hume claims that when we step back from our ordinary belief that we can observe power or necessary connexion in the objects, we realize that the belief is not correct, and that the truth of our epistemic situation, critically assessed, is as follows:

---

[37] *Correspondence*, ed. H. W. Turnbull *et al.*, 3 vols. (Cambridge: Cambridge University Press, 1959–77), iii. 240.

All events seem entirely loose and separate. One event follows another; but we never can observe any tye between them. They seem *conjoined*, but never *connected*. And as we can have no idea of any thing, which never appeared to our outward sense or inward sentiment, the necessary conclusion *seems* to be, that we have no idea of connexion or power at all, and that these words are absolutely without any meaning . . .

It follows, according to him, that

When we say . . . that one object is connected with another, we *mean only*, that they have acquired a connexion in our thought . . . A conclusion, which is somewhat extraordinary; but which seems founded on sufficient evidence. (*E* 76, my emphasis)

In other words, we try to talk about the real force or energy in the world, but these words, in our use, only manage to (positively-contentfully) mean their impression-source: i.e. a feeling of determination in the mind, derived from experience of regular succession or constant conjunction.

But Hume does not say that regular succession is all that causation is. Once again, his point is that this is all we can know or comprehend of causation. He admits that it seems 'somewhat extraordinary' that when we talk of causal connexion between two objects we do not really manage to mean the real causal connexion between them (which of course exists), but mean only that they have acquired a connexion in our thought on account of having been observed to be constantly conjoined. But he doesn't take this as grounds for any sort of ontological assertion that this is all that causation (really) is, but rather as an occasion for an epistemological remark about the *profound limitations on the human capacity to grasp the nature of reality*:

what stronger instance can be produced of the surprizing ignorance and weakness of the understanding, than the present [one]? (*E* 76)

That is, in our unreflective moments (or excessively exalted philosophical moments) we are pretty sure we know about causal power in the objects if we know about anything. But in fact human understanding is so restricted that it cannot even 'comprehend' the nature of causal power, in so far as it involves something more than observable regular succession. The 'somewhat extraordinary' conclusion, then, is not that there is really no such thing as Causation. That would certainly be an extraordinary conclusion, but I don't think that it ever crossed Hume's mind.[38] His point is this: it is truly extraordinary that

---

[38] It is an elementary error to suppose that Hume's frequent remarks to the effect that 'Any thing may produce any thing' (e.g. *T* 173, *E* 164) provide any support for the claim that he considered the idea that there might be no such thing as Causation. The view he is endorsing, in making such remarks, is simply this: that so far as *reason* (or a priori thought) is concerned, there is no *logical* contradiction in the idea that any one thing may produce any other thing, however disparate the two things may seem to us. This view is correct, and is entirely compatible with the view (which he also holds) that given the way things actually are in reality (considered independently of anything that reason has to say about it), nothing can

despite the fact that causal power is all-pervasive, governing our thoughts and actions and our world in all respects, still human understanding is utterly incapable of grasping its true nature in any way. That's how limited we are:

> Our thoughts and enquiries are . . . every moment employed about this relation. Yet so imperfect are the ideas which we form concerning it, that it is impossible to give any just definition of *cause*, except what is drawn from something extraneous and foreign to it. (*E* 76)

It concerns us at every moment, and yet we cannot grasp its true nature at all. This purely epistemological point is what the philosophers Hume was arguing against could not believe.[39]

XI

The view that Hume's point is epistemological is further confirmed by what he goes on to say about his two 'definitions' of cause. When he says that 'the ideas which we form concerning' cause are

> so imperfect . . . that it is impossible to give any just definition of *cause*, except what is drawn from something extraneous and foreign to it (*E* 76),

he is referring to the two definitions that immediately follow, which specify the content that the idea of cause has given its impression-sources: they tell us what we can legitimately manage to mean, on the terms of the theory of ideas, when we talk about causes. The first defines causation as constant conjunction or regular succession and the second defines it in terms of a feeling of determination in the mind (*E* 76–7, *T* 170, 172), but both are held to be imperfect because

---

possibly happen any differently from the way it does happen. Consider the quotation from the *Dialogues* on p. 248 above.

[39] 'When a man speaks as do others, that does not always signify that he is of their opinion. But when he positively says the opposite of what is commonly said, though he might say it only once, we have reason to judge that it is his view' (N. Malebranche, *The Search afer Truth* (1674–5), trans. T. M. Lennon and P. J. Olscamp (Ohio: Ohio State University Press, 1980), 672–3). Broackes ('Did Hume Hold a Regularity Theory of Causation?') cites this passage as support for the standard view of Hume, and is right to think that Hume is saying the opposite of what is commonly said: for Hume is saying that we have no (legitimate) positive conception of the nature of causation. He is not, however, saying what the standard view has him say; *that* idea hasn't occurred to him, and the claim that the Malebranche quotation supports the standard view is scuppered by the points made in §II above. It must also be offset by two true remarks of Kant's: 'many historians of philosophy, with all their intended praise . . . attribute mere nonsense . . . to past philosophers. They are incapable of recognizing, beyond what the philosophers actually said, what they really meant to say' ('On a Discovery', in *The Kant–Eberhard Controversy* (1790), trans. H. Allison (Baltimore: Johns Hopkins University Press, 1973), 160). 'If we take single passages, torn from their context, and compare them with one another, contradictions are not likely to be lacking, especially in a work that is written with any freedom of expression . . . but they are easily resolved by those who have mastered the idea of the whole' (Preface to the Second Edition of the *Critique of Pure Reason* (1787), trans. N. Kemp Smith (London: Macmillan, 1933), Bxliv).

they cannot representationally encompass causation or power 'as it is in itself' (*E* 77 n.). They can define it only by reference to something other than itself.

An enormous amount has been written about the content of the two definitions, but here I am concerned only with Hume's view of what they achieve: his view that it is actually impossible for us to give anything other than an 'imperfect' definition of cause. Some deny that Hume thinks his definitions are imperfect, pointing out that in the *Treatise* he says that they are 'exact' and 'precise' (*T* 169). But we can allow this (though both these words disappear from the corresponding passage in the *Enquiry*). We can allow that he thinks his definitions are 'just', or as just as any definitions of cause can be (*E* 76, *T* 170). For the present point is then this: Hume says that the definitions are imperfect *in spite of* the fact that he thinks they are entirely exact, precise, and just. So what can he mean by 'imperfect'?

He is very clear about it. He means that the definitions do not really capture the true nature of causation at all. The trouble is that

we cannot remedy this inconvenience, or attain any more perfect definition, which may point out *that circumstance in the cause, which gives it a connexion with its effect* (*E* 77, my emphasis).

The trouble, in other words, is that although there is something about the cause-event in virtue of which it is connected with its effect, in any particular case, we cannot form any genuine descriptively contentful conception of it, on the terms of the theory of ideas.

Note that this quotation suffices by itself to refute the view that Hume held a regularity theory of causation. For if causation in the objects were just regular succession or constant conjunction, there would be *no inconvenience or imperfection in the first definition at all*. And in giving the first definition, we could hardly be said to be in the position of finding it 'impossible to give any just definition of *cause*, except what is drawn from something extraneous and foreign to it'.[40]

Some may say that all that Hume means, when he says that one has to refer to circumstances foreign to the cause, is that one has to go beyond the individual cause-event considered on its own: one has to mention the effect-event, and other events of the same type as the cause-event and effect-event, and even the human mind. But let us suppose that this is at least part of what he meant.[41] The present point retains its full force. For Hume says that the definitions are imperfect specifically because they cannot 'point out that circumstance in the cause,

---

[40]   Many still reject the present interpretation of Hume, but no one as far as I know has made any sort of reply to this point. (I discuss the strongest prima facie evidence for the opposite view of Hume in Strawson, *The Secret Connexion*, chs. 14 and 15.)

[41]   See Wright, 'Hume's Causal Realism'.

which [actually] gives it a connexion with its effect' (*E* 77; cf. *E* 67–8). There is something about the cause itself which the definitions cannot capture or represent: they leave out the essential thing. The imperfection in question is the imperfection that definitions have when they do not fully capture the nature of the thing that they are meant to be definitions of. We can't give a perfect definition of cause because of our ignorance of its nature. All we can encompass in our definition are its observable manifestations—its regular-succession manifestations (first definition), and the feelings of necessity or determination or habits of inference in the mind to which these give rise (second definition).

There has been a lot of speculation about the differences between Hume's use of the word 'definition' and our present-day use,[42] and in this context Edmund Burke's remarks about definition are illuminating, for they were made in 1757, nine years after the publication of the first edition of the first *Enquiry*, in a work which Hume read.[43] 'When we define', Burke writes,

we seem in danger of circumscribing nature within the bounds of our own notions, which we often . . . form out of a limited and partial consideration of the object before us, instead of extending our ideas to take in all that nature comprehends, according to her manner of combining . . . A definition may be very exact, and yet go but a very little way towards informing us of the nature of the thing defined.[44]

Here, I propose, Burke uses 'definition' in exactly the same way as Hume. A definition of a natural phenomenon, as opposed to a definition of a geometrical figure, records human understanding's best take on that phenomenon. As such, it may be very 'exact' and 'precise' (*T* 169) while also being very 'imperfect', 'limited and partial' in its representation of the nature of the phenomenon defined.[45]

Hume restates his position as follows:

If we examine the operations of body, and the production of effects from their causes, we shall find, that all our faculties can never carry us farther in our knowledge of [the] relation [of cause and effect] than *barely* to observe, that particular objects are *constantly conjoined* together [see the first definition], and that the mind is carried, by a *customary transition*, from the appearance of one to the belief of the other [see the second definition]. (*E* 92, first emphasis mine)

---

[42] Craig has a good discussion of differences between Hume's use of 'definition' and ours (*The Mind of God and the Works of Man*, ch. 2 §4, and this volume, ch. 7 §2).

[43] He called it 'a very pretty Treatise' (*NHL* 51).

[44] E. Burke, *A Philosophical Enquiry into the Origin of our Ideas of the Sublime and Beautiful* (1757), ed. Adam Phillips (Oxford: Oxford University Press, 1999), 12.

[45] The practice is not restricted to the 18th century. Russell uses 'define' in exactly the Hume–Burke sense when discussing the nature of matter: 'all that we ought to assume is series of groups of events, connected by discoverable laws. These series we may *define* as "matter". Whether there *is* matter in any other sense, no one can tell' (B. Russell, *An Outline of Philosophy* (first pub. 1927; London: Routledge, 1992), 93). Russell makes it very clear that to give a definition is not to make an ontological declaration.

That is, all we can get to know of causation is the content of the two imperfect definitions. That is, we can't get very far. We can 'barely' (merely) observe this much. So these two definitions do not say what causation actually is; they just express all we know of it. And

this conclusion concerning human ignorance [is] the result of the strictest scrutiny of this subject . . . we know nothing farther of causation . . . than *merely* the *constant conjunction* of objects, and the consequent *inference* of the mind from one to another (first emphasis mine).

The conclusion, then, is a conclusion about human ignorance. There is more to causation, but we are ignorant of it.[46]

XII

Hume's principal targets are those philosophers (mechanists or mentalists) who think that they mean or know more than it is possible to mean or know; those who think that the intrinsic nature of causation is 'intelligible' (whether partly or wholly), and that they have some sort of genuine understanding of it. Hume thinks that it is dangerous to use words like 'power', 'force', and 'energy' without continual stress on our ignorance, for the use of these terms is likely to delude us into thinking that we do after all have some positively contentful or 'perfect' grasp of the nature of causation—a grasp that goes beyond what is given in experience of regular succession and the feeling of determination to which regular succession gives rise in human minds. This, just this, is, he insists, a mistake. Our best grasp of causation is very imperfect. We are ignorant of its nature. This ignorance is what has to be shown and argued for from all sides.

That's what Hume believed. At no point in the *Enquiry*, which must 'alone be regarded as containing his philosophical sentiments and principles', does he even hint at the thesis for which he is so unjustly famous: the thesis that all there is to causation in the world is regular succession; the thesis that there is (provably) nothing at all in the nature of things in virtue of which reality is regular in the way that it is, so that the regularity of the world is, from moment to moment, and knowably, an 'outrageous run of luck'.[47]

---

[46] Here again Hume follows Newton, who was criticized by Leibniz and Huygens—and even by Berkeley—for disrupting the existing mechanist world-picture by reintroducing 'inexplicable qualities' into nature. Blackburn calls some of these inexplicable qualities 'straitjacketing facts', and claims that Hume's attitude to them is 'contemptuous' (p. 268 n. 18 in this volume), but this is a mistake. Hume's contempt is for people who attempt to elaborate positive *theories* about the nature of these facts. He has no contempt for the facts themselves, any more than Newton does.

[47] Cf. Strawson, *The Secret Connexion*, 26. Reid loves criticizing Hume for adopting views contrary to common sense, and attacks him at length for denying that we can know a priori that 'every thing that begins to exist, must have a cause of its existence', but never criticizes him for holding a view apocalyptically contrary to common sense—the ontological regularity theory of causation. Why not? Because he

One might summarize the dispute about Hume as follows. Two things in Hume are incompatible: (1) the theory of ideas, strictly and literally interpreted, and (2) the view that a straightforwardly realist view of objects and causation is at least coherent and intelligible ('it is a question of fact . . .'; *E* 153). Most people have argued that Hume's adherence to (1) proves his rejection of (2), but this is the wrong way round. His adherence to (2) proves his rejection of (1). And he not only thinks that a straightforwardly realist view of objects and causation is coherent and intelligible; he standardly takes it for granted that such a view is true.[48]

reads Hume correctly, attributing to him the same view as Priestley: ' "a cause cannot be defined to be any thing, but *such previous circumstances as are constantly followed by a certain effect*, the constancy of the result making us conclude, that there must be a *sufficient reason, in the nature of things*, why it should be produced in those circumstances" . . . This is Mr. Hume's definition [NB definition] of a cause' (T. Reid, *Essays on the Active Powers of the Human Mind* (first pub. 1788; Cambridge, Mass.: MIT Press, 1969), 282, quoting Priestley; my emphasis on 'in the nature of things'). See also *T* 212 and the commentary on it in Strawson, *The Secret Connexion*, 166–7.

[48] This paper abridges, supplements, and adjusts arguments in *The Secret Connexion*. I wrote it in 1992–3, and have made minor adjustments to it since then. Until 1995 I tried to answer any objection that I came across and that seemed to me to need a reply; but publication has been long delayed and I have not been able to keep up (Winkler's enjoyable and influential paper 'The New Hume' raised no new objections; it seriously misrepresented the standard view by suggesting that it did not ascribe the ontological regularity theory to Hume, and many pages would have been needed to straighten out the tangles it contains). I would like to thank John Wright and Peter Millican for their comments, and audiences at Birmingham, Bristol, Cambridge, Lund, Oxford, and University College London.

9

Hume and Thick Connexions

Simon Blackburn

1. TWO APPROACHES

Recently there has been a pronounced shift in the interpretation of Hume on causation. The previous weight of opinion took him to be a positivist, but the new view is that he is a sceptical realist.[1] I hold no brief for the positivist view, but I believe it needs replacing by something slightly different, and that at best it shows an error of taste to make sceptical realism a fundamental factor in the interpretation of Hume.

Let us call any concept of one event producing another, or being necessarily a cause or consequence of another, and that involves something in the events beyond their merely being kinds of events that regularly occur together, a *thick* concept of the dependence of one event on another. Then on the positivist account, Hume believes that no thick notion is intelligible. On the positivist view there is very little that we can ever understand and mean by a causal connexion between events. All we can understand and properly mean by talk of causation is that events fall into certain regular patterns, and the positivist interpretation is that Hume offered this as a reductive definition of causation. This is the famous regularity theory, summed up in the 'philosophical' definition: 'an object, followed by another, and where all the objects, similar to the first, are followed by objects similar to the second' (*E* 76). The sceptical realist view denies that Hume offered any such reduction or analysis of the notion of causation. It takes seriously the many passages in which Hume appears to allow that we are

This paper was first published in *Philosophy and Phenomenological Research*, 50 (special half-centenary suppl., 1990), 237–50; repr. in revised form as chapter 5 in Simon Blackburn, *Essays in Quasi-Realism* (New York: Oxford University Press, 1993), 94–107.

[1] I have in mind Edward Craig, *The Mind of God and the Works of Man* (Oxford: Clarendon Press, 1987); Galen Strawson, *The Secret Connexion* (Oxford: Clarendon Press, 1989); and John Wright, *The Sceptical Realism of David Hume* (Manchester: Manchester University Press, 1983).

talking of some thick notion of dependence of one event on another, going beyond regular succession. It takes it that Hume acknowledges that there is some such thick relation, even if it will be one about whose nature and extent we are doomed to ignorance. Hence, in John Wright's phrase, sceptical realism.

At first sight the difference between positivism and sceptical realism is reasonably clear, and it is plausible that if these are the only two options then Hume is better seen as tending towards the second. But, as proponents of the sceptical realist interpretation realize, there is one big problem, arising from Hume's theory of meaning. Sceptical realism seems to demand that we understand what it would be for one event to depend thickly upon another, even if we are ignorant of the nature of this relation; Hume seems to insist that we have no impression and hence no idea of any such dependence.

The problem here is a problem for any interpretation and can be focused on a contradiction, to which Hume seems to be committed:

(1) We have no ideas except those that are preceded by suitably related impressions.

(2) There are no impressions that are suitably related to the idea of a thick necessary connexion between distinct events.

(3) We have an idea of a thick necessary connexion between distinct events.

The 'suitable relation' spoken of includes direct copying, in the case of simple ideas, and whatever is covered by 'compounding' in the case of complex ideas that are compounded out of simple ones.

The positivist interpretation takes Hume to be claiming that when we talk of causation we mean only something that strips out the thick element of necessity and substitutes regular contiguous succession. So (3) is false. The difficulty is that Hume apparently denies this:

Shall we then rest contented with these two relations of contiguity and succession, as affording a compleat idea of causation? By no means. An object may be contiguous and prior to another, without being consider'd as its cause. There is a NECESSARY CONNEXION to be taken into consideration; and that relation is of much greater importance, than any of the other two above-mention'd. (T 77)

The central problem in interpreting Hume is coping with the contradiction. The sceptical realist strategy is to downplay the importance of the theory of understanding, so that even if Hume officially said (2), it played a negligible part in his view of causation.

2. A DOUBTFUL DISTINCTION

How then does the sceptical realist deal with the problem of meaning? Edward Craig and Galen Strawson draw attention to a distinction that occurs in Hume's writings.[2] When the theory of ideas threatens our idea of external existence or 'body', it is said that Hume invokes a distinction between what we can 'suppose' and what we can 'conceive', the idea being that we can coherently suppose that there are things of some sort (external objects) even when strictly we have no idea of what it is that we are supposing. Another way of putting it is that we have a 'relative' idea of things whose 'specific' difference from other things we cannot comprehend. We could say that we have no representative idea of what we talk about, but a relative or relational idea, locating it by its role. We would talk of a 'something-we-know-not-what' that does something or bears some relation to an aspect of the world of which we do have an idea. This distinction solves the contradiction by distinguishing between the terminology of (2) and (3). Hume thinks we have no representative idea of causation: we have no impression of it, and in some important sense it remains incomprehensible, and we cannot represent to ourselves what it is. What we do have, however, is a relational idea of it: it is whatever it is that issues in regular successions of events or upon which such patterns depend, or whatever forces such regularities. The negative side is given in (2) but the positive side in (3).

The texts, however, give no direct support to this interpretation of Hume. While he does indeed use both a 'relative' versus 'specific' distinction and the possibility of 'supposing' what we cannot 'conceive', he uses them very sparingly indeed. In fact he never uses either, nor mentions either, in connexion with causation. He never uses or mentions either in the *Enquiry* or in the *Dialogues* in any context at all. This alone makes them unlikely candidates for a central role in understanding his mature philosophy.[3] But worse, there are warning signs to be noticed when they occur in the *Treatise*. There are four occurrences: on *T* 67–8, *T* 188 referring back to them, *T* 218, and *T* 241. In none of these cases is Hume actually contrasting a specific versus a relative idea of any one property or relation, enjoining us that we can understand a property or object by its relations even if we cannot understand it by some stricter standard derived from the theory of ideas. On the contrary, in each context it is the impossibility of conceiving a 'specific difference' between external objects and perceptions that is the focus of attention. 'Specific' qualifies the properties supposedly differentiating external objects from ideas, and of these specific qualities we know and understand nothing by any standard at all. Here are the two major passages with enough surrounding context to matter:

---

[2] Craig, *The Mind of God and the Works of Man*, 124, and Strawson, *The Secret Connexion*, ch. 12 (cf. pp. 239–41 above).

[3] It is particularly odd that Strawson relies upon them, since he conceives of the *Enquiry* as embodying Hume's official theory of causation.

Now since nothing is ever present to the mind but perceptions, and since all ideas are deriv'd from something antecedently present to the mind; it follows, that 'tis impossible for us so much as to conceive or form an idea of any thing specifically different from ideas and impressions. Let us fix our attention out of ourselves as much as possible: Let us chace our imagination to the heavens, or to the utmost limits of the universe; we never really advance a step beyond ourselves, nor can conceive any kind of existence, but those perceptions, which have appear'd in that narrow compass. This is the universe of the imagination, nor have we any idea but what is there produc'd.

The farthest we can go towards a conception of external objects, when suppos'd *specifically* different from our perceptions, is to form a relative idea of them, without pretending to comprehend the related objects. Generally speaking we do not suppose them specifically different; but only attribute to them different relations, connexions and durations. But of this more fully hereafter. (*T* 67–8)

Philosophers deny our resembling perceptions to be identically the same, and uninterrupted; and yet have so great a propensity to believe them such, that they arbitrarily invent a new set of perceptions, to which they attribute these qualities. I say, a new set of perceptions: For we may well suppose in general, but 'tis impossible for us distinctly to conceive, objects to be in their nature any thing but exactly the same with perceptions. What then can we look for from this confusion of groundless and extraordinary opinions but error and falshood? And how can we justify to ourselves any belief we repose in them? (*T* 218)

It requires some daring to take these passages as a model for sceptical realism. Hume is far—about as far as can be—from saying that we actually possess a going idea of the external world that allows us to understand, by some weak standard, what the externality is that we do not know about. Each of the two passages gives the strongest contrary impression. The first affirms idealism ('we never really advance a step beyond ourselves'). The second introduces the 'supposes' versus 'conceives' distinction only while he simultaneously dismisses its effect out of hand. Its dismissal justifies Hume in describing his Philosophers (the culture whose spokesman is Locke) as actually inventing new *perceptions*, rather than inventing new things different from perceptions. This is the very opposite of the view a sceptical realist Hume should take. He should admit that a Lockean succeeds in introducing a (relative) notion of an external object as something that has various relations to our perceptions, and then go on to worry how much we know about such objects. Hume does not do this: he simply dismisses the idea that we have a set of determinate, intelligible, propositions about which, unfortunately, we shall never know the truth. It is not that we understand something, but cannot know whether it is true; it is that we give ourselves explanations that seemed to introduce an intelligible concept, but in fact fail (the demands put upon an external world independent of perception are simply inconsistent). We are in the domain of a 'confusion of groundless and extraordinary opinions' where our only hope is to abandon reason altogether. So, even when it is used, the 'specific' versus 'relative' distinction is not used as Craig and Strawson would have it used in the different area of causation, to which, as I have said, Hume never applies it.

3. ANOTHER DISTINCTION

Before proceeding it is necssary to have in mind two things that might be asked of 'thick' causation. When we think of a causally connected pair of events, such as the impact of the first billiard ball causing the motion of the second, we want there to be a further fact than (mere) succession, or even mere regular succession of these kinds of event. We want there to be a dependency or connexion, a fact making it so that when the first happens the second must happen. Call this the desire for a causal *nexus*. But now suppose we shift our gaze to the whole ongoing course of nature. Again, we may want there to be a further fact than mere regular succession. We feel that the ongoing pattern would be too much of a coincidence unless there is something in virtue of which the world has had and is going to go on having the order that it does. We want there to be some secret spring or principle, some ultimate cause, 'on which this regular course and succession of objects totally depends' (E 55). This is whatever it is that ensures the continuation of the natural order, that dispels the inductive vertigo that arises when we think how natural it might be, how probable even, that the constrained and delicate pattern of events might fall apart. Call the desire for this further fact the desire for a *straitjacket* on the possible course of nature: something whose existence at one time guarantees constancies at any later time.[4]

A fact alleviating this vertigo has to be a very peculiar fact, for the following reason. It has to be something whose own continued efficacy through time is subject to no possibility of change or chance of failure. For otherwise the fact that it keeps on as it does would itself be a case of coincidence or fluke, another contingency crying out for explanation and engendering inductive vertigo. Some think they can point us towards a fact with this potency. Some draw comfort from God's sustaining will (as if anything understood on the analogy of our own mental states could be timeproof!). David Armstrong believes that a kind of necessary, timeless, gridlock of universals will do.[5] Galen Strawson takes comfort in fundamental forces constitutive of the nature of matter.[6]

---

[4] At least. It may be that its existence at one time should entail its existence at any previous time as well. But one way of gesturing at what is wanted is to imagine God creating it by some kind of fiat or act of law-giving, whose writ would run only into the future.

[5] *What is a Law of Nature* (Cambridge: Cambridge University Press, 1983), 88 ff.

[6] e.g. *The Secret Connexion*, 91, 254–5.

It is easy to conflate the desire for a nexus, case by case, with the desire for a straitjacket. But Hume (sometimes—but see below) is clear that they are different. They are different because whatever the nexus between two events is at one time, it is the kind of thing that can in principle change, so that at a different time events of the same kind may bear a different connexion. Thus suppose we grant ourselves the right to think in terms of a thick connexion between one event and another: a power or force whereby an event of the first kind brings about an event of the second. Nevertheless, there is no contradiction in supposing that the powers and forces with which events are endowed at one time cease at another, nor in supposing that any secret nature of bodies upon which those powers and forces depend itself changes, bringing their change in its wake. Hume emphasizes this point in both the *Enquiry* and the *Treatise* (*T* 90–1, *E* 37). It is his reason for denying that the problem of induction can be solved by appeal to the powers and forces of bodies. But it is equally a reason for separating the question of a nexus from that of a straitjacket. Nexuses by themselves do not provide a straitjacket. The ongoing regularity and constancy even of a thick nexus between one kind of event and another is just as much a brute contingent regularity as the bare regular concatenation of events.[7] In each case we have something that can engender the inductive vertigo, or whose continuation through time might be thought to demand some kind of ground or ultimate cause or straitjacket.

The difference between a nexus holding on some particular occasions and a straitjacket guaranteeing the continuation of a pattern of connexions is easy to overlook. This is because of a lurking epistemological difficulty. Suppose one thinks that a particular nexus can be known for what it is, for instance by some observation whose content is more than the mere succession of events. One might report this by claiming to have seen that the one event *had to* happen, given the other. But if you see a 'must' in one pair of events, would you not thereby see that it will hold for every pair of some kind that the original pair enables you to identify? How could you see it without seeing something with general implications, and ones that are immune to temporal change? In other words, you will take yourself to have seen a time-proof connexion: one that rigidly governs how things could ever fall out. To put it the other way round, if things were not to fall out as expected, the original claim to have seen that the one event had to follow the other is refuted. This in turn makes it hard to see how a particular nexus could be an object of observation. Observation extends

---

[7] One might seek to avoid this by the verbal manoeuvre of identifying kinds of events by their causal powers, in which case it will follow that events of the same kind will bear the same causal connexions. But as Hume in effect points out, inductive vertigo then transfers itself to the contingent question of whether future events with the same sensory appearance will turn out to be of the same kind.

only to limited periods of space and time: how could we have within our view something that *essentially* casts its net over the whole of space and time?

This problem probably explains one puzzling feature of Hume's procedure. He repeatedly affirms that someone who has a full apprehension of a thick causal connexion would be in a position to make an a priori claim about the way events will fall out and what kind of event will be caused by another. He argues that because we cannot have this time-proof knowledge we do not apprehend the causal connexion, for instance in the exercise of our own will (*E* 63–9). The argument seems initially to be, as Craig describes it, a muddle, since there is no evident reason why someone apprehending a nexus on one occasion should thereby know that the same nexus will obtain on another—the very point Hume himself emphasizes when arguing that powers and forces will not solve the problem of induction.[8] I suspect that Hume sees that nothing would really count as apprehension of a particular 'must' unless it carried with it implications of uniformity for the general case. It is to be (*per impossibile*) a particular apprehension, but one with the consequences of apprehending a straitjacket. Someone apprehending a straitjacket for what it is will as a consequence know its immunity to time and chance: he will know the timeless 'must' that it guarantees. He will be apprehending the impossibility that events should ever transpire otherwise. He has therefore a piece of knowledge that, although it took an empirical starting-point in the apprehension of an individual thick necessary connexion, can be seen a priori to have implications for all other places and times. And it is this that Hume treats as his target, even when the issue ought to be the apparently lesser one of the particular nexus.[9]

There may be some room for manoeuvre over the lesser claim to have apprehended a particular, but not necessarily time-proof, thick connexion. One might try allowing the particular apprehension not to carry any implications for what might be present on other occasions.[10] The difficulty will be that an apprehension of a mutable thick connexion does not gives us quite what we want from knowledge of causation. That knowledge has to have a *consequence*: the subject possessing it must be prepared to foretell the one kind of event on the appearance of the other. It is not at all clear how apprehension of a particular relation obtaining at a particular place and time could automatically carry any such consequence: one might, as it were, say that this is how events are connected today, and form no expectation, and not know what to expect to happen tomorrow.

---

[8] *T* 91, *E* 37–8, and Craig, *The Mind of God and the Works of Man*, 97 (cf. p. 219 in this volume).

[9] On these issues, see also Peter Millican, 'Natural Necessity and Induction', *Philosophy*, 61 (1986), 395–403.

[10] G. E. M. Anscombe, 'Causality and Determination', in *Metaphysics and the Philosophy of Mind: Collected Philosophical Papers*, ii (Oxford: Blackwell, 1981).

Sceptical realism might characterize Hume's position on either the nexus or the straitjacket. But unless we understand the extraordinary demands on a straitjacket we shall fail to see that realism concerning it is hardly important compared to his scepticism. Thus when Strawson opposes the Regularity Theory, with its ongoing flukes, by citing 'fundamental forces' essentially constitutive of 'the nature of matter', and invokes these to soothe away inductive vertigo, he is surely forgetting Hume's point.[11] Even if forces are taken 'to latch on to real, mind independent, observable-regularity-transcendent facts about reality',[12] they need something further in order to serve as a straitjacket. They need *necessary* immunity to change; they need to be things for which the inductive vertigo does not arise. Equally, if the 'nature of matter' is to help, then the continuation of matter must not be just one more contingency, whose falling out the same way instant after instant, time after time, is a cosmic fluke. The force that through the green fuse drives the flower might falter, and so might the fuse and the flower, but a straitjacket must not. Its immunity to change must be necessary, for if it is contingent then either it is a fluke—of any changes that might occur, none ever does—or else this regularity is itself not brute but demands some further straitjacket in the background, of which we have even less inkling. The point is that we will not locate it by ordinary talk of 'force' and its cognates. For even if Hume can countenance understanding of a thick nexus, the theoretical pressures on a straitjacket are a great deal more demanding.[13]

Hume's main interest in causation is to destroy the idea that we could ever apprehend a straitjacketing fact: we have no conception of it, nor any conception of what it would be to have such a conception, nor any conception of how we might approach such a conception. In particular we must not think of the advance of science as targeted on finding such a thing. The lesson drawn from Newton is that just as *Principia* gives us the operation of gravitational force but does not tell us what it is, so any conceivable advance in science can do only more of the same. It can put events into wider and more interesting and exception-free patterns, and that is all. 'The most perfect philosophy of the natural kind only staves off our ignorance a little longer' (*E* 31).[14]

[11] Stawson, *The Secret Connexion*, 91.   [12] Ibid.

[13] Strawson is probably betrayed into this conflation by using the one term 'Causation' (with a capital 'C') equally for a thick nexus and a thick straitjacket.

[14] This is the famous point where Newton said 'hypotheses non fingo', and the point that left contemporary scientists such as Huygens and Leibniz, who had wanted to know what gravity *was* and not merely how bodies moved under its influence, feeling badly let down. Newton was quite within his rights to want more scientific understanding of gravitational attraction, and Hume does not oppose the goal. But if Newton and his contemporaries wanted a different thing—an understanding of the impossibility that events should ever fall out otherwise—then Hume stands in his way. Hume does not magnify the difference between himself and Newton, but if Newton was aiming at this superlative piece of understanding

Would it be easy for Hume to allow us a 'relative' idea of a straitjacketing fact—a something-we-know-not-what that governs/brings about/explains the continuing order of nature? We understand this only in so far as we understand the relation of governing or bringing about. But can we understand the relation? Can Hume say the relation part of the relational idea is intelligible? The question is whether we know what governing or bringing about would be when we have no example, and indeed no conception, of the kind of fact alleged to be doing it. Hume, given his endorsement of Berkeley's theory of ideas, must say that we cannot take relational ideas (governing, forcing, grounding, issuing in, bringing about) out of the context within which they have intelligible application, and apply them without blush in contexts in which they do not.[15] We can generate the general idea only if we have particular examples. Otherwise, comprehension fails.

Nevertheless, it will be said, even if this shows that we have no idea at all of what would count either as a straitjacket, or as knowledge that some kind of fact provides one, it seems plain that Hume allows that there is one, even while insisting on scepticism about its nature. Sceptical realists might be right that he allows us a 'relative' idea of such a fact, silently betraying the Berkeleian background. Even if this were technically correct—and we have seen how far it stretches the texts—it would still misplace the stress; this is why I originally described it as an error of taste rather than an outright mistake. The point is that Hume is utterly contemptuous of any kind of theorizing conducted in terms of such a thing. We are at the point where anything we say 'will be of little consequence to the world' (T 168),[16] or in the world of 'notion[s] so imperfect, that no sceptic will think it worth while to contend against [them]' (E 155). His attitude must be the same as that he holds to an equally noumenal substratum, supporting the qualities of matter:

But these philosophers carry their fictions still farther in their sentiments concerning *occult qualities*, and both suppose a substance supporting, which they do not understand, and an accident supported, of which they have as imperfect an idea. The whole system, therefore, is entirely incomprehensible . . . (T 222)

and thought that the methods of natural science might give it, then Hume is clearly opposed. He was the first to see that what Newton did was the only kind of thing that could ever be done.

[15] Berkeley's rigour on this is apparent in his constant polemic against 'abstraction' and in such matters as his embargo on taking causal relations away from the domain of the will, given that it is this that is the basis of our understanding of them. More directly relevant is his insistence that if you try to introduce a 'relative notion' of matter as whatever it is that supports various properties, you mean nothing. As well as the passage quoted in the text, see *Principles of Human Knowledge*, p. 1 sect. 80.

[16] 'I am, indeed, ready to allow, that there may be several qualities both in material and immaterial objects, with which we are utterly unacquainted; and if we please to call these *power* or *efficacy*, 'twill be of little consequence to the world.'

He is here directly echoing Berkeley:

Lastly, where there is not so much as the most inadequate or faint idea pretended to: I will not indeed thence conclude against the reality of any notion or existence of any thing: but my inference shall be, that you mean nothing at all: that you imply words to no manner of purpose, without any design or signification whatsoever. And I leave it to you to consider how mere jargon should be treated.[17]

Craig especially makes the case that there is importance in the positive claim that something-we-know-not-what exists, and the importance is sceptical: it enables Hume to destroy any pretension to finding what we might antecedently have hoped to understand about nature. I agree entirely that this critical aim is essential to Hume, and at least as important as the theory of understanding itself. But Hume enjoys this realignment without himself making any positive claim about the existence of any mysterious, straitjacketing fact or facts. The realignment of our self-image, our philosophy of what real discovery and understanding might be, is independent of any such assertion. We do not our-selves have to think the other side of the line to learn how tightly the line defin-ing the limit of all possible empirical enquiry is drawn. The point is that our real engagement with the world, in our understanding and our science, and our self-image or philosophical understanding of the notions we actually use, must sail on in complete indifference to any facts transcending our ideas. 'Relative' ideas of such facts play no role any more than relative ideas of many things: Cartesian egos (simple, indivisible entities whose permanence ensures the identity of the self); the substratum in which properties inhere; objective goods commanding the will of all those who apprehend them, and so on. Since the actual business of making judgements about the identity of the self, or the possession of proper-ties by things, or what is good or bad, goes on in complete indifference to these things, they play no role in our real understanding.[18] They have no use at all: nothing will do just as well as something about which nothing can be said.

4. THE NEXUS

Perhaps the same is not true of individual thick connexions, that is, the par-ticular causal nexus obtaining between specific events at a time. Don't we give every employment to such a notion? And if sceptical realists are right that Hume is not giving us a positivist reduction, do they remain in possession of the field here at least? I do not think so, for there is a third option: a truer description of Hume on ordinary empirical causation would be that he is neither a positivist

---

[17] Berkeley, *Three Dialogues between Hylas and Philonous*, Dialogue 2 para. 121.
[18] Strawson is at pains to show that not all Hume's references to straitjacketing facts are ironic, but I do not think he shows that they are not contemptuous.

nor a sceptical realist, but rather a not-so-sceptical anti-realist.[19] That is, he gives us a story explaining and even justifying our use of the vocabulary of causation, while denying that we represent a real aspect of the world to ourselves as we use it.

The outline of Hume's positive theory of causation is well known. The mind's perceptions, which form the material with which it must work, reveal only a regular succession of events. However, upon experience of such a regular succession the mind changes. It does not change by forming an impression or idea of any external property invisible in one instance alone. It changes functionally: it becomes organized so that the impression of the antecedent event gives rise to the idea of the subsequent event. No new aspect of the world is revealed by this change: it is strictly non-representative, just like the onset of a passion, with which Hume frequently compares it.[20] But once it takes place we think of the events as thickly connected; we become confident of the association, we talk of causation, and of course we act and plan in the light of that confidence.

There are two separate components in this story: the contribution of the world to our apprehension, and the functional change in the mind itself.[21] These are the two aspects separated in the famous two 'definitions' of cause:

an object, followed by another, and where all the objects, similar to the first, are followed by objects similar to the second.

an object followed by another, and whose appearance always conveys the thought to that other. (*E* 76–7)

The first 'philosophical definition' (cf. I 170) describes the contribution of the world, in so far as we can apprehend it, and the second 'natural' definition describes the non-representative, functional difference in the mind that apprehends the regularity. The parallel with Hume's philosophy of ethics is so far complete: again, there is a neutral starting-point in the mind's apprehension of some non-ethical facts, and then the onset of non-representative passions ready to be voiced in our moralizing.

It is only now that complexities start, but unfortunately Hume gives less help with them than one would wish. The theory so far tells us of a non-representative change, a change in the structure of our expectations, that gets expression when we deem two events to be causally connected. But it has not yet conjured up a full theory of the content of propositions about cause. It does not

---

[19] Or, quasi-realist, in the sense I have tried to give to the term.

[20] Norman Kemp Smith, *The Philosophy of David Hume* (London: Macmillan, 1942), chs. 1 and 2, present convincing evidence that this comparison was the prime mover of Hume's theory of causation. It opened up the 'new Scene of Thought' of which he speaks in the 1734 letter to an unnamed physician (HL i 12–18).

[21] As clear a statement as any is Hume's recapitulation, *E* 78–9.

tell us, for example, what we are bothered about when we wonder if *A* caused *B*, what we are saying when we say that every event has a cause, or whether we can sensibly talk of unknown causes. We need more detail about the way in which cause becomes objectified so as to be spoken of as a feature of the real world, if its origin is in a feature of our own minds. Hume shows little interest in such questions, and indeed against the background of the theory of ideas, he can point only in misleading directions. He says, for example, that by a necessary connexion we 'mean' a connexion in the mind, leaving himself open to interpretation as a kind of Berkeleian, taking the idea of necessity to be a representation of some thick connexion we are aware of in our own minds. He then has to spend Part i of Section VII of the *Enquiry* averting this misunderstanding.[22] In his theory of morality he similarly seems unclear whether he is saying that virtue and vice are 'nothing in the objects', but only sentiments in us, or that they are the qualities of objects that tend to arouse those sentiments.[23] What he lacks is a link between the real functional difference and the thick content to give causal judgements: the way we talk and think in terms of a projected property of things.[24] A telling point here is that in both the *Treatise* and the *Enquiry* he produces the 'two definitions' only at the end of the discussion, and in each place he does so apologetically, in effect telling us that they are not to be regarded as strict definitions. On the view I am recommending this is right: they separate the two different *aspects* of the matter—the contribution of the world, and the change in us. But they do not give us a lexicographer's analysis, and we should not expect one. There is no way of moralizing without using a moral vocabulary, and no way of causalizing without using the vocabulary of cause, efficacy, or power.

Notice, however, how many cards Hume holds in his hands. The basic theory is flexible enough to accommodate many points that are usually raised against him. Our reactions to nature are subtle: not all regularities betoken cause, and sometimes we attribute cause after minuscule experience of regularity.[25] Well and good: the basic theory need put no limits on the input to our causalizing, any more than his theory that in moralizing we voice a passion puts a limit on

[22] An interesting scholarly question, to which I do not know the answer, is why he took such elaborate care in the *Enquiry*, Section VII, to distinguish his theory from Berkeley's, when the *Treatise* contains no corresponding passages. It is one of the very few cases where the *Enquiry* is fuller than the *Treatise*. Did some review or correspondence make the need evident to him?

[23] His lists of virtues (e.g. at *M* 277 in the second *Enquiry*) specify the properties of people, such as benevolence, serenity, and so on, that make us love them; his official position (e.g. *T* 471, 614) identifies the virtue with the sentiment itself.

[24] Hume is quite prepared to allow that our common notion of cause contains defective elements— see *E* 77 n. But overall he is perfectly friendly to the way we think.

[25] Hume discusses these complexities in *Treatise* I. iii. 15, 'Rules by which to judge of causes and effects'; cf. *E* 107 n.

the input to our moralizing. On the output side, the change in the structure of our thought after we have deemed a sequence to be causal may also be complex. Its heart is that we 'make no longer any scruple of foretelling' one event upon the appearance of another. But there may be other changes. We may become willing, for example, to hold the sequence constant as we think about what would have happened if something else had happened, or what would happen if something else were to happen. Once we view a sequence as causal, it is held fixed as we conduct counterfactual and conditional deliberations. Well and good: the basic theory puts no limits on such consequences either. The theory also happily predicts the 'intuitions' that lead people to detest the positivistic 'regularity' theory of the content of our causal sayings. Someone talking of cause is voicing a distinct mental set: he is by no means in the same state as someone merely describing regular sequences, any more than someone who appreciates some natural feature as good is in the same state of mind as someone who merely appreciates the feature. The difference in this case is in the sentiment or passion that the feature arouses, and, in the causal case, in the fixity that the sequence of events takes in our thinking. Finally, the contradiction I identified at the beginning of this essay is sidestepped by distinguishing a representative idea of a connexion, which we do not have, from a capacity to make legitimate use of a term whose function is given non-representatively, which we can have.

There are, I believe, only two ways in which this kind of theory could be opposed. One is to deny that a Humean could forge the missing links between the functional difference we are expressing and the surface content of our causal judgements. The other is to deny that we have here a distinctive position, by assailing the limits on 'representation' under which Hume operates. The first attack presses the point that Hume needs to tell us what happens not just when we think that *A* causes *B*, but also when we think that there exist unknown causal connexions, that regardless of whether we had ever existed there would still have been causal connexions, and so on. We think in terms of causation as an element of the external world, and there remains a real question of how much of this thought Hume can explain and how much he has to regret. However, his prospects for deflecting this first criticism must be quite bright. For as we have seen, he is working with exactly the same ingredients in the case of ethics. Here too there is the task of explaining the apparently objective content of moral judgements given their source in the passions, but here it is much harder to believe that the problem is insoluble, and Hume certainly did not believe it to be so.

The second attack need not deny Hume his ingredients. It simply claims that we can cook with them in a different way, awarding ourselves the right to a genuinely representative concept of causation. For when should we say that we have a representative idea of a property or relation? One answer would be: when we can picture it holding, or exhibit to ourselves in imagination a scene in which the property or relation is visibly instanced. This is a natural empiricist answer and the one that leaves Hume poised to argue that we have no representative idea of thick causal connexions. For a view (or succession of other experiences: sounds, felt pressures, and so on) in which there is given a certain succession of events, and in which one event causes another, need be no different from a view in which the one event does not cause another, but in which the same succession happens anyhow. This is why we have to *interpret* sequences as causal, and, however automatic this act is, it is still one that needs to be performed. But empiricism nowadays sounds like prejudice: why should we not have a *theoretical* concept of a thick causal connexion, allowing that there is a step from the raw appearance of a scene to the belief that it instances such and such connexions, but also insisting that we know what it is for such connexions to exist? We have a theoretical idea of them, and the idea represents the way the world is when they are present.

The real problem with this is that it only works if we also understand the relation between the thick connexions and the ongoing pattern of events. Thick connexions make events happen; they guarantee outcomes, they issue in patterns of events, and so on. But these are terms of dependency or causation, so we understand the theory only if we understand them. And this understanding in turn is queried by the problems described above: any realist theory needs to tell us how the 'musts' present on one occasion throw their writ over others. Otherwise it fails to give us what we want from a causal understanding of the world. For all the story goes, someone might be a virtuoso at detecting particular thick connexions, yet have no idea what to expect or how to conduct counterfactual and conditional reasoning.

The net result is that any such realist theory looks extravagant. It asks from us more than we need. To see this, imagine a character we might call the Bare Humean. The Bare Humean misses out this capacity for apprehension or theory, so does indeed lack the representative idea of thick connexions that these are supposed to give us. But she goes through the functional change that Hume describes, and conducts her expectations and actions accordingly. She can be an enthusiastic natural scientist, finding concealed features and concealed patterns in nature to aid prediction. She can understand that finding ever more simplicity and ever more general patterns may be 'set us as a task', so that there will always be more to know about nature. She will need a vocabulary to express her confidences and her doubts, and to communicate them to others; she will be a virtuoso at the salient features that are usable day by day to control her world. What else does she need? Are we sure she is missing anything at all— isn't she a bit like you and me?

POSTSCRIPT

I write this postscript in a mood of benign paternity. Revisiting my essay has caused me to admire it once more rather than wish to unsay any of it. But I think I can offer one or two comments that may, perhaps, cast a little light on the debate. These comments were inspired by hearing Galen Strawson and John Wright presenting their views at a conference on Hume and pragmatism that Huw Price and Steve Buckle organized in Sydney in August 1997. Although I was not myself talking about just these issues, they forced me to reflect once more upon them.

These days, in any debate about 'realism', we must be sure that we all know what we mean. In the old days this was easier. There were realists, and there were reductionists. And if these are the interpretative options, since Hume is now agreed by all serious interpreters not to be a reductionist about causation, out he comes as a realist. But there are currently many more options in front of us, and unfortunately many more ways of distributing the title 'realist'. I think that to begin to understand Hume, we need at least to know just how many intepreta-tive options we have. Of course, I have a fairly large stake in this. Since one of the options is my own pet creation, I become quite despondent when it is ignored. But without indulging this lament, let me sketch at least the two major families of options that seem to me to lie in front of us. Consider this distinction:

(1) *Face-value or default realism (lower-case realism)*. Take any area of dis-course whose participants say *p*. Suppose we agree with them that *p*. Then if we cannot reduce the content of *p* we must be realists about the entities and properties and relations ostensibly referred to. Our only anti-realist options are either to find other terms, or to stop saying *p* (reductionism or eliminativism).

(2) *Theoretical or ontological Realism (upper-case Realism)*. Take any area of discourse whose participants say *p*. Suppose we agree with them that *p*. Suppose we cannot understand what is going on except in terms of our responding to a world whose entities and properties and relations are the ones ostensibly referred to. In that case we have to be realists about those entities and properties and relations. But anti-Realist options would include explaining what is going in other ways than in terms of such a response.

There are many areas that illustrate the difference here. Consider colours. Many philosophers would want to hold what is, in these terms, the combina-tion of lower-case realism, and upper-case anti-Realism. They would say that propositions ascribing colours do not permit of reduction. You cannot say what they say in interestingly different terms. But you can understand perfectly well what is going on without supposing that we respond to a world in which things are coloured. Such philosophers think, rightly or wrongly, that colour science shows that we should not think this. Some might hold the same combination of views about mathematics and set theory. Some (myself included) would hold the same combination of views about ethics. Others (myself included) would hold the same about propositions apparently mentioning different possible worlds. These people would be face-value, lower-case realists, but anti-Realists.

Obviously, if we ourselves can only see the issues in lower-case terms, so that anti-Realism is invisible to us, we will lose a lot of interpretative options. Philosophers who want to be lower-case realists but upper-case anti-Realists will in fact seem to contradict themselves. Someone like Hume, a paradigm realist and anti-Realist in the case of causation as in the case of ethics, becomes an exegetical nightmare. But the problem would lie with the impoverished options we are offering him.

If we only see lower-case realism, it will be easy to cite the many passages rightly and repeatedly quoted by the 'causal realist' school of interpretation, to allow them to claim Hume. But if we look at the entire context, in which Hume's explanatory interests become visible, everything changes. It is easiest to see this, of course, in the case of ethics. Hume is a moderately strict moralist. He makes many assertions about what counts as virtue, what counts as human flourishing, and what counts as vice or misery. He shows no temptation to reductionism, as if we could moralize in other terms than those that are designed for the purpose. So he is a lower-case realist, and indeed says as much on the first page of the second *Enquiry*. But the work of the anatomist shows us what is going on, and it shows us this without making any appeal to a 'response' or a receptivity to an order of nature that includes virtues, vices, duties, rights, and the rest. That is the point of the sentimentalist tradition that he absorbed from Hutcheson. And it is this that he applied to causation. Causalizing—seeing regularities in terms of necessities—is exactly analagous to moralizing, seeing human affairs in terms of good and bad, right and wrong.

Once the issue is seen in this way, it is simply no good citing one more time the places where Hume shows sympathy with unknown causes, hidden springs and principles, the propriety of thinking of matter as containing within itself the power to initiate motion, and so on. Hume was regrettably uninterested in the natural sciences of the Edinburgh of his day, but it is not as if he was some kind of armchair opponent of physics or chemistry (as I have actually heard said). This is like staring at passages where he says, for instance, that ingratitude is horrid, and claiming him for moral realism, or alternatively staring at the passages where he talks about vice being in the breast, and supposing that he cannot really mean that ingratitude is horrid. But the real Hume endorses the first-order sayings. He has no quarrel with the mental habits that lead us to them. In fact, in the case of causation, he characteristically celebrates the fact that nature has implanted our fixed propensities to causalizing in us. But these, in his view, are active mental responses to perceived regularities, rather than passive mental representations of an order of properties and relations that cannot be perceived, and so ones of which we can have no idea. Hence, realism together with anti-Realism.

It is important in the current climate, when 'minimalism' is very much the vogue, to be careful to separate two issues. A minimalist may strike at the way in which upper-case Realism is staged. He may say that it depends, ultimately, on an untenable view of what is possible to philosophy, or metatheory. He may 'minimalize' all the terms in which debate about explanation can be conducted. He might insist on giving the blandest reading to 'responds' or 'represents', so that it becomes merely a part of first-order, everyday discourse to say, for example, that colour vision represents the colours of things, or that we respond to those colours when we talk of them. Equally, on this tack, we respond to numbers when we talk of them, or possibilities and possible worlds when we talk of them. We might even say that in moralizing we represent the moral aspects of things, and respond to them. But (according to the minimalist) we should not find these sayings shocking or uncomfortable. They just go with the first-order turf. In other words, minimalism tries to close off the space for explanatory philosophical theory. It does this by kidnapping, for the first-order discourse, all the terms we might have used in order to try to get a philosophical take on it.

One issue is whether minimalism succeeds. The other is whether, if it does, this closes off the space for understanding Hume. It could do so among some philosophers. Not making space for an enterprise themselves, they become unable to understand those who thought they were pursuing it. But it should not make understanding impossible. We know, because he tells us, that Hume thought of himself as the anatomist, delving into the structures of mind and of world that end up with our thoughts and sayings being the way they are. We may be less sanguine about his enterprise than he was, without failing to understand that it was after all his enterprise. And in fact, in the case of ethics if not in the case of causation, most philosophers do understand this. They see that his expressivism and the sentimentalist tradition in general provide a distinctive explanation of human moralizing, and then they rail ineffectually against it.

Obviously, what I have called 'realism' and 'Realism' can subdivide. We are dealing with families of positions, depending on how we construe understanding what is going on, what strikes us as a good or bad explanation, what content we think we have managed to give to first-order p, and so on. I do not claim at all that my simple distinction remains simple. What I do claim is that until it is entrenched in our minds, any attempt to discuss whether Hume was a realist about this or that is hopeless.

10

Hume on Liberty and Necessity

George Botterill

Hume was certainly tackling a 'long disputed question' under his heading 'Of Liberty and Necessity'. If our actions are causally determined, can we still maintain that we are capable of acting freely? Or does our deeply rooted commitment to regarding other people as morally responsible agents also commit us to regarding them as exceptions to the general order of nature and, at some level, somehow exempt from the operation of causal laws? By now this has been disputed even longer, whether we call it the Problem of Free Will and (or versus) Determinism, or the topic of Moral Responsibility and Causal Determination. The basic issue is familiar enough to be referred to as an 'old chestnut'—which, in my view, implies we ought to have cracked it by now.

Actually, I do believe that the position usually referred to nowadays as *Compatibilism* provides a solution to this problem, and no doubt this influences the view I take of Hume's treatment of the topic. In order to relate Hume's contribution to subsequent discussions and to the accumulated terminology of the debate, it will be useful to have a general scheme of the main positions in mind.

Call the assumption that people—at any rate, normal adults—do have the capacity to act freely and are therefore morally responsible for their actions the *Free Will Assumption*. Evidently this is an assumption that we implicitly make in many different ways. For example, if a Rottweiler attacks and injures a child, we may be shocked by the injuries and loathe and fear the dog that inflicted them. But we don't *blame* the dog, because such an animal is not an appropriate target for that attitude: it cannot help the savagery which is part of its nature. And if the dog is put down, this is for reasons of safety, to prevent a repetition of the attack. It is not an *execution*. We take a different attitude to the dog's owner, who should perhaps have foreseen the possibility of such an attack, and who in any case has a responsibility to control so dangerous a pet.

What Hume calls 'the doctrine of necessity' is the *Principle of Determinism*, according to which all events (including all human actions) are entirely the result of prior causes. So now we go on to ask: can the Free Will Assumption and the Principle of Determinism both be true?

That they can both be true, because they are logically consistent, is the answer given by Compatibilism. Those who hold that the Free Will Assumption and the Principle of Determinism cannot both be true are *Incompatibilists*. For these people there arises the further question: If they cannot, on grounds of logical consistency, both be true, then which is false? *Libertarians* maintain that we have free will, and that we must therefore conclude that the Principle of Determinism is false, or at any rate does not apply to human actions and decisions. *Hard Determinists* maintain that the Principle of Determinism is true, and that therefore we are making a metaphysical error when we assume that people have free will. The diagram below represents the general structure of the debate to show how the parties stand.

In discussions of free will and causal determination conducted outside the confines of academic philosophy, compatibilism still remains little known and largely ignored. Indeed, non-philosophers and undergraduate beginners in

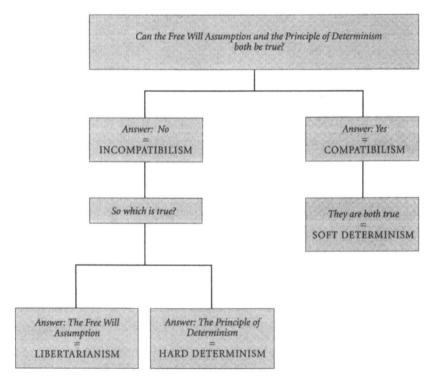

The relations between the Free Will Assumption, the Principle of Determinism, Libertarianism, Hard Determinism, and Soft Determinism–Compatibilism

philosophy seem to find compatibilism highly paradoxical, when first introduced to it. But within the history of philosophy the compatibilists can point to
a dynasty of champions stretching from Hobbes through Hume to Ayer. For
example, in one of his papers Donald Davidson announces that 'Hobbes, Locke,
Hume, Moore, Schlick, Ayer, Stevenson, and a host of others have done what can
be done, or ought ever to have been needed, to remove the confusions that can
make determinism seem to frustrate freedom.'[1] With such a tradition behind it,
it is only natural to assume there has been some cumulative development in the
compatibilist case, that it did not spring complete and perfectly formed from
the head of Thomas Hobbes.

In fact I think it is preferable to think of the case for compatibilism as composed of a battery of arguments, some much more forceful than others. Yet if
one were looking for a single main argument that might be strengthened, the
obvious and most popular candidate is one that derives from the thought that

(1) the concept of freedom is *contrastive*, since there is a genuine distinction
     to be drawn between actions that are freely performed and those that are
     not,

but that

(2) it is a mistake to suppose that the contrast is with causation in general.

I shall refer to this argument as the Contrastive Argument.[2] The tricky bit, of
course, is to say exactly what it is that acting freely *is* to be contrasted with. The
favoured options are the other three 'C's—coercion, compulsion, and constraint. How exactly we are to capture this contrast—between, on the one hand,
cases in which people may be said to act freely, or voluntarily, or of their own
free will and, on the other hand, cases in which they do not—is something that
may still, after all these years, need a bit of working up. However, there is a presumption that a Humean account of causation cannot but be helpful to the
Contrastive Argument, if only on the grounds that the less we pack into the
general causal relation, the more will be available for the purposes of distinguishing those special causes that do frustrate the freedom of an agent. Whether
or not a Humean account of causation aids the Contrastive Argument, I want
to make it quite clear that Hume himself does not advance that argument. If
we look carefully at what Hume says on this subject, we will hesitate to think of

---

[1] 'Freedom to Act', in Davidson, *Essays on Actions and Events* (Oxford: Clarendon Press, 1980), 63.

[2] Its most influential statements have been Hobbes, *Leviathan* (1651), ch. xxi: 'Liberty, or Freedome,
signifieth (properly) the absence of Opposition . . .'; M. Schlick, *Problems of Ethics*, trans. D. Rynin (New
York: Prentice-Hall, 1939), 150: 'Freedom means the opposite of compulsion; a man is *free* if he does not
act under *compulsion*, and he is compelled or unfree when he is hindered from without in the realization
of his natural desires'; and A. J. Ayer, *Philosophical Essays* (London: Macmillan, 1954), 278: 'For it is not, I
think, causality that freedom is to be contrasted with, but constraint.'

him as fitting into a single overall case for compatibilism based on the Contrastive Argument.[3] That will be just as well, not only in order to report Hume's position correctly, but also in order to appreciate the strength of the case for compatibilism.

The biggest question is whether compatibilism provides a solution to the traditional problem of free will and determinism. Many philosophers have maintained that it does, and have acknowledged that Hume made an important, if not decisive, contribution to the development of compatibilism. So the further question arises: What exactly was the contribution that Hume made to compatibilism? In attempting to answer this question we need to look closely at the two places where Hume wrote about 'liberty and necessity' in the *Treatise* and the first *Enquiry*. On reading through these passages we will observe that although they are in many respects closely similar, there is one striking difference between them. So we are led on to the further questions: What accounts for that striking difference? And is it more, or less, important than the similarities? I shall start with the last two questions, by analysing the similarities and differences between Hume's two treatments. §1 describes the major difference between what Hume has to say on the topic in the *Treatise* and in the *Enquiry*. §§2 and 3 examine the similarities. In §4 I shall explain why it is a mistake to attribute the Contrastive Argument to Hume. Finally, in §5 I will offer an evaluation of Hume's contribution to the development of compatibilism.

1. THE STRIKING DIFFERENCE

The striking difference between *Treatise* II. iii. 1–2 and *Enquiry* VIII is that in the former Hume is a partisan for the 'doctrine of necessity' and against the 'doctrine of liberty', whereas in the latter he presents himself as a peacemaker who will heal the breach between the two sides to this ancient dispute. In the *Treatise* he says that 'there are always the same arguments against liberty or free-will' (*T* 407) and describes the doctrine of liberty as a 'fantastical system' (*T* 404), as 'absurd . . . in one sense, and unintelligible in any other' (*T* 407), and as having 'odious consequences' (*T* 412). His conclusion is that he 'cannot doubt of an entire victory'—i.e. for necessity and against liberty. In sum, the author of the *Treatise* advises his readers plainly enough that there is no such thing as free will. Hume has become, by contrast, completely emollient in the *Enquiry*. After a couple of introductory paragraphs on the theme of how an apparently intractable controversy can be resolved if we will only avail ourselves of 'a few

---

[3] Paul Russell ('On the Naturalism of Hume's "Reconciling Project"', *Mind*, 92 (1983), 593–600) has also emphasized this point. In 'Causation, Compulsion, and Compatibilism', *American Philosophical Quarterly*, 25 (1988), 313–21, he even argues that a regularity account of causation weakens the Contrastive Argument (which he calls the 'compulsion argument').

intelligible definitions', he declares that 'all men have ever agreed in the doctrines both of necessity and of liberty' (E 81). He repeats this claim in what is perhaps the most frequently quoted passage of this section, where he describes his present discussion as a 'reconciling project':

But to proceed in this reconciling project with regard to the question of liberty and necessity; the most contentious question, of metaphysics, the most contentious science; it will not require many words to prove, that all mankind have ever agreed in the doctrine of liberty as well as in that of necessity, and that the whole dispute, in this respect also, has been hitherto merely verbal. (E 95)

To borrow the terminology introduced by William James, it would seem, then, that Hume was a *hard determinist* in the *Treatise* and a *soft determinist* in the *Enquiry*. However, although those categories are useful for some purposes, they are rather too crude to help us in the present case. In particular, hard determinism can come in different grades of toughness. The hardest form would insist that it is wrong to hold people accountable for their actions, and that moral attitudes to others based upon their supposed role as agents are all equally without any real foundation. It is clear that even in the *Treatise* Hume is not a hard determinist of that stamp. So in what does the reconciling softness of the first *Enquiry* consist? In order to assess the significance of the striking difference, we had better place it within the context of the similarities between *Treatise* II. iii. 1–2 and *Enquiry* VIII.

The similarities are extensive and involve the overall argumentative structure of the two passages. In both Hume divides the topic of 'liberty and necessity' into two sections. In the first of these he attempts to establish that human conduct is no less the product of causal necessity than other events. In the second he argues that, so far from causal necessity being inimical to morality, we need actions to be caused in order for moral sentiments to be directed upon their proper objects.

2. THE DOCTRINE OF NECESSITY

In comparing the two treatments of these two sections it seems appropriate to start, as Hume does, with his arguments for the doctrine of necessity (*T* 399–407, *E* 82–94). It is here, in arguing the case for determinism, that Hume employs his new account of the idea of causal necessity. The point deserves emphasis: *Hume uses his account of causation to argue that determinism is true of actions as well as other events, not in order to argue that determinism is compatible with actions being freely performed and justly subject to moral appraisal.* In this respect his procedure is exactly the same in the *Enquiry* as in the *Treatise*. Moreover, when in the *Abstract* he (if it is he, as I am presuming it is) claims to have put 'the whole controversy in a new light, by giving a new definition of necessity', he does not follow this up by claiming that we should now be able to see that there is no inconsistency between an action's being caused and being freely performed. Instead, he immediately proceeds to explain that what must be accepted, even by 'the most zealous advocates of free-will', is that actions exhibit causal necessity in his sense, because we know from experience that there are constant conjunctions between motives and actions, and because we do in fact confidently infer the latter from the former. He leaves to his opponents (the advocates for free will) what he takes to be the impossible task of showing that there is anything more to causal necessity than constant conjunction and consequent inferential habits to be discovered in 'the actions of matter'.

Since Hume reproduces in the *Enquiry*, with ingenious illustrative variation, the case he had made out for determinism in the *Treatise*, and since he had also advertised it in the *Abstract* as one of the philosophically useful results to be obtained from his definition of causation, we must judge that he was himself fairly well satisfied with his arguments for determinism. However, this part of his treatment of the topic of liberty and necessity cannot be described as having made a lasting contribution to the development of compatibilism, if only because a modern compatibilist need not be, as Hume was, a convinced determinist. Modern science has certainly not delivered the unequivocal verdict in favour of determinism that appeared to be indicated by Newtonian mechanics. This, however, does not rob compatibilism of its philosophical interest. Perhaps we should preserve a cautious agnosticism on the speculative metaphysical issue of whether the universe is deterministic or not. So long as it is supposed that there is at least a possibility that determinism is true, and in particular that human actions are causally determined, it will remain important to be able to show that this possibility would neither make our moral attitudes entirely groundless nor have the consequence that people could never justly be held responsible for what they have done.

In fact, it would surely be very surprising (to put it mildly) if Hume, or anyone else, could establish the truth of determinism simply by appealing to our ordinary everyday experience of the world and of human conduct. Hume does not set himself this task in its full generality. In closely parallel passages in the two treatments he invites his readers to accept determinism with respect to the physical world as something that has already been established:

'Tis universally acknowledg'd, that the operations of external bodies are necessary, and that in the communication of their motion, in their attraction, and mutual cohesion, there are not the least traces of indifference or liberty. (*T* 399–400)

It is universally allowed, that matter, in all its operations, is actuated by a necessary force, and that every natural effect is so precisely determined by the energy of its cause, that no other effect, in such particular circumstances, could possibly have resulted from it. (*E* 82)

He therefore sets himself the slightly more modest objective of showing that we have much the same evidence for causal necessity with regard to motives and actions as we have with regard to events in the external material world and their causes. This is where the new definition of causal necessity is deployed. For, by Hume's account of the twofold experiential root of our idea of necessity, such evidence can only consist in constant conjunctions between similar motives and similar actions, and an observer's consequent disposition to infer actions from past experience of such regularities.

In both treatments Hume concludes that experience does reveal constant conjunctions: 'No union can be more constant and certain, than that of some actions with some motives and characters . . .' (T 404); 'the conjunction between motives and voluntary actions is as regular and uniform, as that between the cause and effect in any part of nature' (E 88). There are, however, major problems concerning the claim of a constant conjunction between motives and actions.

Hume is well aware of one of these, namely that it simply is not the case that experience manifestly reveals *exceptionless* regularities linking circumstances, character, and conduct: different people may react differently to the same circumstances, and a given individual may on occasion act out of character. A critic of the doctrine of necessity might feel entitled to point to this as contrary evidence. Hume formulates the objection pithily: 'Necessity is regular and certain. Human conduct is irregular and uncertain. The one, therefore, proceeds not from the other.' (T 403). In the *Treatise* he devoted only about a page (T 403–4) to explaining away this contrary evidence, and the guarded formulation of the conclusion cited above (in which he only claims a constant union 'of *some* actions with *some* motives and characters', my emphasis) might indicate a degree of reservation over whether he had actually succeeded in defeating the objection. He returned to the point in the *Abstract*, offering a memorable analogy designed to show that while psychological regularities are not invariably reliable, they are no worse in this respect than other regularities: 'Thirty grains of opium will kill any man that is not accustomed to it; tho' thirty grains of rhubarb will not always purge him. In like manner the fear of death will always make a man go twenty paces out of his road; tho' it will not always make him do a bad action.' (A 661)

In the *Enquiry* the treatment of this difficulty is considerably expanded (E 85–8). The line Hume takes here is that any apparent exceptions to causal regularities should be attributed to undetected differences in the causes. While 'the vulgar', on the one hand, attribute a lack of regularity 'to such an uncertainty in the causes as makes the latter often fail of their usual influence' (E 86), on the other hand 'philosophers' (I suppose we may take it that Hume means *scientists*) 'form a maxim, that the connexion between all causes and effects is equally necessary, and that its seeming uncertainty in some instances proceeds from the secret opposition of contrary causes' (*E* 87).

There are several reasons why this method of explaining away apparent irregularity should raise the reader's eyebrows. The first is that it is flatly inconsistent with what Hume claims at the beginning of Section VIII, namely that 'all men have ever agreed in the doctrines both of necessity and of liberty' (*E* 81). For it now appears that *the vulgar do not agree in the doctrine of necessity*, at least not in regard to all actions, since such agreement depends upon a philosophical (or scientific) insight into the possibility of 'the secret operation of contrary causes' (*E* 87). The second reason for unease is that Hume's subsequent appeal to 'this *inference* from motives to voluntary actions; from characters to conduct' (*E* 90)—the second requisite for our idea of causal necessity to be applicable to actions—is severely weakened. For we surely cannot be determined to form inferences by the secret operation of contrary causes, and yet awareness of this possibility ought to (and presumably would) weaken the confidence of any expectations concerning conduct in a rational student of human nature. The third reason for surprise at Hume's way of defending determinism derives from the fact that *Treatise* II. iii. 1 and *Enquiry* VIII come as close as Hume ever approached to redeeming the promissory note issued at the end of *Treatise* I. iii. 3, entitled 'Why a cause is always necessary'. In that section Hume asserts that he has refuted the claim that it is either intuitively or demonstratively certain that 'whatever has a beginning has also a cause of existence'. One might have expected that Hume would then proceed to explain how belief in the causal principle is derived from experience. Instead he says, 'it will be more convenient to sink this question in' an examination of why we think that particular causes must have particular effects (*T* 82). It sinks all right. The difficulty is to see whether it ever emerges again, except in the sections that we are now considering. Yet does he here show that experience alone either supports or induces a belief in universal causation? Hardly. When he says that 'From the observation of several parallel instances, philosophers form a maxim, that the connexion between all causes and effects is equally necessary' (*E* 87), this looks (in spite of the thin veil drawn by the first clause) very much like the active adoption of a regulative or methodological principle. It is actually an echo of the sixth of his *rules by which to judge of causes and effects*: 'The difference in the effects of two resembling objects must proceed from that particular, in which they differ. For as like causes always produce like effects, when in any instance we find our expectations to be disappointed, we must conclude that this irregularity proceeds from some difference in the causes.' (*T* 174). But whatever the status of this rule might be,[4] its employ-

---

[4] For discussion of the puzzle as to how Hume could have thought that methodological rules were derived from experience, see J. Passmore, *Hume's Intentions*, 3rd edn. (London: Duckworth, 1980), 52–60.

ment in the present case cannot be anything more than question-begging. Given that the issue is whether all actions are the result of antecedent causes, it cannot be admissible to argue that *since they are effects*, they must therefore be the result of *unknown causes*, in any case in which they are not instances of a regularity manifest to experience.

My review of the way that Hume wrestles with this problem concerning the regularity of the connexion between motives and actions is sufficient to show that he fails to make out a convincing case either for the claim that the doctrine of necessity applies to actions as to other events, or, for that matter, for the claim that everyone in practice assumes this to be so. But I implied above that there are other major objections to the alleged constant conjunction between actions and motives. It hardly needs to be remarked that the claim that an agent's motives are causes of his actions has been the subject of a protracted controversy in modern analytical philosophy. I cannot enter into that controversy here, and hope I will not be accused of dogmatism if I restrict myself to observing that Hume's view that motives are causes of action seems to me perfectly defensible and indeed correct.[5] But there are three objections to the way Hume argues for the doctrine of necessity that we do need to consider.

The first is that Hume's procedure gives a very misleading impression of how common-sense psychology (often referred to by modern philosophers and psychologists as 'folk psychology' or 'theory of mind') actually works. Hume thinks that we arrive at expectations about conduct as a result of inferential habits formed by previously experienced regularities. Yet this could only be true if we started with an awareness of a person's motives and then subsequently observed his actions. But how do we come to have beliefs about the motives of others? The answer must surely be: through interpreting their actions. In other words, the ascription of motives and reasons to agents is theory-laden: at least some part of the theory of mind (common-sense psychology) must already be in place if we are ever to get started on the interconnected projects of interpreting and predicting the actions of other human agents. An argument in the style of Chomsky that inductive learning (and thus, a fortiori, simple induction by repetition) is not sufficient to account for acquisition seems to apply with at least as much force to theory of mind as to linguistic competence.[6]

The second and third objections concern the point that Hume is in fact arguing for *psychological determinism*: that the doctrine of necessity applies to

---

[5] We might return the compliment on behalf of Hume *et al.* by saying that Davidson has removed the confusions that can make *rationalization* seem inconsistent with causation. See D. Davidson 'Actions, Reasons, and Causes', *Journal of Philosophy*, 60 (1963), 685–700; also in Davidson, *Actions and Events* (Oxford: Clarendon Press, 1980), 3–19.

[6] See P. Carruthers, *Human Knowledge and Human Nature* (Oxford: Oxford University Press, 1992), chs. 6–8, for the development of such an argument. Also G. Botterill and P. Carruthers, *The Philosophy of Psychology* (Cambridge: Cambridge University Press, 1999), chs. 3–4.

the connexion between motives (internal states described in a psychological vocabulary) and actions. There are two difficulties here. The first (and, hence, second major objection to Hume's procedure) is that in explaining away apparent failures of constant conjunction by appealing to unknown causes Hume offers no justification for the assumption that those unknown causes *are psychological in character.*[7] It is doubtful whether any such justification can be provided and therefore doubtful whether psychological determinism is true. When two people with apparently similar motivation act in different ways, there is presumably some difference between them that accounts for this. But folk psychology is not a sufficiently tightly knit and fundamental theory to ensure that such a difference must be capturable within its own explanatory and predictive resources. It could, for example, be the case that the crucial difference between these two people is a difference in the level of a certain hormone within their bodies, or a difference in the release of some neurotransmitter within their brains. This point has implications for the second half of Hume's argument. If determinism in general is true (i.e. if every event results from previous factors in accordance with exceptionless causal laws), but psychological determinism in particular is *not*, then the way an agent acts on a particular occasion may be due to some internal state without that internal state being part of the agent's *character.*

The third objection concerns the *relevance*, to the traditional problem of free will, of psychological determinism, in so far as such a determinism concentrates solely on psychological causes and their effects on action (the output side, as one might say). Hume does at times mention *circumstances* as well as character and conduct, but for the most part he maintains causal necessity in relation to action only in so far as the connexion between motives and actions is concerned. An incompatibilist might well point out that it is not causal links that go back only as far as the psychological level that generate the problem of free will. For if determinism is true without restriction, then those psychological antecedents will have their necessitating causes in turn, and so we are driven back to acknowledge a causal origin for actions in events and states that lie outside the agent's body and before his birth. Hence the ultimate causes of an agent's actions are surely beyond his control, if determinism is true. Hume appears to confess, frankly and rather alarmingly, that he has no answer to this problem:

I pretend not to have obviated or removed all objections to this theory . . . It may be said, for instance, that, if voluntary actions be subjected to the same laws of necessity with the operations of matter, there is a continued chain of necessary causes, pre-ordained and

---

[7] Mill makes the same assumption and equally fails to provide any justification for it. See *A System of Logic* (1843), VI. ii. 2.

pre-determined, reaching from the original cause of all, to every single volition of every human creature. No contingency any where in the universe; no indifference; no liberty. While we act, we are, at the same time, acted upon. (*E* 99)

He proceeds to convert this into a theological discussion on whether God is responsible for all wrongdoing. But he should have seen that the problem is more general than that, and that the objection needs to be met, whether or not God is supposed the first cause of everything.

3. MORALITY REQUIRES NECESSITY

Hume's overall strategy is to argue (1) that determinism is true, but (2) that this, so far from making attributions of responsibility problematic, is actually a pre-condition for moral sentiments to be directed towards their proper objects. We have seen that the first half of his case turns out to be an unconvincing, and indeed misconceived, attempt to establish the truth of psychological determinism. We have also noted that a compatibilist need not be convinced of the truth of determinism: in other words, that while a compatibilist must of course not be a hard determinist, he need not be a soft determinist either.

So it is the second half of Hume's position (to be found in *T* 407–12 and *E* 96–103) that promises to be of more lasting relevance to the development of compatibilism. And in fact what Hume says here has often been reworked and re-presented.[8]

In reading Hume's two presentations of the second half of his case one can hardly fail to notice that in the *Enquiry* he has greatly improved the organization of his material. For in the *Treatise* the important argument that attributions of responsibility require us to see actions as causally determined by motives figures most awkwardly as the response to the third of three reasons 'for the prevalence of the doctrine of liberty' (*T* 409–12). The first two reasons both concern the relevance of introspection to the debate. They are: (1) that we are reluctant to allow that our own actions have been 'govern'd by necessity', and (2) that 'there is a *false sensation or experience* even of the liberty of indifference; which is regarded as an argument for its real existence'. In part the reorganization of his material is forced on Hume by 'the reconciling project'. Whereas in the *Treatise* he was arguing for the doctrine of necessity and against the doctrine of liberty, in the *Enquiry* he is arguing that both are true, so he will hardly want to begin Part ii of Section VIII by explaining why we are

[8] Two well-known and influential examples are Schlick, *Problems of Ethics*, 151–4, and R. E. Hobart, 'Free Will as Involving Determination and Inconceivable Without It', *Mind*, 43 (1934), 1–27. Hobart's summary of his main thesis would serve equally well as an epitome of the second half of Hume's case: 'absence of determination, if and so far as it exists, is no gain to freedom, but sheer loss of it; no advantage to the moral life, but blank subtraction from it'.

mistakenly attached to the doctrine of liberty. But, of course, I hope it will by now have become clear that the phrase 'the doctrine of liberty' does not bear the same meaning in the *Enquiry* as it did in the *Treatise*. In the *Treatise* 'the doctrine of liberty' is a metaphysical position. It is what would nowadays be referred to as *Libertarianism*—the view that human agents have a contra-causal freedom of the will. Hume never retreats from his opposition to this view, but in the *Enquiry* he is quite happy to join with others in subscribing to 'the doctrine of liberty', according to all that anyone can actually succeed in referring to when talking of the liberty involved in agency. This he defines as 'a power of acting or not acting, according to the determinations of the will' (*E* 95), and of course in this formulation the phrase 'the determinations of the will' is to be taken in a passive as well as an active sense. He intends it to be understood that the will is just as much determined as determining, that it is a causal intermediary between motives and actions. But, quite apart from this shift in usage of the phrase 'the doctrine of liberty', it was rather careless in the *Treatise* to lump together the three reasons for the prevalence of the doctrine. For the first two reasons both invoked alleged introspective evidence against psychological determinism. So in the *Enquiry* he is quite right to relocate their treatment to a footnote to the first half of the case in Part i of Section VIII (*E* 94).

We come now to what had appeared in the *Treatise* as the third reason for the prevalence of the doctrine of liberty, which is rightly elevated in the *Enquiry* to the status of the focal point for the discussion of Section VIII Part ii. This is the charge that determinism (the doctrine of necessity) is subversive of religion and morality. He enters verbatim exactly the same protest in both treatments against any attempt to refute a hypothesis by appealing to 'its dangerous consequences to religion and morality':

When any opinion leads to absurdities, it is certainly false; but it is not certain that an opinion is false, because it is of dangerous consequence. Such topics, therefore, ought entirely to be forborne; as serving nothing to the discovery of truth, but only to make the person of an antagonist odious. (*E* 96; there are only minor stylistic changes from the parallel passage in *T* 409)

Nevertheless, Hume is ready to meet this challenge because he believes he can show that the doctrine of necessity is 'not only consistent with morality', but even 'absolutely essential to its support' (*E* 97). In the *Treatise* he had claimed that 'the doctrine of necessity, according to my explication of it, is not only innocent, but even advantageous to religion and morality' (*T* 409). It is interesting, and surely significant, that in the *Enquiry* he no longer pretends that determinism is 'advantageous to religion'. Indeed, the final five paragraphs of Section VIII should surely tend to make the reader think that, if we are to accept the doctrine of necessity, then the existence of evil is a very severe problem for Christian belief. Hume camouflages this conclusion with a final paragraph which is a very masterpiece of ironic disingenuity. Admitting that he cannot explain 'how the Deity can be the mediate cause of all the actions of men, without being the author of sin and moral turpitude', he makes a show of conceding that 'These are mysteries, which mere natural and unassisted reason is very unfit to handle' and that philosophy should be 'sensible of her temerity, when she pries into these sublime mysteries' (E 103). The camouflage is so flamboyantly disingenuous that we are left in no real doubt that Hume was more concerned that his real opinion on the subject should be discernible to the unprejudiced reader, than that he should escape personal odium from those apt to complain of consequences dangerous to religion.

Our present concern, however, is not Hume's views on religious belief, but rather how he argues for the contention that the doctrine of necessity is essential to the 'support' of morality. The same argument is advanced, for the most part in the very same words, in the *Treatise* (*T* 410–12) and in the *Enquiry* (*E* 97–9). Actions in themselves may be 'blameable', but a person is not 'answerable' for them unless they proceed from something 'in him, that is durable and constant'.[9] In other words, Hume thinks that it is a necessary condition of moral responsibility for anything that has been done that the actions should be attributable to 'some *cause* in the character and disposition of the person who performed them'. He advances the following considerations, which may be taken as counting either in favour of the view that this is a necessary condition for moral responsibility, or alternatively as evidence that people do in practice subscribe to this view:

(1) People are not blamed for actions performed ignorantly and casually, 'because the principles of these actions are only momentary, and terminate in them alone'.

Presumably, Hume's thought is that in such cases we realize that if the agent were better informed he would act otherwise, and therefore the actions do not reveal anything blameworthy in his character.

(2) People are less blamed for hasty and unpremeditated than for deliberated actions, because a hasty temper 'infects not the whole character'.

---

[9] We can only wonder how Hume might have thought he could reconcile this with his celebrated pronouncement that persons are 'nothing but a bundle or collection of different perceptions, which succeed each other with an inconceivable rapidity, and are in a perpetual flux and movement' (*T* 252). Lacking, as he confessed in the Appendix to the *Treatise*, any satisfactory account of 'the principles, that unite our successive perceptions in our thought or consciousness' (*T* 636), it was prudent of Hume not to reopen the discussion of personal identity in the *Enquiry*.

(3) People are not blamed for something they have done once they have repented and reformed, because 'actions render a person criminal, merely as they are proofs of criminal principles in the mind' and after genuine repentance and reform the objectionable principles of conduct are no longer present.

Paul Russell has urged[10] that we should interpret Hume's argument here in a 'naturalistic' way. His claim is that Hume's thesis is that it is a matter of psychological fact that the moral sentiments of approval and disapproval are only aroused in us by persons or their characters. Regarding a person as morally responsible is, therefore, a matter of our feelings with regard to his character. Knowledge of character, however, requires inference from actions to motives, and such inference in turn requires causal necessity. The conclusion is that 'it is an empirical psychological fact that without necessity morality would be impossible'.[11] This cannot be quite right, since the psychological fact must be, not that characters directly arouse our moral sentiments, but rather that our *beliefs* about them do. So it would not be *psychologically impossible* for people to hold the moral attitudes involved in regarding others as responsible agents if beliefs about character failed to constitute knowledge, because they failed to track any genuine causal connexions between actions and persistent internal states of the agent. If, however, that really were the case, then morality would certainly be ill-founded, because it would be based upon false and unreliable beliefs about people's characters. That conclusion is quite sufficient to vindicate Hume's contention that the doctrine of necessity is essential to the support of morality.

Hume, of course, does not think that we should seriously entertain the nightmarish possibility of a general mismatch between our beliefs about character and the actual origins of conduct. For he has already remarked that by 'liberty' we 'cannot surely mean, that actions have so little connexion with motives, inclinations, and circumstances, that one does not follow with a certain degree of uniformity from the other, and that one affords no inference by which we can conclude the existence of the other' (*E* 95).

What we need to be clear about in relation to *Enquiry* VIII. ii is the question whether Hume's account of causation plays any essential role in his argument that causal necessity is essential to the support of morality. He does begin (*E* 97) by recapitulating his claim that necessity 'consists either in the constant conjunction of like objects, or in the inference of the understanding from one object to another'. Hume thought this was a correct account of causal necessity, and, after all, there were then no rival accounts of causation as an instance of

---

[10] Russell, 'On the Naturalism of Hume's "Reconciling Project" ', esp. 596–9.   [11] Ibid. 599.

general lawlike connexion that he could have been expected to introduce into the discussion. So it is understandable that he should have thought it a unique distinction of his view of causation that it enabled him to explain how our beliefs about causation enter into our moral thinking and the formation of our sentiments towards other agents. However, all he actually does in Part ii of Section VIII is to point out that we believe in the causal efficacy of rewards and punishments and that we depend on causal inference in attributing responsibility for an action to an agent. Any account of causation that (i) takes particular causal relations to be instances of general lawlike connexions, (ii) allows inference from effect to cause on the basis of knowledge of causal generalizations, and (iii) represents causes as of such a kind that psychological states can enter into causal relations with actions, would serve equally well. You do not need to be a Humean about causation—except in the loose sense that all those who accept the nomological character of causality are Humeans—in order to appreciate the force of Hume's arguments in *Enquiry* VIII. ii.

4. THE CONTRASTIVE ARGUMENT AND THE THREE LIBERTIES

Most commentators attribute the Contrastive Argument to Hume. One way of doing so is by concentrating on the confusion that he alleges between 'the liberty of *spontaneity*' and 'the liberty of *indifference*' (*T* 407), because the latter involves contra-causal freedom of the will, whereas the former only requires that the agent should encounter no hindrance in doing what he wants to do.[12] Penelhum, for example, describes this diagnosis of a confusion as 'the major argument' and explains that liberty of spontaneity 'is not opposed to the existence of causes, but is opposed to "violence"', and that, therefore, according to Hume: 'to be free is not to be prevented from doing that which you choose to do'.[13] Árdal gives a similar summary of Hume's compatibilism:

When we remember that all the necessity involved in the causal relation belongs to the mind thinking about or observing sequences, one may see that, to Hume, causal necessity would not, in any sense, restrict human freedom. It is because people have held erroneous views about necessity that they have failed to realize this. The error stems from confusing liberty of spontaneity and liberty of indifference. The first has as its opposite *violence*, the second has as its opposite necessity and causes.[14]

---

[12] This, at least, is all that I think these two pieces of technical terminology are doing. Beyond that they hardly serve to introduce any additional clarity or precision to the debate, and in so far as they may suggest that there are only two kinds of 'liberty' that are relevant to the discussion, they are positively mischievous.

[13] T. Penelhum, *Hume* (London: Macmillan, 1975), 120.

[14] P. S. Árdal, *Passion and Value in Hume's 'Treatise'*, 2nd edn. (Edinburgh: Edinburgh University Press, 1989), p. 87.

Moritz Schlick credits Hume with having been 'especially clear' on the point that 'morality is interested only' in freedom of conduct, not in freedom of the will. He goes on to add: 'And this is quite correct. Freedom means the opposite of compulsion; a man is *free* if he does not act under *compulsion*, and he is compelled or unfree when he is hindered from without in the realization of his natural desires.'[15]

Barry Stroud does at least notice that Hume does not repeat in the *Enquiry* the *Treatise*'s allegation concerning a confusion between the liberty of indifference and the liberty of spontaneity. But he does claim that in the *Enquiry* 'The "liberty of spontaneity" is said to be the only kind there is.' This claim carries a substantial load of interpretation, since Hume does not once use the phrase 'liberty of spontaneity' in *Enquiry* VIII. Stroud presumes that Hume's statement that by liberty we can only mean 'a power of acting or not acting, according to the determinations of the will' is intended to express the liberty of spontaneity, which he now sees as the only intelligible idea of liberty. I suppose this might be taken as a characterization of the liberty of spontaneity. But whether it is or not is indeed a merely verbal issue concerning the definition of a piece of scholastic terminology. What is of real importance is that an agent may possess such a power of acting *even when he acts under compulsion*.

Stroud takes this to be a defect in Hume's account of liberty:

[I]t can hardly be described as a subtle or profound analysis of the concept. A man from whom money is demanded with a gun at his head certainly has 'a power of acting or not acting, according to the determinations of the will'. If he chooses not to give the money, he may, and if he chooses to give it, he may. The penalties will be much greater on the one alternative than on the other, but which alternative is realized now depends on his will. So this example would seem to count as a case of liberty, given Hume's explanation of it, although it is clearly a case in which the kind of liberty Hume says it most concerns us to preserve is absent.[16]

The point is intended as a criticism of Hume's treatment of liberty. Seen in a true light, it is no such thing. On the contrary, it is one of the strengths of Hume's position that, since he does not rely on the Contrastive Argument, he can say of such a case of coercion that the agent has liberty, in one sense, and yet lacks that liberty which 'it concerns us most to preserve'.

There is a muddle here which badly needs to be cleaned up, if we are ever to arrive at a reasonable view as to whether a compatibilist solution to the problem of free will and determinism is possible—whether Hume's reconciling project can be successfully completed. Hume himself avoids the muddle, but the different senses in which he uses the term 'liberty' have certainly helped to entangle

---

[15]   Schlick, *Problems of Ethics*, 150.
[16]   B. Stroud, *Hume* (London: Routledge & Kegan Paul, 1977), 145–6.

others. Schlick remarked that it was unfortunate that Hume used the same word in two different senses.[17] In fact, it is absolutely vital to see that in the passages and commentaries we are considering 'liberty' carries *three* different senses, which can be distinguished as follows:

> *liberty*$_1$ is libertarian liberty. It is a contra-causal freedom of the will. Hume sometimes marks this sense of 'liberty' by saying that it is 'opposed to necessity'.

> *liberty*$_2$ is that in virtue of which a person is an agent in respect of what he does, and it is therefore a condition of responsibility. It is what is present in intentional action and absent in such things as hiccuping and snoring.

> *liberty*$_3$ is the absence of unwelcome restrictions affecting choice of action. It is what you have when you act without being subject to coercion, compulsion, or an influence that is resented. The dominant species of *liberty*$_3$ is sociopolitical freedom, although it is also true that circumstances can compel you to do something you would otherwise prefer not to do.

Liberty$_1$ is the liberty of indifference. Hume has the same opinion about it in both the *Treatise* and the *Enquiry*: there is no such thing, and that is just as well because, if there were, then we would either be incapable of holding moral attitudes to others (at any rate, to others, *qua* agents), or else if we held them they would be based on false beliefs. It is *liberty*$_2$ that he identifies as 'a power of acting or not acting, according to the determinations of the will'. It is the actualization of this power that makes someone an agent in respect of anything done, and so it is a necessary (though not sufficient) condition for moral responsibility. The power is realized in the causal influence of an agent's character on his actions, and that is why the causal determination of action is a requisite for morality. What he referred to in the *Treatise* as 'the liberty of spontaneity' (not altogether happily, as he seems to have appreciated in revising his treatment of the topic for the *Enquiry*) may be identified with *liberty*$_3$. This is 'that species of liberty, which it concerns us to preserve'. It should be remarked that *liberty*$_3$ is obviously a matter of degree, since what restricts our freedom in social and political life is the threat of some penalty consequent upon action or inaction, and threats can be more or less severe.

The division of the three liberties enables us to highlight some of the major mistakes so often perpetrated in the freewill debate. The libertarian

---

[17] The 1939 English translation of *Schlick's Problems of Ethics*, p. 150, actually says that it is 'freedom' that is inappropriately used to signify both freedom of the will and freedom of conduct.

incompatibilist insists on identifying *liberty₁* with *liberty₂*. This is quite definitely an error, for reasons I shall go into in the final section. That is a familiar enough theme. Yet the compatibilist who relies on the Contrastive Argument is also at fault. For that argument amounts to little more than the contention that *liberty₃* is not to be identified with *liberty₁*. This is quite true, but it is also neither very interesting nor very enlightening, and the libertarian is fully entitled to protest that it misses the whole point of *his* concern that the truth of determinism would make human beings nothing more than conduits through which causal forces operate. For it is just as serious a mistake to identify *liberty₃* with *liberty₂* as it is to identify *liberty₁* with *liberty₂*.

Hume himself does not commit the mistake of identifying *liberty₃* with *liberty₂*, though his text does not assist the reader to distinguish them. But notice this significant point: it would be completely fatuous to describe *liberty₂* as 'even the most common sense of the word' or the sort of liberty 'which it concerns us to preserve', as Hume describes the liberty of spontaneity (here *liberty₃*) at *T* 407–8. In the first place, so far from it being a common sense of the word, there is *no* ordinary English word for *liberty₂*. We could call it *genuine agency*, or *intentional agency*, or *moral agency*, but those are all philosophical coinage.[18] Secondly, we are not concerned to preserve it. This is not because it is unimportant to us, but rather because we are in little danger of losing it, so long as we continue to live, unless some extraordinary and incapacitating calamity befalls, such as total paralysis or being transformed into a zombie. As Hume says, 'this hypothetical liberty is universally allowed to belong to every one, who is not a prisoner and in chains' (*E* 95).

Strictly speaking, even a prisoner in chains still possesses *liberty₂* so long as he retains the power to rattle his chains or not, as he thinks fit. Yet the example (like that of someone in a straitjacket) is apt in so far as it comes as close as possible to providing an imaginable case of losing *liberty₂* while still remaining a person. It is crucial here to observe the distinction between compulsion and constraint,[19] and indeed even between two different kinds of constraint. If I am *constrained to do* something, then I am forced or obliged to do it, and so I act, though in a way I would prefer not to in the absence of the constraint. But if I am *being held under constraint*, then I am being prevented from acting—e.g. by someone sitting on top of me, or pinning my arms behind my back. A severe and lasting form of constraint, such as being closely confined, shackled, or put in a straitjacket, would still leave an agent with *liberty₂*, but only as a potential which the unfortu-

---

[18] This absence of a substantive should not be supposed to prevent us from talking or thinking about *liberty₂*. We talk about its presence or absence on particular occasions through descriptions of *actions* as voluntary or involuntary, intentional or unintentional, deliberate or accidental.

[19] This is one of the reasons why I find it advisable to introduce the label 'the Contrastive Argument'. Some writers call it 'the compulsion argument', others 'the constraint argument'.

nate agent has no (or very little) opportunity to exercise. I think there can be little doubt that this was what Hume had in mind when writing of a liberty 'universally allowed to belong to every one' who is not *both* a prisoner *and* in chains.

Hume does *not* say—please note—that this is a liberty allowed to belong to every one except when compelled or coerced to act in a way they would rather not. He does well not to, for those who say it fail to discern the difference between *liberty*₂ and *liberty*₃, and in consequence confound the question of whether an agent is responsible with the question of whether he acts freely. Consider, for example, Ayer's influential discussion of the topic:

If I am constrained, I do not act freely. But in what circumstances can I legitimately be said to be constrained? An obvious instance is the case in which I am compelled by another person to do what he wants. In a case of this sort the compulsion need not be such as to deprive one of the power of choice. . . . Thus, if the man points a pistol at my head I may still choose to disobey him: but this does not prevent its being true that if I do fall in with his wishes he can legitimately be said to have compelled me. And if the circumstances are such that no reasonable person would be expected to choose the other alternative, then the action that I am made to do is not one for which I am held to be morally responsible.[20]

Ayer is accurate on the question of choice. We might say the bank clerk with a gun at his head had no choice, but chose the lesser evil. This sounds paradoxical, but in fact is not. The appearance of paradox derives from the fact that when we say we have 'no choice but to . . .', what we usually mean is that we *do* have a choice but that it is *quite clear* what choice we ought to make. 'No choice' is like 'no contest'. What is 'no contest' is not something that is not a contest: it is, rather, a contest that is very one-sided.

But what Ayer says about responsibility (in a case of someone acting under this sort of compulsion) is much less satisfactory. He makes it sound as if the poor clerk with a gun at his head is let off because we all yield to that sort of 'persuasion'. We can all agree that in this situation the clerk is not to be blamed for handing over the money. A manager who blamed the clerk for having done this would be more than (and worse than) stern and exacting. However, this is not because the clerk was not morally responsible for handing over the money, but rather because *he did not do anything wrong*. Faced with a choice of two evils he quite rightly chose the lesser evil. We can see this by altering the case in such a way that the lesser evil becomes the greater evil. Make the robber a terrorist and the subject of his demand something more dangerous than money, such as nerve gas or plutonium. In that case one really does need to enter the plea, on behalf of the victim of coercion, that few of us would be courageous enough to

[20] Ayer, *Philosophical Essays*, 279.

refuse to comply.[21] Aristotle seems to have discerned the correct view of this sort of case when he said that such actions (done from fear of greater evils) are mixed, but are more like voluntary actions.[22] In spite of the horrible threat, the agent still acts intentionally. It is quite obvious that his reason for complying is to avoid the threat being carried out. So what the agent does has the sort of causal origin that is required for responsible agency. But, equally obviously, this is the sort of case in which $liberty_3$ is severely impaired.

The conclusion to be drawn is that the Contrastive Argument is at best a digression from what ought to be the main focus of debate. For all it can show is that it is the presence or absence of compulsion or coercion, rather than causation in itself, that is relevant to the question whether an agent acts freely or not. But it is not whether an agent acts freely, in the sense of having $liberty_3$, that is at issue in concerns over the implications of determinism for morality, but whether anyone can ever have genuine responsibility for their actions.

Lest I be suspected of concocting an interpretation to suit my own purposes, it would be desirable to substantiate the claim that 'liberty' occurs in each of these three senses in Hume's text. The job is easy enough as far as $liberty_1$ is concerned. I think it will be readily accepted that when Hume inveighs against 'the doctrine of liberty' in *Treatise* II. iii. 1–2, it is $liberty_1$ that he has in mind. This is proved by the way he summarizes his argument against the doctrine: 'liberty, by removing necessity, removes also causes, and is the very same thing with chance. As chance is commonly thought to imply a contradiction, and is at least directly contrary to experience, there are always the same arguments against liberty or free-will.' (*T* 407). Throughout *Enquiry* VIII Hume is careful to avoid using 'liberty' in the sense of $liberty_1$, except in the footnote to *E* 94 (which reproduces nearly verbatim a paragraph at *T* 408–9), where he writes:

The prevalence of the doctrine of liberty may be accounted for, from another cause, *viz.* a false sensation or seeming experience which we have, or may have, of liberty or indifference . . . liberty, when opposed to necessity, is nothing but the want of that determination, and a certain looseness or indifference . . . And it seems certain, that, however we may imagine we feel a liberty within ourselves, a spectator can commonly infer our actions from our motives and character . . .

Here, without doubt, 'liberty' means $liberty_1$. The one other use of 'liberty' to mean $liberty_1$ in *Enquiry* VIII comes at *E* 96, and Hume marks the fact that he is

---

[21] Galen Strawson makes much the same point about this sort of case (see G. Strawson, 'On the Inevitability of Freedom (from the Compatibilist Point of View)', *American Philosophical Quarterly*, 23 (1986), 393–400). He thinks it shows that according to 'standard compatibilist accounts of freedom' one acts freely whenever one acts at all. So much the worse for the standard accounts. A more discriminating compatibilism will maintain that whenever one genuinely acts, one has $liberty_2$, but one may not have $liberty_3$.

[22] *Nicomachean Ethics* 3. 1110[a–b].

there using the term in a special sense: 'liberty, when opposed to necessity, not to constraint, is the same thing with chance; which is universally allowed to have no existence'.

It is more difficult to detail occurrences of 'liberty' in the senses of *liberty₂* and *liberty₃* in an uncontroversial way. This is because, if my interpretation is right, when Hume uses 'liberty' in *Enquiry* VIII, he usually means *liberty₂*, and has little to say about *liberty₃*. Yet commentators who cannot resist acribing the Contrastive Argument to Hume generally fail to distinguish *liberty₂* from *liberty₃*. The one exception seems to be Stroud, who, as we have seen, mistakenly reproaches Hume for defining liberty so as to include cases in which *liberty₃* is impaired.

So I will instead try to show that passages in which Hume may be thought to be advancing some form of the Contrastive Argument do not in fact support this interpretation. What textual evidence is there for ascribing the Contrastive Argument to Hume? It is slender indeed and consists in the following two passages:

(A) Few are capable of distinguishing betwixt the liberty of *spontaneity*, as it is call'd in the schools, and the liberty of *indifference*; betwixt that which is oppos'd to violence, and that which means a negation of necessity and causes. The first is even the most common sense of the word; and as 'tis only that species of liberty, which it concerns us to preserve, our thoughts have been principally turn'd towards it, and have almost universally confounded it with the other. (*T* 407–8)

(B) It will be equally easy to prove, and from the same arguments, that *liberty*, according to that definition above-mentioned, in which all men agree, is also essential to morality, and that no human actions, where it is wanting, are susceptible of any moral qualities, or can be the objects either of approbation or dislike. For as actions are objects of our moral sentiment, so far only as they are indications of the internal character, passions, and affections; it is impossible that they can give rise either to praise or blame, where they proceed not from these principles, but are derived altogether from external violence. (*E* 99)

Much has been made of passage (A) and its contrast between the liberty of spontaneity and the liberty of indifference. Yet it should be noted that this passage occurs only in the *Treatise*. Though he repeats many of the arguments of the earlier version almost word for word in *Enquiry* VIII, this is not one of them.[23] I have already pointed out that Hume could hardly have thought that liberty as defined (at *E* 95) as 'a power of acting or not acting, according to the determinations of the will' was 'that species of liberty, which it concerns us to

---

[23] What he does instead (at *E* 92–3) is to give a fuller and less misleading explanation of why the fact that we do not in acting *feel* any necessary connexion between motives and actions is, on his view of causal necessity, no objection to the doctrine of necessity.

preserve', and so 'liberty of spontaneity' seems here to mean *liberty₃*. There is one further, and quite decisive, consideration. This is that passage (A) cannot justly be taken as part of Hume's 'reconciling project'. Quite apart from the fact that Hume did not conceive himself to be engaged in a reconciling project in the *Treatise* (the striking difference), the actual context in which passage (A) occurs is one in which he is anwering a possible objection to the doctrine of necessity. He is not arguing for compatibilism, but defending determinism against assault from alleged deliverances of introspection. The sentence which precedes passage (A) makes this clear enough: 'After we have perform'd any actions; tho' we confess we were influenc'd by particular views and motives; 'tis difficult for us to perswade ourselves we were govern'd by necessity, and that 'twas utterly impossible for us to have acted otherwise; the idea of necessity seeming to imply something of force, and violence, and constraint, of which we are not sensible.' His point is simply that the fact that we have no phenomenological awareness of internal compulsion when we act does not count against the doctrine of necessity. So passage (A) is part of the case for maintaining that determinism is true, *whether or not* the truth of determinism is consistent with (or, as he *subsequently* argues, even required for) our attributions of responsibility.

Passage (B) is certainly part of Hume's contribution to the reconciling project. But it is only the final clause of this passage that could be seen as expressing a version of the Contrastive Argument, and that would be putting the emphasis in the wrong place. Moreover, if Hume were here committed to the Contrastive Argument, he would have to mean that actions 'derived altogether from external violence' were actions *performed through fear of* external violence. But this is not what he says, and we must surely credit him with being astute enough to distinguish between violent external causes and the threat of violence. He would, of course, be aware that Hobbes had maintained that fear and liberty were consistent. Besides, Hume would be the last person to overlook that our 'internal character, passions, and affections' are implicated in our fear of violence and personal injury.

5. HUME'S CONTRIBUTION TO COMPATIBILISM

I conclude that it is a mistake to ascribe the Contrastive Argument to Hume. The idea of a unified Hume–Schlick–Ayer line on compatibilism is, therefore, a myth, since Schlick and Ayer clearly do rely on the Contrastive Argument. In doing so they skew the focus of the discussion, since they are concentrating on the distinction between acting freely and not acting freely (*liberty₃*), and that is not a distinction fundamental enough to give us insight into what an agent's responsibility for his actions consists in. Freedom may be a negative concept, but what distinguishes us as moral agents must reside in some positive power that we possess. Otherwise it would be difficult to explain why the Free Will Assumption applies to human beings and not to members of other species.

Hume, however, has what is of central importance clearly in focus in both *Enquiry* VIII. ii and *Treatise* II. iii. 2. It must be admitted that his discussion of moral responsibility is too brief and sketchy to give full satisfaction. For example, the suggestion that it is really always an agent's character that is the object of our moral sentiments should be questioned, since we can blame a person of generally good character for an occasional misdeed. Also, the claim that 'repentance wipes off every crime, if attended with a reformation of life and manners' is a wildly implausible view of human forgiveness. Yet it would be wrong to dwell too long on these points because what Hume was after was not a detailed account, but the basic necessary condition for responsibility. If we express that by saying that a person can only be responsible for what he does if his doing it is the result of an intentional state that can be attributed to him, we have the essence of Hume's reconciling position on liberty and necessity. And that part of Hume's case seems to me every bit as secure as he confidently proclaimed it was.

So Hume did succeed in showing that what it is about an agent in virtue of which he may be held responsible for his actions (*liberty₂*, or intentional agency) is not only consistent with those actions being caused, but actually requires them to be caused—by psychological states of the agent. He did not, however, follow this up by showing that it is also consistent with a completely unrestricted determinism which applies to an agent's motivational states not only as causes, but also as effects of prior causes. So he did not complete the reconciling project. Concentrating on the agent's intentional states may help us to do that, since the principal reason for supposing determinism inconsistent with attributions of responsibility derives from the thought that if determinism is universally true, then it cannot be that an agent could ever have acted otherwise than he did. Now, it is arguable that the notion of possibility involved here ought to be *epistemic*,[24] so that what is required for responsibility is not that the agent's acting otherwise than he did be consistent with all previous history and the laws of nature, but rather consistent with information cognitively available to the agent at the time of acting. But since we are not here concerned with arguments Hume did not offer that might strengthen the case for compatibilism, this is not the place to pursue this line of thought further.

It may now seem that the striking difference between the *Enquiry* and the *Treatise* is not really so important after all. In a way that is true, since the main argument for regarding the causal determination of action as essential to moral appraisal is the same in both sources (see §3 above). However, in refusing to

---

[24] Cf. D. Dennett, *Elbow Room* (Oxford: Clarendon Press, 1984), 148.

allow his libertarian opponents a proprietary usage even of the word 'liberty', he did see a very important point: 'Whatever definition we may give of *liberty*, we should be careful to observe two requisite circumstances; *first*, that it be consistent with plain matter of fact; *secondly*, that it be consistent with itself.' (*E* 95).

Hume thought that 'liberty' in the sense of *liberty₁*—contra-causal libertarian liberty—failed on both counts to be a permissible meaning of the word. Since we do not share Hume's belief that the truth of determinism is 'plain matter of fact', we cannot put the objection to libertarianism in exactly the same way as he does. However, a slight amendment to Hume's point, designed to accommodate agnosticism as to the truth of determinism, is sufficient to show why it is a mistake to identify *liberty₁* with *liberty₂*, the liberty which grounds attributions of responsibility. For we cannot know an action, or any other event, to be uncaused. So we surely must not base our attributions of responsibility upon a contra-causal freedom that we can never in any single instance know that an agent possesses.

My conclusion is that Hume's contribution to compatibilism was not only very considerable, but also considerably better than has usually been thought. Although his rather casual and shifting usage of the term 'liberty' makes his discussion of the topic more difficult to follow than it need have been, his most important argument in both the *Treatise* and the *Enquiry* (the argument of *T* 410–12 and *E* 97–9) is clearly directed at the fundamental issue of the conditions for responsible agency. Nor does he succumb to the tempting trap, into which many later compatibilists have fallen, of supposing that responsible agency is merely a matter of acting in the absence of coercion or constraint.

11

Hume on Testimony concerning Miracles

Don Garrett

The Scientific Revolution not only posed questions about the relation between nature and human actions; it also posed questions about the relation between nature and divine action, and about the existence of divine actions in or along-side nature. In the face of a mechanistic universe from which God appeared to stand aloof, many theologians claimed that the historical occurrence of miracles in conjunction with divine revelation, as established by the testimony of scripture, was a primary source of evidence for the truth of Christianity.

Section X of *An Enquiry concerning Human Understanding*—entitled 'Of Miracles'—is surely the most famous philosophical treatment of the credibility of reports of miracles ever written. Hume divides the section into two parts. Part i provides his most general argument concerning assent to miracles, an argument that appeals prominently to claims about 'proof', 'probability', 'experience', 'laws of nature', 'miracles', and the relations among them. Part ii goes on to raise four separate and specific objections to the credibility of testimony for miracles, concerning (i) the quality of existing testimony for miracles, (ii) the psychological factors contributing to the offering and acceptance of testimony for miracles, (iii) the frequent origination of testimony for miracles among ignorant peoples, and (iv) the conflicts posed by the testimony for miracles of different religions. Because of the contrast between the generality of the premisses of Part i and the specificity of the premisses of Part ii, commentators sometimes refer to the argument of Part i as Hume's 'a priori argument' concerning miracles, and to the four arguments of Part ii as his 'a posteriori arguments'.

This paper is adapted from D. Garrett, *Cognition and Commitment in Hume's Philosophy* (Oxford: Oxford University Press, 1997), ch. 7.

There is general consensus among Hume's readers concerning the structure of the arguments and the content of the conclusions of the more specific and 'a posteriori' Part ii. Furthermore, if there is not quite universal consensus about the precise degree of success that those arguments achieve, there is general agreement that the arguments are appropriate and establish at least a prima-facie case against the credibility of testimony for miracles. In contrast, however, there is no consensus concerning the argument, the conclusion, or the success or failure of the more general, but crucial, Part i.

That there is no consensus about Hume's *argument* in Part i is evident from a survey of the literature. Commentators have offered a wide variety of principles as 'central premisses' in Hume's argument, few of which occur either in Hume's text or in the reconstructions of other commentators. These proposals for tacit or implied premisses include the following: 'a violated law of nature is no longer a law of nature';[1] 'if *E* is a highly improbable event, no evidence is sufficient to warrant our belief that it occurred';[2] 'to evaluate testimony that *p*, one must compare the [prior] probability of *p* with the probability that the testifiers are lying or mistaken, and take the greater probability';[3] 'we cannot have an impression of a supernatural cause';[4] 'empirical reason includes the principle that for every event there is a law that explains it';[5] 'if in one case the occurrence of an event within the natural causal order were not sufficient to establish that the event had natural causes, then there would be no reason for believing it would be sufficient in any case';[6] and 'sensory evidence is always stronger than testimonial evidence'.[7]

There is no greater consensus concerning Hume's *conclusion* in Part i. On the contrary, some commentators characterize Hume as arguing that miracles are impossible or *cannot occur*;[8] others, that one cannot *reasonably believe* that a miracle has occurred;[9] still others, that one cannot reasonably believe *on the*

---

[1] D. F. Norton, *David Hume: Common-Sense Moralist, Sceptical Metaphysician* (Princeton: Princeton University Press, 1982); F. J. Beckwith, *David Hume's Argument against Miracles: A Critical Analysis* (Lanham, Md.: University Press of America, 1989).

[2] Beckwith, *David Hume's Argument against Miracles*.

[3] R. Hambourger, 'Belief in Miracles and Hume's *Essay*', *Nous*, 14 (1980), 587–604.

[4] M. P. Levine, *Hume and the Problem of Miracles: A Solution* (Dordrecht: Kluwer, 1989).

[5] F. Wilson, 'The Logic of Probabilities in Hume's Argument against Miracles', *Hume Studies*, 15/2 (Nov. 1989), 255–75.

[6] D. Ahern, 'Hume on the Evidential Impossibility of Miracles', in N. Rescher (ed.), *Studies in Epistemology* (Oxford: Blackwell, 1975).

[7] K. E. Yandell, *Hume's 'Inexplicable Mystery': His Views on Religion* (Philadelphia: Temple University Press, 1990).

[8] Beckwith, *David Hume's Argument against Miracles*; Norton, *David Hume*; R. J. Fogelin, 'What Hume Actually Said about Miracles', *Hume Studies*, 16/1 (Apr. 1990), 81–6.

[9] R. A. Sorenson, 'Hume's Skepticism concerning Reports of Miracles', *Analysis*, 43 (Jan. 1983), 60; D. Coleman, 'Hume, Miracles, and Lotteries', *Hume Studies*, 14/2 (Nov. 1988), 328–46; Yandell, *Hume's 'Inexplicable Mystery'*; and Fogelin, 'What Hume Actually Said about Miracles'.

basis of testimony that a miracle has occurred;[10] and yet others, only that one cannot reasonably believe on the basis of testimony that a miracle has occurred *unless* the falsehood of the testimony would be even more miraculous than the occurrence of the miracle that it allegedly reports—and that even in that case, one can reasonably accept the miracle only with a relatively low degree of assurance.[11]

Finally, there is no consensus about the *success or failure* of Hume's argument in Part i. Some commentators hold that Hume's argument is at least reasonably successful.[12] Others hold that it fails, either because it relies on one or more false premises,[13] because its premises are not adequate to its conclusion,[14] or because it begs the question.[15]

Much of this striking lack of agreement is the result of six apparent inconsistencies in Hume's discussion. Commentators often attribute tacit or implied premises to Hume because they are trying to reconstruct his argument so as to avoid one or more of the inconsistencies. Frequently, when commentators revise or reinterpret Hume's stated conclusion, they do so either in order to avoid one or more of the inconsistencies directly, or in order to accommodate his conclusion to reconstructions of the argument that are themselves motivated by the same goal. Their final evaluations of the argument, in turn, generally depend on the quality of the reconstructed argument, the character of the revised conclusion, or the continuing lack of resolution of one or more of the remaining apparent inconsistencies.

---

[10] C. S. Lewis, *Miracles: A Preliminary Study* (New York: MacMillan, 1947); Ahern, 'Hume on the Evidential Impossibility of Miracles'; T. Penelhum, *Hume* (New York: St Martin's Press, 1975); Hambourger, 'Belief in Miracles and Hume's *Essay*'; Levine, *Hume and the Problem of Miracles*; Wilson, 'The Logic of Probabilities in Hume's Argument against Miracles'.

[11] A. Flew, 'Hume's Check', *Philosophical Quarterly*, 9 (1959), 1–18; *Hume's Philosophy of Belief* (London: Routledge & Kegan Paul, 1961); *David Hume: Philosopher of Moral Science* (Oxford: Blackwell, 1986); R. Swinburne, *The Concept of Miracle* (London: Macmillan, 1970); D. and R. Basinger, *Philosophy and Miracle: The Contemporary Debate* (Lewiston, NY: Edwin Mellen, 1986); J. H. Sobel, 'On the Evidence of Testimony for Miracles: A Bayesian Reconstruction of David Hume's Analysis', *Philosophical Quarterly*, 37/147 (Apr. 1987), 166–86.

[12] J. L. Mackie, *The Miracle of Theism* (Oxford: Clarendon Press, 1982); D. Owen, 'Hume versus Price on Miracles and Prior Probabilities: Testimony and the Bayesian Calculation', *Philosophical Quarterly*, 37/147 (Apr. 1987), 187–202 (Ch. 12 in this volume); Sobel, 'On the Evidence of Testimony for Miracles'; Wilson, 'The Logic of Probabilities in Hume's Argument against Miracles'.

[13] Ahern, 'Hume on the Evidential Impossibility of Miracles'; Hambourger, 'Belief in Miracles and Hume's *Essay*'; R. M. Burns, *The Great Debate on Miracles: From Joseph Glanville to David Hume* (Lewisburg, Pa.: Bucknell University Press, 1981); Beckwith, *David Hume's Argument against Miracles*; Levine, *Hume and the Problem of Miracles*; Yandell, *Hume's 'Inexplicable Mystery'*.

[14] C. D. Broad, 'Hume's Theory of the Credibility of Miracles', *Proceedings of the Aristotelian Society*, NS 17 (1916–17), 77–94; repr. in A. Sesonske and N. Fleming (eds.), *Human Understanding: Essays in the Philosophy of David Hume* (Belmont, NC: Wadsworth, 1965); Swinburne, *The Concept of Miracle*; Burns, *The Great Debate on Miracles*.

[15] Lewis, *Miracles*; Beckwith, *David Hume's Argument against Miracles*; Levine, *Hume and the Problem of Miracles*.

Each of the six inconsistencies is only apparent, and not real. The key to resolving them lies in an understanding of Hume's argument as he actually presents it—in the context of his cognitive psychology and of the conception of probability that he derives from it. In this essay I first describe the six apparent inconsistencies themselves. I then explain several relevant aspects of Hume's cognitive psychology and of his conception of probability before going on to outline the argument of 'On Miracles'. Finally, I draw on the results of the previous sections in order to resolve the six apparent inconsistencies in Hume's discussion and to assess its significance.

SIX APPARENT INCONSISTENCIES

Each of the six apparent inconsistencies raises a fundamental question about Hume's meaning or procedure. I will consider these questions in an order in which they are likely to occur to the reader of Hume's text.

Experience

First, what does Hume mean by 'experience'? Near the beginning of Part i, he argues that any judgement of the probability of human testimony must depend entirely on experience (E 111–12). In making this argument, it seems that he must be referring only and specifically to the experience of the individual who is to judge. For to judge the probability of testimony on the basis of the (merely reported) experiences of *others* would appear to beg the question of the reliability of testimony. A few pages later, however, he claims that an assessment of the testimony for a miracle must take into account what he calls the 'uniform *experience* against every miraculous event' (E 115, my emphasis), and he cites such 'uniform experience' as showing what 'has never been observed, in any age or country'. Yet the fact that something has never been observed *in any age or country* is something that could hardly be established without already relying freely on the testimony of others. Thus it seems that Hume equivocates on the central term 'experience' in such a way as to make it appear that an individual's evidence against the occurrence of a miracle is far more extensive (as involving observations at distant times and places) than it actually could be on his own theory.

Laws of Nature

Second, what does Hume mean by 'laws of nature'? This term plays the crucial role in his main definition of a 'miracle' as 'a violation of the laws of nature' (E 114).[16] Yet he does not explicitly define 'law of nature'; he simply goes on to

---

[16] It also plays the same role in the expanded definition he offers in a footnote: 'a transgression of a law of nature by a particular volition of the Deity, or by the interposition of some invisible agent'

claim that 'a firm and unalterable experience has established these laws' (*E* 114). From this characterization of them, it seems natural to suppose that 'laws of nature' are by definition either (i) universal generalizations to which no exceptions ever *occur*, or (ii) universal generalizations to which no exceptions are ever *observed*. On the former supposition, however, the concept of a miracle occurring would be self-contradictory from the very start; and on the latter supposition, the concept of veridical eyewitness testimony for a miracle would be self-contradictory. In either case, the rest of Hume's arguments concerning the credibility of testimony for miracles would evidently then be superfluous.

Moreover, if either one of these suppositions is correct, Hume will appear to have missed the larger point, for no event—no matter how bizarre—will *be* a miracle unless it (i) fails to occur (given the first supposition), or (ii) fails to be observed (given the second). Defenders of testimony for particular bizarre or supernatural events—such as someone rising from the dead, to take a Humean example, or the parting of the Red Sea—may then easily claim to elude the scope of his negative conclusion, a conclusion that concerns only the credibility of reports of *miracles*. For if laws of nature are universal generalizations to which no exceptions ever *occur*, then to suggest that a particular bizarre event has occurred will be to suggest, *ipso facto*, that it is not a violation of a law of nature, hence not a miracle, and hence that it is outside the scope of Hume's conclusion. Similarly, if laws of nature are universal generalizations to which no exceptions are ever *observed*, then to report that a bizarre event has been observed will be to imply, *ipso facto*, that the event is not a violation of a law of nature, hence not a miracle, and hence that it is, once again, outside the scope of Hume's conclusion. Thus it seems that Hume defines his terms in a way that obviates all of his more specific arguments about testimony for miracles, while at the same time deriving an epistemic principle that could be applied even to the most bizarre kinds of events only by begging the question of their non-existence or failure to be observed.

The Miraculous and the Marvellous

Third, what does Hume mean by the distinction he draws between the 'miraculous' and the merely 'marvellous' (or 'extraordinary')—or, equivalently, between events that would be 'contrary' to one's experience and those that are merely 'not conformable' to it? He draws this distinction in order to emphasize that testimony for the *miraculous* must meet an even higher standard than testimony for the merely *marvellous*. His example is the 'INDIAN prince', who 'reasoned justly' when he 'refused to believe the first relations concerning the effects

(*E* 115 n.). Although the restriction to volitions of the Deity or an invisible agent accurately captures the class of cases in which Hume is most interested, the restriction plays no role in Hume's argument of Part i, which is presumably why it appears only in a footnote.

of frost' (*E* 113). According to Hume, the freezing of water in cold weather would be *marvellous* and *extraordinary* for the Indian prince, and *not conformable* to his previous experience. Nevertheless, Hume insists, it would *not* be *miraculous* for the prince or *contrary* to his experience, because the prince has observed water only in warm weather, and has no experience of water in cold. It thus requires only 'very strong' or 'a pretty strong' testimony to establish for the prince that water has frozen. An event like the raising of the dead, in contrast, would be *a miracle*, and *contrary* to experience, according to Hume, and thus testimony for it must be held to a far more stringent standard.

Yet how are these two cases essentially different? For although Hume may have experience of the death of individuals whom an almighty deity did *not* will to raise from the dead, he has evidently no experience of the death of individuals whom an almighty deity *did* will to raise from the dead. Why does this latter fact not render the raising of the dead—like the freezing of water—at most merely *marvellous* and *not conformable* to previous experience for Hume, and hence subject to the weaker evidential standard that he imposes on testimony for the merely marvellous and extraordinary? It seems that Hume treats these similar cases inconsistently.

Superior Proofs and Greater Miracles

Fourth, what does Hume mean when he writes of 'opposite' and 'superior' proofs of the occurrence or non-occurrence of a particular miracle—or, correlatively, of a miracle that would be 'more miraculous' or a 'greater miracle' than another? Near the end of Part i, he writes that: 'there is here a direct and full *proof*, from the nature of the fact, against the existence of any miracle; nor can such a proof be destroyed, or the miracle rendered credible, but by an *opposite proof, which is superior*' (*E* 115, second emphasis mine). Yet he has already defined 'proofs' as 'such arguments from experience as leave no room for doubt or opposition' (*E* 56 n.); and it seems that one proof could not be opposite and superior to another when neither would leave any room for doubt or opposition.

Similarly, he concludes that 'no testimony is sufficient to establish a miracle, unless the testimony be of such a kind, that its falsehood would *be more miraculous*, than the fact, which it endeavours to establish' (*E* 115–16, my emphasis). And he ends Part i by reporting that, when considering testimony of a miracle:

I weigh the one miracle against the other; and according to the superiority, which I discover, I pronounce my decision, and always reject *the greater miracle*. If the falsehood of his testimony would be *more miraculous*, than the event which he relates; then, and not till then, can he pretend to command my belief or opinion. (*E* 116, my emphasis)

Yet as we have seen, Hume defines a 'miracle' as a 'violation of a law of nature'; and he himself insists in a footnote that:

The raising of a house or ship into the air is a visible miracle. The raising of a feather, when the wind wants ever so little of a force requisite for that purpose, is *as real a miracle*, though not so sensible with regard to us. (*E* 115 n., my emphasis)

Since an event either violates a law of nature or it does not, it seems that no miraculous event could be a *greater* miracle, or *more* miraculous than any other. Thus it seems that Hume contradicts his own definitions.

Absolute Impossibility

Fifth, what does Hume mean when he refers, in Part ii, to 'the absolute impossibility' of certain miraculous events? Commenting on the witnesses to a recent series of alleged Jansenist miracles, he writes: 'And what have we to oppose to such a cloud of witnesses, but the *absolute impossibility* or miraculous nature of the events, which they relate? And this surely, in the eyes of all reasonable people, will alone be regarded as a sufficient refutation.' (*E* 125, my emphasis). Treating miracles as an 'absolute impossibility' appears to be inconsistent with his repeated denials (e.g. in *Treatise* I. iii. 14 and *Enquiry* VII) that we can have any insight into necessary connexions in nature. It appears to be even more directly in conflict with his Conceivability Criterion of Possibility, namely that 'whatever we *conceive* is possible, at least in a metaphysical sense' (*A* 650).[17] Moreover, it seems to conflict with his own approach throughout Part i of Section X. For in Part i he appears to take the metaphysical possibility of miracles for granted even while arguing that testimony for their occurrence must be epistemically problematic. Indeed, he concludes Part i by asserting only that testimony cannot establish a miracle unless the falsehood of the testimony would be even more miraculous; and he illustrates the point by citing his own willingness to weigh one alleged miracle against another. Yet nothing in the 'a posteriori' arguments of Part ii seems to warrant any shift in attitude on the question of the absolute impossibility of miracles from Part i to Part ii. Thus it seems that Hume both violates his own general metaphysical principles and equivocates on the question of what Part i actually establishes.

The Uniformity of Nature

Finally, regardless of his other arguments, how can Hume himself *criticize* beliefs in miracles—as he clearly does throughout both Part i and Part ii—in light of his own views about what we would call 'inductive inferences' and he

---

[17] See also *T* 32, 241, *E* 25–6, 164; and D. Garrett, *Cognition and Commitment in Hume's Philosophy* (New York: Oxford University Press, 1997), ch. 1.

calls 'inferences from experience'? To treat past experience as providing a legitimate 'proof' against the occurrence of a miracle seems to presuppose that the course of nature is uniform, and that instances one has not observed will resemble instances one has observed. Yet Hume vigorously maintains that this thesis of the uniformity of nature cannot be defended by any argument that does not presuppose it (*Treatise* I. iii. 6; *Enquiry* IV). Moreover, he holds that all inferences that go beyond the content of present experience and personal memory are 'not determin'd by reason' (*T* 92) and 'are *not* founded on reasoning, or any process of the understanding' (*E* 32). Thus, given these views, it seems that Hume is inconsistent in treating beliefs in miracles as worse than other beliefs about matters of fact that go beyond present experience and memory.

COGNITIVE PSYCHOLOGY AND PROBABILITY

In order to understand Hume's argument in 'On Miracles', and so to resolve these apparent inconsistencies, it is necessary to understand (i) his distinction of arguments into demonstrations, proofs, and probabilities; and (ii) his account of the species of probability.

Demonstration, Proof, and Probability

'Demonstrations', according to Hume, are arguments depending only on the intrinsic relations among ideas, arguments in which the denial of the conclusion involves a contradiction (*E* 35). As such, they do not depend on experience. 'Proofs' are not demonstrations, but rather 'such arguments *from experience* as leave no room for doubt or opposition' (*E* 56 n., my emphasis). 'Probabilities' constitute the *remainder* of arguments from experience—i.e. those that produce a lower degree of assurance.

Proofs and probabilities thus differ in the degree of assurance they produce. But they resemble each other, Hume holds (*Enquiry* V–VI), inasmuch as the degree of assurance involved in both proof and probability is nothing more than the degree of a fundamental psychological magnitude that constitutes 'belief' or 'assent'. In the *Treatise* Hume explicitly identifies this psychological magnitude as 'force and vivacity', the same magnitude that, when present in an even higher degree, also serves to distinguish impressions from ideas. In the first *Enquiry*, however, Hume does not explicitly make this identification of belief with a lower degree of 'force and vivacity', although he does characterize belief as 'nothing but a more vivid, lively, forcible, firm, steady conception' (*E* 49). In what follows, I will refer to the psychological magnitude that constitutes Humean belief simply as 'vivacity'. Both the *Treatise* and the *Enquiry* emphasize that, in both proof and probability, the characteristic constituting belief or assent is produced in an idea by an impression, ultimately as a causal consequence of an association derived from some amount of uniformity in the judger's past experience. In the case of a proof, this experience has been 'entirely regular and uniform' (*E* 58), whereas in the case of probability, such entire regularity and uniformity is in some way lacking.[18]

Species of Probability

Section VI of the *Enquiry* ('Of Probability') describes two species of probability, the first of which is the probability of *chances*. In this species of probability, the projection of past experience assures us that one out of a certain set of alternatives will be realized in a given circumstance. At the same time, however, this experience gives no greater expectation of one rather than another of these alternatives. Hence, an idea, or 'view', of each alternative acquires a certain and similar degree of vivacity, as one of the alternatives suggested by past experience. When some of these views happen to *concur* in some characteristic, their force is combined in that respect, giving greater vivacity (and hence belief or assent) to the idea of an outcome possessing that characteristic. This greater vivacity varies with the number of concurring views. At the same time, however, views of those possibilities that do not concur in that characteristic will *oppose* or *conflict with* the concurring views. Accordingly, these opposing views will lessen the vivacity of the idea of an outcome possessing the characteristic in question. This lessening effect will vary with the number of opposing views. The final result is a degree of vivacity for the idea of a particular kind of outcome that corresponds to the proportion of concurring views among all of the views. In Hume's example, if a die has one number marked on four of its faces, and another number marked on the other two, we expect that the first number will come up on a roll of the die—with more assurance than if that number had only been on, say, three out of six sides, but with less than if it had been on 999 out of 1,000.

The second species of probability that Hume discusses in *Enquiry* VI is the probability of *causes*. In the most common form of this species of probability, the projection of past experience once again provides us with a set of alternatives, one of which is to be realized in a given set of circumstances.[19] As before,

---

[18] In contrast, it is not entirely clear from Hume's discussion (*T* 95–7) whether the assurance produced by a *demonstration* is a matter of an idea coming to possess vivacity at all (and hence whether it is a matter of 'belief' in Hume's technical sense), or whether it is just a matter of coming to *conceive of* (or recognize that one is conceiving of) particular ideas standing in those relations that the conclusion of the demonstration describes.

[19] In the *Treatise* Hume mentions 'several kinds' of probability of causes. That described here is the only kind he discusses in the *Enquiry*, however; and it is—not coincidentally—the only kind that bears directly on his treatment of miracles. The other kinds depend not on comparing different views derived from experiments, but on an imperfection in the *habit* or custom by which we make inferences

the vivacity that constitutes belief or assent is derived from the concurrence in some characteristic of various different ideas or views, while the diminished vivacity that is characteristic of mere probability is the result of a conflict of opposing views. And as before, this vivacity increases with the number of concurring views and decreases with the number of opposing views, with the final result that the vivacity of the idea of a particular kind of outcome corresponds to the proportion of concurring views among all of the views. In the probability of causes, however, each different view is the result of a distinct past experience, which Hume calls an 'experiment'. In his example, if we have experience that nineteen out of twenty ships sent out have returned safely, the twenty experiments produce nineteen concurring views in which a ship returns safely, and we expect that the next will return safely as well—with more assurance than if, say, only eighteen of twenty had returned safely, but with less than if 999 out of 1,000 had done so.

Enquiry IX ('Of the Reason of Animals') begins with a brief discussion of a third species of probability, that of *analogy*, which the *Treatise* explains at greater length. Whereas the probabilities of chances and of causes involve imperfect *uniformity*, the probability of analogy derives from a different kind of irregularity—namely, a lack of full *resemblance* between the circumstances under consideration and those involved in one's past experiments. This lack of resemblance weakens the vivacity, and hence the belief and assurance, of the conclusion. Thus, Hume writes:

The vivacity of the first impression cannot be fully convey'd to the related idea, either where the conjunction of their objects is not constant, or where the present impression does not perfectly resemble any of those, whose union we are accustom'd to observe. In those probabilities of chance and causes above-explain'd, 'tis the constancy of the union, which is diminish'd; and in the probability deriv'd from analogy, 'tis the resemblance only, which is affected. Without some degree of resemblance, as well as union, 'tis impossible there can be any reasoning: but as this resemblance admits of many different degrees, the reasoning becomes proportionably more or less firm and certain. An experiment loses of its force, when transferr'd to instances, which are not exactly resembling; tho' 'tis evident it may still retain as much as may be the foundation of probability, as long as there is any resemblance remaining. (*T* 142)

In the *Treatise* Hume also describes four kinds of 'unphilosophical probability'. These include (i) the variations in vivacity that result from the temporal distance of the relevant experiments; (ii) the additional vivacity derived from whatever happens to be the most recent experiment; (iii) the variations of

___

concerning an unobserved case—that is, on an imperfection in the ability of the impression to produce a full measure of vivacity in the idea that constitutes our conclusion. This imperfection is due either to an insufficient *number* of experiments, or to a variability in the *outcome* of those experiments.

vivacity that result from the mere length of arguments; and (iv) the rashly formed 'general rules' (such as national or ethnic prejudices) that result from applying the probability of analogy even to circumstances of resemblance that have already been determined to be causally irrelevant (*Treatise* I. iii. 13). Whereas the probabilities of chances, causes, and analogy 'are receiv'd by philosophers, and allow'd to be reasonable foundations of belief and opinion', unphilosophical probability comprises those kinds of probability that 'have not had the good fortune to obtain the same sanction'. They lack this good fortune because they involve cognitive mechanisms that, upon reflection, we find we do not approve. Those who do reflect on these mechanisms—i.e. the 'philosophical'—reject the first kind of unphilosophical probability, for example, because they observe that, if it were accepted, 'an argument must have a different force to day, from what it shall have a month hence' (*T* 143). Similarly, they reject the fourth kind of unphilosophical probability because it conflicts with those positive general 'rules by which to judge of causes and effects' that we formulate for ourselves on the basis of reflection on our cognitive mechanisms and their inductive successes and failures (*T* 149), and which Hume details in *Treatise* I. iii. 15. Thus, he writes:

when we take a review of this act of the mind [i.e. the fourth kind of unphilosophical probability, concerning rashly formed general rules], and compare it with the more general and authentic operations of the understanding, we find it to be of an irregular nature, and destructive of all the most establish'd principles of reasonings; which is the cause of our rejecting it. (*T* 150)

THE ARGUMENT AGAINST TESTIMONY
FOR MIRACLES

With this understanding of Humean probability as background, we can now understand his arguments concerning testimony for miracles. His argument in Part i may be usefully divided into three sections. The first concerns epistemological principles of proof and probability in general; the second concerns human testimony; and the third concerns testimony for miracles in particular. I will outline these sections in order using Hume's own words. For purposes of comparison, I will then go on to outline Hume's argument as it continues in Part ii.

Epistemological Principles of Proof and Probability

The first section of Hume's argument (*E* 110–11) seeks to establish three general epistemological principles on the basis of three initial premises. It may be outlined as follows:

(1) [E]xperience [is] our only guide in reasoning concerning matters of fact.

(2) Some events are found, in all countries and all ages, to have been constantly conjoined together: Others are found to have been more variable, and sometimes to disappoint our expectations.

(3) A wise man . . . proportions his belief to the evidence.

(4) In such conclusions as are founded on an infallible experience, [a wise man] expects the event with the last degree of assurance, and regards his past experience as a full *proof* of the future existence of that event. [from (1), (2), and (3)]

(5) In other cases [i.e. where conclusions are not founded on an infallible experience, a wise man] proceeds with more caution: He weighs the opposite experiments: He considers which side is supported by the greater number of experiments: To that side he inclines, with doubt and hesitation; and when at last he fixes his judgment, the evidence exceeds not what we properly call *probability*. [from (1), (2), and (3)]

(6) In all cases [of reasoning concerning matters of fact], we must balance the opposite experiments, where they are opposite, and deduct the smaller number from the greater, in order to know the exact force of the superior evidence. [from (1), (2), and (3)]

(1), which states that experience is our only guide in reasoning concerning matters of fact, is a direct consequence of Hume's previous analysis of causal reasoning. (2) characterizes that experience: some kinds of events are found to be conjoined with complete constancy, while others are often conjoined but with less constancy and more variability. (3) characterizes the response of the 'wise man' to this experience: he proportions his belief to the evidence. Hume's first conclusion from these premises is (4), which affirms that the wise man expects the pattern of an infallible experience to be continued in the future with 'the last degree of assurance' and regards the experience itself as constituting a 'proof'. His second conclusion, (5), is that, where experience is more mixed or variable, the wise man 'proceeds with more caution . . . weighs the opposite experiments . . . considers which side is supported by the greater number of experiments', and inclines to that side 'with doubt and hesitation', so that the evidence 'exceeds not what we properly call probability' (and, more specifically, the probability of causes). Given Hume's cognitive psychology, (4) and (5) imply that the amount of vivacity characterizing the conclusions of the wise is a function of the uniformity of their experience concerning similar circumstances. That is, where that experience is completely uniform, the vivacity is of the highest degree (in proof); and where that experience is less uniform, the degree of vivacity varies with the degree of uniformity (in probability). The third conclusion, (6), is that in all cases of reasoning concerning matters of fact, 'we must balance the opposite experiments, where they are opposite, and deduct the smaller number from the greater, in order to know the exact force of the superior evidence'. For example, we must allow the opposing experiments to decrease the vivacity of the conclusion in a way that varies with the number of opposing experiments, so that the final belief in the conclusion will be a function of the proportion of positive experiments or views among the class of all relevant experiments or views.

Human Testimony

The second section of Hume's argument (*E* 111–12) seeks, as he says, to 'apply these principles'—that is, (4), (5), and (6)—'to a particular instance'. That instance is, of course, the case of human testimony. Thus, he argues as follows:

(7) [N]o objects have any discoverable connexion together, and . . . all the inferences, which we can draw from one to another, are founded merely on our experience of their constant and regular conjunction.

(8) [The connexion of] human testimony . . . with any event seems, in itself, as little necessary as any other.

(9) Were not the memory tenacious to a certain degree; had not men commonly an inclination to truth and a principle of probity; were they not sensible to shame, when detected in a falsehood: Were not these . . . discovered by *experience* to be qualities, inherent in human nature, we should never repose the least confidence in human testimony.

(10) . . . [O]ur assurance in any argument [derived from the testimony of men and the reports of eyewitnesses and spectators] is derived from no other principle than our observation of the veracity of human testimony, and of the usual conformity of facts to the reports of witnesses. [from (7), (8), and (9)]

(11) . . . [T]he evidence, derived from witnesses and human testimony . . . varies with the experience, and is regarded either as a *proof* or a *probability*, according as the conjunction between any particular kind of report and any kind of object has been found to be constant or variable. [from (4), (5), and (10)]

(7) is a consequence of Hume's account of causal inference: that there are no discoverable necessary connexions in nature, and that all inferences about matters of fact are based instead on the experience of constant conjunction. He then observes more specifically, in (8), that we find no necessary connexion between testimony, on the one hand, and the truth of the claims made by that testimony, on the other; and he adds in (9) that if we did not find the truth of testimony to be *conjoined* with its being offered, we would not repose any faith in it at all. He concludes at (10) that the inference from any human testimony of an event to the actual occurrence of the event is based on the experienced conjunction of similar testimony with the events reported. He then appeals to his general epistemological principles concerning proof and probability. From (4), (5), and (10), he concludes, at (11), that where the conformity between facts and testimony has been constant and unalterable, we have proof; where it has not been, we have only probability.

Testimony for Miracles

The third section of Hume's argument (*E* 114–16) goes on to consider the particular case of testimony for miracles, given two additional premisses, and may be outlined as follows:

(12) A miracle is a violation of the laws of nature. [definition]

(13) . . . [A] firm and unalterable experience has established these laws [of nature].

(14) There must, therefore, be a uniform experience against every miraculous event, otherwise the event would not merit that appellation. [from (12) and (13)]

(15) . . . [T]here is here a direct and full *proof*, from the nature of the fact, against the existence of any miracle; nor can such a proof be destroyed, or the miracle rendered credible, but by an opposite proof, which is superior. [from (4), (5), and (14)]

(16) [Where] the testimony of witnesses [affirms something that] instead of being only marvellous, is really miraculous; and . . . the testimony, considered apart and in itself, amounts to an entire proof; in that case, there is proof against proof, of which the strongest must prevail, but still with a diminution of its force, in proportion to that of its antagonist. [from (6), (11), and (15)]

(17) . . . [N]o testimony is sufficient to establish a miracle, unless the testimony be of such a kind, that its falsehood would be more miraculous, than the fact, which it endeavours to establish: And even in that case, there is a mutual destruction of arguments, and the superior only gives us an assurance suitable to that degree of force, which remains, after deducting the inferior. [from (15) and (16)]

The first additional premiss is (12), the definition of a miracle as a 'violation of the laws of nature'. The second is (13), the claim that 'a firm and unalterable experience has established these laws'. From these premisses Hume concludes at (14) that there must be a uniform experience against every miraculous event. From this together with the characterization of 'proof' in (4), and the implication of (4) and (5) that proofs are always stronger arguments than probabilities, he concludes at (15) that there is a 'direct and full proof' against the existence of any miracle, and that such a proof cannot 'be destroyed, or the miracle rendered credible, but by an opposite proof, which is superior'. At (16) he considers the special case in which testimony for a miracle is of a kind that, considered in itself, would make the testimony a proof. He concludes, from (6), (11), and (15), that in such a case 'there is proof against proof, of which the strongest must prevail, but still with a diminution of its force, in proportion to that of its antagonist.'[20] This conclusion may plausibly be regarded as a special second-order application, to (11) and (15), of the 'balancing' principle enunciated in (6), with conflicting proofs themselves playing the role of compound 'experiments'.

---

[20] Step (16) actually occurs in Hume's text in the sentence prior to (12). However, since its claim about 'proof against proof' clearly depends on (15), I have placed it here.

From (15) and (16) Hume reaches his final conclusion of Part i, (17), that 'no testimony is sufficient to establish a miracle, unless the testimony be of such a kind, that its falsehood would be more miraculous, than the fact, which it endeavours to establish', and that 'even in that case, there is a mutual destruction of arguments, and the superior only gives us an assurance suitable to that degree of force, which remains, after deducting the inferior'.

'A Posteriori' Arguments

In Part ii of 'On Miracles' Hume seeks to establish two further main conclusions about testimony for miracles. In order to do so, he provides four additional considerations, arguing as follows (E 116–27):

(18) [T]here is not to be found, in all history, any miracle attested by a sufficient number of men, of such unquestioned good sense, education, and learning, as to secure us against all delusion in themselves; of such undoubted integrity, as to place them beyond all suspicion of any design to deceive others; of such credit and reputation in the eyes of mankind, as to have a great deal to lose in case of their being detected in any falsehood; and at the same time, attesting facts, performed in such a public manner, and in so celebrated a part of the world, as to render the detection unavoidable: All of which circumstances are requisite to give us a full assurance in the testimony of men.

(19) . . . [P]assions . . . incline the generality of mankind to believe and report, with the greatest vehemence and assurance, all religious miracles.

(20) It forms a strong presumption against all supernatural and miraculous relations, that they are observed chiefly to abound among ignorant and barbarous nations; or if a civilized people has ever given admission to any of them, that people will be found to have received them from ignorant and barbarous ancestors, who transmitted them with that inviolable sanction and authority, which always attend received opinions.

(21) . . . [I]n matters of religion, whatever is different is contrary [in such a way that] it is impossible the religions of [e.g.] ancient ROME, of TURKEY, of SIAM, and of CHINA should, all of them, be established on any solid foundation.

(22) Every miracle . . . pretended to have been wrought in any . . . [religion], as its direct scope is to establish the particular system to which it is attributed; so has it the same force, though more indirectly, to overthrow every other system. [from (21)]

(23) In destroying a rival system, [a miracle] likewise destroys the credit of those miracles, on which that system was established.

(24) [A]ll the prodigies of different religions are to be regarded as contrary facts, and the evidences of these prodigies, whether weak or strong, as opposite to each other. [from (22) and (23)]

(25) . . . [I]t appears, that no testimony for any kind of miracle has ever amounted to a probability, much less to a proof; and that, even supposing it amounted to a

proof, it would be opposed by another proof; derived from the very nature of the fact, which it would endeavour to establish. [from (4), (5), (15), (18), (19), (20), and (24)]

(26) It is experience only, which gives authority to human testimony; and it is the same experience, which assures us of the laws of nature. [from (1), (10), and (13)]

(27) When . . . these two kinds of experience [i.e. that for a kind of human testimony and that for a law of nature] are contrary, we have nothing to do but to subtract the one from the other, and embrace an opinion, either on one side or the other, with that assurance which arises from the remainder. [from (6) and (26)]

(28) . . . [T]his subtraction, with regard to all popular religions, amounts to an entire annihilation. [from (4), (5), (13), (19), (20), (24), and (27)]

(29) . . . [N]o human testimony can have such force as to prove a miracle and make it a just foundation for any such system of religion. [from (4), (12), and (28)]

First, Hume claims at (18) that none of our actual historical testimony for miracles satisfies the conditions required to give us 'a full assurance in the testimony of men'. These conditions demand a sufficient number of witnesses (i) 'of such unquestioned good sense, education, and learning, as to secure us against all delusion in themselves'; (ii) 'of such undoubted integrity, as to place them beyond all suspicion [of deceit]'; (iii) 'of such credit and reputation in the eyes of mankind, as to have a great deal to lose in case of their being detected in any falsehood'; and at the same time, (iv) 'attesting facts performed in such a public manner and in so celebrated a part of the world, as to render the detection unavoidable'.

Second, Hume claims at (19) that 'passions . . . incline the generality of mankind to believe and report, with the greatest vehemence and assurance, all religious miracles'. Among the passionate mechanisms that Hume details (E 117–19) are (i) the direct tendency of the pleasant feelings of surprise and wonder associated with miracles to enliven belief in them; (ii) the indirect tendency of these same pleasant feelings to encourage the relating of miracles, as a result of the sympathetic pleasure that results from producing the pleasant feelings of surprise and wonder in others; (iii) the tendency of the 'spirit of religion' to make us suspend our critical faculties and even our honesty for the sake of a supposedly holy cause; and (iv) the tendency of the 'spirit of religion' to increase the usual idea-enlivening effects of eloquence, thus producing credulity in the auditors, the perception of which increases the impudence of the reporter, which in turn overwhelms the credulity of the auditors.

Third, Hume claims at (20) that 'supernatural and miraculous relations' are 'observed chiefly to abound among ignorant and barbarous nations'; or, if they are accepted among civilized people, 'that people will be found to have received them from ignorant and barbarous ancestors, who transmitted them with that inviolable sanction and authority, which always attends received opinions'. This, he asserts, forms a strong presumption against all such relations.

Fourth, Hume argues at (21) that rival religions make incompatible claims. He infers from this at (22) that, to whatever extent any miracle tends to establish one religion, it tends at the same time to overthrow other religions to the same extent. But, he claims at (23), to the extent that a miracle would establish a particular religion, it must to that extent be overthrown by any miracle that would overthrow that particular religion. Thus, he concludes at (24) that 'all the prodigies of different religions are to be regarded as contrary facts, and the evidence of those prodigies, whether weak or strong, as opposite to each other'.

From these four considerations—i.e. from (18), (19), (20), and (24)—together with his epistemological principles (4) and (5) concerning proof and probability, Hume concludes at (25) that, to the present time, 'no testimony for any kind of miracle *has ever* amounted to a probability, much less to a proof' (my emphasis). And, given (15), he adds that 'even supposing it amounted to a proof, it would be opposed by another proof; derived from the very nature of the fact, which it would endeavour to establish'. Step (25) constitutes one of the two main conclusions of Part ii.

The second, third, and fourth considerations, however, bear not only on the credibility of *extant* testimony for miracles, but on the credibility of *future* testimony for miracles as well, at least to the extent that the alleged miracle would tend to 'establish a religion'. Thus, Hume remarks at (26) that it is experience alone that gives authority both to human testimony and to laws of nature, a claim that follows from (1), (10), and (13). At (27) he applies the balancing principle of (6) to conflicts between the experience for testimony and that for laws of nature, inferring that when 'these two kinds of experience are contrary', we must 'subtract the one from the other, and embrace an opinion, either on one side or the other, with that assurance which arises from the remainder'. But (13) states that the experience for a law of nature is always a proof; while the considerations about passions, barbarous civilizations, and conflicts among miracles of different religions—i.e. (19), (20), and (24)—show that human testimony for a miracle of a kind that would establish a religion *can never* amount to a proof. It should be noted that Hume here treats (4) and (5) as implying that probabilities lose *all* their force in the face of proof. This is a reasonable way to interpret (4) and (5), since (5) is explicitly limited to 'other cases'—i.e. cases in which proof is not present. Thus, by (27), he infers at (28) that in the case of 'all popular religions' this subtraction 'amounts to an entire annihilation'. From (28), the characterization of proof at (4), and the characterization of miracles at (12), he concludes that 'no human testimony *can* have such force as to prove a miracle and make it a just foundation for any such system of religion' (my emphasis).

This is the second main conclusion of Part ii. Hume emphasizes that this last conclusion is restricted to the proof of miracles 'so as to be the foundation of a system of religion' (*E* 127), remarking that otherwise it may well be possible for human testimony to provide a proof of the occurrence of a miracle—even though, as he has already concluded at (25), no human testimony has in fact ever provided such a proof.

THE SIX APPARENT INCONSISTENCIES RESOLVED

We are now in a position to answer the six questions posed earlier, so as to resolve the six apparent inconsistencies.

Experience Reconsidered

What does Hume mean by 'experience'? When he argues at (7)–(11) that judgements of the probability of testimony must depend entirely on experience, he must indeed mean that such judgements depend ultimately on the experience of the *individual judger*, since one could not use the experiences of other persons as evidence without already effectively judging the probability of their testimony. When he writes of the uniform experience against a miracle as showing what 'has never been observed, in any age or country', on the other hand, he clearly intends the scope of the term 'experience' to include at least some of the experiences of others. But there is no inconsistency here. For Hume makes it clear in (11) that it is possible for *particular kinds of testimony* to achieve the level of 'proof'. The process by which a first particular kind of testimony comes to achieve this status must, of course, involve only the individual's own confirmations of that kind of testimony. Once the reliability of that kind of testimony has achieved the level of proof, however, testimony of that kind will bestow 'full assurance', and hence it may well function itself to provide vicarious experiments and views in the cognitive process of probable judgement that Hume describes as the probability of causes. That is why Hume asserts in Section IX of the *Enquiry*—in the course of listing nine reasons why some persons so exceed others in reasoning, despite their having the same basic cognitive faculties—that '*After we have acquired a confidence in human testimony*, books and conversation *enlarge* much more the sphere of *one man's experience* and thought than those of another.' (*E* 107 n., my emphasis).[21] Thus, Hume need not be equivocating on the scope of 'experience'. The probability of any given kind of testimony is ultimately dependent on the judger's own experience; but once that experience has validated a kind of testimony, the experience of others—when it is the object of that kind of testimony—can then function cog-

---

[21] Annette Baier first called the relevance of this passage to my attention.

nitively very much as if it were one's own. Indeed, such testimony may even be brought to bear as part of the proof against a proposition that is supported by a *second* kind of testimony that has *not* achieved the status of proof—as occurs in the case of testimony for miracles.

Laws of Nature Reconsidered

What does Hume mean by 'laws of nature'? Although Hume does not define the term, a good deal can be inferred from his use of it. First, the choice of the term itself suggests that laws of nature have the form of universal causal generalizations. Second, according to (12), a violation of a law of nature is by definition a miracle. Third, (13) requires that there must be a 'firm and unalterable experience' in favour of any law of nature.[22] Finally, (14) requires, via (12)'s definition of 'miracle', that there be a direct and full *proof* of every law of nature. I conclude, therefore, that a law of nature is a universal causal generalization, whose violation is by definition a miracle, supported by a 'firm and unalterable experience'—i.e. a universal causal generalization for which there is a *proof*, in Hume's technical sense of that term.

But what does it mean to say that there is a 'firm and unalterable experience' or 'proof' for something having the form of a universal causal generalization? Do we mean that there is, objectively, an exceptionless uniformity, and hence (the basis for) a proof, whether anyone knows it or not? Or do we mean only that the individual judging has an exceptionless and uniform experience, something that therefore functions as a proof for that individual?

In *Treatise* I. iii. 14, and again in *Enquiry* VII, Hume offers two different definitions of the term 'cause', the first in terms of the constant conjunction of resembling events, and the second in terms of association and inference in the mind. Each of these two definitions of 'cause' is ambiguous between a 'subjective' reading and an 'absolute' reading. (The two definitions are coextensive on their subjective readings, and again coextensive on their absolute readings.[23] Hume's theory of abstract ideas prevents him from distinguishing these two readings more clearly.) On the subjective reading, two things are related as cause and effect for an observer if and only if they have been observed to be constantly conjoined in the observer's experience, so that they lead to association and

---

[22] It has been objected that, because he denies our access to, or conception of, any real necessary connexions in nature, and defines 'cause' in terms of constant conjunction, Hume has no right to the modal notion of 'unalterable' experience. Presumably, however, he would simply define causal modalities themselves in terms of constant conjunction. When he writes of an 'unalterable' experience, he may simply mean that, however we try, we find that we—and others whose testimony about such matters has achieved the status of proof—are unable to produce a counter-example.

[23] D. Garrett, 'The Representation of Causation and Hume's Two Definitions of "Cause" ', *Nous*, 27/2 (June 1993), 167–90; *Cognition and Commitment in Hume's Philosophy*, ch. 5.

inference in the mind of the observer. On the absolute reading, two things are related as cause and effect if and only if they have actually been constantly conjoined in all times and places, so that they would lead to association and inference in the mind of an idealized observer. Both the subjective and the absolute readings have their uses for Hume, in different contexts. For sometimes when he discusses causes, he is interested in events that are related by 'absolute' or 'objective' causation, while at other times he is interested in events whose ideas function psychologically as ideas of cause and effect in the cognitive organization of an individual judger, whether the events are objectively related as cause and effect or not.

Not only the term 'cause', but also such related terms as 'proof', and hence also 'law of nature' and 'miracle', are susceptible to the same kind of subjective–absolute ambiguity in Hume. In the context of 'On Miracles', however, it is clear from the structure of the argument that Hume is appealing to *subjective* senses of 'proof', 'laws of nature', and 'miracle'. For if a law of nature were understood as a completely uniform constant conjunction, or something for which an idealized observer had a firm and unalterable experience, the very notion of an exception to a law of nature would be contradictory, as we have already seen. Rather, as Hume uses the terms in 'Of Miracles', something has the status of 'law of nature'—i.e. plays the cognitive role of a 'law of nature'—for an individual judger if it has the form of a universal generalization, is regarded by the judger as causal, and is something for which the judger has a firm and unalterable experience—i.e. a proof. This is, of course, compatible with there actually being exceptions to it, so long as none of those exceptions have, for the judger, the status of experiments within his or her experience.

Thus, Hume is not arguing that the wise reject testimony for miracles because they recognize that miracles are impossible by definition. Nor is he claiming that no one could ever *observe* a miracle. He is not missing the point by defining 'miracle' in such a way that any event which actually occurs or is observed, no matter how bizarre, would fail to be a miracle. Rather, he is claiming at (14) and (15) that, if something is to have the status of 'miracle' *in an individual's cognitive organization*, then by definition it is something for which the individual has, within his or her experience, a *proof*. Hence the 'miracle' must be—prior to the consideration of the new testimony in favour of it—something of whose denial the individual rightly has *full assurance*.[24]

---

[24] It may be suggested that Hume relies on an absolute, rather than a subjective, sense of 'miracle' in his previously cited footnote, when he claims that 'the raising of a feather, when the wind wants ever so little of a force requisite for that purpose, is as real a miracle, though not so sensible with regard to us' (*E* 115 n.). To this suggestion I have two replies. First, it would not be surprising if Hume did occasionally use the term in an absolute sense, since he does not clearly distinguish the absolute sense of 'cause' (and related terms) from the subjective sense, for reasons having to do with his theory of abstract ideas. The

The Miraculous and the Marvellous Reconsidered

What does Hume mean by the distinction he draws between the 'miraculous' and the merely 'marvellous' (or 'extraordinary')—or, equivalently, between events that would be 'contrary' to one's experience and those that are merely 'not conformable' to it? As we have seen, events that are miraculous or contrary to experience for an individual judger are events that would violate 'a law of nature'—i.e. a generalization, universal and causal in form, for which the individual judger has a proof. Marvellous or extraordinary events, events not conformable to experience, are—as Hume explains them—events that, while occurring in circumstances of which the judger has no experience or proof, are *contrary to 'analogy'* (*E* 114 n.). Analogy, as we have already seen, is the species of probability that arises from an *imperfect resemblance* between past experiments and the circumstance presently under consideration.

But can Hume offer any principled basis for his claim that frost is merely *marvellous* for the Indian prince while the raising of the dead is *miraculous* for us? There is indeed a difference between the two cases, as Hume understands them. For although the prince has not experienced cold climates, considerable evidence suggests that there are such climates, and even that temperature is sometimes relevant to the state and behaviour of substances (as the boiling of water and the cooling of heated metals suggest). The Indian prince must therefore allow that, although there may be a high *probability of analogy* against the sudden hardening of water even in cold climates, he has no *proof* that water does not harden in cold climates; and he must also grant that there is at least some probability that *cold climates exist*. In the case of raising the dead by divine volition, in contrast, it may be denied that there is any degree of probability that any

---

important point, for our purposes, is that we can and must interpret the terms 'proof', 'law of nature', and 'miracle' as being consistently used in the subjective sense throughout the course of his *argument*. The footnote in question does not contribute any premises to the argument. Second, however, the use of 'miracle' in the footnote is entirely compatible with a subjective reading. For Hume's point is that 'A miracle may either be discoverable by men or not'—i.e. that an event's being a miracle does not entail either that the event is easily observable or that it is not. On a subjective reading, Hume would thus be claiming that a proposed motion of a feather under certain circumstances could rightly play the cognitive role of a miracle if it would violate a 'law of nature' (concerning the sufficiency of forces) for which we have a proof, whether the motion itself would be easily detectable by us or not. In contrast, the most obvious versions of an absolute reading would be incompatible with Hume's use of the term in the footnote, since on those versions, as we have seen, no miracles can be 'discoverable by men'.

I do not claim that Hume could not *develop* a version of an absolute sense in which miracles would sometimes be discoverable. For example, he might define a 'law of nature' as a regularity for which there is at most one exception, objectively speaking, and a 'miracle' as a violation of such a law. However, the fact that he makes no effort to develop such a definition in 'Of Miracles' suggests that his thinking is being governed throughout that section by the subjective sense. The subjective sense is also strongly suggested by the context provided by the rest of the footnote, which is concerned with the question of what can be 'denominated' or 'esteemed' a miracle. Tom Reed brought home to me the need to reconcile this footnote from *Enquiry* 115 n. with my claim that Hume uses 'miracle' subjectively in 'Of Miracles'.

almighty deity ever *does* will to raise persons from the dead. This may be denied on either of two grounds: (i) that there *is* no such almighty deity; or (ii) that no such deity, even if existing, ever wills to raise persons from the dead.

It is important to note that Hume does not *argue*, in Part i, that the raising of the dead is a miraculous event for us; he merely gives it as one example among many (such as the raising of houses into the air) along the way to arguing for a much more general claim about the relation between testimony and miraculous events, *whatever* events may ultimately prove to fall within the latter class. And nothing in the argument of Part i requires that all—or even any—alleged *divine actions* be miraculous. However, Hume does indicate in Part ii what his strategy would be for treating various alleged divine actions as miraculous rather than merely marvellous. He writes:

> Though the Being, to whom the miracle is ascribed, be, in this case, Almighty, it does not, upon that account, become a whit more probable; *since it is impossible for us to know the attributes or actions of such a Being, otherwise than from the experience which we have of his productions, in the usual course of nature.* This still reduces us to past observation . . . (*E* 129, my emphasis)

Although Hume gives some grounds elsewhere in his writings (and even, somewhat obliquely, in Section XI of the *Enquiry*) for doubting the existence of an almighty intelligent deity, here his strategy is more restricted: he argues that we could know whether such a deity performs particular kinds of action only on the basis of experience. The implication of this argument for the case of raising the dead is that our experience of various deaths (of individuals good and bad, pious and impious, important and unimportant, in a wide variety of circumstances, from a wide variety of causes) provides a *proof* for the claim that persons are not raised from the dead by the volitions of an almighty deity. Although there is indeed some testimony, as Hume must admit, to the effect that such a deity has done so, this testimony is not of a kind that constitutes a *proof*, and hence does not furnish an *experiment*, in Hume's technical sense of that term. On the contrary, he holds that such testimony belongs to a class of testimony that is easily discountable—on specific grounds provided in Part ii— and so it does not give rise to an opposing *view* serving to lessen our proof that such volitions do not occur. In other words, no raising of the dead enters into the judger's experience, where 'experience' is understood in the way explained previously. Thus, although we can specify circumstances—such as a volition of an almighty deity—in which a raising of the dead would presumably occur, this does not prevent the raising of the dead from being a miracle for us, *if* we have (what is for us) a proof that such circumstances are themselves miraculous.

Of course, it is likely that every death occurs in a specific set of circumstances that is not completely duplicated in any other death. And it is also likely that we can specify a concatenation of specific circumstances under which no deaths have yet happened to be observed, even though some future death may well occur under them. It might therefore be argued that our confidence that no one will ever be raised from the dead by divine volition is only a matter of analogy, and not of proof. But a similar claim could equally well be made about any other sort of event. *If* we have a proof that none of these circumstances is *individually* of a kind that is relevant to a divine volition for a raising of the dead, then once again this fact need not prevent the raising of the dead from being a miracle for us. Our understanding of the difference between life and death is connected with our knowledge of many other laws of nature, laws that rule out a huge number of circumstances as causally irrelevant to the difference between life and death. Similarly, our experience of the world appears to rule out a huge number of circumstances as causally irrelevant to the production of divine volitions. And, as we have seen, it is precisely the tendency to attach continuing weight to circumstances already shown to be causally irrelevant that reflective and philosophical persons reject in the fourth species of unphilosophical probability (namely, that drawn from hasty general rules). Thus, by appealing implicitly to an experiential proof that divine volitions to raise the dead do not occur, Hume appears to have at least the basis for a principled distinction between (i) frost in cold climates, as assessed by the Indian prince, and (ii) the raising of the dead by divine volition, as assessed by ourselves.

Superior Proofs and Greater Miracles Reconsidered

What does Hume mean when he writes of 'opposite' and 'superior' proofs of the occurrence or non-occurrence of a particular miracle—or, correlatively, of a miracle that would be 'more miraculous' or a 'greater miracle' than another? First, we must understand how proofs can be 'opposite', when both are by definition such as to leave no room for 'doubt or opposition'.

How can a proof *oppose* another proof that leaves no room for *opposition*? We have already seen that, where past experiments involving a given kind of circumstance provide incompatible *views* of what has happened or will happen in such a circumstance, these incompatible views do indeed prevent proof, and instead produce mere probability. In the case of proofs for two different laws of nature, however, the experiments do not all present views of *the same circumstances*. The experiments against raising the dead, for example, all produce views of dead persons and the subsequent behaviour of their bodies. If these experiments are uniform, the result is a proof. The experiments in favour of a certain species of testimony, in contrast, produce views of testimony of that kind being given in conjunction with the experienced or proven truth of the testimony. If *these* experiments are uniform, the result is *another* proof. Because of the difference in kinds of circumstance, views of the first kind do not *directly* conflict with views of the second. They produce an (unexpected) conflict only when an instance of the particular kind of testimony occurs *for the claim that a dead person has risen*. This certainly produces a cognitive conflict; but it is not a *direct* opposition between those views supporting the law of nature and those views supporting the testimony, for these are still not opposing views of the *same* circumstance, but of two different circumstances—namely deaths and testimonies. Rather, the views supporting the law of nature produce a *further* idea, with a maximal degree of assurance, that the raising of the dead reported did *not* occur, while the views supporting the testimony produce a *further* idea, with a maximal degree of assurance, that the raising of the dead *did* occur. It is these composite or *second-level* ideas or views, *resulting* from the initial experiments and views, that are in opposition or conflict, because they are incompatible projections from past experiences into the present case. The resolution of this conflict may indeed prevent these two second-order views from maintaining their maximal degrees of assurance, but that does not mean that both did not result from what were, in themselves, proofs.

How are such conflicts to be resolved? When a proof conflicts with a probability, Hume in effect concludes at (15), the proof will always be superior.[25] But conflict resolution can only take this form when the conflict is between a proof and a probability. Where the conflict is between opposing proofs, some other means must be employed to resolve the conflict. Hume holds, at (16), that in a conflict between proofs, each must lose a 'considerable' portion of its vivacity from the conflict. But this does not entail that each will lose the *same* portion. On the contrary, there are at least two ways in which one proof can be superior to another and so be better able to maintain a relatively greater amount of vivacity.

First, one proof may include more experiments than another. We may perhaps read Hume as allowing that proofs supported by more experiments and views have greater initial vivacity than proofs supported by fewer experiments and views. For although he writes of proof as providing a *maximal* degree

---

[25] Indeed, as we have noted, he appears in his deduction of (28) to go further, holding that proofs entirely obviate, or 'annihilate', considerations of probability. Such a position has considerable plausibility. For example, if we are told only that a fairly weighted six-sided die with four blue faces and two red faces was thrown, we will affirm (with probability) that a blue face turned up. If we are then shown a videotape of the throw resulting in a red face turning up, however, and our past experience provides us with a proof of the reliability of videotapes, then we will regard it as *proven* that a red face turned up, the prior probability of a blue face notwithstanding; for the basis of our previous belief was merely probability, whereas now we have a proof. In terms of Humean cognitive psychology, the firm belief resulting from the proof would simply destroy the hesitating belief resulting from the probability. This may occur even when the number of concurring experiments for the probability exceeds the number of experiments supporting the proof. For the cognitive conflict will be between the *outcomes* of the proof and the probability, and by hypothesis, the proof produces a higher degree of vivacity for its outcome than the probability does.

of belief or assent, perhaps he means only that the vivacity of a 'proof' must fall somewhere above a certain line that divides the assent of proof from the assent of probability. Even if he does not mean this, however—so that the assent produced by every proof is initially of the very same degree—the number of experiments may *still* help to determine the ability of a proof to *resist loss* of vivacity to another proof. (In a similar way, the ability of a set of previously uniform experiments to resist the loss of vivacity resulting from a new *direct* opposing experiment is, for Hume, a function of the number of uniform experiments to which it is opposed.) As already suggested, allowing the number of experiments to play this role would be a plausible application of Hume's 'balancing' principle of (6) to the special case of competing proofs.

Second, other experiments besides those contributing directly to the two opposing proofs may nevertheless contribute to the ability of one to resist the force of the other. In particular, this will be so if some additional experiments support the conclusion of one of the proofs *by analogy*. Thus Hume writes— concerning a hypothetical conflict between a proof that there cannot be eight days of total darkness, on the one hand, and a proof of the veracity of very extensive and uniform human testimony, on the other—as follows: 'The decay, corruption, and dissolution of nature, is an *event rendered probable by so many analogies*, that any phænomenon, which seems to have a tendency towards that catastrophe, comes within the reach of human testimony, if that testimony be very extensive and uniform.' (*E* 128, my emphasis). As Hume indicates, this strengthening of one proof, in its conflict with another, by a consideration of somewhat resembling experiments is an instance of what he calls the probability of analogy. It is another plausible second-order application of the 'balancing principle' of (6) to the special case of opposing proofs.

Thus, some Humean proofs can indeed be *opposite* and *superior* to others. Furthermore, the same considerations also explain how one miracle can be a *greater* miracle, or *more miraculous*, than another. For a miracle will be a greater miracle, or more miraculous, than a second if and only if the proof against the first is superior to the proof against the second. Hume is not contradicting his own definitions of 'proof' and 'miracle' in writing of opposite and superior proofs and greater miracles; rather, he is alluding to what he believes is the greater ability of some proofs to resist loss of vivacity in cases where proofs derived from views of different circumstances come into unexpected conflict.

Absolute Impossibility Reconsidered

What does Hume mean when he refers, in Part ii, to 'the absolute impossibility' of certain miraculous events? As we have seen, Hume's Conceivability Criterion of Possibility holds that 'whatever we *conceive* is possible, at least in a metaphysical sense' (*A* 650; cf. *E* 25–6, 164). Thus, he cannot consistently hold that miracles are impossible 'in a metaphysical sense' unless he holds that they are inconceivable. But his own cognitive psychology demands that, in order to treat them as inconceivable, he would have to argue that the concept of a miracle is somehow contradictory—and this, we have seen, he does not do. In his *Treatise* discussion of the probability of causes, however, he writes that 'there is no probability so great as not to allow of a *contrary possibility*; because otherwise 'twou'd cease to be a probability, and *wou'd become a certainty*' (*T* 135, my emphasis). He goes on to argue that the 'component parts of this possibility and probability are of the same nature, and differ in number only' (*T* 136). That is to say, the 'possibility' opposed to every probability of causes is itself a compound of one or more different *views*, derived from opposing *experiments*.

Thus, there is a second sense of 'possibility' in Hume, one derived not from mere conceivability but rather from the lack of uniformity in experience. Hence, there is a correlative kind of impossibility that is opposed not to the knowledge produced by intuition or demonstration (which shows the denial of a conclusion to be a contradiction) but rather to the certainty of *proof*. (These dual senses of 'possible' and 'impossible' correspond to dual senses of 'separable' and 'inseparable'.[26]) When Hume claims, in Part ii, that the alleged Jansenist miracles he mentions are 'impossible', he is alluding to a consequence of Part i: namely, that in the nature of the case we have an experiential *proof* against them. In adding that they are 'absolutely' impossible, he is likely also thinking of his argument, given earlier in Part ii, that because of their religious character, no testimony in *favour* of them can itself ever amount to another, contrary, proof. Since he is pronouncing the miracles impossible, not in the 'metaphysical sense' in which their existence is a *contradiction* but in the practical sense in which their existence is ruled out by a *proof*, he is neither violating his metaphysical principles nor equivocating on his earlier conclusion.

The Uniformity of Nature Reconsidered

Finally, regardless of his other arguments, how can Hume himself criticize beliefs in miracles—as he clearly does throughout both Part i and Part ii—in light of his own views about what we would call 'inductive inferences', or what he calls 'inferences from experience'? When Hume argues that the thesis of the uniformity of nature cannot be 'produced by any argument or process of the understanding', he is not thereby denying or doubting the thesis of the uniformity of nature, nor passing a negative epistemic judgement on inductive inferences from experience.[27] Rather, he is making a claim in cognitive psychology about the causal origin of such inferences: namely, that it is not as a result of any

---

[26] Garrett, *Cognition and Commitment in Hume's Philosophy*, ch. 3.   [27] Ibid., ch. 4.

prior or intermediary argument or operation of our inferential faculty that we are caused to engage in them. (See the Appendix to this essay, pp. 332–4.) Deflating and discomforting as the intense contemplation of this claim may admittedly be, acceptance of it does not preclude Hume, logically or psychologically, from engaging in such inferences or from accepting the thesis of the uniformity of nature. On the contrary, he holds that he, like every other human being, *must* perform such inferences and accept the thesis in practice, given his and our shared inductive cognitive mechanisms. Moreover, he holds that when these cognitive mechanisms are turned reflectively on themselves and the consequences of their own operations, they generate a set of 'rules by which to judge of causes and effects' (*T* 149, 173–6). He and other human beings who so reflect will be causally determined, he thinks, to come to *approve* of inferences that conform to those rules as constituting the best way to the truth about matters of fact that go beyond our present perceptions and memories.

Indeed, Hume not only approves *epistemically* of those who make inductive inferences from experience in accordance with the rules for judging of causes and effects; he also approves of them *morally*. According to Hume's general theory of virtue or personal merit, as set out in *Treatise* Book III and again in *An Enquiry concerning the Principles of Morals*, virtues are mental characteristics that are useful or agreeable to their possessors or others, producing a pleasing sentiment of approbation in those who consider them. Among these virtues is that of 'wisdom', as he indicates explicitly in *Treatise* III. iii. 4 (*T* 611). As we have already seen, Humean wisdom involves, among other things, 'proportioning one's belief to the evidence' in the way described in (4)–(6). Because his reflectively supported conclusion is that wisdom leads to truth, which he regards as generally useful (especially to its possessor, but surely also to others), Hume himself approves morally of wisdom, and he holds that other reflective individuals will do so also. It is because he holds that inductive proportioning of belief to the evidence is typically productive of truth that he endorses it as true and draws a conclusion about what is and is not (epistemically) 'sufficient' to establish a miracle. But it is his view that wisdom is a virtue that gives this conclusion its ultimate practical force.

Just as his claims in cognitive psychology about the causal origin of inductive inferences from experience do not preclude Hume from engaging in such inferences or from accepting the thesis of the uniformity of nature, so those claims do not preclude him from disapproving of those cognitive mechanisms that, upon reflection, appear to be distortions of those inferences, hindering or preventing reasoning from operating in accordance with the philosophical rules for judging of causes and effects. He disapproves epistemically of such mechanisms as obstacles to the pursuit of truth, and he disapproves morally of those whose beliefs are frequently produced or coloured by them. Among these distorting mechanisms are the four kinds of unphilosophical probability that he describes in the *Treatise*. Also among them, he finds, are the passionate mechanisms that he describes—in Part ii of 'Of Miracles'—as contributing to belief in miracles despite the weight of contrary experiments. To let these distorting mechanisms govern one's beliefs is, in Humean terminology, not wisdom but 'folly'.

There should be no misunderstanding about the basis of Hume's position. He does not have, and does not believe that anyone has, an argument that would convince beings with a cognitive nature radically different from ours to engage in inductive inferences from experience, or to accept the thesis of the uniformity of nature, or, *ipso facto*, to adopt our philosophical rules for judging of causes and effects. Nor does he believe that *we* are caused to engage in such inferences or to accept that thesis as the result of argument (although arguments presupposing the uniformity of nature may serve to confirm us in them and will lead the philosophical among us to the rules for judging of causes and effects). Similarly, Hume does not have, and does not believe that anyone has, an argument that would convince beings with a *moral* nature radically different from ours to value wisdom as a *virtue*—even if they were already convinced that it was the most effective way to truth. Nor does he believe that we are caused to value wisdom as a virtue solely as the result of argument (although argument may convince us of its utility); moral sentiments of approval must also occur in order to produce that result.

But arguments binding on beings with radically different cognitive or moral natures are not required for Hume's purposes, since his readers all share the same fundamental human cognitive and moral mechanisms. When these mechanisms are turned upon our cognitive mechanisms themselves—at least in a world like ours—they produce an epistemic and moral valuing of wisdom. Reflective individuals will thus come to desire to proportion their belief to the evidence, just as Hume desires to do.[28] Such individuals are Hume's intended primary audience in 'Of Miracles', as he indicates early in Part i:

Nothing is so convenient as a decisive argument of this kind, which must at least *silence* the most arrogant bigotry and superstition, and free us from their impertinent solicitations. I flatter myself, that I have discovered an argument of a like nature, which, if just, will, *with the wise and learned*, be an everlasting check to all kinds of superstitious delusion, and consequently, will be useful as long as the world endures. (*E* 110, second emphasis mine)

---

[28]   Given human psychology as Hume understands it, it would be a *miracle* if *reasonable and reflective* individuals did *not* do so. This is the point of his ironic concluding remark that 'the CHRISTIAN religion not only was at first attended with miracles, but even at this day cannot be believed by any *reasonable* person without one' (*E* 131, my emphasis).

Moreover, because even foolish and unreflective human beings share these same fundamental cognitive and moral mechanisms, Hume holds that his arguments should at least silence their impertinence, even if it does not change the way they manage their beliefs.

Hume is thus not guilty of inconsistency in condemning belief in miracles, even though he holds that the thesis of the uniformity of nature cannot be defended by any argument that does not presuppose it and that any inferences that go beyond the content of present experience and personal memory are 'not determin'd by reason'. In nevertheless accepting the thesis of the uniformity of nature and performing inductive inferences from experience, he is consistently instantiating his own theory of human cognitive psychology. In seeking to govern his inferences 'wisely', by proportioning his belief to the evidence in accordance with philosophical rules for judging of causes and effects, he is seeking to be the kind of person of whom he can epistemically and morally approve; and in arguing that others should do the same, he is appealing to premisses that—if his human cognitive and moral psychology is correct—should be shared or shareable by all of his readers.

THE PROBABILITY OF MIRACLES

The six apparent inconsistencies in Hume's discussion of miracles in *Enquiry* X Part i can each be resolved by careful attention to the theory of proof and probability that Hume derives from his more general cognitive psychology. We can now look again at the nature of Hume's argument, the content of his conclusion, and the success or failure of his undertaking in Part i.

Hume's argument in Part i proceeds from a set of premisses about the cognitive functioning of the wise man to a set of general epistemological principles concerning proof and probability. It then applies these principles to the case of human testimony in general. From this application, in turn, together with a general characterization of the role of 'laws of nature' and 'miracles' in human cognitive organization, he reaches a conclusion concerning the kind of testimonial evidence that would be required to establish the occurrence of a miracle. That argument is complete as he presents it in Part i and does not require supplementation by any of the additional premisses proposed by commentators.

Hume's intended conclusion in Part i is precisely the one he states:

[N]o testimony is sufficient to establish a miracle, unless the testimony be of such a kind, that its falsehood would be more miraculous, than the fact, which it endeavours to establish: And even in that case, there is a mutual destruction of arguments, and the superior only gives us an assurance suitable to that degree of force, which remains, after deducting the inferior. (*E* 115–16)

In that conclusion, the term 'miracle' should be understood 'subjectively', as relative to an individual's own cognitive organization—that is, as referring to a universal generalization, regarded by the individual judger as causal, and for which the individual judger has a *proof*. The long qualification concerning 'opposing' miracles is an essential part of that conclusion and is not merely an ironic superfluity, as some commentators have suggested. And although one might guess what Hume's attitude would be towards apparent personal sensory experience of a miracle—namely, that one should be sceptically alert to the likelihood of illusion or delusion—his own argument in Part i concerns only testimonial evidence. Finally, it is important to realize that the argument of Part i does not, by itself, show that all or any *divine actions* would be miracles. Hence it does not, by itself, establish that no testimony is sufficient to establish the occurrence of a divine action, or even that the occurrence of such actions would be epistemologically problematic. Hume does suggest grounds in Part ii, however, for thinking that our experience includes proofs against the occurrence of a wide variety of divine actions. He also provides several arguments in Part ii for thinking that testimony of divine actions will always be of especially low evidential quality.

Hume's argument is careful, detailed, and coherent. It does not beg the question in any way, and its premises, if true, provide strong support for the conclusion. On the other hand, the argument's premises depend on his cognitive psychology, which is not only outdated in its general over-reliance on images but is also questionable in its details.

One unintended consequence, for example, of Hume's description of these mechanisms is that the *sufficiency* of evidence can depend on the order in which it is received. Suppose that person A testifies to the occurrence of an event, E, that would violate regularity R, and suppose that person A's testimony is of a kind T. Suppose that no other examples of violations of R are ever perceived by anyone and that no other examples of false testimony of kind T are ever discovered by anyone. Is A's testimony credible? If the recipient has had enough experience of veridical instances of T to establish that kind of testimony as proof, but has not *yet* observed enough instances of R, then A's testimony will constitute an *experiment* against R, and R can at best achieve probability, not proof, no matter how much further experience accumulates for it. On the other hand, if the recipient has observed enough instances of R to establish it as a law of nature, but has not *yet* observed enough instances of T, then the proof of R will provide an *experiment* against the reliability of T, and T can at best achieve probability, not proof, no matter how much further evidence accumulates for its reliability. Finally, if the recipient has already had enough experience of R and of T to render them *both* sources of proof, then the recipient will experience the conflict between proofs that Hume describes in the case of the 'eight days of darkness'. Yet this variability of evidential force with the order in which evidence is received is closely related to the second kind of 'unphilosophical probability' (in which the most recent experiment carries extra weight), a kind of probability of which Hume disapproves. Clearly, some additional reflection on ways to correct this consequence is called for within Hume's epistemology.

Somewhat more generally, it might be argued that Hume's distinction between proofs and probabilities is artificially sharp and that he is wrong to maintain that proofs should always outweigh probabilities. In his defence, however, it should be emphasized that 'proof' may be a very difficult status to achieve, and that it is likely to characterize only or chiefly our most *fundamental* beliefs about the ways in which the world works—beliefs that serve to organize all of our thinking, and which are typically supported by enormous amounts of human testimony, among other kinds of evidence. It is precisely because reports of miracles violate *these* beliefs that they are so striking. Surely the burden of proof lies with those who claim that it can be wise to abandon these beliefs on the basis of individual human testimony. Hume is not arguing that testimony should never lead us to revise our conception of what the laws of nature *are*; repeated independent testimony might well lead us to abandon one conception of a regularity instantiated by our past experience for an alternative conception. Hume's quarrel is only with the practice of believing, on testimony, an event that *simultaneously* retains the status of *miracle* in the cognitive organization of the believer.

Hume's overall project in the *Treatise* and in the first *Enquiry* was to understand human cognitive functioning in such a way as to improve our ability to arrive together at a reflective assessment concerning which features of that functioning we wish to approve and encourage, and which we do not. That assessment, he hoped, would lead us to recognize the cognitive mechanisms supporting what he regarded as 'superstitious' religion—including belief in miracles—as irregular and pernicious ones, deserving to be classified as a species of 'unphilosophical probability'. Certainly—as Hume himself would have expected—reflection about probability has advanced considerably since he wrote. To take one example, Bayesianism now explicitly informs our thinking about probability. Nevertheless, his overall project of seeking reflective assessments about probability in general, and miracles in particular, remains attractive. Hence, it is still worth examining how, and to what extent, we may be in a position to go beyond Hume in our own reflective judgements about the cognitive processes that are involved in the evaluation and acceptance of miracles. Indeed, over 250 years after he wrote, such a comparison of our standpoint with Hume's remains one of the most rewarding ways to begin one's own attempt to assess the praiseworthy wisdom or blameable folly of believing in miracles. In his humbler moments, at least, Hume would have hoped for no more than this for his discussion of miracles—and also, no less.

APPENDIX

The Meaning of Hume's Conclusion concerning 'Inductive' Inferences

ARGUMENT, INFERENCE, AND REASON

There are serious objections to both the traditional 'sceptical' and the more contemporary 'non-sceptical' readings of Hume's argument.[29] Although Hume does *more* than simply attack a narrow rationalistic conception of reason's role in inductive inference, at the same time he does *less* than pronounce all inductive inference to be completely lacking in evidentiary value.

We can find one important clue to Hume's intentions in his characterization of his own argument as showing that we can give 'no reason' for making inductive inferences. Compare this characterization with his statement of the argument's main conclusion in the *Abstract*:

even after I have had experience of many repeated effects of this kind, *there is no argument, which determines me to suppose*, that the effect will be conformable to past experience . . . what *reason* have we to think, that the same powers will always be conjoined with the same sensible qualities?

'Tis not, therefore, reason, which is the guide of life, but custom. (*A* 652, first emphasis mine)

The same conclusion in *Enquiry* IV reads as follows:

even after we have experience of the operations of cause and effect, our conclusions from that experience are *not founded on reasoning, or any process of the understanding*. (*E* 32, last nine words my emphasis)

Consider, too, the following passages:

'tis impossible to satisfy ourselves by our reason, why we shou'd extend that experience beyond those particular instances, which have fallen under our observation. We *suppose, but are never able to prove*, that there must be a resemblance betwixt those objects, of which we have had experience, and those which lie beyond the reach of our discovery. (*T* 91–2, my emphasis)

What logic, what *process of argument* secures you against this supposition [i.e., the falsity of the Uniformity Principle]? (*E* 38, my emphasis)

This appendix is adapted from Garrett, *Cognition and Commitment in Hume's Philosophy*, ch. 4, pp. 91–3.

[29] Peter Millican calls these the 'deductivist' and 'anti–deductivist' interpretations respectively (pp. 155–6 in this volume), advancing strong objections to them with which I broadly agree.

it is not *reasoning* which engages us to suppose the past resembling the future, and to expect similar effects from causes, which are, to appearance, similar. This is the proposition which I intended to enforce in the present section. . . . if I be wrong, I must acknowledge myself to be indeed a very backward scholar; since I cannot now *discover an argument*, which, it seems, was perfectly familiar to me, before I was out of my cradle. (*E* 39, my emphasis)

Hume should be interpreted quite literally, as making a specific claim, within cognitive psychology, about the underlying causal mechanism that gives rise to inductive inferences: namely, that it is not itself dependent on any reasoning or inference. This is established, he thinks, by the utterly sufficient reason that there *is* no argument or inference ('reasoning' or 'process of the understanding') that could have this effect. There can be no such relevant demonstrative argument, because the denial of the conclusion remains conceivable; and there can be no such probable argument, because probable arguments are effective only to those who *already* engage in inductive inference. Because these are the only two kinds of arguments, it follows that no argument at all could cause or '*determine*' us to engage in induction. As a result, we find that we can literally '*give no reason*' for our making inductive inferences. (We can, however, specify the cause: 'CUSTOM or HABIT'; *E* 43.)

It must be emphasized that this does not mean that inductive inferences are not themselves *instances* of argumentation or reasoning; indeed, Hume continually refers to them as both 'reasonings' and 'inferences' in the course of the very passages in question. His point is rather that they are reasonings which are not themselves *caused* by any piece of reasoning (including, of course, themselves). Inductive inferences require that we bridge a gap between observation and prediction, and for someone not already disposed by nature to bridge that gap, no argument for doing so would be persuasive. Hence, in just this sense, inductive inferences are a class of 'reasonings' (inferences or arguments) that 'reason' (the faculty of making inferences or giving arguments) does not itself 'determine' (cause) us to make. 'Reason', here as elsewhere for Hume, is neither a normative epistemic term (as proponents of the sceptical interpretation have assumed) nor a term for some narrow aspect or conception of reasoning that Hume intends to denigrate or abuse (as proponents of the non-sceptical interpretation have supposed). Instead, it is simply the name that Hume, as cognitive psychologist, consistently employs for the general faculty of making inferences or producing arguments—just as it was for Locke.[30]

---

[30] In *Hume's Skepticism in 'A Treatise of Human Nature'* (London: Routledge & Kegan Paul, 1985), Robert Fogelin describes Hume as employing a 'no-argument argument'—that is, an argument that there is no argument of a certain character—as part of his defence of inductive scepticism. On my interpretation, the *conclusion* of Hume's famous argument is a 'no-argument conclusion'. It should be noted that the characterization I have given here of Hume's famous conclusion is slightly broader than that provided in *Cognition and Commitment in Hume's Philosophy* (New York: Oxford University Press, 1997). There, I implied that Hume was specifically concerned to rule out the production of inductive inferences by means of prior arguments about the *reliability* of inductive inferences. While such arguments are certainly within the scope of Hume's conclusion, I no longer think it correct to suggest that such arguments were his exclusive focus. I have come to think this as a result of discussion with Peter Millican and David Owen. For further discussion of these matters, see 'Ideas, Reason, and Skepticism: Replies to My Critics [Margaret Wilson, Peter Millican, and Robert Fogelin]', *Hume Studies*, 24/1 (Apr. 1998), 177–94 and a symposium on *Cognition and Commitment in Hume's Philosophy* in *Philosophy and Phenomenological Research*, 62/1 (Jan. 2001), 185–215.

REASON AND SCEPTICISM

This absence of an argument or arguments leading to the performance of inductive inferences and the acceptance of inductive reasonings is, Hume implies, initially surprising. He is well aware that it leaves room for us to raise a theoretical *question* about the legitimacy of inductive inference. But it does not itself entail that induction must be without evidentiary value, and Hume does not ever write as though he thinks that it does. In *Treatise* I. iii. 6 itself, and in its correlates in the *Enquiry* and the *Abstract*, he concludes only that we are not led to make inductive inferences by a supporting inference or argument, on the quite sufficient grounds that there is no such argument that could move us unless we were *already* inductive thinkers—and so already moved without it. Whether and in what sense induction is 'reasonable' or provides 'evidence' or increases 'probability' in spite of this lack remains, at the close of the famous argument, an as yet unanswered question. Indeed, at least in the *Treatise* version of the argument, it is an as yet *unraised* question. At no point does Hume argue, assert, or imply that inductive inferences could have evidentiary value *only* if we were caused to perform or accept them by prior arguments. We can observe such potentially disconcerting facts as induction's dependence on instinct and the apparent conflict between inductive reasoning and the belief in 'continu'd' and 'distinct' bodies (*T* 188), and these facts can give us some pause. But the inevitability of our commitment to the practice of induction places severe constraints on the kind of psychological effects the recognition of these facts can have. Hume explores these constraints in the final section of Book I of the *Treatise* and in the final section of his first *Enquiry*.

This interpretation of Hume's conclusion—as a claim that we are not caused to engage in induction by a prior inference or argument—has a number of advantages over both the traditional 'sceptical' and the contemporary 'non-sceptical' interpretations. It construes Hume's use of 'reason' as consistently referring to *all* argument and inference, demonstrative and probable, throughout his works. It squares with Hume's own later characterizations of his conclusion as concerned with an absence of 'reasons'. It accounts for the structure of Hume's main line of argument, which is equally concerned to rule out demonstrative and probable justifications. In addition, it explains why Hume seems not to treat his argument as directly entailing that induction lacks evidentiary value, and why he goes on in the *Treatise* for many pages without offering any explicit defence for his continuing use of induction.

12

Hume versus Price on Miracles and Prior Probabilities: Testimony and the Bayesian Calculation

David Owen

I

Hume's essay on miracles is one of his most celebrated arguments. It is also, perhaps, the second most discussed and argued-over of his sceptical positions.[1] Reading it in the light of a recent controversy over Bayesianism and the appropriateness of taking prior probabilities into account when judging the likelihood of an event's occurrence on the basis of reliable testimony,[2] I have been struck by the thought that Hume can best be seen as applying a proto-Bayesian argument to a celebrated eighteenth-century controversy. There is some evidence[3] that it struck Hume's critics that way as well, yet none of the recent major commentators (e.g. Broad, Flew, Gaskin) mention Bayes[4] or Hume's contemporary critic Richard Price, who most clearly discussed Hume's argument in

This chapter was first published in the *Philosophical Quarterly*, 37/147 (Apr. 1987).

[1] First place being taken by his famous argument concerning induction, presented in Section IV of the *Enquiry*.

[2] See L. J. Cohen, 'Can Human Irrationality be Experimentally Demonstrated?', and replies, *Behavioral and Brain Sciences*, 4 (1981).

[3] Richard Price, *Four Dissertations*, 3rd edn. (1772); Bernard Peach, 'Miracles, Methodology and Metaphysical Rationalization', *International Journal for Philosophy of Religion*, 9 (1978), 69–74; David Raynor, 'Hume's Mistake—Another Guess', *Hume Studies*, 8 (1981), 164–6. Raynor rightly pleads for an examination of Hume and Price on miracles. This paper can be seen, I hope, as a start.

[4] Although Hume's *Dialogues concerning Natural Religion* have been discussed in the light of Bayes (see e.g. W. C. Salmon, 'Religion and Science: A New Look at Hume's Dialogues', *Philosophical Studies*, 33 (1978), 177–83 and Raynor's reply, *Philosophical Studies*, 38 (1980), 105–6) Hume's arguments about miracles are not mentioned. Raynor suggests that Hume may have come to know Bayes's Theorem through Price.

this light. This is doubly unfortunate; not only does it make difficult a clear appreciation of what Hume was up to in the argument about miracles, but it also insulates the modern debate about prior probabilities from its history.[5] In this paper I should like to do a little to rectify this and, in passing, to make some independent observations about Hume's argument as well.

II

In Part i of Section X of the *Enquiry* Hume formulates a position about judging probabilities according to the available evidence. He distinguishes, perhaps misleadingly, between proofs and probabilities in just the way he has already done in the footnote to Section VI, 'Of Probability'. 'Proofs' are those arguments from 'infallible experience' that provide 'the last degree of assurance' (*E* 110) concerning an event. Such arguments from experience 'leave no room for doubt or opposition' (*E* 56 n.). Events supported by such arguments, such as the sun's rising tomorrow, are expected with the highest degree of probability for Hume. What Hume calls 'probabilities' as opposed to 'proofs' are those arguments where past experience concerning whether or not a particular sort of event has occurred is mixed. We expect the event in proportion to how many times it has occurred in these circumstances and how many times it has not. 'In all cases, we must balance the opposite experiments, where they are opposite, and deduct the smaller number from the greater, in order to know the exact force of the superior evidence.' (*E* 111). In such cases, the probability that such an event will occur, according to the evidence, will be less than the full assurance given by proofs.

Hume then argues that our assurance concerning testimony is to be calculated in the same way. Our assurance concerning testimony should vary as past experience dictates. 'And as the evidence, derived from witnesses and human testimony, is founded on past experience, so it varies with the experience, and is regarded either as a *proof* or a *probability*, according as the conjunction between any particular kind of report and any kind of object has been found to be constant or variable.' (*E* 112). What is interesting is that Hume insists that *more than a person's general propensity to tell the truth* (or speak falsely) needs to be taken into account. It is true that 'A man delirious, or noted for falsehood and villany, has no manner of authority with us' (*E* 112), but such considerations are not exhaustive. Hume claims that the 'contrariety of evidence . . . may be derived

---

[5] Although both Blackburn and Mackie in their replies to Cohen, 'Can Human Irrationality be Experimentally Demonstrated?', mention Hume on miracles as relevant to the modern debate, neither of them mention Price or his criticisms of Hume, which can to some extent be seen as precursors of Cohen's position on when to take prior probabilities into account.

from several different causes' (*E* 112), and he mentions 'opposition of contrary testimony', 'the character or number of the witnesses', 'the manner of their delivering their testimony' as well as 'many other particulars of the same kind' (*E* 112–3). Of course the particular Hume is most interested in is the case when 'the fact, which the testimony endeavours to establish, partakes of the extraordinary and the marvellous; in that case, the evidence, resulting from the testimony, admits of a diminution, greater or less, in proportion as the fact is more or less unusual' (*E* 113). So here is his central case. Although many factors are relevant when judging the likelihood of the occurrence of a reported event (and Hume discusses some of these factors in great detail in Part ii) Hume is mainly concerned about weighing the conformity we are accustomed to find 'between testimony and reality' as against the likelihood of an event 'as has seldom fallen under our observation' (*E* 113).

How are we to weigh up these two competing considerations? Hume, typically, first gives us a quasi-mechanical account: 'here is a contest of two experiences; of which the one destroys the other, as far as its force goes, and the superior can only operate in the mind by the force, which remains' (*E* 113). After he has characterized a miracle as a violation of a law of nature, Hume considers the case of testimony which 'considered apart and in itself, amounts to an entire proof' (*E* 114) that affirms the occurrence of a miracle. Now since a miracle is a violation of a law of nature, and the evidence in favour of a law of nature is exceptionless, i.e. constitutes a 'proof', we have a stand-off. One proof destroys the other, and we are left indifferent as to whether the event testified to occurred or whether the testimony is false. Given the nature of miracles, no testimony can be good enough to command our assent.

Hume, at this stage, is a little careless. He talks as if the proof in favour of the law of nature and against its violation, i.e. the occurrence of a miracle, could be overcome 'by an opposite proof, which is superior' (*E* 115). But since a proof, by his own account, provides *full* assurance based on exceptionless experience, the notion of a superior proof seems incoherent.[6] But the general point remains.

---

[6] See J. H. Sobel, 'On the Evidence of Testimony for Miracles: A Bayesian Reconstruction of David Hume's Analysis' (*Philosophical Quarterly*, 37/147 (Apr. 1987), 166–86) for an interesting but technical way of retaining the notion of a 'superior proof' and a literal reading of 'testimony . . . of such a kind, that its falsehood would be more miraculous, than the fact, which it endeavours to establish' (*E* 116). Sobel treats our assurance in a law of nature as having probability infinitely close to one, and the corresponding violation as infinitely close to zero. I prefer to think of Hume's notion of proof as being simply an argument with very high probability indeed. This allows there to be such a thing as a superior proof without resort to the un-Humean notion of 'infinitely close to', and thus allows one to treat seriously Hume's important example of the real possibility of being rationally convinced that the earth was covered in darkness for eight days (*E* 127–8). It is entirely in line with Hume's motivation for introducing 'proof' as well as 'probability', which is simply to avoid the oddness of saying 'that it is only probable all men must die, or that the sun will rise to-morrow' (*E* 56 n.). One bit of evidence that this reading concurs with Hume's intentions is mentioned by I. Hacking in another context ('Hume's Species of Probability', *Philosophical*

Hume is simply talking about greater and lesser probabilities in a graphic way. No matter how reliable the testimony, it cannot in general overcome the intrinsic improbability of a violation of a law of nature. Suppose that the testimony is as reliable as possible; the case is still a stand-off. The two proofs destroy each other, and we have no more reason to believe that the miracle occurred than that the testimony is false. And furthermore suppose, *per impossibile*, that the reliability of the testimony that a miracle occurred is slightly greater than our assurance of the relevant law of nature. We should not then believe that the miracle occurred with the same degree of assurance that we have in the reliability of the testimony. Rather, Hume says, 'even in that case, there is a mutual destruction of arguments, and the superior only gives an assurance suitable to that degree of force, which remains, after deducting the inferior' (*E* 116). (Again, notice the mechanical metaphor.) The general rule is clear. We should only believe that the miraculous or unlikely event occurred, on the basis of testimony, if the likelihood of the testimony's being false is less than the likelihood of the law of nature's being violated. In Hume's words, 'The plain consequence is (and it is a general maxim worthy of our attention), "That no testimony is sufficient to establish a miracle, unless the testimony be of such a kind, that its falsehood would be more miraculous, than the fact, which it endeavours to establish . . ."' (*E* 115–16). Given the nature of miracles, this situation can never occur. And even if, *per impossibile*, it did occur, the strength of our belief that the miracle occurred would be substantially less than the strength of our belief in the reliability of the testimony.

It is this last point that may appear puzzling. If we believe in the reliability of the testimony with a certain degree of assurance, surely we believe that the event reported by the testimony occurred with exactly the same degree of assurance. How could the likelihood of the event lessen that already held belief? As long as there is *some* probability that the event occurred, surely our belief in the reliability of the testimony is exactly the same as our belief that the event occurred. This is the point that puzzled Price and, apparently, Cohen. It is easy enough to make the point in terms of the mechanical metaphor. If the argument in favour of the belief is of a certain force, and the argument against the event's occurring is of an opposite force, even if one ends up believing that the event occurred, the degree of assurance will be lessened proportionately to the amount of the

Studies, 33 (1978), 21–37). Hacking points out (pp. 27–8) that while Hume allows, in theory, a species of probability connected with exceptionless uniformities, he further claims that in fact 'no one, who is arriv'd at the age of maturity, can any longer be acquainted with it' (*Treatise of Human Nature* I. iii. 12, *T* 131). So unless in maturity we also lose our acquaintance with proofs, proofs cannot be based on exceptionless experience and have probability infinitely close to one. We must be content with proofs yielding simply very high probabilities indeed. Nothing in the subsequent argument hinges on the exact interpretation of 'proof' as long as it is understood that it does not mean 'demonstrative proof'.

countervailing force. But in order to pursue this, let us recast Hume's argument in the light of Bayes's Theorem.

III

The relevant application of Bayes's Theorem which I shall use[7] states that if p is the prior probability of a certain event, and if t is the probability that a certain witness tells the truth, i.e. the probability that the witness asserts that the event took place, given that it did take place, then the probability that the event did take place, given that the witness asserts that it has taken place, is as follows.

$$\frac{pt}{pt + (1-p)(1-t)}$$

It is easily seen that this formula gives just the results that Hume asserts. For instance, consider the claim that we should be indifferent (or judge with probability of 0.5) when the probability that the witness speaks falsely is the same as the probability that the unlikely event occurred. Suppose that both these probabilities are 0.1. In this case, since p, the prior probability that the event did take place, is 0.1, and t, the probability that the witness tells the truth, is $1 - 0.1 = 0.9$, then the probability that the event did take place, given that the witness asserts that it did take place, is, according to our formula,

$$\frac{(0.1)(0.9)}{(0.1)(0.9) + (1 - 0.1)(1 - 0.9)} = 0.5.$$

In fact, it is easily seen that for any $p = 1 - t$,

$$\frac{pt}{pt + (1-p)(1-t)} = 0.5.$$

Similarly, if it is more probable that the witness speaks falsely than that the unlikely event occurred, i.e. if $(1 - t) > p$, the relevant probability is less than 0.5, and if it is more probable that the event occurred than that the witness spoke

---

[7] The formula is given by Niiniluoto in his reply to Cohen, 'Can Human Irrationality be Experimentally Demonstrated?', 349. He claims that it was known as early as 1785 to Condorcet. For doubts, see Sobel, 'On the Evidence of Testimony for Miracles'. It is important to remember that the formula gives the conditional probability that an event took place, given that a witness said it took place. Let us symbolize this as $Pr(e/\text{says } e)$. Bayes's Theorem then gives us his formula:

$$Pr(e/\text{says} e) \equiv \frac{Pr(e) \times Pr(\text{says} e/e)}{[Pr(e) \times Pr(\text{says} e/e)] + [Pr(\neg e) \times Pr(\text{says} e/\neg e)]}$$

If $p = Pr(e)$ and $t = Pr(\text{says } e/e)$, then our formula is derivable from the long formula as long as $Pr(\text{says } e/e) = Pr(\text{says} \neg e/\neg e)$. Where that assumption does not hold, the long formula can be used instead of our short one.

falsely, i.e. if $p > (1 - t)$, then the relevant probability is greater than 0.5. Furthermore, it is interesting to see how much less the probability that the event occurred, given that the witness said it occurred, is than the reliability of the witness, even when it is less likely that the witness spoke falsely than that the event occurred. Suppose the witness is 99 per cent reliable, so that there is only a 1 per cent chance that he spoke falsely, and that the likelihood of the event is 2 per cent. Then with $p = 0.02$ and $t = 0.99$, our formula yields:

$$\frac{(0.02)(0.99)}{(0.02)(0.99) + (1 - 0.02)(1 - 0.99)} = 0.67.$$

This is a surprising result, but in accordance with Hume's view that when 'the fact, which the testimony endeavours to establish, partakes of the extraordinary and the marvellous; in that case, the evidence, resulting from the testimony, admits of a diminution, greater or less, in proportion as the fact is more or less unusual' (*E* 113).[8]

IV

Price finds Hume's results on testimony and prior probabilities 'contrary to all reason'.[9] He argues, partially by example and partially by appeal to general principles, that Hume is wrong to allow prior probabilities any impact at all on our judgements concerning whether the event reported by the witness actually occurred.[10] Part of his point is that our assent to testimony is not based on induction, because 'One conversation with a man may convince us of his integrity and induce us to believe his testimony, though we never, in a single instance, experienced his veracity' (p. 399). As a result, Price thinks, testimony for miracles is *not* a matter of using a feebler experience to overthrow another of the same kind which is stronger. Rather, it is proof of an event which at best, prior to its happening, would have appeared to have a presumption against its

---

[8] The surprising result is that $Pr(e/\text{says } e)$, the probability that the event took place, given that the witness said it took place, is only 0.67, while $Pr(\text{says } e/e)$, the probability that the witness said it took place, given that it took place, is 99%. The figure of 0.67, however, should also be contrasted with the prior probability of the event's occurring, i.e. 2%. Hume certainly didn't intend to argue that testimony should have *no* effect on our belief, but rather that in certain circumstances it might have less effect than we might at first think.

[9] Richard Price, *Four Dissertations*, fourth dissertation entitled 'On the Importance of Christianity, the Nature of Historical Evidence, and Miracles', 407. Subsequent page references to Price will be given in the body of the paper.

[10] Not allowing prior probabilities to have any effect at all is the same as using our formula, but stipulating that p always equals 0.5. Then the formula results in $Pr(e/\text{says } e)$ being simply equal to t, i.e. to $Pr(\text{says } e/e)$. According to Diaconis and Freedman in their reply to Cohen, 'Can Human Irrationality be Experimentally Demonstrated?' (p. 334 n. 4), this is an application of Laplace's Principle of Insufficient Reason, first published around 1780.

happening (p. 401). This is a weak point, and does not show that likelihood of testimony being correct is not calculated in the same manner as induction. Hume himself admits that a single instance can serve as an inductive basis for a causal belief.[11] Price further argues that we *never* have an absolute proof that a very probable sort of event will happen again, nor the *least reason* to believe that it will *always* happen (pp. 394–5). But there is nothing in this to bother Hume, and at most it shows only that Price has not noticed that Hume is using a reasonably well-defined technical sense of 'proof' in the section on miracles.

After this unpromising start, Price has some most interesting things to say about prior probabilities. Concerning a case where the probability of the truth of testimony is ten to one, and the event attested to is the success of a person engaged in a pursuit against the success of which there was a probability of a hundred to one, Price says,

> The truth is, that the testimony would give the probability of ten to one to the event, unabated by the supposed probability against it . . . [because] the very experience which teaches us to give credit to testimony, is an experience by which we have found, that it has informed us rightly concerning facts, in which there would have appeared to us, previously, a great improbability. (pp. 407–8)

The argument here is that in making judgements about the likelihood of an event's occurring, on the basis of testimony, we should ignore the prior probability of the likelihood of the event, because our judgement about the reliability of the testimony (in this case ten to one) is a judgement about testimony *concerning unlikely events*. In other words, the likelihood of the event's occurring has *already been taken into account* when we make the judgement about the reliability of testimony. It would be double counting if we then proceeded to further calculate probabilities in the way Hume, and our application of Bayes's Theorem, suggests.

Price then proceeds to give a series of apparently persuasive examples.[12] Suppose a newspaper is generally accurate two out of three times, and suppose it reports, separately and individually, the occurrence of nine quite improbable events. Hume, Price claims, would reject all nine reports, i.e. he would say, 'that what, by supposition, reports truth six times in nine, does not report truth once in nine times' (p. 409). Or suppose that the same newspaper reported the loss of

---

[11] *Treatise* I. iii. 8; cf. *E* 107 n.

[12] Including the lottery example, a favourite in the 19th century and also mentioned by Cohen. Here is Cohen's formulation (p. 329): 'A witness of 99% reliability asserts that the number of the single ticket drawn in a lottery of 10,000 tickets was, say, 297; ought we really to reject that proposition just because of the size of the lottery?' The lottery problem is different from the other problems discussed here as there is not just one way of being wrong about 297, but 9,999 ways. Proper application of Bayes's Theorem does not result in rejecting the witness's testimony because of the size of the lottery. See Diaconis and Freedman, reply to Cohen, and Sobel, 'On the Evidence of Testimony for Miracles'.

a ferry boat during a crossing it had previously made safely 2,000 times. In this case, Price asserts, testimony that is accurate only two out of three times would overcome odds of thousands to one against.

Later (p. 418) Price admits that prior probabilities should *sometimes* be taken into account. We should not, for example, believe reports, however reliable the bearers of such reports are in general, of impossibilities. It remains unclear at this stage when prior probabilities are relevant, and when they are not. Price could say consistently with his argument so far, that our previous experience concerning the accuracy of testimony has presented us with cases of accurate testimony concerning improbable events, but never of accurate testimony concerning impossible events. This, however, might well just simply give the game away to Hume concerning miracles. But in a footnote at the end of his dissertation Price gives a better reason, and strengthens his argument about the usual irrelevance of prior probabilities (p. 444). Price says that two events are independent when the happening of one of them has no influence on the happening of the other, and with this account of independence he goes on to enunciate the principle that the improbabilities of independent events are the same whether they are considered jointly or separately. As it stands, this point does not seem to amount to much of an argument against Hume. Testimony that an event occurred is, when accurate, related both causally and logically to the occurrence of the event. However, it is easy enough to reformulate the point in an apparently telling way against Hume. One could argue that the *likelihood* of the event reported, or the distribution of past occurrences or non-occurrences, is independent of the accuracy of the testimony, so that when we are to consider whether or not to believe testimony, only its accuracy should be taken into account. Alternatively, if we want to retain the generality of Bayes's Theorem, we should treat the prior probability of the event as 0.5 when we judge the known prior probability of that event to be irrelevant to the accuracy of the testimony we are considering (see note 10). If sound, this point entirely undermines Hume's use of prior probabilities in his discussion of the rationality of belief in miracles based on testimony.

V

In the article already cited, L. J. Cohen, during the discussion of empirical tests of rationality, comes to conclusions remarkably similar to Price's, and for apparently similar reasons.

First of all, let me outline two examples Cohen mentions (pp. 328–9). In one case, subjects were told that, in a certain town where blue and green cabs operated in a ratio of 85 to 15 respectively, a witness identified a cab in a crash as green. The court is told that in the relevant light conditions such a witness can distinguish blue from green cabs 80 per cent of the time. The subjects were then asked, what is the probability that the cab involved in the accident was blue? The usual answer was 0.2, indicating that the subjects were ignoring the prior probability based on the distribution of cabs in the town. But if that probability were taken into account, the right answer, according to our formula, would be

$$\frac{(0.85)(0.2)}{(0.85)(0.2)+(1-0.85)(1-0.2)} = 0.59.$$

An 80 per cent reliable witness, sincerely claiming that the cab was green, would be judged to have 0.59 chance of misidentifying the colour of the cab.[13]

Cohen's second example, concerning diagnosis, is this. Suppose you are suffering from symptoms which indicate that you have either disease A or disease B, which require different treatments. Disease A is nineteen times as common as B, but you take a test, which always distinguishes A and B, and in the past has been right 80 per cent of the time. The test results indicate that you have disease B. Should you opt for treatment for B, on the grounds that the probability that you have B is, as Price would apparently calculate it, $^4/_5$, or should you opt for treatment for A, on the grounds that the probability that you have A is, as Hume would apparently calculate it, $^{19}/_{23}$? If you decide with Hume, of course, you need not have taken the test at all.

Cohen admits, as Price probably would not, that if one were concerned only with long-term frequencies or instances thereof, one should calculate as we have claimed Hume would. But, Cohen argues, if we are concerned with the likelihood of a particular witness correctly identifying a particular cab, or if a patient is concerned with successful diagnosis in his own particular case, then we should ignore prior probabilities, i.e. treat them as 0.5 in the Bayesian calculation. And his reason for this seems to be precisely Price's: since the distribution of past instances has no causal efficacy on, i.e. is independent of, the individual event (the witnessing, the taking of the test) then the prior probability based on such chance distribution is irrelevant.[14]

VI

How are we to decide between Hume and standard statistical methods, on the one hand, and Cohen and the eighteenth-century theologians on the other? To

---

[13] Again, note that while the prior probability that the cab was green is only 15%, the probability that the cab was green, given that the witness said it was green, is 0.41.

[14] See also Cohen's interesting discussion of this point in terms of detaching unconditional probabilities from conditional probabilities only when the conditions include, not just the knowledge we have (i.e. in the examples mentioned, chance distribution) but 'a substantial amount of the causally relevant factors' (p. 365).

what extent does the modern debate deepen our understanding of what is at issue between Hume and Price, or vice versa? These are large questions, and only a partial unravelling of the issues will be attempted here. My main purpose has been to show that Hume's argument has a larger significance than is generally realized, that Price saw this and has been unjustly neglected, and that their debate is extremely similar to an important modern issue. The parallel between the two debates is significant, I think, and not merely of historical interest. It indicates that the issue is a long-standing one, and that there are unresolved divisions (some would say 'persistent cognitive illusions'[15]) over what constitutes a rational decision concerning prior probabilities. Which side one comes down on could be of profound importance. The patient has to decide whether to believe the result of the test; the doctor has to decide whether even to administer it: both might be risking the patient's life. Or suppose that the likelihood of a nuclear attack is one in a thousand, but that the accuracy of one's radar or other early warning devices is only 99.8 per cent. Would it be rational to act on the information given by one's equipment, or more rational not to set up such warning devices at all? If one in a hundred new foodstuffs is carcinogenic, but one's tests are only 90 per cent accurate, should one bother to carry out the tests or not? There are no easy answers to these questions, and apparently good arguments can be provided on both sides.[16]

On first pass, one's intuitions seem to side with Price and Cohen, and for the reasons they give. If the prior probabilities are not causally relevant to the actual case of visual perception that grounds the witness's testimony, why should we take them into account when deciding whether or not to believe him? As Cohen says, 'if the green cab company suddenly increased the size of its fleet relative to that of the blue company, the accuracy of the witness's vision would not be affected, and the credibility of his testimony would therefore remain precisely the same in any particular case of the relevant kind' (p. 329).[17] Similarly, it is hard not to side, at least initially, with Price concerning the particular examples that he gives.

On the other hand, consider this way to formulating the diagnosis case. One *could* argue that, given the 19 to 1 distribution of the disease, and the 80 per cent accuracy of the test, the test will indicate that an individual has disease B 4.75 times more often when he has A than when he has B. Consider a population of 20,000 who take the test. 19,000 will have A and 1,000 will have B. Out of the

---

[15] See Diaconis and Freedman, reply to Cohen.

[16] It is of interest that most of those who replied to Cohen seemed to think that he was clearly right (and that his point had been obvious since the early days of probability theory) or clearly, perhaps even dangerously, wrong.

[17] It is significant, surely, that the median answer given by the people to whom the cab problem was posed chose to answer with Cohen.

19,000 who have A, the test will indicate that 3,800 of them have B. Out of the 1,000 who have B, the test will indicate that 800 of them have B. So out of 4,600 instances of the test indicating B, 3,800 of them will actually have A. The 80 per cent accurate test will be right in only 800 cases out of 4,600 indications of B, or only 17.39 per cent of the time.[18] But how could a test of 80 per cent accuracy be right in only 17.39 per cent of B-indicating cases? We need to make a distinction between two claims:[19]

(1) Concerning people who have disease B, the test is right 80 per cent of the time.
(2) Concerning people whom the test indicates as having B, it is right 80 per cent of the time.

It is clear that the above line of reasoning, which is simply another way of advocating taking prior probabilities into account in the way our formula recommends, requires that we treat the 80 per cent accuracy claim as equivalent to claim (1) above. And if that is what the claim did mean, we would be wise not to trust the results of the test. But given the way we have outlined the example, there is no reason whatsoever to treat the claim as meaning (1) rather than (2), or for that matter as (2) rather than (1). But any company that marketed such a test, and claimed that it was 80 per cent accurate, had better mean, by 80 per cent accuracy, claim (2), or they would, I suspect, be deluged by lawsuits.

Throughout this paper I have talked of 'accuracy of testimony', 'probability that the witness tells the truth', 'reliability of testimony', 'probability of the truth of testimony', 'general accuracy of a newspaper', and the like, and used the value of t to reflect what such expressions meant when using the formula

$$\frac{pt}{pt + (1 - p)(1 - t)}$$

to calculate the probability that an event did take place, given that the witness said that it took place. Strictly speaking, for this formula to operate at all, t must be the probability that the witness said that the event took place, given that the event did take place. Let us symbolize the former probability as $Pr(e/\text{says } e)$ and the latter probability as $Pr(\text{says } e/e)$.[20] Our discussion of the diagnosis case, and the distinction between claim (1) and claim (2), shows that the terms 'accuracy', 'reliability', etc. are ambiguous. Though we have treated them throughout as giving $Pr(\text{says } e/e)$, and hence giving a value for t, it may be the case, as our

---

[18] See Krantz's reply to Cohen, p. 341, for this line of reasoning. Note that the same figures can be arrived at by using our formula and that the 17.39% figure contrasts also with the one in twenty prior probability.

[19] See Mackie's reply to Cohen, p. 346.

[20] See n. 7.

discussion of claim (2) shows, that sometimes they are meant instead to indicate $Pr(e/\text{says } e)$. But $Pr(e/\text{says } e)$ is just what our formula was meant to calculate. If a degree of accuracy or reliability is given, and is meant to give $Pr(e/\text{says } e)$, then it would be a gross mistake to treat it as $Pr(\text{says } e/e)$ and use it as a value for t in our formula. On the other hand, if the reliability figure gives $Pr(\text{says } e/e)$, it would be an equally bad mistake not to use our formula in deciding on a value for $Pr(e/\text{says } e)$ when a value for the prior probability $Pr(e)$ (i.e. p in our formula) is available. Although no ordinary language expression unequivocally expresses the distinction between $Pr(e/\text{says } e)$ and $Pr(\text{says } e/e)$, for the remaining discussion let us mean by 'credibility of testimony' the former and by 'reliability of the witness' the latter. Then our formula is a means of calculating credibility of testimony in terms of the reliability of the witness and the prior probability of the event reported.

It is my contention that Hume argued, rightly, that the credibility of testimony in favour of miracles would never be high enough to command our assent, even if the reliability of the witnesses was high. Price thought otherwise, and argued so both by means of general principles and by example. It is obvious, I think, that neither was absolutely clear about the distinction between credibility and reliability that has just been drawn and in terms of which the dispute between them can be adjudicated. But in the end, I think, Hume's insistence on the distinction between our degree of belief in the occurrence of an event on the sole grounds that a witness reported its happening, and our degree of belief in the reliability of the witness,[21] shows him to have a better grip on the matter, and to be the better proto-Bayesian.

What of Price's arguments, and the other examples mentioned? As has already been said, the diagnosis case is underdescribed; but it would be grossly irresponsible of those marketing the test not to mean 'credibility' rather than 'reliability' by their 80 per cent accuracy figure. The cab example is also underdescribed. The crucial datum was given as, 'a witness can distinguish blue from green cabs 80 per cent of the time'. Does this mean credibility or reliability? It is charitable to assume that the subjects of the experiment took it to mean credibility, as that interpretation shows their answer to be correct, though one would have to look at details of the original experiment to see whether their taking it that way was correct. In any event, a close look at the original data on which the 80 per cent figure in the cab case (or, for that matter, the diagnosis case) was reached would reveal how to disambiguate that figure. It should not be a difficult matter to determine whether the data support an 80 per cent probability that the cab was blue, given that the witness said it was blue (credibility)

---

[21] Most graphically expressed by his quoting, 'I should not believe such a story were it told me by Cato' (*E* 113).

or an 80 per cent probability that the witness said that the cab was blue, given that it was blue (reliability).

What of Price's persuasive newspaper example? Again, everything hinges on what is meant by the claim that a newspaper is accurate two out of three times. Does it mean that, given that the newspaper said the event happened, it has a two out of three chance of being right, or rather that, given that it happened, the newspaper has a two out of three chance of being right? To the extent that we are persuaded by Price's example, we are taking him to be making the former claim. Intuitively the two-thirds figure for newspaper accuracy does seem more likely to mean credibility ($Pr(e/\text{says } e)$) rather than reliability ($Pr(\text{says } e/e)$) as we would normally come up with that figure by starting with the newspaper reports, and then checking to see whether what it reported actually occurred.

Although Price at some points seems near to grasping the distinction between what we have called credibility and reliability,[22] in the end it seems to elude him. Most of his examples and his argument concerning 'double counting' make sense only if he is thinking of credibility. If the figure we are given is a value for $Pr(e/\text{says } e)$ then of course we cannot use that as a value for t (i.e. $Pr(\text{says } e/e)$) in our formula. On the other hand, his argument from independence is only plausible if he is talking about reliability. The argument was that, unless the prior probability was causally operative on the accuracy of the witness's testimony, it had no effect on that accuracy. If accuracy here means reliability, the point may stand. But if accuracy here means credibility, i.e. $Pr(e/\text{says } e)$, the prior probability $Pr(e)$ is crucial, as we have seen.[23]

Price's arguments and examples do not add up to a coherent position as a result of his confusion concerning crucial terms such as 'accuracy'. Hume's admirable insistence on the distinction between the degree of belief we should have concerning the occurrence of a reported event and the degree of belief we should have in the veracity of the reporter stands in marked contrast. However, there is a very simple point that might be made, on grounds adduced by Price, against Hume on miracles. Why, it might be asked, should we not treat the evidence based on testimony in favour of miracles as a matter of credibility, rather than reliability, just as we should in the newspaper example? Hume's answer is, I think, clear. Given the incredibly high odds against the occurrence of a miracle (it is, after all, a violation of a law of nature), what possible grounds could there be for treating the evidence based on testimony as a matter of credibility rather

---

[22] See, for instance, pp. 417–18, where he claims that though prior probabilities *as such* should not be considered as invalidating counter-evidence to testimony (or, as he puts it on p. 413, do not 'lessen the capacity of testimony to report truth') they none the less may affect the *credit* of testimony.

[23] The passage already quoted from Cohen about the irrelevance of the green cab company's increasing the size of its fleet merits similar treatment. It is irrelevant if we are concerned about the witness's reliability, but not at all irrelevant if it is the credibility of witnesses' testimony that is at issue.

than reliability? One who argues in such a way should be challenged to defend his attribution of credibility to the witness's testimony. If it is to be a matter of *credibility*, then the reliability of the witness must be greater than the probability that the law of nature holds. And what witness is so reliable?

A this point Hume's argument leaves the realm of abstract probability theory. As is little noted, Hume does admit that it is conceivable that the reliability of testimony may exceed the evidence in favour of a law of nature, and hence that the credibility of testimony may exceed 0.5. This is shown by his example of the earth being covered in darkness for eight days (*E* 127–8). What he denies is that such a possibility should ever be 'proved, so as to be the foundation of a system of religion' (*E* 127). A miracle is not simply a violation of a law of nature, but must also be 'by a particular volition of the Deity, or by the interposition of some invisible agent' (*E* 115 n.). It is conceivable that reliability of witnesses may be enough to render credible the violation of a law of nature: 'The decay, corruption, and dissolution of nature, is an event rendered probable by so many analogies, that any phœnomenon, which seems to have a tendency towards that catastrophe, comes within the reach of human testimony, if that testimony be very extensive and uniform.' (*E* 128). Hume thinks that no such instance is to be found 'in all the records of history' (*E* 127). But even if it were found, and the violation were credible, what possible grounds could be adduced so that it became plausible to treat the phenomenon as owing to a particular volition of the Deity rather than as an instance of the already experienced dissolution of nature? If one *already* believed in the God of the Christian religion, then if the sort of evidence envisaged became available, it might be rational to treat the violation as a result of God's volition. But if one was not already a believer, then even if such evidence obtained, one would still have no good reason to change one's mind.

Hume argued that the evidence of testimony in favour of miracles could never be good enough to provide a rational basis for the foundation of a religion. His argument was designed not, as Price thought (p. 379), as an objection to Christianity, but as an argument against a certain way of trying to rationally ground belief in Christianity. Given the difficulties we have discussed, it surely must be admitted that he succeeded in this limited task.[24]

[24] An ancestor of this paper was read at the University of Calgary, where I received many helpful comments, especially from T. Hurka and J. Heintz. Correspondence with P. Maher and L. J. Cohen was also most useful. A shorter version was read at the 28th Annual Congress of the Canadian Philosophical Association, Guelph, Ontario, 11 June 1984. J. H. Sobel replied. His paper 'On the Evidence of Testimony for Miracles' and his subsequent discussion with me greatly contributed to the revision of my paper. Ian Hacking was also of great help.

13

Religion: The Useless Hypothesis

J. C. A. Gaskin

Section XI of the *Enquiry* ('Of a Particular Providence and of a Future State') is concerned with religion and the existence of a deity. It is designed both to show that the supposition of God's existence is useless as an hypothesis for explaining the phenomena of the universe or the vicissitudes of human life, and to show that belief in a provident God is not an essential part of the functioning of morality.

These designs were flatly contrary to the received and powerful religious beliefs of Hume's day and are by no means universally accepted in our own. We should therefore not be surprised to find that Hume cautiously (and slightly confusingly) places what he says in the section at several removes from himself. A friend 'who loves sceptical paradoxes' makes a speech on behalf of Epicurus while Hume (mostly) voices objections. What does cause surprise to some people (e.g. to Selby-Bigge, see *E* xix) is that this section, which foreshadows the comprehensive critique of religion carried out by Hume in the 1750s, should appear in the *Enquiry* at all. Noting the real and important ways in which Section XI connects philosophically and strategically with the rest of the *Enquiry* is thus a primary requirement for understanding what Hume is about. The second task is to analyse the structure of the section. The worth and implications of its main arguments can then be examined.

1. WHAT IS ARGUED: CONNEXIONS

The title under which the *Enquiry* first appeared in 1748, and continued to appear until the edition of 1758, was *Philosophical Essays concerning Human Understanding*. This would have led the reader to expect what in fact we still have: not a systematically developed thesis in which every move comes from previously established positions and leads to those that follow, but a sequence of essays clustered round a central topic and employing common presuppositions and arguments. Within that expectation, I shall argue, Section XI is not only a natural companion to the earlier essays, but also a crucial complement to the essay which immediately precedes it, 'Of Miracles', that scandalous outcast from the *Treatise* whose surprise appearance in the *Enquiry* would indeed have had little justification were it not coupled with 'Of a Particular Providence and of a Future State'.[1]

There are thus two questions. The first asks how Section XI complements Hume's thoughts on miracles to make a unity of anti-religious argument, a unity not immediately obvious to the modern reader. The second asks to what extent Section XI relies upon and shares arguments and positions elsewhere evident in the *Enquiry*.

The short answer to the first question is that Section X, 'Of Miracles', challenges the claim that the Christian revelation is validated by good evidence. Section XI completes the attack by arguing that belief in a provident God (i.e. one exerting control, guidance, or forethought in the moral affairs or physical processes of the world) is not justified by arguments of the sort generally employed. Thus *taken together* the two sections make up a concerted attempt to show that there are no sound reasons for affirming any popular religious belief. I say the sections *taken together* complete the attack because, as an outcome of the long progression of Christian apologetic that preceded Hume, religious belief had come to be commended to the *rational* man (Hume's 'wise man' who 'proportions his belief to the evidence'; *E* 110) on precisely the *two* grounds considered successively in Sections X and XI, namely that the Christian revelation is validated by miracles, and that the existence of a theistic God (more precisely the provident Christian God) is established by sound arguments. But it is worth noting that the distinction between the credentials of revelation and the rational grounding of a general theistic belief in God (and the appeal to both) has biblical justification. Thus in John 3: 2 we read, 'We know that you are a teacher come from God; for no one can do these signs that you do, unless God is with him', and in Romans 1: 20, 'Ever since the creation of the world [God's] invisible nature, namely, his eternal power and deity, has been clearly perceived in the things that have been made.' (RSV; the New English Bible has 'visible to the eye of reason'.) The attempt to give a rational basis of some sort for religious belief is therefore not the eighteenth-century aberration it is sometimes made out to be. Hume is not merely attacking contemporary religious errors. He is attacking things appealed to at source by Christianity.

---

[1] We know from a letter written by Hume in 1737 that some version of his observations on miracles had originally been intended for inclusion in the *Treatise*: 'Having a frankt Letter I was resolv'd to make Use of it, & accordingly enclose some Reasonings concerning Miracles, which I once thought of publishing with the rest, but which I am afraid will give too much Offence even as the World is dispos'd at present.' (*NHL* 2).

The reliance on miracles was both traditional and popular. It is, for instance, unequivocally expressed by Samuel Clarke in his Boyle Lecture of 1705: 'The Christian Revelation is positively and directly proved, to be actually and immediately sent to us from God, by the many infallible *Signs and Miracles*, which the Author of it worked publicly as the Evidence of his Divine Commission.' Hume's reply in Section X (and it is a reply which gathers together many strands from previous controversy concerning miracles[2]) is that for an event to be called a miracle it must be regarded as contrary to the laws of nature. But our proper incredulity about such events is too great to be overcome by historical testimony of the suspect sort provided by ancient documents. Therefore, reports of miracles, including the crucial case of the Resurrection,[3] cannot be used by the wise man as 'a just foundation for any [popular] system of religion'. In short the credentials of revelation are suspect.

The appeal to natural theology (or to 'natural religion', as was the commoner eighteenth-century usage), that is to say to allegedly sound arguments to prove the existence of God, can be found in philosophical and theological writers from Xenophon to Alvin Plantinga, but was particularly evident in the Enlightenment. Thus even an untypically cautious apologist like Joseph Butler wrote: 'As the manifold appearances of design and of final causes, in the constitution of the world, prove it to be the work of an intelligent mind; so the particular final causes of pleasure and pain distributed amongst his creatures, prove that they are under his government.' And again: 'to an unprejudiced mind ten thousand thousand instances of design cannot but prove a designer'.[4]

In general the existence of an entity having many of the essential characteristics of the provident Christian God was held to be proved, or at the very least made highly probable, by certain ancient arguments. The principal among these, in the eighteenth century and for long before and afterwards, were varieties of a priori argument to a first cause (i.e. arguments independent of experience), and the ever-popular a posteriori Design Argument (an argument dependent upon experience). The former had already been dealt

---

[2] The controversy is most readably documented by Sir Leslie Stephen in his *History of English Thought in the Eighteenth Century* (1876), IV. iv. The area has been more thoroughly and more recently worked over by R. M. Burns in *The Great Debate on Miracles* (London: Associated University Presses, 1981).

[3] I have argued elsewhere (*Hume's Philosophy of Religion*, 2nd edn. (Basingstoke: Macmillan, 1988), ch. 8) that Hume's comparatively circumspect conclusion that 'no human testimony can have such force as to prove a miracle, and make it a just foundation for any [popular] system of religion' (*E* 127), when divested of prudential reticence, would read: 'no human testimony can have such force as to prove the Resurrection, and make it a just foundation for the Christian religion'. An interesting attempt to rebut Hume's argument is in R. A. H. Larmer's *Water into Wine? An Investigation of the Concept of Miracle* (Montreal: McGill-Queen's University Press, 1988; repr. 1996).

[4] Butler, *The Analogy of Religion* (1736), from, respectively, ch. 3 and the Conclusion.

with by Hume elsewhere in his writings.[5] The latter is the butt of his criticisms in Section XI.

So in effect Hume is saying in Sections X and XI that neither of the supposed—and main—rational justifications for Christian belief do their job properly. Read against a background of religious apologetics, Section XI is thus tightly connected with Section X. But is Section XI legitimately connected with the rest of the *Enquiry*?

The *Enquiry* as a whole contains a positive empiricist and a negative sceptical thesis. The positive thesis holds that matters of fact and real existence can only be established by experience, and that experience is the sole guide to what causes what. This thesis is developed in Section IV. It is also the basis of most of the argument in Section XI and is explicitly appealed to more than once in this section: 'But allowing you to make experience (as indeed I think you ought) the only standard of our judgment concerning this, and all other questions of fact; I doubt not but, from the very same experience, to which you appeal, it may be possible to refute this reasoning . . .' (*E* 142; see also *E* 136 and 148). It is, however, the negative thesis of the *Enquiry* that most strongly infuses Section XI. This thesis appears in three modes: as an emphasis on the limitations of our understanding, as a consequential hostility to grandiose metaphysical speculation, and (a particular application of the last) as a vigorous rejection of metaphysical rationalizations of religious beliefs.

The source for Hume's emphasis on the limitation of our understanding is, fairly obviously, his positive thesis concerning the source of our knowledge of facts, real existence, and causes, together with his empiricist theory of meaning (see *Treatise* I. i. 1 and *Enquiry* II), which locates the meaning of terms (i.e. words or phrases) in experience. The appeal to both of these is widely evident in the *Enquiry*: 'Our line [i.e. the reach of our understanding] is too short to fathom such immense abysses.' (*E* 72); 'if men attempt the discussion of questions, which lie entirely beyond the reach of human capacity, such as those concerning the origin of worlds, or the œconomy of the intellectual system or region of spirits, they may long beat the air in their fruitless contests' (*E* 81); a species of mitigated scepticism which may be of advantage to us 'is the limitation of our enquiries to such subjects as are best adapted to the narrow capacity of human understanding' (*E* 162); and in Section XI itself: 'It is uncertain; because the subject lies entirely beyond the reach of human experience.' (*E* 142).

The consequent hostility to metaphysical speculation is declared in no uncertain terms in the manifesto which forms Section I of the *Enquiry*:

---

[5] e.g. in the section of Book I of the *Treatise* called 'Why a cause is always necessary' (I. iii. 3) and in *A Letter from a Gentleman to his Friend in Edinburgh* (1745), *L* 22–3.

Here indeed lies the justest and most plausible objection against a considerable part of metaphysics, that they are not properly a science; but arise either from the fruitless efforts of human vanity, which would penetrate into subjects utterly inaccessible to the understanding, or from the craft of popular superstitions, which, being unable to defend themselves on fair ground, raise these intangling brambles to cover and protect their weakness. (*E* 11)

A little later the particular application of all this—dissolution of the union of metaphysics (or 'abstruse philosophy') with superstition (or 'popular religion')—is emphasized as a main objective of the *Enquiry*:

And still more happy, if, reasoning in this easy manner, we can undermine the foundations of an abstruse philosophy, which seems to have hitherto served only as a shelter to superstition, and a cover to absurdity and error! (*E* 16)

It is perhaps scarcely necessary to point out that the famous sentences with which the *Enquiry* concludes proclaim the outcome of the whole anti-metaphysical, anti-religious, enterprise:

If we take in our hand any volume; of divinity or school metaphysics, for instance; let us ask, *Does it contain any abstract reasoning concerning quantity or number?* No. *Does it contain any experimental reasoning concerning matter of fact and existence?* No. Commit it then to the flames: For it can contain nothing but sophistry and illusion. (*E* 165)

Now one of the most conspicious parts of the 'philosophical religion' (the union of metaphysics and superstition) to which Hume so strongly objects was the a priori argument for God's existence (made famous by al-Kindi, Maimonides, Anselm, Aquinas, Descartes, Leibniz, and Samuel Clarke among many others, and including both what we would now call the ontological argument and several types of cosmological argument). The other was the a posteriori argument for God's existence known as the Design Argument (the argument that the purposes and/or order discernible in the physical world can only be explained as being the result of a transcendent active intelligence imposing such purposes and/or order).

The main a priori argument (the argument from a regress of physical causes to a necessarily existent being) had already been indirectly dismantled by Hume in his discussion of causation in both the *Treatise* and earlier sections of the *Enquiry* (see note 5). It was to be the object of renewed attacks in Part IX of the *Dialogues*, and is destroyed root and branch if we take seriously anything like his epistemological distinction between matters of fact and relations of ideas ('Hume's Fork', as Antony Flew calls it; see *E* 25–6). The result, for the main a priori argument, of combining Hume's Fork with his account of causation is spelled out in the final section of the *Enquiry*: 'Whatever *is* may *not be*. No negation of a fact can involve a contradiction . . . The existence, therefore, of any being can only be proved by arguments from its cause or its effect; and these arguments are founded entirely on experience.' (*E* 164).

But the Design Argument is not so readily swept aside with an epistemological brush. It is not only the most popular and enduring reason for belief in a deity (and the core of 'philosophical' religion). It is also an argument from effects to causes and, moreover, an argument based upon experience. It thus requires separate treatment from the a priori argument: partly because (for Hume) it is an example of the generally condemned reasoning concerning matters remote and abstruse and beyond the limits of our understanding; partly on its own terms as an argument from experience. The full treatment is given in Hume's *Dialogues concerning Natural Religion*. But it is begun in *Enquiry* XI. Indeed it is difficult to see how Hume's anti-religious and anti-metaphysical programme in the *Enquiry* could be regarded as in any way complete if he had *not* confronted what he there calls 'the chief or sole argument for a divine existence' (*E* 135).

So Section XI is an integral part of the programme of the *Enquiry*. It employs the arguments, methods, and assumptions elsewhere developed in that work. But the aim of showing that popular religion lacks rational support would be only half done without the arguments in 'Of Miracles': hence the coupling of Sections X and XI, and their joint inclusion in the *Enquiry*. Section X sheds doubt upon the credentials of revelation. Section XI sheds doubt upon the main argument of natural religion that is derived from experience.

2. WHAT IS ARGUED: ANALYSIS

Section XI is in the form of a quasi-dialogue between Hume and 'a friend who loves sceptical paradoxes'. For the most part Hume casts himself as a defender of the 'religious hypothesis', but at the last moment he hazards a direct attack upon it. The discussion, in the order in which Hume presents it, can be divided into four moves. Of these, the second and fourth are concerned with defects in the Design Argument, the first and third deal with the practical consequences (or lack of consequences) for social morality implied by these defects. Hume's four moves are as follows.

1. The opening exchanges concern the possible consequences of religious scepticism (*E* 132 ff.). Hume first draws attention to the tolerance with which Athens and Rome, despite their multiple civic superstitions, treated every sect of philosophy, including the Epicureans (who denied the activity and providence of gods and the reality of a future life). His sceptical friend then points out that the bigotry that is fatal to philosophy is not a product of unlearned or natural superstition, but of superstition underpinned by metaphysical arguments and systematized in creeds. But, replies Hume, religion has a political

(meaning a social and moral) dimension, and certain philosophers, typically the Epicureans, by 'denying a divine existence,[6] and consequently a providence and a future state [a life after death], seem to loosen, in a great measure, the ties of morality, and may be supposed, for that reason, pernicious to the peace of civil society' (E 133–4). The sceptical friend then undertakes to show that Epicurus' denial of providence and a future state has no 'political' consequences because it merely denies a metaphysical species of religion which itself can make no well-founded claim to any 'political' application.

2. Discussion of the limitations of the Design Argument begins in the speech on behalf of Epicurus (E 134–42). In this the sceptical friend identifies a crucial difficulty for 'the chief or sole argument for a divine existence'. The difficulty is that even if accepted, the argument provides no good evidence for a god exercising *providence*. The 'chief or sole argument' is that the religious philosophers 'paint, in the most magnificent colours, the order, beauty, and wise arrangement of the universe; and then ask, if such a glorious display of intelligence could proceed from the fortuitous concourse of atoms, or if chance could produce what the greatest genius can never sufficiently admire' (E 135). The difficulty identified by the sceptical friend is that this is an argument from effects (the world) back to causes (gods) or to a single cause (God). As such it allows no inference concerning the nature of the cause beyond what is actually discernible in the effect. But the appearance in the effect is of moral neutrality in both nature and human affairs, and such neutrality is not evidence for the existence of a supreme governor who designed things for our convenience or 'punishes the vicious with infamy and disappointment, and rewards the virtuous with honour and success' (E 140). Rewards and punishments, argues the sceptical friend, except where contrived by civil society, are no more and no less than those found in the natural world, and those are random and arbitrary. We have no evidence from *this* world about rewards and punishments in another world to which this one is imagined to be 'a porch, which leads to a greater, and vastly different building' (E 141), and the evidence from revelation about the supposed *other* world is, as Hume had already argued in Section X, profoundly suspect.

A counter to Epicurus (E 142 ff.) is then urged by Hume. In certain circumstances we *can* infer more in the cause than is apparent in the effect. For example, when we see a half-finished building we can infer that it has a builder and that it will be finished later. But, the sceptical friend replies (E 143–7), there is a vast difference between houses and their causes on the one hand, and the

---

[6] Hume is not strictly correct here. The Epicureans denied a life after death on all manner of grounds (see e.g. Lucretius, *On the Nature of the Universe* 3) and they certainly denied that the gods exercised providence. *Consequently,* Hume takes it that they deny the existence of God as that entity would normally be understood in the theistic tradition which concerns him (and us).

universe and its cause or causes on the other. '[M]an is a being, whom we know by experience'. Saying that something is caused by a man thus leads to all sorts of legitimate expectations and knowledge beyond that inferable from the thing itself. The Deity, on the other hand, 'is a single being in the universe, not comprehended under any species or genus, from whose experienced attributes or qualities, we can, by analogy, infer any [additional] attribute or quality in him' (*E*144). 'No new fact can ever be inferred from the religious hypothesis; no event foreseen or foretold; no reward or punishment expected or dreaded, beyond what is already known by practice and observation.' (*E* 146). Hence (a final return to the alleged consequences of religious scepticism) 'philosophical disputes concerning metaphysics and religion' (*E* 147) have no connexion with the interests of society.

3. Discussion of these interests. All this may be so, replies Hume, but you overlook the fact that men *believe* that the Deity will reward virtue and punish vice more than is here apparent, and to destroy that belief (however ill-founded it may be) frees men from one restraint upon their conduct. Nevertheless, the state ought to tolerate all philosophies since restraints upon reasoning pave the way 'for persecution and oppression in points, where the generality of mankind are more deeply interested and concerned' (*E* 147).

4. But, concludes Hume, there is a further difficulty with regard to the Design Argument (*E* 148). A cause and effect relation can only be identified where *two* species of objects are constantly conjoined. Since the universe is not a species but a unique object, 'I do not see, that we could form any conjecture or inference at all concerning its cause'.

3. WHAT IS ARGUED: COMMENTS

Hume tried two titles for Section XI. In the first edition of the *Enquiry* it appeared with the provocative title 'Of the Practical Consequences of Natural Theology'—provocative because the burden of his argument is that metaphysical religion has *no* practical consequences. The second title, 'Of a Particular Providence and of a Future State', draws more attention to the doubts which are aired in the section about evidence for the providence of God, and the moral significance of an afterlife. If one were to invent a third title it might be 'From World to God and Back Again'. But however the section is described, Hume's main concerns are (A) the two difficulties with the Design Argument identified at 2 and 4 in the above analysis, and (B) the relations between religion and morality identified at 1 and 3. His contentions, in the order I shall now examine them, are thus:

(A1)   God's *providence* is not established by the 'chief or sole argument for a divine existence' (the Design Argument).

(A2) The Design Argument may be *per se* invalid due to causal relations only being establishable between two species of objects constantly conjoined.

(B) The denial of God's providence and of an afterlife does not undermine social morality.

(A1) God's Providence is Not Established by the Design Argument

Hume's contention is that the Design Argument, even if structurally and conceptually sound, does not entitle us to infer the existence of a *provident* God (a God morally concerned with us, and active in the world) of the sort that is the object of popular theistic religions.

When we infer a cause from its effect, Hume argues,[7] we can infer more about the cause than is required to produce the given effect if and only if we are operating in the usual conditions: namely, when the cause can be identified as a member of a species known other than via the effect under consideration. But when the cause is *only* inferred from its effect, and falls under no otherwise known species, then, argues Hume, we can *only* ascribe to the cause whatever characteristics are required to produce the given effect. The universe is just such an effect. Its supposed cause falls under no known or apparently knowable species. Hence if we cannot discern, for example, benevolent providence in the effect, we cannot ascribe benevolent providence to the cause. (It would be even more absurd, according to Hume, to postulate *perfectly* benevolent providence in the cause, and then 'torture your brain' (*E* 139) with trying to show why such providence is not evident in the effect we experience.) Let us look at Hume's argument in the light of three examples.

The first is supplied by Hume himself. It is intended to illustrate inference under the normally prevailing conditions when we can readily infer *more* about the cause than would be just sufficient to produce the effect. Discovery of a half-finished house, says Hume, entitles us to infer that it is the incomplete project of some human person or persons, and *from what we already know about human persons*, we can infer, for example, an intention to finish the house, or that the builders were very probably possessed of the normal physical properties of human beings. '[M]an is a being, whom we know by experience' (*E* 143).

A second example, similar in form, permits a more limited and uncertain inference about the nature of the cause. In the late 1980s the cause (or causes) of the disease of cattle bovine spongiform encephalopathy (BSE) were not known. Symptoms occurred, and a pathology was observed which was analogous to

---

[7] As we have seen, the arguments are divided between Hume, his sceptical friend, and the friend speaking on behalf of Epicurus. But since philosophical discussion of the arguments does not depend upon to whom they are nominally assigned, I shall simply refer to Hume from now on.

that associated with scrapie—a long-familiar disease of sheep. But no causal agent had been identified for BSE. Nevertheless, given the analogy with the scrapie syndrome, and the possibility of chemically poisoned feed having been dismissed, it was initially presumed that the causal agent would be found to be some sort of virus or quasi-virus, and would therefore have at least some of the characteristics of that species of entity (being partly composed of protein, invisible under any form of ocular magnification, operating inside the host cell, etc.). Thus from the hypothesis that the cause would turn out to be a member of a known species, some further effects of the presumed cause could be conjectured to guide research. In the case of BSE it was, for example, conjectured that the disease would be transferable to other cattle and possibly to other animals in ways in which toxic chemical invasion would not be transferable.

Let us now imagine a third example. Suppose all the human beings in a particular remote area (call it Umbopoland) die suddenly and apparently causelessly. However, subsequent pathological examination shows that the entire physical structure of their nervous systems has uniformly collapsed, without trace of invasive organism, and without trace of abnormal chemical addition or subtraction. That is to say, there exists no indication of what species of entity the cause could have been, and, moreover, nothing like it has ever before been recorded. In such a case, I would suggest, medical and scientific faith in the universality of causation (used as no more than a guide to investigation) would express itself thus: 'Something must have caused this disorder. Something powerful enough to produce the pathological effects observed. Let us for the time being call this something P. As yet we have no idea what P is, or what further effects or manifestations it may have. Investigations are continuing. But we shall have to be very careful. It looks nasty!' Or, in more Humean terms, 'Our determination to believe in causation leads us to infer a cause, P, sufficient to produce this effect. But our complete ignorance of the species to which P belongs prevents us from forming any inference or expectation about what its effects could be or will be beyond those we have already observed.' Notice that even here, where what can be inferred about the cause is most limited, the scientist retains a philosophical conviction and a guide from previous experience. The philosophical conviction is that P, some cause of the unique syndrome, exists; that causality is indeed universal, and hence that P is there to be found, and found, moreover, not as a unique entity, but in the usual way as a member or members of a known or knowable species. The guide from previous experience comes, as with BSE, from the context, and from the accumulation of experience that in the context in question certain causes seldom or never occur. Thus the researcher is far more likely to look for the cause of the Umbopoland deaths in areas of chemical or viral activity than in the ill-wishing of the Umbopolanders by a neighbouring human community.

Now it is Hume's contention that the Design Argument, or argument from the order of the universe (or the purposes seeable in it) to the theistic nature of its cause, is not at all like the first case—inference from a house to its builder(s). The universe's cause is not a member of a species like *Homo sapiens*, from whose experienced attributes and qualities we can confidently infer more than is evident from the single effect. We simply have no idea what causes of universes are like. To put it another way: Hume argues that, having designated the cause of *this* universe in some way (say as *X*), we know nothing more about *X* than can be inferred from *this* universe. So inference to *X* by means of the Design Argument is not like an ordinary causal inference to a known species. Nor is it like inferring the cause of BSE, where context and comparison with other known diseases and their aetiology suggest that the cause will be found within a certain area, the suggestion then setting up lines of enquiry about future effects: in Hume's terms where, with caution, we can 'mount from the effect to the cause; and descending again from the cause, infer alterations in the effect' (*E* 144). The universe has no 'context' or possibility of comparison with anything beyond itself.[8]

The Design Argument is thus closest to the third case: inferring the cause of a unique human pathology (unique in the sense that it has never before been observed). In both cases it is assumed that the enormous range of events (Hume tends to use the even wider word 'objects') which have causes leads to the presumption that all events ('objects') have causes. Therefore, it is argued, the unique human deaths have *some* cause. And, by parity of reasoning, the (unique) universe has *some* cause.

But even allowing what Hume evidently doubts (see below, pp. 363–4), namely that the same conviction in the universality of causation justifies the postulation of *P*, a cause for the deaths in Umbopoland (a cause *within* the natural system of the universe), and the postulation of *X* (an external cause *of* the natural system of the universe), the guide provided by previous experience is different. As already pointed out, the context of the Umbopoland deaths gives, from previous experience, some indication of the areas in which the cause will probably be found, and gives strong indications of the areas where research will almost certainly be fruitless—the phases of the moon, ill-wishing by a neighbour, and so on. But in the inference to the nature of *X*, the cause or causes of the universe, no guides from general experience are available. To paraphrase Hume again: we have *no* experience of searching for the cause or causes of universes from which we can learn to expect anything about the cause or causes of this one. All we have is the single monocosmic effect to which we apply the

---

[8] Cosmologists do indeed speak of 'other universes', but this is misleading since the reference of such talk is always to *parts* (however large) of what is properly called *the* universe ('universe' from the neuter form of the Latin adjective *universus* used as a noun to mean 'all taken as one' or, more literally, 'turned into one').

supposedly universal principle of causation. The inferred cause is of no known species, and thus has no typical characteristics. It is simply whatever might be sufficient to produce the unique effect. And since the unique effect comprehends everything, the inferred cause explains and predicts no one thing as opposed to any other thing. In fact our degree of understanding of 'the effect' (for example, its internal causes and regularities), remains exactly as it was before X was postulated as its cause.

But are things really as bad as that? Surely X can be put under some sort of genus or species. Thus X as an active intelligent agent or god (an X with theistic characteristics) is supposedly identified by the Design Argument, and 'agents' are a species of entity. Or it might be argued that the search for any X is futile because the universe is an actually infinite temporal regress of physical events admitting no possible cause. Or X might be identified with the Big Bang of modern cosmology as one of several possible naturalistic Xs.

There can be no doubt that in some of his works Hume does give serious attention to radical alternatives to the traditional theistic X supposedly identified by the Design Argument,[9] and in that sense he seems to admit at least the possibility that there might be no X, or that X might be brought under a naturalistic rather than theistic description. But in Section XI of the *Enquiry* his main objective is to restrict inference to any divine author of nature. He is explicit about this: 'Allowing, therefore, the gods to be the authors of the existence or order of the universe; it follows, that they possess that precise degree of power, intelligence, and benevolence, which appears in their workmanship' (*E* 137). It is what follows, not what is allowed, that Hume is so concerned to restrict. Indeed, with the exception of the final page, the whole discussion in Section XI is carried on, not under the presumption that the Design Argument is formally invalid, or that some naturalistic X is to be preferred, but in pursuit of the conclusion that the Design Argument, with its conclusion in terms of a theistic X, is useless; and useless not merely and only in predicting natural phenomena, but also and particularly in accounting for human weal and woe: 'No new fact can ever be inferred from the religious hypothesis; no event foreseen or foretold; no reward or punishment expected or dreaded, beyond what is already known by practice and observation.' (*E* 146). The failure to predict 'new facts' from 'the religious hypothesis' exactly accords with the way in which the cause of the universe has been inferred from the totality of all observed facts in the universe. At most, and in an entirely redundant way, X could be used to predict the discovery of causal relations where at first sight there appear to be none. I say 'redundant' because the same prediction is directly available from an inductively attained principle of universal causation. We are not assisted by having the

---

[9] Note particularly the discussion in Parts VI to VIII of the *Dialogues*.

universality of causation deduced from an entity whose existence is in the first place inferred from that very universality. But it is not the failure of X as a useful hypothesis for the natural scientist which most concerns Hume. What most concerns him is the failure of the Design Argument to permit us to infer in X (when X is identified with God) any concern for individual men and women, any guidance of the affairs of this world, or of the universe at large, i.e. any *providence*, over and above the apparent indifference which we observe. The conclusion Hume implies is most vividly expressed by Philo in Part XI of the *Dialogues concerning Natural Religion*:

The whole presents nothing but the idea of a blind nature, impregnated by a great vivifying principle, and pouring forth from her lap, without discernment or parental care, her maimed and abortive children. . . . The true conclusion is, that the original source of all things is entirely indifferent to all these principles, and has no more regard to good above ill than to heat above cold . . . (*D* 211–12)

In the *Enquiry* Hume's challenge to the evidence for God's (i.e. the theistic X's) providence is forthright. If we do not find 'any marks of a distributive justice in the world' (*E* 141), we cannot *from this world* infer them in the author of nature (any more than we can infer that this world is not 'very faulty and imperfect, compared to a superior standard, and was only the rude essay of some infant deity who afterwards abandoned it, ashamed of his lame performance'; *Dialogues* v, *D* 169). If we find limited marks of distributive justice, then, to the extent warranted by those limited marks and no further, we can infer providence in the author of nature. What is particularly absurd, according to Hume, is finding weal and woe distributed in a morally perverse or random way, and then concluding, from what we *supposedly* know, or believe, about the author of nature, that the apparent perversity or randomness will be compensated in some future state of which we have absolutely no experience, and no assurance beyond the tenuous historical evidence already criticized in 'Of Miracles'.

The last point is worth emphasizing. The knowledge of God's providence, his love, fatherly concern, and justice, comes, for the Christian, from assurances in the scriptures and from the somewhat contorted theology of the Atonement based upon them. That is to say, it comes from precisely those sources whose credentials Hume has just dismissed in 'Of Miracles'. If we take seriously his arguments in that section (as in effect most modern biblical scholarship does), then the Design Argument cannot be augmented by the 'supposed' knowledge of God's providence derived from evidence outside the scope of the Design Argument itself.

Apart from the implied rejection of such external evidence, there is clearly a second (and, I believe, unobjectionable) assumption implicit in Hume's restrictions on inference from the world to a provident God. The assumption—

derived from common experience—is that the world does not display nice or even very general moral providence or 'distributive justice'. In Section XI Hume does not make this assumption explicitly, but it is clear from the tone of the whole discussion that both speakers accept the commonplace that good fortune is distributed in a morally perverse or random way. The perversity is as evident to, for example, the pagan Plautus—'Ye gods, how will the guilty be marked out by you if this is the way you honour the innocent!' (*The Rope* 1. 3)—as to, for example, the writer of Ecclesiastes: 'All things come alike to all: there is *one* event to the righteous, and to the wicked' (9:2, KJV). In short, *from observation of the world and the events of human life alone* it always seems to have been acknowledged that it is not possible to infer a perfect benevolence in the author of nature. But Hume is more precise and radical: it is not possible to infer any degree of benevolence beyond what we actually experience.

I have elsewhere called the point Hume is here making the Inference Problem of Evil in order to distinguish it from the more commonly discussed Consistency Problem of Evil.[10] The Inference Problem is that the nature of the world, taken as something *in toto* by God, inhibits inference to a benevolent providence. He who proportions his belief to the evidence, in the absence of privileged information of the biblical type, and in the absence of predisposing prejudices, is indeed very unlikely to *infer* from the phenomena of the world benevolent providence in its cause. If things were otherwise, the modern cosmologist arguing to a cause of the universe might be expected to argue from the nature of the world to the benevolence or providence of the Big Bang. The most, the very most, that a modern scientist could be justified in claiming as a conclusion from the Big Bang cosmology is that it leads us back to a beginning, which might indeed be called 'the cause of all that is'; but is otherwise utterly and unknowably different from the personal, just, loving, concerned, and participating Deity of advanced Judaism, Christianity, or Islam.

In sum: granted the apparent moral improvidence of human affairs, and granted that no evidence that would convince a 'wise man' is available from scripture, the Inference Problem indentified by Hume in Section XI of the *Enquiry* constitutes a real and serious restriction upon any ascription of providence to 'the author of nature' via the Design Argument.

The Consistency Problem, the other and more usually discussed problem of evil, is concerned with attempting to show that the existence of moral and physical evil in the world is *consistent* with the presumed existence of a provident God. It is very much Hume's concern in Parts X and XI of the *Dialogues concerning Natural Religion*. But there he also reminds us emphatically that,

---

[10] See my *Hume's Philosophy of Religion*, ch. 3. A very much more thorough discussion of the Design Argument than is possible in the present context will also be found in chs. 2 and 7.

while it may be possible to show that the appearances of evil are consistent with belief in a provident God, it is glaringly impossible to *infer* belief in a provident God given the appearances of evil in the world. In the *Enquiry* the force of the Consistency Problem is affirmed more gently, but no less comprehensively: 'Why torture your brain to justify the course of nature upon suppositions, which, for aught you know, may be entirely imaginary, and of which there are to be found no traces in the course of nature?' (*E* 139). Part of the answer to Hume's rhetorical question is that certain views of morality require that God exhibit moral providence towards mankind. Rejection of this view is Hume's other main contention in Section XI. I shall return to it under heading B.

(A2) The Design Argument may be per se Invalid

In the final paragraph of Section XI Hume proposes 'without insisting on' a much more serious difficulty with the Design Argument than the one so far discussed. It is not merely that the inference is limited because the cause of the universe can belong to no known species, but, Hume suggests, causal relations in general can only be established 'when TWO *species* of objects are found to be constantly conjoined' (*E* 148, my capitalization). Since neither the universe nor its cause are species, let alone constantly conjoined species, 'I do not see, that we could form any conjecture or inference at all concerning its cause'. The same difficulty is discussed at greater length in Part II of the *Dialogues*:

> When two *species* of objects have always been observed to be conjoined together, I can *infer*, by custom, the existence of one whenever I *see* the existence of the other: And this I call an argument from experience. But how this argument can have place, where the objects, as in the present case, are single, individual, without parallel, or specific resemblance, may be difficult to explain . . . To ascertain this reasoning, it were requisite, that we had experience of the origin of worlds . . . (*D* 149–50)

The new question is whether a causal relation can hold at all between two objects when *both* of them are unique, and they are *productively conjoined only once*. Surely the answer is yes, if (but only if) we understand 'cause' in a very weak sense as 'whatever has to exist, or to have existed, before what we call the effect could exist or have existed'. We would then be saying that the universe as a whole exists because something else, *X*, exists or has existed in such a way as to produce it. But there are difficulties here. One is provided by Hume himself. If his account of causal relations (given in the *Treatise* and the *Enquiry*) as repeated conjunctions of events is correct, then this one-off relation of 'production' certainly does not qualify as a causal relation. The alleged 'cause' would, in Humean terms, merely be the antecedent of the universe, not something that we could understand as causally related to it in any more informative sense. Another difficulty is that even if we accept the unique conjunction as a 'causal' relation, such a 'causal' relation is purely formal. It tells us nothing. It asserts nothing we can look for or find again. It explains nothing and predicts nothing, being no more than a contentless instance of some version of the universal law of causation. But surely, someone will reply, we can and do talk about, and scientists think they understand, at least one causal statement which concerns precisely the unique object and the unique conjunction Hume is worried about. The cosmologists' Big Bang is the unique productive antecedent related once only to a unique effect which is the universe as a whole. It is, moreover, the currently favoured candidate for what, in the terms I have used, would be called a naturalistic X. It is arrived at via the history of the physical universe as the initial physical cause or primary event. It is, as it were, the vanishing-point into which all causal histories can theoretically be traced, and out of which all emerge. No causal histories beyond those already used to establish it can be inferred from the initial vanishing-point, and all future causal sequences will be no more than the extrapolation into the future of those same causal histories that were used to establish the initial vanishing-point. But this vanishing-point has no assignable qualities. It is no species of thing. Why then is it cosmically interesting, and in a certain respect informative?

Because it is a way of saying that there is empirical evidence that the physical history of the universe had a beginning (as opposed to being infinite, as the ancient Greeks usually supposed). But, it will be noticed, at this stage nothing whatever has been established about the existence or nature of a God. 'God' is not a redundant name for the vanishing-point of the physical universe. 'God' in the great religions of the world is the name of what is claimed to be a unique entity with qualities (particularly providential ones) above and beyond that of being the vanishing-point of physical histories. But even if it is agreed that God and the Big Bang are not identical, why should we accept Hume's argument that the 'religious hypothesis' of a God is useless, in the sense that it can tell us nothing new about the phenomena from which it is inferred, and then *not* accept that Hume's argument applies to such a naturalistic hypothesis as the Big Bang?

I cannot develop a full reply here, but I think the basic move must be an attempt to distinguish external and internal causes, and then to argue that the naturalistic Big Bang is an internal cause, while the theistic God is an external 'cause': talk of internal causes being within our understanding, talk of an external 'cause' being an illicit transplant of the word to areas where it cannot be applied with the same understanding. The argument in outline would be as follows.

A statement about the internal development of the universe, even if it contains or appears to contain statements about the origin of a unique collection of objects such as all there is, is arrived at by extrapolation from known regularities which are themselves derived from repeated or repeatable observations. A statement about the external origin of the universe is not arrived at in this way. Thus, the cosmologists' conclusions about the origins of the universe as a whole must, and do, depend upon extrapolations from known scientific regularities, for example from the speed of light or the calculated rate of expansion of the observable universe. I say 'must' because if they do not, then any one hypothesis, Big Bang, continuous creation of matter, or the cyclic cosmos of the Stoics, will not, for scientists, be differently supported from any other hypothesis. In this way, although the universe is a unique object, the scientists' accounts of its origins are generated from within it by extrapolation from regularities which are far from unique. This is what distinguishes a seriously presented scientific cosmology from a religious account of the origin of the universe. The latter is given in terms of an external 'cause'—God, the great spider (*D* 180), or whatever—which *does* make the universe a unique effect in just that sense which entitled Hume to distinguish it as 'not comprehended under any known *species*', and to conclude that we cannot 'form any conjecture or inference at all concerning its cause' (*E* 148). What Hume is saying, surely correctly in this context, is that the Design Argument, because it leads to an external or transcendent object as the 'cause' (special sense) of the universe, employs the familiar and experience-based concept of cause (normal sense) in a meaningless way. The theistic God is a transcendent entity, not identical with the naturalistic Big Bang, not accessible like the Big Bang via the history of the physical universe, and not providing well-evidenced assurance that the physical history of the universe had a beginning. In short, and in contrast to naturalistic accounts of the origin of the universe, in Hume's terms, God is a useless hypothesis.

(B) The Denial of God's Providence and of an Afterlife does not Undermine Social Morality

There are really two claims to be established here: the first apparently innocuous, the second fundamental. Both point in the end to the same practical problem. The first follows directly from Hume's discussion of the limited inference possible in using the Design Argument. It is that if recourse to the Design Argument does not establish, on a sound basis, the moral providence of the author of nature, then criticism of the argument (criticism of at least that aspect of philosophical religion) cannot be damaging to morality on any view. You cannot damage *Y* by attacking *Z* if *Y* is in no way derivable from *Z*. In general 'the political [i.e. moral and social] interests of society' have no 'connexion with the philosophical disputes concerning metaphysics and religion' (*E* 147).

But this is somewhat disingenuous. All that has really been established is that finding fault with the Design Argument cannot damage whatever dependence on God's providence morality might be supposed to have. But there could still be other 'philosophical disputes' capable of damaging the dependence of morality on religion *if there is any such dependence*. That there is no such dependence is Hume's fundamental claim. However, before turning to it, note that if the members of a society believe (even falsely) that the Design Argument establishes the providence of God, and further believe (even falsely) that the providence of God is one of the necessary conditions for a coherent morality, then any effective criticism of the Design Argument could, in practice, damage people's adherence to morality. Hume might here answer, and might well answer, that irrespective of such practicalities the wise man will not be guided in his policy by errors like supposing that the Design Argument provides worthwhile evidence for the providence of God. But not all of us are wise. That is part of the practical problem which Hume's second and fundamental claim exacerbates.

His fundamental claim is that the 'wise magistrate' reasons falsely if he thinks that 'certain tenets of philosophy, such as those of EPICURUS' that deny 'a divine existence, and consequently a providence and a future state' loosen the ties of morality (*E* 133–4). In the *Enquiry* (mainly *E* 140–1) the uncoupling of morality from religious suppositions is done in a very summary fashion. It consists mainly in an affirmation of certain features of our experience which serve the objectives of morality irrespective of religious beliefs or truths:

I acknowledge, that, in the present order of things, virtue is attended with more peace of mind than vice, and meets with a more favourable reception from the world. I am sensible, that, according to the past experience of mankind, friendship is the chief joy of human life, and moderation the only source of tranquillity and happiness. I never balance between the virtuous and the vicious course of life; but am sensible, that, to a well-disposed mind, every advantage is on the side of the former. (*E* 140)

Let us unpack this further. It is at least arguable that a distinction can be made between moral principles (rules or action-guiding general principles that state what ought to be done) and the reasons or motives that induce us to do what ought to be done. The moral principles may be arrived at in a variety of ways. For example, they may be seen as the outcome of the historical accumulation of experience that certain actions are better, more conducive to general welfare and happiness, than their contraries. Thus promise-keeping is better than promise-breaking, respect for life is better than murder, and so on. Now the question arises: when adhering to a moral principle is contrary to my selfish calculations or inclinations, what is there to interest me in adhering to it? Hume gives a very limited version of his answer in the passage from the *Enquiry* just quoted. In the *Enquiry concerning the Principles of Morals* (the second *Enquiry*) he takes the matter very much further. Apart from his utilitarian analysis of the way in which we arrive at and justify the principles of morals, the second *Enquiry* contains an account of what Hume calls the '*interested* obligation' of virtue (*E* 278).

This interested obligation is the natural (in the sense of commonly found) and normally operating conjunction of influences which relates our own best interests to the 'political' interests of society. It is a combination of many factors: our participation in the feelings of others through sympathy or fellow feeling, our concern to be well thought of in society and live at ease with ourselves and others, our aversion to criminal punishment and disgrace, our calculation of our own interest in the sense that there are occasions when my interest in seeing that other people observe a moral code towards me can only be served by my observing a similar code towards them, and so on. In short, according to Hume, moral principles enshrine what is perceived to be conducive to happiness for individuals, and to usefulness for society; observing these principles accords with a man's best interests, and is in harmony with his normal personality. On this showing, morality is social, utilitarian, and secular. There is no reference to the providence of God or the rewards and punishments of an afterlife.

Now it is this sort of analysis of the nature of morality which provides the more substantial backing to Hume's position than is evident in Section XI of the *Enquiry* taken in isolation. His completed position is that morality has a social and practical source which is sufficient for its purposes, and which depends upon neither the dubious and obscure functioning of God's providence nor the rewards and punishments of a future life for its (interested) obligation.

There is of course a practical problem here, and it is the one already noted. Even if the principles of social morality can be arrived at, and our interested obligation in observing them felt and understood, without reference to God or the afterlife, if some people *believe* in God's providence or *believe* in an afterlife, then such religious beliefs will *in practice* augment the 'interested obligation' to virtue for those people. Hume himself makes the point with vigour and clarity towards the end of Section XI:

You conclude, that religious doctrines and reasonings *can* have no influence on life, because they *ought* to have no influence; never considering, that men reason not in the same manner you do, but draw many consequences from the belief of a divine Existence, and suppose that the Deity will inflict punishments on vice, and bestow rewards on virtue, beyond what appear in the ordinary course of nature. Whether this reasoning of theirs be just or not, is no matter. Its influence on their life and conduct must still be the same. And those, who attempt to disabuse them of such prejudices, may, for aught I know, be good reasoners, but I cannot allow them to be good citizens and politicians; since they free men from one restraint upon their passions, and make the infringement of the laws of society, in one respect, more easy and secure. (*E* 147)

In the *Enquiry* Hume offers no direct reply to this beyond a plea for toleration even of apparently subversive philosophical ideas which, unlike religion's, are 'not very alluring to the people'. But he does reply in the last part of the *Dialogues concerning Natural Religion*. There, Cleanthes, who defends the reasonableness of belief in God, is made to remark, 'For if finite and temporary rewards and punishments have so great an effect, as we daily find: How much greater must be expected from such as are infinite and eternal?' To which Philo, the sceptic, replies two paragraphs later:

> Your reasonings are more easily eluded than my facts. The inference is not just, because finite and temporary rewards and punishments have so great influence, that therefore such as are infinite and eternal must have so much greater. Consider, I beseech you, the attachment, which we have to present things, and the little concern which we discover for objects so remote and uncertain. (*D* 220)

It is sometimes said that Hume discounts the hopes and fears of a future life because he himself rejects the possibility of such a life:[11] religious doctrines 'can have no influence on life, because they *ought* to have no influence'. But his actual position is that religious doctrines *ought* to have influence on life, but *in practice* have very little. The reason Hume identifies for this is the remoteness and uncertainty of the future life. He might also have cited the point made by that remarkable Roman emperor Julianus Caesar (Julian the Apostate) that Christianity *weakens* the obligations of social morality by holding ever available the promise of absolution to square the account, whatever one has done, providing only that the sinner is truly repentant, the absolution being available again and again after each new transgression (provided there is true repentance).

Hume's comments in the *Enquiry* on the relation between morality and religion are thus radical, but incompletely developed. His full thesis is (*a*) that since the Design Argument does not establish the providence of God, criticism of it cannot disturb the obligations of morality even if these do depend on divine providence; (*b*) that anyway the important sources of obligations to morality do *not* depend upon divine providence here and now (which in our experience is obscure and limited, if it exists at all), or upon retributive providence later and hereafter (which is remote and uncertain, and totally without foundation in our experience); (*c*) finally, and irrespective of (*a*) and (*b*), philosophical speculation will never damage the interests of society because it only influences 'the learned and wise' (*E* 133) and 'there is no enthusiasm [roughly, "fanaticism"] among philosophers' (*E* 147). The plea for toleration is the more understandable

---

[11] There is overwhelming circumstantial and direct evidence that Hume identified with Epicurean unbelief concerning an afterlife. See in particular Boswell's account of his last interview with Hume, reprinted at *D* 76–9.

when we remember that although his account of secular morality saw the light of print in the polished and urbane second *Enquiry*, his thoughts on immortality and on suicide were suppressed, and his full-scale attack on the Design Argument did not appear until after his death.[12]

I first read 'Of a Particular Providence and of a Future State' in defiance and in hope: in defiance of an Oxford whose fastidious philosophy seemed designed to avoid first-order moral or political or religious issues, and in hope of finding arguments to resolve the issue between religion and atheism. The defiance has been justified by subsequent changes in the concerns of philosophy. The hopes were, at the time, disappointed. Hume's arguments at first reading seem on a level of abstraction far removed from any personal commitment to religion. The section's radical consequences for social morality and religion are easily missed, and the Augustan style and quasi-dialogue form deliberately obscure Hume's subversive purposes. What is more, it was and remains all too easy to be misguided by Selby-Bigge's Introduction (*E* xix) and to see both 'Of Miracles' and Section XI as intruded chapters which form no coherent part of the main philosophical plot of the *Enquiry*.

I now believe that my original hopes were indeed justified. 'Of a Particular Providence and of a Future State' contains at least some arguments good enough to shake and go on shaking 'the chief or sole argument for a divine existence'. Its attempts to separate religion from philosophy, and social morality from religion, are both salutary. As a whole the section foreshadows Hume's formidable assault upon any reasoned commitment to religion—the assault carried out in the second *Enquiry*, the *Dialogues*, the *Natural History of Religion*, and the suppressed essays of 1757 ('Of Suicide' and 'Of the Immortality of the Soul'). Within the confines of the *Enquiry* itself the section, with its predecessor, 'Of Miracles', is an integral part of the sceptical enterprise; so much so that Selby-Bigge's judgement must be reversed. He should have written: 'Their insertion into the *Enquiry* is a fundamental application of the main principles employed throughout the work. Excise them, and you have an emasculated work of abstract sceptical epistemology. Include them, and the revolutionary application, and real, practical focus of the whole, is apparent.'

---

[12] The essay 'Of the Immortality of the Soul' (together with the essay 'Of Suicide') was to have appeared in the volume eventually published in 1757 as *Four Dissertations*. But Hume, alarmed at the risks involved in publishing such pieces, withdrew them before publication. For the text of both essays as finally corrected by Hume, see my *Varieties of Unbelief, from Epicurus to Sartre* (New York: MacMillan, 1989). Hume died in 1776. The *Dialogues*, having been first written in the 1750s, were not published until 1779.

14

Of the Academical or Sceptical Philosophy

David Fate Norton

I

At the beginning of Section V of the *Enquiry concerning Human Understanding* Hume expresses his admiration for the academical or sceptical philosophy. This species of philosophy has, he says, a clear advantage over all other kinds: by its very nature it protects those who adopt it from the excesses that are characteristic of alternative forms of philosophy. The academic sceptic, noting the dangers of hasty and dogmatic judgement, emphasizes continually the advantages of 'doubt and suspence of judgment . . . of confining to very narrow bounds the enquiries of the understanding, and of renouncing all speculations which lie not within the limits of common life and practice'. In this way these sceptics avoid the arrogance, pretension, and credulity of the dogmatists, but their philosophy, because it 'gains few partizans' while yet 'opposing so many vices and follies', is itself left vulnerable to enemies who attack it as 'libertine, profane, and irreligious' (5.1, *E* 41).[1]

As a start, we may read Section XII as a defence of the academic philosophy.[2] Hume begins this defence by pointing out that the critics of scepticism are, very much like some critics of atheism, confused. They cannot decide whether to attack scepticism as harmful and dangerous, or to dismiss it as too ridiculous and untenable to be believed. The obvious thing to do, then, is to try to

---

[1] References are to section and paragraph of *An Enquiry concerning Human Understanding*, ed. T. L. Beauchamp, Oxford Philosophical Texts (Oxford: Oxford University Press, 1999), followed by page numbers of *E*.

[2] The philosophical position that Hume calls the *academical philosophy* and which is now more likely to be referred to as *academic scepticism* is so named because it was first articulated (in the 3rd century BC) at the Academy earlier founded by Plato.

determine 'What is meant by a sceptic? And how far it is possible to push these philosophical principles of doubt and uncertainty?' (12.2, *E* 149). The answer requires that some distinctions be made.

There is, first, *antecedent scepticism*, one extreme and untenable form of which is associated with Descartes, and which we may, falling in with the prevailing oxymoron, call *Cartesian scepticism*. Antecedent scepticism is antecedent in so far as it calls on us, prior to any further use we may make of them, to raise doubts not only about our opinions, but also about the faculties of mind that are responsible for these opinions. According to Hume, a moderate form of antecedent scepticism is a 'necessary preparative to the study of philosophy', for it enables us to set aside ill-founded prejudices and attain a suitable impartiality of judgement. It achieves these salutary ends by requiring us 'To begin with clear and self-evident principles, to advance by timorous and sure steps, to review frequently our conclusions, and examine accurately all their consequences', a simple, but hard-won, method. On the other hand, antecedent scepticism in the form recommended by Descartes (in, notably, his *Meditations*) is simply incoherent and unworkable. It calls for us to question not only all our opinions, but also all our faculties. No faculty of the mind is to be used until we can, by a proper deduction from some obviously unassailable first principle, assure ourselves of its veracity. But, responds Hume, there is in the first place no such obviously unassailable starting-point, and even if there were it would be impossible to deduce anything from it without relying on one or more of those faculties whose use has been suspended until their veracity has been established. Cartesian scepticism is untenable—it calls for us to doubt everything at once, something we clearly cannot do, and from which we would never recover if we could do it. It is also inconsistent—its demands regarding the use of our faculties, particularly our reason, are contradictory (12.2–4, *E* 149–50).

Hume turns next to a species of scepticism that is '*consequent* to science and enquiry', or that arises after it is discovered that our mental faculties are, if not entirely unreliable, noticeably unable to provide us with settled opinions regarding 'all those curious subjects of speculation' which are of common interest. This species of scepticism also appears to come in untenable and tenable forms. Thus one group of philosophers (Hume later identifies these as Pyrrhonians) goes so far as to raise doubts about the senses, and subjects 'the maxims of common life' to doubt no different from that aimed at 'the most profound principles or conclusions of metaphysics and theology' (12.5, *E* 150). As this scepticism is found in at least a few philosophers, and is refuted by even more, it merits further attention.

Very little time is spent on the familiar sceptical arguments ('trite topics') against the senses. Organized by the ancient Greek sceptics into *tropes*, or what one might think of as patterns of procedure, these arguments had focused on the relativity of sense-perceptions: they point out that (what we take to be) the same object may have different appearances at different times, in different circumstances, and to different observers or kinds of observer. According to Hume, these arguments show only that 'the senses alone are not implicitly to be depended on', and that we must correct them (or, more accurately, correct our perceptual judgements) by taking into account those factors (distance, media, disposition of the perceiving organ) which (as we have presumably learned) affect our perception. Once we have done so, the senses, if confined 'within their sphere', function as 'proper *criteria* of truth and falsehood' (12.6, *E* 151).

There are, however, deeper and seemingly unanswerable arguments against the senses; Hume outlines two of these. In the most general terms, these arguments reveal our inability to give a satisfactory account of the causes of our sense-perceptions or of the beliefs we hold about the objects of the senses.

We seem instinctively led, Hume suggests, to trust our senses. So much so that without the least reflection we come to believe that there is an independently existing external world, a world that would exist even if there were no sensible beings to experience it. Even animals seem to share this belief. It also appears that when we fall in with this 'blind and powerful instinct of nature' we suppose that we directly perceive aspects of this independently existing world. If we see a table, we suppose that the eye has presented this table directly to the mind, and not only that the table exists independently of us, but also that it exists exactly as we perceive it. We suppose, as Hume puts it, 'the very images, presented by the senses, to be the external objects'. The ordinary, unreflective person is, in other words, some kind of direct or naive realist about perception and its objects (12.8, *E* 151–2).

It takes but little thought to see that this opinion, however widespread and instinctive it may be, cannot be correct. We can easily be brought to notice, to use Hume's somewhat confusing way of putting the matter, that the table 'which we see, seems to diminish, as we remove farther from it', while 'the real table' undergoes no such change. He means, of course, that our *perception* of the table (the image of it before the mind) alters as we move away from the table, while (presumably) the independently existing object, the table, undergoes no corresponding alteration. But the moment we begin to think like that, the moment we distinguish between an independently existing *object* and our *perception* of that object, we have obviously given up the common-sense view that our senses present external objects to us directly. Our reason has led us to exchange that form of *direct realism* which is the 'universal and primary opinion' of humankind for a very different *representative realism*. We now deny that our sense-impressions are identical with independently existing objects, and say only that these perceptions *represent* these objects, thinking that we will in this way account for perceptual variation and even for perceptual error (12.9, *E* 152).

We find, however, that as a consequence of accepting this seemingly justified change of view we have opened ourselves to a sceptical objection that is both profound and insurmountable. We no longer say that perceptions and objects are identical; the former merely represent the latter. But if this representational account is correct, it then follows that we can never have any direct experience of an object. If the theory is correct, then what we know, what we have before our minds, is never more than the representation of an object. But if all we ever experience are representations, how do we know that there are corresponding objects that are the source of these representations, or, should there be such, that the representations actually resemble the objects that give rise to them? Our situation is something like Dorothy's as she listens to the unseen Wizard of Oz. We receive perceptual messages, but we don't know the reality behind these messages. We don't even know that there *is* anything beyond the message. Perhaps, as George Berkeley had argued, the message is all there is; perhaps the perception is the reality? Unfortunately, we have no Toto to pull aside the curtain and reveal what, if anything, stands behind it. We simply go on seeing and hearing without any hope of directly experiencing whatever lies behind or causes such perceptions. Are they caused by something external that resembles them? Are they merely the result of systematic hallucination? Are they, as Descartes had asked, the effect of a systematic deception by some 'invisible and unknown spirit'? (12.11, *E* 153).

This issue is, as Hume sees, a question of fact or experience. The insurmountable difficulty is that the representative theory of perception, adoption of which is forced upon us by reason and experience, denies access to the relevant experience. If, as that account concludes, our minds never have anything present to them but perceptions, then, given what Hume had earlier shown us about causal connexions, we can see that we shall never be able to establish that any perception is causally dependent on any independently existing object or, for that matter, on any particular cause. Consequently, assuming that the representational theory of perception is correct, we are left without any way of knowing anything about any external and independently existing reality—neither *what* that reality is, nor even *that* it is.[3] On the other hand, should we refuse to adopt the representative theory, clinging to the pre-philosophical view

---

[3] Some philosophers (and Hume again seems to have Descartes and his followers in mind) have attempted to avoid the force of this conclusion by appealing to the 'veracity' of the Deity, but such an appeal is of no philosophical merit. More fundamentally, it begs the question in so far as it assumes what is at issue, namely, whether anything other than experienced perceptions does or does not exist. In addition, the appeal seems inconsistent. If it is argued that we can safely rely on our senses because of the veracity of the supreme Being, why is it that we cannot always rely on them? It won't do to say that we know that we can rely on our senses because God is not a deceiver, for in that event we should always be able to rely on our senses—we should never make perceptual errors of any sort. That, of course, is contrary to fact, and hence it must be that the initial assumption is unsound.

that 'the very perception or sensible image is the external object', we would find ourselves committed to the view that objects, although external, are apparently not independent entities. That is, on the pre-philosophical view, objects appear to change with every change we make (they become smaller, for example, as we move away from them), and hence appear to be entirely unstable entities. Our pre-philosophical realism may derive from 'the instincts and propensities of nature', but it is obviously untenable. As Hume sees it, the sceptic triumphs because we are forced by reason to give up our untenable pre-philosophical theory in favour of another, equally unsatisfactory theory which entails that we will never be able to make a single well-founded claim about the nature or existence of external objects (12.14, *E* 153–4).

Hume treats more briefly the second of the seemingly unanswerable arguments against the senses. He reminds us that modern philosophers such as Descartes and Locke distinguish between those qualities of objects (extension and solidity, for example) that are said to exist in objects themselves, and those sensible qualities (hardness and softness and colour, for example) that are merely 'perceptions of the mind, without any external archetype or model, which they represent'. He argues, following such earlier philosophers as Simon Foucher, Pierre Bayle, and Berkeley, that this commonplace and apparently necessary distinction, widely known as the *primary–secondary quality distinction*, leads to a profoundly sceptical conclusion: The same arguments that establish that our ideas of colour and softness are only mind-dependent ideas of sense will, if uniformly applied, lead to the same conclusion regarding the idea of extension.[4] All ideas are in the mind and all ideas are acquired by the senses. Our idea of extension is wholly dependent upon and thoroughly infected by the ideas of merely 'secondary' qualities. But 'if all the qualities, perceived by the senses, be in the mind, not in the object', then we must also conclude that extension and the other allegedly 'primary' qualities are only in the mind. In short, all qualities, or at least all intelligible qualities, are in the mind. If we accept the arguments of the modern philosophers, the most that we can say about external and independently existing existence, about objects or *matter*, is that there may be 'a certain unknown, inexplicable *something*, as the cause of our perceptions'—a conclusion so 'imperfect', so hesitant, so tenuous, so vague, that no sceptic will bother to challenge it (12.15–16, *E* 154–5).

By their use of these arguments, says Hume, 'the profounder and more philosophical sceptics will always triumph' in their efforts 'to introduce an universal doubt into all subjects of human knowledge and enquiry'. The first argument leaves us to wonder about the reality of external existence by pitting reason

---

[4] Hume here uses *idea* in the wider sense in which it is used by Descartes and Locke, a sense that is equivalent to the term *perception* as this is understood in Section II of the *Enquiry*.

against natural instinct. The second achieves the same effect by showing that belief in external objects is contrary to reason. No sceptic need labour to improve on these results. None the less, we must be careful not to exaggerate the advantage Hume is prepared to concede to the sceptic who would use these arguments against the senses. These arguments, like Berkeley's notorious argument against the existence of matter (indeed, the second is an abbreviated version of Berkeley's argument), may produce a 'momentary amazement and irresolution and confusion'. But they by no means *convince* us of their sceptical conclusions. These arguments may well leave us at a philosophical loss in so far as they leave us wondering how to justify an unabated belief in external objects, but they are not, as we shall see, the central components of the academic scepticism Hume has undertaken to explain and defend (12.14, n. 32; *E* 153–4, 155 n.).

In the second part of Section XII Hume makes still further distinctions. Just as the objects of human enquiry may be divided into two kinds, *relations of ideas* and *matters of fact* (4.1, *E* 25), so does sceptical activity divide along these same lines. The sceptic who would undercut our confidence in our ability to reason abstractly (to reason only about the relations of ideas) will focus on problems that arise from an analysis of our ideas of space and time. In ordinary circumstances, these ideas seem 'very clear and intelligible', but when they are examined more closely they appear, by the 'clearest and most natural' reasoning, to entail conclusions 'which seem full of absurdity and contradiction' and which shock our common sense. Any quantity of extended matter, no matter how minute, even if 'infinitely less' than some other quantity of matter, may, our reason tells us, be infinitely divided. Moreover, these new infinitesimals (a term Hume does not use) can be infinitely divided into still smaller ones, and so on *in infinitum*. The situation with time is, if possible, even more puzzling. Any moment of time, no matter how brief, may be infinitely divided into further moments, leaving us to wonder how an 'infinite number of real parts of time', requiring, presumably, an infinite (and therefore inexhaustible) number of moments, could ever have passed (12.18–19, *E* 156–7). And yet we must grant that an infinite number of such inexhaustible moments has already passed. Shall we not grow old waiting for a single moment to pass? How much confidence can we have in a faculty that, starting with something everyone appears to understand, lands us in such a muddle?

The sceptic, it seems, can triumph without even turning up for the contest. Reason has confounded and amazed herself, and shown her inability to 'pronounce with certainty and assurance' concerning any subject. Once again, however, the sceptic is brought up short. If our reason is so dubious a tool, or if in our clear and intelligible ideas it finds implications that are 'absolutely incomprehensible . . . as absurd as any proposition, which can be formed', then we must indeed be diffident about our reason. But then the scepticism that arises so naturally from the paradoxical conclusions of our abstract reasoning must itself be 'full of doubt and hesitation'; it is a scepticism that must distrust its own conclusions and remain sceptical even about itself (12.18, 20; *E* 156–8).

Continuing his ever-lengthening catalogue, Hume next turns to scepticism regarding matters of fact, and immediately distinguishes between *popular* and *philosophical* versions thereof. His comments about the latter, sandwiched between two slightly longer comments about the former, are brief: Hume recommends that the sceptic base his attack on reasoning about matters of fact on a linked set of arguments derived from some of our 'more profound researches'. The sceptic could begin by showing us that our evidence for any matter of fact of which we have had no experience depends entirely on the relation of cause and effect. He could then show that the relation of cause and effect itself depends upon experience. And he could conclude by showing us that it is only 'custom or a certain instinct . . . which, like other instincts, may be fallacious and deceitful' that leads us to believe similar objects have been or will be similarly conjoined in instances not experienced. These arguments, Hume says, forcefully demonstrate the limitations of our factual reasoning (including that of the sceptic), and 'might be displayed at greater length, if any durable good or benefit to society could ever be expected to result from them' (12.22, *E* 159). As Sections IV–VII of the first *Enquiry* are in fact devoted to displaying just these arguments at very considerable length, it seems safe to conclude that Hume imagined that the sceptical analyses constituting these earlier sections might well have durable and beneficial effects. I return to this point later.

About the *popular* objections to factual reasoning Hume has, initially, nothing positive to say. Associating these objections with 'Pyrrhonism or the excessive principles of scepticism' (probably because he supposed they were intended to lead us to suspend belief in matters of fact by establishing the 'natural weakness of human understanding'), Hume insists that this kind of scepticism is simply powerless before our natural, everyday reactions. It is easy enough for the Pyrrhonian to pass before us the vast and contradictory variety of human opinion, and to derive from this variety doubts about both factual reasoning and matters of fact themselves. But though these doubts may flourish in the sheltered environment of the philosophical schools, the moment such theoretical doubts are removed from this artificial environment and come face to face with 'real objects', they 'vanish like smoke, and leave the most determined sceptic in the same condition as other mortals'. In the presence of the real world the Pyrrhonian cannot help but become a believer in objects, causal connexions, other minds—in the entire shipment of common-sense freight. And well it is for humanity that this should be the case. Were such excessive scepticism to be adopted and consistently maintained, it would destroy human life; were Pyrrhonism to prevail, humanity would perish: 'All discourse, all action would immediately cease; and men remain in a total lethargy, till the necessities of nature, unsatisfied, put an end to their miserable existence' (12.21, 23; *E* 158–60).

Pyrrhonism as propounded by the Pyrrhonians is neither durable, nor beneficial, and, both because our nature is too strong for it and because it would destroy life if it were to prevail, it cannot be lived. It does not follow, however, that Hume finds Pyrrhonism to be without value. After reminding us once again of the obstinately and even violently dogmatical character of the 'greater part of mankind', Hume goes on to suggest that an acquaintance with Pyrrhonism would have a salutary effect on all 'dogmatical reasoners', illiterate or learned, for it would reveal to the former the 'strange infirmities of human understanding', and remind the latter that their advantages over the ignorant 'are but inconsiderable, if compared with the universal perplexity and confusion, which is inherent in human nature'. In brief, a moderate dose of Pyrrhonian doubt should clear the system of false confidence, and prepare it to accept the first rule of Hume's scepticism: Be prepared to doubt, be cautious, be modest. In his own words, 'there is a degree of doubt, and caution, and modesty, which, in all kinds of scrutiny and decision, *ought* for ever to accompany a just reasoner' (12.24, *E* 161–2, my emphasis).

Hume's academic scepticism also enjoins us to stick to our proper business— enjoins us, that is, to limit 'our enquiries to such subjects as are best adapted to the narrow capacity of human understanding'. The human imagination, uncontrolled, runs wild in its search for new and exciting matters on which to speculate, and new gods, even philosophical gods, to adulate. In contrast, a correctly disciplined mind leaves all such lofty marvels to poets and priests and politicians, and restricts itself to the study of those matters of which we have had experience. 'To bring us to so salutary a determination, nothing can be more serviceable, than to be once thoroughly convinced of the force of the PYRRHON-IAN doubt, and of the impossibility, that any thing, but the strong power of natural instinct, could free us from it.' Having come to this understanding, we may well choose to indulge our propensity for philosophy (whether natural or moral), but we will not be tempted to engage in speculations that carry us beyond the range of experience. As long as 'we cannot give a satisfactory reason, why we believe, after a thousand experiments, that a stone will fall, or fire burn; can we ever satisfy ourselves concerning any determination, which we may form, with regard to the origin of worlds, and the situation of nature, from, and to eternity?' (12.25, *E* 162).

II

What, Hume asks, is meant by *sceptic*? As we have seen, he answers his own question by means of an annotated catalogue of the types or species of scepticism. In the course of this discussion there are explicit references to *antecedent* and to *consequent* scepticism; the former has both a *Cartesian* and a *moderate* form. There are equally explicit references to *academic*, to *Pyrrhonian*, and to *mitigated* scepticism, while some sceptical arguments are denominated *popular*, and others *philosophical*. The term *sceptic*, it seems, means substantively different things and, despite the comprehensiveness of Hume's discussion, it is difficult to say just how many species of scepticism have been identified. The difficulty arises from the fact that the several categories overlap—the scepticism Hume defends appears to be a mitigated and philosophical version of consequent scepticism, the effect of which will be to make its adherents moderate antecedent sceptics as well. Fortunately, deciding precisely how many *distinct* species of scepticism there are (or how many Hume supposes there are) seems not to be of pressing importance.

But Hume's answer to the second of his original questions—'how far it is possible to push these philosophical principles of doubt and uncertainty?' (12.2, *E* 149)—is important. From the discussion found in Section XII one can readily conclude that there is nothing, no substantive matter and no faculty, that some sceptic has not doubted or tried to doubt. Hume, however, has countered this popular view of the sceptic as one who doubts anything and everything by pointing out that some 'principles of doubt and uncertainty' are untenable or ineffective. Descartes's version of antecedent scepticism, for example, counsels an impossible doubt (doubt everything at once and continue to do so until a foundation of knowledge is found), which, once entered into, could not be escaped. The familiar arguments (those regarding sense variations) of certain consequent sceptics are too trivial to merit attention. The more profound consequent sceptic can adduce insurmountable arguments showing us that we know nothing about the nature of external objects, and even that there may be no such objects, but these sceptical arguments, although they cannot be answered, produce no conviction, and are of only momentary effect and no durable good. Similarly, the doubts the Pyrrhonians direct at the objects of common life are as evanescent as smoke, and, fortunately for us, of no effect as far as our belief in those objects is concerned. And even those sceptics of whom Hume speaks positively are warned: every sceptic must recognize that even his most significant doubts are the product of the very faculties he has criticized as weak and unreliable.

And yet Hume continues to recommend scepticism and doubt. The academic sceptics, who themselves emphasize the advantages of 'doubt and suspence of judgment', are presented as model philosophers (5.1, *E* 41). Academic scepticism is found to be both durable and useful. We are told that there is a degree of doubt that ought to be standard equipment for every enquirer. How are we to reconcile these remarks, how fit Hume's criticisms and recommendations into a coherent defence of scepticism? We can do so by placing Hume's distinctions between *kinds of doubt* in the wider context of two contrasting accounts of belief and doubt.

The two accounts are those of Descartes's *Meditations*, and Hume's own. Descartes, apparently concerned about the state of learning in general and about the reliability of his own beliefs, hit upon his now famous method of doubt. Consider any belief, any claim whatsoever, Descartes said. Is it conceivable that this belief could be false? If not, if the belief is indubitable, it may be accepted as true. But if the belief *could* be false, it is to be taken to *be* false. 'Anything which admits of the slightest doubt', says Descartes, 'I will set aside just as if I had found it to be wholly false.'[5] It was in this manner that Descartes considered his beliefs about the existence and nature of physical objects, mathematical propositions, and even the existence of God. About each such kind of belief he finds some possible flaw, some reason to think that kind of belief could be false, and so, exercising his will, he treats all beliefs of these several kinds as false.

In one of his explanations of his enterprise Descartes compares his method with the actions of a person who is concerned that his entire basket of apples may spoil because some of his apples are already rotten. It is perfectly understandable, he says, that such a person would tip all the apples out of the basket, so that he could inspect each in turn, and return only sound apples to the basket.[6] In fact, Descartes's method is more radical than this comparison suggests. He is more nearly like a person who, concerned about the state of his apples, discards not merely those that are spoiled, but also those that could spoil. Of course Descartes has also generalized his procedure: he does not have to inspect each belief individually because he applies his method of doubt to the very faculties that produce belief—to the senses, to reason, and to consciousness itself. Having thus made matters doubly easier (he need find only one doubtful belief of each type), he is poised to cast off every belief and every faculty. It is as if the apple inspector, having noticed that some coloured fruit of determinate shape has spoiled, decided to discard all his apples because they too, being coloured fruit of a determinate shape, could spoil.

Descartes's antecedent scepticism, then, takes any belief that is not perfectly indubitable to be false. This suggests that Descartes supposes that belief and doubt are in one important sense incompatible, a suggestion confirmed by his account of error. Many people hold common-sense beliefs that Descartes takes

    [5] *Meditations on First Philosophy*, in *The Philosophical Writings of Descartes*, trans. J. Cottingham, R. Stoothoff, D. Murdoch, and A. Kenny, 3 vols. (Cambridge: Cambridge University Press, 1984), ii. 16; cited hereafter as *Meditations*.

    [6] Seventh Set of Objections and Replies, in *The Philosophical Writings of Descartes*, ii. 324.

to be false (many people believe, for example, that apples are really coloured, whereas Descartes argues that colour is not a quality of apples themselves), but, although we owe our existence and our faculties to God, he insists that God is not to be blamed for the fact that these erroneous beliefs are held. God is not responsible for our errors, no matter how natural these may seem, because he has given us a faculty of *judgement*, or a faculty by which we may control the *will*, and it is this latter faculty that is immediately responsible for our beliefs. Error arises only because we allow our will to outrun this faculty of judgement and to cause us to believe before truth has been established. If we put our minds to it, if we rigorously exercise our will, we can avoid believing anything that can be doubted, anything that we do not yet know to be true.

The sense in which Descartes suggests that belief and doubt are incompatible is now clear. On his account, it is clearly not possible for someone to doubt something and at the same time claim that she cannot avoid believing (or believing in) that same thing. On this account of the matter to say that one *doubts P* is just to say that one *disbelieves P*, or that, either involuntarily or voluntarily, one has come to the conclusion that *P* is false. On the other hand, when one's understanding has supplied one with a clear and distinct idea of something, one then has justification for ceasing to doubt or to withhold assent—justification for, in other words, allowing oneself to believe about this particular matter. In short, Descartes suggests that individuals can exercise complete control over any belief that is not founded on perfect knowledge itself. Consequently, he can argue that an individual should permit belief only when he or she has such knowledge: 'If, however, I simply refrain from making a judgement in cases where I do not perceive the truth with sufficient clarity and distinctness, then it is clear that I am behaving correctly and avoiding error.' To believe in the absence of knowledge is to permit the relatively powerful will to overrun the weaker understanding and to lay oneself open to the possibility of error. It is also in itself blameworthy. Even if, lacking knowledge, I by accident 'arrive at the truth . . . I shall still be at fault since it is clear by the natural light that the perception of the intellect should always precede the determination of the will'.[7]

Two further and closely related features of this account are relevant here. According to the *Meditations*, there can never be, once one has attained grounds for legitimate belief, any need to continue to doubt. If the preconditions of responsible belief have been met, there can be no further grounds for withholding assent or for any form of restraint. Belief is justified only when knowledge is perfect, but knowledge can be perfect, and when it is one need not restrain one's

---

[7] *Meditations*, ii. 41.

commitment. Neither hesitation nor even modesty is required. Moreover, once one does have knowledge of any particular matter, further doubt about that matter is in fact impossible. That which is known is, according to Descartes, indubitable. Knowledge not only makes doubt unnecessary, but also makes it impossible. As Descartes puts it, 'Whatever is revealed to me by the natural light—for example that from the fact that I am doubting it follows that I exist, and so on—cannot in any way be open to doubt.'[8]

Hume's account of these matters is significantly different. For one thing, he maintains that belief is proximately involuntary. In Hume's view, belief arises as a consequence of what he characterizes as natural causes and not as the result of an act of the will. We can wilfully join or separate ideas (the units of thought, as it were), and these wilful acts may indirectly influence our beliefs, but the proximate and direct causes of beliefs are outside our immediate control. 'Nothing is more free than the imagination of man', he writes, and though the imagination cannot of itself produce entirely new ideas, it has an 'unlimited power of mixing, compounding, separating, and dividing' ideas and 'can feign a train of events, with all the appearance of reality . . . that belongs to any historical fact, which it believes with the greatest certainty' (5.10, E 47).[9] There is, however, an essential difference between even the most credible *fiction* (a feigned or imagined idea or sequence of ideas) and a *belief*. Nor does this difference depend on some distinctive idea which, when added to a fiction, causes the resulting mixture to command our assent. If that were the case, we could believe at will; if that were the case we could believe simply by adding this distinctive idea to any other idea that came to mind. On the contrary, the difference between fictional conceptions not believed, and any conception that is believed or that 'commands our assent', depends on

some sentiment or feeling, which is annexed to the latter, not to the former, and which depends not on the will, nor can be commanded at pleasure. *It must be excited by nature, like all other sentiments; and must arise from the particular situation, in which the mind is placed at any particular juncture.* Whenever any object is presented to the memory or senses, it immediately, by the force of custom, carries the imagination to conceive that

---

[8] *Meditations*, ii. 27.

[9] In his *Treatise* Hume argues that the word *relation* is used in two very different senses. There are *natural* relations, or instances of one idea (or perception) 'naturally' introducing another, and *philosophical* relations, or instances of 'the arbitrary union of two ideas in the fancy' whenever 'we may think proper to compare them' (1.1.5.1, i.e. Book 1 Part 1 Sect. 5 para. 1 of *A Treatise of Human Nature*, ed. D. F. and M. J. Norton, Oxford Philosophical Texts (Oxford: Oxford University Press, 2000); *T* 13). The freedom of the imagination spoken of in the first *Enquiry* is the freedom to consider a wide range of philosophical relations and their negations. Although Hume does not seem explicitly to have said so, he apparently supposes that the philosophical doubt which he recommends is made possible by our imaginative freedom, and is, in fact, constituted by some particular forms which the exercise of this freedom may take.

object, which is usually conjoined to it; and this conception is attended with a feeling or sentiment, different from the loose reveries of the fancy. In this consists the whole nature of belief. (5.11, *E* 48, my emphasis)[10]

Hume is also content that we should believe on grounds other than the one singled out in the *Meditations*, namely, the possession of indubitable knowledge. Indeed, it is an obvious implication of the account of belief just sketched that we will have a great many unjustified beliefs. We simply cannot respect the philosopher's injunction that we should refrain from believing until we have the perfect illumination provided by an infallible natural light. Even many apparently unavoidable beliefs appear to be unjustified. According to Hume, we find it impossible not to believe that there are independently existing objects or that particular causes will in the future be followed by the same effects that have followed them in the past, and yet, as we have already seen, these beliefs cannot be rationally justified.

On Hume's account, then, there are beliefs that are both unavoidable and unjustified. Consequently, there may also be beliefs that are both unavoidable and false; even the most stubborn or ineradicable, the most *natural*, of our beliefs may be false, although there may be virtually no likelihood of establishing that falsity. The persistent strength—the indubitability—of a belief is of itself not proof, nor even evidence, that the belief is true. In short, Hume has driven an unexpected wedge between belief and truth. It is not just that I can doubt the veracity of your beliefs, whatever those may be; I can, and according to Hume, I should, doubt my own beliefs.

These conclusions leave us, however, with some serious questions. Hume argues that belief is fundamentally involuntary. What then are we to make of his injunctions to doubt? Is it really up to us? How can we doubt beliefs that may be forced upon us against our wills even as we hold those same beliefs?

The answer to these questions lies, ultimately, in Hume's account of the imagination. As we have already seen, Hume ascribes to this faculty the 'unlimited power of mixing, compounding, separating, and dividing' ideas. It is this voluntary facility that enables us to doubt as Hume enjoins. Circumstances and custom cause our ideas to be accompanied with that particular feeling called belief, but we none the less retain the ability to entertain, at least on occasion, any manner of possibility, including possibilities that are contrary to our expectations and beliefs. Custom and the propensities of the imagination lead us to the conviction that the sun will certainly rise again tomorrow. But that same

---

[10] Hume's discussion of belief in the *Enquiry*, and particularly that found in Section V, is focused on the belief that characterizes causal inference, or a process that involves the transfer of attention from a present impression to an associated idea. His *Treatise* (see esp. 1.3.4–10 and App. 2–9, *T* 82–123 and 623–9) and *Abstract* (paras. 17–25, *A* 649–56) provide the more generalized account of belief outlined here.

imagination, in a more reflective mode, can conceive the contrary of this conviction, and even discover that, whatever its psychological force, the conviction is epistemologically suspect. Hume, contradicting the claim of Descartes's *Meditations*, insists that belief is involuntary. Doubt, however—doubt in a form Hume supposes to be both viable and valuable—is voluntary.

This last may seem a surprising possibility. Certainly it has not occurred to a host of philosophers who have undertaken to refute scepticism, *all* scepticism, by pointing out that the sceptic cannot *live* his doubts: sooner rather than later, this argument goes, the sceptic himself, although he urges us to doubt, will find that he cannot maintain his own doubt. He will, willy-nilly, jump out of the paths of onrushing vehicles, he will eat the food on the table, he will go out the door and not the window (see *D* 132). But those who have claimed to refute the sceptic in this way have not noticed that, in counselling doubt, the sceptic need not be aiming to put us in a state of mind characterized by some form of palpable uncertainty or puzzlement (a distinctive psychological state), or even to lead us to adopt an attitude or disposition characterized by suspension of belief about such common things as vehicles, tables, and doors. The sceptic may, as Hume certainly did, recommend doubt of a significantly different form: he may recommend what may be aptly called *philosophical* (in contrast to *psychological*) doubt.

The form of doubt that Hume recommends may be understood as a cognitive activity or as a philosophical method. When Hume speaks positively about the moderate form of antecedent scepticism, he represents this as a 'necessary preparative', a method of enquiry that calls for us 'To begin with clear and self-evident principles, to advance by timorous and sure steps, to review frequently our conclusions, and [to] examine accurately all their consequences' (12.4, *E* 150). The '*mitigated* scepticism, or ACADEMICAL philosophy' (12.24, *E* 161) he recommends is very similar. It calls for us to use one form of our imaginative freedom, reflective reason, to challenge our beliefs, even those beliefs that appear most natural or are most cherished. We are to *doubt*: that is, we are to attend to the counter-evidence and counter-arguments; we are to avoid precipitate decisions on the issues before us; we are to take note of the inherent limitations on our faculties; we are to confine our enquiries to those subjects of which we have had, or can yet have, experience.[11] It is not intended, however, that this

---

[11] By now it will be clear that Hume distinguishes between the suspension of *belief*, that impossible task urged on us (so he thought) by the Pyrrhonians, and the suspension of *judgement* (which includes avoidance of the precipitate decisions just mentioned) recommended by the academics. But that Hume thought the suspension of judgement possible does not mean that he thought it equally likely at every moment. In the final paragraph of Book I of the *Treatise* he says that it is not only proper that 'we shou'd in general indulge our inclination in the most elaborate philosophical researches, notwithstanding our sceptical principles, but also that we shou'd yield to that propensity, which inclines us to be positive and

philosophical doubt should turn us into neurotics forever having bones set because we do not know what to believe about oncoming traffic. Hume himself is clear about this. There is, he says, no danger that *philosophical* doubt 'should ever undermine the reasonings of common life, and carry its doubts so far as to destroy all action, as well as speculation. Nature will always maintain her rights, and prevail in the end over any abstract reasoning whatsoever' (5.2, *E* 41).

But, although nature will always prevail over all forms of abstract reasoning, philosophical doubt included, engaging in such doubt is not without beneficial effect. Philosophical doubt is intended only (as if this is not enough) to 'inspire' us to 'more modesty and reserve', to a diminution of our blind biases in favour of our own views and against those who disagree with us (12.24, *E* 161). It accomplishes this valuable goal by indirection. Realizing that virtually nothing will be gained by a direct attack on our ordinary, common-sense views, the Humean sceptic seeks rather to alter 'the particular situation, in which the mind is placed' when belief arises (5.11, *E* 48). Belief arises naturally and involuntarily as the effect of certain causes or intellectual conditions. The effective and valuable sceptic does not seek to arrest this involuntary effect *per se*. He seeks rather to alter the intellectual *conditions* in which belief arises, thus changing the character of the relevant effect, or, at least, the manner in which belief is held. Hume supposes that beliefs may be stronger or weaker or vary by degree. Voluntary doubt, although it may not be able to extinguish any given belief, may none the less prevent any such belief from rising to the height of dogmatic and intolerant certainty. Voluntary doubt can serve to moderate or mitigate belief.

Alternatively, we may say that on Hume's account belief is *contextual*. We do not conclude that a pinpoint of light in a darkened sky is a comet and not a star without further information, including the knowledge that there is a difference between stars and comets.[12] Consequently, many individuals, including many relatively expert observers, may, on seeing some such pinpoint of light, defer from concluding that it is a comet and not a star (or a star and not a comet) because, even though they know that there are unmistakable differences between these two astronomical phenomena, they are not in a position to say

---

certain in *particular points*, according to the light, in which we survey them in any *particular instant*. 'Tis easier to forbear all examination and enquiry, than to check ourselves in so natural a propensity, and guard against that assurance, which always arises from an exact and full survey of an object. On such an occasion we are apt not only to forget our scepticism, but even our modesty too; and make use of such terms as these, '*tis evident*, '*tis certain*, '*tis undeniable*; which a due deference to the public ought, perhaps, to prevent. I may have fallen into this fault after the example of others; but I here enter a *caveat* against any objections, which may be offer'd on that head; and declare that such expressions were extorted from me by the present view of the object, and imply no dogmatical spirit, nor conceited idea of my own judgment, which are sentiments that I am sensible can become no body, and a sceptic still less than any other' (1.4.7.15, *T* 273–4).

[12] We can safely ignore the fact that certain 'stars' are actually galaxies and other such complications.

which it is they are experiencing at this particular time and place. Others, less well informed about the possibilities, may simply assume that the phenomenon is a star. The point is simple: the relatively expert observer recognizes that her faculties and information provide an inadequate basis on which to make a definitive claim about the phenomenon being experienced. This observer has learned, from personal experience or from the experience of others—likely from both—and perhaps even from reading Hume, about our limitations and our proneness to error, and hence is not only cautious in her pronouncements, but even in her very thoughts about the matter.

Whether our hypothetical observer's belief about the phenomenon she is experiencing has been affected by considerations of exactly the type that constitute philosophical doubt is unimportant. The point is, rather, that Hume saw that we would benefit from the kind of philosophical activity that adds an appreciation of our limitations to the conditions in which belief is formed— that adds an appreciation of the narrow range of the human understanding and of the fanciful speculations and dogmas that have attended its unrestricted use, and of its history of error even when restricted within its appropriate sphere. Seeing that belief is itself involuntary, Hume does not attempt to lead us, as he supposed the Pyrrhonians had, to a suspension of belief.[13] Instead, he attempts to add to the conditions that give rise to belief the salutary and mitigating influence of properly distinguished, philosophical doubts. Philo, often thought to be Hume's spokesman in his *Dialogues concerning Natural Religion*, suggests that scepticism may have a result very much like that just described:

if a man has accustomed himself to sceptical considerations on the uncertainty and narrow limits of reason, he will not entirely forget them when he turns his reflections on other subjects; but in all his philosophical principles and reasoning, I dare not say, in his common conduct, he will be found different from those, who either never formed any opinions in the case, or have entertained sentiments more favourable to human reason. (*D* 134)[14]

---

[13] Contrary to the impression Hume gives, the Pyrrhonists did not recommend a wholesale suspension of belief. They did not, as they put it, doubt appearances. They accepted, for example, that the honey now being eaten tastes sweet or that the oar now seen appears bent. They only engaged in those doubts that lead to suspension of belief about non-evident things—about any form of theoretical explanation. As Sextus Empiricus puts it, 'we do not deny those things which, in accordance with the passivity of our sense-impressions, lead us involuntarily to give our assent to them; and these are appearances. . . . Hence not the appearance is questioned, but that which is predicated of the appearance.' The predications in question concern, of course, the non-evident things about which the Pyrrhonist makes no assertions, a point Sextus later underscores by saying, 'One must also remember that, as for dogmatic assertions about the non-evident, we neither affirm nor deny them' (*Outlines of Pyrrhonism*, 1. 10, 1. 20, in *Sextus Empiricus: Selections from the Major Writings on Scepticism, Man and God*, ed. P. P. Haillie, trans. S. G. Etheridge (Indianapolis: Hackett, 1985), 38, 81).

[14] The goal of philosophical scepticism is also well stated in *A Letter from a Gentleman*, a work to which Hume contributed: 'In Reality, a Philosopher who affects to doubt of the Maxims of *common Reason*, and

III

I have argued that the fundamental aim of Hume's academical scepticism is not disbelief, but mitigated belief. For just that reason Humean scepticism is a viable scepticism. To see that this is so we must consider the manner in which this mitigating scepticism works. This we can do by turning again to an earlier section of the first *Enquiry*.

After certain preliminaries the *Enquiry* settles down to the business of cautioning us about the fundamental limitations of the human understanding, and of challenging philosophical and theological pretension. In Section IV, for example ('Sceptical Doubts concerning the Operations of the Understanding'), Hume shows us that neither abstract reasoning nor reasoning from experience can provide a secure or adequate foundation for the apparently universal and essential belief that similar effects will follow from similar causes, and hence that the future will resemble the past. Neither a rationalistic nor an empirical philosophy can provide a foundation for our causal reasonings. He grants, of course, that it is by experience that we come to have what we call 'knowledge' of cause and effect, and to this extent accepts the empiricist account of the matter. But when he goes on to ask a new and difficult question, 'What is the foundation of all conclusions from experience?', it is clear that empiricism, too, is to undergo sceptical scrutiny. If empiricists 'give themselves airs of superior wisdom', then they too must be pushed from every pretended haven until the embarrassing inadequacy of their position is apparent to all, and their claims are put forward with an appropriate modesty. The best course, however, is to incorporate this modesty into our enterprise from the start so that it can mitigate our conclusions: 'The best expedient to prevent this confusion, is to be modest in our pretensions; and even to discover the difficulty ourselves before it is objected to us. By this means, we may make a kind of merit of our very ignorance.' (4.14, *E* 32).

In the balance of Section IV Hume undertakes first what he describes as an 'easy task', namely, showing that our causal beliefs 'are *not* founded on reasoning, or any process of the understanding'. He argues that nature is deep and secretive, and our knowledge of it so superficial, that we simply cannot connect the sensible qualities of the objects we experience with any of the real and hidden powers of these objects. Even this purely 'negative argument' could in

even of his *Senses*, declares sufficiently that he is not in earnest, and that he intends not to advance an Opinion which he would recommend as Standards of Judgment and Action. All he means by these Scruples is to abate the Pride of *mere human Reasoners*, by showing them, that even with regard to Principles which seem the clearest, and which they are necessitated from the strongest Instincts of Nature to embrace, they are not able to attain a full Consistence and absolute Certainty. *Modesty* then, and *Humility*, with regard to the Operations of our natural Faculties, is the Result of *Scepticism*' (*L* 19).

time, he suggests, become 'altogether convincing': if, despite concerted effort, no one is 'ever able to discover any connecting proposition or intermediate step' establishing that particular causes will always have particular effects, then eventually we will be (by custom, of course) convinced that this fundamental ignorance is endemic (4.15–17, *E* 32–4).

Those who do not wish to draw so important a conclusion from the simple fact that they have as yet been unable to find an argument which establishes that the future must resemble the past are invited to follow Hume in the more difficult task of showing that no existing branch of human knowledge can possibly establish this link. Reasoning, he argues, is either 'demonstrative' or 'moral'. It concerns either relations of ideas, or matter of fact. Given that sound demonstrative arguments are characterized by the fact that we cannot conceive the contrary of their conclusions, and that we can conceive that the contrary of any causal claim is true, it is obvious that there can be no demonstrative arguments establishing that, with respect to any particular cause, the future will always be like the past. The contrary of any such conclusion is readily conceivable.[15]

On the other hand, moral or probable arguments concerning matters of fact depend upon our knowledge of causal relations, a knowledge that depends upon the conclusions we draw from experience. But 'all our experimental conclusions proceed upon the supposition, that the future will be conformable to the past' (4.19, *E* 35). To attempt by the use of probable arguments to prove that the future will resemble the past entails an obvious begging of the question. This supremely important and universal belief lacks a secure foundation in both reason and experience. However uniform the past may have been, no intuition, no logic, no probable argument, secures us against the possibility that all may, in a moment, be changed.

Hume's practice, our practice, may appear to refute such doubts. We all act as though the future will resemble the past—humans are nothing if not planning animals—and consequently this doubt about the future must be mistaken. Those who pose this objection misunderstand the issue. 'As an agent, I am quite satisfied in the point', says Hume, 'but as a philosopher, who has some share of curiosity, I will not say scepticism, I want to learn the foundation of this inference.' But why? What possible value in knowing the foundation of an inference we cannot in any event avoid making? And what possible benefit can arise from showing that this universal inference is unfounded? 'We shall at

---

[15] This argument is briefly restated near the end of Section XII: 'matter of fact and existence . . . are evidently incapable of demonstration. Whatever *is* may *not be*. No negation of a fact can involve a contradiction. The non-existence of any being, without exception, is as clear and distinct an idea as its existence. The proposition, which affirms it not to be, however false, is no less conceivable and intelligible, than that which affirms it to be. The case is different with the sciences [of quantity and number] . . . Every proposition, which is not true, is there confused and unintelligible.' (12.28, *E* 163–4).

least, by this means, be sensible of our ignorance, if we do not augment our knowledge' (4.21, *E* 38). And once we are aware of this fundamental ignorance? Then, surely, the conditions of belief will have changed. Belief will be mitigated, and pretension, dogmatism, and intolerance will, to the extent of our new sensibility, be reduced or eliminated. Hume's sceptical arguments, thus displayed at greater length, do offer the prospect of a durable good or benefit to society: the benefit of modesty and an attendant open-mindedness and tolerance.

IV

Having in *Enquiry* IV demonstrated to us what appears to be a fundamental limitation of our faculties, Hume later in the work marshals sceptical arguments against religious apologists and theologians, or against the claims of those individuals who, in his experience, represent all too well the dangers of pretension and dogmatism.

Hume first focuses his attention on miracles, and then on the Argument from Design, two allegedly empirical supports of particular religious views. Miracles are putative facts of a special kind which were (and are) used by some religious thinkers to justify their commitment to one creed or another. And, as Hume very well knew, these commitments were all too often maintained with both a mind-numbing tenacity and a dangerous and disruptive intolerance towards contrary views. Hume attempts to undermine such superstition and arrogance by providing us with an argument that will, at least 'with the wise and learned, be an everlasting check to all kinds of superstitious delusion' and which, consequently, 'will be useful as long as the world endures' (10.2, *E* 110). In brief, Hume does not undertake to show that the evidence for any particular miracle is inadequate. Neither does he attempt to show us that no miraculous event could possibly occur. He does, however, show us that there is something inherently problematic about miracles themselves (the then current conception of them, he suggests, is incoherent), about the evidential status of miracles (the evidence for even the most likely miracle will always be counterbalanced by the masses of evidence establishing the law of nature the miracle is said to violate), and about the evidence that may be adduced in support of any given miracle (such evidence is always tainted). Those who have carefully attended to this discussion are unlikely ever again to accept uncritically even well-authenticated accounts of miracles. Hume may well have hoped that most of his readers would cease to believe in miracles, but he could also hope that *even those who continue to believe in them* would be changed for the better. These individuals, despite having been exposed to Hume's argument, will continue to believe in particular miracles, but the effective intellectual conditions in which their belief arises may have been changed, and, as a consequence, their beliefs will have been mitigated, and they themselves significantly changed.

Hume's strictures against the Argument from Design, outlined in Section XI ('Of a Particular Providence and of a Future State'), and elaborated in his posthumously published *Dialogues concerning Natural Religion*, have much the same effect. As commonly formulated, the Argument from Design purports to show that so orderly a world as that we inhabit could only be the effect of a supremely intelligent and benevolent cause, and then goes on to claim that each aspect of this divine creation is well designed to fulfil an essentially beneficial function. Hume's criticisms of the argument are designed to show that the conclusions drawn run well ahead of the evidence available. In the first place, it is not obvious that the world is so very well designed. It certainly includes pleasant and well-ordered features, but these are balanced by a good measure of the unpleasant and the plainly botched. Secondly, in so far as the argument supposes that the universe is the unique effect of a unique cause, it paints itself into a corner. Hume had argued that what we claim to be *knowledge* of causal connexions depends on experience, on, more specifically, the repeated experience of particular entities or events of some type A, spatially and temporally contiguous to, and followed by, particular events of another type B (4.6, E 27). When we have repeated and constant experience of such associations or conjunctions, we come to call events of type A *causes*, and to call the contiguous and following entities or events of type B *effects* (7.27, E 74–5). If we lack the requisite experience, if a particular entity u, for example, is both unique and has never been conjoined with and contiguous and successive to some other entity or type of entity, then we have no grounds for assigning a cause to u.[16]

The Argument from Design entirely ignores this finding. The universe, for which that argument attempts to provide a causal explanation, is, so far as any of us can determine, a unique entity. It follows that none of us has had repeated experience of distinct universes and thus we obviously have not had experience of entities of type U constantly conjoined with entities of some other type, type D, let us say. We lack, in other words, experiential grounds for concluding that universes generally are produced by any given type of cause, deities included. Moreover, although it may be reasonable to suppose our universe is the effect of some cause, it is clear that this supposed effect antedates all human experience of it. Not even in this one case of a universe-effect, then, do we have experience

---

[16] Hume also repeats this argument near the end of Section XII: 'The existence, therefore, of any being can only be proved by arguments from its cause or its effect; and these arguments are founded entirely on experience. If we reason *a priori*, any thing may appear able to produce any thing. The falling of a pebble may, for aught we know, extinguish the sun; or the wish of a man controul the planets in their orbits. It is only experience, which teaches us the nature and bounds of cause and effect, and enables us to infer the existence of one object from that of another.' (12.29, E 164).

of some entity or event that preceded and was contiguous to the effect for which the Argument from Design claims to provide an explanation. In short, if we limit ourselves to our experiential grounds, the most we can say is that we find ourselves in the midst of this large and mixed effect, and, as we have through experience come to believe that effects have causes, it *seems* likely to us that this effect has a commensurately large and mixed cause. And, given that this effect is remotely like some products of human design and construction, it also may seem likely 'that the cause or causes of order in the universe probably bear some remote analogy to human intelligence'.[17] Given that we have formed the habit of supposing that effects have causes, it is reasonable to suppose that the unique effect we inhabit has a cause—but this reasonable conclusion is far removed from that of the theologians who put so much stock in the Argument from Design. Once we realize this fact, we will also find that the belief the argument engenders has been significantly modified. We may still, when we look up at the stars, feel the awe and wonder that occasions the idea of an intelligent creator, but we will recognize that this so-called *argument*, as it provides no rational, and very little experiential, ground for such an inference, cannot possibly provide the kind of certainty that justifies or in any way supports sectarian pretension or dogmatic intolerance. Hume's analysis of the causal relation, his philosophical doubts about causation, have changed the conditions in which the Argument from Design functions to bring about belief. If we understand this analysis, we ourselves will be modified, and our belief in an intelligent creator mitigated.

V

The careful reader of Section XII will likely have wondered how to reconcile Hume's battle against intolerance with the notorious conclusion of this section and of the *Enquiry* itself. How can a philosopher who tells us that certain books (those judged to contain nothing but sophistry and illusion) should be committed to the flames be a champion of tolerance? Is not Hume guilty of the very intellectual rigidity his mitigated scepticism is designed to overturn?

Perhaps he is. Perhaps Hume's final remark is inconsistent with the scepticism he has recommended. In that event one could look for an explanation of this inconsistency, or one could simply accept it as further evidence of a deeply seated human propensity to be, in Hume's own words, 'affirmative and dogmatical'. In any case, the charge of inconsistency as it arises here is a charge *ad hominem*; it is a charge against the philosopher, not the philosophical position he sought to articulate. An inconsistency on Hume's part does not itself entail that the scepticism he recommends is neither viable or valuable, although it

---

[17] This is the concession of Philo in the *Dialogues concerning Natural Religion*; see D 227.

does remind us just how difficult it is to keep our affirmative tendencies within proper bounds. More importantly, Hume's broad programme of mitigation, the programme that leads to mitigation of belief, can also be directed at this very recommendation or at any other hasty determination to which the sceptic may be naturally drawn. The sceptical programme that Hume outlines shows us how to mitigate any pronouncement by showing us what he describes as 'the whimsical condition of mankind'. That is, we 'must act and reason and believe' even though we are unable, even by the most careful enquiry, to satisfy ourselves concerning 'the foundation of these operations, or to remove the objections, which may be raised against them' (12.23–4, *E* 160–1). Such a programme can be directed also at scepticism and at itself: the sceptic's beliefs about scepticism and about belief itself and the conditions in which it arises can themselves be mitigated. Humean sceptics may have their rash moments, but these moments need not betray any entrenched dogmatical spirit or any desire to put oneself and one's views beyond the scope and influence of scepticism.[18]

It can also be argued that Hume's closing injunction is to be understood in a significantly different way. We can connect this injunction to the reference with which Section XII begins, the reference to atheists. Hume may have been suggesting that the public hangman had been burning the wrong books. The literature that constitutes a danger to society, that, as experience so readily shows, threatens to provoke sectarian strife and even outright warfare, is not the work of the atheist, but that of the believer. Epicurus could easily have shown, we have been told, that his principles were 'as salutary as those of his adversaries'. The dangerous books in Hume's view were those containing the 'Speculative dogmas of religion' which are 'the present occasions of such furious dispute' (11.3, 5; *E* 133–4). These particular books meet neither of Hume's tests. They contain no abstract reasoning about quantity or number; they contain no experimental reasoning concerning matters of fact. To suggest that it is these empty and disruptive works that deserve the attention of the hangman is once again to attempt to change the conditions of belief. Hume's readers will think again when they hear that some heterodox work should be burned or banned. They will remember that society needs protection, not from sceptics, but from dogmatists.

---

[18] Hume had already faced this issue in his *Treatise*; see above, n. 11.

My Own Life

David Hume

1   It is difficult for a man to speak long of himself without vanity; therefore, I shall be short. It may be thought an instance of vanity that I pretend at all to write my life; but this Narrative shall contain little more than the History of my Writings; as, indeed, almost all my life has been spent in literary pursuits and occupations. The first success of most of my writings was not such as to be an object of vanity.

2   I was born the 26th of April 1711, old style, at Edinburgh. I was of a good family, both by father and mother: my father's family is a branch of the Earl of Home's, or Hume's; and my ancestors had been proprietors of the estate, which my brother possesses, for several generations. My mother was daughter of Sir David Falconer, President of the College of Justice: the title of Lord Halkerton came by succession to her brother.

3   My family, however, was not rich, and being myself a younger brother, my patrimony, according to the mode of my country, was of course very slender. My father, who passed for a man of parts, died when I was an infant, leaving me, with an elder brother and a sister, under the care of our mother, a woman of singular merit, who, though young and handsome, devoted herself entirely to the rearing and educating of her children. I passed through the ordinary course of education with success, and was seized very early with a passion for literature, which has been the ruling passion of my life, and the great source of my enjoyments. My studious disposition, my sobriety, and my industry, gave my family a notion that the law was a proper profession for me; but I found an unsurmountable aversion to every thing but the pursuits of philosophy and general learning; and while they fancied I was poring upon Voet and Vinnius, Cicero and Virgil were the authors which I was secretly devouring.

4   My very slender fortune, however, being unsuitable to this plan of life, and my health being a little broken by my ardent application, I was tempted, or rather forced, to make a very feeble trial for entering into a more active scene of life. In 1734, I went to Bristol, with some recommendations to eminent merchants, but in a few months found that scene totally unsuitable to me. I went over to France, with a view of prosecuting my studies in a country retreat; and I there laid that plan of life, which I have steadily and successfully pursued. I resolved to make a very rigid frugality supply my deficiency of fortune, to

maintain unimpaired my independency, and to regard every object as con-
temptible, except the improvement of my talents in literature.

5   During my retreat in France, first at Reims, but chiefly at La Fleche, in Anjou,
I composed my *Treatise of Human Nature*. After passing three years very agreeably in that country, I came over to London in 1737. In the end of 1738, I published my Treatise, and immediately went down to my mother and my brother,
who lived at his country house, and was employing himself very judiciously and
successfully in the improvement of his fortune.

6   Never literary attempt was more unfortunate than my Treatise of Human
Nature. It fell *dead-born from the press*, without reaching such distinction, as
even to excite a murmur among the zealots. But being naturally of a cheerful
and sanguine temper, I very soon recovered the blow, and prosecuted with great
ardour my studies in the country. In 1742, I printed at Edinburgh the first part of
my Essays: the work was favourably received, and soon made me entirely forget
my former disappointment. I continued with my mother and brother in the
country, and in that time recovered the knowledge of the Greek language, which
I had too much neglected in my early youth.

7   In 1745, I received a letter from the Marquis of Annandale, inviting me to
come and live with him in England; I found also, that the friends and family of
that young nobleman were desirous of putting him under my care and direction, for the state of his mind and health required it. I lived with him a twelvemonth. My appointments during that time made a considerable accession to
my small fortune. I then received an invitation from General St. Clair to attend
him as Secretary to his expedition, which was at first meant against Canada,
but ended in an incursion on the coast of France. Next year, to wit, 1747, I
received an invitation from the General to attend him in the same station in his
military embassy to the courts of Vienna and Turin. I there wore the uniform of
an officer, and was introduced at these courts as aid-de-camp to the general,
along with Sir Harry Erskine and Captain Grant, now General Grant. These two
years were almost the only interruptions which my studies have received in
the course of my life: I passed them agreeably and in good company; and my
appointments, with my frugality, had made me reach a fortune, which I called
independent, though most of my friends were inclined to smile when I said so;
in short, I was now master of near a thousand pound.

8   I had always entertained a notion, that my want of success in publishing the
Treatise of Human Nature, had proceeded more from the manner than the
matter, and that I had been guilty of a very usual indiscretion, in going to
the press too early. I, therefore, cast the first part of that work anew in the
Enquiry concerning Human Understanding, which was published while I was
at Turin. But this piece was at first but little more successful than the Treatise of
Human Nature. On my return from Italy, I had the mortification to find all
England in a ferment, on account of Dr. Middleton's Free Enquiry, while my

performance was entirely overlooked and neglected. A new edition, which had been published at London, of my Essays, moral and political, met not with a much better reception.

9   Such is the force of natural temper, that these disappointments made little or no impression on me. I went down in 1749, and lived two years with my brother at his country-house, for my mother was now dead. I there composed the second part of my Essays, which I called Political Discourses, and also my Enquiry concerning the Principles of Morals, which is another part of my treatise that I cast anew. Meanwhile, my bookseller, A. Millar, informed me, that my former publications (all but the unfortunate Treatise) were beginning to be the subject of conversation; that the sale of them was gradually increasing, and that new editions were demanded. Answers by Reverends, and Right Reverends, came out two or three in a year; and I found, by Dr. Warburton's railing, that the books were beginning to be esteemed in good company. However, I had fixed a resolution, which I inflexibly maintained, never to reply to any body; and not being very irascible in my temper, I have easily kept myself clear of all literary squabbles. These symptoms of a rising reputation gave me encouragement, as I was ever more disposed to see the favourable than unfavourable side of things; a turn of mind which it is more happy to possess, than to be born to an estate of ten thousand a year.

10   In 1751, I removed from the country to the town, the true scene for a man of letters. In 1752, were published at Edinburgh, where I then lived, my Political Discourses, the only work of mine that was successful on the first publication. It was well received abroad and at home. In the same year was published at London, my Enquiry concerning the Principles of Morals; which, in my own opinion (who ought not to judge on that subject), is of all my writings, historical, philosophical, or literary, incomparably the best. It came unnoticed and unobserved into the world.

11   In 1752, the Faculty of Advocates chose me their Librarian, an office from which I received little or no emolument, but which gave me the command of a large library. I then formed the plan of writing the History of England; but being frightened with the notion of continuing a narrative through a period of 1700 years, I commenced with the accession of the House of Stuart, an epoch when, I thought, the misrepresentations of faction began chiefly to take place. I was, I own, sanguine in my expectations of the success of this work. I thought that I was the only historian, that had at once neglected present power, interest, and authority, and the cry of popular prejudices; and as the subject was suited to every capacity, I expected proportional applause. But miserable was my disappointment: I was assailed by one cry of reproach, disapprobation, and even detestation; English, Scotch, and Irish, Whig and Tory, churchman and sectary, freethinker and religionist, patriot and courtier, united in their rage against the man, who had presumed to shed a generous tear for the fate of Charles I. and the

Earl of Strafford; and after the first ebullitions of this fury were over, what was still more mortifying, the book seemed to sink into oblivion. Mr. Millar told me, that in a twelvemonth he sold only forty-five copies of it. I scarcely, indeed, heard of one man in the three kingdoms, considerable for rank or letters, that could endure the book. I must only except the primate of England, Dr. Herring, and the primate of Ireland, Dr. Stone, which seem two odd exceptions. These dignified prelates separately sent me messages not to be discouraged.

12   I was, however, I confess, discouraged; and had not the war been at that time breaking out between France and England, I had certainly retired to some provincial town of the former kingdom, have changed my name, and never more have returned to my native country. But as this scheme was not now practicable, and the subsequent volume was considerably advanced, I resolved to pick up courage and to persevere.

13   In this interval, I published at London my Natural History of Religion, along with some other small pieces: its public entry was rather obscure, except only that Dr. Hurd wrote a pamphlet against it, with all the illiberal petulance, arrogance, and scurrility, which distinguishes the Warburtonian school. This pamphlet gave me some consolation for the otherwise indifferent reception of my performance.

14   In 1756, two years after the fall of the first volume, was published the second volume of my History, containing the period from the death of Charles I. till the Revolution. This performance happened to give less displeasure to the Whigs, and was better received. It not only rose itself, but helped to buoy up its unfortunate brother.

15   But though I had been taught by experience, that the Whig party were in possession of bestowing all places, both in the state and in literature, I was so little inclined to yield to their senseless clamour, that in above a hundred alterations, which farther study, reading, or reflection engaged me to make in the reigns of the two first Stuarts, I have made all of them invariably to the Tory side. It is ridiculous to consider the English constitution before that period as a regular plan of liberty.

16   In 1759, I published my History of the House of Tudor. The clamour against this performance was almost equal to that against the History of the two first Stuarts. The reign of Elizabeth was particularly obnoxious. But I was now callous against the impressions of public folly, and continued very peaceably and contentedly in my retreat at Edinburgh, to finish, in two volumes, the more early part of the English History, which I gave to the public in 1761, with tolerable, and but tolerable success.

17   But, notwithstanding this variety of winds and seasons, to which my writings had been exposed, they had still been making such advances, that the copy-money given me by the booksellers, much exceeded any thing formerly known

in England; I was become not only independent, but opulent. I retired to my native country of Scotland, determined never more to set my foot out of it; and retaining the satisfaction of never having preferred a request to one great man, or even making advances of friendship to any of them. As I was now turned of fifty, I thought of passing all the rest of my life in this philosophical manner, when I received, in 1763, an invitation from Lord Hertford, with whom I was not in the least acquainted, to attend him on his embassy to Paris, with a near prospect of being appointed secretary to the embassy; and, in the meanwhile, of performing the functions of that office. This offer, however inviting, I at first declined, both because I was reluctant to begin connexions with the great, and because I was afraid that the civilities and gay company of Paris, would prove disagreeable to a person of my age and humour: but on his lordship's repeating the invitation, I accepted of it. I have every reason, both of pleasure and interest, to think myself happy in my connexions with that nobleman, as well as afterwards with his brother, General Conway.

18   Those who have not seen the strange effect of modes, will never imagine the reception I met with at Paris, from men and women of all ranks and stations. The more I recoiled from their excessive civilities, the more I was loaded with them. There is, however, a real satisfaction in living at Paris, from the great number of sensible, knowing, and polite company with which that city abounds above all places in the universe. I thought once of settling there for life.

19   I was appointed secretary to the embassy; and in summer 1765, Lord Hertford left me, being appointed Lord Lieutenant of Ireland. I was *chargé d'affaires* till the arrival of the Duke of Richmond, towards the end of the year. In the beginning of 1766, I left Paris, and next summer went to Edinburgh, with the same view as formerly, of burying myself in a philosophical retreat. I returned to that place, not richer, but with much more money, and a much larger income, by means of Lord Hertford's friendship, than I left it; and I was desirous of trying what superfluity could produce, as I had formerly made an experiment of a competency. But, in 1767, I received from Mr. Conway an invitation to be Undersecretary; and this invitation, both the character of the person, and my connexions with Lord Hertford, prevented me from declining. I returned to Edinburgh in 1769, very opulent (for I possessed a revenue of 1,000 pounds a year), healthy, and though somewhat stricken in years, with the prospect of enjoying long my ease, and of seeing the increase of my reputation.

20   In spring 1775, I was struck with a disorder in my bowels, which at first gave me no alarm, but has since, as I apprehend it, become mortal and incurable. I now reckon upon a speedy dissolution. I have suffered very little pain from my disorder; and what is more strange, have, notwithstanding the great decline of my person, never suffered a moment's abatement of my spirits; insomuch, that were I to name the period of my life, which I should most choose to pass over

again, I might be tempted to point to this later period. I possess the same ardour as ever in study, and the same gaiety in company. I consider, besides, that a man of sixty-five, by dying, cuts off only a few years of infirmities; and though I see many symptoms of my literary reputation's breaking out at last with additional lustre, I know that I had but few years to enjoy it. It is difficult to be more detached from life than I am at present.

21   To conclude historically with my own character. I am, or rather was (for that is the style I must now use in speaking of myself, which emboldens me the more to speak my sentiments); I was, I say, a man of mild dispositions, of command of temper, of an open, social, and cheerful humour, capable of attachment, but little susceptible of enmity, and of great moderation in all my passions. Even my love of literary fame, my ruling passion, never soured my humour, notwithstanding my frequent disappointments. My company was not unacceptable to the young and careless, as well as to the studious and literary; and as I took a particular pleasure in the company of modest women, I had no reason to be displeased with the reception I met with from them. In a word, though most men any wise eminent, have found reason to complain of calumny, I never was touched, or even attacked by her baleful tooth: and though I wantonly exposed myself to the rage of both civil and religious factions, they seemed to be disarmed in my behalf of their wonted fury. My friends never had occasion to vindicate any one circumstance of my character and conduct: not but that the zealots, we may well suppose, would have been glad to invent and propagate any story to my disadvantage, but they could never find any which they thought would wear the face of probability. I cannot say there is no vanity in making this funeral oration of myself, but I hope it is not a misplaced one; and this is a matter of fact which is easily cleared and ascertained.

April 18, 1776.

Abstract of the *Treatise*

A N

ABSTRACT

O F

A BOOK lately PUBLISHED;

ENTITULED,

A

TREATISE

O F

Human Nature, &c.

WHEREIN

The CHIEF ARGUMENT of that
BOOK is farther ILLUSTRATED and
EXPLAINED.

L O N D O N:
Printed for C. BORBET, at *Addison's Head,*
over-against St. *Dunstan's Church,* in *Fleet-
street.* 1740.
[Price fix Pence.]

Preface.

1 MY *expectations in this small performance may seem somewhat extraordinary, when I declare that my intentions are to render a larger work more intelligible to ordinary capacities, by abridging it. 'Tis however certain, that those who are not accustomed to abstract reasoning, are apt to lose the thread of argument, where it is drawn out to a great length, and each part fortified with all the arguments, guarded against all the objections, and illustrated with all the views, which occur to a writer in the diligent survey of his subject. Such Readers will more readily apprehend a chain of reasoning, that is more single and concise, where the chief propositions only are linkt on to each other, illustrated by some simple examples, and confirmed by a few of the more forcible arguments. The parts lying nearer together can better be compared, and the connexion be more easily traced from the first principles to the last conclusion.*

2 *The work, of which I here present the Reader with an abstract, has been complained of as obscure and difficult to be comprehended, and I am apt to think, that this proceeded as much from the length as from the abstractedness of the argument. If I have remedy'd this inconvenience in any degree, I have attain'd my end. The book seem'd to me to have such an air of singularity, and novelty as claim'd the attention of the public; especially if it be found, as the Author seems to insinuate, that were his philosophy receiv'd, we must alter from the foundation the greatest part of the sciences. Such bold attempts are always advantageous in the republic of* *letters, because they shake off the yoke of authority, accustom men to think for themselves, give new hints, which men of genius may carry further, and by the very opposition, illustrate points, wherein no one before suspected any difficulty.*

3 *The Author must be contented to wait with patience for some time before the learned world can agree in their sentiments of his performance. 'Tis his misfortune, that he cannot make an* appeal to the people, *who in all matters of common reason and eloquence are found so infallible a tribunal. He must be judg'd by the* FEW, *whose verdict is more apt to be corrupted by partiality and prejudice, especially as no one is a proper judge in these subjects, who has not often thought of them; and* such *are apt to form to themselves systems of their own, which they resolve not to relinquish. I hope the Author will excuse me for inter-meddling in this affair, since my aim is only to encrease his auditory, by removing some difficulties, which have kept many from apprehending his meaning.*

4 *I have chosen one simple argument, which I have carefully traced from the beginning to the end. This is the only point I have taken care to finish. The rest is only hints of particular passages, which seem'd to me curious and remarkable.*

An Abstract of a Book lately Published, entituled, [645]
A Treatise of Human Nature, &c.

David Hume

1   THIS book seems to be wrote upon the same plan with several other works that have had a great vogue of late years in *England*. The philosophical spirit, which has been so much improved all over *Europe* within these last fourscore years, has been carried to as great a length in this kingdom as in any other. Our writers seem even to have started a new kind of philosophy, which promises more both to the entertainment and advantage of mankind, than any other with which the world has been yet acquainted. Most of the philosophers of antiquity, who treated of human nature, have shewn more of a delicacy of sentiment, a just sense of morals, or a greatness of soul, than a depth of reasoning and reflection. They content themselves with representing the common sense of mankind in the strongest lights, and with the best turn of thought and expression, without following out steadily a chain of propositions, or forming the several truths into a regular science. But 'tis at least worth while to try if the science of *man* will not admit of the same accuracy which several parts of natural philosophy are found susceptible of. There seems to be all the reason in the world to imagine that it may be carried to the greatest degree of exactness. If, in examining several [646] phænomena, we find that they resolve themselves into one common principle, and can trace this principle into another, we shall at last arrive at those few simple principles, on which all the rest depend. And tho' we can never arrive at the ultimate principles, 'tis a satisfaction to go as far as our faculties will allow us.

2   This seems to have been the aim of our late philosophers, and, among the rest, of this author. He proposes to anatomize human nature in a regular manner, and promises to draw no conclusions but where he is authorized by experience. He talks with contempt of hypotheses; and insinuates, that such of our countrymen as have banished them from moral philosophy, have done a more signal service to the world, than *my Lord Bacon*, whom he considers as the father of experimental physicks. He mentions, on this occasion, *Mr. Locke, my Lord Shaftsbury, Dr. Mandeville, Mr. Hutchison, Dr. Butler*, who, tho' they differ in many points among themselves, seem all to agree in founding their accurate disquisitions of human nature intirely upon experience.

3   Beside the satisfaction of being acquainted with what most nearly concerns us, it may be safely affirmed, that almost all the sciences are comprehended in the science of human nature, and are dependent on it. *The sole end of* logic *is to explain the principles and Operations of our reasoning faculty, and the nature of our ideas*; morals and criticism *regard our tastes and sentiments*; *and* politics

consider men as united in society, and dependent on each other. This treatise therefore of human nature seems intended for a system of the sciences. The author has finished what regards logic, and has laid the foundation of the other parts in his account of the passions.

4   The celebrated *Monsieur Leibnitz* has observed it to be a defect in the common systems of logic, that they are very copious when they explain the [647] operations of the understanding in the forming of demonstrations, but are too concise when they treat of probabilities, and those other measures of evidence on which life and action intirely depend, and which are our guides even in most of our philosophical speculations. In this censure, he comprehends *the essay on human understanding, le recherche de la verité,* and *l'art de penser.* The author of the *treatise of human nature* seems to have been sensible of this defect in these philosophers, and has endeavoured, as much as he can, to supply it. As his book contains a great number of speculations very new and remarkable, it will be impossible to give the reader a just notion of the whole. We shall therefore chiefly confine ourselves to his explication of our reasonings from cause and effect. If we can make this intelligible to the reader, it may serve as a specimen of the whole.

5   Our author begins with some definitions. He calls a *perception* whatever can be present to the mind, whether we employ our senses, or are actuated with passion, or exercise our thought and reflection. He divides our perceptions into two kinds, *viz. impressions* and *ideas.* When we feel a passion or emotion of any kind, or have the images of external objects conveyed by our senses; the perception of the mind is what he calls an *impression,* which is a word that he employs in a new sense. When we reflect on a passion or an object which is not present, this perception is an *idea. Impressions,* therefore, are our lively and strong perceptions; *ideas* are the fainter and weaker. This distinction is evident; as evident as that betwixt feeling and thinking.

6   The first proposition he advances, is, that all our ideas, or weak perceptions, are derived from our impressions, or strong perceptions, and that we can never think of any thing which we have not seen without us, or felt in our own minds. [648] This proposition seems to be equivalent to that which Mr. *Locke* has taken such pains to establish, *viz. that no ideas are innate.* Only it may be observed, as an inaccuracy of that famous philosopher, that he comprehends all our perceptions under the term of idea, in which sense it is false, that we have no innate ideas. For it is evident our stronger perceptions or impressions are innate, and that natural affection, love of virtue, resentment, and all the other passions, arise immediately from nature. I am perswaded, whoever would take the question in this light, would be easily able to reconcile all parties. *Father Malebranche* would find himself at a loss to point out any thought of the mind, which did not represent something antecedently felt by it, either internally, or by means of the external senses, and must allow, that however we may compound, and mix,

and augment, and diminish our ideas, they are all derived from these sources. *Mr. Locke*, on the other hand, would readily acknowledge, that all our passions are a kind of natural instincts, derived from nothing but the original constitution of the human mind.

7   Our author thinks, 'that no discovery could have been made more happily for deciding all controversies concerning ideas than this, that impressions always take the precedency of them, and that every idea with which the imagination is furnished, first makes its appearance in a correspondent impression. These latter perceptions are all so clear and evident, that they admit of no controversy; tho' many of our ideas are so obscure, that 'tis almost impossible even for the mind, which forms them, to tell exactly their nature and composition.' Accordingly, wherever any idea is ambiguous, he has always recourse to the impression, which must render it clear and precise. And when he suspects that any philosophical term has no idea annexed to it (as is too common) he always asks *from what impression that pretended idea is derived?* And if no impression can be   [649] produced, he concludes that the term is altogether insignificant. 'Tis after this manner he examines our idea of *substance* and *essence*; and it were to be wished, that this rigorous method were more practised in all philosophical debates.

8   'Tis evident, that all reasonings concerning *matter of fact* are founded on the relation of cause and effect, and that we can never infer the existence of one object from another, unless they be connected together, either mediately or immediately. In order therefore to understand these reasonings, we must be perfectly acquainted with the idea of a cause; and in order to that, must look about us to find something that is the cause of another.

9   Here is a billiard-ball lying on the table, and another ball moving towards it with rapidity. They strike; and the ball, which was formerly at rest, now acquires a motion. This is as perfect an instance of the relation of cause and effect as any which we know, either by sensation or reflection. Let us therefore examine it. 'Tis evident, that the two balls touched one another before the motion was communicated, and that there was no interval betwixt the shock and the motion. *Contiguity* in time and place is therefore a requisite circumstance to the operation of all causes. 'Tis evident likewise, that the motion, which was the cause, is prior to the motion, which was the effect. *Priority* in time, is therefore another requisite circumstance in every cause. But this is not all. Let us try any other balls of the same kind in a like situation, and we shall always find, that the impulse of the one produces motion in the other. Here therefore is a *third* circumstance, *viz.* that of a *constant conjunction* betwixt the cause and effect. Every object like the cause, produces always some object like the effect. Beyond these three circumstances of contiguity, priority, and constant conjunction, I can discover   [650] nothing in this cause. The first ball is in motion; touches the second; immediately the second is in motion: and when I try the experiment with the same or like balls, in the same or like circumstances, I find, that upon the motion and

touch of the one ball, motion always follows in the other. In whatever shape I turn this matter, and however I examine it, I can find nothing farther.

10   This is the case when both the cause and effect are present to the senses. Let us now see upon what our inference is founded, when we conclude from the one that the other has existed or will exist. Suppose I see a ball moving in a streight line towards another, I immediately conclude, that they will shock, and that the second will be in motion. This is the inference from cause to effect; and of this nature are all our reasonings in the conduct of life: on this is founded all our belief in history: and from hence is derived all philosophy, excepting only geometry and arithmetic. If we can explain the inference from the shock of two balls, we shall be able to account for this operation of the mind in all instances.

11   Were a man, such as *Adam*, created in the full vigour of understanding, without experience, he would never be able to infer motion in the second ball from the motion and impulse of the first. It is not any thing that reason sees in the cause, which make us *infer* the effect. Such an inference, were it possible, would amount to a demonstration, as being founded merely on the comparison of ideas. But no inference from cause to effect amounts to a demonstration. Of which there is this evident proof. The mind can always *conceive* any effect to follow from any cause, and indeed any event to follow upon another: whatever we *conceive* is possible, at least in a metaphysical sense: but wherever a demonstration takes place, the contrary is impossible, and implies a contradiction. There is no demonstration, therefore, for any conjunction of cause and effect.   [651] And this is a principle, which is generally allowed by philosophers.

12   It would have been necessary, therefore, for *Adam* (if he was not inspired) to have had *experience* of the effect, which followed upon the impulse of these two balls. He must have seen, in several instances, that when the one ball struck upon the other, the second always acquired motion. If he had seen a sufficient number of instances of this kind, whenever he saw the one ball moving towards the other, he would always conclude without hesitation, that the second would acquire motion. His understanding would anticipate his sight, and form a conclusion suitable to his past experience.

13   It follows, then, that all reasonings concerning cause and effect, are founded on experience, and that all reasonings from experience are founded on the supposition, that the course of nature will continue uniformly the same. We conclude, that like causes, in like circumstances, will always produce like effects. It may now be worth while to consider, what determines us to form a conclusion of such infinite consequence.

14   'Tis evident, that *Adam* with all his science, would never have been able to *demonstrate*, that the course of nature must continue uniformly the same, and that the future must be conformable to the past. What is possible can never be demonstrated to be false; and 'tis possible the course of nature may change,

since we can conceive such a change. Nay, I will go farther, and assert, that he could not so much as prove by any *probable* arguments, that the future must be conformable to the past. All probable arguments are built on the supposition, that there is this conformity betwixt the future and the past, and therefore can never prove it. This conformity is a *matter of fact*, and if it must be proved, will admit of no proof but from experience. But our experience in the past can be a proof of nothing for the future, but upon a supposition, that there is a resem-   [652] blance betwixt them. This therefore is a point, which can admit of no proof at all, and which we take for granted without any proof.

15   We are determined by CUSTOM alone to suppose the future conformable to the past. When I see a billiard-ball moving towards another, my mind is immediately carry'd by habit to the usual effect, and anticipates my sight by conceiving the second ball in motion. There is nothing in these objects, abstractly considered, and independent of experience, which leads me to form any such conclusion: and even after I have had experience of many repeated effects of this kind, there is no argument, which determines me to suppose, that the effect will be conformable to past experience. The powers, by which bodies operate, are entirely unknown. We perceive only their sensible qualities: and what *reason* have we to think, that the same powers will always be conjoined with the same sensible qualities?

16   'Tis not, therefore, reason, which is the guide of life, but custom. That alone determines the mind, in all instances, to suppose the future conformable to the past. However easy this step may seem, reason would never, to all eternity, be able to make it.

17   This is a very curious discovery, but leads us to others, that are still more curious. *When I see a billiard-ball moving towards another, my mind is immediately carried by habit to the usual effect, and anticipates my sight by conceiving the second ball in motion.* But is this all? Do I nothing but CONCEIVE the motion of the second ball? No surely. I also BELIEVE that it will move. What then is this *belief*? And how does it differ from the simple conception of any thing? Here is a new question unthought of by philosophers.

18   When a demonstration convinces me of any proposition, it not only makes   [653] me conceive the proposition, but also makes me sensible, that 'tis impossible to conceive any thing contrary. What is demonstratively false implies a contradiction; and what implies a contradiction cannot be conceived. But with regard to any matter of fact, however strong the proof may be from experience, I can always conceive the contrary, tho' I cannot always believe it. The belief, therefore, makes some difference betwixt the conception to which we assent, and that to which we do not assent.

19   To account for this, there are only two hypotheses. It may be said, that belief joins some new idea to those which we may conceive without assenting to them.

But this hypothesis is false. For *first*, no such idea can be produced. When we simply conceive an object, we conceive it in all its parts. We conceive it as it might exist, tho' we do not believe it to exist. Our belief of it would discover no new qualities. We may paint out the entire object in imagination without believing it. We may set it, in a manner, before our eyes, with every circumstance of time and place. 'Tis the very object conceived as it might exist; and when we believe it, we can do no more.

20　　*Secondly*, The mind has a faculty of joining all ideas together, which involve not a contradiction; and therefore if belief consisted in some idea, which we add to the simple conception, it would be in a man's power, by adding this idea to it, to believe any thing, which he can conceive.

21　　Since therefore belief implies a conception, and yet is something more; and since it adds no new idea to the conception; it follows, that it is a different MANNER of conceiving an object; *something* that is distinguishable to the feeling, and depends not upon our will, as all our ideas do. My mind runs by habit from the visible object of one ball moving towards another, to the usual effect of motion in the second ball. It not only conceives that motion, but *feels*　　[654] something different in the conception of it from a mere reverie of the imagination. The presence of this visible object, and the constant conjunction of that particular effect, render the idea different to the *feeling* from those loose ideas, which come into the mind without any introduction. This conclusion seems a little surprizing; but we are led into it by a chain of propositions, which admit of no doubt. To ease the reader's memory I shall briefly resume them. No matter of fact can be proved but from its cause or its effect. Nothing can be known to be the cause of another but by experience. We can give no reason for extending to the future our experience in the past; but are entirely determined by custom, when we conceive an effect to follow from its usual cause. But we also believe an effect to follow, as well as conceive it. This belief joins no new idea to the conception. It only varies the manner of conceiving, and makes a difference to the feeling or sentiment. Belief, therefore, in all matters of fact arises only from custom, and is an idea conceived in a peculiar *manner*.

22　　Our author proceeds to explain the manner or feeling, which renders belief different from a loose conception. He seems sensible, that 'tis impossible by words to describe this feeling, which every one must be conscious of in his own breast. He calls it sometimes a *stronger* conception, sometimes a more *lively*, a more *vivid*, a *firmer*, or a more *intense* conception. And indeed, whatever name we may give to this feeling, which constitutes belief, our author thinks it evident, that it has a more forcible effect on the mind than fiction and mere conception. This he proves by its influence on the passions and on the imagination; which are only moved by truth or what is taken for such. Poetry, with all its art, can never cause a passion, like one in real life. It fails in the original conception of its objects, which never *feel* in the same manner as those which command our belief and opinion.

23   Our author presuming, that he had sufficiently proved, that the ideas we assent to are different to the feeling from the other ideas, and that this feeling is more firm and lively than our common conception, endeavours in the next place to explain the cause of this lively feeling by an analogy with other acts of the mind. His reasoning seems to be curious; but could scarce be rendered intelligible, or at least probable to the reader, without a long detail, which would exceed the compass I have prescribed to myself.   [655]

24   I have likewise omitted many arguments, which he adduces to prove that belief consists merely in a peculiar feeling or sentiment. I shall only mention one. Our past experience is not always uniform. Sometimes one effect follows from a cause, sometimes another: In which case we always believe, that that will exist which is most common. I see a billiard-ball moving towards another. I cannot distinguish whether it moves upon its axis, or was struck so as to skim along the table. In the first case, I know it will not stop after the shock. In the second it may stop. The first is most common, and therefore I lay my account with that effect. But I also conceive the other effect, and conceive it as possible, and as connected with the cause. Were not the one conception different in the feeling or sentiment from the other, there would be no difference betwixt them.

25   We have confin'd ourselves in this whole reasoning to the relation of cause and effect, as discovered in the motions and operations of matter. But the same reasoning extends to the operations of the mind. Whether we consider the influence of the will in moving our body, or in governing our thought, it may safely be affirmed, that we could never foretel the effect, merely from the consideration of the cause, without experience. And even after we have experience of these effects, 'tis custom alone, not reason, which determines us to make it the standard of our future judgments. When the cause is presented, the mind, from habit, immediately passes to the conception and belief of the usual effect. This belief is something different from the conception. It does not, however, join any new idea to it. It only makes it be felt differently, and renders it stronger and more lively.   [656]

26   Having dispatcht this material point concerning the nature of the inference from cause and effect, our author returns upon his footsteps, and examines anew the idea of that relation. In the considering of motion communicated from one ball to another, we could find nothing but contiguity, priority in the cause, and constant conjunction. But, beside these circumstances, 'tis commonly suppos'd, that there is a necessary connexion betwixt the cause and effect, and that the cause possesses something, which we call a *power*, or *force*, or *energy*. The question is, what idea is annex'd to these terms? If all our ideas or thoughts be derived from our impressions, this power must either discover itself

to our senses, or to our internal feeling. But so little does any *power* discover itself to the senses in the operations of matter, that the *Cartesians* have made no scruple to assert, that matter is utterly deprived of energy, and that all its operations are perform'd merely by the energy of the supreme Being. But the question still recurs, *What idea have we of energy or power even in the supreme Being?* All our idea of a Deity (according to those who deny innate ideas) is nothing but a composition of those ideas, which we acquire from reflecting on the operations of our own minds. Now our own minds afford us no more notion of energy than matter does. When we consider our will or volition *a priori*, abstracting from experience, we are never able to infer any effect from it. And when we take the assistance of experience, it only shows us objects contiguous, successive, and [657] constantly conjoined. Upon the whole, then, either we have no idea at all of force and energy, and these words are altogether insignificant, or they can mean nothing but that determination of the thought, acquir'd by habit, to pass from the cause to its usual effect. But who-ever would thoroughly understand this must consult the author himself. 'Tis sufficient, if I can make the learned world apprehend, that there is some difficulty in the case, and that who-ever solves the difficulty must say some thing very new and extraordinary; as new as the difficulty itself.

27   By all that has been said the reader will easily perceive, that the philosophy contain'd in this book is very sceptical, and tends to give us a notion of the imperfections and narrow limits of human understanding. Almost all reasoning is there reduced to experience; and the belief, which attends experience, is explained to be nothing but a peculiar sentiment, or lively conception produced by habit. Nor is this all, when we believe any thing of *external* existence, or suppose an object to exist a moment after it is no longer perceived, this belief is nothing but a sentiment of the same kind. Our author insists upon several other sceptical topics; and upon the whole concludes, that we assent to our faculties, and employ our reason only because we cannot help it. Philosophy wou'd render us entirely *Pyrrhonian*, were not nature too strong for it.

28   I shall conclude the logics of this author with an account of two opinions, which seem to be peculiar to himself, as indeed are most of his opinions. He asserts, that the soul, as far as we can conceive it, is nothing but a system or train of different perceptions, those of heat and cold, love and anger, thoughts and sensations; all united together, but without any perfect simplicity or identity. *Des Cartes* maintained that thought was the essence of the mind; not this thought or that thought, but thought in general. This seems to be absolutely [658] unintelligible, since every thing, that exists, is particular: And therefore it must be our several particular perceptions, that compose the mind. I say, *compose* the mind, not *belong* to it. The mind is not a substance, in which the perceptions

inhere. That notion is as unintelligible as the *Cartesian*, that thought or perception in general is the essence of the mind. We have no idea of substance of any kind, since we have no idea but what is derived from some impression, and we have no impression of any substance either material or spiritual. We know nothing but particular qualities and perceptions. As our idea of any body, a peach, for instance, is only that of a particular taste, colour, figure, size, consistence, &c. So our idea of any mind is only that of particular perceptions, without the notion of any thing we call substance, either simple or compound.

29   The second principle, which I proposed to take notice of, is with regard to Geometry. Having denied the infinite divisibility of extension, our author finds himself obliged to refute those mathematical arguments, which have been adduced for it; and these indeed are the only ones of any weight. This he does by denying Geometry to be a science exact enough to admit of conclusions so subtle as those which regard infinite divisibility. His arguments may be thus explained. All Geometry is founded on the notions of equality and inequality, and therefore according as we have or have not an exact standard of those relations, the science itself will or will not admit of great exactness. Now there is an exact standard of equality, if we suppose that quantity is composed of indivisible points. Two lines are equal when the numbers of the points, that compose them, are equal, and when there is a point in one corresponding to a point in the other. But tho' this standard be exact, 'tis useless; since we can never compute the number of points in any line. It is besides founded on the supposition of finite divisibility, and therefore can never afford any conclusion against it. If we [659] reject this standard of equality, we have none that has any pretensions to exactness. I find two that are commonly made use of. Two lines above a yard, for instance, are said to be equal, when they contain any inferior quantity, as an inch, an equal number of times. But this runs in a circle. For the quantity we call an inch in the one is supposed to be *equal* to what we call an inch in the other: And the question still is, by what standard we proceed when we judge them to be equal; or, in other words, what we mean when we say they are equal. If we take still inferior quantities, we go on *in infinitum*. This therefore is no standard of equality. The greatest part of philosophers, when ask'd what they mean by equality, say, that the word admits of no definition, and that it is sufficient to place before us two equal bodies, such as two diameters of a circle, to make us understand that term. Now this is taking the *general appearance* of the objects for the standard of that proportion, and renders our imagination and senses the ultimate judges of it. But such a standard admits of no exactness, and can never afford any conclusion contrary to the imagination and senses. Whether this reasoning be just or not, must be left to the learned world to judge. 'Twere certainly to be wish'd, that some expedient were fallen upon to reconcile philosophy and

common sense, which with regard to the question of infinite divisibility have wag'd most cruel wars with each other.

30   We must now proceed to give some account of the second volume of this work, which treats of the PASSIONS. 'Tis of more easy comprehension than the first; but contains opinions, that are altogether as new and extraordinary. The author begins with *pride* and *humility*. He observes, that the objects which excite these passions, are very numerous, and seemingly very different from each other. Pride or self-esteem may arise from the qualities of the mind; wit, [660] good-sense, learning, courage, integrity: from those of the body; beauty, strength, agility, good mein, address in dancing, riding, fencing: from external advantages; country, family, children, relations, riches, houses, gardens, horses, dogs, cloaths. He afterwards proceeds to find out that common circumstance, in which all these objects agree, and which causes them to operate on the passions. His theory likewise extends to love and hatred, and other affections. As these questions, tho' curious, could not be rendered intelligible without a long discourse, we shall here omit them.

31   It may perhaps be more acceptable to the reader to be informed of what our author says concerning *free-will*. He has laid the foundation of his doctrine in what he said concerning cause and effect, as above explained. ' 'Tis universally acknowledged, that the operations of external bodies are necessary, and that in the communication of their motion, in their attraction and mutual cohesion, there are not the least traces of indifference or liberty.'—'Whatever therefore is in this respect on the same footing with matter, must be acknowledged to be necessary. That we may know whether this be the case with the actions of the mind, we may examine matter, and consider on what the idea of a necessity in its operations are founded, and why we conclude one body or action to be the infallible cause of another.

32   'It has been observed already, that in no single instance the ultimate connexion of any object is discoverable either by our senses or reason, and that we can never penetrate so far into the essence and construction of bodies, as to perceive the principle on which their mutual influence is founded. 'Tis their constant union alone, with which we are acquainted; and 'tis from the constant union the necessity arises, when the mind is determined to pass from one object to its usual attendant, and infer the existence of one from that of the other. Here then [661] are two particulars, which we are to regard as essential to *necessity*, *viz.* the constant *union* and the *inference* of the mind, and wherever we discover these we must acknowledge a necessity.' Now nothing is more evident than the constant union of particular actions with particular motives. If all actions be not constantly united with their proper motives, this uncertainty is no more than what may be observed every day in the actions of matter, where by reason of the mixture and uncertainty of causes, the effect is often variable and uncertain.

Thirty grains of opium will kill any man that is not accustomed to it; tho' thirty grains of rhubarb will not always purge him. In like manner the fear of death will always make a man go twenty paces out of his road; tho' it will not always make him do a bad action.

33   And as there is often a constant conjunction of the actions of the will with their motives, so the inference from the one to the other is often as certain as any reasoning concerning bodies: and there is always an inference proportioned to the constancy of the conjunction. On this is founded our belief in witnesses, our credit in history, and indeed all kinds of moral evidence, and almost the whole conduct of life.

34   Our author pretends, that this reasoning puts the whole controversy in a new light, by giving a new definition of necessity. And, indeed, the most zealous advocates for free-will must allow this union and inference with regard to human actions. They will only deny, that this makes the whole of necessity. But then they must shew, that we have an idea of something else in the actions of matter; which, according to the foregoing reasoning, is impossible.

35   Thro' this whole book, there are great pretensions to new discoveries in philosophy; but if any thing can intitle the author to so glorious a name as that of an *inventor*, 'tis the use he makes of the principle of the association of ideas, which enters into most of his philosophy. Our imagination has a great author- [662] ity over our ideas; and there are no ideas that are different from each other, which it cannot separate, and join, and compose into all the varieties of fiction. But notwithstanding the empire of the imagination, there is a secret tie or union among particular ideas, which causes the mind to conjoin them more frequently together, and makes the one, upon its appearance, introduce the other. Hence arises what we call the *apropos* of discourse: hence the connexion of writing: and hence that thread, or chain of thought, which a man naturally supports even in the loosest *reverie*. These principles of association are reduced to three, *viz. Resemblance*; a picture naturally makes us think of the man it was drawn for. *Contiguity*; when *St. Dennis* is mentioned, the idea of *Paris* naturally occurs. *Causation*; when we think of the son, we are apt to carry our attention to the father. 'Twill be easy to conceive of what vast consequence these principles must be in the science of human nature, if we consider, that so far as regards the mind, these are the only links that bind the parts of the universe together, or connect us with any person or object exterior to ourselves. For as it is by means of thought only that any thing operates upon our passions, and as these are the only ties of our thoughts, they are really *to us* the cement of the universe, and all the operations of the mind must, in a great measure, depend on them.

FINIS.

CRITICAL SURVEY OF THE LITERATURE ON HUME AND THE FIRST ENQUIRY

Peter Millican

This survey aims to provide useful suggestions for further reading related to the first *Enquiry*, focused especially on the philosophical and scholarly issues discussed in this volume, and supplemented by references to contemporary works on the same themes. It starts with a short discussion of selected current editions of the *Enquiry* itself, then of Hume's other relevant works, before moving on to philosophical and interpretative topics, mostly organized according to the sections of the *Enquiry* where those topics are addressed, and making reference where appropriate to the papers in this volume (reserving the capitalized 'Chapter' for this purpose). Wherever a topic is not only of scholarly interest, but also of continuing philosophical or scientific relevance, I have tried to suggest some useful points of access into the modern literature, so that those whose interest is stimulated by the reading of Hume can follow this through into some of the many fascinating areas of contemporary debate.

Since Beauchamp's student edition of the *Enquiry* (referenced in §1.1 below) already contains a useful and reasonably up-to-date annotated bibliography (in its 'Supplementary Reading' section), I have tried as far as possible to complement it rather than to overlap. Hence there is no special section here on historical sources or bibliographic materials, nor on introductory surveys of Hume's thought, nor on general anthologies and collections of essays; in all of these areas my own recommendations (except in the case of the recent general collections mentioned in §3.1 below) would correspond closely with those made by Beauchamp. Instead, I have tried to give more specific advice for students or scholars working through the issues discussed in this volume, often under pressure of time, and needing to make decisions which more wide-ranging bibliographies typically leave open, such as which Hume edition(s) they are best advised to purchase, and which particular articles or sections of books will most repay study on each of the various issues (and in which order). To this end I have summarized the most salient points of the majority of the items listed (excepting those that are too wide-ranging to make this feasible), and these summaries are often quite extensive where this has enabled me to spell out how the discussions fit together as parts of a continuing debate, or where the issues are particularly complex. In the case of some very recent items to which appropriate responses have not yet appeared, I have also added some personal suggestions regarding promising lines of criticism.

The whole field of Hume studies is blossoming, with interest in his philosophy stronger than ever and high-quality contributions appearing every year. This has enabled me to include here many very recent works, whose citations can therefore in turn be used to identify further topical material for those with time to move beyond my recommendations. Such readers will find some additional suggestions in Beauchamp's bibliography, which in particular lists a number of books that I have omitted not from any adverse judgement on their quality, but usually because they are relatively unfocused on the topic in question. Also useful for older references will be 'Some Notes on the Hume Literature' which appears as an appendix to Terence Penelhum's *David Hume: An Introduction to his Philosophical System* (see §3.2 below).

In the future I intend to provide updates to this survey through the Leeds Electronic Text Centre Hume Project website which hosts my electronic edition of the *Enquiry* (at www.etext.leeds.ac.uk/hume/). This site will also give access to freely available electronic copies of some of the works listed here, especially where these are difficult to obtain (e.g. because they are out of print or in journals of limited circulation). Any authors or other copyright holders willing to provide such electronic copies are invited to contact the Electronic Text Centre through the website. Readers will, I hope, find this an increasingly useful resource for gaining unrestricted access to some of the best available work on Hume and the *Enquiry*.

1. EDITIONS OF THE ENQUIRY

1.1 *Printed Editions*

For many years the standard edition of the *Enquiry*, used for page references in the vast majority of philosophical and scholarly works on Hume, has been the edition published by Oxford University Press, originally edited by Selby-Bigge and more recently revised by Nidditch:

> David Hume, *Enquiries concerning Human Understanding and concerning the Principles of Morals* (1777), ed. L. A. Selby-Bigge, 3rd edn. rev. P. H. Nidditch (Oxford: Clarendon Press, 1975).

The text is based on the 1777 edition, which was the last to contain new authorial corrections (Hume having died in 1776). However, it is far from perfect, containing well over 1,000 small inaccuracies, mostly of punctuation. Moreover, Selby-Bigge's editorial additions are generally best ignored, with the possible exceptions of the analytical index and the comparative table of contents with the *Treatise*. In particular, his Introduction is dated and totally misrepresents Hume's intentions, while the marginal numbers which he inserted within the text simply invite misunderstanding because they are so easily confused with page numbers.

The page numbering of the Selby-Bigge edition will continue to be important for the foreseeable future, given the sheer number of books and articles on Hume (including those in the current volume) which use it to make reference to the two *Enquiries*. Readers of other editions are therefore well advised to write the Selby-Bigge page numbers at the relevant points in the margin of whatever edition they use themselves—the location of the Selby-Bigge page breaks can be found not only from the printed edition itself, but also from the appropriate version of the Leeds electronic edition of the *Enquiry*, available freely on the World Wide Web from the address www.etext.leeds.ac.uk/hume/ (see §1.2 below).

Most printed editions of the *Enquiry* are textually even less accurate than the Selby-Bigge, but a number of them have useful editorial notes to supplement the text, such as elucidations of Hume's terms and explanations of his references. Though by now rather dated, the one by Hendel is particularly worthy of mention, because it also contains details of the various editions of the *Enquiry* that appeared in Hume's lifetime, together with the text of footnotes and other passages that were omitted from the 1777 edition:

David Hume, *An Inquiry concerning Human Understanding* (1777), ed. Charles W. Hendel (Indianapolis: Bobbs-Merrill Educational Publishing, 1955).

By far the best printed edition of the *Enquiry* currently available, however, has only recently appeared in the Oxford Philosophical Texts series:[1]

David Hume, *An Enquiry concerning Human Understanding* (1772), ed. Tom L. Beauchamp (Oxford and New York: Oxford University Press, 1999).

Beauchamp's editorial material is in general first-rate. It includes a detailed introduction describing the background to the *Enquiry* and giving an outline of each section, an excellent survey of supplementary reading, an extensive and well-organized appendix of annotations to the text, and a useful glossary. The text is also highly reliable, though based on the 1772 edition, which is arguably less authoritative than the 1777 preferred by most other editors. The main difference between the two is Hume's deletion from the latter of the majority of Section III, which he presumably excised from the edition left to posterity because he appreciated its lack of philosophical relevance to the main project of the *Enquiry* as a whole. Beauchamp notes the deletion,[2] so in this respect readers are free to take their choice, but it is perhaps a shame that other significant deletions, from previous editions of the *Enquiry*, are not also noted by him (hence the continuing value of Hendel's edition, which does record them). The last and major criticism of Beauchamp's edition is its lack of Selby-Bigge page numbering. No doubt from a purist point of view the strict paragraph numbering introduced in Beauchamp's edition (as in the other new Oxford editions of Hume's works) is superior, but the inclusion of Selby-Bigge numbers in the margin would have greatly facilitated the usefulness of this edition for study, given that they have for so long been the de facto standard for references to the *Enquiry* in philosophical and scholarly works. Again, however, the solution is straightforward, and readers who wish to remedy this omission in their copy of the Beauchamp edition can easily do so by hand.

---

[1] Note that this is Beauchamp's *student* edition of the *Enquiry*, joined even more recently by a Clarendon *critical* edition with the same editor and based on the same text, which will be of particular interest to specialist scholars but is significantly more expensive.

[2] In his note on the text (p. 80) Beauchamp calls it 'a major and unexplained deletion', thereby perhaps suggesting doubt regarding its authority. My own view is that the deletion was entirely judicious, and totally in line with the sort of streamlining outlined in §6 of Chapter 1 of this volume, 'The Context, Aims, and Structure of Hume's First *Enquiry*'.

1.2 Electronic Editions

For students and scholars, the two most obvious potential virtues of electronic texts are cheapness and ease of manipulation (the latter including ease of reproduction, distribution, excerpting, and searching). Many free versions of the *Enquiry* are available from the World Wide Web, but most are of dubious quality, being based on old printed editions that are now in the public domain. There is, however, a highly reliable version of the 1777 edition published by the University of Leeds Electronic Text Centre, and made freely available for non-profit academic purposes:

> David Hume, *An Enquiry concerning Human Understanding* (1777), ed. Peter Millican (Leeds Electronic Text Centre, 2000), from Web address www.etext.leeds.ac.uk/hume/

This site is the home page of a recently established but long-term project devoted to works on, and by, Hume, focusing on the publication of high-quality texts and bibliographic materials together with search and other facilities. These facilities include the ability to display the texts in a number of formats, for example unpaginated, paginated as in Hume's original edition, or paginated according to the standard editions. The last of these is particularly useful in the current context, since it enables the Selby-Bigge pagination to be freely consulted over the Web.

Currently the best search facilities available for Hume's works in general are provided by

> *Complete Works & Correspondence of David Hume*, CD-ROM in the Past Masters series, published by InteLex Corporation, Charlottesville, Virginia; Web address www.nlx.com

The texts used by InteLex are not of high quality (e.g. the *Enquiry* is taken from the 1898 Green and Grose edition), and the CD-ROM is far too expensive for most students, but the search facilities make it invaluable for those engaged in serious research on Hume, especially as it includes not only Hume's philosophical works, but also his *History of England* and his correspondence.

2. HUME'S OTHER WORKS

2.1 A Treatise of Human Nature

Exactly as with the two *Enquiries*, the standard edition of the *Treatise* has for many years been the Oxford University Press edition originally edited by Selby-Bigge, and more recently revised by Nidditch:

> David Hume, *A Treatise of Human Nature* (1739–40), ed. L. A. Selby-Bigge, 2nd edn. rev. P. H. Nidditch (Oxford: Clarendon Press, 1978).

Thanks to Nidditch, the text is of high quality. And Selby-Bigge's analytical index remains useful, though just as with the *Enquiries*, his edition has recently been effectively supplanted (for all purposes other than text references) by a new edition in the Oxford Philosophical Texts series:

David Hume, *A Treatise of Human Nature* (1739–40), ed. David Fate Norton and Mary J. Norton (Oxford and New York: Oxford University Press, 2000).

David Norton's introduction is particularly valuable, providing an excellent outline of this complex and difficult work. Other useful editorial material includes a section of comprehensive annotations to the *Treatise* and to the *Abstract* (the text of which is included with the *Treatise* in both the editions mentioned here), and a glossary of 'potentially puzzling words and phrases'. Again the major criticism of the new Oxford edition is its lack of Selby-Bigge page numbering, but again this can easily be remedied by hand.

2.2 An Enquiry Concerning the Principles of Morals

Hume's second *Enquiry* is included with the first in the Selby-Bigge edition discussed in §1.1 above, but yet again the best modern edition is in the Oxford Philosophical Texts series:

David Hume, *An Enquiry concerning the Principles of Morals* (1751), ed. Tom L. Beauchamp (Oxford and New York: Oxford University Press, 1998).

This has similar virtues to Beauchamp's companion edition of the first *Enquiry* (see §1.1 above), and is therefore highly recommended.

2.3 Dialogues Concerning Natural Religion

For understanding the *Enquiry*, Hume's posthumously published *Dialogues* have an importance surpassed only by the *Treatise*. They are also the most cleverly constructed and entertaining of all his works, and perhaps the funniest truly great work of philosophy ever written by anyone. The standard edition referred to in most articles and books on Hume is the one edited by Kemp Smith:

David Hume, *Dialogues concerning Natural Religion* (1779), ed. Norman Kemp Smith, 2nd edn. (Edinburgh: Nelson, 1947).

This edition is particularly highly respected for two reasons. First, Kemp Smith carefully examined Hume's manuscript (even to the extent of studying the watermarks of the sheets on which it is written), and in his edition highlights his conclusions regarding the important changes that Hume made to the *Dialogues* between its original composition (in the early 1750s) and his death in 1776 (when he evidently took great care in preparing it for posthumous publication). Secondly, Kemp Smith provides a great deal in addition to Hume's text, including sections on various aspects of Hume's general views on religion, a short discussion of Sections X and XI of the *Enquiry*, a famous interpretative essay entitled 'The Argument of the *Dialogues concerning Natural Religion*', a detailed critical analysis of the argument of the *Dialogues*, and some further appendices and textual supplements of related historical material. It is a great shame that at the time of writing this excellent and standard edition (though reprinted by Bobbs-Merrill of Indianapolis from 1962 to 1980) is out of print.

   Those seeking a reasonably priced and reliable modern edition of the *Dialogues* are probably best advised to choose one of the following:

David Hume, *Dialogues concerning Natural Religion* (1779) and *The Natural History of Religion* (1757), ed. J. C. A. Gaskin (Oxford and New York: Oxford University Press, 1993).

David Hume, *Dialogues concerning Natural Religion* (1779), ed. Martin Bell (Harmondsworth: Penguin, 1990).

Gaskin uses Kemp Smith's text, and also his footnotes, which highlight what he took to be Hume's most significant manuscript alterations. Hence this edition will particularly appeal to those with interest in these scholarly issues, and it also has the very significant benefit of including Hume's *Natural History of Religion* together with a short editorial introduction and useful explanatory notes on both works. Bell's edition seems to be targeted more at the general reader—it is, for example, less densely printed and hence much easier on the eye, while its introduction weaves major themes from the philosophy of the *Treatise* and *Enquiry* into the discussion of Hume's life and his views on religion so as to provide a context for readers unfamiliar with his general epistemology. The editorial notes likewise provide helpful references to quotations from Hume's other writings and from the works of related philosophers and historical sources.

2.4 Hume's Essays

Of Hume's many essays, the ones most directly relevant to the topics of the *Enquiry* are those on religion, in particular 'Of Superstition and Enthusiasm' and 'Of the Immortality of the Soul'. But a number of others, for example 'Of the Dignity or Meanness of Human Nature', 'The Sceptic', 'Of the Standard of Taste', 'Of Essay Writing', and 'Of Suicide', also cover themes that are pertinent to the *Enquiry*, in respect of either its philosophical content or the context and manner of its composition. The standard modern edition of Hume's *Essays* is the following:

David Hume, *Essays, Moral, Political, and Literary* (1741–83), ed. Eugene F. Miller, 2nd edn. (Indianapolis: Liberty Classics, 1987).

Most of the essays, including all those mentioned above, are also included in a companion volume to Gaskin's edition of the *Dialogues*, in Oxford's World's Classics series:

David Hume, *Selected Essays* (1741–83), ed. Stephen Copley and Andrew Edgar (Oxford and New York: Oxford University Press, 1993).

2.5 Other Writings by Hume

Apart from Hume's major works dealt with above, and the *Abstract* and 'My Own Life' reprinted in this volume, his writings most relevant to the *Enquiry* are

David Hume, *A Letter from a Gentleman to his Friend in Edinburgh* (1745), ed. Ernest C. Mossner and John V. Price (Edinburgh: Edinburgh University Press, 1967).

The Letters of David Hume, ed. J. Y. T. Greig, 2 vols. (Oxford: Clarendon Press, 1932).

New Letters of David Hume, ed. R. Klibansky and E. C. Mossner (Oxford: Clarendon Press, 1954).

Only two other significant works remain to be mentioned, namely the largely forgotten *Dissertation on the Passions*, which currently has no modern printed edition,[3] and the *History of England*, which fortunately does:

> David Hume, *The History of England* (1754–62), ed. William Todd, 6 vols. (Indianapolis: Liberty Classics, 1983).

Full of historical insight and wry humour, *The History of England* will be particularly fascinating for the Hume scholar attuned to his characteristic comments and turns of phrase. However, it was written for a more leisured age, and its six volumes will probably strike most modern readers as rather heavy going.

3. GENERAL SECONDARY LITERATURE ON HUME AND THE ENQUIRY

3.1 Recent General Collections of Scholarly Work on Hume

Four of the best-known collections of advanced papers on Hume—edited by Chappell (1968), Livingston and King (1976), Morice (1977), and Norton, Capaldi, and Robison (1979)—are now all more than twenty years old, though still well worth consulting. Relevant papers from them are listed in the sections that follow, as also from the 1990 collection *Studies in the Philosophy of the Scottish Enlightenment*, edited by Stewart. Of far more general interest for the study of the *Enquiry* is another recent Stewart volume:

> Stewart, M. A., and Wright, John P. (eds.), *Hume and Hume's Connexions* (Edinburgh: Edinburgh University Press, 1994),

whose twelve papers include discussions of Hume's attempts to become a professor, the influences on his thought, his conception of 'the science of the mind' and of 'probable reasoning', his early attacks on the Design Argument, his treatment of miracles, and his other writings on religion.

The papers in *Hume and Hume's Connexions* all present new research, and are therefore not ideally suited for students. A less scholarly but far more systematic overview of Hume's philosophy, at a relatively introductory level, is provided by

> Norton, David Fate (ed.), *The Cambridge Companion to Hume* (Cambridge: Cambridge University Press, 1993).

This contains extremely useful papers by a number of distinguished authors, covering a wide range of topics including Hume's overall approach to philosophy, his science of the mind, his philosophy of science, his scepticism, and his view of religion, as well as others

---

[3] The *Dissertation on the Passions*, like most of Hume's other works, is available in *The Philosophical Works of David Hume* edited by T. H. Green and T. H. Grose, 4 vols. (London: Longmans, 1882–6), which has recently been reprinted in facsimile (Bristol: Thoemmes, 1996). Like other works the *Dissertation* is also destined to appear in the Clarendon Hume series of critical editions from Oxford University Press. In the meantime, the best practical source for Hume's more obscure works is probably the InteLex electronic edition mentioned in §1.2 above.

less relevant to the *Enquiry* (e.g. on Hume's moral, political, aesthetic, and historical work).

Two other recent collections are particularly useful for the purposes of this survey, and will be mentioned frequently below. Unfortunately both are expensive, and targeted for library rather than for individual purchase, but both include a wide range of important reprints which are well worth consulting and are sometimes hard to obtain elsewhere. In what follows, these will be referred to as 'Tweyman (ed.), *Hume*' and 'Owen (ed.), *Hume*' respectively:

> Tweyman, Stanley (ed.), *David Hume: Critical Assessments*, 6 vols. (London and New York: Routledge, 1995).

> Owen, David W. D. (ed.), *Hume: General Philosophy* (Aldershot and Burlington, Vt.: Ashgate, 2000).

Tweyman's massive collection aims to cover the whole range of Hume's philosophy including, among many others, sections devoted to Hume's views on epistemology (17 papers), reason (7 papers), induction (7 papers), scepticism (9 papers), naturalism (7 papers), causality (19 papers), the external world (4 papers), and religion (34 papers). Many of the papers are well-known 'classics', but a high proportion date from the 1980s or later, and although the editor's selection is inevitably controversial in parts, the collection as a whole undoubtedly provides the most valuable single resource currently available for articles on Hume.

Owen's collection is a single volume of 'facsimile' reprints, divided into eight sections, of which all but the one on personal identity have immediate relevance to the *Enquiry* (being respectively on methodology, ideas and impressions, logic and demonstrative reasoning, belief and probable reasoning, miracles, causation and the 'New Hume', and scepticism). For each section the editor has selected between two and four papers, aiming to give good coverage of major areas of recent scholarly debate, and with particular points of interest and disagreement being highlighted by his introduction. The papers are of a very high standard, and the collection is highly topical (with only three of the twenty-one selections pre-dating 1985). It is therefore likely to prove particularly useful for readers wishing to get up to date with recent scholarship on Hume's epistemology and metaphysics, and to acquaint themselves in reasonable detail with some of the major issues that are currently exciting most controversy.

To keep abreast with ongoing developments in Hume scholarship, by far the most valuable resource is the journal of the Hume Society:

> *Hume Studies*, published by the Hume Society twice yearly (Apr. and Nov.).

Most of the major contributors to the Hume literature have presented at least some of their work through *Hume Studies*, which is now highly respected in the philosophical community. Moreover, it attracts papers not only from specialist scholars, but also from notable contributors to contemporary thought—one recent issue, for example, included articles by Annette Baier, Simon Blackburn, David Pears, and Barry Stroud.

3.2 *General Introductory Books on Hume's Philosophy in the* Enquiry

The only major single-author work devoted to the philosophy of the *Enquiry* is still Antony Flew's classic:

Flew, Antony, *Hume's Philosophy of Belief* (London: Routledge & Kegan Paul, 1961).

Though extremely dated, and therefore to be treated with caution, this still repays reading on topics where Hume's purposes have long been well understood. The book as a whole is difficult for beginners, partly because Flew engages in so many detours to point out (often in characteristically forthright terms) the anti-metaphysical and anti-theological implications of Hume's views. However, these detours themselves give the book a distinctive value, especially in Flew's chapters on Hume's Fork (ch. 3), on liberty and necessity (ch. 7), and on the Design Argument (ch. 9), in all of which his broad sympathy with Hume's views are very evident. Also worth consulting are his chapters on 'the objects of the exercise' (ch. 1), on belief (ch. 5), on scepticism (ch. 10), and on the Copy Principle (ch. 2), in the last of which he takes a somewhat similar line to Bennett in Chapter 3 of this volume. The book is weakest where Flew has least sympathy with what he takes to be Hume's position, most notably in the case of his deductivist interpretation of the famous argument concerning induction (which also unfortunately distorts his otherwise useful treatment of miracles—hence my preference in §9.1 below for his 1959 article on the topic).

An engaging introduction to most of the central aspects of Hume's philosophy in the *Enquiry*, which combines the text of Sections II, III, IV, VII, and XI (and of two second *Enquiry* appendices) with editorial commentary at a level suitable for beginners, is

> Penelhum, Terence, *David Hume: An Introduction to his Philosophical System* (West Lafayette, Ind.: Purdue University Press, 1992).

Penelhum's account of Hume's motivations (which he developed in the article cited in §10.3 below) will be of interest to scholars as well as students: he identifies the essence of Hume's 'sceptical' view as being that philosophy itself should not be taken too seriously, since so far from bringing inner peace and tranquillity—as often traditionally claimed—it can instead lead to bewilderment and despair. Penelhum's discussions of the theory of ideas, cause and effect, and the Design Argument are less distinctive, but are all very clear and philosophically well informed. His appendix 'Some Notes on the Hume Literature' is also useful, if rather dated (containing very few references beyond 1985).

3.3 *Hume's Life, His Aims in the* Enquiry, *and Its Relation to the* Treatise

The standard biography of Hume, which is thorough, generally accurate, and provides valuable discussion concerning the background to his publications, is

> Mossner, Ernest Campbell, *The Life of David Hume*, 2nd edn. (Oxford: Clarendon Press, 1980).

The traditional accusation that Hume was led to write the *Enquiry* for vulgar motives of popular notoriety (discussed in §4 of Chapter 1 of this volume) has long since been thoroughly disposed of, the two best-known refutations being

> Kemp Smith, Norman, *The Philosophy of David Hume* (London: Macmillan, 1941), ch. 24.

Mossner, Ernest Campbell, 'Philosophy and Biography: The Case of David Hume', *Philosophical Review*, 59 (1950), 184–201; repr. in V. C. Chappell (ed.), *Hume* (London and Melbourne: Macmillan, 1968), 6–34.

More recently the same ground has been covered by

Buckle, Stephen, 'Hume's Biography and Hume's Philosophy', *Australasian Journal of Philosophy*, 77 (1999), 1–25.

Buckle presents the *Enquiry* as a coherent and unified work, distinguished from the *Treatise* primarily in its greater focus on an 'experimentalism' inspired by Newtonian science. Humean experimentalism involves a preference for mechanistic explanations and an eschewal of speculation about ultimate causes, both of which are prominent themes in the *Enquiry*, from the theory of association of ideas with which it begins (in Sections II and III) to the mitigated scepticism with which it ends (in Section XII).

Although Buckle seems to suggest that the move from the *Treatise* to the *Enquiry* is primarily a change of focus rather than of philosophical position, he approvingly mentions (p. 17) an article by Immerwahr whose aim is to provide a deeper account:

Immerwahr, John, 'A Skeptic's Progress: Hume's Preference for the First *Enquiry*', in David Fate Norton, Nicholas Capaldi, and Wade L. Robison (eds.), *McGill Hume Studies* (San Diego: Austin Hill Press, 1979), 227–38.

Immerwahr draws attention to Hume's distinction in the *Treatise* between the 'general and more establish'd properties of the imagination' and the 'trivial properties of the fancy' (*T* 225, 267–8). The latter are the dubious source of much theology and rationalist metaphysics, but in the *Treatise* Hume is unable consistently to condemn them, because (as made clear at *T* 185–6 and 268) they also play a crucial role in avoiding the corrosive scepticism to which the 'general properties' give rise in *Treatise* I. iv. 1. Immerwahr sees the *Enquiry* as providing Hume with a more satisfactory basis for his critical purposes, avoiding radical scepticism not by reliance on the 'trivial properties', but instead by limiting the 'general properties' to the subjects appropriate for human investigation. Other writers too—notably Penelhum, Norton, and Fogelin—have viewed the sceptical outlook of the two works as significantly different, contrasting the calm mitigated scepticism of the *Enquiry* (discussed at length by Norton in Chapter 14) with the unstable 'on-again-off-again' Pyrrhonism of the *Treatise* (the works of all three authors are considered in §10.3 below). But this picture has recently been contested by

McCormick, Miriam, 'A Change in Manner: Hume's Scepticism in the *Treatise* and the First *Enquiry*', *Canadian Journal of Philosophy*, 29 (1999), 431–47.

McCormick stresses instead the continuity between the *Treatise* and the *Enquiry*, by arguing that the sceptical attitude of the *Treatise* is (despite some appearances to the contrary) virtually identical to that which is expressed much more clearly in the *Enquiry*.

Differences between the *Treatise* and the *Enquiry* are not, of course, confined to Hume's account of scepticism. One very significant change in the *Enquiry*, to which Noxon draws attention, is the separation of philosophical from psychological theorizing, which in the *Treatise* were densely intertwined:

Noxon, James, *Hume's Philosophical Development* (Oxford: Clarendon Press, 1973), esp. 12–26, 153–65, 180–7.

On Noxon's account, Hume's later works quite generally separate the critical from the constructive elements of his philosophy, a separation most evident in his later moral and political writings which (unlike the *Treatise*) tend to establish their positions on the basis of direct observation rather than psychological theory. This separation leaves the *Enquiry* focusing on the critical aspects of Hume's philosophy, with little attempt to forge any connexion (e.g. through the theory of association; cf. Dauer's paper in §4.1 below) with the psychological complexities that had figured so prominently in the *Treatise*, but which had ultimately, and inevitably, proved incapable of providing a criterion for distinguishing science from superstition. Noxon sees Hume in the *Enquiry* as adopting a new criterion, a 'Principle of Methodological Consistency', based on the idea that legitimate science is a development of the methods 'of common life, methodized and corrected' (*E* 162). Such a principle obviously harmonizes well with the mitigated scepticism emphasized by Buckle and Immerwahr, but its adoption need not in itself imply any doubts about the psychological theories of the *Treatise*, even if Hume now sees them as largely irrelevant to his main critical purposes. Nelson, however, argues that the divide between the *Treatise* and the *Enquiry* goes deeper still, with Hume's repudiation of the earlier work being motivated by the recognition that it is contaminated with metaphysics of the very kind that he would later famously condemn in *Enquiry* XII:

Nelson, John O., 'Two Main Questions concerning Hume's *Treatise* and *Enquiry*', *Philosophical Review*, 81 (1972), 333–7.

Nelson's theory is itself forcefully repudiated by

Cummins, Phillip D., 'Hume's Disavowal of the *Treatise*', *Philosophical Review*, 82 (1973), 371–9,

who argues that the *Enquiry* differs from the *Treatise* in respect of its psychology rather than its metaphysics. Indeed the only major Humean metaphysical doctrine whose absence from the *Enquiry* Cummins acknowledges (p. 379 note 35) is the bundle theory of the self, though he downplays even this by suggesting that Hume's famous difficulties with that theory (expressed in the Appendix to the *Treatise*) are relatively superficial, concerning only the explanation of *our belief* in personal identity. Flage, by contrast, takes Hume's difficulties with the bundle theory to be fundamental, even to the extent of providing the main reason for his dissatisfaction with the theory of mind in the *Treatise*, and motivating his move in the *Enquiry* to a far less ambitious theory which aspires only to lawful description of the mind's operations and makes no attempt to draw conclusions about the nature of the mind itself:

Flage, Daniel E., *David Hume's Theory of Mind* (London and New York: Routledge, 1990), ch. 8; also available from the website www.etext.leeds.ac.uk/hume/

Flage's account also implies that Hume's problems with personal identity were the primary reason for his apparent loss of confidence in associationism (as documented in §4 of Chapter 1 of this volume). However, Broackes (in Chapter 6) argues that despite these problems the bundle theory continued to underlie Hume's psychological theorizing, while Bell (in Chapter 5) suggests that much of Hume's associationism may simply have been omitted from the *Enquiry* rather than rejected. As this wide range of different views testifies, we are still some way from any consensus on what lies behind the differences between the *Treatise* and the *Enquiry*. Nor should we restrict our attention here to philosophical considerations, for as Stewart makes clear in Chapter 2, at least some aspects of the *Enquiry* were significantly influenced not only by literary considerations, but also by some more personal and historical concerns.

4. THE NATURE AND ORIGIN OF IDEAS

4.1 *Impressions and Ideas, Force and Vivacity*

An excellent introduction to Hume's theory of ideas, and also his theory of belief, appears in a volume aimed at pre-university students. In this paper Craig also explicitly relates these theories to his 'Image of God' interpretation as discussed in Chapter 7:

Craig, Edward, 'Hume on Thought and Belief', in Godfrey Vesey (ed.), *Philosophers Ancient and Modern* (Cambridge: Cambridge University Press, 1986), 93–110.

Stroud's well-known book provides a rather more advanced discussion of the main features of Hume's theory of ideas, though it is generally focused far more on the *Treatise* than on the *Enquiry*:

Stroud, Barry, *Hume* (London and Boston: Routledge & Kegan Paul, 1977), ch. 2.

Hume's fundamental distinction between impressions and ideas is founded on the notion of 'force and vivacity', which Stroud—like Bennett in Chapter 3—interprets in the most straightforward way, as phenomenological intensity. Both Bennett and Stroud accordingly find Hume's distinction inadequate to capture the difference he intends, between feeling and thinking. Govier suggests that a more satisfactory position can be developed by recognizing forcefulness and vivacity as two distinguishable characteristics of Humean perceptions, with a forceful perception being one that has a sustained causal influence, and a vivacious perception being one that is clear and intense. Then 'force' corresponds to distinctions related to degrees of belief, and 'vivacity' to the distinction between impressions and ideas:

Govier, Trudy, 'Variations on Force and Vivacity in Hume', *Philosophical Quarterly*, 22 (1972), 44–52.

Govier thus differs from Stroud and Bennett in taking 'force and vivacity' to be functional as much as phenomenological. Everson goes even further, arguing that Humean 'force and vivacity' should be interpreted exclusively in functional rather than phenomenological terms:

Everson, Stephen, 'The Difference between Feeling and Thinking', *Mind*, 97 (1988), 401–13; repr. in Tweyman (ed.), *Hume*, i. 10–24 and in Owen (ed.), *Hume*, 57–69.

However, a functional interpretation of force and vivacity makes its availability to consciousness problematic, and therefore seems hard to square with Hume's use of the notion. A recent discussion of the issue, proposing an alternative account according to which the 'force and vivacity' of impressions involves their sense of 'presentedness', is provided by

> Dauer, Francis W., 'Force and Vivacity in the *Treatise* and the *Enquiry*', *Hume Studies*, 25 (1999), 83–99.

Dauer's account has the implication that the 'force and vivacity' of impressions, memories, and beliefs, though somewhat analogous, are nevertheless distinct. He sees this as motivating Hume's move away from the 'hydraulic' model of belief (as outlined in §7 of Chapter 1) and therefore having significance in respect of the philosophical differences between the *Treatise* and the *Enquiry*.

Hume's hydraulic language may itself have even more direct relevance to the interpretation of his conception of force and vivacity (at least in the *Treatise*), for Wright draws on eighteenth-century physiology to suggest that he may have intended such language to be understood quite literally:

> Wright, John P., *The Sceptical Realism of David Hume* (Manchester: Manchester University Press, 1983), §19.

In the wake of twentieth-century philosophy it is natural to dismiss such a literalistic account as too crude to be worth considering. But a striking corrective is provided by recent work on neurophysiology, which suggests that Hume's admittedly simplistic theories of mental activity may contain a germ of truth. As Damasio, a prominent neurologist, puts it (p. 108): 'The images reconstituted from the brain's interior are less vivid than those prompted by the exterior. They are "faint", as David Hume put it, in comparison with the "lively" images generated by stimuli from outside the brain. But they are images nonetheless.'

> Damasio, Antonio R., *Descartes's Error*, Papermac edn. (London and Basingstoke: Macmillan, 1996), ch. 5.

Later in his book (especially chapters 8, 9, and 11), Damasio emphasizes another more fundamental respect in which Hume anticipated modern neuroscience: his insistence on the essential role of feeling within human reasoning, evident in his theory of belief in *Enquiry* V (and even more so in the *Treatise*, e.g. *T* 103 and 183). There is, of course, an intimate connexion between Hume's theory of ideas and his theory of belief, as brought out in a rich discussion by Flage which takes the 'force and vivacity' issue close to the territory covered by Broackes in Chapter 6:

> Flage, Daniel E., *David Hume's Theory of Mind* (London and New York: Routledge, 1990), app.: 'Force and Vivacity'; an adapted version appears in Tweyman (ed.), *Hume*, i. 56–74.

To explore further in this direction, see the items listed in §6.1 below (most notably MacNabb's chapter and the end of the chapter by Bricke, both of which discuss the 'force and vivacity' of beliefs).

4.2 *The Copy Principle*

Bennett, in Chapter 3, casts serious doubt on the arguments that Hume presents for his Copy Principle, but nevertheless finds philosophical value in it by fundamentally reinterpreting it away from the idiom of 'ideas'. A recent book which spells out Bennett's approach at a more elementary level is

> Dicker, Georges, *Hume's Epistemology and Metaphysics* (London and New York: Routledge, 1998), 5–14.

Others have attempted to defend Hume in ways that do less violence to his professed philosophical foundations. Garrett, in a thought-provoking examination of the whole issue, maintains that Hume consistently treats the Copy Principle as a well-confirmed empirical generalization, and counters Bennett's negative assessment of Hume's arguments for it when thus interpreted:

> Garrett, Don, *Cognition and Commitment in Hume's Philosophy* (Oxford and New York: Oxford University Press, 1997), ch. 2.

One notorious puzzle for making sense of Hume's position is posed by his dismissive reaction to an apparent counter-example to the Copy Principle, the 'missing shade of blue' (*E* 20–1). Bennett's reinterpretation of the principle may seem to explain this away, but the adequacy of such a solution is challenged by

> Cummins, Robert, 'The Missing Shade of Blue', *Philosophical Review*, 87 (1978), 548–65,

who interprets the having of a Humean idea not as *understanding* a term, but as the possession of a *recognitional capacity*. Garrett's alternative solution is based on the natural resemblances which Hume acknowledges between simple ideas. For those seeking a summary of some of the main points in this debate, Bennett's approach and that of Fogelin (which is similar to Garrett's) are outlined by Noonan:

> Noonan, Harold W., *Hume on Knowledge* (London and New York: Routledge, 1999), ch. 2, esp. 65–70.

However, Noonan's chapter is valuable more as an introduction to the general topic than as an account of Hume's thinking in the *Enquiry*, for it focuses as least as much on the philosophical as on the scholarly issues, and is explicitly concerned with the *Treatise*. Another work devoted to the *Treatise* provides a philosophically deep discussion of the Copy Principle, aiming to steer a course between the positivist approach favoured by Bennett, and the naturalism exemplified by Garrett:

> Pears, David, *Hume's System* (Oxford and New York: Oxford University Press, 1990), chs. 1 and 2.

Noxon takes a very different view of the Copy Principle, proposing an 'instrumentalist' interpretation according to which the principle is a 'rule of procedure for analysis' rather than a universal generalization:

> Noxon, James, *Hume's Philosophical Development* (Oxford: Clarendon Press, 1973), 138–48.

Livingston provides yet another perspective, relating the Copy Principle, as a criterion of 'internal' conceptual mastery, to a general interpretation of Hume which sees him primarily as a historically rather than scientifically oriented philosopher:

Livingston, Donald W., *Hume's Philosophy of Common Life* (Chicago and London: University of Chicago Press, 1984), chs. 3 and 4.

Livingston does not accept any need for the sort of rational reconstruction undertaken by Bennett, for on his account, Hume's understanding of language is already far more sophisticated than the simplistic traditional interpretation—according to which Hume takes word meanings to be images copied from impressions—from which Bennett begins. In challenging this traditional interpretation Livingston draws on an influential paper by Árdal, which discusses Hume's account of abstract ideas and moral conventions (though this obviously moves the discussion a long way from the direct concerns of the *Enquiry*):

Árdal, Páll S., 'Convention and Value', in George P. Morice (ed.), *David Hume: Bicentenary Papers* (Edinburgh: Edinburgh University Press, 1977), 51–68; repr. in Tweyman (ed.), *Hume*, iv. 61–77.

Those wishing to follow up these issues through contemporary discussions in the philosophy of language will find that much recent work is fearsomely difficult. However, Blackburn and Miller provide two relatively accessible introductions, which take highly contrasting approaches while both giving significant attention to Humean issues:

Blackburn, Simon, *Spreading the Word* (Oxford and New York: Clarendon Press, 1984).

Miller, Alexander, *Philosophy of Language* (London: UCL Press, 1998).

Blackburn's treatment of the general problem of meaning occupies his first four chapters, with chapter 2 explaining the inadequacies of the Locke–Hume theory of ideas in this context. But whereas Blackburn starts from the empiricists and takes a broadly Gricean 'convention-belief' (or 'communication-intention') approach, Miller starts from Frege and prefers the more fashionable 'truth-conditional' style of meaning theory, explicitly opposing (in ch. 7) some of Blackburn's arguments. Miller's chapter 3 is of particular interest for its discussion of the verification principle, around which the logical positivists—claiming inspiration from Hume's Copy Principle—built their theory of meaning (however, their claim to be Hume's heirs is certainly disputable, as made clear for example by Craig's book mentioned in §7.3 below).

5. REASON AND INDUCTION

5.1 *Hume's Philosophical Logic*

Though fundamental to his philosophy, there has been relatively little detailed discussion of Hume's distinction between 'relations of ideas' and 'matters of fact'. Flew's chapter in his 1961 book remains valuable for a general introduction to the status and philosophical point of what he named 'Hume's Fork':

Flew, Antony, *Hume's Philosophy of Belief* (London: Routledge & Kegan Paul, 1961), ch. 3.

A thorough recent discussion of the distinction appears in an introductory text:

Dicker, Georges, *Hume's Epistemology and Metaphysics* (London and New York: Routledge, 1998), ch. 2.

Both Flew and Dicker relate Hume's Fork to Kant's analytic–synthetic distinction;
indeed Dicker gives Hume's position a surprisingly Kantian flavour, by suggesting that
it leaves room for synthetic a priori principles (including, on his account, Hume's Fork
itself), since he interprets Hume's 'matters of fact' as being restricted to propositions that
either assert or deny existence. Most have instead taken Hume's Fork to correspond to
the analytic–synthetic distinction as understood by the logical positivists such as Ayer,
according to whom 'a proposition is analytic when its validity depends solely on the definitions of the symbols it contains [or in Humean language, the nature of the ideas], and
synthetic when its validity is determined by the facts of experience' (p. 105):

> Ayer, A. J., *Language, Truth and Logic*, 2nd edn. (Harmondsworth: Penguin, 1971),
> ch. 4.

The analytic–synthetic distinction, thus understood, was famously criticised by Quine
and then defended by Grice and Strawson:

> Quine, Willard Van Orman, 'Two Dogmas of Empiricism', in *From a Logical Point of
> View* (Cambridge, Mass.: Harvard University Press, 1953), 20–46; repr. in Paul K.
> Moser (ed.), *A Priori Knowledge* (Oxford and New York: Oxford University Press,
> 1987), 42–67.

> Grice, H. P., and Strawson, P. F., 'In Defense of a Dogma', *Philosophical Review*, 65
> (1956), 141–58; repr. in Paul Grice, *Studies in the Way of Words* (Cambridge, Mass., and
> London: Harvard University Press, 1989), 196–212.

Miller provides an up-to-date commentary on this debate, also introducing some
important related issues (notably Quine's thesis of the indeterminacy of translation)
and giving advice for further reading:

> Miller, Alexander, *Philosophy of Language* (London: UCL Press, 1998), ch. 4.

Also of particular interest is the 'pragmatic' approach to analyticity taken by Aune, in his
attempt to develop a 'reformed' Humean empiricism on the way to solving the problem
of the external world:

> Aune, Bruce, *Knowledge of the External World* (London and New York: Routledge,
> 1991), 57–9, 86–90, 144–56.

Along with the famous Quinean objections, some more recent issues in the theory of
reference—associated with the work of Kripke—pose new difficulties for any simple
binary distinction such as Hume's Fork. Since, however, these technical difficulties are
unlikely to carry significant implications for Hume's philosophical purposes, it will
suffice here to mention one article that usefully introduces the logical issues, reprinted
within a topical collection which provides a good starting point for those wishing to dig
deeper:

> Swinburne, R. G., 'Analyticity, Necessity, and Apriority', *Mind*, 84 (1975), 225–43; repr.
> in Paul K. Moser (ed.), *A Priori Knowledge* (Oxford and New York: Oxford University
> Press, 1987), 170–89.

A potentially more serious problem for Hume concerns the adequacy of his famous maxim that whatever is conceivable is possible—the Conceivability Principle—which serves as his principal criterion for distinguishing between relations of ideas and matters of fact (*A* 650, *E* 25–6, 35, 48). Hume has often been supposed to accept in addition the (far more questionable) Inconceivability Principle, that whatever is inconceivable is impossible, which would have significant implications for his views on such things as the possibility of alternative senses (*E* 20), causal realism (*E* 33, 67–8), the external world (*E* 154–5), and infinite divisibility (*E* 155–8). Lightner argues forcefully that such an attribution would be incorrect:

> Lightner, D. Tycerium, 'Hume on Conceivability and Inconceivability', *Hume Studies*, 23 (1997), 113–32.

But the Conceivability Principle is itself controversial. Tidman considers various possible interpretations of 'conceivable', concluding that none of them can justify Hume's maxim because 'merely conceiving of a state of affairs gives us no reason whatsoever to think that state of affairs to be possible' (p. 298):

> Tidman, Paul, 'Conceivability as a Test for Possibility', *American Philosophical Quarterly*, 31 (1994), 297–309.

Tidman attributes the appeal of the maxim to a confusion between conceiving of a state of affairs, and having a modal intuition (which sometimes accompanies such conceiving). Yablo implicitly disputes, however, whether this is indeed a confusion if 'conceiving' is interpreted in the appropriate manner:

> Yablo, Stephen, 'Is Conceivability a Guide to Possibility?', *Philosophy and Phenomenological Research*, 53 (1993), 1–42.

On this account, 'I find *p* conceivable if I can imagine . . . a situation . . . *of* which I truly believe that *p*' (p. 26), and 'to imagine an *X* is *thereby* to enjoy the appearance that an *X* could exist' (p. 30). Hence conceivability itself (in the appropriate sense) involves modal intuition, though Yablo concedes that such intuition is not infallible. Nor is it always available, and his corresponding account of inconceivability—as inability to imagine a situation 'that I don't take to falsify *p*' (p. 29)—leaves room for states of affairs that are neither conceivable nor inconceivable, and hence can be classed as 'undecidable'. This provides a straightforward way of dealing with alleged counter-examples to the Conceivability Principle including mathematical propositions (e.g. Goldbach's Conjecture) whose necessary truth or necessary falsehood is currently unknown. An alternative approach to such mathematical objections (which were first raised by Thomas Reid) is suggested by Casullo, who recommends revising the Conceivability and Inconceivability Principles in a way that harmonizes with Hume's distinction between intuition and demonstration:

> Casullo, Albert, 'Reid and Mill on Hume's Maxim of Conceivability', *Analysis*, 39 (1979), 212–19.

Casullo's proposal is to treat inconceivability as a criterion of impossibility only in the case of propositions knowable by intuition (those simple enough to enable the mind to 'see' directly the relationship between the ideas involved). More complex propositions—those knowable only by demonstration—will then be necessarily true (and hence classed as relations of ideas) if and only if they are 'derivable from other propositions whose denials describe inconceivable states of affairs, using only principles of inference whose denials are inconceivable' (p. 215).

Despite all these complications, Hume's distinction between 'analytic' relations of ideas and 'synthetic' matters of fact is widely accepted and taken for granted, at least for the general run of propositions (leaving aside, for example, difficult problem cases involving theoretical terms whose meaning can evolve as science develops). However, other aspects of Hume's philosophical logic are far more problematic, partly because his evident contempt for scholastic syllogism in particular seems to have given him a mistakenly dismissive attitude to formal rigour in general. Two searching discussions of his 'logic' are now rather dated, but still extremely helpful for highlighting some of the resulting difficulties:

> Bennett, Jonathan, *Locke, Berkeley, Hume: Central Themes* (Oxford: Clarendon Press, 1971), ch. 10.
>
> Passmore, John, *Hume's Intentions*, 3rd edn. (London: Duckworth, 1980), ch. 2.

Fortunately, many of the issues to which Bennett and Passmore draw attention (e.g. in Hume's theory of relations) impact more on the *Treatise* than on the *Enquiry*, but a notable exception is Hume's distinction between 'demonstrative' and 'probable' reasoning, which plays a fundamental role in *Enquiry* IV and XII. My own attempt to clarify Hume's understanding of this distinction is most concisely presented in §2 of

> Millican, P. J. R., 'Hume's Argument concerning Induction: Structure and Interpretation', in Tweyman (ed.), *Hume*, ii. 91–144; repr. in Owen (ed.), *Hume*, 165–218,

and more extensively developed in Chapter 4 of the current volume (§§3.1 and 7.1). Here I argue—against the general trend—that Hume's distinction corresponds quite closely to the modern distinction between 'deductive' and 'inductive' reasoning, where the former is understood in an *informal* (i.e. semantic rather than syntactic) manner. The most thorough recent discussions on the other side of this debate are

> Owen, David, 'Hume on Demonstration', in Patricia Easton (ed.), *Logic and the Workings of the Mind: The Logic of Ideas and Faculty Psychology in Early Modern Philosophy*, North American Kant Society Studies in Philosophy 5 (Atascadero, Calif.: Ridgeview, 1997), 153–74; repr. in Owen (ed.), *Hume*, 109–30.
>
> Owen, David, *Hume's Reason* (Oxford and New York: Oxford University Press, 1999), ch. 5.

However, it is important to note that Owen tends to interpret 'deductive' as meaning *formally* deductive, a concept admittedly quite foreign to Hume's philosophy given his contempt for formal logic.

5.2 The Structure of Hume's Argument Concerning Induction

For many years Stove's analysis of Hume's famous argument, which interpreted it as relying on the implicit premiss of deductivism, was commonly taken to be authoritative:

Stove, D. C., 'Hume, Probability, and Induction', *Philosophical Review*, 74 (1965), 160–77; repr. in V. C. Chappell (ed.), *Hume* (London and Melbourne: Macmillan, 1968), 187–212 and in Tweyman (ed.), *Hume*, ii. 29–43.

Stove, D. C., *Probability and Hume's Inductive Scepticism* (Oxford: Clarendon Press, 1973).

Detailed criticisms of Stove's interpretation, together with alternative accounts of the structure of Hume's argument, are provided by

Morris, William Edward, 'Hume's Refutation of Inductive Probabilism', in James H. Fetzer (ed.), *Probability and Causality* (Dordrecht: Reidel, 1988), 43–77.

Millican, P. J. R., 'Hume's Argument concerning Induction: Structure and Interpretation', in Tweyman (ed.), *Hume*, ii. 91–144; repr. in Owen (ed.), *Hume*, 165–218.

Both focus mainly on the *Enquiry*, and although broadly similar in spirit, they differ significantly both in the points made and in the structure diagrams they propose for Hume's argument. Morris concentrates his fire on Mackie and Stove before presenting his own analysis. My own article is more wide-ranging in its criticisms of earlier authors, but says virtually nothing about Mackie and gives less textual detail on Stove. However, it includes (in §11) a discussion of Stove's probabilistic account of Hume's conclusion, arguing that this is implausible quite independently of the defects of his structural analysis. Note that there is no need to consult this paper for my own structural analysis of Hume's argument, which Chapter 4 repeats in an improved form (in other respects the papers are very different, and only the detailed textual commentary—most of which I saw no reason to change—contains a high proportion of material in common).

5.3 Interpretations of Hume on Reason and Induction

Together with the work listed in §5.2 above, Chapter 4 of the current volume, and the appendix to Don Garrett's Chapter 11 (which develops two sections from his 1997 book, cited later in this section), the following represent the main contemporary currents of thought in the interpretation of Hume's argument concerning induction:

Beauchamp, Tom, and Rosenberg, Alexander, *Hume and the Problem of Causation* (Oxford and New York: Oxford University Press, 1981), ch. 2.

Broughton, Janet, 'Hume's Skepticism about Causal Inferences', *Pacific Philosophical Quarterly*, 64 (1983), 3–18; repr. in Owen (ed.), *Hume*, 149–64.

Noonan, Harold W., *Hume on Knowledge* (London and New York: Routledge, 1999), 110–34.

Owen, David, *Hume's Reason* (Oxford and New York: Oxford University Press, 1999), ch. 6.

Winkler, Kenneth, 'Hume's Inductive Skepticism', in Margaret Atherton (ed.), *The Empiricists* (Lanham, Md.: Rowman & Littlefield, 1999), 183–212.

All those listed here except Winkler interpret Hume's argument as non-sceptical, and therefore depart radically from the traditional view of his intentions. Winkler aims to re-establish the traditional sceptical view with reference both to the writings of Hume's contemporaries and to other parts of the *Treatise* and *Enquiry* (including in particular Section XII).

Beauchamp, Rosenberg and Broughton see Hume as opposing only a narrowly rationalist conception of induction; so when he denies that induction is founded on reason, they take him to be understanding 'reason' in a deductivist sense. But since elsewhere Hume frequently operates with a notion of reason that embraces 'probable' as well as 'demonstrative' inference, this implies an ambiguity in his use of the term, as spelled out in the following well-known article:

> Winters, Barbara, 'Hume on Reason', *Hume Studies*, 5 (1979), 20–35; repr. in Owen (ed.), *Hume*, 133–48.

However, an anti-deductivist conception of Hume's argument is vulnerable to objections of a fairly straightforward kind, as presented in §14 of my 1995 paper (cited in §5.2 above) and developed at greater length in

> Garrett, Don, *Cognition and Commitment in Hume's Philosophy* (Oxford and New York: Oxford University Press, 1997), 83–91.

§13 of my own paper suggests a different ambiguity, interpreting 'reason' within Hume's argument as a notion involving quasi-perceptual insight, and detecting two other notions of reason elsewhere in Hume's writings (for further development of the perceptual notion, but without discussion of the ambiguity thesis, see §2 of Chapter 4). Garrett and Noonan deny any ambiguity in Hume's notion; Owen disagrees on this point, but concurs with them in seeing the intention of Hume's argument as being to deny the dependence of inductive inferences on *ratiocination*, rather than to prove such inferences' unreasonableness (on *any* conception of 'reason').

As the dates of many of these contributions make clear, this is a very active area of current debate among Hume scholars. Part of that ongoing debate can be found in the pages of *Hume Studies*, which remains the obvious place to look for further developments:

> Millican, Peter, 'Hume on Reason and Induction: Epistemology or Cognitive Science?', *Hume Studies*, 24 (1998), 141–59.
>
> Garrett, Don, 'Ideas, Reason, and Skepticism: Replies to my Critics', *Hume Studies*, 24 (1998), 171–94 esp. 177–88.

Here Garrett mounts a spirited and uncompromising defence against my attack on his 1997 interpretation, and moreover goes onto the offensive against my 1995 paper. My latest response to his and to Noonan's and Owen's recent work is, of course, to be found in Chapter 4 of the current volume, §10.3 of which develops detailed logical objections to all non-sceptical interpretations of Hume's argument.

5.4 Inductive Scepticism

An undemanding but philosophically deep introduction to the general issue of inductive scepticism, eminently suitable for beginning students but entertaining at any level, is:

Salmon, Wesley, *An Encounter with David Hume*, in Joel Feinberg (ed.), *Reason and Responsibility*, 3rd edn. (Encino and Belmont, Calif.: Dickenson, 1975), 190–208.

Whether Hume was himself an inductive sceptic is, as we have seen, a very controversial issue, but whatever his own views, the famous 'problem of induction' is probably his most celebrated philosophical legacy. A good background for exploring the issues, starting with the editor's introduction, is provided by

Swinburne, Richard (ed.), *The Justification of Induction* (Oxford: Oxford University Press, 1974).

Swinburne considers three traditional methods of attempting to justify induction—the 'analytic', the 'pragmatic', and the 'inductive'—and the same three methods are also discussed by Skyrms's book mentioned in §6.2 below (which is particularly useful for its detailed treatment on pp. 28–37 of the inductive justification, perhaps the most challenging of the traditional methods and of particular recent interest because of its application to 'abduction' or 'inference to the best explanation', for which see Psillos's book in §10.1 below). Neither Swinburne nor Skyrms, however, considers attempts to justify induction by appeal to a priori probability, which (for reasons explained in §7.2 of Chapter 4) would neatly sidestep Hume's negative argument if only they could be made to work. They would also pose an unambiguous challenge to Hume, unlike the 'analytic' and 'pragmatic' justifications, which both contain elements of similarity with Hume's own views. Two interesting attempts to develop such a probabilistic justification of induction, which combine accessibly presented technical ideas with illuminating philosophical discussion, are provided by

Blackburn, Simon, *Reason and Prediction* (Cambridge: Cambridge University Press, 1973), ch. 7.

Mackie, J. L., 'A Defence of Induction', in G. F. Macdonald (ed.), *Perception and Identity* (Ithaca, NY: Cornell University Press, 1979), 113–30; repr. in *Logic and Knowledge* (Oxford and New York: Clarendon Press, 1985), 159–77.

Both Blackburn and Mackie aim to justify induction through the extrapolation of general uniformity, but historically a more popular way of attempting a probabilistic justification is by applying a statistical 'law of large numbers' to specific events. Such attempts date back to Laplace, and the most persuasive are perhaps those of De Finetti and D. C. Williams. Stove has recently developed Williams's argument further, and presented it in a form suitable for a non-technical audience. (But note that Stove gives two distinct probabilistic arguments against Hume, the first of which—in chapter 5 of his book—is far less interesting, depending as it does on his questionable analysis of Hume's conclusion mentioned in §5.2 above.)

Stove, D. C., *The Rationality of Induction* (Oxford and New York: Clarendon Press, 1986), ch. 6.

Although most modern philosophers would be highly sceptical about the possibility of any such justification of induction, no clear refutation of Blackburn, De Finetti, or Williams–Stove has yet been published (for criticism of Mackie, see P. J. R. Millican, 'Mackie's Defence of Induction', *Analysis*, 42 (1982), 19–24). The question of whether

Humean inductive scepticism can be overcome using probability theory remains open.

6. BELIEF, PROBABILITY, RATIONALITY, AND THE REASON OF ANIMALS

This section covers four aspects of Hume's thought which are quite closely interrelated and a full understanding of which requires reference to the *Treatise*, where Hume's theories of the mechanics of belief, and of the criteria for acceptable and unacceptable probable inference, are far more elaborate than in the *Enquiry*. In the *Treatise* belief is explained using an explicit 'hydraulic' model which in the *Enquiry* is quietly dropped (see the reference to Dauer's paper in §4.1 above). Partly as a result of this, the detailed sections on 'the probability of chances' (I. iii. 11), 'the probability of causes' (I. iii. 12), 'unphilosophical probability' (I. iii. 13), and 'rules by which to judge of causes and effects' (I. iii. 15), which together constitute about a third of the central part of Book I of the *Treatise*, are reduced in the *Enquiry* to the small Section VI, 'Of Probability', and the long footnote in Section IX, 'Of the Reason of Animals'. Apparently Hume considered these details inessential to his main philosophical purposes in the *Enquiry*, and although many would agree—especially in respect of his simplistic theory of the mechanics of belief—nevertheless his treatment of the criteria for correct probable reasoning remains of great importance in assessing the implications of the mitigated scepticism which he develops in Section XII.

6.1 Hume's Theory of Belief

A dated but still philosophically interesting overview of Sections V and VI of the *Enquiry* is provided by

> Flew, Antony, *Hume's Philosophy of Belief* (London: Routledge & Kegan Paul, 1961), ch. 5.

The essays in this volume by Bell and Broackes (Chapters 5 and 6) dig deeper, addressing changes in Hume's account of belief between the *Treatise* and the *Enquiry*, and drawing attention to many relevant interpretative and philosophical issues. For further investigation of these issues the following are helpful, though they pay relatively little attention to the development of Hume's thought:

> Hodges, M., and Lachs, J., 'Hume on Belief', *Review of Metaphysics*, 30 (1976), 3–18; repr. in Tweyman (ed.), *Hume*, i. 144–57.

> Gorman, Michael M., 'Hume's Theory of Belief', *Hume Studies*, 19 (1993), 89–101.

> MacNabb, D. G. C., *David Hume: His Theory of Knowledge and Morality*, 2nd edn. (Oxford: Blackwell, 1966), ch. 5.

> Pears, David, *Hume's System* (Oxford and New York: Oxford University Press, 1990), chs. 4 and 5.

> Bricke, John, *Hume's Philosophy of Mind* (Edinburgh: Edinburgh University Press, 1980), ch. 6.

Hodges and Lachs, like Broackes, find systematic inconsistencies in Hume's theory, but relate these to his need for an effective critique of religious belief (e.g. alleged lively perceptions of God) rather than to his view on personal identity. They also see the problems as symptomatic of an underlying tension in his philosophy between two empiricist tendencies, one phenomenological and the other naturalistically realist. Gorman disagrees with them, claiming that a more charitable reading of Hume's (admittedly poorly expressed) words reveals a consistent view of belief as 'a perception that has a certain feeling to the mind, which is the same as saying that it is a perception that is conceived in a certain manner' (p. 99). MacNabb also accepts that belief may involve a characteristic feeling, but argues that what is really essential to Humean belief is firmness and steadiness (cf. the issue of force and vivacity in §4.1 above, and Loeb's use of steadiness as a criterion of rational belief in his papers mentioned in §6.3 below, a use anticipated by MacNabb in §3 of his chapter 6). Pears's fourth chapter provides a philosophical critique of Hume's theory in the *Treatise*, generally treating it as a unified whole; his next chapter then addresses a problem highlighted by Bell (pp. 179–80 above), of why causation is the only one of Hume's three associative relations able to generate belief. Finally, Bricke discusses Hume's treatment of belief in the context of his theory of thought and judgement, and thereby raises additional issues similar to some of those dealt with by Passmore's chapter referenced in §5.1 above (note also that Passmore's fifth chapter, especially from page 92 onwards, is highly relevant here).

Smith and Jones's introduction to the philosophy of mind provides an accessible link between Hume's theory of belief and modern discussions of the topic, in a chapter that focuses on Hume and Ryle:

Smith, Peter, and Jones, O. R., *The Philosophy of Mind* (Cambridge, New York, and Melbourne: Cambridge University Press, 1986), ch. 10.

In subsequent chapters they go on to develop a functionalist account of belief, drawing particularly on the influential work of Armstrong, but also making connexions with adjacent areas in the philosophy of mind.

6.2 Probability of Chances and Probability of Causes

For an initial outline of Hume's treatment of probability, see Garrett's section entitled 'Cognitive Psychology and Probability' in Chapter 11 of this volume (pp. 308–11). Given the importance of the topic and its close historical association with the celebrated Humean problem of induction, there have been surprisingly few significant discussions in the literature, the following being among the most notable exceptions:

Kemp Smith, Norman, *The Philosophy of David Hume* (London: Macmillan, 1941), ch. 19.

MacNabb, D. G. C., *David Hume: His Theory of Knowledge and Morality*, 2nd edn. (Oxford: Blackwell, 1966), ch. 6.

Hacking, Ian, 'Hume's Species of Probability', *Philosophical Studies*, 33 (1978), 21–37.

Gower, Barry, 'Hume on Probability', *British Journal for the Philosophy of Science*, 42 (1991), 1–19.

Kemp Smith provides a useful critical introduction to the account of probability in the *Treatise*, highlighting some of its crucial defects (Hume's awareness of which, he suggests, may account for the brevity of the *Enquiry* account), and explaining how Hume's theory of belief leads him to treat both 'probability of chances' and 'probability of causes' as involving the same associationist mechanism. MacNabb likewise focuses on the *Treatise*, but gives more attention to the philosophical issues than to the details of Hume's own account, being (understandably) dismissive of some of its intricacies. Hacking praises Hume for noting the distinction between the two species of probability, but regrets that this insight was then erased by his conflation of the two, and was not pursued further either by Hume himself or by subsequent pioneers of the theory of probability. Gower, unlike these other commentators, takes seriously the additive account of probability measures suggested by Hume's talk (at *T* 138 and *E* 127) of *subtracting* the weight of evidence against a hypothesis from that in favour (so that a probability of zero represents indifference rather than certain falsehood). As Gower points out, this distinctive approach to probability tends to be overlooked given the modern enthusiasm for analysing some of Hume's arguments in standard Bayesian terms, but those responsible would no doubt see such analysis as charitable interpretation rather than oversight, given that Hume in the relevant contexts (e.g. *T* 127–42 and *E* 56–8) also uses terms implying proportionality, while the literal additive account is dubiously coherent (however, Gower discusses its application to Hume's essay on miracles in 'David Hume and the Probability of Miracles', *Hume Studies*, 16 (1990), 17–31).

Contemporary philosophy of probability tends to be fearsomely technical, and additionally complicated by the multiplicity of different interpretations of the relevant concepts, some of which also go together with different formal treatments. For an informal philosophical discussion of probability concepts, see

Mackie, J. L., *Truth, Probability, and Paradox* (Oxford: Clarendon Press, 1973), ch. 5.

A straightforward classification of different formal approaches to probability, together with a sketch of some influential previous taxonomies, is given by

Weatherford, Roy, *Philosophical Foundations of Probability Theory* (London, Boston, and Melbourne: Routledge & Kegan Paul, 1982), ch. 1.

Those with the technical competence to dig deeper will find a useful survey of modern developments in:

Howson, Colin, 'Theories of Probability', *British Journal for the Philosophy of Science*, 46 (1995), 1–32.

To explore the relationship between probability and induction, a useful start is Gillies's encyclopaedia article, which outlines the historical development of theories of probability, introducing some of the influential technical issues (such as the paradoxes of indifference, Dutch book arguments, Bayesian conditionalization, and the Carnap–Hesse thesis) and relating them to the philosophy of induction:

Gillies, Donald A., 'Induction and Probability', in G. H. R. Parkinson (ed.), *An Encyclopaedia of Philosophy* (London and New York: Routledge, 1988), 179–204.

Application of the probability calculus to inductive inference is problematic not only for Humean reasons (i.e. the apparent impossibility of a priori probability assignments, and sceptical doubts about inductive uniformity), but also because any such 'inductive logic' presupposes a grasp of 'natural kinds' or real uniformities in nature and therefore cannot—unlike deductive logic—be purely formal. The classic presentation of this 'new riddle of induction' is

> Goodman, Nelson, *Fact, Fiction, and Forecast*, 4th edn. (Cambridge, Mass., and London: Harvard University Press, 1983), ch. 3.

Skyrms's introduction to inductive logic provides a useful discussion of Goodman's 'riddle', as also of Mill's methods of induction and of modern responses to Humean inductive scepticism. However, in a brief discussion on the interpretation of probability he acknowledges the uncertain basis of the entire enterprise of inductive logic, given the resilience of the fundamental problems of induction:

> Skyrms, Brian, *Choice and Chance* (Belmont, Calif.: Dickenson, 1966).

6.3 Probability and Rationality in the Treatise and the Enquiry

Traditionally there has been little interest in those sections of the *Treatise* (notably sections 9–13 of Book I Part iii) where Hume discusses probabilistic inferential processes, including a number that he considers dubious. A fairly detailed survey of the various Humean belief-forming mechanisms is provided by §1 of Falkenstein's paper listed later in this section, but for a brief review, see

> Fogelin, Robert, *Hume's Skepticism in the 'Treatise of Human Nature'* (London, Boston, and Melbourne: Routledge & Kegan Paul, 1985), ch. 5.

The most interesting of the mechanisms that Hume discusses is our tendency to seek and apply 'general rules', which though often leading to unwarranted prejudices also provides the only solution to such prejudices through reflection upon them (a point expressed dramatically at *T* 150). Hearn's well-known article surveys Hume's treatment of general rules, showing how they perform an important role not only in his epistemology, but also in his philosophy of the passions and of morals:

> Hearn Jr., Thomas K., ' "General Rules" in Hume's *Treatise*', *Journal of the History of Philosophy*, 8 (1970), 405–22.

The recent growth of interest in *Treatise* I. iii. 9–13 has resulted from an appreciation that neither Hume's scepticism nor his naturalism are undiscriminating—within these sections but also elsewhere (e.g. *Enquiry* VIII–XII), he repeatedly endorses certain factual beliefs and methods of enquiry (notably those characteristic of empirical science), while dismissing others as spurious (e.g. those characteristic of superstition). As long as the orthodox interpretation took Hume to be a deductivist sceptic regarding induction, such judgements were themselves typically dismissed as mere inconsistencies on his part, but once it became generally accepted that he is no crude deductivist (see §§5.2 and 5.3 above), the question of whether his philosophy can sustain a plausible theory of normative discrimination came to prominence. However, the suggestion that it might do so is in some tension not only with his inductive scepticism, but also with his central thesis that belief is involuntary. In Chapter 14 Norton seeks to alleviate this latter tension, by showing how even if beliefs are indeed 'proximately involuntary', it is still possible for reflective philosophical doubt to alter the context in which they arise and thus to influence what we believe. Norton develops this position further in his book, arguing that a proper recognition of the role of reflective thought in Hume's philosophy comprehensively undermines Kemp Smith's influential claim that the fundamental theme of Hume's philosophy is the subordination of reason to feeling:

> Norton, David Fate, *David Hume: Common-Sense Moralist, Sceptical Metaphysician* (Princeton and Guildford: Princeton University Press, 1982), ch. 5 part 2.

Passmore's paper 'Hume and the Ethics of Belief' takes a similar approach, explaining how Hume's theory of belief, while implying its involuntary nature, can nevertheless allow us to have some control over what we believe by adopting a 'belief policy' involving such things as attention to and critical examination of evidence. Hence normative recommendations become at least a meaningful possibility, though the third chapter of Passmore's book casts doubt on whether such recommendations can be given any adequate basis using the resources at Hume's disposal in the *Treatise* (in particular his notion of general rules):

> Passmore, John, *Hume's Intentions*, 3rd edn. (London: Duckworth, 1980), ch. 3 and the appendix entitled 'Hume and the Ethics of Belief', whose original version appeared in George P. Morice (ed.), *David Hume: Bicentenary Papers* (Edinburgh: Edinburgh University Press, 1977), 77–92.

Other discussions of the *Treatise* treatment of probability are more optimistic, seeing it as providing not only a rich source of apparently normative judgements, but also a plausible Humean attempt at a theoretical foundation for such judgements based on the empirical assessment of our reasoning methods. However, as the following summaries make clear, there is relatively little agreement regarding the nature of this empirical assessment, and the criteria to which it answers:

> Winters, Barbara, 'Hume's Argument for the Superiority of Natural Instinct', *Dialogue*, 20 (1981), 635–43; repr. in Tweyman (ed.), *Hume*, iii. 262–70.

Winters takes Hume's problem to be that of justifying a preference for the 'general and more establish'd properties of the imagination' over the 'trivial properties of the fancy' (cf. Immerwahr's paper in §3.3 above). Hume's preference for the former, she suggests, is founded on two main considerations, namely their relative efficiency (deriving from their immediacy, irresistibility, and durability) and their naturalness (which makes them easy and satisfying to apply).

> Costa, M. J., 'Hume and Justified Belief', *Canadian Journal of Philosophy* 11 (1981), 219–28; repr. in Tweyman (ed.), *Hume*, i. 174–82.

Costa shares Winters's conception of Hume's problem, but sees his preference for disciplined causal reasoning (that which conforms to his 'rules by which to judge of causes and effects') as founded on its superior reliability compared with other inferential mechanisms. He ends by suggesting that Hume's philosophy thus contains the seeds of modern 'externalist' or 'reliabilist' epistemology, which likewise assesses epistemic justification according to the reliability of the belief-forming mechanisms involved.

> Baier, Annette C., *A Progress of Sentiments: Reflections on Hume's 'Treatise'* (Cambridge, Mass., and London: Harvard University Press, 1991), ch. 4.

Baier, in tune with the overall theme of her book, takes Hume's approval of causal norms of reasoning to derive from their reflexive application, whereby causal reasoning is applied to vindicate the very causal norms that it employs. Pithily summarized, '*Successful reflexivity is normativity*' (pp. 99–100). (The third part of Winkler's paper referenced in §5.3 above follows Baier in emphasizing the role of reflection in Hume's '*normalising of the natural*' (p. 204), but in Winkler's view Hume fails to resolve the underlying tension between his inductive scepticism and his desire for normative discrimination.)

> Loeb, Louis E., 'Hume on Stability, Justification, and Unphilosophical Probability', *Journal of the History of Philosophy*, 33 (1995), 101–32.

> Loeb, Louis E., 'Instability and Uneasiness in Hume's Theories of Belief and Justification', *British Journal for the History of Philosophy*, 3 (1995), 301–27.

Loeb views Hume's discussions of 'unphilosophical probability' as fitting into a general framework of inductive assessment of inferential processes, but differs from Baier in taking the appropriate criterion to be stability of belief rather than successful reflexivity. In his second paper he explains the motivation for seeking such stability as being the avoidance of uneasiness, and thus attributes Hume with a theory of justification which has close affinities to Peirce's theory of belief.

> Wilson, Fred, 'Hume's Defence of Causal Inference', *Dialogue*, 22 (1983), 661–94.

> Wilson, Fred, *Hume's Defence of Causal Inference* (Toronto, Buffalo, and London: University of Toronto Press, 1997), esp. ch. 2 §3.

Wilson, on Hume's behalf, appeals to the (arguable) principle that 'must implies ought' to justify the basic practice of inductive causal reasoning over which we have no choice. He then interprets Hume's discussion of the various particular mechanisms of causal inference—and the formulating of 'general rules' about these mechanisms—as intended to yield an inductive assessment of their capacity to satisfy the natural passion of curiosity, this passion providing our motive for reasoning in accordance with those mechanisms that have proved most reliable.

> Falkenstein, Lorne, 'Naturalism, Normativity, and Scepticism in Hume's Account of Belief', *Hume Studies*, 23 (1997), 29–72; repr. in Owen (ed.), *Hume*, 219–62.

Falkenstein follows Wilson in focusing on Hume's appeal to general rules, but puts particular emphasis on the formulation of second-order rules that assess the reliability of first-order rules. Such second-order reflection requires time and effort, suggesting that the relatively weak passion of curiosity may be insufficient to motivate it. Instead, Falkenstein argues (pp. 54–9), Hume sees such reflection as being induced by the contemplation of sceptical arguments, which initially undermine all our beliefs but from which some beliefs—notably those that are frequently reinforced in common life—are quickly able to recover. Thus it is that the Pyrrhonian arguments lead naturally to both normative discrimination and mitigated scepticism.

All of the above summarized accounts imply that at least some of the material of *Treatise* I. iii. 9, 10, and 13 is crucial for the understanding of Hume's attitude to science and scepticism, and hence that a fundamental constituent of his philosophy is almost entirely absent from his later writings. Relatively few commentators have tried to avoid this uncomfortable conclusion by finding an adequate basis for normative discrimination within the text of the *Enquiry* and *Dialogues*, something which I attempt in §11 of Chapter 4 of this volume (a similar account, but focusing more on the *Treatise* and stressing common elements with several of the discussions above, is in §13 of my paper mentioned in §5.2 above). What I take to be the key passage from the *Enquiry* is Hume's suggestion that science involves 'nothing but the reflections of common life, methodized and corrected' (*E* 162), a passage which is—perhaps significantly—very clearly echoed in the *Dialogues* (*D* 134), and which Noxon likewise sees as expressing a general 'Principle of Methodological Consistency' (see the reference to his book in §3.3 above). A quite different approach, but one which also draws on both the *Treatise* and the *Enquiry*, is taken by

Ferreira, M. Jamie, 'Hume's Naturalism—"Proof" and Practice', *Philosophical Quarterly*, 35 (1985), 45–57; repr. in Tweyman (ed.), *Hume*, iii. 271–83.

Ferreira argues that Hume's distinction between 'proofs' and mere 'probabilities' (*T* 124, *E* 56 n.) is epistemologically very significant, separating those beliefs which in Hume's view can reasonably be doubted from those which cannot. She thus places Hume within a tradition of 'reasonable doubt' naturalism, a tradition whose progress from Wilkins to Newman she recounts in her book *Scepticism and Reasonable Doubt* (Oxford and New York: Clarendon Press, 1986), and which she there contrasts (p. 234) with both 'sceptical' naturalism and 'justifying' naturalism. Her interpretation has the implication that Hume is rather close to Reid—the central representative of this tradition—in ruling out any reasonable ground for doubt about the fundamental beliefs derived from our natural faculties. For a strongly contrasting view, to which Ferreira herself alludes, see part 1 of Norton's chapter mentioned earlier in this section.

Moving on to contemporary discussions of human rationality, the question of how far our natural inferential methods conform to theoretical ideals has attracted much attention since the work of Kahneman and Tversky, who devised a range of experiments revealing various 'heuristics' that we use in our thinking, and 'biases' to which these lead. Their main papers are collected in

Kahneman, D., Slovic, P., and Tversky, A. (eds.), *Judgement under Uncertainty: Heuristics and Biases* (Cambridge: Cambridge University Press, 1982).

There is, however, debate over how some of the results of Kahneman and Tversky should be interpreted (as exemplified by Cohen's criticism of their taxicab example, discussed by Owen in Chapter 12). Both their results and some of this debate are summarized in the chapter on probability in a book whose theme is precisely what Hume addressed in the sections of the *Treatise* that I have been discussing—the subtle interplay between rational norms and our inferential practices:

Manktelow, K. I., and Over, D. E., *Inference and Understanding: A Philosophical and Psychological Perspective* (London and New York: Routledge, 1990), ch. 7.

6.4 The Reason of Animals

Despite its importance for his anti-rationalist and naturalizing philosophical project, very little has been written on Hume's discussion of animals (indeed not one paper out of nearly 200 in Tweyman's six volumes is devoted to the topic!). What little has been written, moreover, has tended to focus on the moral rather than the epistemological aspects of Hume's position. With this reservation, a useful recent paper is

Pitson, Antony E., 'The Nature of Humean Animals', *Hume Studies*, 19 (1993), 301–16.

Hume's view of animal and human reason as differing in degree rather than in their essential nature obviously fits very comfortably with the theory of evolution, and it is interesting to note that *Enquiry* IX is explicitly mentioned by Darwin in a manuscript dating from the time when he was developing that theory:

Huntley, William B., 'David Hume and Charles Darwin', *Journal of the History of Ideas*, 33 (1972), 457–70.

In this context it is understandable that the book on Hume which most emphasizes the topic was written over a century ago by the man known as 'Darwin's bulldog':

Huxley, T. H., *Hume* (London: Macmillan, 1886), ch. 5, 'The Mental Phenomena of Animals'.

Since then the overwhelming success of evolutionary theory as an explanatory framework for biology has, of course, led to its almost universal acceptance in scientific circles. Yet perhaps surprisingly, Hume's bold claim that animals can reason in a way closely analogous to ourselves remains controversial. For an engaging account of some striking recent evidence in favour of Hume's position, see

Dawkins, Marian Stamp, *Through our Eyes Only?* (Oxford, New York, and Tokyo: Oxford University Press, 1998).

7. CAUSATION

7.1 Hume's Account of Causation

In Chapter 7 Craig describes Hume's hunt for the impression of necessary connexion, and introduces some of the complex issues raised by it and by Hume's notorious two definitions of cause. Two other useful discussions of Hume's corresponding account in the *Treatise*, providing different perspectives on some of the same issues but also raising some new ones, are

Stroud, Barry, *Hume* (London and Boston: Routledge & Kegan Paul, 1977), ch. 4.

Noonan, Harold W., *Hume on Knowledge* (London and New York: Routledge, 1999), 140–57.

In the course of his discussion Stroud influentially takes on the question of what Hume's elusive impression of necessary connexion might be, concluding that it is just a certain feeling that accompanies our causal inferences, which because of its simplicity must be indefinable. His view is critically examined at length, in the context of a general treatment of Hume's theory of causation, by

> Pears, David, *Hume's System* (Oxford and New York: Oxford University Press, 1990), ch. 7.

Stroud responds to Pears in a paper which considers the more general issue of whether any Humean internal impression (such as of necessity, or of moral sentiments) can coherently be projected onto the world in the way that Hume supposes (the problem being that such projection takes for granted the prior availability within the mind of something which in fact seems to make sense only after the projection has taken place):

> Stroud, Barry, ' "Gilding or Staining" the World with "Sentiments" and "Phantasms" ', *Hume Studies*, 19 (1993), 253–72; repr. in Rupert Read and Kenneth A. Richman (eds.), *The New Hume Debate* (London and New York: Routledge, 2000), 16–30.

Hume's notorious 'two definitions of cause' have provoked numerous discussions over many years because the two apparently conflict. Craig's response is to demote them from the status of strict *definitions* of causation, and to see them instead as general encapsulations of two different aspects of Hume's conclusions about our causal beliefs. A less compromising approach is taken by Beauchamp, who sees Hume's definitions as capturing two different theories of causation, which Hume tries in vain to reconcile:

> Beauchamp, Tom, 'Hume's Two Theories of Causation', *Archiv für Geschichte der Philosophie*, 55 (1973), 281–300; repr. in Tweyman (ed.), *Hume*, iii. 303–21.

In his later book with Rosenberg the development of this position is more extensive, and provides useful detailed discussion of a number of previous commentators' views:

> Beauchamp, Tom, and Rosenberg, Alexander, *Hume and the Problem of Causation* (Oxford and New York: Oxford University Press, 1981), ch. 1.

A different perspective is brought to the issue by Russell, who sees Hume's two definitions as giving accounts of causation as it exists in the material world and in our perceptions respectively:

> Russell, Paul, 'Hume's "Two Definitions" of Cause and the Ontology of "Double Existence" ', *Hume Studies*, 10 (1984), 1–25; repr. in Tweyman (ed.), *Hume*, iii. 416–33.
>
> Russell, Paul, *Freedom and Moral Sentiment* (Oxford and New York: Oxford University Press, 1995), ch. 2.

Another insightful recent analysis first gives an overview of the various types of position that commentators have taken on the two definitions, and the general evidence for and against them. It then presents Hume as having a thoroughly coherent position based around his theory of abstract ideas and their definition:

> Garrett, Don, *Cognition and Commitment in Hume's Philosophy* (Oxford and New York: Oxford University Press, 1997), ch. 5.

Perhaps the most obvious objection to Garrett is that Hume does not explicitly mention his theory of abstract ideas in the context of his two definitions; moreover, that theory does not feature at all in the *Enquiry* (except in a footnote at *E* 158), although the two definitions are just as prominent there as in the *Treatise*. Much of what Garrett says, however—in particular, his claim that the two definitions are coextensive if properly understood (reiterated on pp. 319–20 in this volume)—is plausible quite independently of any such connexion with abstract ideas.

It should be noted that Beauchamp, Rosenberg, Russell, and Garrett all focus predominantly on the *Treatise*, so parts of their discussions are less directly appropriate to the *Enquiry* where Hume's two definitions are somewhat different. Perhaps their most important omission is any mention of the puzzle concerning Hume's 'other words' appended to his first definition in the *Enquiry* ('Or in other words, *where, if the first object had not been, the second never had existed.*'; *E* 76), which have often been interpreted (e.g. by Vesey in the article listed in §8.2 below, p. 122) in a counterfactual manner that seems straightforwardly to conflict with the definition they supposedly paraphrase. For a statement of the simplest solution to this puzzle, which interprets the conditional as merely tensed rather than counterfactual, see p. 157 of

Jacobson, Anne Jaap, 'From Cognitive Science to a Post-Cartesian Text', in Rupert Read and Kenneth A. Richman (eds.), *The New Hume Debate* (London and New York: Routledge, 2000), 156–66.

In addition to her comments on the two definitions, Jacobson raises important criticisms of Stroud's view of the impression of necessity (p. 160). Her more general thesis that the *Enquiry* is to be read in a postmodern fashion, as developing different (and incompatible) perspectives rather than seeking determinate conclusions, is interestingly provocative but likely to be seen by most Hume interpreters as a premature counsel of despair.

7.2 *Humean Theories of Causation*

Hume's theory of causation has become so influential that philosophical discussions of his views tend at the same time to be contributions to the contemporary philosophy of causation. This can make entry into the literature rather daunting, but fortunately a recent student text provides a relatively gentle introduction to some of the major issues:

Dicker, Georges, *Hume's Epistemology and Metaphysics* (London and New York: Routledge, 1998), ch. 4.

The outstanding modern contribution to the philosophy of causation in the Humean tradition is

Mackie, J. L., *The Cement of the Universe* (Oxford and New York: Clarendon Press, 1974).

The paperback edition (published in 1980) adds a useful preface, summarizing Mackie's position and the book's contents. Though inspired by Hume, Mackie departs significantly from what he takes to be the Humean position (but his detailed analysis of Hume's arguments is questionable—see Morris's article in §5.2 above). Another major book, more textually sensitive and faithful to Hume than Mackie's though less philosophically groundbreaking, has already been mentioned in §§5.3 and 7.1 above:

> Beauchamp, Tom, and Rosenberg, Alexander, *Hume and the Problem of Causation* (Oxford and New York: Oxford University Press, 1981).

Beauchamp and Rosenberg present a rational reconstruction of Hume's view (ridding him of the 'two definitions' inconsistency that they ascribe to him), which they then defend against Mackie's criticisms and others. One author discussed both by them and by Mackie is Anscombe, whose Cambridge inaugural lecture is probably the best-known radical attack on the entire Humean position:

> Anscombe, G. E. M., *Causality and Determination* (Cambridge: Cambridge University Press, 1971); repr. in *Metaphysics and the Philosophy of Mind: Collected Philosophical Papers*, vol. ii (Oxford: Blackwell, 1981), 133–47.

Anscombe's lecture is also reprinted in a collection which starts from Mackie's seminal paper 'Causes and Conditions' (1965) and contains other important articles on the nature of causation:

> Sosa, Ernest, and Tooley, Michael (eds.), *Causation* (Oxford and New York: Oxford University Press, 1993).

7.3 Causal Realism and the 'New Hume'

In Chapter 8 of this volume Galen Strawson presents a summarized account—with particular reference to the *Enquiry*—of the substantial case for Hume's causal realism which he made at far greater length in

> Strawson, Galen, *The Secret Connexion* (Oxford and New York: Clarendon Press, 1989).

Strawson's book is given an elegant summary and a judicious critical assessment by

> Broackes, Justin, 'Did Hume Hold a Regularity Theory of Causation?', *British Journal for the History of Philosophy*, 1 (1993), 99–114.

Broackes packs a multitude of points into his fifteen pages, making this a particularly efficient introduction to the issues which, while generally disputing the evidence for the causal realist interpretation, nevertheless expresses sufficient sympathy with it to conclude that Hume probably had no completely settled view (a conclusion interestingly similar to the one Broackes draws about Hume's theory of belief in Chapter 6).

Although he developed his position quite independently of these other authors, Strawson's book acknowledges that similar views had already been presented (albeit in very different style) by

> Wright, John P., *The Sceptical Realism of David Hume* (Manchester: Manchester University Press, 1983), ch. 4.

> Livingston, Donald W., *Hume's Philosophy of Common Life* (Chicago and London: University of Chicago Press, 1984), ch. 6.

Less detailed but perhaps more widely known than the earlier work of Wright and Livingston, Craig's chapter on Hume (from parts of which his essay in Chapter 7 of this volume is developed) presents a general picture of his thought which is particularly congenial for the causal realist interpretation:

> Craig, Edward, *The Mind of God and the Works of Man* (Oxford and New York: Clarendon Press, 1987), ch. 2.

The first chapter of Craig's book is also of great interest, giving a survey of rationalist writings prior to Hume that exemplify the 'Image of God' conception of human reason which Craig sees as Hume's principal target. The upshot of Craig's thesis is that the traditional reading of Hume as a positivist is totally wrong-headed; far preferable is the kind of 'sceptical realism' attributed to him by Wright and Strawson.

Together with Blackburn's article in Chapter 9, which defends a 'projectivist' reading of Hume, the most influential critique of the causal realist interpretation is

> Winkler, Kenneth P., 'The New Hume', *Philosophical Review*, 100 (1991), 541–79; repr. in Owen (ed.), *Hume*, 347–85 and in Rupert Read and Kenneth A. Richman (eds.), *The New Hume Debate* (London and New York: Routledge, 2000), 52–74.

The reprint of Winkler's paper in *The New Hume Debate* adds a postscript entitled 'Intelligibility and the Theory of Ideas' (pages 74–87). Also in this recent collection are a number of new papers, including a direct reply to many of the points made by Winkler:

> Wright, John P., 'Hume's Causal Realism: Recovering a Traditional Interpretation', in Rupert Read and Kenneth A. Richman (eds.), *The New Hume Debate* (London and New York: Routledge, 2000), 88–99.

Three other new papers in the collection, by Craig, Bell, and Flage, are of more specific interest in the causal realism debate:

> Craig, Edward, 'Projectivist *and* Realist?', in Rupert Read and Kenneth A. Richman (eds.), *The New Hume Debate* (London and New York: Routledge, 2000), 113–21.

Craig here suggests that Hume may be *both* a projectivist *and* a realist about causation—projectivist about our everyday understanding of it (founded on 'the Imagination'), but realist about causes in nature. He then, however, goes on to question whether such realism may be just as incompatible with Hume's epistemology as it apparently is with his theory of ideas, because neither 'Reason' nor 'the Senses' can provide it with any basis ('Reason' here being rejected as a basis simply because uncaused regularity is conceivable). But since Craig detects traces, at the end of *Enquiry* V, of a *non*-demonstrative argument for realism based on the regularity of nature, his negative conclusion might be avoidable by adopting one of the non-rationalistic conceptions of reason favoured by most of the works discussed in §5.3 above.

> Bell, Martin, 'Sceptical Doubts concerning Hume's Causal Realism', in Rupert Read and Kenneth A. Richman (eds.), *The New Hume Debate* (London and New York: Routledge, 2000), 122–37.

Bell attacks both Strawson's book and Wright's response to Winkler. Against Strawson he alleges a conflict between causal realism and Hume's inductive scepticism, given

Strawson's apparent endorsement of the idea (alluded to by Craig) that realist causation can explain, and hence can be reasonably inferred from, the regularity of nature (but see my Introduction note 15 for doubts whether Strawson is indeed committed, as Bell implies on p. 126, to what Blackburn in Chapter 9 calls a 'straitjacket'). Against Wright, Bell continues a debate on the interpretation of Hume's divergences from Malebranche, which started with

> Wright, John P., 'Hume's Criticism of Malebranche's Theory of Causation: A Lesson in the Historiography of Philosophy', in Stuart Brown (ed.), *Nicolas Malebranche: His Philosophical Critics and Successors* (Assen: Van Gorcum, 1991), 116–30.

> Bell, Martin, 'Hume and Causal Power: The Influences of Malebranche and Newton', *British Journal for the History of Philosophy*, 5 (1997), 67–86.

Wright (like Strawson in Chapter 11 of his book) sees Hume as adopting Malebranche's aprioristic criterion of causation—as what would license a priori inference from cause to effect—and takes his divergence from Malebranche to involve (sceptical) realism about causes so conceived. Bell sees Hume as rejecting Malebranche's entire notion, and replacing it with one that can be applied only on the basis of experience and whose instances are metaphysically quite distinct. However, Bell ends his later paper by observing a resulting tension in Hume's thought, since such distinctness sits uneasily with the generality that is characteristic of necessity. This tension, Bell suggests, may explain the acknowledged imperfection in Hume's two definitions of cause (*T* 170, *E* 76–7), which New Humeans have taken as strong evidence of causal realism.

> Flage, Daniel, 'Relative Ideas Re-Viewed', in Rupert Read and Kenneth A. Richman (eds.), *The New Hume Debate* (London and New York: Routledge, 2000), 138–55.

If Hume believes in truly *objective* causal powers, then he must maintain a belief about something for which—as he shows in *Enquiry* VII—there is no corresponding impression (and hence, according to his Copy Principle, no idea). New Humeans have seen the solution to this puzzle in his notion of 'relative ideas' (cf. the discussion of Wright in §10.1 below, and pp. 237–47, 261–3 above), but Flage, author of earlier articles on the notion, here argues that it is inadequate to play such a role. He draws attention to similar notions in the work of Locke, Berkeley, Arnauld, and Reid, which, however, require clear understanding of the relation involved, something unachievable in the current case. He also argues that there is no evidence that Hume's 'relative ideas' can support a belief, for in the *Treatise* and *Enquiry* force and vivacity attach only to positive ideas.

8. LIBERTY AND NECESSITY

8.1 Hume's Treatment of Liberty and Necessity

Given its enormous importance for Hume, it is surprising that the literature on his treatment of liberty and necessity is so meagre. Moreover, what little has been written has tended to focus on his discussion in the *Treatise*, which (as Botterill explains in Chapter 10) is significantly different from that in the *Enquiry* and in some ways quite misleading. In particular, the distinction between two types of liberty in the *Treatise* has encouraged many past commentators (for example, Stroud in Chapter 7 of his 1977 book, cited in

§7.1) to interpret Hume as a straightforward classical compatibilist, a view exploded both by Botterill and by Russell (see his 1995 book below). Kemp Smith's short but influential chapter on the topic, though useful as an account of Hume's main points in the *Treatise*, exemplifies this misleading emphasis on the two liberties:

Kemp Smith, Norman, *The Philosophy of David Hume* (London: Macmillan, 1941), ch. 20.

For the student of the *Enquiry*, perhaps the most interesting of the traditional compatibilist accounts is

Flew, Antony, *Hume's Philosophy of Belief* (London: Routledge & Kegan Paul, 1961), ch. 7.

The recent recognition that Hume's compatibilism is more distinctive and subtle than previously assumed, and rooted at least as much in his naturalist project as in conceptual concerns, is due largely to Russell's work, brought together in what is undoubtedly the most important book on the topic:

Russell, Paul, *Freedom and Moral Sentiment* (Oxford and New York: Oxford University Press, 1995).

Most relevant for the interpretation of the *Enquiry* are chapters 1, 3, 4, and 7 (chapter 2 has already been mentioned in §7.1 above). Rejecting, like Botterill, the traditional focus on the contrast between the two types of 'liberty' mentioned in the *Treatise*, Russell emphasizes instead Hume's analyses of necessity and of the conditions for moral responsibility. His densely argued work provides the most comprehensive available account of how all these important strands in Hume's philosophy weave together. For another perspective on Hume's view of the relationships between liberty, necessity, and moral responsibility, see

Bricke, J., 'Hume, Freedom to Act, and Personal Evaluation', *History of Philosophy Quarterly*, 5 (1988), 141–56; repr. in Tweyman (ed.), *Hume*, iv. 175–91.

Garrett's recent book provides a general problem-orientated discussion of liberty and necessity, nicely complementing Russell's approach (though unfortunately not discussing it) by focusing in turn on specific interpretative difficulties rather than explicitly developing an integrated overall perspective:

Garrett, Don, *Cognition and Commitment in Hume's Philosophy* (Oxford and New York: Oxford University Press, 1997), ch. 6.

Garrett highlights a range of apparent inconsistencies and other problems that various commentators have identified in Hume's account, and then with characteristic ingenuity proceeds to explain them away.

8.2 Free Will and Determinism

There is, of course, a far wider range of material on the general philosophical topic of free will and determinism than on the detailed interpretation of Hume's position. A brief introduction, approaching the topic through Hume's *Enquiry* in a (now rather dated) Wittgensteinian spirit, is provided by

Vesey, Godfrey, 'Hume on Liberty and Necessity', in Godfrey Vesey (ed.), *Philosophers Ancient and Modern* (Cambridge: Cambridge University Press, 1986), 111–27.

A particularly clear defence of Humean compatibilism, which helpfully introduces the contributions of contemporary philosophers such as Van Inwagen and Frankfurt, occurs in a chapter (of a book on artificial intelligence) whose aim is to refute the general claim that a robot could not be free:

Copeland, Jack, *Artificial Intelligence: A Philosophical Introduction* (Oxford and Cambridge, Mass.: Blackwell, 1993), ch. 7.

Honderich provides a more detailed but still introductory discussion, which (though misinterpreting Hume in the traditional manner) sets out many of the surrounding issues with great clarity while developing his own 'theory of determinism', a theory which rejects both compatibilism and incompatibilism:

Honderich, Ted, *How Free are You?* (Oxford and New York: Oxford University Press, 1993).

The concept of free will is intimately connected with that of intentional action, and both impinge on moral theory. Mackie provides an accessible general treatment of these issues, from the viewpoint of a broadly Humean approach to morality:

Mackie, J. L., *Ethics: Inventing Right and Wrong* (Harmondsworth: Penguin, 1977), ch. 9.

Turning now to more detailed treatments, the following are among the most influential book-length presentations of the case for compatibilism and for libertarianism respectively:

Dennett, Daniel C., *Elbow Room: The Varieties of Free Will Worth Wanting* (Oxford: Clarendon Press, 1984).

Van Inwagen, Peter, *An Essay on Free Will* (Oxford: Clarendon Press, 1983).

A contrasting and very uncompromising approach can be found in Galen Strawson's book on the topic, which rejects both Humean compatibilism and traditional libertarianism on the ground that *irrespective* of the truth or falsity of determinism, our belief that we are truly free and responsible agents is false:

Strawson, Galen, *Freedom and Belief* (Oxford and New York: Clarendon Press, 1986).

Other contemporary approaches are represented in Watson's useful collection, including two of the best-known compatibilist contributions, 'Freedom of the Will and the Concept of a Person' by Harry Frankfurt, and 'Freedom and Resentment' by Peter Strawson (the latter of which is discussed at some length in chapter 5 of Russell's book, finding illuminating parallels with Hume):

Watson, Gary (ed.), *Free Will* (Oxford and New York: Oxford University Press, 1982).

Understanding how all these different views relate to each other is a complex matter, but the first part of a recent book—written from a libertarian perspective—draws the threads of contemporary debate into a coherent pattern:

Kane, Robert, *The Significance of Free Will* (Oxford and New York: Oxford University Press, 1996), pt. 1.

Hume ends his section on liberty and necessity by hinting that his compatibilist account leaves God as the author of sin. Kenny provides a contemporary discussion of this issue, with the same conclusion:

Kenny, Anthony, *The God of the Philosophers* (Oxford and New York: Clarendon Press, 1979), ch. 6.

9. HUME'S PHILOSOPHY OF RELIGION

The best general account of Hume's philosophy of religion is

Gaskin, J. C. A., *Hume's Philosophy of Religion*, 2nd edn. (Basingstoke and London: Macmillan, 1988).

The same author provides an excellent overview in Norton's *Cambridge Companion*:

Gaskin, J. C. A., 'Hume on Religion', in David Fate Norton (ed.), *The Cambridge Companion to Hume* (Cambridge: Cambridge University Press, 1993), 313–44.

Two other important general resources are Kemp Smith's editorial material in his standard edition of the *Dialogues*, discussed in §2.3 above, and a book which is unfortunately hard to obtain in Europe:

Yandell, Keith E., *Hume's 'Inexplicable Mystery': His Views on Religion* (Philadelphia: Temple University Press, 1990).

Penelhum's 1975 book on Hume is unusual in giving explicit attention to the arguments of *Enquiry* XI as well as those of *Enquiry* X, offering a convenient summary and a brief philosophical discussion of each:

Penelhum, Terence, *Hume* (London and Basingstoke: Macmillan, 1975), ch. 8, esp. 175–80.

When reading Hume's writings on religion, it is important to remain alert to the possibility of irony in his apparent declarations of theistic belief (e.g. in the concluding paragraph of *Enquiry* VIII and X). Berman's discussion of contemporary deist writings sets Hume in context, showing how widely practised—and widely recognized—was the art of 'theological lying':

Berman, David, 'Deism, Immortality, and the Art of Theological Lying', in J. A. Leo Lemay (ed.), *Deism, Masonry, and the Enlightenment* (London and Toronto: Associated University Presses, 1987), 61–78.

Fieser illustrates how this context was taken for granted by Hume's early critics, who clearly recognized the need to 'decode' his writings in order to reveal their hidden meaning:

Fieser, James, 'Hume's Concealed Attack on Religion and his Early Critics', *Journal of Philosophical Research*, 20 (1995), 83–101.

Given this background, it is a genuine puzzle to identify Hume's real views on religion, a puzzle which has generated a great deal of literature especially in relation to the interpretation of his *Dialogues* (as discussed in §9.2 below). It seems clear that Hume himself held at most a very minimal deism, which raises the question of why he should have devoted so much attention to the topic. Noxon suggests that his fascination with it derived from his perception of religious belief itself as an extraordinary phenomenon:

Noxon, James, 'Hume's Concern with Religion', in K. R. Merrill and R. S. Shahan (eds.), *David Hume: Many-Sided Genius* (Norman: University of Oklahoma Press, 1976), 59–82; repr. in Tweyman (ed.), *Hume*, v. 3–25.

The most obvious alternative explanation—that Hume was motivated by the desire to oppose superstition—is rejected by Noxon (following Wollheim) by appeal to Hume's pessimism and conservative temperament. Hume was indeed pessimistic about the power of philosophy to undermine the religious commitments of 'the vulgar', but this does not imply that he had no such reformative ambition in respect of his more discerning readers. Quite the contrary is suggested by his manifesto in *Enquiry* I, which explicitly advocates that we 'cultivate true metaphysics . . . in order to destroy the false and adulterate' (*E* 12), and also by his posthumously published essay 'Of Suicide', whose first paragraph describes philosophy as a 'sovereign antidote . . . to superstition and false religion' (see §3 of Chapter 1 of this volume for other relevant references). Moreover, his concern with religion was very far from being the relatively detached curiosity suggested by Noxon, though as Siebert shows, his passionate moral opposition to religion is more clearly manifested in the *History of England* than in his philosophical writings:

Siebert, Donald T., *The Moral Animus of David Hume* (London and Toronto: Associated University Presses, 1990), ch. 2.

9.1 Miracles

The historical context of Hume's essay on miracles has become much better understood over recent years. Chapter 8 of Gaskin's book (listed above) is useful, but the most detailed treatment of both the prior debate and of Hume's arguments is

Burns, R. M., *The Great Debate on Miracles* (London and Toronto: Associated University Presses, 1981).

Two recent articles are also particularly noteworthy:

Wootton, David, 'Hume's "Of Miracles": Probability and Irreligion', in M. A. Stewart (ed.), *Studies in the Philosophy of the Scottish Enlightenment* (Oxford and New York: Clarendon Press, 1990), 191–229.

Stewart, M. A., 'Hume's Historical View of Miracles', in M. A. Stewart and John P. Wright (eds.), *Hume and Hume's Connexions* (Edinburgh: Edinburgh University Press, 1994), 171–200.

Gaskin locates Hume's essay within an ongoing English debate centring around Thomas Sherlock's famous *Tryal of the Witnesses of the Resurrection*, in which Sherlock defended the Gospel resurrection stories as historically well founded. Burns discusses a wider variety of English authors, finding parallels to the arguments of both Sherlock and Hume which make it harder to identify Sherlock as Hume's specific target, and also suggest that Hume's arguments may be less original than is often supposed (with similarities to those of deists such as William Wollaston). Wootton stresses the influence on Hume's thinking of less familiar French sources, which Hume may well have encountered during his time in France working on the *Treatise*. Stewart, while acknowledging both French and English sources, argues that Locke was the primary influence on Hume's thinking about the topic. Locke's views are put into context by Jones, who surveys how the topics of testimony and miracles were treated by British philosophers from Bacon to Hume:

Jones, Peter, *Hume's Sentiments* (Edinburgh: Edinburgh University Press, 1982), 45–56.

There are numerous discussions of the philosophical merits of what has been, ever since its publication, one of Hume's most controversial arguments. Some early responses and relevant reviews have recently become easily available in a useful collection (see *Hume Studies*, 24 (1998), 198 for details):

Tweyman, Stanley (ed.), *Hume on Miracles* (Bristol: Thoemmes Press, 1996).

One particularly entertaining piece, unfortunately long since out of print and not included in Tweyman's collection, is a spoof by Archbishop Richard Whately which was initially published (anonymously) in 1819. Here Whately aims to demonstrate the absurdity of Hume's criteria for judging miracle stories by showing that the history of Napoleon's exploits would, on these criteria, appear equally incredible:

Whately, Richard, *Historic Doubts relative to Napoleon Buonaparte* (London: John W. Parker & Son, 1859).

Moving on to modern interpretations and assessments of Hume's argument, the first section of Garrett's Chapter 11 gives some indication of their large number and considerable variety, and his footnoted references can easily be used to identify works which diverge from his interpretation in particular respects. Rather than duplicate this resource, I here pick out only a few highlights from the immense literature. To begin with those that have attained 'classic' status, the following short general discussions of Hume's essay are still well worth reading, even though they may look slightly dated in the light of more recent scholarship:

Broad, C. D., 'Hume's Theory of the Credibility of Miracles', *Proceedings of the Aristotelian Society*, 17 (1916–17), 77–94; repr. in Tweyman (ed.), *Hume*, v. 444–55.

Flew, Antony, 'Hume's Check', *Philosophical Quarterly*, 9 (1959), 1–18.

Mackie, J. L., *The Miracle of Theism* (Oxford and New York: Clarendon Press, 1982), ch. 1.

Broad is sympathetic but ultimately critical of the strength of Hume's conclusion, and sees it as inconsistent with his inductive scepticism (see §6.3 for suggested reading on this crucial issue). Flew takes Hume to be less ambitious, aiming to provide only a 'check' to the 'impertinent solicitations' of 'bigotry and superstition' addressed to 'the wise and learned' rather than a more general offensive criterion; however, he too sees the essay as inconsistent with Hume's account of induction. Mackie is less textually focused, and therefore less faithful to the details of Hume's treatment, but his discussion—which generally supports a Humean point of view—is philosophically interesting in its own right (for criticism, see Bruce Langtry, 'Mackie on Miracles', *Australasian Journal of Philosophy*, 66 (1988), 368–75).

Perhaps not surprisingly, the most substantial contributions are on the theistic side of the debate, with two books being particularly noteworthy:

Swinburne, Richard, *The Concept of Miracle* (London and Basingstoke: Macmillan, 1970).

Swinburne's well-known study starts by analysing how the notions of 'miracle' and 'law of nature' should be understood (criticizing Hume for ignoring the relevance of an event's religious significance), then considers the appropriate criteria for weighing of evidence and for preferring a purposive to a scientific explanation. Overall Swinburne finds Hume's conclusion simplistic, in that it fails to take into account both the full range of possible evidence, and also how miracles can fit into a pattern of explanation within a theistic world-view in which miracles and other evidence for God's existence are mutually supporting.

Houston, J., *Reported Miracles: A Critique of Hume* (Cambridge: Cambridge University Press, 1994).

Houston's book is more theologically informed than Swinburne's, but just as philosophically sensitive, reaching conclusions in a similar spirit but adding more incisive criticism of Hume. It starts with a historical survey of views on the miraculous, ranging through Augustine, Aquinas, Locke, Hume, Bradley, and Troeltsch, and ends with two chapters on the epistemological and theological implications of taking miracles seriously. But the heart of the book consists of two chapters on the concept of a miracle (one on theological conceptions, the other on Hume's) followed by three in which 'Hume's case' is assessed. Houston's primary criticism (ch. 9) questions Hume's assumption 'that the evidence for the relevant law(s) of nature is, in the overall dialectical context, undeniably relevant to an assessment of the probability (or improbability) that a reported putative miracle actually took place' (p. 133). This threatens to undercut Hume's entire argument in Part i of his essay, the point being that if the theist himself takes the reported event to be a *violation* of what, in other instances, has been a universal law, then the evidence for that law garnered from those other instances is exactly in accord with what the theist claims—Hume is apparently simply begging the question against the possibility of a miracle by presuming that the general rule must extend to the event in question. Houston follows up with a secondary objection (ch. 10), against Hume's aprioristic assumption that a report of an improbable event must itself inherit that improbability. For it would be perfectly possible that mankind in general—like the proverbial Edinburgh solicitor to whom Houston alludes—should be *more* reliable when reporting unusual events than when reporting relatively everyday happenings. Of course Hume, in Part ii of his essay, argues strongly that the facts of human nature are otherwise, but the point remains that on Hume's own principles such facts can be known only a posteriori. For his argument is founded on an inductive conception of testimony, according to which its reliability can be known only through experience; hence experience alone can tell us under what circumstances different types of testimony are more, or less, reliable.[4]

Hume's inductive conception of testimony is itself attacked by Coady in an article and in a subsequent book:

Coady, C. A. J., 'Testimony and Observation', *American Philosophical Quarterly*, 10 (1973), 149–55.

Coady, C. A. J., *Testimony* (Oxford and New York: Clarendon Press, 1992), esp. chs. 4 and 10.

The tenth chapter of Coady's book deals with the topic of 'astonishing reports', describing some of the complexities of assessing such evidence and concluding that no simple rule of assessment, such as Hume's, is likely to be universally applicable. But he addresses more basic concerns in his fourth chapter (as in his article), attacking Hume's 'reductive approach' whereby testimony is viewed as simply a species of inductive evidence, which therefore needs to be grounded on an observed correlation between reports and facts if it is to provide an adequate basis for belief. He argues for the incoherence of this view (which, for example, seems to imply the possibility of testimony's existing in a community but yet having no connexion with reality), and concludes that testimonial evidence must instead be seen as a fundamental category of evidence that is not reducible to other kinds. Hume is defended against this attack in

Traiger, Saul, 'Humean Testimony', *Pacific Philosophical Quarterly*, 74 (1993), 135–49,

where Traiger argues that the traditional attribution to Hume of an epistemically individualist and purely inductivist conception of testimony is incorrect.

Yet another book-length attack on Hume, which has appeared very recently, has the merit of giving detailed attention not only to Hume's own argument, but to four 'reconstructions' of it by Mackie, Mill, Flew, and Sobel:

Johnson, David, *Hume, Holism, and Miracles* (Ithaca, NY, and London: Cornell University Press, 1999), esp. 5–33.

---

[4] Houston's book has yet to receive a substantial answer, and he efficiently dismisses the various Humean responses that he himself considers. Hence it may be helpful to suggest some other possible lines of reply. One response to his primary criticism may be implicit in Hume's comment that 'it is impossible for us to know the attributes or actions of such a Being [i.e. God], otherwise than from the experience which we have of his productions, in the usual course of nature. This still reduces us to past observation, and obliges us to compare the instances of the violations of truth in the testimony of men with those of the violation of the laws of nature by miracles, in order to judge which of them is most likely and probable.' (E129). Thus the postulation of divine intentions that go beyond what is manifest in common experience will be gratuitous (a message spelled out explicitly in *Enquiry* XI), undermining any attempts to use the theistic hypothesis to go further than the conclusions of ordinary induction from experienced regularities. Development of this debate is likely to move beyond the single issue of miracles to the general explanatory value of a theistic world-view (including the Problem of Evil), somewhat confirming the moral drawn by both Swinburne and Houston. Houston's secondary objection is less fundamental, for although his logical point is well made, from a Humean point of view it remains plausible that inductive evidence for the reliability of *any* testimony can never exceed the evidence for a law of nature.

Johnson provides forceful criticisms of many distinctive points—made by Mill and Flew in particular—that are somewhat distant from Hume's own words and so tend not to be addressed by other authors. However, his principal criticism of all five versions of Hume's argument is that they ultimately beg the question against the miraculous, either by defining miracles out of existence (e.g. as exceptions to an exceptionless law of nature), or by taking for granted without argument that the inductive balance of evidence against any miracle cannot be outweighed by testimony on the other side. Johnson maintains that the inductive evidence can be so outweighed, even in principle by the testimony of a single witness, and he supports this claim with illustrations involving selection of marbles from an urn (pp. 25, 56) and reports of unusual weather (p. 31). These illustrations indeed appear initially very convincing, but it is a shame that Johnson does not consider some possible objections, for which we must turn to another strand of recent debate.

As Owen makes clear in Chapter 12, illustrations in a similar spirit to those used by Johnson—often involving lotteries, urns, and other probabilistically calculable scenarios—date right back to Hume's contemporary Richard Price. But after many years of relative neglect they have recently inspired great interest in the formal analysis of Hume's argument, largely with the aim of clarifying their true force against it. The standard lottery example involves a report (e.g. from a newspaper which is normally 99 per cent reliable in such matters) that the winning ticket in a lottery of, say, 10,000 tickets was ticket number 297 (or whatever). In this situation it seems that Hume's argument would advise us to reject the report, on the ground that it is more probable that the report should be false (probability 1 per cent) than that ticket 297 should really have won the lottery (probability 0.01 per cent). But intuitively this seems quite wrong—if the newspaper is 99 per cent reliable in such matters, then surely we should have 99 per cent confidence that the winning ticket was indeed 297. As Hambourger shows, such points can also be made in respect of many other types of report, even something as mundane as someone's reporting their own name:

Hambourger, Robert, 'Belief in Miracles and Hume's Essay', *Noûs*, 14 (1980), 587–604.

Owen hints (in his footnote 12) that this problem for Hume is solvable by taking into account that in such a lottery an incorrect report of the winning number can be wrong in 9,999 different ways (hence if some ticket other than 297 actually won but the newspaper reported it wrongly, the chance that it would report the particular number 297 is only 1 in 9,999). However, a formal treatment of this solution requires a Bayesian analysis more complex than Owen's simplified version—two such treatments (the first involving non-standard infinitesimals and the second more straightforward) are presented by

Sobel, Jordan Howard, 'On the Evidence of Testimony for Miracles: A Bayesian Interpretation of David Hume's Analysis', *Philosophical Quarterly*, 37 (1987), 166–86.

Dawid, Philip, and Gillies, Donald, 'A Bayesian Analysis of Hume's Argument concerning Miracles', *Philosophical Quarterly*, 39 (1989), 57–65.

However, Olin points out that matters are not quite this straightforward, because an exactly parallel move is possible with respect to miracle reports on the basis that if the reported event did not happen, then it would be extremely unlikely that *this* particular thing would be reported:

Olin, D., 'Hume, Miracles, and Prior Probabilities', in Tweyman (ed.), *Hume*, v. 416–26.

Nevertheless, there remains, as Hambourger stresses, an evident disanalogy between the case of the lottery and the miracle—in the lottery the *particular* event reported may be initially improbable, but the *type* of event reported is not. Schlesinger provides a formal analysis which is able to take this into account, by explicitly giving a low value to the probability that *any kind* of miracle has occurred in a specific situation:

Schlesinger, George N., 'Miracles and Probabilities', *Noûs*, 21 (1987), 219–32; repr. in Owen (ed.), *Hume*, 265–78.

Schlesinger goes on to argue that miracle reports can nevertheless raise the probability of God's existence (though highly paradoxically, he suggests that on the assumption that God exists, such reports need not raise the probability of the miracle itself!).

The continuing debate over lottery and related examples is not of merely technical interest, for it has brought into the open many issues of more general relevance. Olin, for example, lays the blame for Hume's problems on his failure to distinguish statistical from epistemic probability, and on his key presumption that evidence is additive. Hambourger too sees Hume's treatment of evidence as simplistic, in particular his supposition that the likelihood of the reported event can be factored out separately from the credibility of the report (a point which also seems to lie behind some criticisms that Johnson makes in his book, for example in chapter 7). If indeed the two cannot be separated, then the only coherent way of interpreting Hume's rule for the assessment of miracle reports may be to reduce it to a triviality, though arguably this need not be objectionable (for a sketch of this issue, and some implications for attempts to formalize Hume's position, see Peter Millican, '"Hume's Theorem" concerning Miracles', *Philosophical Quarterly*, 43 (1993), 489–95).

9.2 Hume on the Design Argument

In terms of their direct impact on the secondary literature, Sections X and XI of the *Enquiry* could hardly be further apart. With Section X the problem is one of selection from a vast range of critiques and replies; with Section XI the problem is to find even a handful of contributions that directly address the specific issues that Hume raises there. A notable exception is the relevant chapter of Flew's classic book:

Flew, Antony, *Hume's Philosophy of Belief* (London: Routledge & Kegan Paul, 1961), ch. 9.

Flew generally supports Hume's contention that it is illegitimate to infer qualities in the cosmic Designer beyond those that are manifested in the experienced cosmos, and he also agrees with Hume's closing hint that the supposed Deity's uniqueness is a decisive obstacle to viewing theism as a hypothesis open to confirmation from the empirical evidence. Both principles are challenged forcefully by Swinburne, who argues that they are contrary to standard criteria of scientific inference:

Swinburne, R. G., 'The Argument from Design', *Philosophy*, 43 (1968), 199–212; repr. in Tweyman (ed.), *Hume*, v. 197–209 (see esp. Swinburne's itemized points 1 to 3).

These general issues are explored by Gaskin in Chapter 13 of this volume, and a detailed reply to Swinburne has recently appeared in a new journal published by the Council for Secular Humanism, which is named after Philo, Hume's sceptical spokesman in the *Dialogues*:

> Beaudoin, John, 'On Some Criticisms of Hume's Principle of Proportioning Cause to Effect', *Philo*, 2 (1999), 26–40; also available from the website www.etext.leeds.ac.uk/hume/

We must now turn to the *Dialogues* themselves, which have attracted the vast majority of scholarly interest regarding Hume's criticisms of the Design Argument. What follows is only a very brief review of a massive debate, for the puzzle of how far the *Dialogues* reveal Hume's own views on religion has for many years been one of the most discussed issues of Hume interpretation. There are several detailed commentaries on the *Dialogues* available, of which Kemp Smith's (referred to in §2.3 above) is certainly the most influential. Two others of particular interest are

> Pike, Nelson, 'Hume on the Argument from Design', in Pike (ed.), *David Hume: Dialogues concerning Natural Religion* (Indianapolis: Bobbs-Merrill, 1970), 125–238.

> Tweyman, Stanley, introduction to Tweyman (ed.), *David Hume: Dialogues concerning Natural Religion in Focus* (London and New York: Routledge, 1991), 1–94.

Kemp Smith's uncompromising interpretation provides the background to the subsequent debate: 'I shall contend that Philo [the sceptic], from start to finish, represents Hume; and that Cleanthes [the advocate of the Design Argument] can be regarded as Hume's mouthpiece only in those passages in which he is explicitly agreeing with Philo, or in those other passages in which, while refuting Demea [the mystically inclined a priori theist], he is also being used to prepare the way for one or other of Philo's independent conclusions' (D 59). Pike (pp. 224–34) disputes this sceptical reading, highlighting Cleanthes' rejoinder in Part III, where he says to Philo that if he contemplates the structure of an eye, the idea of a designer will 'immediately flow in upon you with a force like that of sensation' (D 154). Philo makes no reply at this point, but Pike suggests that it is his acceptance of this 'irregular' but 'irresistible' argument that forms the basis for his famously puzzling 'confession' at the beginning of Part XII (D 214–7). Tweyman develops this idea further, relating it to Hume's discussion of scepticism in the *Enquiry*. He suggests that Philo's argumentation itself exemplifies the Humean transition, discussed by Norton in Chapter 14 of this volume, from Pyrrhonian scepticism (which though unsustainable performs the useful service of undermining our initial dogmatic confidence) to mitigated scepticism (which corrects the Pyrrhonian doubts with 'common sense and reflection'; E 161). According to Tweyman, in Parts I to VIII Philo argues as a Pyrrhonian, aiming for suspense of judgement, but thereafter he mitigates his scepticism and by Part XII is prepared to acknowledge the natural force of Cleanthes' 'irregular' argument.

Since Hume is famous for affirming the power of nature to compel belief beyond the reach of reason, it is not surprising that many commentators have seen a similar pattern in the *Dialogues*, with Cleanthes' irresistible inference of Part III and Philo's confession of Part XII indicating that theism may be a Humean 'natural belief' (the term is Kemp Smith's) alongside those in inductive uniformity, the reliability of our senses, and the independent continuity of the external world. Butler and Penelhum have been perhaps the strongest advocates of this idea, and Gaskin its most resolute opponent, with the following works (in order) giving the essence of their debate:

Butler, R. J., 'Natural Belief and the Enigma of Hume', *Archiv für Geschichte der Philosophie*, 42 (1960), 73–100.

Gaskin, J. C. A., 'God, Hume and Natural Belief', *Philosophy*, 49 (1974), 281–94; repr. in Tweyman (ed.), *Hume*, v. 150–63; this article is reproduced, largely verbatim, in his book *Hume's Philosophy of Religion*, 1st edn. (London and Basingstoke: Macmillan, 1978), 129–39.

Penelhum, Terence, 'Natural Belief and Religious Belief in Hume's Philosophy', *Philosophical Quarterly*, 33 (1983), 266–82; repr. in Tweyman (ed.), *Hume*, v. 164–80.

Gaskin, J. C. A., *Hume's Philosophy of Religion*, 2nd edn. (Basingstoke and London: Macmillan, 1988), 116–31.

Gaskin objects to the classification of theism as a 'natural belief' on the grounds that it does not seem to be a belief of common life, is not irresistible and independent of reasoning, is not necessary for action in the world, and is not universal. In response to these criticisms, Penelhum suggests a modified position according to which the belief in God, though potentially requiring reasoning to bring it about (and hence not 'natural' in the strict sense) nevertheless is like the natural beliefs in being, *once acquired*, beyond the power of reason to dislodge. But given the very minimal theism which Penelhum ascribes to Hume, his difference from Gaskin reduces to the question of whether, in Hume's view, such 'attenuated deism' may be, after all, a reasonable conclusion to draw from the Design Argument. Gaskin maintains that it is, though since this reasonable belief is easily conflated with a natural and non-rational *feeling for design*, the psychological upshot of Penelhum's and Gaskin's positions may ultimately be hard to distinguish. Another subtle variation on the same general theme is provided by

Yandell, K. E., 'Hume on Religious Belief', in Donald W. Livingston and James T. King (eds.), *Hume: A Re-evaluation* (New York: Fordham University Press, 1976), 109–25; repr. in Tweyman (ed.), *Hume*, v. 36–55,

who seeks illumination by starting from the *Natural History of Religion* instead of the highly ambiguous *Dialogues*. Yandell's Hume accepts that some minimal religious principle is part of human nature, though it is not irresistible and is often intermixed with more primitive religious feelings arising from ignorant hopes and fears. Although the Design Argument is unsound, contemplation of the order of the world can trigger our innate propensity to believe in a designer, and Yandell maintains that this propensity— despite its instinctive nature—is appropriately judged to be part of our *rational* capacity (p. 118). *Why* such an instinct should be appropriately called 'rational' is, however, unclear, and one might suspect that Yandell has here gone too far in attempting to find a genuine reconciliation between Hume's refutation of the Design Argument and his endorsements of the design hypothesis in the *Natural History* and elsewhere. For a more straightforward explanation of Hume's position suggests itself—that his declarations of belief are simply instances of the 'theological lying' discussed by Berman and Fieser in their essays mentioned in §9 above. Faced with this possibility, the only way of revealing

Hume's true opinions seems to be to follow where his most forceful arguments lead, and to try to identify the targets at which they are aimed.

With this in mind, many authors have attempted to identify the real archetypes behind the characters of the *Dialogues*. Pakaluk takes all three to be representative of abstract philosophical 'types', with Philo being a mitigated sceptic or 'true philosopher', Cleanthes a 'false philosopher', and Demea a 'vulgar reasoner'. Like Tweyman, Pakaluk sees Philo's eventual acceptance of the design hypothesis as exemplifying a Humean transition of thought, though not a change of theory so much as a change of temper, when the natural sentiments of the mind that have hitherto been suppressed return after the sceptical duelling ceases. In developing this account, he also draws various interesting parallels between the *Dialogues* and *Enquiry* XII (especially, at pp. 127–9, Hume's discussion of the external world in *Enquiry* XII Part i):

> Pakaluk, Michael, 'Philosophical "Types" in Hume's *Dialogues*', in V. Hope (ed.), *Philosophers of the Scottish Enlightenment* (Edinburgh: Edinburgh University Press, 1984), 116–32; repr. in Tweyman (ed.), *Hume*, v. 323–38.

A more concrete identification of Hume's characters was influentially made by Mossner very soon after the first appearance of Kemp Smith's edition. Accepting Kemp Smith's identification of Philo with Hume, Mossner argues that Cleanthes and Demea represent respectively Joseph Butler and Samuel Clarke:

> Mossner, Ernest C., 'The Enigma of Hume', *Mind*, 45 (1936), 334–49.

All three of Mossner's identifications are challenged, however, by a comprehensive comparative study of Hume and Butler:

> Jeffner, Anders, *Butler and Hume on Religion* (Stockholm: Diakonistyrelsens Bokförlag, 1966), esp. 131–43, 169–71, 180–209.

According to Jeffner, although Butler is indeed a primary target of the *Dialogues*, he is not represented directly by any of the characters. Instead, Cleanthes is modelled on a type of scientific theologian associated with the Royal Society (most famously Boyle and Newton, but also John Wilkins, John Ray, William Derham, George Cheyne, and Colin Maclaurin), who were enthusiastic advocates of the analogical Design Argument. Here Jeffner draws on

> Hurlbutt III, R. H., 'David Hume and Scientific Theism', *Journal of the History of Ideas*, 17 (1956), 486–97,

who quotes passages from Cheyne and Maclaurin strikingly similar to Cleanthes' words (including his famous appeal to the 'force like that of sensation' in Part III which has inspired so much interest in the natural belief interpretation). Jeffner goes on to suggest that Demea is modelled on the theological school of Peter Browne, William King, and William Law, who denied that we have understanding of the supposed analogical similarity between God's and man's attributes and who were accordingly inclined to prefer the aprioristic reasoning of Samuel Clarke. Finally, Jeffner identifies Philo not with Hume himself but with Bayle, combining scepticism and mysticism with apparently devout fideism. On this reading, it is the combinations of the characters rather than their individual positions that display Hume's true views and spell defeat for

Butler's theism. Philo and Demea combine to portray the evil of the world and the impossibility of an analogical argument for a good God; Cleanthes and Philo combine to reject a priori natural theology; while Cleanthes and Demea combine to insist that faith, if it is to be intellectually respectable, should be founded on reason. Taken together, these results imply the impossibility of any defensible theism.

9.3 The Contemporary Design Argument

Although for many years the Design Argument lay under the cloud of Hume's critique, and perhaps even more influentially the undermining of its biological aspect through the theory of evolution, it has recently enjoyed something of a renaissance. The first wave of this rebirth came from philosophers who advocated treating the argument not as decisive in itself, but as part of a *cumulative case* in which a wide range of considerations are adduced to show the overall plausibility of a theistic world-view. The roots of this approach go back to Hume's contemporary Joseph Butler, but its modern pioneer was Mitchell, soon to be followed by Swinburne:

> Mitchell, Basil, *The Justification of Religious Belief* (London and Basingstoke: Macmillan, 1973), esp. chs. 2 and 3.

> Swinburne, Richard, *The Existence of God* (Oxford and New York: Clarendon Press, 1979), esp. ch. 8 (chs. 10 and 11 consider the Problem of Evil).

The best-known critique of Swinburne is by Mackie, who starts by explicitly following Hume's objections to the logic of the Design Argument. He then—like Philo in Parts X and XI of the *Dialogues*—presses home his attack by emphasizing the Problem of Evil, which aims to turn the tables by confronting the theist with empirical evidence that is far less favourable to his optimistic conclusions:

> Mackie, J. L., *The Miracle of Theism* (Oxford and New York: Clarendon Press, 1982), chs. 8 and 9.

The revised edition of Swinburne's book adds a direct reply to Mackie in a new appendix:

> Swinburne, Richard, *The Existence of God*, rev. edn. (Oxford and New York: Clarendon Press, 1991), app. A.

The second wave of the Design Argument's renaissance has come, perhaps surprisingly, from the same arena that inspired the Enlightenment vision of a divine clockmaker, namely the heavens. Modern discoveries in physics and cosmology suggest that the universe began with a 'Big Bang', and that the initial conditions of this Big Bang, and the laws of nature that have governed the universe since, must have been impressively 'finely tuned' to permit the evolution of stars, planets, and hence—ultimately—life. For a fairly detailed (and moderately technical) outline of this apparent 'fine tuning', see

> Davies, P. C. W., *The Accidental Universe* (Cambridge, New York, and Melbourne: Cambridge University Press, 1982), esp. chs. 3 and 4.

Less detailed overviews are provided by two philosophical discussions from strong advocates of the Fine Tuning Argument, who draw the inference that unless the universe were designed with life in mind, the existence of this favourable fine tuning would be vanishingly improbable:

> Swinburne, Richard, *The Existence of God*, rev. edn. (Oxford and New York: Clarendon Press, 1991), app. B.

> Craig, William Lane, 'The Teleological Argument and the Anthropic Principle', in W. L. Craig and M. McLeod (eds.), *The Logic of Rational Theism: Exploratory Essays* (Lewiston, NY: Edwin Mellen, 1990), 127–53.

All three of these writers make reference to the (rather unfortunately named, and variously interpreted) 'Anthropic Principle', which has been used to explain away the apparent fine tuning—or 'anthropic coincidences'—as a selection effect. This idea can be summed up as a retort to the theist: 'You shouldn't find it surprising to observe that the universe is "fine tuned" for life, because if it weren't, you wouldn't be here to observe anything'. As the discussions above make clear, however, this retort seems dubious unless there is a 'population' of universes for the selection effect to work on, for if there is only one universe, then it does indeed appear surprising (and hence crying out for explanation) that this sole universe should happen to be 'finely tuned' in a way that makes possible the existence of observers. (The atheist's retort conflates the unsurprising fact that we *fail to observe* a universe *unsuitable* for life with the surprising fact that we *observe* a universe *suitable* for life—indeed that we are here to observe anything at all.) This constitutes a serious problem for the atheist, for it seems to put the boot of metaphysical extravagance—traditionally one of the very strongest objections to theism—on the other foot. For if the only reasonable alternative to the hypothesis of a divine Fine Tuner is a massive ensemble of universes, with life emerging only in the minute proportion that happen to be 'finely tuned', then arguably theism has now become the more modest and metaphysically economical of the available hypotheses. All of these themes are engagingly developed at length in the most extensive philosophical treatment of the issue so far published:

> Leslie, John, *Universes* (London and New York: Routledge, 1989).

Leslie is not, however, a conventional theist, for the 'God' to whose action he attributes the creation of the Universe is a Neoplatonic 'ethical requiredness' rather than a divine person.

The recent discovery of the Fine Tuning Argument is perhaps the most significant development in natural theology since Hume's *Dialogues*, and it is too early yet to attempt any general assessment of its merits (not least because the physical theory on which it is based is very far from being solidly established). One notable advantage that it has over traditional versions of the Design Argument is to point unambiguously to *advance planning* as the ultimate source of order in the universe, thus bypassing Hume's objection (*D* 147–8, 170–85) that it is mere bias to prefer intelligence over the other potential sources of order that we experience, such as vegetation, generation, and the emergence of patterns from chaos. The cosmological scale of the argument also seems to lend support to the theist's desired conclusions about the Designer's unity and supremacy (cf. *D* 166–8). But other Humean objections remain strong, particularly his insistence (*E* 143–8, *D* 149–50) that, without experience of the origin of worlds, we are unable to make any proper assessment of the probability that a life-favouring universe (whether like ours or profoundly different) might exist without being expressly designed. Indeed this point gains even more force in the light of modern physics, which has repeatedly demonstrated the unreliability of our intuitive judgements when applied beyond the human scale of things, to atoms and the cosmos. Another Humean objection (*D* 191) highlights our ignorance of the underlying structure of the world, suggesting that for all we know there may be some deep reason why it *has to be* structured as it is. Applied to the Fine Tuning Argument, this draws attention to the possibility of a future theory that will provide a clear explanation for what at present seem surprising coincidences. Such objections, like those made by Philo to the traditional Design Argument a century before the theory of evolution, may appear 'mere cavils and sophisms' (*D* 202), being based on promissory notes and appeals to ignorance rather than offering any explicit alternative theory. But just like Philo, the atheist can effectively force his adversary onto the defensive by turning instead to the ancient Problem of Evil, where the anthropic coincidences are of no help to the theist. A malevolent spirit, just as much as a benevolent one, can be expected to favour a universe conducive to life, because, as Smith points out, life is a prerequisite of moral evil as well as of moral good:

> Smith, Quentin, 'The Anthropic Coincidences, Evil and the Disconfirmation of Theism', *Religious Studies*, 28 (1992), 347–50.

For an extended development of this 'antitheistic' strategy, which applies it to a wide range of traditional theistic arguments and to Swinburne's Design Argument in particular detail, see

> Millican, P. J. R., 'The Devil's Advocate', *Cogito*, 3 (1989), 193–207; also available from the website www.etext.leeds.ac.uk/hume/

Presumably Hume himself—like Philo—viewed the Problem of Evil as the theist's most formidable obstacle, obliging him 'to tug the labouring oar, and to support [his] philosophical subtilties against the dictates of plain reason and experience' (*D* 202). To explore the prospects for a successful theistic defence, see (in addition to the books by Mitchell and Swinburne mentioned above)

> Taliaferro, Charles, *Contemporary Philosophy of Religion* (Oxford and Malden, Mass.: Blackwell, 1998), ch. 9.

> Adams, Marilyn McCord, and Adams, Robert Merrihew (eds.), *The Problem of Evil* (Oxford and New York: Oxford University Press, 1990).

Taliaferro gives a wide-ranging overview of contemporary approaches, while the Adamses' collection contains many of the most important pieces, including a number discussed by Taliaferro.

10. SCEPTICISM

Section XII of the *Enquiry* is particularly complex, since as Norton makes clear in Chapter 14 it not only discusses a wide range of sceptical positions and arguments, but also makes reference (either implicitly or explicitly) to many other aspects of Hume's philosophy. Any proper understanding of Hume's scepticism must therefore take account of a number of important issues discussed earlier, most notably the relationship between the *Enquiry* and the *Treatise* (§3.3), Hume's argument concerning induction (§§5.2 and 5.3), and his discussions of philosophical and unphilosophical probability (§6.3), but also his alleged causal realism (§7.3) and his religious scepticism (§9).

Though seriously dated in some matters of interpretation, each of the following provides a stimulating discussion of the wide range of issues that arise in this complex section:

Flew, Antony, *Hume's Philosophy of Belief* (London: Routledge & Kegan Paul, 1961), ch. 10.

Passmore, John, *Hume's Intentions*, 3rd edn. (London: Duckworth, 1980), ch. 7.

The most prominent of the topics raised for the first time in *Enquiry* XII are scepticism with regard to the external world and with regard to infinite divisibility. The literature on each of these is sufficiently rich to merit separate consideration before we turn to discuss more general perspectives on Hume's scepticism.

10.1 *Scepticism regarding the External World*

The first major sceptical topic in Section XII is the external world, which also incorporates the primary–secondary quality distinction, though this *Enquiry* discussion (*E* 151–5) is drastically scaled down from that in the *Treatise* (*T* 187–231). No doubt for this reason, most commentators have focused almost exclusively on the far more sophisticated *Treatise* account, the interpretation of which poses severe problems not only because of its complexity but also because Hume's ultimate view has proved so elusive. Good presentations of this *Treatise* account have appeared in a number of general books on Hume:

Stroud, Barry, *Hume* (London and Boston: Routledge & Kegan Paul, 1977), ch. 5.

Noonan, Harold W., *Hume on Knowledge* (London and New York: Routledge, 1999), ch. 4.

Pears, David, *Hume's System* (Oxford and New York: Oxford University Press, 1990), chs. 10 and 11.

Fogelin, Robert, *Hume's Skepticism in the 'Treatise of Human Nature'* (London, Boston, and Melbourne: Routledge & Kegan Paul, 1985), chs. 6 and 7.

Stroud, whose entire book follows Kemp Smith in stressing Hume's naturalism in opposition to his scepticism, interprets the discussion of *Treatise* I. iv. 2 as an attempt to explain the origin of our idea of continued and distinct existence, with the aim of showing that this idea is not innate. The apparently sceptical outcome of the discussion may be unsettling, but again its point is naturalistic, 'to show that reason, as traditionally understood, is not the dominant force in human life' (pp. 116–17). Noonan starts his chapter in a similar spirit, by emphasizing the naturalistic purposes of Hume's sceptical arguments, but unlike Stroud he goes on to consider the deeper sceptical problems raised by *Treatise* I. iv. 4 (concerning the primary–secondary quality distinction; cf. *E* 154–5), and ends with the comment that Hume's sceptical conclusions here undermine his earlier attempt to give a consistent account of the distinction between the principles of the understanding and those of the narrow imagination: 'Thus our common belief in an external world is indubitable, but in no way justified and, being false, incapable of any justification' (p. 186). Pears restricts his attention to *Treatise* I. iv. 2, dissecting Hume's arguments in detail and blaming his conclusion 'that our belief in body is intellectually indefensible' (p. 196) on an inadequate recognition of the distinction between impressions and physical objects, both in Hume's own view and in that which he attributes to the vulgar. Pears thus interprets Hume as seriously sceptical about (both the tenability and content of) our belief in body even before the primary–secondary quality objection of *Treatise* I. iv. 4 which according to the *Enquiry* 'goes farther' (*E* 155). Fogelin sees all this scepticism as fundamental to Hume's intentions, taking him to be a committed Pyrrhonian who deliberately aims to highlight irreconcilable differences between the various points of view described in his 'natural history' of philosophy, with none of these providing a stable outcome. (Fogelin very clearly spells out this position—which he calls 'radical perspectivism'—in a later critique of Garrett: 'Garrett on the Consistency of Hume's Philosophy', *Hume Studies*, 24 (1998), 161–9.)

Probably the two best-known discussions of these sections of the *Treatise* are

Price, H. H., *Hume's Theory of the External World* (Oxford: Clarendon Press, 1940).

Bennett, Jonathan, *Locke, Berkeley, Hume: Central Themes* (Oxford: Clarendon Press, 1971), ch. 13 and pp. 91–4.

Neither of these is particularly scholarly by modern standards, but both are serious and illuminating attempts to address the philosophical issues. Price's book is very dated, relating Hume's views to positions that were influential at the time such as those of Kant, Russell, and the logical positivists. But this in itself gives the book a distinctive value, because Price's elegant writing makes its age no obstacle to comprehension, while some parts of Hume's theory (e.g. his claim that perceptions can exist independently) can be usefully illuminated by being put alongside their early twentieth-century descendants (e.g. Russell's notion of sensibilia). Bennett's discussion is far shorter, and probably for that reason more intense as he grapples philosophically with Hume's problems in an effort to avoid his apparently despairing conclusion. Though rewarding this makes for difficult reading, but Bennett's views are given a relatively simple critical discussion in an introductory book which also provides its own analysis of Hume's argument:

Dicker, Georges, *Hume's Epistemology and Metaphysics* (London and New York: Routledge, 1998), ch. 6.

Dicker's chapter ends with a sketch of the Kantian response to this form of scepticism, which again will prove useful for students needing a straightforward introduction to a very complex issue.

From the point of view of a student of the *Enquiry*, perhaps the three most thought-provoking recent discussions of Hume's scepticism about the external world are

Bricke, John, *Hume's Philosophy of Mind* (Edinburgh: Edinburgh University Press, 1980), ch. 1.

Garrett, Don, *Cognition and Commitment in Hume's Philosophy* (Oxford and New York: Oxford University Press, 1997), ch. 10, esp. 209–20.

Wright, John P., *The Sceptical Realism of David Hume* (Manchester: Manchester University Press, 1983), ch. 2 and §11.

Bricke is unusual in giving serious attention to the *Enquiry* as well as to the *Treatise*, and he provides a careful and philosophically sensitive discussion of both. However, he concurs with other commentators in finding Hume's position ultimately unstable, showing sympathy with the perspectival view championed by Fogelin before finally concluding that Hume is himself probably a representative realist, whose sceptical attack on such realism is intended not to refute it outright but only to undermine our confidence in building theories that stray too far from the vulgar perspective. Garrett goes further in attempting to develop a consistent Humean position, based on his view of Hume as primarily a cognitive scientist rather than a sceptical philosopher. He does this by thoroughly downplaying the apparent extreme scepticism which has proved so puzzling for Stroud and other previous commentators in the 'naturalist' tradition: 'Nowhere does Hume claim that most of our beliefs in the existence of continued and distinct existences are unworthy of assent, nor that such beliefs should be rejected or suspended.' (p. 220). This claim involves some delicate interpretation of Hume's statements, some of which superficially appear to tell strongly in the opposite direction. But at least some of this appearance can be explained away, as Wright also does in an account which considers the background to Hume's views in physiological theories of perception deriving in large part from Malebranche. According to Wright, most of Hume's *Treatise* discussion is devoted to explaining—in terms that are at least implicitly physiological—the 'vulgar' belief in external objects that are supposedly identical to our perceptions. *This* belief Hume takes to be clearly false, though it importantly paves the way *psychologically* for representative realism by setting the scene for the 'obvious' argument from sensory variation that is presented most clearly at *E* 152 (cf. *T* 193). Representative realism is thus an example of those 'reflections of common life, methodized and corrected' (*E* 162) which Hume commends, and he can consistently endorse it because its dependence on the false vulgar view is psychological rather than logical. Such realism might seem to be contradicted (as Fogelin and Noonan suppose) by Hume's scepticism concerning the primary–secondary quality distinction. But although this indeed implies that we are unable to conceive distinctly of objects 'specifically different from our perceptions', it does not prevent our forming a bare 'relative idea' of them (*T* 68) and thus maintaining a form of realism even though we lack any distinct conception of the objects concerned. As we have seen in §7.3 above, this notion of relative ideas also plays a major role in Wright's account of Hume's 'sceptical realism' with regard to causation; indeed it is the similarity between the two cases which provides much of the attraction for his interpretation.

Unfortunately neither Garrett nor Wright says much about Hume's discussion in the *Enquiry*, but both suggest the possibility of a non-sceptical reading. And if, like Garrett, we are prepared to entertain the possibility that some of Hume's statements have an import rather different from their superficial impression, then this may cast new light on, for example, the crucial final paragraph of Section XII Part i. This contains both the conditional clause: 'at least, if it be a principle of reason, that all sensible qualities are in the mind, not in the object'; and also a concluding comment that the notion of 'a certain unknown, inexplicable *something*' is 'so imperfect, that no sceptic will think it worth while to contend against it'. These have generally been read in what is probably the most natural way, as respectively *endorsing* the 'principle of reason' and *rejecting* the imperfect notion, but they can be read in a very different way, as *raising a genuine question* about the alleged principle (which fits well with the agnosticism about objects' natures implied by both Garrett and Wright) and as *accepting* the admittedly imperfect notion of an 'unknown, inexplicable *something*'. There is no doubt that Hume was capable of artful composition (as witnessed supremely by his *Dialogues*), but why might he wish to present these views in such an obscure and misleading manner? Perhaps this too can be explained given the context in which he wrote and his purposes in the *Enquiry*. For a prominent theme in British philosophy at the time was the pursuit of metaphysics based on supposed insight into the nature of matter. An accessible discussion of this tradition is in a book by Yolton:

> Yolton, John W., *Thinking Matter* (Minneapolis: University of Minnesota Press, 1983), ch. 5,

which particularly singles out Andrew Baxter as an influential exponent of this style of metaphysics, who like others in the tradition maintained the intrinsic inertness of matter as a means of drawing religious conclusions. Hume knew Baxter's work, and it has even recently been argued that Baxter's influence may lie behind the vitriolic attack which, as Stewart explains in Chapter 2 (pp. 83–6), ruined Hume's attempt to gain appointment to an Edinburgh chair at just the time when he was writing the *Enquiry*:

> Russell, Paul, 'Wishart, Baxter and Hume's *Letter from a Gentleman*', *Hume Studies*, 23 (1997), 245–76.

In this context Hume may have seen good reason for stressing the sceptical implications of his arguments concerning matter, so as to wreck the prospects for any attempt to build a solid metaphysics on insight into its nature (which the primary–secondary quality distinction was supposed by some to exemplify). As suggested in §12 of Chapter 4, a confused and obscure notion of matter would leave empirical induction as the only remaining basis for scientific progress, a result which seems to harmonize perfectly with the overall intention and design of the *Enquiry* as interpreted in Chapter 1 (see especially pp. 62–5).

Contemporary attacks on scepticism regarding the external world have tended to avoid disputing with Hume on his own ground, preferring to rely on more fundamental objections to the very coherence of the sceptical position. For example, both Hookway, and Bell and McGinn (referenced in §10.3 below) follow Wittgenstein's *On Certainty* in seeing the existence of external objects as a 'framework' judgement presupposed by our thinking, rather than as a potentially questionable factual statement in need of evidential support. Nevertheless, there are exceptions to this general trend, in particular two discussions in a Humean spirit, one on each side of the sceptical debate:

> Mates, Benson, *Skeptical Essays* (Chicago and London: Chicago University Press, 1981), ch. 3.

> Aune, Bruce, *Knowledge of the External World* (London and New York: Routledge, 1991), esp. chs. 3, 6, and 7.

Mates engagingly elaborates Humean objections to the external world, concluding that they are ultimately unanswerable. Aune sets out to answer them, based on 'reformed' empiricist principles that in part claim inspiration directly from Hume. At the end of his discussion Aune touches on issues of scientific realism, which are central to modern philosophy of science. To explore these issues further, see

Psillos, Stathis, *Scientific Realism: How Science Tracks Truth* (London and New York: Routledge, 1999).

Particularly relevant here are Psillos's fourth and ninth chapters. The former provides a defence of 'abduction' or 'inference to the best explanation' which is strongly reminiscent of the 'inductive' justification of induction mentioned in §5.4 above. The latter defends scientific realism against Van Fraassen's 'constructive empiricism' largely on grounds that echo the Humean claim that science is 'nothing but the reflections of common life, methodized and corrected' (*E* 162).

10.2 *Scepticism regarding Infinite Divisibility*

Few would argue that Hume's work in the philosophy of mathematics is of great lasting significance, for here his confident and sometimes almost heroic commitment to empiricism leads him to draw conclusions well beyond the bounds of his technical expertise. Confirmation of this assessment can be drawn from the minor role which Hume is given in a relatively accessible guide to the history and philosophy of the infinite (one which ultimately advocates a finitist position, though on Wittgensteinian rather than Humean grounds):

Moore, A. W., *The Infinite* (London and New York: Routledge, 1990), esp. 80–3, 205.

Perhaps not surprisingly, most authors of books on Hume have ignored the topic, a notable exception being Fogelin, who also followed up his book with an article explaining both the proposed proofs of infinite divisibility to which Hume alludes and also his debt to Berkeley's earlier critique:

Fogelin, Robert, *Hume's Skepticism in the 'Treatise of Human Nature'* (London, Boston, and Melbourne: Routledge & Kegan Paul, 1985), ch. 3.

Fogelin, Robert, 'Hume and Berkeley on the Proofs of Infinite Divisibility', *Philosophical Review*, 97 (1988), 47–69.

Fogelin's book concentrates entirely on the *Treatise* and his article says relatively little about the *Enquiry*, whose treatment of infinite divisibility is significantly different. Fortunately a recent paper is able to fill the gap:

Jacquette, Dale, 'Infinite Divisibility in Hume's First *Enquiry*', *Hume Studies*, 20 (1994), 219–40.

This is one of a number of useful papers on the topic to have appeared recently in *Hume Studies*. Another aims to assess the philosophical value of Hume's contribution:

Franklin, James, 'Achievements and Fallacies in Hume's Account of Infinite Divisibility', *Hume Studies*, 20 (1994), 85–101.

Though disagreeing with Hume's would-be refutation of infinite divisibility, Franklin is broadly sympathetic even to the extent of maintaining (p. 87) that Hume's conclusions about the discreteness of space are consistent with standard geometry. (For a contrary view, see H. Mark Pressman, 'Hume on Geometry and Infinite Divisibility in the *Treatise*', *Hume Studies*, 23 (1997), 227–44, esp. 239–41.) However, Franklin is dismissive of Hume's attempts to draw conclusions about space from the nature of our ideas, which he sees as involving the crude fallacy 'it is not conceivable by the human mind, therefore it cannot be' (p. 93; cf. Lightner in §5.1 above). Hume is defended against this charge of crudeness by

> Waxman, Wayne, 'The Psychologistic Foundations of Hume's Critique of Mathematical Philosophy', *Hume Studies*, 22 (1996), 123–67,

who finds Hume's argument to be a consistent following-through of his theories of relations and abstraction from *Treatise* Book I Part i and of his Separability Principle. However, neither the theory of relations nor the Separability Principle figure explicitly in the later work, while the theory of abstraction appears only at *E* 158 n., in a role for which it is not used in the *Treatise* (as Jacquette observes). There is work to be done on how far the truncated *Enquiry* account can make sense without the metaphysical commitments of the *Treatise*—whether, for example, the argument at *E* 156 n. is intended to involve a conclusion beyond what Waxman calls the 'perceptible manifold', in which case the Separability Principle would seem to be required (note that the reference to 'physical points' does not decide this issue in the way that might be expected, given Hume's only other uses of the phrase, at *T* 40 and *T* 112).

10.3 The Nature of Hume's Scepticism

Many discussions of Hume's scepticism draw comparisons between his views and those of the ancient sceptics, either the Pyrrhonists (whose pre-eminent spokesman was Sextus Empiricus) or the Academics (whose doctrines became known primarily through the works of Cicero). The views of both of these schools and their relationship to Hume are outlined in the final chapter of Norton's book, which also provides the basis for some of his discussion in Chapter 14 of this volume:

> Norton, David Fate, *David Hume: Common-Sense Moralist, Sceptical Metaphysician* (Princeton and Guildford: Princeton University Press, 1982), 255–69 (on Pyrrhonism) and 269–79 (on Academic scepticism).

Popkin charts the Renaissance rediscovery of Greek scepticism and its influence on subsequent thinkers in his well-known history, which fostered the now general appreciation of the sceptical tradition's immense impact on modern thought:

> Popkin, Richard H., *The History of Scepticism from Erasmus to Spinoza* (Berkeley and London: University of California Press, 1979).

Popkin is also the author of what is probably the best-known discussion of Hume's scepticism, referred to by a number of the works discussed below:

> Popkin, Richard H., 'David Hume: His Pyrrhonism and his Critique of Pyrrhonism', *Philosophical Quarterly*, 1 (1951), 385–407; repr. in V. C. Chappell (ed.), *Hume* (London and Melbourne: Macmillan, 1968), 53–98 and in Tweyman (ed.), *Hume*, ii. 161–87.

Although Hume himself in *Enquiry* XII repeatedly describes Pyrrhonism as 'excessive' and criticizes it as unlivable (*E* 159–61), Popkin points out that his understanding of it is incomplete, failing to take into account the Pyrrhonian principles—expounded by Sextus Empiricus—of living according to nature and accepting 'evident' appearances undogmatically. However, Sextus can still be criticized for not going far enough, and Popkin argues that Hume's position, which goes much further in accepting the natural inevitability of *almost all* our beliefs, is in fact the only consistent development of Pyrrhonism. The Pyrrhonian should admit that both our beliefs and our doubts are determined by nature, and might well vary, according to our mood or situation, quite independently of their epistemological merit. Nature does not allow us to suspend judgement, even about non-evident things, just because a belief is shown to lack rational warrant. So ironically, ancient Pyrrhonism is too dogmatically rationalistic in failing to separate the issue of warrant from that of belief. Popkin believes that Hume is right to criticize it as unlivable, and as a recipe for madness rather than a path to the *ataraxia* (i.e. quietude or unperturbedness) which is its avowed aim. A more detailed discussion of the livability of traditional Pyrrhonism comes to a similar conclusion:

> Burnyeat, M. F., 'Can the Skeptic Live his Skepticism?', in Malcolm Schofield, Myles Burnyeat, and Jonathan Barnes (eds.), *Doubt and Dogmatism* (Oxford and New York: Clarendon Press, 1980), 20–53; repr. in Myles Burnyeat (ed.), *The Skeptical Tradition* (Berkeley and London: University of California Press, 1983), 117–48.

Burnyeat starts by criticizing Hume for assuming without argument 'that it is impossible to live without reason and belief' (a charge which seems unfair given Hume's extensive account of how belief arises quite involuntarily—cf. Norton's discussion at pp. 382–3 above). But after a close examination of Sextus' views, including his crucial distinction between belief and merely accepting 'appearances', Burnyeat concludes that this distinction breaks down for 'appearances' that are non-perceptual. The sceptic cannot plausibly deny that *these* 'appearances'—which he himself accepts to be part of a natural life—are epistemic and therefore instances of belief. Living without such beliefs would involve a radical self-detachment which does indeed seem humanly impossible.

The sceptical tradition is given a historically informed though predominantly philosophical treatment by Hookway, who agrees with Popkin in seeing Hume's position as essentially a development of Pyrrhonism, but a development that makes room not only for belief, but also for science:

> Hookway, Christopher, *Scepticism* (London and New York: Routledge, 1990), ch. 5.

On Hookway's account, Hume accepts that Pyrrhonian arguments are unanswerable and, like Sextus, rejects 'the prospect of achieving an active rational control over our reasonings' (p. 106); instead we must simply yield passively to the beliefs that we naturally find ourselves holding. Hume also follows Sextus in recommending the virtues of detachment from our cognitive faculties on practical grounds, though whereas Sextus sees such detachment—and consequent abandonment of belief and theoretical enquiry—as a route to tranquil *ataraxia*, Hume differs in taking both belief and theoretical enquiry to be part of our nature, so that Pyrrhonian tranquillity is unattainable. The best we can achieve is to make our speculations more tentative, to limit their scope, and—by leaving their most worrying conclusions behind when we quit our study—to prevent them from impinging undesirably on common life. Many similar themes are explored in a rich paper which has as much to say about Hume's scepticism as it does about the *Dialogues* in particular:

> Penelhum, Terence, 'Hume's Skepticism and the *Dialogues*', in David Fate Norton, Nicholas Capaldi, and Wade L. Robison (eds.), *McGill Hume Studies* (San Diego: Austin Hill Press, 1979), 253–78; repr. in Tweyman (ed.), *Hume*, v. 126–49.

Penelhum, like Hookway, sees Hume as advocating a limitation on 'distant and high enquiries' (*E* 162) not on the ground that they are unnatural (for on the contrary, they are all too natural), but rather, to avoid the anxiety that such enquiries can cause. However, he finds a major contrast between Hume's response to this problem in the *Treatise* and the *Enquiry*—in the *Treatise* the damaging effects of excessive scepticism are to be limited by being confined to the study (thus implying the 'on-again-off-again' scepticism which McCormick's paper in §3.3 above argues is a misinterpretation), whereas in the *Enquiry* Hume recommends instead a limitation of subject-matter. The only justification Penelhum can discern for this later limitation is the notion that our cognitive faculties are so imperfect that we should avoid any reliance on them wherever we are able to do so. However, he finds this justification objectionably ad hoc, for some people might find speculation about theological and metaphysical matters psychologically unavoidable, and as much a part of their nature as more down-to-earth theoretical enquiry. This 'consistency problem' for the mitigated scepticism of the *Enquiry* seems particularly hard to evade if Hume takes theism to be a natural belief, as Penelhum goes on to maintain (though he slightly modifies this view in a later paper—for discussion, see §9.2 above).

Fogelin answers Penelhum's consistency problem by arguing that Hume does not intend his mitigated scepticism to be *justified* at all—no such justification could possibly be available, because from a theoretical point of view Hume's scepticism is wholly unmitigated (as demonstrated in particular by his 'scepticism with regard to reason' of *Treatise* I. iv. 1). Instead, the mitigation is simply a *causal* outcome of our confrontation with Pyrrhonism, in that when we come to appreciate the force of the sceptical arguments, this will naturally have the *effect* of instilling us with modesty, and inducing us to restrict our enquiries in accordance with Hume's recommendation:

> Fogelin, Robert J., 'The Tendency of Hume's Skepticism', in Myles Burnyeat (ed.), *The Skeptical Tradition* (Berkeley and London: University of California Press, 1983), 397–412.

Stroud takes a similar approach, interpreting Hume's mitigated scepticism as 'a state we can find ourselves in, when the reflections leading to excessive scepticism have been tempered or mitigated by our natural inclinations' (p. 280):

> Stroud, Barry, 'Hume's Scepticism: Natural Instincts and Philosophical Reflection', *Philosophical Topics*, 19 (1991), 271–91; repr. in Owen (ed.), *Hume*, 471–91.

However, Stroud emphasizes that Hume's mitigated sceptic is not simply the Pyrrhonian slave of nature described by Popkin. An unreflective peasant can equally well live naively in accordance with our natural instincts, and what distinguishes the Humean sceptic is a reflective appreciation and acceptance of our subservience to these instincts. Such an acceptance (like the 'mitigated belief' emphasised by Norton in Chapter 14, pp. 384–6) can be an enduring state, very different from the 'on-again-off-again' scepticism seen by Popkin and others as the essence of Hume's scepticism. Moreover, this state can lead to something like the *ataraxia* sought by the ancient Pyrrhonians, thus providing a basis for the pragmatic recommendation of Humean philosophy which Stroud finds in the *Treatise* but even more clearly in the *Enquiry* (Sections I, V, and XII). This pragmatic theme is developed at greater length by

Owen, David, 'Philosophy and the Good Life: Hume's Defence of Probable Reasoning', *Dialogue*, 35 (1996), 485–503.

Owen, David, *Hume's Reason* (Oxford and New York: Oxford University Press, 1999), ch. 9, esp. 205–6, 211–23.

Owen takes very seriously Hume's recommendation in the *Treatise* that since we cannot help pursuing enquiries beyond the realm of common life (a premiss which seems in some tension with the mitigated scepticism of the *Enquiry*), 'we ought only to deliberate concerning the choice of our guide, and ought to prefer that which is safest and most agreeable' (*T* 271). He interprets Hume's earlier discussions of probable reasoning—and even his apparently approving descriptions of the inferential practices of 'wise' and 'reasonable' people and of 'philosophers'—as having nothing whatever to do with questions of justification or warrant (cf. §§5.3 and 6.3 above). They are normative only in the sense of clarifying what 'correct' probable reasoning involves, and it is then a quite different question whether such reasoning is to be preferred to any alternatives (e.g. Roman augury by the inspection of a sacrificed sheep's entrails, which can also be done either 'correctly' or 'incorrectly'—see Owen's book, p. 206). Hume's justification of 'philosophy' comes later and is purely pragmatic, based on the observation that such philosophy is more useful and agreeable than superstition, and therefore conforms to the Humean conception of the virtues. Owen, like Stroud, puts particular weight on Section I of the *Enquiry* in developing his pragmatic interpretation. For a contrasting view, see §4 of Chapter 1 of this volume, which interprets that section as arguing for 'abstruse philosophy' more on the basis of a search after *truth* than a quest for calm.

Most of the works discussed above stress Hume's continuity with the sceptical tradition and with Pyrrhonism in particular. However, Hume left his own mark on that tradition, and in summing up this distinctive contribution Hookway (pp. 104–5) emphasizes three particular aspects of his thought, namely his emphasis on the irresistibility of belief, his ambition to develop a naturalistic science of man, and his conceptual concern with the limits of our ideas. We have already seen that the first of these plays a central role in several of the works mentioned above, but the second and third have figured less prominently in discussions of his scepticism. However, Hume's naturalistic ambitions assume centre-stage in a paper which contends that although his *conclusions* were sceptical, his *aims* were not:

Bell, Martin, and McGinn, Marie, 'Naturalism and Scepticism', *Philosophy*, 65 (1990), 399–418.

Bell and McGinn argue that Hume's philosophy is intended not so much as a *development* of scepticism as a *rejection* of it, with his fundamental objective being to achieve a naturalistic understanding of our ordinary beliefs that would allow us to see them as entirely legitimate. In the case of induction, they maintain, he succeeds: his account of why we are convinced by causal inferences enables us to see that we are neither absurd nor arbitrary in founding our beliefs on such inferences, and paves the way for a confident endorsement of inductive method. But the anti-sceptical project misfires when Hume's explanation of our belief in the continued and distinct existence of body leads him to the conclusion that this belief is not only unsupported by reason but is actually false, and hence is a belief that we ought not to hold (cf. §10.1 above). Bell and McGinn therefore interpret the apparent dismay provoked by this result in the *Treatise* (e.g. *T* 217–18, 265–6) as entirely genuine, and not merely a dialectical prelude to a premeditated pragmatic resolution, nor a dramatic wallowing in the excesses of scepticism. However, the contrast they draw, between Hume's constructive treatment of causal reasoning on the one hand and his destructive conclusions with regard to the external world on the other, is implicitly contested by Robison, who focuses on the third distinctive feature of Hume's scepticism identified by Hookway, namely its conceptual aspect:

> Robison, Wade L., 'David Hume: Naturalist and Meta-Sceptic', in Donald W. Livingston and James T. King (eds.), *Hume: A Re-evaluation* (New York: Fordham University Press, 1976), 23–49; repr. in Tweyman (ed.), *Hume*, v. 36–55.

Robison sees the core of Hume's scepticism as involving the realization that the human mind is *essentially incoherent*: we cannot help applying to our experience various concepts—notably that of continuing objects distinct from our perceptions, and objective necessary connexions between those objects—which his analyses demonstrate to have no legitimate application to it. Even Hume himself, after undertaking these analyses and proving that the concepts in question are illegitimate, cannot help applying them, so there is no philosophical solution to this 'meta-scepticism': all we can do is resort to 'carelessness and inattention' (*T* 218; cf. *T* 268) and ignore the problem.[5] This indeed seems to be Hume's prescription in some relevant parts of the *Treatise*, but obviously such an account fits less comfortably with the *Enquiry*, which ends not on a note of despair, but with a positive endorsement of empirical science within the bounds of a relatively mild mitigated scepticism. However, the principal sources of Hume's conceptual scepticism—his Copy Principle, and his attack on the supposed abstract ideas of primary qualities—are still present, so how are we to explain his apparent equanimity in the later work? Assuming that this is not a mere ignoring of inconsistency, we seem to have three main possibilities. The simplest is to follow Stroud in seeing Hume as calmly accepting 'the whimsical condition of mankind' (*E* 160), now that the initial anxiety of his sceptical enquiries in the *Treatise* has subsided. The second is to find ways in which

---

[5] Robison's paper is accompanied in both collections by a response to his views from Páll S. Árdal ('Some Implications of the Virtue of Reasonableness in Hume's *Treatise*', in Livingston and King (eds.), 91–106; Tweyman (ed.), *Hume*, iv. 398–416), which has since been influential on writers such as Beauchamp and Rosenberg, Baier, and Owen (cf. above §§5.3, 6.3, and 10.3 respectively). Árdal himself says little about the *Enquiry*, but views Hume's sceptical quandaries from the perspective of *Treatise* II and III (on which most of his paper is focused). He finds a resolution in the quest for *reasonableness*, an acceptance of beliefs according to their utility, in preference to the narrowly truth-seeking *reason* of Book I. Although not explicitly discussed by Hume, such a notion would satisfy his account of the virtues, being itself justified by its utility and thus giving a pragmatic basis for accepting the natural 'vulgar' beliefs and ignoring their underlying incoherence. Hence in contrast to Robison, Árdal sees Hume's prescription of 'carelessness and inattention' not as an admission of failure on the part of *reason*, but rather, as the affirmation of a *reasonable* 'remedy'.

the conceptual scepticism of the *Enquiry* can coexist with that work's endorsement of science; I have tried in §§9.2 and 12 of Chapter 4 to sketch how such an account might go, accepting the *legitimacy* of causal concepts despite the subjective origin of the relevant idea, and mitigating the negative impact of the confused notion of matter by seeing this confusion as in part a *help* to inductive science (in revealing the lack of any alternative) rather than as a hindrance. The third possibility is to downplay Hume's conceptual scepticism, so that a notion's failure to conform to his theory of ideas remains compatible with that notion's acceptability; as we have already seen in §§7.3 and 10.1 above, this is the essence of the 'sceptical realism' championed by Wright:

> Wright, John P., 'Hume's Academic Scepticism: A Reappraisal of his Philosophy of Human Understanding', *Canadian Journal of Philosophy*, 16 (1986), 407–35; repr. in Tweyman (ed.), *Hume*, ii. 222–47 and in Owen (ed.), *Hume*, 303–31.

Wright forcefully rejects Popkin's Pyrrhonist interpretation, arguing that Hume's writings in fact exemplify only one prominent Pyrrhonist theme, namely the conflict between our natural judgements (the 'noumena') and the way things appear to us (the 'phenomena', including the nature of our impressions and ideas). In other respects—his denial that suspension of belief is possible or that it would lead to tranquillity, his quest for a science of man, and his approval of probabilities—Hume leans instead towards Cicero's 'academic' scepticism, a tendency which becomes fully explicit in the *Enquiry*. All of these threads come together in Hume's account of how the imagination leads us mechanically to accept probable beliefs and to make natural judgements beyond the realm of our ideas. These natural judgements include the inconceivable 'suppositions' of causal power and external existence, which Wright discusses briefly in this article but at much greater length in his book (see §§7.3 and 10.1 above).

Leaving aside the specific topics of induction and the external world (§§5.4 and 10.1 above), most contemporary discussions of scepticism have moved far from specific Humean concerns. Hookway's book mentioned above provides a useful general overview, but says relatively little about some specific issues that have recently come to prominence, such as Putnam's semantic externalism (which can ground an argument from the theory of reference that some sceptical claims can be meaningful only if they are false) and Goldman's reliabilism (which can be used to deny the inference from 'internalist' doubt to lack of knowledge—see Costa's paper in §6.3 above for the suggestion that such reliabilism has roots in Hume's own thought). These developments, and others, are explored from a variety of perspectives in

> DeRose, Keith, and Warfield, Ted A., *Skepticism: A Contemporary Reader* (Oxford and New York: Oxford University Press, 1999).

Particularly helpful is DeRose's introduction, which briefly sketches the issues and thus provides a context for the subsequent papers together with a summary of their main themes.

ADDENDA

A number of new works on Hume have appeared while this volume has been in press, and although it has not been possible to incorporate discussion of them within the body of the Critical Survey as printed here, they will in due course be added to the Web version (at address www.etext.leeds.ac.uk.hume/). Recent books that are particularly relevant to the concerns of this volume include the following:

Bennett, Jonathan, *Learning from Six Philosophers*, 2 vols. (Clarendon Press, 2001)

> The Introduction to Bennett's first volume is a manifesto for his conception of 'collegial early modern studies', which involves studying an author's works in the spirit of a contemporary colleague, antagonist, or student, seeking primarily for philosophical insights rather than historical scholarship (my own introduction to his Chapter 3 in the current collection aims to encapsulate this spirit, but Bennett's manifesto gives numerous further illustrations). His second volume is devoted to Locke, Berkeley, and Hume (the first is on Descartes, Spinoza, and Leibniz), and contains much important new material, together with further developments of the ideas originally presented in his well–known study *Locke, Berkeley, Hume: Central Themes* (Clarendon Press, 1971). As the title of his new book suggests, it provides an excellent starting point for those who wish to use discussion of the early modern philosophers as a platform for exploring philosophical issues of continuing importance.

Buckle, Stephen, *Hume's Enlightenment Tract: The Unity and Purpose of* An Enquiry Concerning Human Understanding (Clarendon Press, 2001)

> The first full single–author study on the *Enquiry* since Flew's *Hume's Philosophy of Belief* in 1961, and therefore a particularly significant addition to the literature, especially in respect of the historical background that it provides. Buckle's overall conception of the *Enquiry* contrasts sharply with that developed in Chapter 1 of the current volume, where Hume's views are presented in direct opposition to those of Descartes and later 'metaphysicians' (*E* 73 n.) such as Malebranche and Baxter (see pp. 29–31, 49–51 above). Buckle instead takes Hume to have a 'relative lack of interest in distinctively rationalist theses', and to view the rationalists primarily as 'misguided fellow–travellers' on the Enlightenment road rather than as targets (p. 49). Accordingly he sees Hume's arguments as directed primarily against the combination of scholasticism and Roman Catholicism—the 'divinity or school metaphysics' of *E* 165. The main part of his book devotes one chapter each to useful and fairly detailed discussions of the twelve sections of the *Enquiry*, with a strong emphasis on understanding Hume in relation to his predecessors rather than engaging in contemporary scholarly debates. However Buckle is strongly partisan in one such debate, expressing enthusiastic support for the 'New Hume' interpretation championed by Craig, Livingston, Strawson, and Wright.

Earman, John, *Hume's Abject Failure: The Argument Against Miracles* (Oxford University Press, 2000)

> As the title indicates, Earman sets out to refute Hume's argument against miracles in *Enquiry* Section X, and his stature as a philosopher of science demands that this attack be taken seriously by anyone who would defend Hume. Earman's critique—which centres around probabilistic considerations—occupies significantly less than half the book, however; the remainder provides a useful compendium of early responses to Hume's notorious argument.

Howson, Colin *Hume's Problem: Induction and the Justification of Belief* (Clarendon Press, 2000)

> Howson's main focus is not so much Hume's argument concerning induction (which he regards as a complete success), but rather, its implications for scientific reasoning. He favours a Bayesian approach, maintaining that this can vindicate a conception of sound inductive inference that is perfectly compatible with Hume's conclusion. Just as is the case with deduction, however, sound inductive argument can only draw substantial conclusions if it is given synthetic premises to start from, and in the case of Bayesian induction, such premises must include the stipulation of appropriate prior probabilities.

O'Connor, David, *Hume on Religion* (Routledge, 2001)

> Like other titles in the 'Routledge Philosophy GuideBook' series (e.g. Noonan's on the *Treatise*), this book aims to provide a fairly comprehensive but accessible guide to a single great work, in this case, Hume's *Dialogues Concerning Natural Religion*. It is therefore particularly relevant to the interpretation of *Enquiry* Section XI, but also of more general interest for the understanding of Hume's philosophy of religion.

Penelhum, Terence, *Themes in Hume: Self, the Will, Religion* (Clarendon Press, 2000)

> Most of Penelhum's essays in this book are reprints of his various (highly respected) papers on Hume, and these should prove particularly useful for anyone who is unable to get hold of the original versions as featured in the sections on religion and scepticism in the Critical Survey of the Literature. But the most important part of Penelhum's book for present purposes is the previously unpublished chapter 11, where he sets out his most current views on Hume's philosophy of religion in an essay which is constructed around a discussion of Sections X and XI of the *Enquiry*. Penelhum concludes that Hume is probably a 'closet atheist', but one who is content to have ascribed to him (e.g. by his friends among the moderate clergy) the minimal deism advocated by Philo in the *Dialogues*.

All of these works will be dealt with at greater length on the website, and ultimately incorporated within the electronic edition of the Critical Survey. Authors or publishers wishing to have books or articles considered for discussion there are invited to send review copies or offprints to Dr Peter Millican, School of Philosophy, University of Leeds, LS2 9JT, England.

INDEX

a priori 121–3, 126 n. 31, 129–30, 135 n. 41,
    136, 137 n. 46, 218, 458–9
  criterion for necessary connexion
    12–13, 215–18, 221, 265, 446
  see also experience; mind not knowable
    a priori; probability: a priori
*Abstract of . . . A Treatise of Human
    Nature* 3, 33, 42–3, 69, 72, 107 nn. 1, 3,
    118, 122, 125 nn. 30, 31, 131, 177, 282,
    283, 332, 334, 399–411, 417, 418
  'chief argument' outlined and
    compared with *Enquiry* 52–63
abstract ideas 5 n. 3, 17, 47, 70, 192,
    203 n. 28, 319, 408–9, 427, 442–3,
    467, 471
  see also general ideas
abstract reasoning 134
  see also reasoning: demonstrative;
    scepticism about abstract reasoning
'abstruse' philosophy 3–4, 46–7, 53, 76,
    87–90, 92, 184–5, 353, 401, 470
  see also metaphysics
academic freedom 94
  see also toleration and intolerance
Adams, M. M. 461
Adams, R. M. 461
Addison, Joseph 72 n. 14, 78 n. 26, 88, 184
'Advertisement' to the *Enquiry* volume of
    Essays and *Treatises* 2, 40, 41, 81,
    232–3
afterlife, see immortality
agency 20, 82, 277, 293, 294, 298–300, 448
  see also liberty
Ahern, D. 302 n. 6, 303 nn. 10, 13
analogies:
  among operations of the mind 43, 56,
    190–1, 407, 411; see also hydraulic
    model

anatomy and painting 70–2, 73, 76,
    88–90, 184, 274–5, 401
  between animals and humans 60, 441
  see also Design Argument; probability
    of analogy; reasoning: analogical
analytic-synthetic distinction 428, 430
  see also Hume's Fork
anatomy, see analogies: anatomy and
    painting
animal spirits, see hydraulic model
animals:
  humans distinct from, see 'Image of
    God' doctrine
  Hume vs. Descartes on 29–30
  instinct in 31, 60, 373
  reason of 6 n. 4, 60, 86, 145–6, 158 n. 76,
    434, 441
  see also analogies between animals and
    humans
Annandale, George Johnstone, Marquis
    of 68, 394
Anscombe, G. E. M. 265 n. 10, 444
Anselm, Saint 353
Anthropic Principle 460
anti-realism 269, 273–4, 275
  see also realism
antiquity 401
  liberty of thought in 92, 354
  see also toleration and intolerance
apologetics, see Christianity
Appendix, see *A Treatise of Human
    Nature*
Aquinas, Saint Thomas 353, 452
Arbuckle, James 72 n. 15
Árdal, P. S. 291, 427, 471 n. 5
argument from design, see Design
    Argument
'argument', meaning of 155 n. 70